Oracle Press

Oracle Enterprise Manager Cloud Control 12*c* Deep Dive

Oracle Press™

Oracle Enterprise Manager Cloud Control 12*c* Deep Dive

Michael New
Edward Whalen
Matthew Burke

New York Chicago San Francisco Athens
London Madrid Mexico City Milan
New Delhi Singapore Sydney Toronto

Cataloging-in-Publication Data is on file with the Library of Congress

McGraw-Hill Education books are available at special quantity discounts to use as premiums and sales promotions, or for use in corporate training programs. To contact a representative, please visit the Contact Us pages at www.mhprofessional.com.

Oracle Enterprise Manager Cloud Control 12*c* Deep Dive

1 2 3 4 5 6 7 8 9 0 DOC DOC 1 0 9 8 7 6 5 4 3

ISBN 978-0-07-179057-4
MHID 0-07-179057-8

Sponsoring Editor
Paul Carlstroem

Editorial Supervisor
Janet Walden

Project Editor
LeeAnn Pickrell

Acquisitions Coordinator
Amanda Russell

Technical Editor
Gary Parker

Copy Editor
Margaret Berson

Proofreader
Paul Tyler

Indexer
James Minkin

Production Supervisor
George Anderson

Composition
Cenveo® Publisher Services

Illustration
Cenveo Publisher Services

Art Director, Cover
Jeff Weeks

To my wife Aimee, and our daughters Leah and Ali.
—Michael New

To my parents.
—Ed Whalen

To Mia, Avery, & Gerianne. Thank you for your patience.
—Matthew Burke

About the Authors

Michael New is a former Technical Manager for Oracle Consulting. He founded New DBA Solutions (www.ndbas.com) in 2008, a technology services company offering remote and onsite Oracle Applications DBA and core Oracle DBA consulting and training. He is a senior information systems architect and Oracle Certified Professional (OCP) with 24 years of experience in the software industry. After receiving his B.S. in Aeronautics and Astronautics from the Massachusetts Institute of Technology, he began his IT career as a software engineer, and for the past 17 years, has been an Oracle Applications DBA. In addition to his extensive EBS project work, Michael has implemented many core Oracle products for clients, in conjunction with and independent of EBS, including RAC, Data Guard, RMAN, Application Server, and Oracle Enterprise Manager, in which he is a recognized authority. Michael New authored *Oracle Enterprise Manager 10*g *Grid Control Implementation Guide* in 2009 (McGraw-Hill Education), has written many white papers on Oracle products, and has been a presenter at Oracle OpenWorld.

Edward Whalen is Chief Technologist at Performance Tuning Corporation (www.perftuning.com), a consulting company specializing in database performance, administration, virtualization, and disaster recovery solutions. Prior to Performance Tuning Corp., he worked at Compaq Computer Corporation as an OS developer and then as a database performance engineer. He has extensive experience in database system design and tuning for optimal performance. His career has consisted of hardware, OS, and database development projects for many different companies. Edward Whalen has written five other books on the Oracle RDBMS and five books on Microsoft SQL Server. He has also worked on numerous benchmarks and performance tuning projects with both Oracle and MS SQL Server. Edward Whalen is recognized as a leader in database performance tuning and optimization and an Oracle ACE.

Matthew Burke is director of a group focusing on remote database administration: implementation, monitoring, backup and recovery, tuning, and high availability (Implicit Technical Solutions, Remote Management Services: http://www.implicit-its.com). The group is currently servicing the needs of numerous clients in both domestic and international locations. He is recognized within the firm as a technical leader in the areas of Real Application Clusters, Parallel Query, and Replication. Matthew Burke has over two decades of Oracle database administration and development experience. He specializes as an Oracle Applications DBA in managing all technical aspects of the Oracle E-Business Suite.

About the Technical Editor

Gary Parker is a senior Oracle consultant with Performance Tuning Corporation. Gary is an Oracle Certified DBA and has extensive experience in consulting, database administration, and system administration. His experience includes more than 18 years tuning and administering Oracle databases and implementing Oracle RAC, Grid Control, Data Guard, Oracle VM, and Oracle applications running on UNIX, Linux, and Windows operating systems on both physical and virtual platforms.

Contents at a Glance

PART III
Notable Management Packs

Contents

PART III
Notable Management Packs

Acknowledgments

The authors acknowledge Sam Alapati for his exceptional work on Chapter 10 on Middleware Management with OEM Cloud Control. Sam is extremely professional and did an excellent job on that chapter.

I am indebted to my wife, Aimee, for helping me finally put pen to paper. After many weeks of listening to me agonize about how to start, she just began writing the first chapter herself, hoping that I would eventually feel sorry for her and take it over. It worked. And she accomplished this feat with mere "conversational DBA" credentials gained from having endured hundreds of hours of my work-related calls from home.

Thanks to the McGraw-Hill Education publishing team for their patience and high standards; Ed Whalen for his generosity in letting me be a co-author, and for a decade of friendship and unwavering professional support; Matt Burke, my mentor these past 13 years; Ily Zislin for his IT wisdom; and my brother Jon and long-time friends Adam Bierman, Brad Stonberg, and Dan Stillit for supporting me in this endeavor and countless other ways.

—Michael New

I would like to thank Gary Parker for his hard work technical editing this book. He not only did a great job editing but offering suggestions along the way as well. Good technical editors can either make or break a book. Gary put in a lot of effort to make this book what it turned out to be. I would also like to thank Sam Alapati for his work on Chapter 10.

Finally, I would like to thank the staff of Oracle Press/McGraw-Hill Education for their hard work and professionalism. This is my third book as an author with Oracle Press/ McGraw Hill Education and all three experiences were great. This publishing company is a pleasure to work with.

—Edward Whalen

I could not even begin to consider this effort without the support, assistance, and camaraderie of Michael New—thank you.

—Matthew Burke

Introduction

Today's system administrators and database administrators can be tasked with the administration and management of hundreds or even thousands of systems. In order to maintain these systems and to be quickly and efficiently alerted in the event of a problem, sophisticated tools must be employed. Oracle Enterprise Manager Cloud Control 12*c* is just such a product, and it can be used to monitor and manage entire data centers with both Oracle and non-Oracle systems. OEM Cloud Control 12*c* is scalable and reliable. This book will teach you how to install and take advantage of the features of OEM Cloud Control 12*c*.

With this book, you will learn how to perform the following tasks:

- Install OEM Cloud Control 12*c*
- Install and administer Management Agents
- Manage hosts, databases, and middleware with OEM Cloud Control 12*c*
- Deploy patches (database and OS)
- Manage Oracle VM environments

This book contains 13 chapters, as described in the following sections.

Chapter 1: Overview of Cloud Control Architecture

In this chapter, you'll learn about the architecture of Oracle Enterprise Manager Cloud Control 12*c*, beginning with architectural developments in the OEM product since Release 10*g*, followed by an examination of the different OEM 12*c* components and how they work together.

Chapter 2: Cloud Control Preinstallation

Here you will see how to prepare for the OEM Cloud Control 12*c* installation. You will be guided through the key architectural design decisions, then provided with all the network configuration, hardware, and software prerequisites for Cloud Control installation.

Chapter 3: Building a Preconfigured Management Repository Database

In this chapter, you'll learn how to use the DBCA template released for Cloud Control 12.1.0.2 to install an Oracle 11*g*R2 Database with a preconfigured Cloud Control Management Repository. You will then finish configuring the database for the installation of the Oracle Management Server (OMS) and to comply better with Maximum Availability Architecture (MAA) best practices.

Chapter 4: Cloud Control Installation and Configuration

In this chapter, you'll learn about the options for installing and upgrading to Cloud Control, how to install and configure a new Cloud Control system, and how to deploy an additional OMS, if needed for high availability or scalability.

Chapter 5: Installing and Configuring Management Agents

You'll learn how the Management Agents are installed and configured, and how they are modular and can be deployed via Cloud Control itself.

Chapter 6: Cloud Control Console Configuration

You'll learn how to configure the Cloud Control Console. The Console is the central port through which Cloud Control is managed and configured. The major features and functions of this interface are addressed.

Chapter 7: Cloud Control Security and User Management

In this chapter, you'll learn how to configure users and security features of OEM Cloud Control. This includes privilege delegation, administrators, and firewall prerequisites for OEM.

Chapter 8: Cloud Control Maintenance and Tuning

In this chapter both maintenance and tuning are covered. Maintenance is addressed from two different perspectives: operational and physical. Operational maintenance concerns the steps or procedures for effectively implementing Cloud Control within the Enterprise. Physical maintenance relates to maintaining the computing resources for the supporting services. Tuning recommendations are also provided to maintain peak performance of your Cloud Control system. Routine care is discussed, such as collecting baselines, removing superfluous tasks, monitoring metrics, modifying parameters and objects, and testing the results.

Chapter 9: DBAs: Manage Databases with Cloud Control

You'll learn how to monitor, administer, and tune databases with OEM Cloud Control. Included are details on how to use SQL Monitoring and ASH Analytics. Database alerting, administration, and advanced processes such as cloning are also covered in this chapter.

Chapter 10: System and Storage Administrators: Manage Infrastructure with Cloud Control

Although databases are, naturally, the primary target of Cloud Control functionality, the product provides a deep wealth of tools for managing both system and storage resources. In this chapter, we take a closer look at these features. Enterprise Manager comes with a comprehensive set of metrics and management tools that support these key back-end components upon which databases rely.

Chapter 11: Middleware Administrators: Manage Middleware with Cloud Control

You'll learn how to manage and monitor middleware with OEM Cloud Control 12*c* in this chapter. You will learn how to discover and manage middleware targets, including WebLogic Server (WLS) and J2EE applications. The chapter then delves into middleware monitoring, including metrics management, system monitoring and notifications, and using the composite application dashboard. Finally, you are shown how to leverage middleware diagnostics, Application Dependency and Performance (ADP), and middleware provisioning through Cloud Control.

Chapter 12: Lifecycle Management Pack

In this chapter, you explore various aspects of the OEM Lifecycle Management Pack to oversee the entire lifecycle of your Cloud Control targets. You'll see how to use this pack to provision the software necessary for running targets, such the OS, database, middleware, and applications. In addition, you'll use this pack for patching, change management, configuration management, and compliance management of these targets.

Chapter 13: Oracle Virtualization Plug-In

You'll learn how to monitor and manage Oracle VM for x86 in this chapter. Oracle VM is Oracle's hypervisor-based virtualization platform. This chapter includes how to create and manage virtual machines as well.

Intended Audience

This book is suitable for the following readers:

- Database administrators
- System and storage administrators who maintain, monitor, or patch with OEM Cloud Control 12*c*.
- Application developers and tuners
- Technical managers or consultants who are responsible for systems

No prior knowledge of Oracle Enterprise Manager is assumed. Everything you need to know to become a competent Cloud Control administrator is contained in this book.

PART I

Implementing and Maintaining Cloud Control 12*c*

CHAPTER 1

Overview of Cloud Control Architecture

Oracle Enterprise Manager Cloud Control 12*c* (hereafter referred to as Cloud Control, CC, or CC 12*c*) is Oracle's solution for managing your complete IT environment—Oracle and non-Oracle products alike. Cloud Control gathers information about your enterprise computing systems, consolidating their management in a central repository. Cloud Control displays this information to administrators from its Web console and sends them alerts on threshold conditions of interest. Administrators can then use this information to have Cloud Control perform tasks for the computing systems it monitors.

Cloud Control is built upon the Oracle technology stack, an Oracle database back end, and a WebLogic Server middle tier that hosts the Oracle Management Service (OMS) application. In a nutshell, an Oracle database hosts the Oracle Management Repository (OMR), which stores alert and metric data for managed targets that is collected and uploaded by local Oracle Management Agents (Agents or OMA). These Agents upload the data to the OMS, which in turn uploads to the Repository. The OMS also renders a Web-based Console for CC administrators and brokers their communications with the Repository. To help you better understand the architecture of Grid Control (GC) beyond this high-level description, so as to architect a Cloud Control infrastructure to meet your needs, this chapter aims to answer the following questions:

- What are the principal architectural developments from Oracle Enterprise Manager (OEM or EM) Grid Control 10*g* and 11*g* to OEM Cloud Control 12*c*? This will help orient those familiar with earlier EM releases to the new CC design.
- What are the main Cloud Control 12*c* components and their function?
- What is the interaction between CC components to allow them to work together to render the Console and process alerts and metric data from monitored targets?

Let's begin with key architectural developments in OEM from the time of GC 10*g*, through GC 11*g* and Cloud Control 12*c*. While this discussion is primarily for the benefit of readers familiar with GC 10*g* and 11*g*, it will also give new Cloud Control users some background on the OEM product, and on how the new 12*c* release is distinguished from earlier releases.

Architectural Developments from GC 10*g* to CC 12*c*

The architecture and installation of Oracle Enterprise Manager GC 10*g*, GC 11*g*, and CC 12*c* differ for all components, and particularly for the OMS and Management Repository:

- **OMS Architecture and Installation** Both the architecture and installation of the OMS diverge between GC 10*g*, GC 11*g*, and CC 12*c*.
    - The 11*g* and 12*c* Oracle Management Service (OMS) is built on Oracle WebLogic Server (WLS) 11*g* Release 1 (version 10.3.5), whereas the 10*g* OMS runs on Oracle Application Server 10*g* (10.1.2.3). This architectural distinction results in an entirely new and vastly improved Console look-and-feel in CC 12*c* than in GC 11*g*/10*g*.
    - The GC 11*g* installation on all platforms except Linux 32-bit requires that you first install Java Development Kit (JDK) 1.6, then install WLS 10.3.2 and apply patch ID WDJ7, whereas on all CC 12*c* platforms, the Installer takes care of WLS 10.3.5 installation and patching for you. CC 12*c* installs WLS, just as GC 10*g* lays down Oracle Application Server 10*g*.
- **Management Repository Installation** As of GC 11*g*, the installation of the database for the Repository was decoupled from the OEM installation itself. In GC 10*g*, one of the Oracle Universal Installer (OUI) options was, in addition to installing the OMS, to create a new 10*g* Database for the Repository. By contrast, the GC 11*g* and 12*c* software distributions do not include a built-in Oracle database for housing the Management Repository; you must preinstall a database in all cases. However, CC 12.1.0.2 offers a template in Database Configuration Assistant (DBCA) that creates a preconfigured Repository database.

The following section provides more details on these key architectural and installation differences between the OEM 10*g*, 11*g*, and 12*c* releases.

OEM 11*g* and 12*c* Use WLS Whereas OEM 10*g* Uses AS 10*g*

Moving from Oracle Application Server 10*g* in GC 10*g* to an Oracle Fusion middleware WLS platform in OEM 11*g* and 12*c* was a radical departure for Oracle, but in line with what is now the foundation of their application infrastructure. Oracle acquired BEA Systems, Inc. for 8.5 billion dollars in April 2008 as a strategic move to overtake IBM's WebSphere platform. Oracle was looking to become the service-oriented architecture (SOA) market leader, by providing complementary middleware products, Oracle OC4J Application Server and BEA WebLogic. Oracle positions WLS 11*g* as the industry's most comprehensive platform for developing, deploying, and integrating enterprise applications.[1] WLS is indeed the top-rated application server in the industry.[2]

---

[1] Oracle Technology Network, Oracle WebLogic Products, http://www.oracle.com/us/products/middleware/application-server/index.html

[2] A recent Gartner worldwide application server market share report shows Oracle at 44 percent, higher than its four closest competitors combined.

In GC 10*g*, the OMS is a Java 2 Platform Enterprise Edition (J2EE) middle-tier application that renders the user interface for the GC Console. (J2EE is an environment for developing and deploying enterprise applications.) The GC 10*g* middle tier, which runs on Oracle Application Server (OAS or Oracle AS) 10*g*, contains three elements: Oracle Application Server Containers for J2EE (OC4J), Oracle HTTP Server (OHS), and OracleAS Web Cache. The OHS deploys the 10*g* Management Service J2EE Web application. The OMS 10*g* is technically part of the OC4J, but the entire GC 10*g* middle tier is usually referred to as the OMS. OracleAS Web Cache provides an additional way to log in to the GC Console.

In contrast to GC 10*g*, the GC 11*g* and CC 12*c* middleware platforms consist of a WLS instance in which an OMS application domain is created (called the GCDomain), rather than the OMS being deployed in its own OC4J container. In addition, OracleAS Web Cache is not used in GC 11*g* and CC 12*c*, as it is in GC 10*g*. This is a boon for GC 11*g*, in our opinion, for at least three reasons. The first is that Web Cache is not terribly useful in GC 10*g*, and provides very little performance advantage over logging in to the Console directly to OHS. Most Console requests, being ad hoc, are for dynamic data with very little cached content, generally limited to icons, menu items, headers, and footers. Secondly, Web Cache complicates the diagnosis of GC 10*g* problems, as many Enterprise Manager analysts at Oracle Support can surely attest. Lastly, Console access via Web Cache is unsecure (on HTTP port 7777) out of the box, and the configuration process to secure such access is nontrivial and undocumented. This is a gaping security hole for sites that want to use Web Cache, but need to enforce secure communications between all GC components.

NOTE

*Web Cache in GC 10*g *acts like a virtual server on behalf of OHS for the Management Service. If any part of the content is in its cache, such as from navigating to a previous page, Web Cache sends that part of the content directly to the Console browser and stores a copy of the page in cache. This is known as a* cache hit. *If Web Cache does not have the requested content, or if the content is stale or invalid, it hands off the request to the OHS, which requests the data from the Management Service. This is known as a* cache miss.

Oracle's direction to use WLS rather than OAS as the middleware platform for the OMS cannot be disputed from the standpoint of technology choice. By all accounts, WLS is a superior product to OAS 10*g* in many respects. Oracle could have taken the direction of using Oracle Application Server (AS) 11*g* for the OMS application. However, AS 11*g* itself uses WLS as its J2EE component. The technological direction came down to whether to build the OMS application in an OC4J container (used in GC 10*g*) or in a WLS instance. While Oracle provides customers with the choice to build their own applications on either OC4J or WLS, it is clear which choice Oracle itself preferred for its own applications, GC 11*g* and CC 12*c*.

Must Preinstall a Database for the Repository in OEM 11*g* and 12*c*

Before installing GC 11*g* or CC 12*c*, you must first install a certified database to house the Management Repository. By contrast, in GC 10*g*, while you had the option to first manually install an Oracle 10*g* or 11*g* Database, you could alternatively choose to have the OUI install a single-instance Oracle 10*g* Database containing the Management Repository. This distinction is more than just a superficial difference in installation choices; it is an architectural diversion between 10*g* and the later 11*g* and 12*c* releases. One can safely assume that the Oracle EM development team recognized that there are too many supported releases (including patch sets) and types of Oracle database installations available in OEM 11*g* and 12*c* to be able to choose just one type or offer multiple installation types through the OEM Installers. Database releases and patch sets include 11.2.0.1+, 11.1.0.7, and 10.2.0.5+, and installation types include Oracle RAC, single-instance, Oracle RAC One-Node (ORON), and Cold Failover Cluster (CFC). The EM development team understandably wanted to get out of the business of having to maintain links in the OEM Installer to one or more Oracle database releases and patch sets certified for the Management Repository.

Even if the EM group chose for the 11*g* and 12*c* Installers only to offer the latest certified database release and patch set for the Repository, this would be a moving target. That is, new database patch sets released and certified with OEM would supersede any earlier database patch set that might be bundled with the OEM software. By not offering to lay down an Oracle database as an option in the OEM 11*g* or 12*c* Installers, the responsibility for selection of a particular Oracle database release, and the database architecture, is left with the DBA performing the EM installation. In our view, this is a good direction for Oracle to have taken, particularly now that CC 12.1.0.2 offers a template for DBCA that creates and configures an 11.2.0.3 Database and preinstalls the Repository in it, before the Cloud Control Installer is run to install the OMS. It was certainly convenient for customers to let the GC 10*g* Installer lay down all GC components, including a database for its Repository. However, we observed that many customers who installed GC 10*g* with the New Database Installation Type never patched, reconfigured, or tuned the seed 10*g* Database that the GC Installer dropped down. These customers made an arguably justifiable assumption that the 10*g* Database installed by GC 10*g* would be patched, configured, and tuned out of the box to support the accompanying Management Repository. Sadly, however, this was not the case. In fact, if you selected the GC New

Database Option in any release or version of GC 10*g* (10.1 or 10.2), the Installer laid down Database 10.1.0.4 for the Repository. This was the case long after 10.2 Database was certified with GC 10*g*—and even after 11.1 Database was certified. Thus, to take advantage of bug fixes and new features afforded by Database Release 10.2 over Release 10.1, customers who chose to let the GC 10*g* OUI install a new database had to subsequently upgrade the Repository database software and database itself from 10.1.0.4 to 10.2.0.1 (including performing post-installation database steps), and then apply the latest Database 10.2.0.*x* Patch Set.

Cloud Control 12*c* Components

Now that you have an idea of how Oracle Enterprise Manager 10*g*, 11*g*, and 12*c* differ architecturally, let's examine the main components, which are common to all releases. The basic Cloud Control topology consists of four core components, as depicted in Figure 1-1: the Cloud Control Console, the Oracle Management Agent, the Oracle Management Service, and the Oracle Management Repository. Each component can be separated by a firewall.

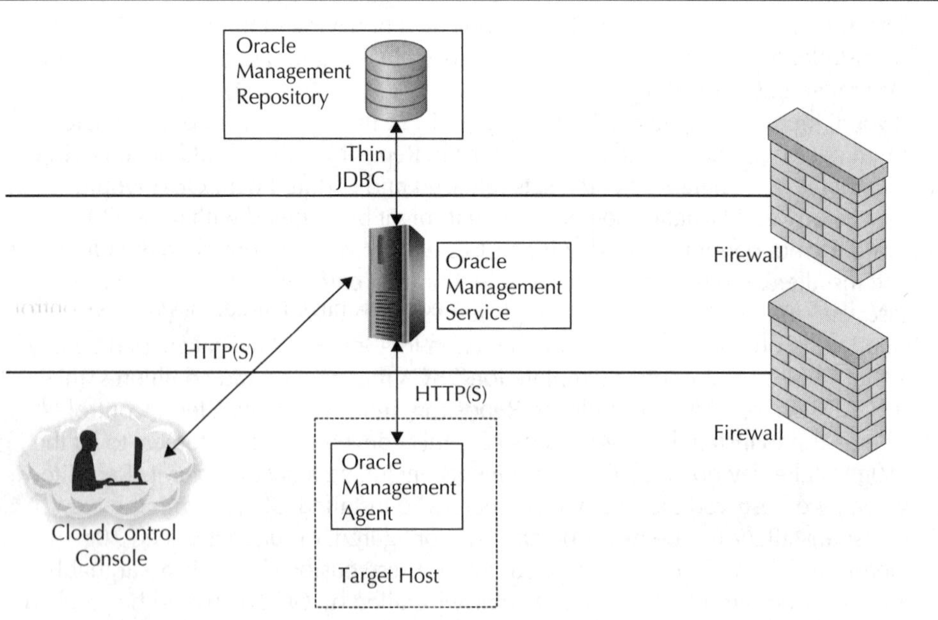

FIGURE 1-1. *Topology of Cloud Control core components*

Following is a brief description of each core component.

- **Cloud Control Console** The Cloud Control Console is a browser-based application through which administrators can centrally manage their entire computing environment. If you had to choose one image to define the big picture for Cloud Control, it would have to be the Console home page:

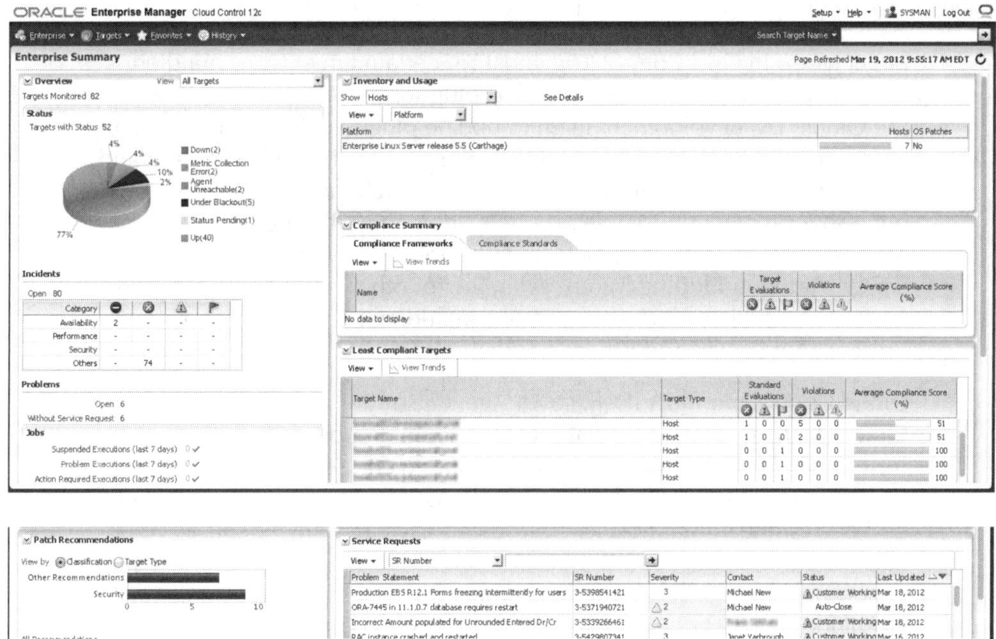

The home page displays an overall view of your managed IT infrastructure from which you can drill down to a specific managed target that Cloud Control administers. The CC Console is certified to run on all popular browsers, including Internet Explorer, Firefox, Safari, and Google Chrome, and to use the Adobe Flash Player plug-in for certain Console functionality. You don't install the Console; the Management Service renders it. You just open a browser and connect to the Console via the Enterprise Manager login URL.

- **Oracle Management Agent** The Management Agent, installed on each managed host, monitors the host and all targets on that host, and communicates information about these targets to the OMS. Targets can be Oracle and non-Oracle components installed on the host. Cloud Control monitors over 200 different target types; each instance of a particular target type counts as a monitored target. Examples of commonly used target types are Database Instance, Listener, Oracle Application Server, and Host.

  Management plug-ins permit monitoring of specific Oracle and non-Oracle target types. In Grid Control 10*g* and 11*g*, certain target types bundled with the product are now packaged as plug-ins in CC 12*c*. This allows the Oracle EM development team to update plug-in software for target types independently of the CC release. Plug-ins are both Oracle-built and partner-built. Oracle-built plug-ins exist for Oracle products, of course, but also for many non-Oracle products, including Microsoft SQL Server, Microsoft Active Directory, NetApp Filer, and IBM WebSphere Application Server. Partner-built plug-ins are available for other non-Oracle components typically found in today's data centers, including F5 BIG-IP LTM, Citrix Presentation Server, and Brocade ServerIron System.

  Cloud Control monitors itself, so an Agent also runs on all nodes hosting the Oracle Management Service and Management Repository. Each managed host (or virtual host) runs one and only one Agent. (Agents in Cold Failover Cluster [CFC] environments run multiple Agents, one for each cluster node, and one for the virtual host itself.) You can have as many Agents as you can scale the Cloud Control infrastructure to support, which is practically capped only by network speeds as limited by geography. Oracle certifies the Agent for the latest current 12*c* release (12.1.0.2) on the most common 32-bit and 64-bit host platforms, including Linux x86-64 and x86 (RHEL, OEL, SLES, and Asianux), Oracle Solaris on SPARC (64-bit), Oracle Solaris on x86-64 (64-bit), IBM AIX on POWER Systems (64-bit), IBM Linux on System z Windows (x64 and x86), and HP-UX (Itanium, PA-RISC).

- **Oracle Management Service** The OMS is a Java 2 Platform Enterprise Edition (J2EE) middle-tier application that renders the user interface for the Console. Agents upload target-related data to the OMS, which then processes this data before uploading it to a data store, the Oracle Management Repository. The Cloud Control middle tier consists of an Oracle WebLogic Server 10.3.5 instance, which deploys the Management Service J2EE Web application.

  You must install the OMS on at least one or more hosts as needed to support your environment for scalability or high availability. Each Management Service must reside on its own host. The OMS and Management Repository can reside on the same host,[3] but for performance reasons, Oracle does not recommend this configuration for a production Cloud Control environment, unless it is small (fewer than 1,000 targets). All physical OMS hosts independently provide the generic Oracle Management Service, though multiple OMS hosts with a Shared Directory can coordinate to process Agent upload files to this directory.

At the time of this writing, the OMS was certified to run on Linux x86-64 and x86, Oracle Solaris on SPARC (x64), Oracle Solaris on x86-64 (64-bit), IBM AIX on POWER Systems, and Windows x86-64. Plans are to certify the OMS on Windows x86 and HP-UX (Itanium, PA-RISC), which are already certified for the Agent.

- **Oracle Management Repository** The Repository (OMR) is the data store for Cloud Control, created either during the CC installation in a preinstalled Oracle database or by the EM template in DBCA when creating the database. The Repository is located in the SYSMAN schema, which contains information on all Cloud Control targets and administrators. The Repository organizes this data so that the OMS can retrieve and display it in the Console for any administrator with privileges to view it. A Cloud Control infrastructure uses just one central Repository database. It can be a single-instance or RAC Oracle database, releases 10gR2 (10.2.0.5), 11gR1 (11.1.0.7.0), or 11gR2 (11.2.0.1+), although Oracle Database 11.2 is recommended.

Console administrators and Agents communicate with the OMS, via ad hoc and batch connections (except alerts), using the following network protocols, respectively:

- An administrator requests content in the Console over HTTP(S) in a browser session, which the OMS renders. The OMS then retrieves the data for the request from the Management Repository and displays it in the Console.
- Agents upload information to the OMS over HTTP(S), and the OMS uploads this data via thin JDBC to the OMR. The OMR sends data back to the OMS over thin JDBC, which is relayed to the Agent via a built-in HTTP listener.

---

[3] In earlier versions of GC 10*g*, it was not supported to install the OMS on a host running Oracle RAC or third-party clusterware. However, in OEM 11*g* and 12*c*, you can install the OMS on one or more RAC nodes hosting the OMR database.

Now that you are familiar with the main components of the Cloud Control architecture, let's examine these components more closely, including their directory structure. We will end by tracing the data flow more closely between components for Console and Agent communications.

Cloud Control Console

The Console provides the user interface to the Cloud Control product. From any location with Web browser access, you can log in to the Console and centrally manage your entire enterprise grid environment. Because the Console interface is rendered in HTML, it uses HTTPS by default (or HTTP if unsecured), making it lightweight, easy to access, and firewall friendly.[4]

The usual way to log in to the Console is at http[s]:*<OMShost>:<port>*/em. The CC installation limits Console browser access to secure communications (SSL), but, after installation, also allows you to open up unsecure (HTTP) access with minimal configuration. (In GC 10*g*, securing Console communications after installation required the reverse manual configuration.)

In GC 10*g*, you could log in via OracleAS Web Cache, which handed you off to Oracle HTTP Server (OHS), or more directly via OHS. In OEM 11*g* and 12*c*, however, you can only log in to the Console through the WLS Apache Web server on default HTTPS port 7799. There is no Web Cache access to the 11*g* or 12*c* Console.

In GC 10*g*, almost all of the capability of Oracle Enterprise Manager 9*i* Java Console was converted to HTML within the GC 10*g* Console. To execute the few leftover 9*i* fat client features not yet available in the GC 10*g* Console, such as management of Oracle Advanced Replication, you had to download the Oracle10*g* Client software and install the Enterprise Manager 10*g* Java Console nondefault component. The Enterprise Manager Java Console only runs in standalone mode; it does not connect to the Management Service. As of GC 11*g*, there is no longer any need for a fat client Java Console. There are no OEM 11*g* or 12*c* features outside of those accessible through the browser Console.

Oracle Management Agent

The Management Agent monitors all Cloud Control targets on a host, including the host itself. It is installed either as a standalone Agent using one of six methods (see Chapter 5) or as part of the first OMS installation, which is known as a "chained" installation. The directory structure of the resulting Agent installation is the same, regardless of the installation method chosen or used (that is, whether chain installed or not), except for a Shared Agent (or NFS Agent), where the Agent binaries are shared

---

[4] EM 10.2 offered wireless device access to Enterprise Manager functionality through its wireless component, EM2Go. However, EM2Go support ended after GC 10.2.0.2. In CC 12*c*, however, you can now log in to the EM full-featured desktop version directly from the Safari browser on any iDevice (iPhone, iPad, or iPod touch). The Cloud Control Mobile app is also available for iDevices as a free app from the iTunes App Store. However, CC Mobile functionality currently provides access only to Incident Manager.

on an NFS file system. The Agent is the distributed portion of the Enterprise Manager framework, and is implemented in the C programming language for performance and resource reasons. It is a multithreaded process that uses Oracle core libraries, the Oracle Call Interface (OCI), and Oracle Secure Sockets Layer (SSL) to secure it by default. A reasonable approach to an overview of the Management Agent architecture is to grasp the concept of Agent target discovery and to look at the Agent file and directory structure.

Target Discovery and Management

You run one and only one Management Agent on each host that has targets to be managed. A properly installed Agent automatically starts monitoring itself, its host, the OMS, if installed along with the Agent on the host, and certain Oracle products (for example, databases, listeners, and Oracle Application Servers) installed on the host. (The Agent and host are targets in their own right; Cloud Control treats them like any other target.) This automatic target discovery begins as soon as the Agent is installed and starts up. Those targets not automatically discovered can be manually discovered in the Console, and new targets can be automatically or manually discovered as well.

Targets are categorized by target type. Cloud Control manages approximately 200 out-of-box target types, and many more target types provided by plug-ins not configured with the OMS. A fair number of plug-ins for GC 11*g* have not yet been updated for CC 12*c*, but it is likely that these plug-ins will be updated in the near term.

The Management Agent uses default monitoring and data collection levels to provide monitoring and management information on discovered targets. The Agent immediately uploads metric alerts and periodically uploads management information to the OMS. The Agent also performs tasks on behalf of the OMS, from running jobs (units of work defined to automate administrative tasks such as backups or patching) to setting blackouts (suspending data collection on targets to perform scheduled maintenance). Blackouts allow for a more accurate picture of a target's performance because Agent downtime can be characterized as planned, thereby not adversely affecting that target's Service Level Agreement (SLA).

Management Agent Files and Directories

The Agent stores its configuration and management information about targets in flat files under the Agent installation base directory (AGENT_BASE), such as /u01/app/oracle/agent/. This directory holds distinctly different information in multiple Homes, for the Agent software, Agent State Home, plug-ins, and setuid binaries. Following is a description of each of these Homes, their default locations, and notable files within them:[5]

---

[5] Much of this information on Agent directory structure is taken from MOS Bulletin 1386113.1.

- **AGENT_HOME** $AGENT_BASE/core/12.1.0.x.0/. Contains all binaries for configuring and running the Management Agent on the host, and is also referred to as the Core Home.
- **AGENT_INSTANCE_HOME (or EMSTATE)** $AGENT_BASE/agent_inst/. Location where the Agent instance files are created, including wrapper scripts to set environment variables, incidents and diagnostic dumps for the Agent, configuration files (principally $AGENT_BASE/agent_inst/sysman/config/emd.properties, the main Agent configuration file), files with target details, and log files. For NFS installations, this directory exists only on remote hosts, and not under $AGENT_BASE.
- **PLUGIN_HOME** $AGENT_BASE/plugins/. Location of plug-ins on the Agent side. Each plug-in directory has its own directories for metric metadata, default collections, and scripts specific to the target types the plug-in supports. The plug-ins installed are listed in $AGENT_HOME/sysman/install/plugins.txt. The status of all plug-in installations is contained in $AGENT_HOME/sysman/install/plugins.txt.status.
- **SBIN_HOME** $AGENT_BASE/sbin/. This is the setuid executable home that contains important binaries (setuid executables) owned by root, such as `nmo`, `nmb`, and `nmhs`.

The most important files and directories in the Management Agent home directory structure are pictured in Figure 1-2. This will give you a general feel for how the Agent organizes itself to monitor targets.

When an Agent is installed on a host, an entry is added to the /etc/oragchomelist file with the $AGENT_HOME, $OMS_HOME, and $AGENT_INSTANCE_HOME directories. However, an entry for the Agent Home is no longer added to the /etc/oratab file, as with GC 10g/11g Agents.

Agent Files Uploaded to OMS

The Agent uploads alerts and monitoring data in XML files to the OMS when any one of the following conditions occurs:

- The Agent needs to send an alert.
- The XML files exceed a predefined size.
- The time since the last upload exceeds a predefined limit (15 minutes by default).

The Agent Upload Manager, also known as the Agent Loader process, is responsible for uploading XML files containing metric data and alerts. The Agent

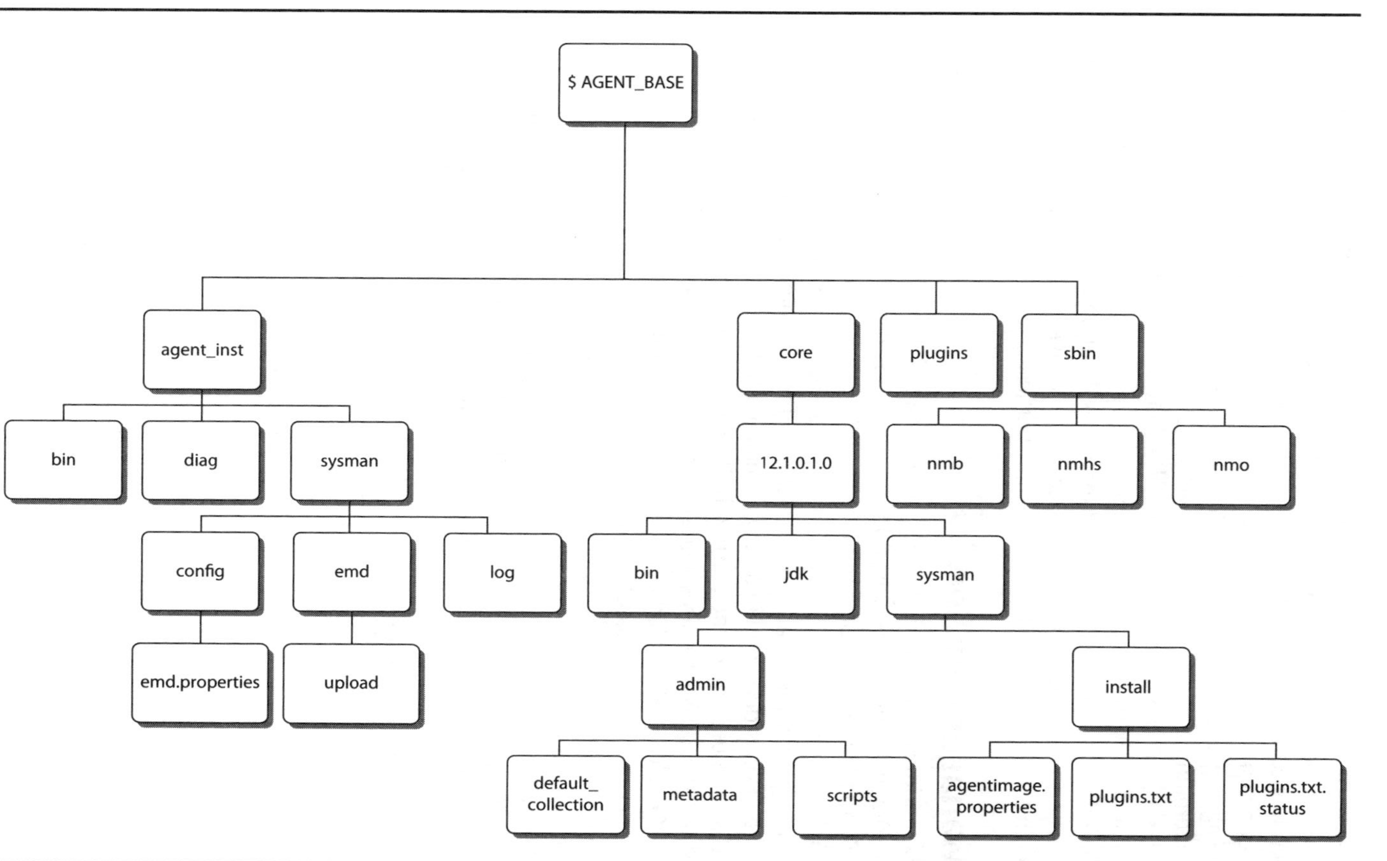

FIGURE 1-2. *Management Agent directory structure*

Loader stores these files in the $AGENT_INST/sysman/emd/upload/ upload directory on the target host, which are uploaded to the OMS. The Upload Manager maintains statistics on pending XML files (files on the Agent host not yet uploaded to the OMS) and disables collections based on the number of files in the upload directory (5,000 by default), the aggregate size of these files (50MB by default), and the percentage of free disk space remaining on the upload file system (2 percent by default). The upload interval is 15 minutes by default, and is the time between scheduled uploads of Agent files that contain metric data, not alerts. The upload interval is dynamic because it is based on an Agent property that increases the upload interval by a certain percentage (20 percent by default) for each successive upload failure. All defaults are set in the Agent properties file emd.properties.

Oracle Management Service

The OMS is the middle tier that renders the user interface for the Console. The OMS is deployed on Oracle WebLogic Server (WLS) 11*g*R1 (10.3.5). As already mentioned, the WLS 10.3.5 installation is bundled with the CC 12*c* Installer. When running the Installer to create a new EM System, a WLS instance is installed in the subdirectory wlserver_10.3 under the Middleware home directory (for example, /u01/app/Middleware). The OMS is deployed in a new domain called GCDomain in this WLS instance, and does not use any of the existing built-in domains. Understanding the architecture of an OMS server requires a grasp of each of its elements. WLS 10.3.5 (which contains Oracle HTTP Server) and the OMS J2EE application in a WLS Fusion domain, together comprise what is collectively referred to as the "OMS."

All OMS components are installed on the same server, regardless of the Cloud Control installation method (via OUI or silent installation). You can deploy multiple Management Services, each on a separate host. However, the OMS on each host must include all OMS components, and must point to the same Repository database for a given Cloud Control environment. Each OMS communicates via thin Java Database Connectivity (JDBC) to the Management Repository. Thin JDBC is a standard Java interface for connecting from Java to relational databases. Also, as mentioned earlier, as of GC 11*g*, Oracle supports a Management Service installation on a node running an Oracle Real Application Clusters (RAC) 10*g* or 11*g* Database that houses a Management Repository.

The OMS directory tree for CC 12*c* is shown in Figure 1-3.

The Middleware home directory includes subdirectories for the EM instance base directory (gc_inst), JDK 1.6 home (jdk16) home, OMS home (oms), Middleware common home (oracle_common), Middleware WebTier home (Oracle_WT), plug-ins installed on the OMS side (plugins), and WebLogic Server home (wlserver_10.3).

The main OMS configuration file, the $OMS_HOME/sysman/config/emoms .properties file used in GC 10*g* and 11*g*, is no longer used in CC 12*c*. Instead, OMS

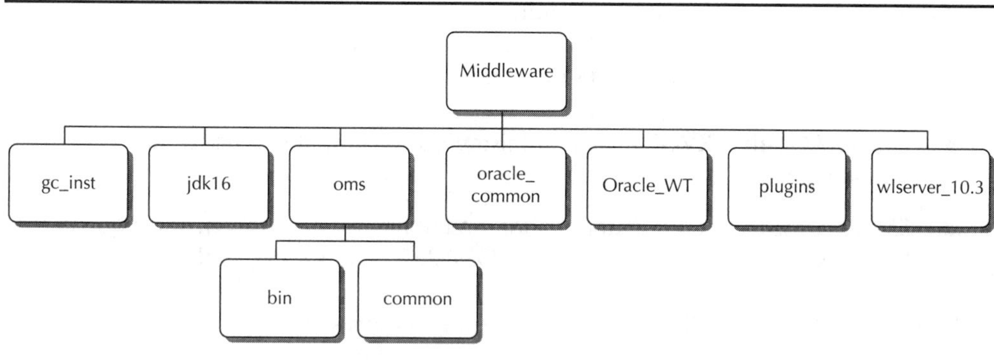

FIGURE 1-3. *OMS directory structure*

properties are modified using `emctl get/set/delete/list` property commands. Once CC is installed, the `emctl` command lists the various configuration options and their syntax.

The WLS installation provides a WebLogic Server Administration Console, which is a full-feature domain administration site available through a WLS instance-specific URL https://*<OMShost>*:7101/console or via a link on the GCDomain target home page in the Console. You log in to the WLS Administration Console as the default *weblogic* user.

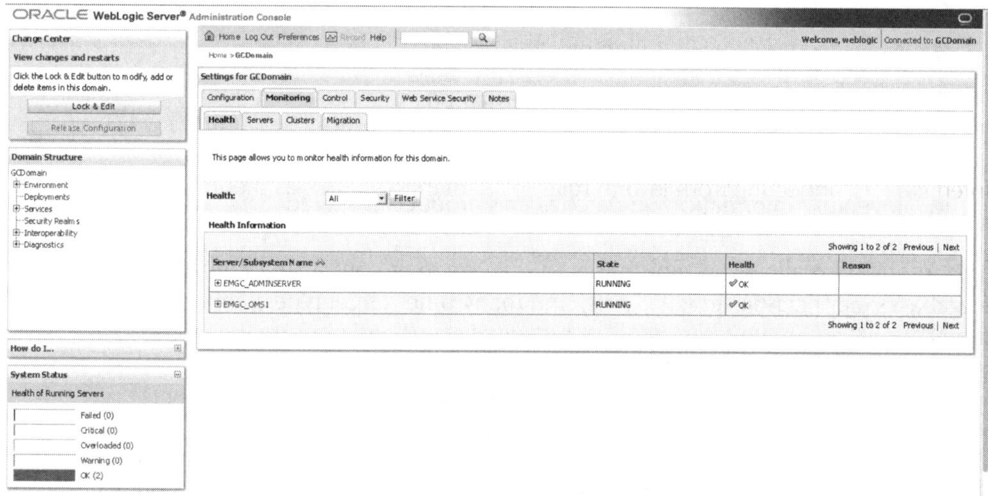

As shown in the illustration, the Administration Console connects to the GCDomain, which after installing CC 12*c*, contains two WLS Managed Servers (and additional servers for each OMS installed):

- **EMGC_ADMINSERVER** The administration server that belongs to the GCDomain.
- **EMGC_OMS1** The OMS application on the first OMS installed. Subsequent OMS installations are named EMGC_OMS2, EMGC_OMS3, and so on.

Both of these two servers will be running when the OMS is started.

Oracle Management Repository

The Oracle Management Repository (OMR) is the comprehensive source for all the management information for Cloud Control. It consists of schema definitions, stored procedures, and RDBMS jobs within an Oracle database, all owned by the SYSMAN database user. A particular Cloud Control implementation employs only one Management Repository. You can install multiple Management Services, but each must use this central Repository as their data store.

All CC Console administrators share the same Management Repository information based on the privileges granted to them. Information in the Management Repository includes:

- Configuration details about the managed targets
- Managed target availability information
- Historical metric data and alert information
- Target response time data
- Inventory information on patches and products installed

This information allows administrators to manage their complete application stack (databases, application servers, hosts, and many other target types), model applications, automate tasks, analyze historical status and performance data, perform Application Service Level Management (ASLM), track and make configuration changes, and carry out many other tasks to manage complex IT systems running a combination of Oracle and non-Oracle technologies.

The Management Repository can reside either on the same host as a Management Service or on a dedicated host. You run the CC Installer on the host where you want the OMS to reside, and in the Installer specify the existing database where you want the Installer to create the Management Repository. Oracle supports running the Repository in either a single-instance or Real Application Clusters (RAC) database,

Release 10gR2, 11gR1, or 11gR2. For specifics on certified database versions, see the Certify page on the My Oracle Support Web site. You must locate the Management Repository in an Enterprise Edition Database. When installing a database for the Repository, you must select the Partitioning Option because Enterprise Manager uses partitioned tables to store management data.

Now let's examine the Management Repository schema, including the schema owner, tablespaces, and objects within that schema. SYSMAN is both the schema owner and the default Super Administrator account. You cannot remove or rename the SYSMAN account. It is used to

- Perform the initial Cloud Control setup, such as creating privileges and roles, administrator accounts, or notification rules
- Discover new targets
- Create generic jobs to run on all databases or hosts

The Installer for Cloud Control creates three default tablespaces to hold its objects:

- **MGMT_TABLESPACE** Holds all target-related monitoring and metrics data
- **MGMT_ECM_DEPOT_TS** Stores configuration data collected from the monitored targets[6]
- **MGMT_AD4J_TS** Stores diagnostics data related to JVM Diagnostics and Application Dependency Performance (ADP)

As for the schema objects, an open Repository schema is the key to one of Cloud Control's most important architectural features: extensibility. An open schema means that it is documented so that you can customize the use of Repository data if the standard configuration does not meet your requirements. The Repository tablespaces contain base tables and indexes that begin primarily with MGMT_ and other data types, including over 600 database views. The views, whose names start mostly with "MGMT$", are particularly handy for mining Repository information that you want to process further. The views are comprehensive so that you can avoid having to directly access the base tables. The inherent advantage to these views is that they insulate custom applications from underlying changes to the base SYSMAN schema due to new releases or patching.

---

[6] Configuration management within Cloud Control includes support for Binary Large Objects (BLOBs). Aside from the benefit of logically isolating configuration data in a separate tablespace, it is a best practice for performance and tuning reasons to locate BLOBs in a separate tablespace like this.

Following are the categories of Cloud Control views that provide access to metric, target, and monitoring data stored in the Management Repository:

- Monitoring views
- Inventory views
- Policy Definition views
- Policy Association views
- Policy Violation views
- Management Template views
- Job views
- Application Service Level Management views
- Configuration views
- Oracle Home Patching views
- Linux Patching views
- Security views
- Configuration Management views
- Database Cluster views
- Storage Reporting views

Views provide the basis for passing alerts on to other System Management products, for customizing new plug-ins, reporting problems, and performing historical analysis and data computation.

Data Flow Between Cloud Control Components

Now that we've reviewed each CC component and its function, let's look at how these components interact, in order to better understand the CC architectural model. The diagram in Figure 1-4 shows how data flows between components for both Console communications and Agent uploads of metric data and alerts.

Let's follow the numbers and arrowed lines in this figure to visualize the flow of management data from one component or subcomponent to another. Default ports

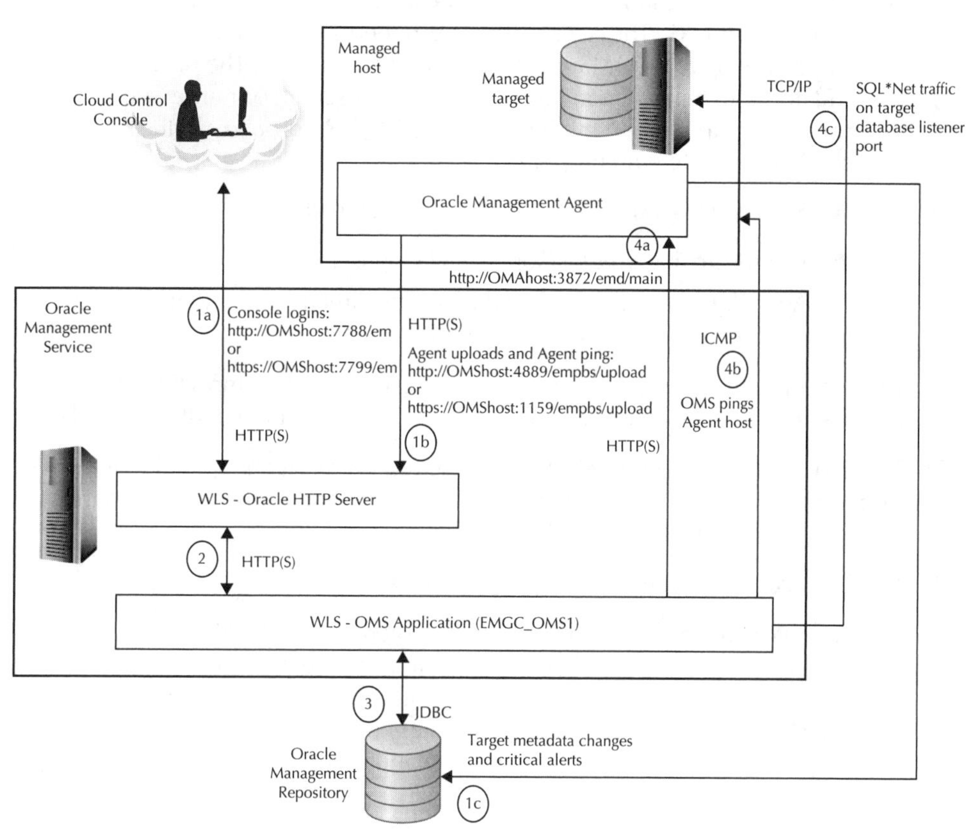

FIGURE 1-4. *Data flow for each type of interaction between Cloud Control components*

are listed in the following explanations. However, an administrator can customize all ports as needed.

1) There are three types of communication for Console requests and Agent uploads:

a) An administrator logs in to the Console at http[s]://<*OMShost*>:<*port*>/em through the Oracle HTTP Server (OHS) of the WLS. The default login URL depends on whether the administrator is using a secure or nonsecure connection:

- Secure: https://<*OMShost*>:7799/em
- Nonsecure: http://<*OMShost*>:7788/em

b) The Agent uploads metric data and warning alerts to the WLS Oracle HTTP Server URL. The Agent also sends a periodic heartbeat called an *Agent ping* to its OMS indicating that it is available. The default URL for both types of communication is via a secure or nonsecure connection, as defined by the REPOSITORY_URL property in the Agent configuration file emd.properties:

- Secure: https://<*OMShost*>:1159/empbs/upload
- Nonsecure: http://<*OMShost*>:4889/empbs/upload

c) The Agent bypasses the OMS and connects directly to the Repository to report target metadata changes and critical alerts.

2) The administrator request in the Console or Agent upload prompts the OHS to pass the request over HTTP or HTTPS to the OMS application (EMGC_OMS1).

3) The OMS application forwards the Console request or Agent upload to the Repository via thin JDBC. Upon receipt, the OMS renders the content in the Console via the same return path.

4) The OMS communicates to the Agent in several ways:

a) The OMS forwards data directly to the Agent over HTTP(S) to the Agent's built-in HTTP listener. It listens on the Agent URL http(s)://<*OMAhost*>:3872/emd/main (https by default), defined by the EMD_URL property located in the Agent configuration file emd.properties. The OMS also submits jobs and other management tasks through this URL.

b) If the OMS-to-Agent communication described in Step 4a is not successful, the OMS checks the status of the target host by pinging the host on which the Agent resides with Internet Control Message Protocol (ICMP) Echo Requests.

c) The OMS sends SQL*Net traffic over TCP ports to target database listeners on Agent hosts, such as when patching database targets through Cloud Control.

Now that you've looked more closely at the internal workings of the Cloud Control engine, you'll have a better understanding of what happens under the hood after CC is installed and operational. This understanding will make it easier to troubleshoot any problems.

Summary

Here is a synopsis of what was covered in this introductory chapter:

- We began with a discussion of the two principal differences between OEM 12*c*/11*g* and GC 10*g*, which were the use of WebLogic Server versus AS 10*g* for the OMS middle tier, and the requirement in OEM 12*c* and 11*g* that you must preinstall an Oracle database in which the Installer can create the Management Repository.
- Next, we introduced the four main Cloud Control components: the Console, Agent, OMS, and Repository.
- We ended this chapter by examining the interaction between Cloud Control components. You saw how these components work together to deliver Console requests and metric data from the Agent on a target host through the OMS to the Repository, how the OMS in turn delivers data back to the Agent, and how Cloud Control performs self-monitoring by using one component to check the status of another.

Now that you understand the basic architecture and concepts of Cloud Control, you are ready to proceed to Chapter 2 to perform CC preinstallation steps. In Chapter 3 you will create the database for the Management Repository, and then, in Chapter 4, you will install Cloud Control.

CHAPTER 2

Cloud Control Preinstallation

In Chapter 1, you learned that, unlike Oracle Enterprise Manager (OEM) Grid Control 11*g*, the OEM Cloud Control 12*c* Installer does not require you to first install Oracle WebLogic Server, which streamlines the installation process. However, unlike Grid Control 10*g*, the CC 12*c* and GC 11*g* installers do not offer an option to create a database for the Management Repository; a database must be installed and configured before running the Cloud Control 12*c* or GC 11*g* installers.

In this chapter, we'll cover preinstallation requirements for installing and operating a Cloud Control environment. We begin with a discussion of key architectural design choices you must make up front, such as how many CC systems to build and the architecture of each component. The remainder of the chapter covers all network, hardware, and software prerequisites for installing CC 12*c*, except those of creating and configuring a database for the Repository, which are presented in Chapter 3.

The prerequisites included in this chapter are for all CC components, which are as follows:

- **Oracle Management Service** An "OMS" is installed on the local host on which the Installer is run.
- **Oracle Management Repository** The Management Repository, or "OMR," is created in a database that you need to preinstall for this purpose.
- **Oracle Management Agents** An Agent, or "OMA," is installed on each managed host you want to monitor with Cloud Control. There are two types of Agents: chain-installed and standalone Agents:
  - **Chain-installed Agents** You do not explicitly install these Agents; their installation is bundled with that of the OMS and is automatically performed by the Installer. Like any Agent, it monitors its host's targets, including the OMS itself, and Repository database, if installed on the same host.
  - **Standalone Agents** You explicitly install standalone Agents on all target hosts except the initial OMS host where Agents are chain-installed. You will deploy standalone Agents after running the CC Installer to install the Management Repository and OMS. You can install standalone Agents using one of six methods, which are presented in Chapter 5.

  Both types of Agents have the same preinstallation requirements, and once installed, are identical. Naturally, you kill two birds with one stone for chain-installed Agents when implementing OMS prerequisites that also apply to Agents. However, these preinstallation steps must be satisfied independently for standalone Agents.

- **CC Console Client** Client workstations are used by CC administrators to access the Console in a browser session. The Console is rendered by the OMS, and does not need to be installed separately. The only preinstallation requirement for CC related to Console clients is network bandwidth and latency requirements between clients and the OMS, as noted later in this chapter.

The preinstallation steps discussed here apply to the hosts where the OMR, OMS, and chain-installed Agents will be installed, hosts where standalone Agents will be deployed, and client workstations that will display the CC Console. These prerequisites, in addition to those for the database to house the Repository presented in Chapter 3, are the sum total of those necessary to install and operate a CC environment.

Preinstallation tasks as organized in this chapter fall into the following four major categories:

- **Architectural design** The first preinstallation step is to design a CC topology, including how many environments to build and OMS servers to install, and taking into account any high availability (HA) or disaster recovery (DR) requirements.
- **Network configuration** After fleshing out the basic CC architecture to employ, you need to satisfy network configuration prerequisites, including host naming rules and constraints, connectivity checks between CC component nodes, and setup specifications for firewall and server load balancer, if used.
- **Hardware requirements** This section provides specifications for OMR, OMS, and Agent hosts with respect to hardware resources (disk space, RAM, swap, and CPU speed) needed to meet CC installation and operating requirements.
- **Software requirements** You need to confirm that the OMS and OMR platforms meet CC certification requirements; create the necessary OS groups, users, and directories; synchronize OS timestamps/time zones between hosts; and satisfy all platform-specific software requirements. (As already mentioned, installing and configuring the database for the Management Repository is covered separately in Chapter 3.)

NOTE
In this chapter, all preinstallation tasks are annotated with OMR, OMS, and/or OMA (applicable to chain-installed and standalone Agents installed via any method) to indicate which CC component(s) the task applies to.

Naturally, you need to perform all OMR and OMS preinstallation requirements before running the Cloud Control Installer, as covered in Chapter 4. However, Agent prerequisites in common with those for the OMS could be deferred for standalone Agents until after installing CC, then performed alongside additional prerequisites relating to the particular standalone Agent installation method(s) chosen, as listed in Chapter 5. Most administrators are anxious to run the CC Installer and don't want to take the time up front to concurrently perform preinstallation steps for standalone Agents on all target hosts. While you can certainly wait to take care of all Agent prerequisites for standalone Agents at once when you get to Chapter 5, it is advisable to at least address Agent preinstallation steps that are in common with the OMS now for standalone Agents because many relate to network connectivity requirements usually performed by a network administrator (NA). Network changes typically take lead time to complete, especially if they must go through a change control process, which is the norm at most CC sites.

While many of the preinstallation steps apply generically to all operating systems, the commands to verify or fulfill some of these steps differ by platform. Where the syntax varies, we generally provide the variations for Windows and all flavors of UNIX.

NOTE
You may want to begin downloading and staging all CC software, beginning with the database server for the OMR, while carrying on with the remaining preinstallation steps, so that the downloads will be finished by the time you're ready to begin the installation. You'll need to stage the CC distribution soon enough anyway, if you'd like to run the EM Prerequisite Kit in standalone mode, as described in Chapter 3. To begin downloading, see the section "Download and Stage CC and Related Software" later in this chapter.

Key Architectural Design Decisions

Before installing Cloud Control, you need to make some key design decisions to ensure that the system will meet all requirements for monitoring your IT infrastructure. How highly available does your CC system need to be? Are there any disaster recovery or scalability considerations? These types of questions must inform your CC architectural choices.

To provide high availability (HA) and disaster recovery (DR), you need to call upon Oracle and/or other technologies, including Oracle Real Application Clusters (RAC), Oracle Automatic Storage Management (ASM), Storage Array Networks (SAN) and Network Attached Storage (NAS), third-party Cold Failover Cluster (CFC) solutions, Oracle Data Guard, Oracle Recovery Manager (RMAN), Oracle Flashback, firewalls, proxy servers, and server load balancers (SLB).

You don't need to integrate these HA and DR technologies when you first install CC, but it may be easier to do so up front if your CC requirements dictate their use. At a minimum, you may need to make a few preliminary design decisions to allow for later incorporation of these technologies. Oracle shops with little or no production monitoring in place understandably want to get Cloud Control up and running as quickly as possible to start monitoring their systems. If you're in this situation, and also need to provide a robust CC system, it may be better to install the base product quickly to reap the benefit of immediate out-of-box monitoring than to continue without monitoring while you design and implement a more HA/DR-compliant CC architecture. You will have to do a cost/benefit analysis to weigh the labor savings in building a fully architected CC system up front against the cost of reconfiguring CC components later to arrive at a final architecture.

There are other benefits than immediate monitoring to waiting until after Cloud Control is operational, then reconfiguring it for HA/DR:

- You can rely on CC functionality itself to boost its own HA and DR capabilities. For instance, you can use CC to help build or convert the Repository database to Oracle RAC, or to create a standby database for the Repository and place it in a Data Guard configuration with the primary database.
- You can use CC to define and track an SLA for itself, then measure its availability and performance against this SLA. From this data, you may determine that your plans to install an additional OMS host or convert the Repository database to RAC aren't necessary after all to ensure compliance with your Cloud Control SLA.
- You can build what will initially be a production CC system (that is, to monitor production targets), then later recommission it as a nonproduction system by removing the production targets from monitoring and discovering and configuring nonproduction targets. In its place, you could install a new HA/DR–compliant production system, which by then you will have had more time to architect and implement, and then rediscover the production targets in this new environment.

Whether you decide to first build a basic Cloud Control engine and leave the high-end setup for later, or to tackle everything up front, you need to make two key topological decisions in order to install Cloud Control:

- How many Cloud Control environments should you build?
- What installation choices should you make?

Decide How Many Cloud Control Environments to Build

OMR, OMS, OMA

A Cloud Control environment is a system consisting of one or more coupled OMS and OMR hosts (single-instance, RAC, or RAC One Node) and related Agents on target hosts. CC environments are independent, by design; they do not intercommunicate, nor can you daisy-chain them. The number of CC environments to build is dictated by several factors:

- Whether to monitor production and nonproduction targets with separate CC environments
- Whether network limitations require multiple CC environments

Production vs. Nonproduction Environments

The overriding factor in determining how many Cloud Control environments to build is whether to monitor production and nonproduction targets using the same, or separate, CC environments. (Most CC sites want to monitor at least some nonproduction targets too, to test the CC monitoring process itself, or because the environment needs to be monitored.) The choice, then, is one of the following instance management strategies:

- Build two CC environments, one for production targets, and the other for nonproduction targets and CC instance management (for example, upgrades, patches, and so on) to test CC infrastructure changes before migrating them to production.
- Build one CC environment for both production and nonproduction management.

NOTE

The instance management strategy at many companies calls for multiple nonproduction environments, such as for staging, development, QA, and UAT. However, one nonproduction CC environment is usually sufficient to test CC infrastructure changes.

A Cloud Control implementation is considered a production environment if it monitors production targets. As such, best practice is the first option: configure a production CC environment to monitor only production targets. This prevents nonproduction targets from adversely impacting a production CC framework.

If you decide on separate production and nonproduction CC environments, it's standard practice to build the nonproduction environment first, just as it would be for any software application. However, if you plan to monitor all targets with one CC environment, then consider this chapter the beginning of a production build. Either way, you need to earmark one or more servers for your installation. It would be best to decide at this point whether these servers are for a production or a nonproduction CC environment. In the following two sections, you will determine the number of OMS and OMR database servers required and whether to co-locate these components on a particular server.

Network Constraints Due to Geography

A question that goes hand in hand with whether to build separate production and nonproduction environments is "How many active environments are geographically required?" (This discussion is limited to OMSs in an Active/Active configuration, as a passive OMS is not subject to online network constraints.) For example, if all production targets are on the east coast of the United States and all nonproduction targets are on the west coast, network bandwidth constraints due to geography may require building two regional CC environments. They would be unrelated to each other; that is, all components—the constituent Agents and OMSs reporting to a Management Repository—for a particular environment would be separate from the other environment. CC has been implemented globally, but only at firms with extremely fast private networks. To calculate whether just one environment would be sufficient from a geographical perspective, you need to know the network requirements for communication between CC components and the performance of the network(s) on which these components will reside. Let's look at each of these factors, in turn.

Cloud Control network error handling is robust, allowing it to tolerate network glitches and outages between components. However, network issues, between Agent and OMS, or between Console browser and OMS, impact overall CC performance much less than those between OMS and OMR tiers. A particular Agent or Console connection to an OMS link can be severed without impacting CC system function at all. However, a network problem between active (not DR) OMS and OMR tiers could significantly reduce overall system performance. Console connection performance could deteriorate, along with monitoring (alerts and notifications), job execution, and almost every other CC function.

NOTE

It is the minimum dedicated network performance requirements between OMS and OMR hosts that usually dictate how far you can "spread" an installation, not any inherent limitations of Cloud Control, which can scale for hundreds of administrators and tens of thousands of targets.

Figure 2-1 depicts the dedicated minimum bandwidth and maximum latency requirements between active OMS, OMR, and OMA tiers, and Table 2-1 summarizes these requirements for easy reference. Network requirements for OMR to its storage are also given and generally come into play when the OMR host is not physically coupled with its storage devices, such as when using cloud hosting or cloud storage.

NOTE
The network requirements discussed here assume that the network is dedicated to CC traffic.

Both Figure 2-1 and Table 2-1 reflect that the minimum bandwidth and maximum latency requirements between OMS and OMR hosts are much more stringent than those between OMA and OMS hosts (10× for latency and over 3000× for bandwidth).

So much for network requirements between CC components. You need to know how they compare to your corporate network speed that can be dedicated to Cloud Control. Due to the necessarily tight network coupling between OMS and OMR tiers, most sites run at least one OMS host from within the same data center as the OMR host. Corporate Local Area Networks (LANs) typically run Gigabit Ethernet (GigE) or higher, so they are typically fast enough to meet the 1Gbps minimum bandwidth requirement between OMS and OMR. Table 2-2 lists bandwidths for the most prevalent LAN devices found in data centers today.

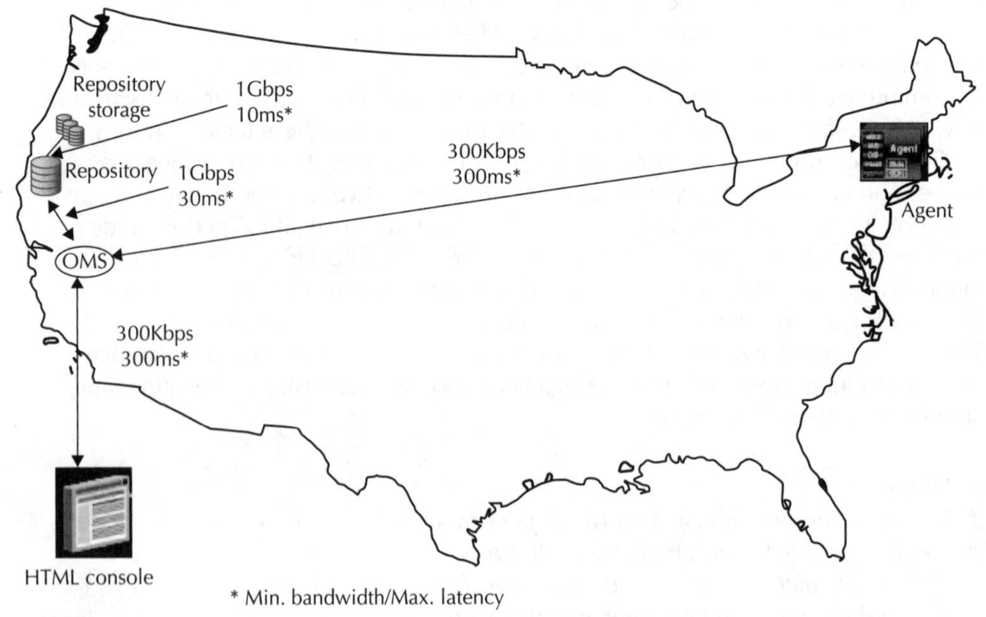

FIGURE 2-1. *Bandwidth and latency specifications between Cloud Control tiers*

Communication Between CC Components	Minimum Bandwidth Required	Maximum Latency Allowed
Console Client <-> OMS	300Kbps	300ms
OMA <-> OMS	300Kbps	300ms
OMS <-> OMR	1Gbps	30ms
OMR <-> OMR Storage	1Gbps	10ms

TABLE 2-1. *Minimum Network Requirements Between Cloud Control Components*

OMS and OMR hosts should perform well if they're on the same GigE LAN. But can you meet Cloud Control network requirements (particularly between OMS and OMR) when using multiple OMSs geographically separated and connected over a Wide Area Network (WAN)? Companies with computing resources located around the country (or even around the world) rely on a private or the public WAN to connect LANs at remote office locations. You cannot guarantee network performance over a public WAN, but to establish whether a private WAN is fast enough to support the OMS locations you are contemplating, let's look briefly at typical WAN speeds. How do they fare in relation to CC network requirements?

WAN bandwidths vary widely by provider, depending upon the underlying device technology. Most U.S. national and international firms run over at least a DS-1 (Tier 1) or DS-3 (Tier 3) WAN. Based on the broadband transmission rates shown in Table 2-3, DS-1 at 1.544Mbps provides substantially more than the required 300Kbps minimum bandwidth for Agent/OMS and Console/OMS communications, provided at least this minimum bandwidth is dedicated to CC.

LAN Device	Bandwidth
Fast Ethernet (100base-X)	100Mbps
FDDI	100Mbps
Gigabit Ethernet (1000base-X)	1Gbps
Myrinet 2000	2Gbps
Infiniband 1X	2.5Gbps
10 Gigabit Ethernet (10Gbase-X)	10Gbps

TABLE 2-2. *LAN Bandwidths for Different LAN Devices*

WAN Connection	Transmission Speed
DS-1 (Tier1)	1.544Mbps
E-1	2.048Mbps
DS-3 (Tier 3)	44.736Mbps
OC-3	155.52Mbps
OC-12	622.08Mbps
OC-48	2.488Gbps
OC-192	9.953Gbps

TABLE 2-3. *Standard Broadband Transmission Rates*

However, not even a dedicated Tier 3 transmission speed of 44.736Mbps would be sufficient to support OMS/OMR network bandwidth requirements, which are over 22 times higher (at 1Gpbs). These requirements, which are usually for a second OMS located far from the OMR and first OMS tiers, would necessitate an OC-48 (2.488Gbps) or higher WAN connection. Such a high-speed broadband network is not uncommon anymore between regional data centers (or between primary and disaster recovery (DR) sites) using expensive leased lines. In this case, network bandwidth could be high enough for the OMR database node(s) and first OMS server to be located at one primary site, with a second active OMS server placed at another site (even the DR site, provided the 30ms latency requirement is also met).

As for CC latency requirements, WANs almost always meet the 300ms latency requirements for Agent/OMS and Console/OMS communications. Even dial-up modem users over the Internet (WAN), if there are any still out there, typically experience only 150–200ms latency. However, while corporate LANs invariably meet the 30ms OMS/OMR maximum latency, WANs may not. Companies with leased lines between data centers may meet this 30ms latency requirement, provided their facilities are located close enough to each other. The speed of light is the limiting factor in meeting a 30ms latency over thousands of miles.

So what does this all mean in terms of the fewest number of environments you can get away with for a particular CC implementation? Companies running a WAN between offices can sometimes get away with a single CC environment for nationwide coverage monitoring both production and nonproduction targets. This is because Agents and Console connections can span large distances to OMS hosts. However, these OMS hosts must be placed geographically close enough to the OMR tier to meet the networking requirements of 1Gbps bandwidth and 30ms latency.

This usually means placing one or more OMS hosts alongside the OMR tier, and if an additional active OMS host is required for scalability reasons, placing it at a remote location (perhaps at the DR data center) within 2,790 miles of the production location. Why 2,790 miles?

The speed of light is 186,000 miles per second. If the second OMS host were separated from the Repository host by 2,790 miles, it would take at least 15 milliseconds for each packet to be sent between hosts. Taking packet acknowledgment into account, the latency doubles to 30 milliseconds.

TIP
To maximize coverage of your Cloud Control environment, separate multiple OMS hosts from the OMR tier geographically, placing OMS hosts on either side of the OMR tier.

With this background, you are now ready to start sketching a picture of your proposed CC topology. You don't need to do this if your site is small and all servers will be located in the same data center. However, if there are several data centers where you might place CC hosts, you'll probably want to go through this exercise.

1. The first decision is how many Cloud Control environments are required. This depends upon whether you need to use separate CC environments to monitor production and nonproduction targets, and on your company's network performance in relation to CC network bandwidth and latency requirements.
2. For each CC environment, map out where its infrastructure and managed targets will reside geographically in the data centers.
3. For each environment, position the OMR tier and active OMS servers at the data centers where you propose to locate them. The host(s) comprising the OMR tier will be co-located and one or more active OMSs can be placed in other locations. Draw a line between each OMS and its associated OMR tier. Draw OMAs to represent where your target hosts are located and connect them to the OMS(s), either each OMA to a particular OMS (manual load balancing), or all OMAs to a server load balancer that will front-end all OMSs using geographical or round-robin load balancing.
4. Do some simple network testing of your own, using `netstat`, `ping`, and `tracert` commands, for example, to estimate the bandwidth and latency that would exist between CC components to see whether the actual network performance meets the network requirements given earlier.

Make Required CC Architectural Choices

OMR, OMS

The Cloud Control architectural choices you need to make include answering the following basic questions regarding Cloud Control topologies:

- What database architecture should you use for the Management Repository?
- What OMS architecture should you deploy?
- Should you co-locate the OMR database and OMS on the same node(s), when OMR and OMS are in the same physical location?

Tackling these questions requires an understanding of the possible CC architectural topologies. We offer a concrete rationale to help you decide on the right topology for your CC environment.

The following table summarizes the answers to the preceding three questions, as to the various OMS and OMR database configurations recommended for small, medium, or large production CC sites, as defined in the Cloud Control documentation by the number of targets, Agents, and Concurrent User Sessions. For each size CC site, the table lists the number of active (see the explanation of Active/Passive after the table) OMR and OMS servers, and total number of servers needed to accommodate them, taking into account whether the OMR and OMS can be co-located on the same server. For all topologies, it is assumed that if you need HA for the OMR database tier, you also need HA for the OMS tier, as both the OMR and OMS must be running for CC to remain operational.

Size of CC Site	Number of Active OMR Nodes	Number of Active OMS Servers	Locate OMR and OMS on Same Host	Total Number of Servers Needed for OMR and OMS
Small <1,000 targets, <100 Agents, <10 Concurrent User Sessions	1 (2-node RAC if HA is required)	1 (2 if HA is required)	Yes	1 (2 if HA is required)
Medium 1,000–10,000 targets, 100–1,000 Agents, 10–25 Concurrent User Sessions	2-node RAC	2	No	4
Large >10,000 targets, >1,000 Agents, >25 Concurrent User Sessions	2-node RAC	3 or more	No	5 or more

The OMR and OMS tiers can be configured as Active/Active or Active/Passive:

- **Active/Active** Active/Active RAC database nodes operate independently and concurrently to process Repository transactions, and Active/Active OMS tiers do the same for Agent uploads and Console requests. An Active/Active configuration for both tiers is a high availability best practice. Active/Active OMS tiers can be individually configured to process uploads from specific Agents (usually based on geographical proximity between OMS and Agent), or all OMS hosts can be pooled to process all Agent uploads via a server load balancer that front-ends the OMS "service."
- **Active/Passive** Active/Passive OMR nodes and Active/Passive OMS nodes are either in a Cold Failover Cluster (CFC) configuration or, in the case of OMR nodes, an Oracle RAC One-Node (ORON) configuration. Only one OMR node and one OMS node are active at any one time. If you're considering configuring the OMR database and/or OMS in an Active/Passive topology, you must follow special installation procedures to concurrently install initial and secondary OMR/OMS nodes. An Active/Passive CFC requires third-party cluster software and shared storage, most commonly NFS, for the OMR database files and OMS home. An Active/Passive OMR setup using ORON requires separate Oracle licensing.

The following section provides an explanation of the reasoning behind the specifications in the preceding table, broken down by each of the three questions from the beginning of this section.

Deciding on Database Architecture for Management Repository

You can install the Management Repository in any database release and version certified for the Repository on your platform, though we suggest using the latest, which is the most recent patch set of Database 11*g*R2. The database architecture depends on high availability requirements and the expected size of the CC site. There are two main database architectural choices: one database instance or multiple database instances. If you need high availability for the OMR (regardless of CC site size), or for medium or large CC sites (that is, more than 1,000 targets), use multiple database instances. Otherwise, just one database instance should suffice.

- **Single database instance** There are several types of database architectures with just one database instance:
  - **Standalone database** A standalone (or single-instance) database instance can be used, with database files located on flat file storage.
  - **Oracle Restart database** A Grid Infrastructure (GI) standalone (or "Oracle Restart") database is an 11*g* Database feature, used only in standalone server (nonclustered) environments. The GI automatically restarts Oracle database-related components (database instance, service, listener, and ASM instance)

after a hardware or software failure, or whenever the database host computer restarts. As far as its application in a CC environment, Oracle Restart, while useful in ensuring all Oracle database-related processes remain running, cannot be considered an HA solution, because there is only one database instance. Therefore, an Oracle Restart database should be treated like a standalone database when it comes to CC sizing and HA requirements.

- **Multiple database instances** Multiple database instances for the Repository allow for a varying degree of HA, depending on whether they employ an Active/Active or Active/Passive architecture. There are three types of architectures for multiple database instances:
  - **RAC database** As the only Active/Active Oracle database architecture, a RAC database is needed even for small sites if they require HA. A two-node RAC database should scale out for bigger (medium and large) CC installations to handle the Repository load, with one qualification. For small-sized CC sites, each of the two OMR RAC database nodes can also accommodate an OMS, whereas for medium or large sites, the nodes should be dedicated just to the Repository.
  - **Standalone database in CFC** A Cold Failover Cluster (CFC) database configuration is an Active/Passive third-party (that is, non-Oracle) hardware solution that allows for Repository HA by relocating an active standalone database on a failed node to another cluster node where the database was running in passive mode. The two nodes must have the same virtual host name and shared storage for the database files. (See My Oracle Support MOS ID 405979.1 for more information on configuring the Management Repository in CFC environments. Though this document says it applies to GC 10*g* and 11*g*, it is equally applicable to CC 12*c*.)
  - **Oracle RAC One-Node (ORON) database** An Oracle RAC One-Node (ORON) database is an Oracle 11*g* licensed[1] feature intended as an all-Oracle alternative Active/Passive technology to compete with CFC third-party hardware-based solutions. ORON provides a single-instance 11*g* Database with a second node configured in cold failover mode. Though it contains the name "RAC", Oracle RAC One-Node is not an Active/Active database architecture, as only one database instance is active at any given time. As far as the Repository database is concerned, ORON is an equivalent HA solution to CFC, though its configuration is different. Consult the Oracle database documentation for how to set up ORON.

For a more in-depth description of these database high availability architectures, consult Section 7.1 of the *Oracle Database High Availability Overview* 11*g* Release 2 (11.2), and see Section 7.2 for help choosing the most appropriate high availability architecture for your CC system.

---

[1] Currently, ORON Perpetual licensing at $10K per Processor is less than half the price of Oracle RAC at $23K per Processor.

Deciding on OMS Architecture

If high availability is needed for the OMS layer, you have several options, depending on the HA needs of the CC system being built ("tier" is used rather than "node" to indicate that the OMS and OMR database may be co-located on a particular node):

- **Single OMS tier** A single OMS tier may suffice, if the CC environment is small (fewer than 1,000 targets) and HA is not needed at the OMS layer.
- **Multiple OMS tiers** If HA is required for the OMS, you need to decide how many OMS tiers are called for, whether they should be placed in an Active/Active or Active/Passive configuration, and where to locate these tiers geographically.
    - For HA at small sites, two OMS tiers are needed, either in an Active/Active or Active/Passive configuration. (Two tiers are needed for HA, and one tier can be passive because small sites don't require additional tiers to handle the load.) For medium and large CC sites, two Active/Active OMS tiers are usually sufficient for scalability purposes. If you need multiple Active/Active OMSs at a medium or large site, but also typically use Active/Passive CFC technology, you can use an Active/Passive configuration for each active OMS. If the active OMSs are geographically separated, a CFC for each active OMS is somewhat redundant (given that active OMSs provide HA themselves), but a CFC will provide local HA capability not afforded by distant, active OMSs.
    - Multiple OMSs may be required for a combination of reasons, including scalability, HA, and geographical coverage to process Agent uploads within network specifications. These specifications for Agent to OMS communication, as listed earlier, are a minimum bandwidth of 300Kbs, and a maximum latency of 300ms.
    - You can run either a Passive or Active OMS from a DR location.
        - You can configure a standby OMS host at a DR location, and leave it down but ready for service to connect to a standby Repository in case of failover.
        - However, you can also run an active OMS (or both an Active and Passive OMS) at a DR location, although you may run one or more other applications in a passive configuration at this DR location. You might decide that an OMS at a DR location should service all administrator and Agent connections on managed targets at the DR center or geographically closer to it than to the production data center, rather than using a server load balancer (SLB) to load-balance these connections to both OMS hosts. Alternatively, you may be able to configure "geographical load balancing" on the SLB to provide the affinity logic for Agents to upload to their local OMS, unless that OMS is down. You will need to determine whether network performance (bandwidth and latency) between primary and DR data centers is fast enough to place an active OMS at each location.

Deciding Whether to Co-locate the OMR Database and OMS

After choosing individual OMR database and OMS architectures, you need to decide whether to install an OMS on the same node as a Repository database instance. There are many variations to this, because the Repository database can be single or multiple instances and you can have one or more OMS tiers. The two major variations are as follows:

- **Install OMS and OMR on separate hosts** Install an OMS on one node, and OMR database on other node(s). This is the appropriate configuration for medium (that is, consisting of more than 1,000 targets) and large CC production environments.
- **Install OMR and OMS on the same node(s)** You can install the OMS and OMR on the same nodes, whether one node, or multiple nodes for HA and/or scalability purposes.
- **Install the OMR and OMS on one host** This option, to place a single OMS on the same host as that running an existing single-instance OMR database, is appropriate for small CC installations of fewer than 1,000 targets that do not require HA.
- **Install OMS and OMR on multiple nodes** Placing the OMS tiers on OMR RAC nodes is a supported configuration in CC 12*c*, appropriate for small CC environments. However, in medium or large CC environments, the danger of this shared topology is that the nodes will not have enough resources for both the OMR and OMS, especially during periods of peak loading. For this reason, at medium or large CC production sites, OMS tiers should be placed on dedicated nodes separate from the OMR database nodes. Following are details on each of these conditions:

TIP

A shared configuration may be a good alternative for large nonproduction environments where server real estate is tight (usually for budgetary reasons), but you want to run a RAC database and multiple OMSs—not necessarily for high availability reasons, but to logically mirror the architecture of a production system.

- **If both the OMR and OMS are certified on your platform** To run on the Repository database server, the OMS must be certified on that server platform. The Repository is certified on certain versions of Database 11gR2, 11gR1, and 10gR2, which, in turn, are certified on certain platforms. The OMS is currently certified on a subset of these database platforms, including UNIX-based 32-bit and 64-bit operating systems. However, the OMS is not currently certified on some platforms for which the OMR database is certified, including Windows 32-bit, and some UNIX 64-bit (including HP-UX and IBM Linux on System z). See the section "Verify Certification Information" later in this chapter for all OMS certified platforms.

- **If the host meets combined OMR and OMS hardware requirements** If OMR and OMS components reside on the same nodes, they must meet the combined hardware requirements for these components on each node, as covered later in this chapter.

  If your CC servers do not meet both of these conditions, plan to install the OMS on different nodes than those for the OMR database.

There you have it. At this point, hopefully you've earmarked whether you're installing separate production and nonproduction CC environments, how many servers you need for the CC installation, and which component topology you will select. Now, let's cover all network configuration, hardware, and software requirements in detail.

Network Configuration Steps

The network configuration steps for Cloud Control involve setting up host name resolution, adhering to certain host naming rules and constraints, using a static IP address for all CC hosts, and confirming connectivity, most importantly between CC hosts. If you abide by the rules described in this section, you will avoid possible problems at installation time, and even more painfully, down the road. While it is not very difficult to deinstall and reinstall CC or any of its components after a failed installation, the cost of doing so rises exponentially once you start using and relying upon the product for your monitoring solution.

NOTE
This heading is so named to distinguish it from the network performance *requirements between CC tiers as covered earlier. Where possible, we distinguish network requirements from recommendations by using words like "must" rather than "should," for instance. However, we suggest adopting all recommendations to maximize your chances of CC installation and operational success.*

You may be questioning why we place CC network configuration steps ahead of all other requirements. The main reason for getting these network steps out of the way now is that it may take some time for your network administrator to make the changes, such as fully qualifying the host name or ensuring that it is registered properly in the Domain Name System (DNS). Your company may have host naming standards that conflict with those presented here, and these conflicts may take time to resolve. At larger corporations, even the simplest network changes can take considerable time to approve and implement, because of their possible ramifications for other applications.

NOTE
One of those network changes to request from your network administrator is to open the necessary firewall ports between hosts to contain CC components. For information on firewall configuration requirements, see Chapter 10 of the Oracle Enterprise Manager Cloud Control Advanced Installation and Configuration Guide*, 12*c *Release 2 (12.1.0.2).*

Set Up Host Name Resolution

OMR, OMS, OMA

The Cloud Control Installer will fail, as will Agent installation, if you do not first configure name resolution on hosts where OMR or OMS components are to be installed. You can set up host names to resolve through the Domain Name System (DNS) through the local hosts file on the server, or both, and set the priority of resolution. Host name resolution is more scalable and centrally manageable via DNS. While resolution via a local hosts file averts a DNS lookup and dependence on DNS, if a CC server's IP address ever needed to be changed, you would need to update the hosts file on every server that contained an entry for that CC server.

NOTE
In this section and throughout the book, the term "local hosts file" or "hosts file" is used to signify /etc/hosts on UNIX and C:\WINDOWS\system32\drivers\etc\hosts on Windows.

On UNIX, to determine whether DNS and/or the local hosts file is used for name resolution, and the order of priority for name resolution, check the "hosts" entry in the /etc/nsswitch.conf file as follows:

```
grep -i hosts /etc/nsswitch.conf
```

The hosts file takes precedence over DNS if the output of this command contains "files" before "dns", similar to the following:

```
hosts: files   dns
```

Conversely, DNS takes precedence over the hosts file if the output from the preceding command contains "dns" before "files".

If the hosts file is configured to take precedence (or is used as DNS backup), verify that it contains at least two entries: one for the localhost loopback address, which should be present irrespective of the resolution method(s) used, and one or more for the IP address to host name mapping for the local host itself and all hosts running CC components, including Agents. For example, the hosts file must contain at least the following two lines:

```
127.0.0.1 localhost localhost.<localdomain>
<IP address>      <hostname>.<domain>      <hostname>      <alias>
```

The localhost entry is a loopback address, and the first alias for it, "localhost," should not be fully qualified.

If DNS is used for name resolution, regardless of its priority, ensure that you configure both forward and reverse DNS for each host name running a CC component (see the section "Fully Qualify the DNS Lookup" later in this chapter).

Fully Qualify Host Name References

OMR, OMS, OMA

OMR and OMS host names, and target hosts running standalone Agents, should be consistently fully qualified wherever they are referenced. A fully qualified host name contains the short host name and domain name (such as omshost.ndbas.com) as opposed to just the short host name (omshost). Host names are populated in CC configuration files, and using a mixture of fully qualified and not fully qualified host names can cause unexpected results, such as CC installation errors and CC Console browser pages not found. Not using the fully qualified host name can also cause confusion in that each host across your enterprise may not be uniquely identified by just its short host name. That said, Cloud Control assigns unique names to each target in the Agent's targets.xml file, even host targets with the same short name and that are not fully qualified.

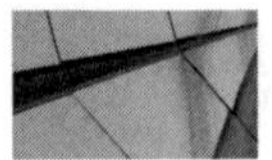

NOTE
Throughout this book, fully qualified host names are used in all explanations and examples.

The main places where host name references ought to be fully qualified are as follows (perform all checks on the local host for itself):

- In the `hostname` command output
- In the local hosts file
- In the DNS

Let's look at each of these host name settings in particular.

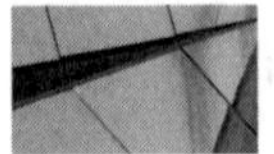

TIP
If your company's network policy is not to use the fully qualified host name everywhere, at least try to be consistent in not using it anywhere (that is, use the short host name) in your CC environment. This may not be possible, though, as a DNS usually returns the fully qualified host name, whereas network policy or other application requirements may dictate returning a short name in the `hostname` *output and/or using the short name as the first alias in the local hosts file. Perhaps you can lobby to change such an inconsistent network policy.*

Fully Qualify the `hostname` Command

Many UNIX networking programs use the `hostname` command to identify the machine. Verify that the `hostname` command returns the fully qualified host name, as follows:

```
hostname
<hostname>.<domainname>
```

On UNIX only, verify that the domain name has not been set dynamically by executing the following command, which displays the name of the Network Information Service (NIS) domain:

```
domainname
```

Verify that no results are returned—the `hostname` command should statically supply both host name and domain name.

If the `hostname` output is not fully qualified for the OMS or OMR hosts, you can both temporarily and permanently change the host name to the fully qualified name, provided your company network policy allows it. To change a host name on UNIX and Windows, you must have root and Administrator privileges, respectively. Temporarily changing the host name avoids your having to restart the network or reboot the server just to change its host name, if required for the change to take effect. You can temporarily change a UNIX host name by issuing the following command as *root*:

```
hostname <hostname>.<domainname>
```

You can then make this change permanent so that it persists across reboot. On Red Hat Linux and Red Hat Enterprise Linux–based systems (including Oracle Linux and Asianux),[2] change the HOSTNAME setting in the file /etc/sysconfig/network. Naturally, do not temporarily change the host name unless you also plan to permanently change it; a temporary host name change would revert to the original name after reboot, which would be out of sync with the host name stored in the CC configuration files if CC were installed after temporarily changing the host name and before the reboot.

Fully Qualify the First Alias in a hosts File

As already mentioned, if a server uses a local hosts file for name resolution (even as a backup method behind DNS), this file should include at least the following two lines:

```
127.0.0.1 localhost localhost.<localdomain>
<DNS IP address>     <hostname>.<domainname>     <hostname>
```

As for the host name, the first alias (after the IP address) should be fully qualified. For example, on a UNIX host named omshost.ndbas.com, the following two lines should be listed in /etc/hosts:[3]

```
127.0.0.1 localhost localhost.ndbas.com
138.2.4.84 omshost.ndbas.com omshost
```

---

[2] For a comprehensive list of Linux distributions, organized by the major distribution or package management system on which they are based, see http://en.wikipedia.org/wiki/List_of_Linux_distributions.

[3] For RAC database nodes, whether for a target or a Repository, in addition to the public IP address entry, you must also include entries for private and VIP addresses. See the Oracle Clusterware documentation for details.

Fully Qualify the DNS Lookup

If a CC host relies upon DNS for name resolution, even as a backup method to a local hosts file, a forward or reverse name server lookup (`nslookup`) of the short name, fully qualified host name, and IP address of a CC host should return the fully qualified host name. Try the following commands on each host running a CC component (OMS, OMR, or OMA), substituting the host name on which you are executing the commands:

```
nslookup
<hostname>.<domainname>
<hostname>
<IP address>
```

Following is the command output from a forward and reverse `nslookup` of the host name omshost.ndbas.com (input is in **bold**):

```
$ nslookup
> omshost.ndbas.com
Server:          138.2.203.16
Address:         138.2.203.16#53

Name:    omshost.ndbas.com
Address: 138.2.4.84
> omshost
Server:          138.2.203.16
Address:         138.2.203.16#53

Name:    omshost.ndbas.com
Address: 138.2.4.84
> 138.2.4.84
Server:          138.2.203.16
Address:         138.2.203.16#53

84.4.2.138.in-addr.arpa name = omshost.ndbas.com.
```

Host Name Constraints

OMR, OMS, OMA

The host names where CC components are installed must adhere to certain naming rules that vary depending upon the component:

- OMR, OMS, and OMA host names cannot be localhost, localhost.localdomain, or an IP address, but must be valid host names. A valid host name is one listed in the local hosts file, or for a virtual host name as discussed next.

- You can use a virtual host name for OMA, OMR, or OMS hosts running in a Cold Failover Cluster (CFC) system. A virtual host name is anything other than the physical host name of the server, as indicated by the `hostname` command output. To use a virtual host name, you need to specify the ORACLE_HOSTNAME argument when running the Cloud Control installer, as covered in Chapter 4 in the section "Choose Desired Installer Options."
- An OMA or OMR host can have multiple aliases registered with the DNS under a single IP address. If this is the case, set the ORACLE_HOSTNAME argument to the alias you want to use as the host name.
- An OMR, OMS, or OMA host can be multihomed, meaning that it can contain multiple network (NIC) cards, each with its own IP address and host name. If you don't specify ORACLE_HOSTNAME as an argument to an OMS or standalone OMA installation using the OUI on a host with multiple NIC cards, then the OUI assigns the first multihomed entry in the hosts file as the host name. (An OMR host can also be multihomed, but the ORACLE_HOSTNAME argument is not used to specify the OMR host name; instead, the first multihomed entry in the hosts file is used.)

Use Static IP Addresses

OMR, OMS, OMA

The hosts on which you are installing the OMR, OMS, and OMA must have unique static IP addresses, not Dynamic Host Configuration Protocol (DHCP) assigned addresses.

Connectivity Checks

OMR, OMS, OMA (vary by subheading)

Perform the following tests to test connectivity to the SMTP server, the Internet, and a proxy server, if used. Also check connectivity to My Oracle Support and check the account credentials Cloud Control will use to download patches and patch information.

SMTP Server Connectivity

OMS, OMA

As part of the configuration process after installing Cloud Control, you will be specifying one or more Outgoing Mail (SMTP) Server names (hereafter referred to in the singular) and Sender's E-mail address for the OMS to send alert notifications to administrators. It is best to confirm SMTP server connectivity up front, before installing Cloud Control, to allow time for troubleshooting in case of connectivity problems from CC hosts to the SMTP server.

Test SMTP Server Connectivity After CC installation and configuring e-mail notifications for alerts, if the SMTP server you specify is not reachable from the OMS host(s), notifications, whether out-of-box or custom, will not be received. For this reason, it is wise to confirm before installing CC that all OMS hosts can reach the SMTP server.

In addition, it is important that the OMS and Agent hosts be able to send an Out of Bound (OOB) notification through the SMTP server. An *OOB notification* is an SOS call sent directly through an SMTP server (not through the OMS application) to a designated e-mail address to relay that no OMS services are online to receive Agent alerts or data uploads (though the OMS host itself may be up). After installing Cloud Control, you can configure OOB notifications as instructed in Chapter 8 under "Out Of Bound (OOB) E-mail Notification."

To ensure that the OMS and OMA hosts will be able to send regular and OOB notifications, make sure now that they can reach (that is, ping) the SMTP server:

```
ping -c 4 <SMTP_Server>
```

Create and Test an Originating E-mail Address for Notifications After installation, you will need to specify a valid originating (that is, "From") e-mail address for Cloud Control that your company SMTP server must recognize to relay outgoing notifications to administrators. This e-mail address should ideally be a generic CC application account, such as oraoem@ndbas.com. Using a particular CC administrator's named e-mail address is less desirable, as it will more likely require periodically changing the username (for example, if the employee leaves the company) or password (according to your company's security policy for named users).

While a CC Sender's E-mail address is required for *outbound* alert notifications, this e-mail account has at least three additional optional uses as an *inbound* e-mail account:

- **A generic Oracle.com account specified in the CC Installer** The CC Installer prompts in the first screen to optionally enter an e-mail address for a MOS username to inform you of security issues and initiate Oracle Configuration Manager (OCM). If you provide a password for the e-mail address, MOS will e-mail security updates to it. Consider using a generic address such as a Distribution List (DL) whose members hold key Oracle roles at your company. Such an address, not belonging to any particular employee, can be perpetually used by whoever holds a particular Oracle IT "office" at the time, such as Cloud Control Administrator, Oracle Team Lead, or MOS Company Administrator.

- **An incoming address for a CC administrator account** You may want to associate this e-mail address with a system-type CC administrator account for receiving notifications, such as the built-in SYSMAN user or a generic username you create, such as OEM_SUPER. This setup can be useful in several ways, such as for specifying an e-mail distribution list (DL) to notify multiple CC administrators on the same CC alerts, or for logging all notifications received, for historical or reference purposes.
- **A designated address for receiving Out of Bound (OOB) notifications** As mentioned earlier in the section "Test SMTP Server Connectivity," OOB notifications report that no OMS hosts are online, as relayed independently of the CC engine from OMS or Agent hosts. You do this by specifying an e-mail address and SMTP server in the OMS or Agent properties files.[4]

TIP
Put in a request now for a new Cloud Control corporate e-mail address to relay notifications. It can take time for corporate IT security to approve such a system-level application e-mail account, and for an e-mail administrator to create and configure it, especially if they need to grant named users access to it.

After an originating CC e-mail address is created on the corporate SMTP server, you can test whether hosts on which you intend to run the OMS can relay e-mail from this address to the SMTP server. On each host where you plan to install an OMS, try to telnet at the command line to the SMTP host on the telnet port (port 25 by default). Following is the output from such a telnet session on the host omshost. In this session, we send a test e-mail from sender oraoem@ndbas.com to the same e-mail address, to also test its use as an incoming address for any of the three additional reasons listed earlier. (You can also send a test e-mail to your own corporate e-mail address.) Input commands are shown in **bold**:

```
$ telnet mail.ndbas.com 25
Trying 138.1.161.138...
Connected to bigip-mail.ndbas.com (138.1.161.138).
Escape character is '^]'.
220 rgmsgw02.ndbas.com ESMTP Mycorp Corporation Secure SMTP Gateway
```

[4] Again, see "Out Of Bound (OOB) E-mail Notification" in Chapter 8, once Cloud Control is installed.

```
Switch-3.1.7/Switch-3.1.7 - Ready at Wed, 3 Apr 2013 11:43:43 -0600 -
Unauthorized Usage Prohibited.
helo
250 rgmsgw02.ndbas.com Hello omshost.ndbas.com [138.2.4.61], pleased to
meet you
mail from: oraoem@ndbas.com
250 2.1.0 oraoem@ndbas.com... Sender ok
rcpt to: oraoem@ndbas.com
250 2.1.5 oraoem@ndbas.com... Recipient ok
data
354 Enter mail, end with "." on a line by itself
Subject: SMTP Test
Hello this is an SMTP test for Cloud Control
.
250 2.0.0 k35HhhOm026568 Message accepted for delivery
quit
221 2.0.0 rgmsgw02.ndbas.com closing connection
Connection closed by foreign host.
```

If you have access to this CC e-mail address, oraoem@ndbas.com, also confirm that you receive the test e-mail in a timely manner.

Connectivity to My Oracle Support

OMS

The OMS must be able to connect to the My Oracle Support Web site at http://support.oracle.com in order to locate and download patches, receive critical security updates, and the like. Open a browser session from the OMS via an X Windows connection, and confirm Internet access to the MOS URL. If the OMS must go through a proxy server to reach the Internet, this test confirms that the browser's proxy server information is correct. Also verify the MOS credentials that the OMS will use for patch-related functionality. As recommended previously, you can use the same e-mail address for the MOS username as for the sender of CC notifications, or create a new MOS username for Cloud Control to use exclusively.

If you cannot install and run a browser on the OMS itself to check MOS connectivity and credentials, at least check that the OMS can access MOS by pinging the URL for downloading updates:

```
ping updates.oracle.com
```

Be aware that this ping will fail if your network administrator disabled ping access from inside the firewall to external sites.

Connectivity Between All CC Hosts

OMR, OMS, OMA

The OMS needs to be able to communicate in both directions with the OMR host via JDBC, and with Agent hosts via HTTP and HTTPS. If a firewall separates the OMS from the OMR hosts or, more likely, if a firewall separates the OMS from the Agent hosts, check that your company's proxy server is configured as required to allow communications between these CC components. First, from the OMS host, ping the proxy server between OMS and OMR node(s), if one exists:

```
ping <proxy_server>
```

Second, from the OMS, ping the OMR and Agent hosts to confirm that they are reachable. Also ping in the reverse direction from the OMR to the OMS hosts, and from the Agent hosts to OMS hosts. Specify fully qualified host names when executing all `ping` commands.

Hardware Requirements

OMR, OMS

Hardware requirements for *installing* Cloud Control versus *operating* Cloud Control for a typical production system can be vastly different. This section covers hardware operating requirements, which encompass those for installation. It seems shortsighted to focus only on hardware installation requirements, when more stringent hardware operating requirements must be met in order to use Cloud Control.

The CC Installer Prereqchecker confirms that your system possesses the minimum hardware resources to install CC. Resources checked include CPU, RAM, and disk space. Neither the Oracle CC Prereqchecker nor associated documentation distinguishes between installation and operating requirements. However, the prerequisite checks really just verify minimum requirements to avoid causing the installation to fail. These checks cannot guarantee that such hardware has enough horsepower to go live with a CC production environment supporting all your managed targets for at least the short term. Therefore, the minimum operating (rather than just installation) requirements are provided here.

If your production Cloud Control environment requires high availability (HA), then you need to design and build in fault-tolerant storage up front for all CC framework components—Management Repository database and software, OMS software, and Agent software. The topic of fault-tolerant storage falls outside the scope of this book. However, you'll find an excellent treatment on best practices for configuring HA storage in Oracle Database High Availability Best Practices, for both Oracle 10*g* Release 2 (10.2) and 11*g* Release 2. These documents identify the following six elements of a fault-tolerant database storage subsystem,[5] but the last three of these elements apply equally to storage for all CC framework components (Repository database, OMS, and Agent), as indicated in the following table:

Element of Fault-Tolerant Storage	Release/Section in Oracle Database HA Best Practices 11.2	Release/Section in Oracle Database HA Best Practices 10.2	Applies To
Evaluate database performance and storage capacity capabilities	Section 4.1	Section 2.1.1	OMR database
Use Automatic Storage Management (ASM) to manage database files	Section 4.2	Section 2.1.2	OMR database
Use a simple disk and disk group configuration	Section 4.3.1	Section 2.1.3	OMR database
Use disk multipathing software to protect from path failure	Section 4.4.1	Section 2.1.4	OMR database, OMS, Agent
Use redundancy to protect from disk failure	Section 4.3.2	Section 2.1.5	OMR database, OMS, Agent
Consider Hardware Assisted Resilient Data (HARD)–compliant storage	Not covered	Section 2.1.6	OMR database, OMS, Agent

Tables 2-4 and 2-5 present a summary of the hardware operating requirements for each OMR host (Table 2-4) and OMS host (Table 2-5), including number of CPUs,[6] RAM, total disk space, temporary disk space, and swap space that Cloud Control needs in a typical production environment to sustain your current IT environment. All requirements are per host, assuming that the OMR and OMS

[5] Only the Oracle Database HA Best Practices for Oracle 10.2 has a write-up on HARD-compliant storage, as reflected in the table.

[6] Expect diminishing performance returns from OMR or OMS hosts running multicore microprocessors. In other words, don't expect double the performance from a dual-core device over a single-core processor.

Deployment Size	Number of OMR Hosts	CPU Cores/ Host (speed)	Physical RAM	Total Disk Space	Temporary Disk Space	Swap Space (UNIX Only)
Small <1,000 targets, <100 Agents, <10 Concurrent User Sessions	2-node RAC if HA is required	2 (3GHz)	8GB	100GB	2GB	4GB
Medium 1,000–10,000 targets, 100–1,000 Agents, 10–25 Concurrent User Sessions	2-node RAC	4 (3GHz)	16GB	400GB	2GB	8GB
Large >10,000 targets, >1,000 Agents, >25 Concurrent User Sessions	2-node RAC	8 (3GHz)	32GB	800GB	2GB	16GB

TABLE 2-4. *Hardware Operating Requirements per Host Dedicated to the OMR*

components reside on different hosts, and that the OMS hosts are in an Active/Active configuration. (The number of recommended hosts for each component, which was listed in an earlier table, is provided again for your convenience.)

NOTE
Again, these requirements assume that the OMR and OMS components reside on different hosts, and are in an Active/Active configuration. However, if these components reside on the same host, which is acceptable for small deployments the combined OMR/OMS requirements are additive.

Deployment Size	Number of Active OMS Hosts	CPU Cores/Host (speed)	Physical RAM	Total Disk Space	Temporary Disk Space	Swap Space (UNIX Only)
Small <1,000 targets, <100 Agents, <10 Concurrent User Sessions	1 (2 if HA is required)	2 (3GHz)	8GB	20GB	256MB	512MB
Medium 1,000–10,000 targets, 100–1,000 Agents, 10–25 Concurrent User Sessions	2	4 (3GHz)	16GB	40GB	256MB	512MB
Large >10,000 targets, >1,000 Agents, >25 Concurrent User Sessions	3 or more	8 (3GHz)	32GB	60GB	256MB	512MB

TABLE 2-5. *Hardware Operating Requirements per Host Dedicated to the OMS*

The range of values correlates with the deployment size (that is, number of targets, Agents, and concurrent user sessions) and, for some hardware resources,[7] significantly exceeds the minimum installation hardware requirements specified in Chapter 2 of *Oracle Enterprise Manager Cloud Control Basic Installation Guide*.

[7] The disk space allotments in particular, for both OMR and OMS, are generous compared with those specified in the Oracle EM documentation, and allow for growth over a system's lifetime. The OMR disk space is sized to handle expected log and trace files, growth in the OMR database tables, and a Fast Recovery Area large enough to hold two days of on-disk RMAN datafile backups and archive logs, a block change tracking file, and 48 hours of flashback data. (Chapter 3 details the OMR database configuration.) The OMS disk space is two to three times that recommended in the EM documentation, based on real-world experience. It allows for centralized storage of patches, preferably on a shared drive accessible by all OMS hosts. This permits administrators to deploy patches when logged in to the Console via any OMS.

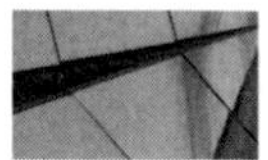

NOTE
All Guides from the the Cloud Control doc set that are referenced in this book are for Release 2 (12.1.0.2), the latest release available at the time of this writing. We refer to Oracle guides in shorthand using the middle part of the actual name of the guide, for example (shown here in bold): "Oracle Enterprise Manager **Cloud Control Basic Installation Guide** *12c Release 2 [12.1.0.2])."*

Table 2-6 lists the commands to check CPU, RAM, swap space, disk space, and temporary disk space requirements for all operating systems currently supported,

	AIX	HP-UX	Linux	Solaris	Windows 7, 2008
Number (speed) of CPUs[8]	`lscfg`[9] `| grep 'proc[0-9]' | awk 'END {print NR}'` `top`	`ioscan -C processor`	`cat /proc/cpuinfo`	`prtconf -v | head`	Right-click Computer Name and select Properties. Environment variable NUMBER_OF_PROCESSORS. WMIC CPU Get NumberOfCores,NumberOfLogicalProcessors /Format:List
Physical RAM	`bootinfo -r` `lsattr -EHl <resource_name> such as mem0`	`grep "Physical:" /var/adm/syslog/syslog.log`	`grep MemTotal /proc/meminfo`	`/usr/sbin/prtconf | grep "Memory size"`	Right-click Computer Name and select Properties.
Swap Space	`swap -s` `lsps -a (for paging info)`	`/usr/sbin/swapinfo -a`	`grep SwapTotal /proc/meminfo`	`/usr/sbin/swap -s`	Right-click Computer Name, select Properties, and then Advanced system settings. Under Performance, click Settings, which brings up Performance Options. On the Advanced tab under Virtual memory, Total paging file size for all drives is listed.
Total Disk Space	`df -h`	`bdf -h`	`df -h`	`df -h`	Right-click on the local disk where CC software will be installed and select Properties.
Temporary Disk Space[10]	`df /tmp`	`bdf /tmp`	`df /tmp`	`df /tmp`	Defaults to C:\Documents and Settings\<*user id*>\Local Settings\Temp. Right-click on drive and select Properties.

[8] For existing databases, you can also look at the initialization parameter CPU_COUNT, which Oracle automatically determines. However, this parameter is not always accurate, as dual and higher CPUs may not be accounted for.
[9] `lscfg` is included in the AIX package called Monitor.
[10] You can supersede the default temporary directory using environment variables TEMP and TMP (set both to be certain).

TABLE 2-6. *Commands to Check Hardware Requirements on All Certified Platforms*

and HP-UX whose certification is, hopefully, forthcoming, for the sake of those Oracle HP-UX-based shops out there.

It is highly recommended to run the OMR on a 64-bit platform. On a host dedicated to an Oracle database, such as the CC Management Repository, 75 percent of the RAM is usually assigned to the Oracle System Global Area (SGA). So for a Small CC site running an OMR on a host with 8GB of RAM, an SGA as large as 6GB could be used. On 32-bit platforms, attaining an SGA above 4GB usually involves implementing the Very Large Memory (VLM) option for that platform. The VLM option introduces complications of its own on all 32-bit platforms. By contrast, if you run the OMR on a 64-bit platform that natively supports large SGAs, you avoid these VLM complications. (Linux 64-bit platforms require implementing HugePages, a VLM option that measurably improves performance.) Also, memory performance on 64-bit platforms is far superior to that of 32-bit platforms running VLM, not to mention the superior performance that 64-bit platforms afford in many other regards.

Software Requirements

This section details the following software requirements for OMR, OMS, and standalone OMA hosts:

- Download and stage Cloud Control and related software
- Verify certification information
- Create required OS groups and users
- Create required directories
- Synchronize OS timestamps/time zones
- Confirm platform-specific software requirements

All supported CC platforms must meet these generic prerequisites (all requirements except platform-specific ones). Such requirements include creating the requisite OS groups, users, and directories that the CC Installer needs.

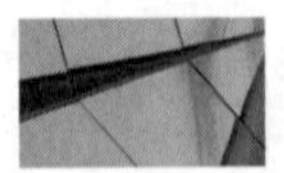

NOTE
Software requirements are defined here much more broadly than in the CC installation guide, limiting them to Oracle software that CC depends upon, such as the Oracle database software required for the OMR. In this section, software requirements also include software configuration steps and platform-specific software requirements.

NOTE
Software requirements for the OMR database are covered in Chapter 3. However, if the OMR database will be located on the same host as the OMS, then satisfying the generic OMS software requirements, "Create Required OS Groups" and "Users and Create Required Directories," will simultaneously satisfy identical preinstallation requirements for the OMR database.

In addition to generic requirements, the section "Confirm Platform-Specific Software Requirements" at the end of this chapter points you to the CC documentation set for unique OMS and Agent package, kernel parameter, and library requirements for each platform and OS version currently certified for CC.

Download and Stage CC and Related Software

OMR, OMS, OMA

This section contains explicit instructions on downloading and staging all CC software, including that for the prerequisite database installation to contain the Repository. (Database information is provided now rather than in Chapter 3, so you can get a jumpstart in downloading the database distribution software.) It is critical to download the correct software for your CC environment, so we provide detailed instructions.

There are two online locations for obtaining the most current prerequisite database software and CC 12*c* distributions for a particular platform: from Oracle Technology Network (OTN) and MOS. The most current distributions are Full Installers of the latest patch set release. You no longer need to download and install the database or CC release first, such as Database 11.2.0.1.0, then apply the latest Patch Set, such as 11.2.0.3.0. (You could also order the respective Media Packs from the Oracle Store, but typically only the base distributions are available, which would require you to manually apply the latest Patch Sets to run the most current versions.) You will need to download the software for these products, as summarized in the following table, and as described after the table.

CC Software Component	Download from OTN	Download from MOS
Oracle Database	No	Yes
OEM Cloud Control 12*c* Full Installer with Latest Bundle Patch	Yes	No

The most direct way would be to open a browser in an X Windows session on the intended database or CC server themselves, if they have Internet access.

Alternatively, you can download the software to a PC with access to the database or CC server. If the server is a Windows platform, open Windows Explorer on your PC after downloading the software, and in the address field enter the \\<*server*>\<*share*> location where you want to copy the software. If the software will run on a UNIX-based platform, use WinSCP or some other third-party SSH tool to transfer the distribution from the PC to the UNIX-based server.

Here's the quickest way to download the 11*g* (or 10*g*) Database Server Full Installation of the latest Patch Set:

1. Open a browser and log in to MOS at http://support.oracle.com.
2. Click the Patches & Updates tab at the top of the page.
3. In the Patching Quick Links region, click Latest Patchsets under Oracle Server and Tools. (If you don't see the Patching Quick Links region, click Customize Page, drag Patching Quick Links on to the page, and click the "x" to close the Customize menu.)
4. In the new window that opens, under Patch Sets for Product Bundles, hover over Oracle database, then over the platform on which the database will run, such as Linux x86-64. The links will expand to include the Patch Set versions. Select the most current Patch Set, which at the time of this writing is 11.2.0.3.0.
5. Click the Patch number link at the bottom of the page.
6. The database distribution consists of a Multi Part Patch. Click the Download button for each file to download it.

To download the OEM CC 12*c* Full Installer software for your platform, do the following:

1. Open a browser and log in to OTN at http://www.oracle.com/technetwork/oem/enterprise-manager/downloads (referred to elsewhere as the OEM Download page). You can also hover over the Downloads tab at the top of the page and select Oracle Enterprise Manager under the Enterprise Management section.
2. Under the Enterprise Manager Base Platform section at the top of the page, select the link for the latest full installation available for your platform. The Full Installers contain the OMS, Agent, Repository, and Management plug-ins.
3. Check Accept License Agreement and download all zip files comprising the Full Installer archives, totaling about 6G in size. Unzip each file into the same staging directory (it creates its own directory structure).

See Chapter 5 for instructions on how to download and install OEM CC 12*c* Agent software for platforms other than that of the OMS. Suffice it to say for now that the Agent 12.1 binaries for other platforms are not available from OTN or MOS; you must use the Self Update feature in the Cloud Control Console.

Once you obtain the prerequisite database software and CC 12*c* software from the sources listed in the table, you can access the software via several methods, depending on whether the target system is local or remote.

If the target system is local, access the CC software directly on that system. On Windows platforms, no further action is required to run the installer locally. On UNIX-based platforms, run the installer either from an X Windows session or from a UNIX workstation.

If the target system is remote, access the CC software using remote access software. If you don't have physical access to a remote system where installing CC, but this system has a local hard drive, you can install CC using remote access software such as Microsoft's built-in Remote Desktop Connection, VNC from RealVNC Ltd., or Hummingbird Exceed. Start the remote access software on both your local computer and the remote system. and install CC in one of the following ways:

- Copy the CC software to a hard drive and install from that hard drive. To do this, share the hard drive, then using the remote access software, map a drive letter on the remote system to the shared hard drive.
- Access CC software from a DVD drive in your local computer. Copy the CC 12*c* distribution to a DVD, insert the DVD into a drive on your local computer, and share the DVD drive. Use the remote access software to map a drive letter on the remote system to the shared DVD drive. You are now set up to run the Oracle Universal Installer (OUI), as described in Chapter 4, from the shared hard drive on the remote host using the remote access software.

On most UNIX systems, a DVD disk mounts automatically when inserted into the disk drive. In case the DVD is not automatically mounted, the following table lists the command to set the mount point for each UNIX platform (execute as *root*):

AIX	**HP-UX**	**Red Hat–based Linux**	**SUSE Linux**	**Solaris**
/usr/sbin/mount -rv cdrfs *<DVD device name>* *<disk mount point directory>*	/usr/sbin/mount -F cdfs -o rr *<DVD device name>* *<disk mount point directory>*	mount -t nfs *<hostname>*:/mnt/*<DVD_path>*	mount -t nfs *<hostname>*:/media/*<DVD_path>*	/usr/sbin/mount -r -F hsfs *<DVD device name>* *<disk mount point directory>*

See the platform-specific CC documentation for more detailed instructions on mounting the product disks.

Verify Certification Information

OMR, OMS, OMA

One of the Cloud Control software preinstallation steps is to check that all components (OMS, Repository, Agents, Console) and Monitoring plug-ins are certified on the intended platforms and for applicable OS, database and browser, and third-party hardware and software versions. To verify that your intended CC environment is supported, click the Certifications tab on MOS.[11] Under the Certifications Search region, on the Search subtab, complete the following three fields:

- **Product** Select Enterprise Manager Base Platform – OMS (Cloud Control, Grid Control, Plug-in, and so on).
- **Release** Choose the latest release (for example, 12.1.0.2.0).
- **Platform** Select your platform, such as Linux x86-64 Oracle Linux 6.

Here is the search screen, using the example inputs from the preceding list:

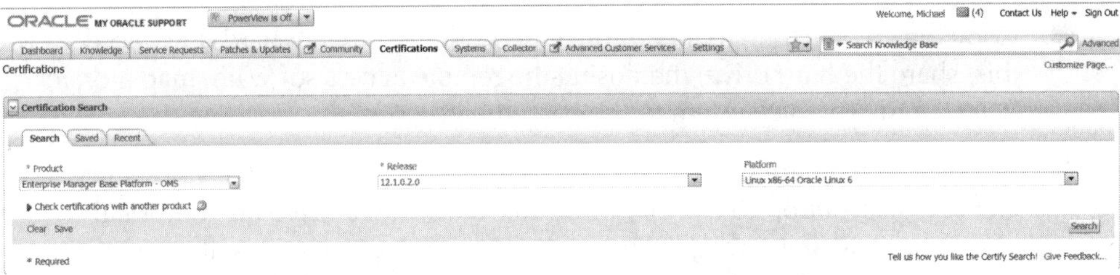

Click Search, and the following search results will be displayed:

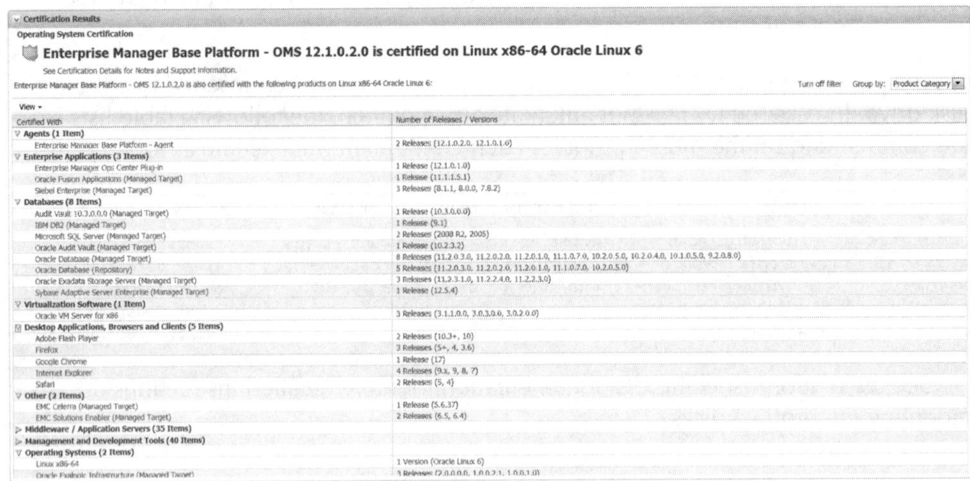

[11] The certifications page replaces the OEM Certification Checker, formerly MOS Note 412431.1.

As shown in the illustration, you can click the Certification Details link for notes and support information on the particular Product, Release, and Platform chosen.

Releases of "Products," which include certified OEM components other than the OMS (that is, Agents, Repository databases, and browsers), have links for drill-down to obtain further details on the particular release.

Create Required OS Groups and Users

OMR, OMS, OMA

Create an OS group and user on the OMS host to own the CC software (and, optionally, the database software, if the Repository will be installed on the same host). Follow a consistent naming convention to simplify administration:

- Oracle inventory group (*oinstall*). This group only applies to UNIX platforms.
- Oracle software owner (*oracle*). This owner is used on UNIX and Windows platforms.

For UNIX platforms in particular, we recommend for consistency's sake that you also use the same user ID (uid), group ID (gid), and supplemental group name for the *oracle* user across all servers where CC components are installed. Hosts containing CC components may actually require that you specify consistent *oracle* user and *oinstall* group names and IDs, to one degree or another, as shown in these examples:

- Choose the same Agent user and groups that own (or predominantly own) existing Oracle targets to be monitored. Additional configuration is sometimes required for Agents to monitor targets installed by a different user.
- All RAC Repository nodes require that you create the same Oracle user name, user ID, group name, and group ID on every RAC node.[12]
- A Repository Data Guard configuration requires that the same Oracle user name, user ID, group name, and group ID be used on all primary and secondary (that is, standby) database nodes.

Create Oracle Inventory Group (*oinstall*)

If you install Cloud Control on a UNIX system with no existing Oracle products, and you have not pre-created a Central Inventory pointer file oraInst.loc on the host, the OUI prompts you to create a new Central Inventory to store information about the CC software and any other Oracle software later installed on the host. You must enter the inventory directory path and OS group name (typically named *oinstall*) with write permission to the inventory directory. The standard name to use for a Central Inventory

---

[12] These requirements are found in the first few chapters of the *Oracle Grid Infrastructure Installation Guide* for your chosen platform and release.

shared by all Oracle software installed on a host is $ORACLE_BASE/../*oraInventory*, such as /u01/app/oraInventory. The OUI then creates the Central Inventory in the specified location. The OUI also creates the oraInst.loc file in a default location to point to the inventory path. The following table shows the default location of this Central Inventory pointer file oraInst.loc file (and the oratab file discussed in the section "Create the Oracle Base Directory" later in the chapter) for all UNIX platforms:

Platform	Location of Configuration Files oraInst.loc and oratab
AIX	/etc
HP-UX	/var/opt/oracle
Linux	/etc
Solaris	/var/opt/oracle

The inventory pointer file consists of two lines following the example format here:

```
inventory_loc=/u01/app/oraInventory
inst_group=oinstall
```

The parameter *inventory_loc* is set to the specified inventory path, and the parameter *inst_group* is set to the specified inventory group owner.

First, determine if there is already an Oracle inventory group by checking whether the oraInst.loc file exists in the default location for your platform. If the oraInst.loc file exists, verify that the group name defined by the parameter *inst_group* is an existing OS group in the /etc/group file, as follows (assuming *oinstall* is the group name):

```
grep oinstall /etc/group
```

If the Oracle inventory group doesn't exist, log in as *root* and create it as follows, which varies by platform:

- On HP-UX, Linux, and Solaris, enter:

  ```
  /usr/sbin/groupadd -g 501 oinstall
  ```

  This example assumes you are creating the *oinstall* group with group id (gid) 501. Specify the same group name and gid on all OMS and OMR hosts, and preferably, all Agent hosts as well.

- On AIX, enter:

  ```
  smit security
  ```

  Choose the appropriate menu commands to create the *oinstall* group, and press F10 to exit.

On Windows platforms, the Cloud Control OUI does not prompt you to create a new Central Inventory, but creates one in the default location, %SystemDrive%\Program Files\Oracle\Inventory. Windows does not use an inventory pointer file, but instead specifies the inventory location in the registry key HKEY_LOCAL_MACHINE\SOFTWARE\ORACLE\INST_LOC. Windows creates an OS group called *OSDBA* to own the Central Inventory.

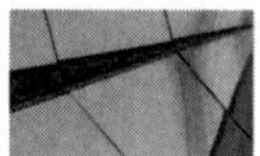

NOTE
Many Oracle shops install all Oracle software, including Cloud Control, with the oracle *user and* dba *(rather than* oinstall*) group because their DBAs manage all Oracle products and therefore need access to all Oracle software. The common* oinstall *group is only absolutely required when installing each Oracle product as a different owner (for example,* oraprod, oratest, oraoem*) and when that software shares the same central Oracle Inventory.*

Create Oracle Software Owner (*oracle*)

The Cloud Control software owner is typically the user *oracle*, and will be so throughout this book. This user should have the Oracle inventory (*oinstall*) group as its primary group.

CAUTION
*If other Oracle software is already installed on the server where you are installing CC, and the Oracle inventory group (*oinstall*) owns the inventory, then this* oinstall *group must be the primary group of the OS user installing the CC software, if CC is to share that inventory.*

It is best practice to run CC on dedicated hosts. However, if the *oracle* user already exists for another Oracle product installed on a server designated for the OMS, and the company policy is to create a different user for each Oracle product installed, then you would need to create a different user to own the CC installation. Check for the existence of whatever username you wish to create as follows (the example assumes it is *oracle*):

```
id oracle
```

If the *oracle* user exists, then the command output will look something like this:

```
uid=200(oracle) gid=500(oinstall) groups=501(dba),502(oper)
```

If the user exists, then decide whether to use the existing user or create another user. To use the existing *oracle* user, confirm as shown earlier that the primary group is the Oracle inventory group (oinstall).

To create a new Oracle software user, either because it doesn't exist or because you require a new one, use the following command syntax as *root*, depending upon the platform:

- On HP-UX, Linux, or Solaris, to create an *oracle* user with the properties shown earlier in this section (assuming the *oinstall* group already exists with the gid listed):

  ```
  /usr/sbin/useradd -u 200 -g oinstall -s /bin/bash -m oracle
  ```

  where

  - `-u` is the numerical value of the user's ID
  - `-g` is the group name of the user's initial login group

Set the password for the *oracle* user as follows:

```
passwd oracle
```

<Enter password>

- On AIX, enter the following command to create the *oracle* user:

  ```
  smit security
  ```

Choose the menu commands to create the *oracle* user as follows:

1. In the Primary GROUP field, specify the Oracle inventory group, *oinstall*. Press F10 to exit.
2. Then set the *oracle* user's password:

   ```
   passwd oracle
   ```

   <Enter password>

If the *oracle* user exists, but its primary group is not *oinstall*, then enter the following command on UNIX-based platforms to modify it (not all *usermod* options in the following example may be necessary):

```
/usr/sbin/usermod -g oinstall -u 200 oracle
```

Create Required Directories

OMR, OMS, OMA

It is best practice that all CC directory structures adhere to the Optimal Flexible Architecture (OFA) guidelines, and that you consistently specify three directories across all OMS, OMR, and Agent hosts. Create, or choose in advance, paths for two such directories that the CC software must use:

- Oracle base directory
- Oracle inventory directory

Using the same directory structure on all CC hosts allows you to more easily find the home or inventory (even hard-code Agent home directory paths into generic Agent scripts if absolutely necessary) and document your Agent installations.

Here is a brief summary of the tasks to perform in this section. Before running the CC Installer, ensure that the Oracle base directory exists and has permissions for the *oracle* user to create the CC Oracle homes below it. Also, decide on Oracle inventory directory specifications, and back up any pre-existing Oracle inventory directory.

CAUTION

The Cloud Control installer and Console cannot process symbolic links or spaces, so don't specify them in CC directory paths, configuration files, or Console.

Create the Oracle Base Directory

The Oracle base directory, defined by the OS environment variable ORACLE_BASE, is the top-level directory for all Oracle software installations, and the location under which the Middleware home should be created. OFA guidelines recommend the following path:

ORACLE_BASE=<*mount_point*>/app/<*oracle_user*>

where <*mount_point*> is the file system to contain the CC software.

For example, ORACLE_BASE could be /u01/app/oracle if the *oracle* user is the owner of the Oracle software, and the Middleware home directory would be /u01/app/oracle/Middleware.[13] You would either use the same Oracle base directory for all installations, if owned by the same user, or separate Oracle base directories for

[13] Many UNIX shops running CC prefer to use "middleware" in all lowercase, as UNIX is case-sensitive and it's easier to remember directory names this way.

each Oracle product, if owned by separate users. Hopefully, you are following best practices, dedicating OMS and OMR hosts to your CC infrastructure, with no other products installed on these hosts. In this case, there will be no pre-existing Oracle base directory. However, if this is not the case, or you're not sure whether an Oracle base directory already exists, you can usually determine what it is by any existing Oracle inventory or Oracle home directories. Directory paths that end with the Oracle software owner are likely candidates for existing Oracle base directories. Check both oraInst.loc and oratab files for such directory paths. For example, the *inventory_loc* value in the oraInst.loc file usually contains some or all of an Oracle base directory path. As an example, in the setting used in the earlier section "Create Oracle Inventory Group (*oinstall*),"

```
inventory_loc=/u01/app/oraInventory
```

the parent directory, /u01/app/, is the beginning of the Oracle base directory /u01/app/oracle. Similarly, if you're using the *oracle* user to install the CC software, and an oratab file exists and contains the following two lines,

```
prod:/u02/app/oracle/product/11.2.0/db_1:Y
*:/u03/app/iasora/product/10.2.0/as10g/:N
```

then /u02/app/oracle would be a viable Oracle base directory to use for CC, if you want the same *oracle* user who owns the Oracle database software under Oracle home /u02/app/oracle/product/11.2.0/db_1 to also own the CC Oracle home. Ideally, you should place this directory on a different file system than that for operating system files, and make sure it has enough free disk space to satisfy Cloud Control as specified in the section "Hardware Requirements" earlier in this chapter.

To create the Oracle base directory with the correct owner, group, and permissions, enter the following commands (you probably need to be logged in as *root*):

```
mkdir -p /u01/app/oracle
chown oracle:oinstall /u01/app/oracle
chmod 775 /u01/app/oracle
```

Choose the Oracle Inventory Directory

If you install Cloud Control on a UNIX system with no existing Oracle products, the OUI prompts you to enter the Oracle inventory directory path and creates the inventory in the specified location with the proper owner, group, and permissions. The installer also creates an oraInst.loc file in the default location for your platform to point to the inventory directory (refer back to the earlier section "Create Oracle

Inventory Group (*oinstall*)" for more background). Do the following now to make sure the OUI can perform these steps when you run the CC Installer in Chapter 4:

1. If the oraInst.loc file does not exist in the default location for your platform, confirm that the Cloud Control user has write permissions to create this file.
2. If the oraInst.loc file does exist in the default location (or you want to pre-create it so as not to be prompted for Inventory information in the CC Installer):

   - Ensure that *root* owns oraInst.loc with 644 permissions, and that *inventory_loc* in this file points to the desired location for the Cloud Control inventory.
   - Ensure that the Cloud Control user (*oracle*) and/or group (*oinstall*) own the inventory directory (the value of *inventory_loc*) with 664 permissions so that the Cloud Control installer can update the inventory. If needed, recursively grant the CC user such access to the inventory directory as follows:

   ```
   chown -R oracle:oinstall <inventory_loc>
   chmod -R 664 <inventory_loc>
   ```

On Windows hosts, you must use a Central Inventory. However, on UNIX systems, you can manage inventories on hosts where Cloud Control components, including Agents, are to be installed using one of two approaches:

- A Central Inventory
- A separate inventory for Cloud Control

Use a Central Inventory for Cloud Control Installing Cloud Control (or any Oracle product) into an existing registered Central Inventory is best practice, and easy to do if you follow another best practice, which is to install the OMS and Repository database on a dedicated host or hosts, devoid of other Oracle or other third-party software. In such a case, no Oracle inventory will exist before installing CC, so the CC Inventory will be, de facto, a Central Inventory.

However, on target hosts where you will deploy Agents, Oracle products will likely already be installed that you want CC to monitor, and these products will use either a Central Inventory or separate inventories. If there are multiple products using a Central Inventory, it makes sense to follow suit and install CC in this Central Inventory; likewise for separate inventories. If only one Oracle product is installed, you need to evaluate it on a case-by-case basis. For example, Oracle E-Business Suite (EBS) Application tier installations use a very specific default inventory location in the EBS software stack. In this case, it is advisable to install the CC Agent software in a separate inventory, particularly because the EBS refresh procedure involves rebuilding the target inventory of the refreshed environment to match that of the source.

Hopefully for you, Oracle products on target hosts use a Central Inventory, because it eliminates the need after installing Agents to configure them to discover separate target inventories. By contrast, Central Inventory information for Oracle target software (and the Agent software itself) will automatically appear in the Console without additional CC configuration required. One possible downside of using a Central Inventory is that, although it's a best practice, it can cause deinstallation, upgrade, and patching problems for Oracle products (including CC components) sharing that inventory, but only if you don't take proper precautions to back up the inventory before running the OUI to perform such maintenance.

In summary, unless you have a good reason to use a separate inventory for Cloud Control installations, we'd recommend using a Central Inventory. If a Central Inventory exists on a host where you plan to install a CC component (likely just the Agent), do the following to validate and back up the inventory on each of these hosts:

1. Confirm the OUI version, accessibility, and validity of the Central Inventory. Run the following command as the owner of the CC component to be installed:

   ```
   opatch lsinventory
   ```

   - Confirm from the value of the OUI version that the pre-existing Central Inventory was created with a version 11.1 Oracle Universal Installer (the same OUI version the CC Installer uses). While a pre-existing inventory created by a 10.*x* installer may work, you're asking for trouble, based on our experience. Unless you want to upgrade your pre-existing OUI to 11.1, we'd suggest using a separate inventory for CC in this case.
   - Verify that the existing Central Inventory is not corrupted and is accessible (that is, "opatch lsinventory" can be run) by the user who owns the CC component to be installed. Confirm that no errors appear in the output from the `opatch` command, and that the last output line says "OPatch succeeded."

2. Prepare to install any CC component on the host by backing up the pre-existing Central Inventory and the corresponding oraInst.loc file pointing to it. If the CC installation fails, you can simply restore the backup of the pre-existing Central Inventory and oraInst.loc file rather than having to detach Cloud Control from it using the OUI.

   - On Windows, back up the Central Inventory at %SystemDrive%\Program Files\Oracle\Inventory\ to another location.
   - On UNIX, back up the inventory as follows:

     ```
     cd <inventory_loc>/..
     cp -Rp <inventory_loc> <backup_loc>
     ```

Use a Separate Inventory for Cloud Control As just described, your site may maintain separate inventories for each Oracle product installed on a particular host. In this case, you may prefer to register the CC installation (likely, the Agent installation, if using dedicated CC hosts for OMS and Repository database) in a new separate inventory in one of the following ways, as illustrated in Figure 2-2:

- **Change the *inventory_loc* value to point to new inventory for CC** Change the *inventory_loc* value in the inventory pointer file oraInst.loc to point to a new location. In Figure 2-2, we are changing *inventory_loc* from /u01/app/oraInventory to /u01/app/oraInventory.CC. First, back up the existing default oraInst.loc file to a meaningful name indicating the corresponding Oracle product already installed (or "pound out" the current entry in the file by entering a "#" as the first character of the line). Then change the *inventory_loc* value in the default oraInst.loc file to point to a new inventory path for the CC installation.

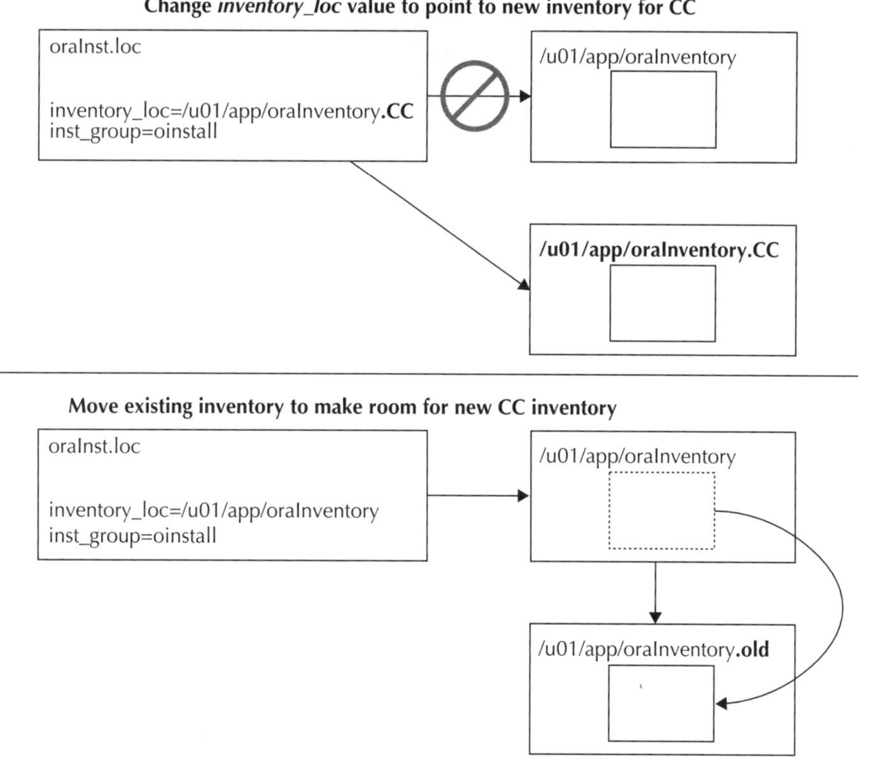

FIGURE 2-2. *The two different methods to use separate Oracle inventories*

- **Move existing inventory to make room for new CC inventory** Move the existing inventory directory containing information on existing Oracle products and specified by *inventory_loc* to an alternate location, and use the existing *inventory_loc* location for the new CC Central Inventory. In Figure 2-2, we move the inventory directory /u01/app/oraInventory to /u01/app/oraInventory.old.

If you decide to use a separate inventory for each product, you will later need to configure Cloud Control to discover each inventory located in a nondefault location (other than that pointed to by the default oraInst.loc file). This configuration process is covered in MOS Note 1386161.1.

Synchronize OS Timestamps/Time Zones

OMR, OMS, OMA

Ensure that the timestamp on the OMS host is synchronized with those on all other Cloud Control hosts, including the Repository database and Agent hosts. Synchronized timestamps are particularly important for the following:

- When viewing CC log files in the Console or at the OS level
- Between RAC Repository nodes to prevent interconnect problems
- On Cluster Agent nodes to avoid Agent installation errors such as "time stamp ... in the future"

You can make minor changes in time on RAC nodes, in the seconds range. To make larger time changes, shut down the instances on all RAC nodes to avoid false evictions. DBMS_SCHEDULER jobs will be affected by time changes, as they use actual clock time rather than System Change Numbers (SCNs). Apart from these issues, the Oracle database server is immune to time changes (for example, transaction and read consistency operations will not be affected).[14]

The recommended approach to synchronize timestamps is to run the Network Time Protocol (NTP)[15] on all hosts containing Cloud Control components. All Cloud

---

[14] Note 200346.1 (Oracle internal only).

[15] Each machine has a different clock frequency and, consequently, a slightly different time drift. NTP computes this time drift within approximately 15 minutes and stores this information in a drift file. NTP adjusts the system clock based both on this known drift and on a chosen time-server for all RAC nodes.

Control and target hosts should use the same NTP server. (Even if you're running the NTP daemon, spot check that timestamps are synchronized across CC hosts by manually running the `date` command as simultaneously as possible on each host.) To check that the NTP daemon is running, check for the presence of the `ntpd` process, which will return output similar to that shown here:

```
ps -ef | grep ntpd | grep -v grep
ntp       1420     1  0 Sep29 ?        00:00:03 ntpd -U ntp -p /var/run/ntpd.pid
```

On Linux, the NTP daemon runs as a service called `ntpd`, so you can execute the following command to see its status:

```
/sbin/service ntpd status
```

If the NTP daemon is not running, start it as *root*. (For details, see your operating system documentation on NTP.) On Linux, you just start the `ntpd` service:

```
/sbin/service ntpd start
```

For Linux hosts, you must add the `-x` flag to this NTP daemon startup command to prevent the clock from going backward.[16]

CAUTION

If you plan to use a RAC Repository database, you must run the NTP or an equivalent service to keep the clocks synchronized across RAC nodes. Otherwise, you may experience unexpected OMS shutdowns, and data collection timestamps may be incorrect.

In addition to timestamps, set the OS time zone (and update the hardware clock) as desired for Cloud Control on the OMS, OMR, and, if possible, on target servers that will run Agents. It is particularly important to set the OS time zone correctly on the node(s) to contain the OMR database, as the database time zone defaults to the OS time zone. If the OS time zone is not a valid Oracle database time zone, the latter defaults to UTC. For instructions on changing the OS time zone, consult your platform-specific documentation.

---

[16] The NTP slewing option (that is, adding the `-x` to the ntpd configuration file ntpd.conf) is a mandatory configuration option when installing 11*g* R2 RAC, per MOS 1344678.1 and MOS 551704.1.

TIP

If your Cloud Control implementation spans multiple time zones and is centrally managed, consider using the UTC time zone for all Cloud Control hosts, including managed target hosts. This will help you avoid having to convert time zones when examining log files and the like.

As an example, on Linux you can change the system time zone in a few short steps. Logged in as *root*, first check which time zone your machine is currently using by executing the following command, whose output will be in the format shown here:

```
/sbin/clock
Thu 14 Feb 2013 05:58:34 AM EST  -0.097270 seconds
```

In this case, EST is the current time zone. Suppose you wanted to change the time zone to UTC. Back up the previous time zone configuration, which for Linux is stored in /etc/localtime. (Don't try to read this file—it contains binary data.)

```
cp /etc/localtime /etc/localtime.bk
```

Next, change to the directory /usr/share/zoneinfo. Here you will find a listing of time zone regions, both files and directories. If appropriate, change to the directory named after the appropriate region. If you live in the United States and want to use local time, you would change to the directory *US* or *America* (the latter is also valid for Canada and the other Americas) and choose your local time zone. In this example, you would not need to change directories because *UTC* is a file under /usr/share/zoneinfo. Copy the appropriate time zone file to /etc/localtime, as shown in this example:

```
cd /usr/share/zoneinfo
cp UTC /etc/localtime
```

If you have the utility `rdate`, update the current system time with this new time zone by executing the following:

```
/usr/bin/rdate -s time.nist.gov
```

Finally, set the hardware clock by executing:

```
/sbin/hwclock --systohc
```

Confirm Platform-Specific Software Requirements

OMS, OMA

OMR, OMS, and standalone OMA hosts have some platform-specific software requirements over and above the generic software requirements already mentioned. These software requirements are listed in Chapter 3 of the *Cloud Control Basic*

Installation Guide. Software requirements for the Repository database are covered next in Chapter 3.

Requirements for OMS and Agents are broken out into three sections:

- Package Requirements
- Kernel Parameter Requirements
- Library Requirements

Refer to the Cloud Control installation guide now to confirm and redress any outstanding software prerequisites for your platform.

Be sure to also comb through the Release Notes for your platform to learn about any known platform-specific installation and upgrade issues, including critical patches to apply.

Summary

This chapter is long because preparation is the key to installing Cloud Control successfully and efficiently. You begin by making some basic architectural design decisions, then address prerequisites related to network configuration, hardware, and software (both generic and platform-specific). Now you're ready to move on to Chapter 3, where you install a database with a preconfigured Management Repository. Prepare to reap the benefits of the thorough preinstallation groundwork you've done in this chapter.

CHAPTER 3

Building a Preconfigured Management Repository Database

This chapter explains the process of installing an Oracle 11gR2 Database "preconfigured" with a Management Repository for Cloud Control, and is organized into two major parts:

- Part I: Provide the steps for building a database preconfigured with a Management Repository, which consists of two major tasks:
  - Perform a software-only installation of the 11gR2 Database server, and apply the latest Patch Set Update (PSU).
  - Create a database in Database Configuration Assistant (DBCA) with the new DBCA template called "DB11.2.0.3 EM seed database" (referred to herein as the "EM template") that preconfigures a Management Repository with all objects.
- Part II: Describe how to finish configuring the database for Repository operations.

In both parts, we supply the steps to set up the database according to Oracle Maximum Availability Architecture (MAA) best practices for an Oracle Database 11gR2.

After completing the steps presented in this chapter, you will be ready to install Cloud Control in Chapter 4. In the CC OUI, you will be selecting the installation option "Create a new Enterprise Manager System" and providing connection details to the preconfigured Repository database you create in this current chapter.

Let's get down to the first order of business, to install and patch Database 11gR2, then use DBCA to create a database preconfigured with a Management Repository.

Part I: Build a Database with a Preconfigured Repository

Before you can install Cloud Control 12*c*, you must first build a database to contain the Management Repository. This database installation consists of two main steps, as covered in Part I of this chapter:

- *Perform a software-only installation of Oracle Database 11gR2.* Install the latest Full Installer Patch Set software distribution of Database 11gR2 (currently 11.2.0.3.0), and apply the latest Patch Set Update (PSU) certified for the Repository (11.2.0.3.6 at the time of this writing). If a later Database PSU and associated EM template have since been made available, you should apply this later PSU instead. If you are using a Grid Infrastructure (GI), you would install and patch the GI Oracle home first, then install and patch the Database Oracle home.

- *Create a new database with a preconfigured Management Repository.* Run DBCA using the new EM template to create a database that contains a preconfigured Repository, containing all Repository structures (schemas, tablespaces, and database objects) and most of the necessary database properties (options, initialization parameters, and storage attributes). We will provide instructions for changing the EM template with the few missing database properties required for the Repository along the way.

Perform a Software-only Installation of Oracle Database 11gR2

For the moment, let's set aside this new feature of creating a preconfigured Repository database with DBCA, as it's covered in the next section. We will begin on more familiar ground with the first step to install and patch the Database 11.2.0.3 software. Little needs to be said about a software-only database installation, as it is the bread and butter for experienced core DBAs, our target audience. Therefore, our coverage is at a high level for a software-only database installation. We reference the appropriate chapters in the Oracle Database 11.2 documentation set, and point out the few database software installation options you must select to support a Management Repository.

Following is the overall GI and database home installation and patching procedure, which applies to standalone and RAC database architectures alike:

- Install a GI Oracle home, then apply the latest GI PSU (if using a Grid Infrastructure architecture).
- Install a Database Oracle home, then apply the latest Database PSU. If using a GI, you would apply the latest GI PSU to the Database Oracle home, as it contains the Database PSU of the same version.

As reflected in the order of this chapter, do not create the database until after you've installed and patched the GI home, then installed and patched the Database home. Patching the database software before creating the database itself streamlines the installation process by letting you circumvent the database postinstallation steps for individual components—standard advice for building any Oracle Database. For those newer DBAs, the way this plays out is to install the latest GI full distribution Patch Set (11.2.0.3.0) but decline to create the database, exit the installer, then patch the GI software home to the latest PSU (currently 11.2.0.3.6). Do the same for the Database home. Then run the Database Configuration Assistant (DBCA) in standalone mode to create the database, as instructed later in this chapter.

TIP

We strongly suggest installing the latest certified database and Patch Set (currently 11.2.0.3.6) for which a DBCA EM template exists, to take advantage of the new 11.2 features, latest Patch Set bug fixes, and the ease of using the EM template. While the Repository is certified to run on certain Oracle 10.2, 10.1, or 9.2 Database releases, there should be no reason to do so. You should be able to use an 11gR2 Database as long as it is dedicated to the Repository (that is, it doesn't support a third-party application not certified on Oracle 11gR2). If for some reason you must use an earlier Oracle database release for the Repository, the syntax still applies for most of the commands and initialization parameters listed in this section, but the section on running DBCA with the EM template would not apply, as it is only available for Database 11.2.0.3.

Hopefully you have decided whether the database will be single-instance (standalone or Oracle Restart) or multiple-instance (RAC, CFC, or ORON). In Chapter 2 the section "Deciding on Database Architecture for Management Repository" provides a clear basis for the higher-level decision of single versus multiple instance, namely, high availability requirements. You can revisit that section if you haven't yet decided. The installation procedures for single-instance versus multiple-instance databases (and variations of each) differ considerably, and we need to get started installing one or the other. The choices of database architectures abound, and we can't cover them all in a book on Cloud Control.

The following list gives the chapters to consult in the Oracle database documentation set available on Oracle Technology Network (OTN) for step-by-step instructions on creating the 11gR2 GI and Database homes.

- **Single-Instance Database** Complete the following chapters listed in the *Oracle Database Installation Guide* for your platform and database release:
    - Chapter 2: Oracle Database Preinstallation Requirements
    - Chapter 3: Oracle Grid Infrastructure (This chapter covers installing a Grid Infrastructure for a standalone server, and includes Oracle Restart and Oracle ASM, as opposed to Grid Infrastructure for a Cluster, which is for RAC databases.)
    - Chapter 4: Installing Oracle Database
    - Chapter 5: Oracle Database Postinstallation Tasks

- **RAC Database** Perform the tasks in the following chapters from the *Grid Infrastructure Installation Guide* and *RAC Installation Guide* for your platform and release:
  - *Oracle Grid Infrastructure Installation Guide*:
    - Chapter 1: Typical Installation for Oracle Grid Infrastructure for a Cluster
    - Chapter 3: Configuring Storage for Grid Infrastructure for a Cluster and Oracle Real Application Clusters
    - Chapter 4: Installing Oracle Grid Infrastructure for a Cluster
  - *Oracle Real Application Clusters Installation Guide*:
    - Chapter 1: Preinstallation Checklist
    - Chapter 2: Installing Oracle Database 11*g* with Oracle Real Application Clusters
    - Chapter 3: Creating Oracle Real Application Clusters Databases with Database Configuration Assistant
    - Chapter 4: Oracle Real Application Clusters Postinstallation Procedures

TIP
MOS Note 169706.1 contains a comprehensive reference list of articles detailing OS requirements for the various Database releases and UNIX platforms.

Next is a brief look at this software-only database installation procedure. Along the way, we point out the few CC-specific requirements for the OMR database software, so you don't have to refer to the Cloud Control 12*c* documentation set for them. It's enough that you have to consult the Oracle Database documentation set, though informed by the CC-specific content in this chapter. (Some of the database installation and configuration points in this chapter differ from or do not appear in the Oracle EM documentation, but are found in My Oracle Support notes or are based on experience in the field.)

Install Grid Infrastructure Software (Conditional)

The procedure to install a GI Oracle home and apply the latest GI PSU pertains to any database architecture you choose that employs a GI:

- A GI home for a standalone server (Oracle Restart), or
- A GI home for a cluster, either for multinode RAC or ORON

Here are the few details on GI installation and patching you need to do to support a Cloud Control Repository database. The operative word is "few" because there are no specific dependencies between a Grid Infrastructure and a CC Repository database, other than to ensure that the database and CC releases are certified together. The only requirements are for the Repository database software itself, which are spelled out in the following instructions.

Install Latest Full Distribution Patch Set of GI 11gR2 Software If you are opting to use a Grid Infrastructure, for either a standalone or RAC database, install the GI portion of the latest Full Distribution Patch Set of Database 11gR2 for your platform (currently 11.2.0.3.0) that is certified with the latest version of Cloud Control 12*c* (currently 12.1.0.2.0), barring some constraint on your end. Also, check the Enterprise Manager Download page on OTN to make sure there is an equivalent EM template for this database release.

There are no other Repository requirements for how to install the GI software home; this is only the case for the Database home, as mentioned in the following instructions.

Apply Latest GI PSU for Database 11.2.0.*x* Software Installed After installing the latest GI Full Distribution Patch Set, apply the latest GI Patch Set Update (GI PSU), which at the time of this writing is 11.2.0.3.6 (Patch 16083653). For a list of the latest GI PSU for your database version, see MOS Note 756671.1 "Oracle Recommended Patches – Oracle Database."

There is not much else to say about installing the GI with respect to supporting the CC Repository database. It is a generic installation step for Oracle Database Server.

Install Database Software

Once the GI has been installed and patched, you can begin installing the database portion of the latest full distribution Patch Set of Oracle 11gR2 Database software for your platform (currently 11.2.0.3.0). The database needs to be installed in a separate Oracle home than the GI home. Install the database software only; do not create the database yet.

Install Latest Full Distribution Patch Set of Database 11gR2 Software We recommend making the following specific choices when installing the latest full Patch Set distribution of the 11gR2 database software, so as to provide the database components necessary for proper CC Repository functionality.

- **Installation Option** Choose "Install database software only." As discussed, do not create the database until you are applying the latest Database PSU (done next).

- **Grid Installation Options** Choose one of the desired database installation options from the three choices given:
  - Single-instance database installation
  - Oracle Real Application Clusters database installation
  - Oracle RAC One Node database installation
- **Product Languages** Select the language(s) you want to use. English must be one of these choices.
- **Database Edition** Choose Enterprise Edition. Click Select Options.
  - Check the box for Oracle Partitioning. This is required for the OMR database, which creates many partitioned tables and indexes in the SYSMAN schema for storing management metrics. The other components listed are not required for a CC Repository database, though you can select them.[1]
- **Installation Location** Specify values for Oracle Base and Software Location, in compliance with Optimal Flexible Architecture (OFA) recommendations, such as:
  - Oracle Base: **/u01/app/oracle**
  - Software Location: **/u01/app/oracle/product/11.2.0/db_1**
- **Operating System Groups** Enter values for OSDBA and OSOPER groups:
  - Database Administrator (OSDBA) Group: **oinstall** or **dba**[2]
  - Database Operator (OSOPER) Group (Optional): **oinstall** or **dba**
- **Summary** Verify that all choices are as desired and click Install.

Apply Latest Database PSU for Database 11.2.0.*x* Software Installed As already mentioned, after installing Database 11.2.0.*x*, apply the latest 11.2.0.*x* Patch Set Unit (PSU) to the database home. For a list of the latest Database PSU for your database version, see MOS Note 756671.1 "Oracle Recommended Patches – Oracle Database."

---

[1] Consider Oracle Real Application Testing (RAT), if you would like to use this option with CC for the Repository database, whether for testing RAT itself or to apply it to tuning of the Repository database. For details, in the Oracle Database documentation set, see *Real Application Testing User's Guide*.

[2] For a discussion of this, see the section "Create Oracle Inventory Group (*oinstall*)" in Chapter 2.

Create a Database with the DBCA EM Template

At this point, you have installed the Grid Infrastructure home (if chosen) and Oracle Database home, and both are at the latest available PSU level. The last step is to actually create a database for the Repository by invoking the Database Configuration Assistant (DBCA) executable under the database $ORACLE_HOME/bin directory. DBCA can create a single-instance or RAC database, as required for the Repository.

To create a single-instance database for the Repository, we recommend using the EM template, which is available for all supported Repository platforms, but only for Database 11.2.0.3. We cover the use of this EM template extensively in this section, as it will be unfamiliar to many DBAs, being new to Cloud Control 12.1.0.2, which itself was only recently released.

Regrettably, the DBCA EM template for Database 11.2.0.3 does not support creation of a RAC database. (Hopefully Oracle will rectify this in the next EM template release.) To create a RAC database for the Repository, we suggest choosing the standard Oracle Custom template in DBCA, and choosing the database parameters listed in the following instructions for the EM template.

While we cover the EM template in detail, as a supplement, for more generic help in using DBCA to create a single-instance or RAC database, see the following guides in the Oracle Database 11.2 documentation set:

- **Single-Instance Database** To create a single-instance database for the OMR using DBCA, see "Creating and Managing a Database with DBCA" in Chapter 2 of *Oracle Database 2 Day DBA* 11*g* Release 2 (11.2).
- **RAC Database** For specifics on running DBCA in standalone mode to create a RAC database, see Chapter 3 of the *Oracle Real Application Clusters Installation Guide* for your platform.

In addition to these references, you can also get online help once you kick off DBCA, by clicking Help on any DBCA installation screen.

This section on using the DBCA EM template to create a preconfigured Repository database is broken down as follows:

- Introduction to the DBCA EM template
- Strategy to preconfigure a Repository database with the EM template
- Staging the EM template
- Creating a listener and net service name for the database
- Running DBCA with the EM template to create a preconfigured Repository database

Introduction to the EM Template

In the initial Cloud Control Release (12.1.0.1), only the CC Installer could install and configure a Management Repository. However, CC 12.1.0.2 offers a DBCA "seeded" template called "DB11.2.0.3 EM seed database," or "EM template" for short, that creates an 11.2.0.3 single-instance database containing a *preconfigured* Repository (Oracle's term). Seeded database templates such as this include structure as well as data, which in this case is the complete Repository containing the required CC database schemas (SYSMAN, SYSMAN_APM, SYSMAN_MDS, SYSMAN_OPSS, and SYSMAN_RO), tablespaces (MGMT_AD4J_TS, MGMT_TABLESPACE, and MGMT_ECM_DEPOT_TS), and their database objects. In addition to creating the database structures, the EM template also specifies properties most aligned with Repository requirements, including database options (such as Oracle Java Virtual Machine or JVM), initialization parameters, and storage attributes.

The EM template is provided in the CC 12.1.0.2 software distribution for you to download and stage under the Database 11.2.0.3 Oracle home, as explained in the following instructions. Once staged, the EM template appears in DBCA on the Database Templates screen alongside the other standard built-in Oracle database DBCA templates with which you are likely familiar (General Purpose or Transaction Processing, Custom, and Data Warehouse). We recommend the EM template over these other templates because they would require many more additional manual configuration changes, both in DBCA and afterward.

This is the first release of the EM template software, which will no doubt be refined in later releases to create a database with even closer compliance to all Repository requirements, perhaps inclusive of some steps presented in Part II of this chapter, entitled "Finish Configuring the Repository Database." Therefore, you should consider using the latest EM template release, in conjunction with Database 11.2.0.3, or a later Patch Set if ever certified with the template.

Strategy to Preconfigure a Repository Database with the EM Template

Before the advent of the EM template for Cloud Control 12.1.0.2, in the initial CC release 12.1.0.1 you needed to select a generic Oracle template in DBCA, such as the Custom template, and then manually configure the database properties to support a Repository, such as initialization parameters and redo log sizes, whether in DBCA or afterward. Now, *most* of the database configuration can be completed by running DBCA with the EM template, which will also pre-create the Repository database structures. However, there are a few additional Repository requirements and database best practices that the EM template does not address. Our suggested strategy for implementing them is to satisfy as many of these shortcomings in DBCA itself (primarily initialization parameter settings), to the extent that the DBCA user interface allows. Then, after creating the database with DBCA, we will close the few remaining gaps, as outlined in the next major section of Part II, "Finish Configuring the Repository Database."

Staging the EM Template

The following steps provide instructions to download and stage the EM template for the Management Repository so that you can select it in DBCA. It is a simple and quick procedure. The EM template can be downloaded from Oracle Technology Network (OTN) on the Enterprise Manager download page, alongside the Cloud Control software distribution itself. As mentioned, the EM template is available for all certified CC platforms, but only for Database 11.2.0.3, which is the latest 11gR2 Patch Set available at the time of this writing.

1. **Download the template file for your OMR database platform.** Hover over Downloads on the OTN home page and click Oracle Enterprise Manager. Expand "Database Template (with EM 12.1.0.2 repository preconfigured) for Installing Enterprise Manager Cloud Control 12*c* Release 2...," click Download DB Templates, accept the OTN License Agreement, and then click on the database template for your platform to download it. Templates are zip archives less than 200MB in size, and named accordingly for each OS, such as DB11.2.0.3_EM_seed_database_linux64.zip for Linux x86-64.
2. **Extract the template zip file under $ORACLE_HOME/assistants/dbca/templates/** on the database node where you will be invoking DBCA. The Oracle home is that laid down in the software-only database installation described earlier in the section "Install Database Software." The zip file contains four files named DB11.2.0.3_EM_seed_database.dbc, DB11.2.0.3_EM_seed_database.ctl, DB11.2.0.3_EM_seed_database.dfb, and shpool.sql, a postinstallation SQL script (explained in the section "Database Content Screen").

Creating a Listener and Net Service Name for the Database

Before kicking off DBCA to create a standalone database, we suggest creating a listener so that you can specify in DBCA that the database register with this listener. (If you're creating a RAC database, do not create a listener, because DBCA configures the Oracle Net services for you.) You specify the listener name in DBCA on the Network Configuration screen, shown in the next section. If you do not pre-create a listener, this screen will not appear in DBCA, and you will need to create the listener afterward. In this case, on database startup, the database PMON process should take care of registering the database with this listener.

Create a Listener for the Database You can create a database listener for the Repository database either in Oracle Net Manager, as Oracle advocates, or manually. To use Oracle Net Manager, start an X Windows session and execute **$ORACLE_HOME/bin/netca** from the database Oracle home you installed earlier. Select "Listener configuration," then Add, and enter the listener name. Typically you would name the listener after the DB_NAME, which in the following example is EMREP. Select the TCP protocol, enter the desired port number, and select No when asked if you would like to configure another listener. Net Manager will create the listener, then start it for you. Do not exit Oracle Net Manager yet, if you also want to use it to create a Net Service name (or alias) for accessing the database server.

Following is the listener entry that will be created in $ORACLE_HOME/network/admin/listener.ora (again, in this example the Repository database name is EMREP):

```
EMREP =
  (DESCRIPTION_LIST =
    (DESCRIPTION =
      (ADDRESS = (PROTOCOL = TCP)(HOST = <hostname>)(PORT = <port>))
    )
  )
ADR_BASE_EMREP = <Oracle_home>
```

where:

<hostname> = database host name

<port> = port for listener

<Oracle_home> = Database Oracle home

To manually configure the listener to produce the same result, create the file *listener.ora* under the ORACLE_HOME/network/admin directory with the preceding listener entry (or add the entry, if the file exists). Then start the listener at the OS command line with:

```
lsnrctl start <listener_name>
```

Earlier releases of Oracle Enterprise Manager required configuration of static service information for remote database startup and other functionality. However, this dynamic service information should be adequate for Cloud Control 12*c*. If you need to statically configure the listener for other reasons, such as remote database startup from a tool other than Cloud Control, append the following to the preceding entry in the listener.ora file (or see the online Help for how to do this in Oracle Net Manager):

```
SID_LIST_EMREP =
  (SID_LIST =
    (SID_DESC =
      (GLOBAL_DBNAME = EMREP)
      (SID_NAME = EMREP)
      (ORACLE_HOME= <Oracle_home>)
    )
  )
```

CAUTION
Make sure the GLOBAL_DBNAME parameter is not set, if using connect-time failover or Transparent Application Failover (TAF), such as in an Oracle RAC database environment.

Create a Net Service Name for the Database After creating and starting the listener, also create a Net Service name (or alias) for accessing the database, on the database server and any other client workstations that require direct access to the database. You do not need to configure the tnsnames.ora file on the OMS server, as the CC Installer will do this for you. As with the listener, you can create this alias using either Oracle Net Manager, the Oracle-supported method, or manually.

If you're using Oracle Net Manager to create a Net Service name, select the Local Net Service Name configuration, click Add, and enter the Service Name to use, usually the global database name (which may be the same as the DB_NAME). Select the TCP protocol, and enter the database host name and listener port (chosen when creating the listener). You could choose to test the connection, but there is no database to test against, so you can then exit `netca`.

To manually create a Net Service name for the database you created, rather than using `netca`, create the file tnsnames.ora under the ORACLE_HOME/network/admin directory with the following entry (or add the entry, if the file exists):

```
EMREP =
  (DESCRIPTION =
    (ADDRESS_LIST =
        (ADDRESS = (PROTOCOL = TCP)(HOST = <hostname>)(PORT = <port>))
    )
        (CONNECT_DATA =
          (SERVICE_NAME = EMREP)
      (UR = A)
    )
  )
```

This entry should be the same as that created by Oracle Net Manager, except for the addition of the "UR = A" parameter when manually creating the alias, which is recommended. This parameter is an Oracle 10*g* feature that allows connection to an unmounted database without receiving an ORA-12528 error, such as when RMAN must connect to an auxiliary instance in a NOMOUNT state. See MOS Note 419440.1 for details.

Running DBCA with the EM Template to Create a Preconfigured Repository Database

Finally, after staging the EM template and creating a listener for the database, it's time to run DBCA with the EM template to create a database with a Management

Repository. Figures 3-1 through 3-18 are screenshots of the DBCA user interface, with recommended installation choices and input provided to help you streamline the installation process and move closer to compliance with 11gR2 database best practices.

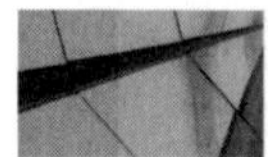

TIP
If you're running a Grid Infrastructure, don't forget to start all GI processes on all cluster nodes now, before launching DBCA to create a database for the Repository.

To invoke DBCA, set ORACLE_BASE (set to /u01/app/oracle in this example), then invoke the DBCA executable if on UNIX, or batch file if on Windows, under the Database Oracle home you installed earlier:

```
export ORACLE_BASE=/u01/app/oracle
```

On UNIX:

```
$ORACLE_HOME/bin/dbca
```

On Windows:

```
$ORACLE_HOME/bin/dbca.bat
```

On the Welcome screen, click Next, and on the Operations screen, select Create a Database.

TIP
Try to advance through each DBCA screen in order, without clicking Back too many times or keeping the X Windows session open too long. The DBCA Java can be temperamental, and we have observed that it can fail to render or hang when it's taxed.

Database Templates Screen (Figure 3-1) Select the template "DB11.2.0.3 EM seed database" (or "EM template") to create a single-instance Repository database. The EM template will only appear if you downloaded and staged it as described earlier.

If you're creating a RAC database, however, you cannot use the EM template, and should select the Custom Database template, as pointed out earlier. This will require making additional changes to those listed in this section to configure the database for a Repository.

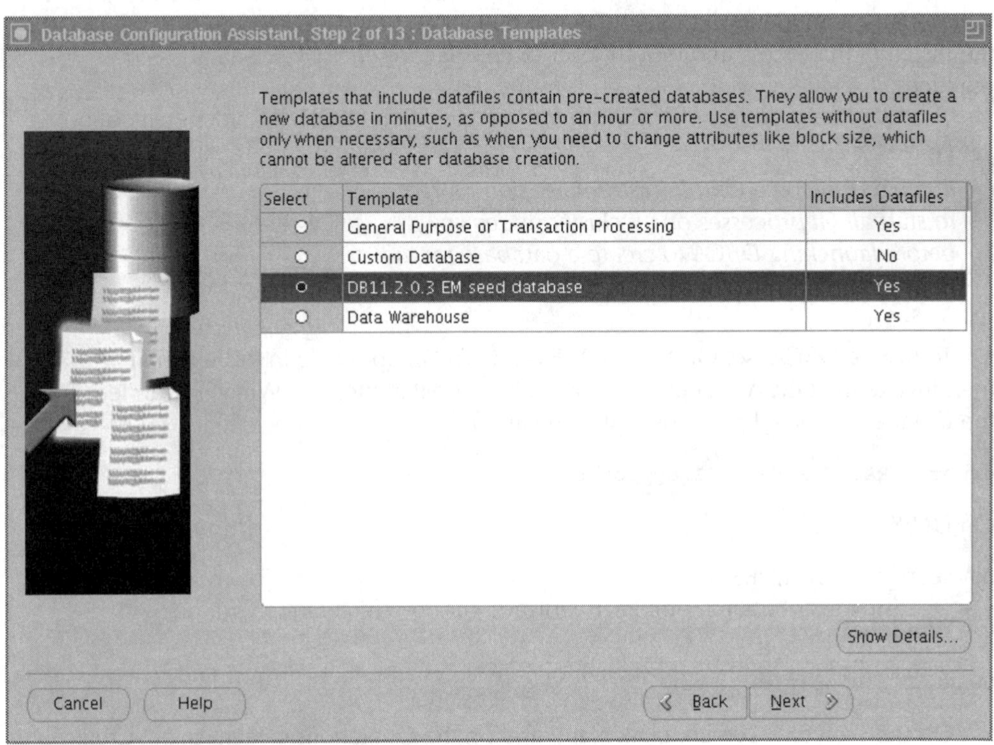

FIGURE 3-1. *Database Templates screen*

Database Identification Screen (Figure 3-2) On this screen, enter the global database name and SID, which may be different, to uniquely identify the database instance.

- **Global Database Name EMREP** (example value). Enter the global database name. Your input in the form of DB_NAME.DB_DOMAIN will determine the values for these initialization parameters. If no domain name is specified here, DOMAIN_NAME will be null.
- **SID EMREP** (example value). Use the same value as for the DB_NAME portion of Global Database Name.

We recommend entering an uppercase name for both the global database name and SID, if you will be choosing Oracle-Managed Files (OMF) as the storage

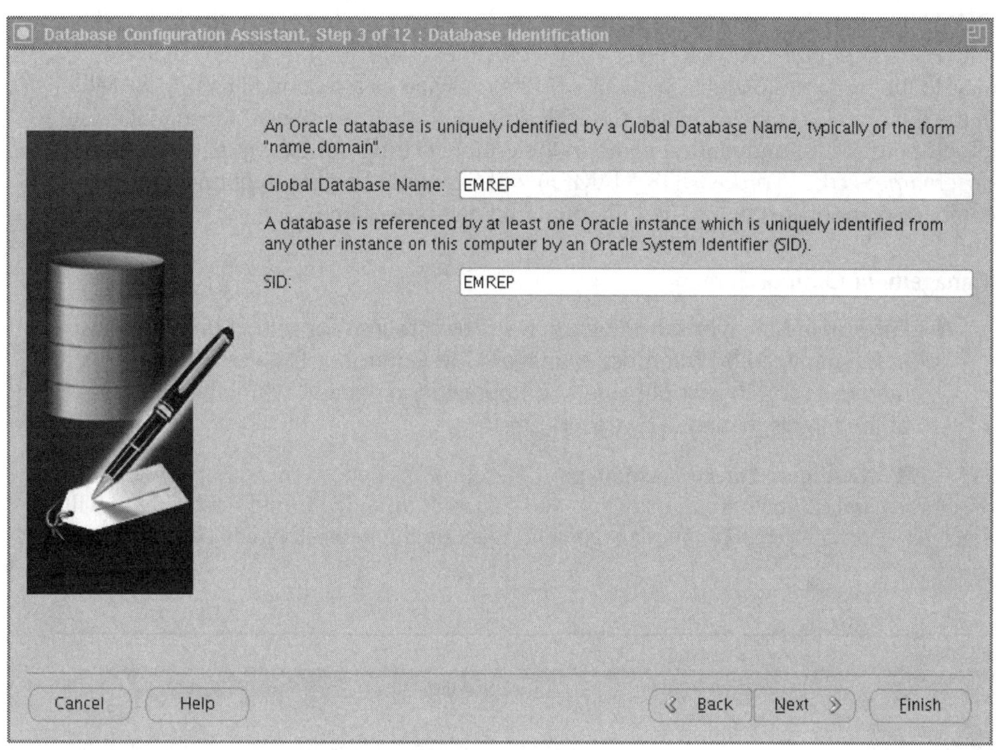

FIGURE 3-2. *Database Identification screen*

location for database files (see Figure 3-7) or fast recovery area (FRA). This will make the SID case consistent with the directory name appended to both the Database Area (see Figure 3-7) and FRA (see Figure 3-8) entered later in DBCA. (Oracle appends these directory names in uppercase even if you enter the SID in lowercase on the Database Identification screen, shown in Figure 3-2.)

The Oracle database documentation rightly suggests that you append a domain name (that is, use DB_NAME.DOMAIN_NAME) to the global database name to distinguish this database from any other in your organization that may have the same DB_NAME but a different DOMAIN_NAME. However, if your company uses unique DB_NAMEs across the enterprise, it is easier to configure the database if you do not fully qualify the global database name, as the value you enter here determines the SERVICE_NAME and global name reflected in the SYS.GLOBAL_NAME view.

If you do specify a DB_DOMAIN, be sure to add **NAMES.DEFAULT_DOMAIN=domain_name** to the sqlnet.ora file on database client hosts (including the database server itself). Also, for even more robustness, add an unqualified database alias to the tnsnames.ora file on client workstations and as a second SERVICE_NAME in the init.ora file on the database server. If none of these three steps is taken, database clients entering an unqualified name in the connect string (for example, connect *<username>*/*<password>*@<DB_NAME>) will likely not be able to connect to the database without specifying the fully qualified database name.

Management Options Screen

- **Enterprise Manager tab** (Figure 3-3) This screen is for setting up a database to be managed by Enterprise Manager Grid Control or Database Control, neither of which is applicable to a Repository database, which will be one of the targets managed by Cloud Control.
  - **Configure Enterprise Manager** Deselect this option. This is not applicable unless you have already installed CC. After installing Cloud Control, you will install a standalone Management Agent on the Repository database server.

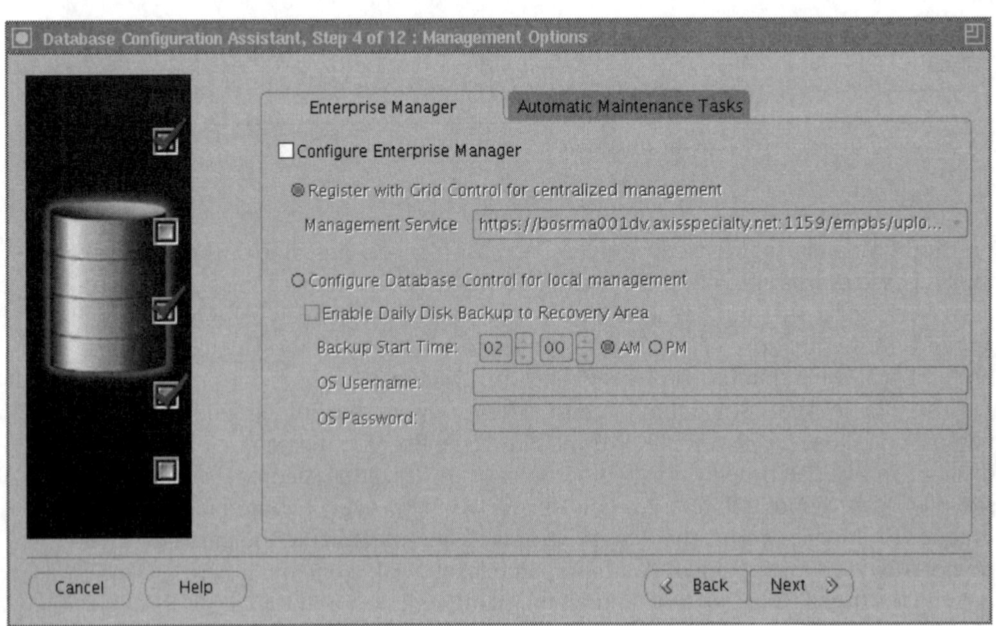

FIGURE 3-3. *Management Options screen: Enterprise Manager tab*

- **Automatic Maintenance Tasks tab** (Figure 3-4) On this screen you choose whether to configure the database to automatically manage maintenance tasks recommended for maintaining any database, including that for the Management Repository.
  - **Enable automatic maintenance tasks** Enable this option. This will set up three database maintenance jobs to run periodically: auto optimizer stats collection, auto space advisor, and sql tuning advisor.

As a Cloud Control installation prerequisite, you will need to temporarily disable the "auto optimizer stats collection" job after creating the database with DBCA, as described later in the section "Disable Auto Optimizer Statistics Collection." In Chapter 4, after installing Cloud Control, we'll remind you to re-enable this job.

Database Credentials Screen (Figure 3-5) Choose the option to set passwords for the administrative database accounts SYS and SYSTEM, as dictated by your corporate IT password policy and database security requirements.

In Figure 3-5, the password was set to be the same for both SYS and SYSTEM.

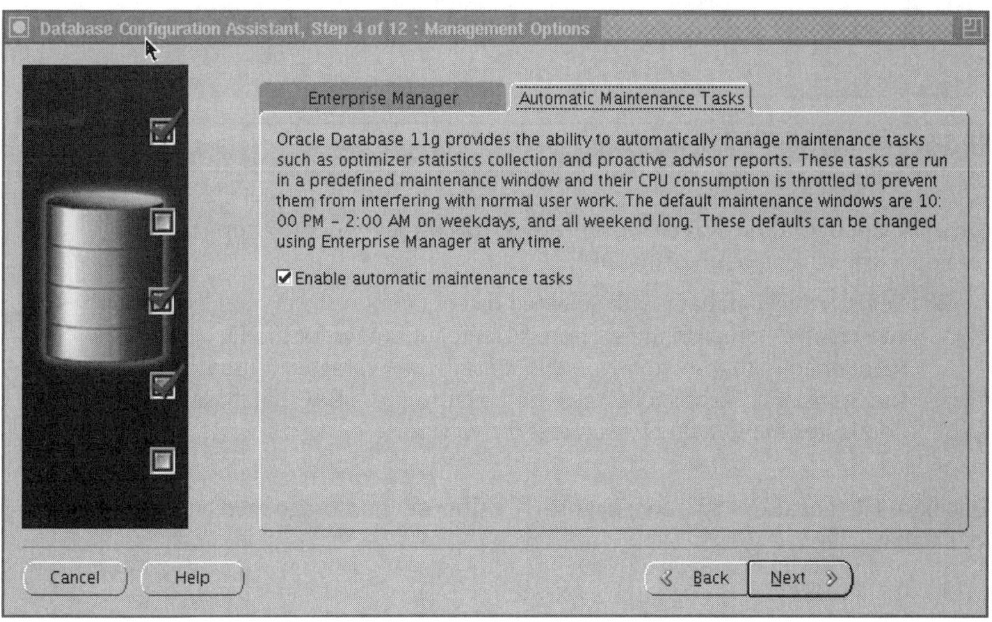

FIGURE 3-4. *Management Options screen: Automatic Maintenance Tasks tab*

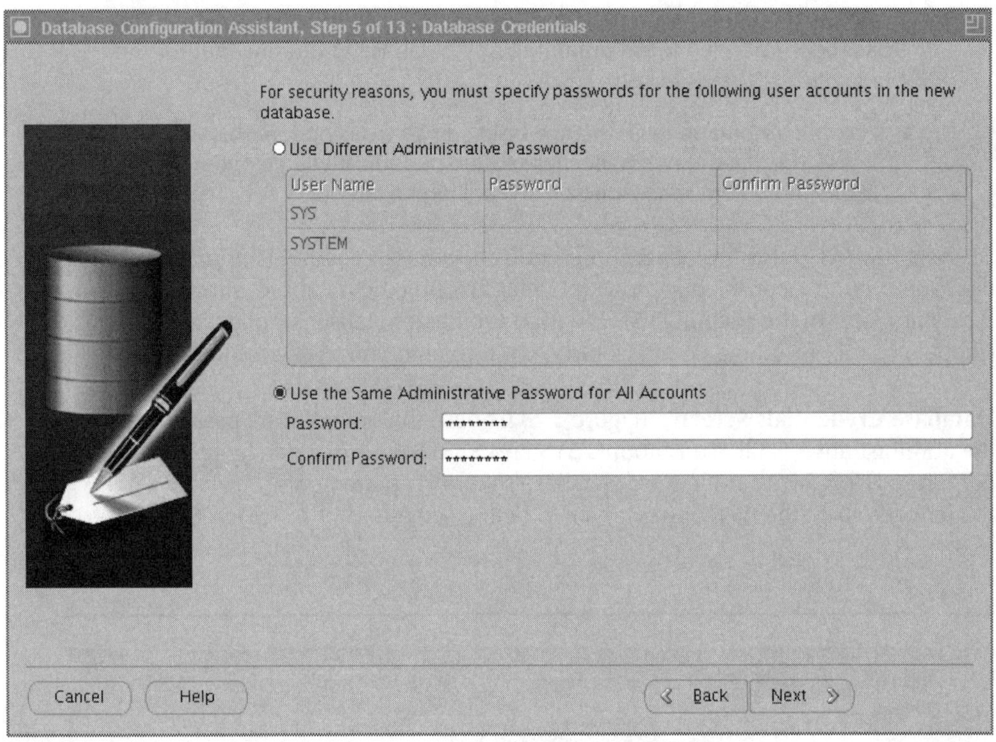

FIGURE 3-5. *Database Credentials screen*

Network Configuration Screen (Figure 3-6) This screen will only appear if you created a listener before invoking DBCA.

- **Register this database with selected listeners only** Select the listener you created earlier in the section, "Create a Listener for the Database." As mentioned in that section, you should only have created a listener for a single-instance Repository database because, for a RAC database, DBCA configures the Oracle Net services for you.[3]

Database File Locations Screen (Figure 3-7) Choose the storage type and locations for database files.

[3] If you did not pre-create a listener, the Network Configuration screen will not appear in DBCA, but you can create the listener (and Net Service name) as instructed earlier after DBCA finishes creating the database and you've exited DBCA. On startup, the database PMON process will register the database with this listener.

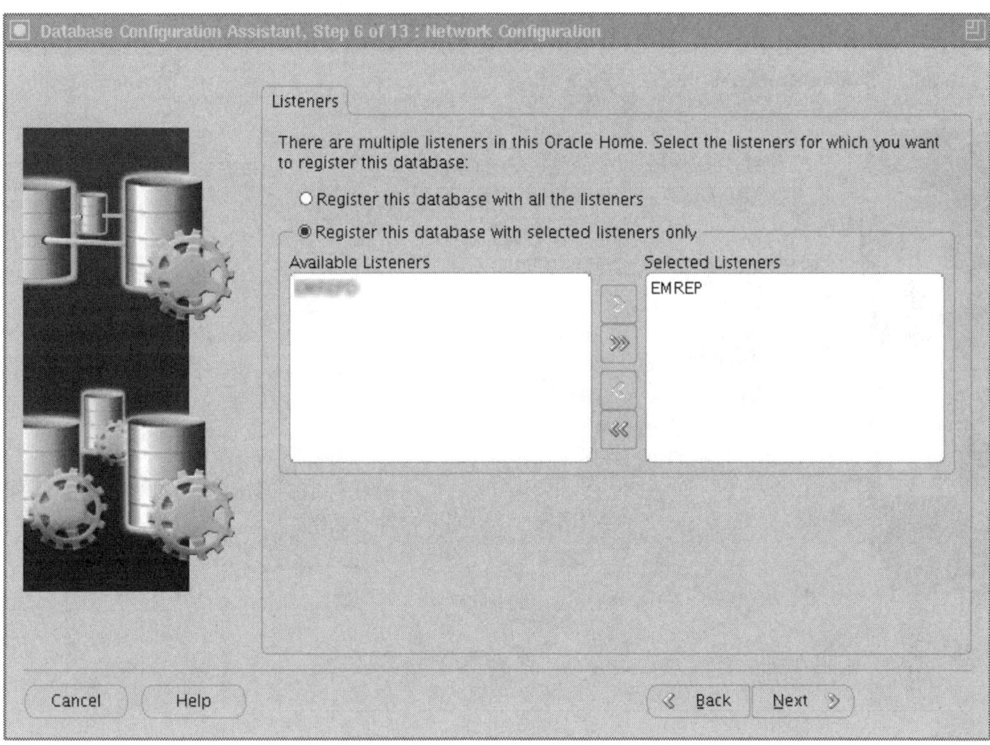

FIGURE 3-6. *Network Configuration screen*

- **Storage Type** Here you can select the kind of storage subsystem you will be using for the database files: File System or Automatic Storage Management (ASM). If you want to use ASM, due to a limitation in the CC Installer (described next under Storage Locations for the option Use Oracle-Managed Files), we advise choosing File System here to install all datafiles on a flat file system. Then after installing CC, assuming you have already prepared the ASM storage, you can migrate the database to ASM. (See MOS Note 252219.1 for the steps.)

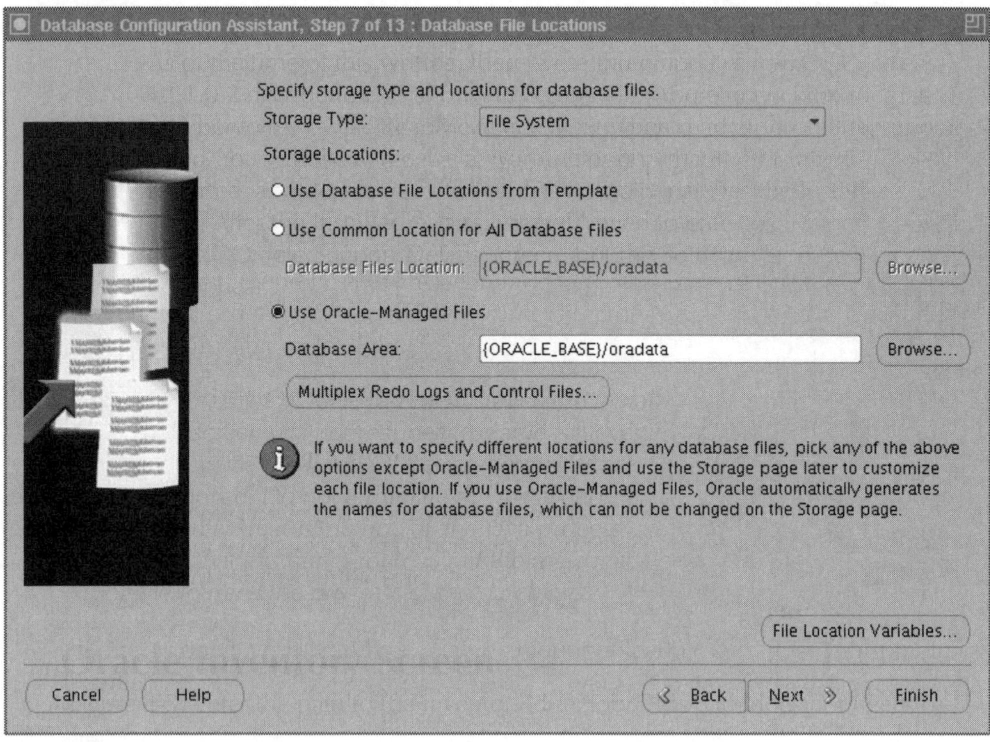

FIGURE 3-7. *Database File Locations screen*

- **Storage Locations** Select either the second or third of the three database storage locations most suitable for your site. DBCA sets the datafile location based on your input here:
  - **Use Database File Locations from Template** Do not choose this option, as you cannot change the EM template names of datafiles created under the directory $ORACLE_BASE/oradata/<*DB_UNIQUE_NAME*> used when selecting this option. (DB_UNIQUE_NAME for the Repository will be the same as DB_NAME.[4]) Instead, if you are not selecting Use Oracle-Managed Files, choose Use Common Location for All Database Files, which places all database files in the same directory as already indicated, but also allows you

[4] DB_UNIQUE_NAME is typically the same value as DB_NAME. The principal reason for them to be different would be to distinguish a primary and standby database, which would have the same DB_NAME but different DB_UNIQUE_NAMEs.

to change a datafile name to be consistent with the default name given in the CC Installer.

- **Use Common Location for All Database Files** Enter the Database Files Location where you want the datafiles to be created, which defaults to $ORACLE_BASE/oradata. The DB_UNIQUE_NAME will be appended to the path you specify. This option will allow you later to correct one datafile name that is not consistent with the default name for this datafile as hard-coded in the CC Installer. See Figure 3-16 in the section "Database Storage Screen" for details.
- **Use Oracle-Managed Files** You can select this option if you want to use OMF and have also selected the File System Storage Type, as shown previously in Figure 3-7. In this case, for the Database Area, use the default directory location, $ORACLE_BASE/oradata. The Database Area will be used to set the initialization parameter DB_CREATE_FILE_DEST. The DB_UNIQUE_NAME (same by default as DB_NAME) will be appended to the Database Area path you specify, and OMF will automatically generate unique names for database files under this path. The DB_UNIQUE_NAME will be appended to the path in uppercase even if the SID is entered in lowercase on the Database Identification screen shown earlier in Figure 3-2 (this is why we recommended using an uppercase DB_NAME on that screen, to be consistent with the case of the DB_UNIQUE_NAME used in this path). When running the CC Installer in Chapter 4, you can then specify these OMF filenames explicitly.

  However, you cannot select this option to use OMF with the Automatic Storage Management (ASM) Storage Type, without encountering the problem when running the CC Installer that the OMF filenames created independently by DBCA would not match those expected by the CC OUI. The reason for this issue is that, when using ASM, the OMF filenames created by DBCA cannot be specified in the CC Installer because it uses only the disk group (for example, +DATA) that you specify (and which should be all that you specify), leaving OMF to name the datafiles. So ironically, while ASM (and OMF, which is used by default with ASM) are database best practices for database storage (and the naming of datafiles), if you used the EM template to pre-create the Repository database, you cannot configure ASM in the CC Installer for database files (though you can configure ASM for the fast recovery area, as explained next). If you want to use ASM for database storage, as mentioned previously we'd suggest selecting the option "Use Common Location for All Database Files" to place all files on a flat file system. Then, after running the CC Installer, you can relocate the datafiles to ASM with OMF.

Recovery Configuration Screen (Figure 3-8) Choose the recovery options for the database.

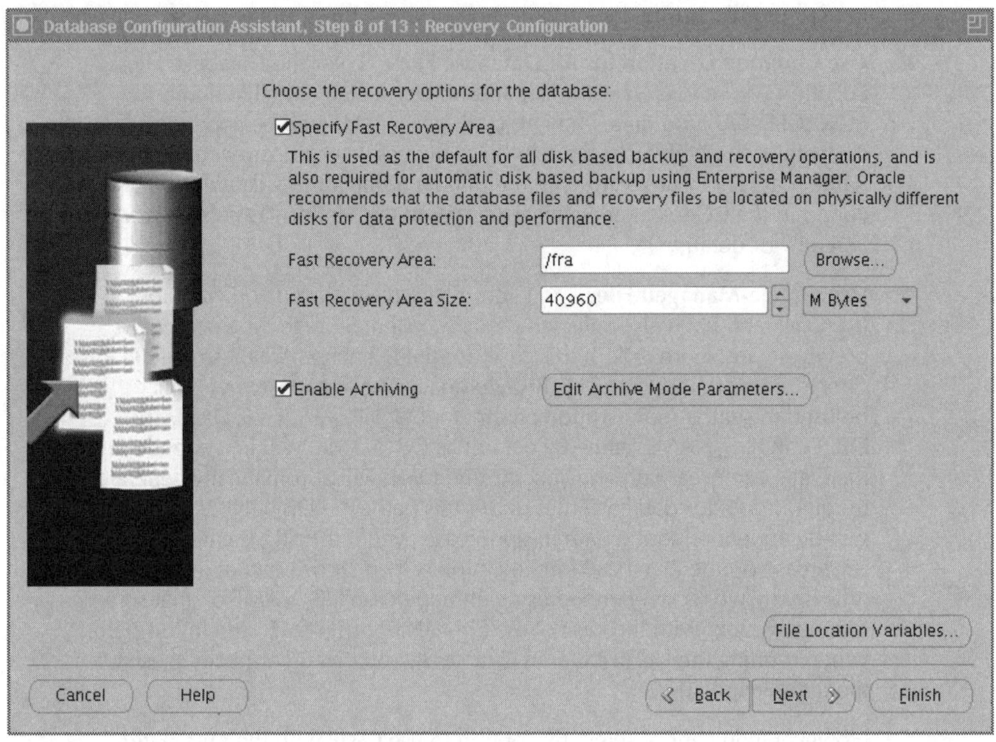

FIGURE 3-8. *Recovery Configuration screen*

- **Specify Fast Recovery Area** Check this option, as a database best practice.
  - **Fast Recovery Area** If using a file system for the FRA, enter the path for the FRA directory, such as **/fra**. If using ASM, specify the recovery disk group you created, such as **+FRA**. The FRA directory, or disk group if using ASM, must be writable by the *oracle* user. The value you enter here sets the initialization parameter DB_RECOVERY_FILE_DEST.

    While there are no issues storing the FRA on ASM, do not use ASM for the database files in DBCA, but migrate them to ASM after running the CC Installer, as recommended in coverage of the previous screen.

    When not using ASM for the datafiles (that is, not setting DB_CREATE_FILE_DEST), when using ASM for the FRA, you need to specify the initialization parameter DB_CREATE_ONLINE_LOG_DEST_*n* (where n=1,2,3...) for the default location of Oracle-managed control files and redo logs. One member of each redo log group is created in each location. At least two locations are recommended, as listed later in Table 3-1, to provide fault tolerance.

- **Fast Recovery Area Size 40960 M Bytes** (example value). The value you enter here is for DB_RECOVERY_FILE_DEST_SIZE. Allocate a FRA size of at least two, and preferably three, times the database size. Even a small CC Repository database can be expected to grow to 20GB or more in the short term, so enter a FRA size of 40GB or more. The minimum FRA size allowed by DBCA is 2749 M Bytes (two times the database size created by the EM template using its default settings).

- **Enable Archiving** Check this box. This is a best practice to allow for database recovery from media failure. If you elected to use a FRA by checking Specify Fast Recovery Area, then archive logs will be stored in the FRA, in addition to control files and redo logs.

Database Content Screen (Figure 3-9) This screen allows you to specify SQL scripts to run after the database is created.

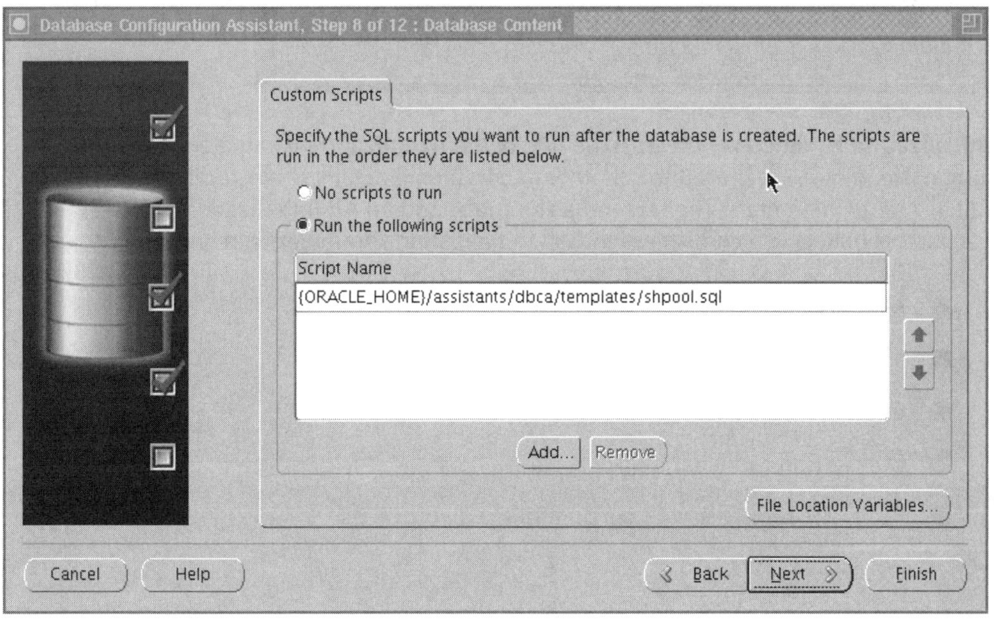

FIGURE 3-9. *Database Content screen*

- **Custom Scripts** Select "Run the following scripts" (Figure 3-9) with script name $ORACLE_HOME/assistants/dbca/template/shpool.sql. This is the default setting chosen by the EM template, which also supplies this SQL script, consisting of the following line to set the SHARED_POOL_SIZE to 286MB after creating the database:

```
alter system set shared_pool_size='300000000';
```

This script is part of the template because, for reasons unknown to us (perhaps a bug), just setting SHARED_POOL_SIZE to a non-zero value on the All Initialization Parameters screen (shown in Figure 3-14) leaves this parameter unset, unless you select to run the script. However, not even the SHARED_POOL_SIZE set in shpool.sql meets the CC installation requirements of 600,000,000 bytes (572MB). Therefore, edit the script shpool.sql now and increase the SHARED_POOL_SIZE from 300,000,000 to the value specified later in Table 3-2, as governed by your CC deployment size.

TIP
It is conceivable that you could perform many of the configuration changes listed in Part II, "Finish Configuring the Repository Database," by specifying a custom SQL script on this screen to run after the database is created. However, such a programmatic effort may not be warranted, unless you are installing multiple CC systems. Regardless, you can manually make these changes easily enough.

Initialization Parameters Screen The title of the Initialization Parameters screen is a bit misleading, as it is used to set other database characteristics in addition to initialization parameters. The screen has four tabs and an All Initialization Parameters button, which displays the All Initialization Parameters screen:

- Memory tab
- Sizing tab
- Character Sets tab
- Connection Mode tab
- All Initialization Parameters button

Two of the tabs, Memory and Sizing, highlight a few key initialization parameters. However, the Character Sets and Connection Mode tabs set other important database characteristics, not initialization parameters.

The following list describes all recommended changes to make to the default EM template settings on the previous five screens, as guided by field experience. Without exception, our "real-world" suggested values, when different, are higher than those populated on this screen by the template, or specified in the CC documentation,[5] which also differs slightly from the default values. We suggest clicking the All Initialization Parameters button and making required changes there *after* inputting changes on the four tabs, so that you can see the default EM template values on these tabs before changing them. (If you were to change the initialization parameters first, the corresponding values in the tabs would change accordingly, and you wouldn't be able to see the default values.) The changes you make on the four tabs will then be reflected in the All Initialization Parameters screen, displayed when you click the All Initialization Parameters button.

- **Memory tab** (Figure 3-10) This tab allows you to choose between Automatic Memory Management (AMM), the Typical option that sets MEMORY_TARGET, and Automatic Shared Memory Management (ASMM), the Custom option that sets SGA_TARGET. Either option is appropriate for managing the Repository instance memory. However, you cannot choose the Typical option if planning to implement HugePages, because it is incompatible with AMM. HugePages, which is configurable on most operating systems, is a best practice for a database with a larger System Global Area (SGA), and will improve memory performance even for Repository databases with the minimum SGA size recommended for a Small CC deployment (2GB). For details see the later section "Implement HugePages."

  Figure 3-10 reflects selection of the Custom option, assuming you are configuring HugePages or want to use ASMM for some other reason.

  As shown previously, if using ASMM, select and enter the following:

  - **Memory Management** This option sets initialization parameters that control how database memory is managed. Leave Automatic Shared Memory Management selected. (The other choice is Manual Shared Memory Management.)
  - **SGA Size** *<SGA_TARGET>*
  - **PGA Size** *<PGA_AGGREGATE_TARGET>*

---

[5] See Section 11.2.2 of the *Cloud Control Advanced Installation and Configuration Guide* for the Oracle-recommended values.

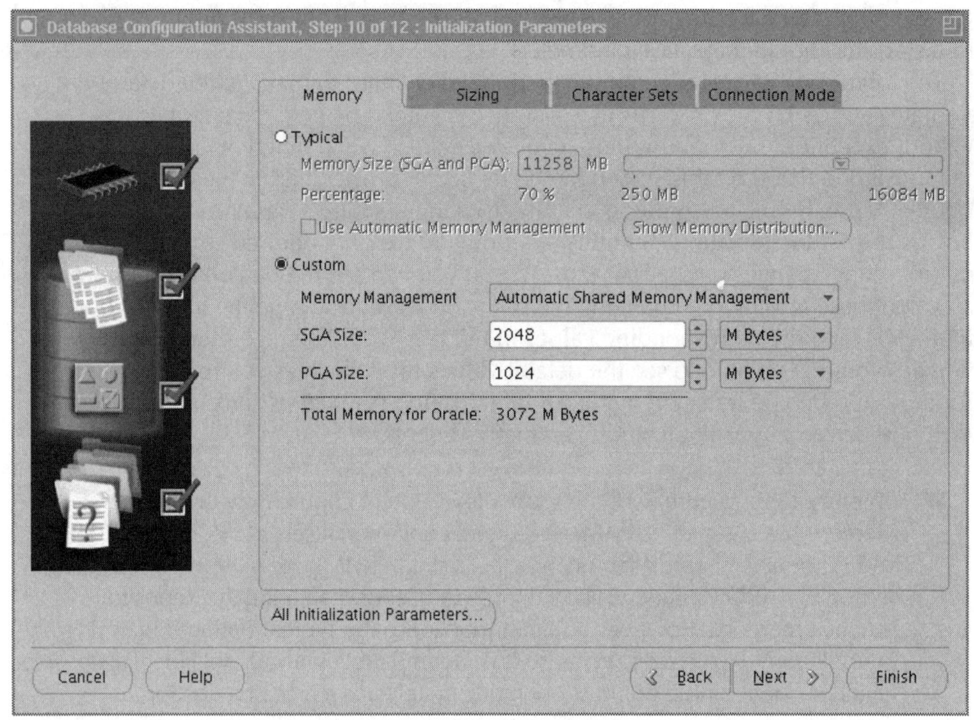

FIGURE 3-10. *Initialization Parameters screen: Memory tab*

NOTE

If, as we recommend, you specify the value for SGA_TARGET here in the SGA Size field (rather than entering the value when clicking the Initialization Parameters button), then you must enter the equivalent value in KB or MB, as DBCA does not accept this large a value in Bytes, due to an apparent bug.

The EM template defaults to Custom, but uses values for SGA and PGA sizes that are too small for even a Small CC deployment. Change the values for SGA Size and PGA Size to those listed for SGA_TARGET and PGA_AGGREGATE_TARGET, respectively in Table 3-2, for your size deployment. (Values that appear in the screen shot are for a Small deployment.)

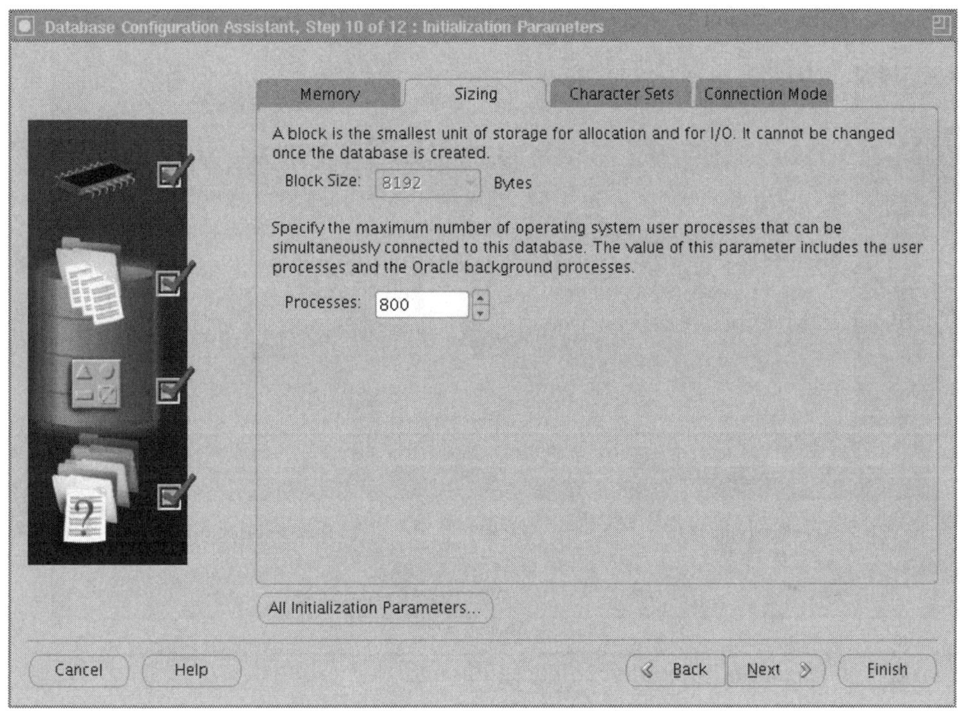

FIGURE 3-11. *Initialization Parameters screen: Sizing tab*

If you would prefer to use AMM rather than ASMM (and are not implementing HugePages, perhaps because the OS for the database server does not support it), select Typical, and for Memory Size (SGA and PGA), enter the value for MEMORY_TARGET listed in Table 3-2 for your size deployment. Also, check Use Automatic Memory Management.

- **Sizing tab** (Figure 3-11) In this tab you specify the database block size (or smallest block size for any tablespace), and the maximum number of OS user processes that can simultaneously connect to the database.
  - **Block Size** The EM template sets Block Size to 8192 bytes, the recommended value for an OMR database, so Block Size is accordingly grayed out.
  - **Processes** PROCESSES defaults to 300 for the EM template, but should be set to at least 800[6] as listed in Table 3-2, depending on the CC deployment

[6] The *Cloud Control Advanced Installation and Configuration Guide*, Section 11.2.2, states that the minimum value for PROCESSES is 300 for Small CC deployments. However, this value is too low even for Small deployments, and the EM Prerequisite Kit run by the CC Installer checks for a minimum value of 600. We recommend a still higher value of 800.

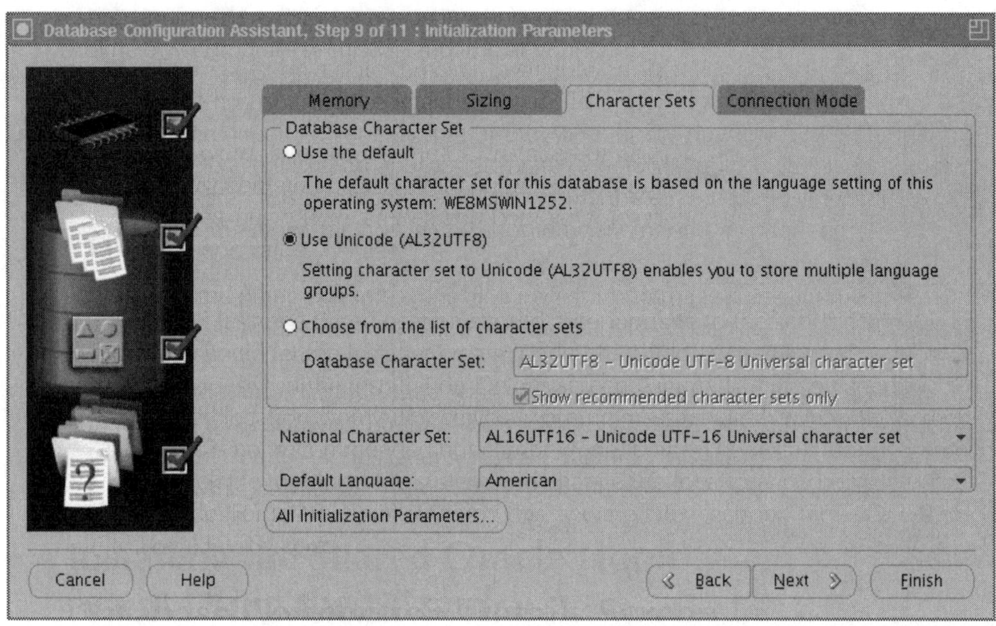

FIGURE 3-12. *Initialization Parameters screen: Character Sets tab*

size. PROCESSES is a static initialization parameter and as such would require bouncing the database to increase, so it is best to use a high enough value to accommodate Cloud Control CPU resource spikes. There is no downside to using a higher value, as it only sets the maximum number of OS processes that can simultaneously connect, and does not pre-spawn any additional processes.

- **Character Sets tab** (Figure 3-12) Use this tab to define the character sets and default language for the database to use.
  - **Database Character Set** The EM template chooses "Use the default" for the Database Character Set. However, Oracle recommends Use Unicode (AL32UTF8), which is the superset for many more languages.[7] Whatever your choice, make sure the chosen database and national character sets store the main language used by CC administrators and any additional language groups desired.

[7] Unicode character sets store Western and non-Western characters. See *Oracle Database Administrator's Guide* 11g Release 2 (11.2), Chapter 2, Considerations Before Creating the Database.

- **National Character Set** If you choose the Database Character Set AL32UTF8, use the accompanying National Character Set to select "AL16UTF16 - Unicode UTF-16 Universal character set," which is selected by default.
- **Default Language** Select the desired language (default American) to support locale-sensitive information such as default sorting sequence and date abbreviations.
- **Default Territory** Select the territory (default United States) name whose conventions are to be followed for day and week numbering, date format, local currency symbols, and so on.

- **Connection Mode tab** (Figure 3-13) This tab allows you to set the mode in which the database will run, either Dedicated Server Mode to spawn a dedicated server process for each user process, or Shared Server Mode to allow a large number of client connections to share a pool of server processes that the database preallocates. Leave the default setting selected, Dedicated Server Mode.

  Shared Server Mode is suitable for applications with thousands of users or database connections, whereas Cloud Control requires only a relatively limited number of simultaneous OMS connections.

- **All Initialization Parameters button** (Figure 3-13) This button displays the All Initialization Parameters screen (Figure 3-14), which provides a list of all database initialization parameters and their current settings.

  Tables 3-1 and 3-2 contain the "fixed" and "variable" initialization parameter values to change, respectively, from the default EM template values. The tables contain all parameters—in addition to those entered on other DBCA screens as covered earlier—whose values we recommend changing from the defaults set by the EM template. These changes are to meet Repository requirements or comply with database best practices. Values for the remaining parameters set by the EM template are already in compliance with Repository database requirements, as will be validated by the EM Prerequisite Kit. For more information on a particular parameter, consult the section of this chapter corresponding to the figure number where the parameter is set, except for those set on the All Initialization Parameters screen itself, shown in Figure 3-14. Figure numbers are listed in the last column in each table, along with names for fields where the parameter value is set (except for Figure 3-14).

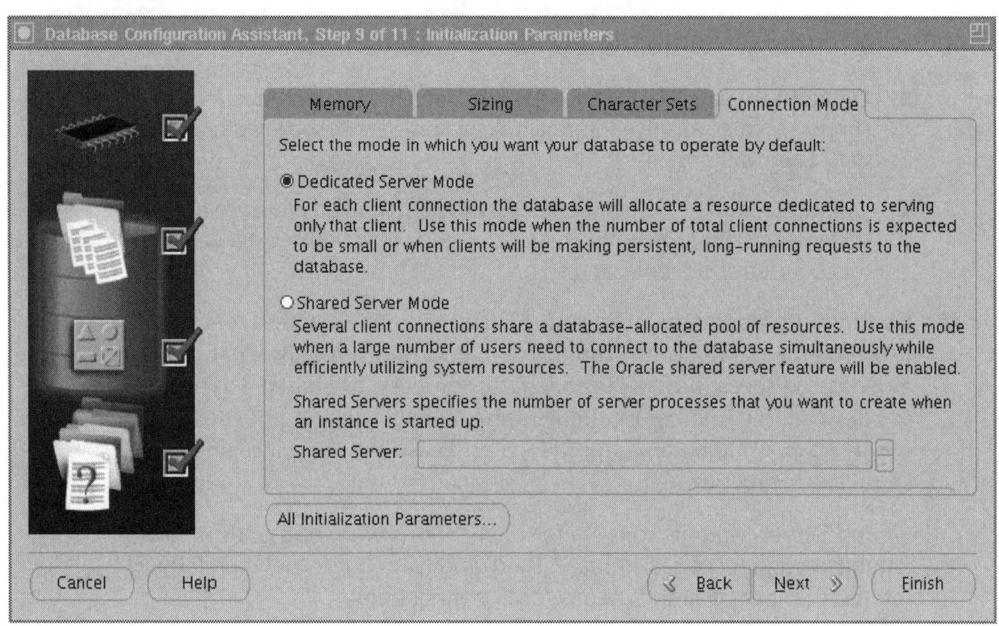

FIGURE 3-13. *Initialization Parameters screen: Connection Mode tab*

Following is generic information about this DBCA screen:

- You must click the Show Advanced Parameters button to display some of these parameters so that you can set them.
- DBCA expects values on this screen to be expressed in Bytes rather than MB or GB for parameters that allow all such units.
- Parameter values specified on previous screens should be reflected on this screen, including those provided in fields not explicitly labeled with their respective parameter names, such as "PGA Size" for PGA_AGGREGATE_TARGET in Figure 3-10.

Set the "fixed" initialization parameter values (that remain the same regardless of the CC deployment size) as shown in Table 3-1.

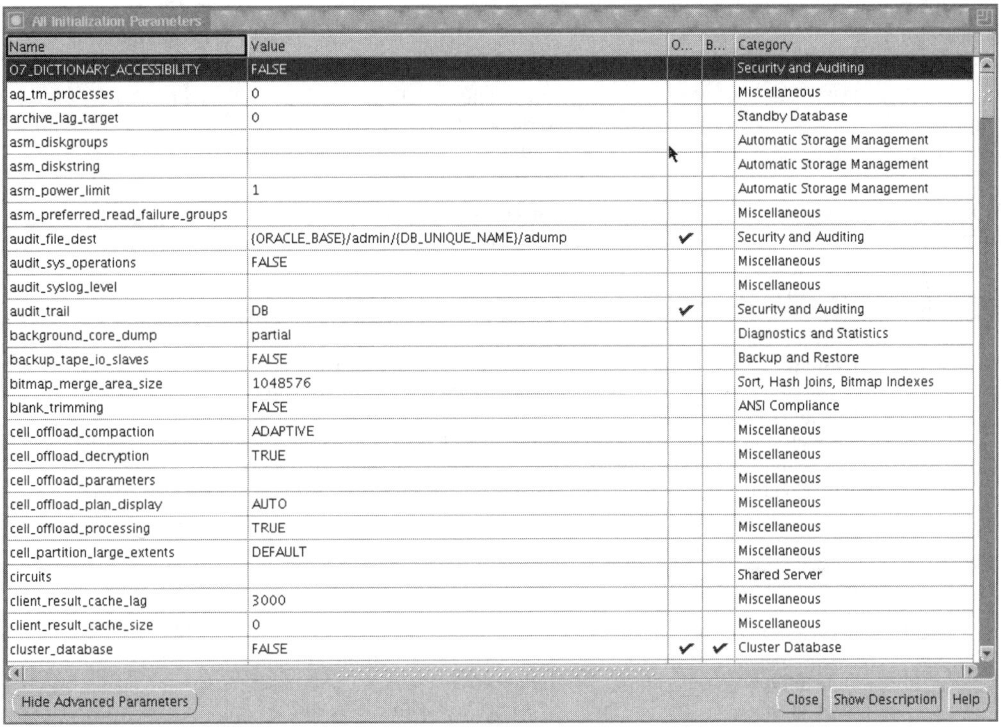

All Initialization Parameters

Name	Value	O...	B...	Category
O7_DICTIONARY_ACCESSIBILITY	FALSE			Security and Auditing
aq_tm_processes	0			Miscellaneous
archive_lag_target	0			Standby Database
asm_diskgroups				Automatic Storage Management
asm_diskstring				Automatic Storage Management
asm_power_limit	1			Automatic Storage Management
asm_preferred_read_failure_groups				Miscellaneous
audit_file_dest	{ORACLE_BASE}/admin/{DB_UNIQUE_NAME}/adump	✔		Security and Auditing
audit_sys_operations	FALSE			Miscellaneous
audit_syslog_level				Miscellaneous
audit_trail	DB	✔		Security and Auditing
background_core_dump	partial			Diagnostics and Statistics
backup_tape_io_slaves	FALSE			Backup and Restore
bitmap_merge_area_size	1048576			Sort, Hash Joins, Bitmap Indexes
blank_trimming	FALSE			ANSI Compliance
cell_offload_compaction	ADAPTIVE			Miscellaneous
cell_offload_decryption	TRUE			Miscellaneous
cell_offload_parameters				Miscellaneous
cell_offload_plan_display	AUTO			Miscellaneous
cell_offload_processing	TRUE			Miscellaneous
cell_partition_large_extents	DEFAULT			Miscellaneous
circuits				Shared Server
client_result_cache_lag	3000			Miscellaneous
client_result_cache_size	0			Miscellaneous
cluster_database	FALSE	✔	✔	Cluster Database

Hide Advanced Parameters   Close   Show Description   Help

FIGURE 3-14. *Initialization Parameters screen: All Initialization Parameters screen*

Set the "variable" initialization parameter values as listed in Table 3-2, so named because values vary based on the size of the CC environment. The EM template sets some parameters correctly for a Small CC deployment, but you need to change their values if your site will be Medium or Large. Parameters for Automatic Memory Management (AMM) and Automatic Shared Memory Management (ASMM), as tagged in the Description column, are mutually exclusive. That is, use AMM to set MEMORY_TARGET and MEMORY_MAX_TARGET, but do not set SGA_TARGET or SGA_MAX_SIZE. However, to use ASMM, do the reverse. See the section on the Memory tab of the Initialization Parameters screen earlier (Figure 3-10) for more information.

Fixed Initialization Parameter	Best Practice Value (Units)	Description	Figure Where Parameter Is Set and Field Label
db_block_checking	FULL	Checks that blocks are logically self-consistent to prevent memory and data corruption. Creates 1% to 10% overhead.	3-14
db_block_checksum	FULL	Detects storage and in-memory corruption. Creates ~5% overhead.	3-14
db_create_file_dest	$ORACLE_BASE/oradata	Sets the default location for Oracle-managed datafiles.	3-7, Database Area
db_create_online_log_dest_1	If using Storage Locations "Use Oracle-Managed Files" with Storage Type "File System," leave unset. If selecting Storage Locations "Use Common Location for all Database Files" with Storage Type "File System," set to hard-coded value of $ORACLE_BASE/oradata.	Sets default location #1 where Oracle-managed control files and redo logs are created. Leave unset if using OMF with File System storage type. Only set if not setting *db_create_file_dest*.	3-14
db_create_online_log_dest_2	If using Storage Locations "Use Oracle-Managed Files" with Storage Type "File System," leave unset). If selecting Storage Locations "Use Common Location for all Database Files" with Storage Type "File System:" set to hard-coded value of the FRA.	Sets default location #2 where Oracle-managed control files and redo logs are created. Leave unset if using OMF with File System storage type. Only set if not setting *db_create_file_dest*.	3-14
db_domain	(leave unset unless needed)	The extension component (that is, after the period ".") of the Global Database Name.	3-2, Global Database Name
db_flashback_retention_target	2880 (minutes)[8]	The upper limit on how far back in time the database may be flashed back. Set to 2× *undo_retention* to meet SLA requirements.	3-14
db_lost_write_protect	TYPICAL	Enables lost write detection.	3-14

TABLE 3-1. *Recommended Changes for Fixed Initialization Parameters* (Continued)

[8] Disk space permitting, enable Flashback Database to 24 hours or more (such as 48 hours as recommended here) for the OMR Database. With a daily disk backup schedule, a setting of 24 hours guarantees that you can perform incomplete recovery from disk using Flashback Database to any time within the past day. See the later section "Enable Flashback Database."

Fixed Initialization Parameter	Best Practice Value (Units)	Description	Figure Where Parameter Is Set and Field Label
db_name	EMREP (example value)	The database identifier.	3-2, SID
db_recovery_file_dest	+FRA or /fra (example values)	Default location for the fast recovery area (FRA).	3-8, Fast Recovery Area
db_recovery_file_dest_size	42949672960 (bytes)	Limit on total space that recovery files can use in the FRA.	3-8, Fast Recovery Area Size
disk_asynch_io	TRUE	Enables asynchronous I/O (AIO) to disk. Set to FALSE if AIO is unstable on your platform.[9]	3-14
fast_start_mttr_target	300 (seconds)	Specifies the number of seconds the database takes to perform crash recovery. Set to a non-zero value that meets your SLA.	3-14
filesystemio_options	setall	Enables direct I/O (DIO). Use setall for asynch I/O (AIO) and DIO, directio for DIO only, or asynch for AIO only, depending on whether your OS, storage subsystem, and file system support AIO or DIO.[10]	3-14
global_names	TRUE	Specifies whether a database link must have the same name as the database to which it connects.	3-14
local_listener	EMREP (example value)	Specify if configuring listener on a port other than default port 1521.[11]	
undo_retention	86400 (seconds)	Allows for retention of undo for at least the time specified. Set to at least 1/2 of *db_flashback_retention_target* to meet your SLA.	3-14

TABLE 3-1. *Recommended Changes for Fixed Initialization Parameters*

[9] This value should already be set correctly by default to TRUE on platforms that support asynchronous disk I/O. See MOS Note 279069.1 for a compatibility matrix between Linux distributions, file systems, and I/O types, including AIO and direct I/O. If AIO is unstable on your platform, you can simulate AIO by setting either DB_WRITER_PROCESSES (preferred) or DBWR_IO_SLAVES (if DB_WRITER_PROCESSES cannot be configured) to twice the number of CPU cores.

[10] Ibid. With DIO, data bypasses the UNIX buffer cache when transferred between SGA and disk. DIO is supported on most file systems, including NFS.

[11] The value for local_listener must match the alias for the connect string specified in the tnsnames.ora file, as described in the section "Create a Net Service Name for the Database."

Variable Initialization Parameter	Value for Small CC Site	Value for Medium CC Site	Value for Large CC Site	Description	Figure Where Parameter Is Set
log_buffer	8388608 (8M)	33554432 (32M)	33554432 (32M)	Specifies the amount of memory used when buffering redo entries to a redo log file. The indicated values are recommended when flashback is enabled.[12]	3-14
memory_max_target	For ASMM: 0 For AMM: 3865470566 (3.6G)	For ASMM: 0 For AMM: 6764573491 (6.3G)	For ASMM: 0 For AMM: 9663676416 (9G)	Allows for dynamic increase in SGA. Set 20% larger than *memory_target*. Only set when using AMM.	3-14
memory_target	For ASMM: 0 For AMM: 3221225472 (3G)	For ASMM: 0 For AMM: 5637144576 (5.25G)	For ASMM: 0 For AMM: 8053063680 (7.5G)	Sets Oracle system-wide usable memory. Only set when using AMM.	3-10
open_cursors	300	350	400	Sets maximum number of SQL cursors per database session. Must be between 300 and 400.	3-14
pga_aggregate_target	For ASMM: 1073741824 (1G) For AMM: 0	For ASMM: 1342177280 (1.25G) For AMM: 0	For ASMM: 1610612736 (1.5G) For AMM: 0	Specifies target aggregate PGA memory available to all server processes. Only set when using ASMM.	3-10

TABLE 3-2. *Recommended Changes for Variable Initialization Parameters* (Continued)

[12] See *Oracle Database High Availability Best Practices* 11g Release 2 (11.2), Section 5.1.8.

Variable Initialization Parameter	Value for Small CC Site	Value for Medium CC Site	Value for Large CC Site	Description	Figure Where Parameter Is Set
processes	800	1200	2000	Specifies maximum number of OS user processes that can simultaneously connect. Must be at least 600 but 800 is recommended.	3-11
session_cached_ cursors	300	400	500	Specifies the number of session cursors to cache for frequently used SQL statements. Must be between 200 and 500.	3-14
sga_max_size	For ASMM: 2576980378 (2.4G) For AMM: 0	For ASMM: 5153960755 (4.8G) For AMM: 0	For ASMM: 7730941133 (7.2G) For AMM: 0	Allows for dynamic increase in SGA. Set 20% larger than *sga_ target*. Only set when using ASMM.	3-14
sga_target	For ASMM: 2147483648 (2G) For AMM: 0	For ASMM: 4294967296 (4G) For AMM: 0	For ASMM: 6442450944 (6G) For AMM: 0	Specifies total size of all SGA components. Only set when using ASMM.	3-10
shared_pool_size	721420288 (688M)	1434451968 (1.33G)	2147483648 (2G)	Set to 1/3 of *sga_target*. Must be greater than 573M.	3-14[13]

TABLE 3-2. *Recommended Changes for Variable Initialization Parameters*

[13] As mentioned under the Database Content screen (Figure 3-9), setting SHARED_POOL_SIZE to a non-zero value on this screen leaves this parameter unset after DBCA completes, unless you select to run the script shpool.sql. However, we'd advise setting SHARED_POOL_SIZE on the All Initialization Parameters screen anyway, in case this bug is ever fixed and so that the value set here is consistent with that set in shpool.sql.

CAUTION
For the moment, leave the value for the initialization parameter COMPATIBLE at the default, which for 11gR2 is the database base release (for example, 11.2.0.0.0), even if you have already applied a Database Patch Set as instructed earlier, such as 11.2.0.3. Otherwise, DBCA will error out. After DBCA completes, you can manually update the COMPATIBLE value. We'll remind you to do this later, after DBCA creates the database.

Database Storage Screen The Database Storage screen allows you to set storage characteristics for the database files, which consist of control files, datafiles, and redo logs.

- **Controlfile** (Figure 3-15) Specify options for the control file.

  The control file options that the EM template specifies are adequate for a CC installation, unless you want more than three redo log members in each redo log group. In this case, increase the value for Maximum Log Members.

- **Datafiles** (Figure 3-16) Specify datafile names for all tablespaces, including the three tablespaces for the Management Repository.

  The EM template creates a different datafile name (mgmt_depot.dbf) for the MGMT_ECM_DEPOT tablespace than the CC OUI creates by default (mgmt_ecm_depot1.dbf). If you selected "Use Common Location for All Database Files" on the Database File Locations screen (see Figure 3-7), then take this opportunity to change the datafile name now in DBCA to mgmt_ecm_depot1.dbf, as shown in Figure 3-16, so that the CC Installer will use this datafile to store configuration management data.

  You cannot change the size of the tablespaces that the EM template creates, and two of the three Repository tablespaces are created significantly smaller than the minimum sizes recommended in the CC documentation.[14] Nevertheless, the datafiles are set to AUTOEXTEND ON, with appropriate NEXT sizes and MAXSIZE UNLIMITED, so they will grow as required for any size deployment. Perhaps this undersizing is serendipitous as it will save disk space and the datafiles will grow only as needed. The EM Prerequisite Kit does not verify tablespace sizes, so it won't complain about the EM template sizes.

---

[14] See *Cloud Control Advanced Installation and Configuration Guide*, Section 11.2.2.4, Table 11-7.

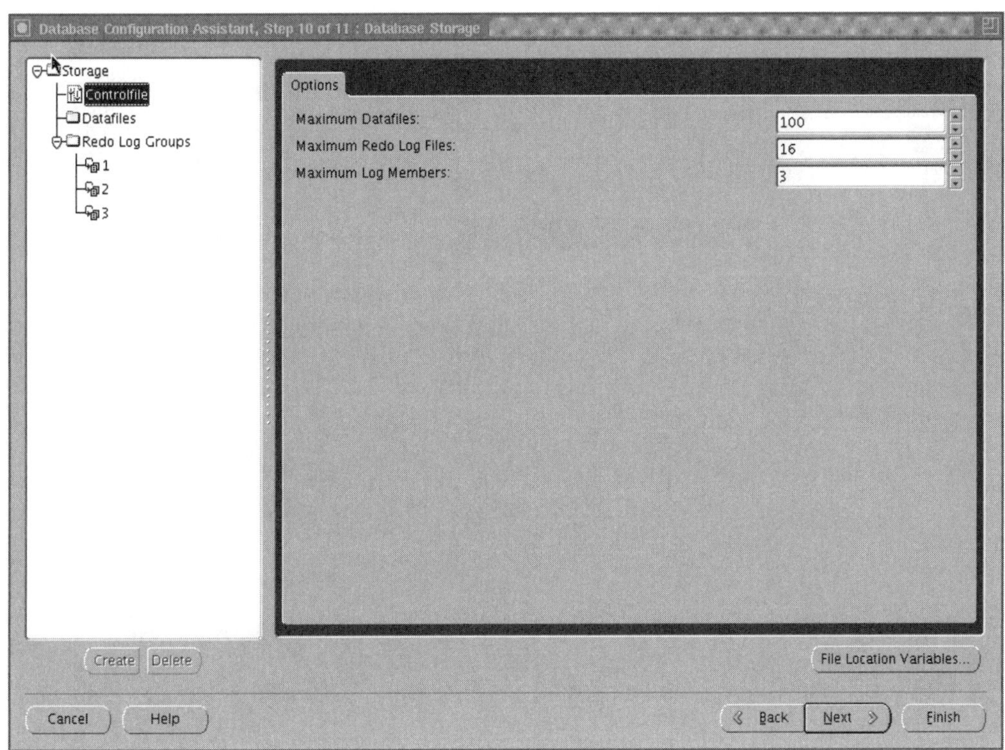

FIGURE 3-15. *Database Storage screen: Controlfile*

For reference only (that is, you don't need to change anything unless you would prefer to), following are the tablespace and NEXT extent sizes the EM template creates listed in comparison to the Oracle-recommended tablespace sizes for Small deployments:

Repository Tablespace Name	Minimum Oracle-Recommended Tablespace Size for Small Deployment (MB)	Tablespace Size Created by EM Template (MB)	Tablespace NEXT Extent Size Created by EM Template (MB)
MGMT_TABLESPACE	51200	200	50
MGMT_ECM_ DEPOT_TS	1024	40	20
MGMT_AD4J_TS	100	850	50

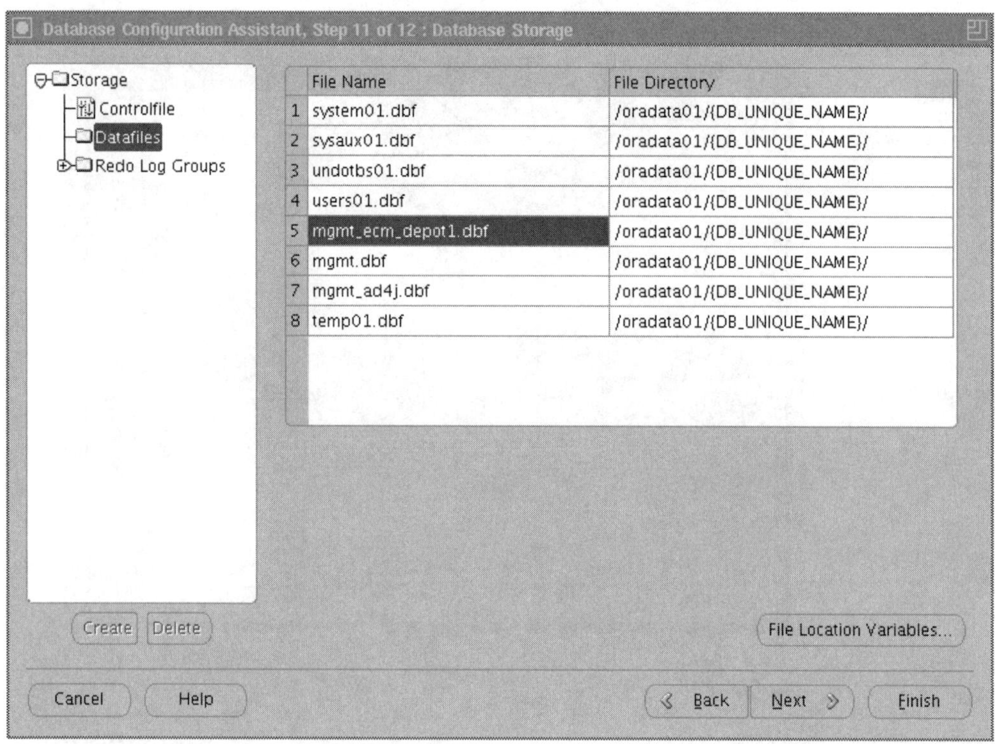

FIGURE 3-16. *Database Storage screen: Datafiles*

- **Redo Log Groups** (Figure 3-17) On this screen you need to specify redo log file sizes, the number of groups to create, and the number of members to use in each group. Following are recommendations for each of these redo log characteristics, presented in the same order as shown in this screen.

  As for the redo log size to use, the EM template specifies creating three groups of redo logs 100MB in size, but this size is too small, according to the Oracle CC documentation,[15] which suggests creating redo logs at least 300MB in size for even a Small CC site. The EM Prerequisite Kit has an even

[15] Redo log sizing is discussed in the *Cloud Control Advanced Installation and Configuration Guide*, Section 11.2.2.

more stringent requirement than the Oracle CC documentation, reporting a failed check if redo log sizes are not greater than 600,000,000 bytes (~573M). This larger redo log size is more in line with the amount of redo that even a small CC site generates, typically resulting in log files switching every 20 minutes. This in turn will keep unnecessary checkpointing to a minimum and thereby optimize database writer and archiver performance. Therefore, specify a minimum redo log size of 600MB for each redo log group to satisfy the EM Prerequisite Kit's minimum specification and CC operating requirements, as shown in Figure 3-17.

It is easier to let DBCA create redo logs with the correct sizes than have to manually resize the redo logs afterward. The redo log sizing recommended depends on the anticipated size of your CC environment, and the suggested

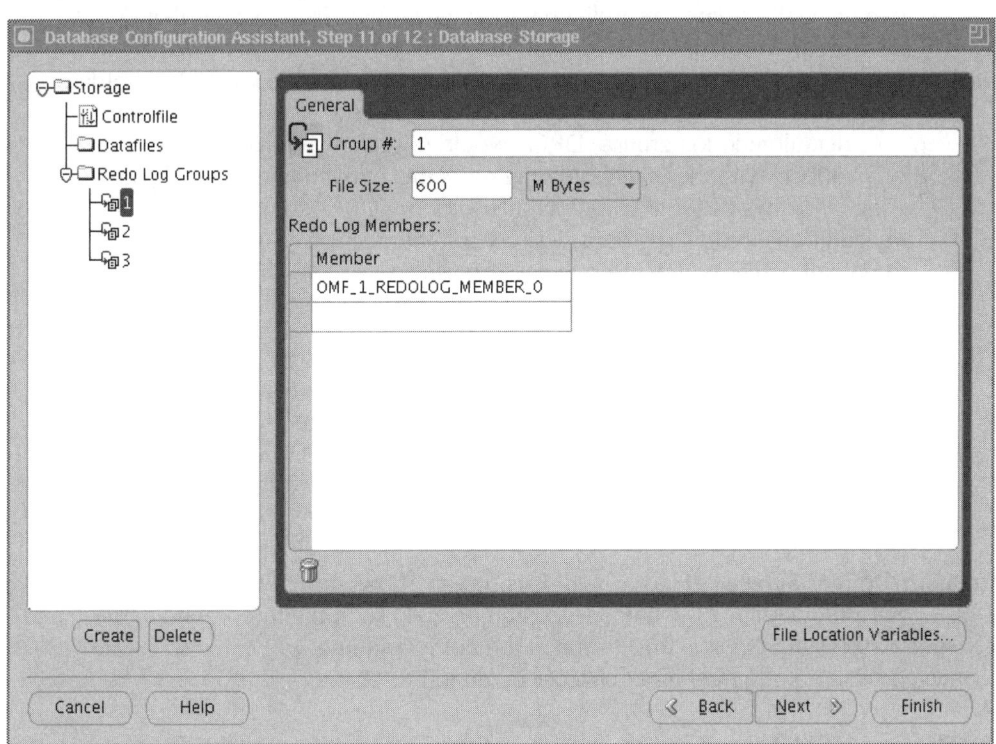

FIGURE 3-17. *Database Storage screen: Redo Log Groups*

values in the following table are larger than those recommended in the Oracle CC documentation:

Deployment Size	**Recommended Redo Log Sizes (MB)**
Small	600
Medium	1024
Large	1536

As for the number of redo log groups to create, the template specifies three groups, the minimum number required for an Oracle database. While this may be sufficient to keep up with redo generation at your site, we'd suggest creating at least one more group as a buffer, even for Small CC deployments, given that a database in ARCHIVELOG mode will hang if a redo log group is needed but cannot be archived. However, if you selected Oracle-Managed Files on the Database File Locations screen (see Figure 3-7), wait until DBCA finishes and then manually create any additional redo log groups. The reason is that DBCA has a problem creating OMF-compliant names for redo log members. If you were to try adding a fourth redo log group in DBCA with the same placeholder name format "OMF_4_REDOLOG_MEMBER_0" used for members of the three default redo log groups, DBCA would mistakenly create the new redo log members with the placeholder name as the actual name. Thus, if you're using OMF, it is better to wait until after running DBCA to manually create any additional redo log groups desired, so that redo log members with OMF-compliant names will be used. If you are using OMF, we will remind you to manually create additional redo log groups later, in part two of this chapter.

Finally, as for the number of redo log members to create in each group, it is an Oracle best practice to multiplex redo logs and control files. If you chose to use OMF on the DBCA screen shown in Figure 3-7, OMF takes care of multiplexing the three default redo log groups. However, if you did not choose OMF, you need to specify additional redo log members for each default group, and for any additional groups you create.

Creation Options Screen (Figure 3-18) This screen allows you to control how DBCA goes about creating the database, whether to do so in the foreground and/or generate database creation scripts to run at the command line. You can also create a new template based on all input choices made in DBCA thus far.

- **Create Database** Check this box to let the DBCA GUI create the database. Otherwise, you need to rely on running scripts that DBCA generates by checking "Generate Database Creation Scripts," as discussed below. (As already mentioned, the EM template cannot be used to create a RAC database. However, for the sake of those who may use DBCA to create a

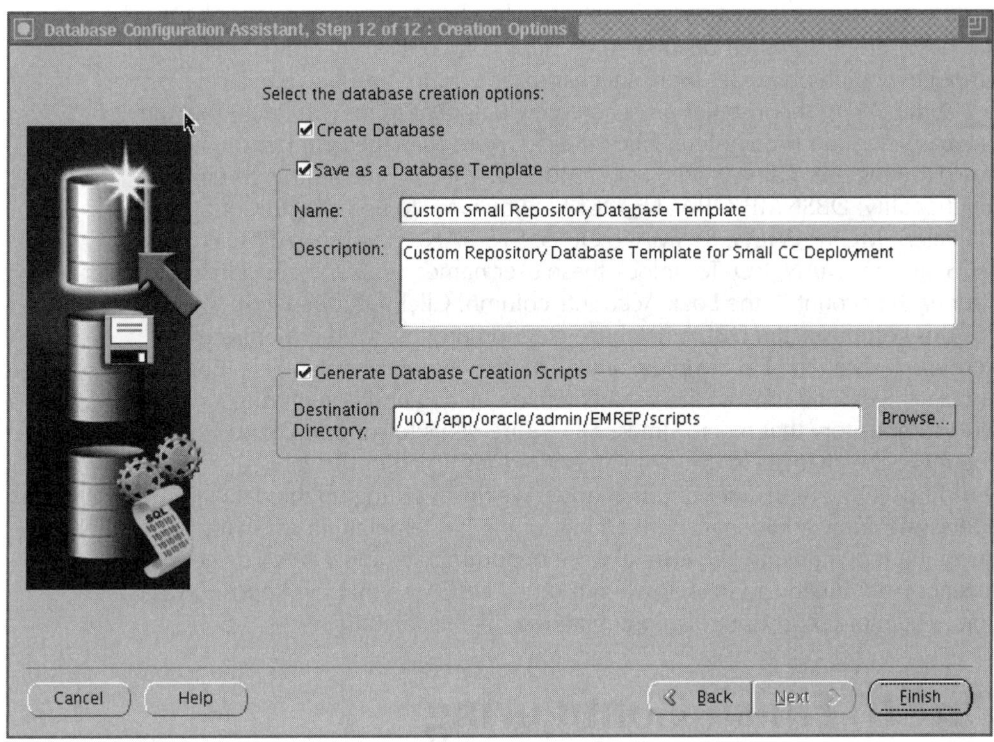

FIGURE 3-18. *Creation Options screen*

RAC database for the Repository or for any other application, it is particularly important to check this box. If you rely instead on DBCA-generated database creation scripts, postinstallation you would need to perform additional manual RAC configuration steps not mentioned in the Oracle Database doc set.)

- **Save as a Database Template** Check this box. This will create a revised EM template customized for your site, so that, if you create another CC system, you can use the customized EM template instead, thereby avoiding having to make the same changes again in the EM template.

- **Generate Database Creation Scripts** Select this option, so that if the database creation fails via the DBCA user interface (UI), you can debug the problem, and then run the scripts instead to create the database, rather than having to rerun DBCA and re-enter all required information. The scripts also serve as a record of the installation process and can be changed directly (such as the SID) to create another Repository database for another CC environment. To display this file later in a browser, specify the extension **.htm** when naming it.

Click Finish, and a Confirmation popup will appear. Click "Save as an HTML file" to save the database configuration details, click Save, and then click OK. The database scripts will then be created. Popups will confirm that the template and script generation processes were successful.

At the end of the installation, a screen will appear to let you know that the database creation is complete. Click the Password Management button, and unlock the following user names, which are required by CC or needed for certain CC functionality: DBSNMP, ORACLE_OCM (if you want to use Oracle Configuration Manager), MGMT_VIEW, SYSMAN_OPSS, SYSMAN, SYSMAN_APM, SYSMAN_MDS, and SYSMAN_RO. To unlock these user names, click the check mark to clear it for each account in the Lock Account? column. Click OK, then Exit.

This completes the DBCA database creation process for the Management Repository using the EM template, and also Part I of this chapter. Selecting the EM template "gets you most of the way there" in creating and configuring a database with a Repository that meets almost all requirements to support Cloud Control, after you make the changes to the template settings as noted in Part I.

In Part II, the remainder of this chapter, we finish setting up the database by addressing a few additional shortcomings of the EM template in satisfying Repository operating requirements. We also take the opportunity to apply MAA database best practices not already addressed when running DBCA, so that the Repository database component of Cloud Control is optimized for high availability.

Part II: Finish Configuring the Repository Database

As you may recall, this chapter is divided into two major parts. This second part picks up where DBCA left off in the first part, to finish configuring the database you just created with a Management Repository. The DBCA EM template creates a database that meets most Repository requirements, and the template's few shortcomings were, for the most part, already corrected in the DBCA user interface (UI) itself, as detailed previously. However, the remaining configuration must be done after running DBCA because it cannot be performed in the DBCA UI. After you complete this configuration, you will be ready to launch the CC Installer, as covered in the next chapter.

NOTE
It is possible to perform at least some of the configuration changes presented in Part II programmatically in a custom SQL script specified in DBCA on the Database Content screen, as shown in Part I (Figure 3-9), to run after the database is created. However, you cannot make these configuration changes in the DBCA user interface itself.

The remaining Repository database configuration after running DBCA begins by renaming CC datafile names to match those expected by the CC OUI, if you chose to use OMF, and disabling automatic optimizer statistics collection, which are the only outstanding prerequisites remaining to running the CC Installer. The other configuration tasks deal primarily with implementing applicable Maximum Availability Architecture (MAA) Database 11.2 high availability best practices that could not (at least not easily) be implemented in DBCA. These best practices are described in the Oracle Database documentation set,[16] and are as relevant for a Repository database as for any Oracle database. These guidelines apply to both standalone and RAC databases, so are applicable even if you created a RAC database and did not use the EM template, which only creates a single-instance database. Many MAA best practices for configuring storage, Clusterware, and RAC are not on our punchlist, due to the limited real estate for such a topic in a book dedicated to Cloud Control.[17]

Here, then, are the additional configuration changes to make in the Repository database, primarily composed of MAA database best practices:

- Rename CC datafiles to align with names expected by the CC Installer.
- Disable auto optimizer statistics collection.
- Set the COMPATIBLE initialization parameter to the "point" release (for example, 11.2.0.3.6) to which you've patched the database.
- Create additional redo log groups (if using OMF—otherwise you can create them when running DBCA).
- Confirm database listeners load balance across RAC nodes.
- Ensure that the OS default locale setting is consistent with the OMR database NLS settings.
- Check that the database and OS time zones match.
- Implement HugePages, if applicable to the OS.
- Enable Flashback Database.
- Enable FORCE LOGGING mode.
- Enable block change tracking for incremental backups.
- Run the EM Prerequisite Kit in standalone mode.

---

[16] The MAA guidelines covered are identified in *Oracle Database High Availability Best Practices* 11g Release 2 (11.2), and are principally found in Chapter 5, "Configuring Oracle Database."

[17] For details on high availability best practices for storage, Clusterware, and RAC, see Chapters 4, 6, and 7, respectively, of *Oracle Database High Availability Best Practices* 11g Release 2 (11.2).

These steps are presented in no particular order because there are no dependencies between them. Some steps require bouncing the database, so you could conceivably streamline the effort by performing all such steps in a row, ending with one database bounce to effect all changes. However, it is highly recommended to bounce the database for each change that requires it, to ensure that the database restarts without error. Otherwise, if a database startup error occurs, you may not be entirely sure which change may have caused the error.

The following sections provide directions on how to complete each of these tasks. Commands are listed, but not their output, unless significant to completing the task. Perform all OS steps as the *oracle* user (the owner of the database software), unless the step must be executed as *root*, as indicated, and execute all database tasks as the SYS user within SQL*Plus.

TIP

Now would be a good time to take a hot or cold backup of the database. A backup will preserve the database creation and configuration you just completed, providing a way to recover and restore to this point should one of the upcoming configuration steps fail with an unrecoverable error, or should the database crash for any other reason.

Rename CC Datafiles If Using OMF

If when creating the database, you selected "Use Oracle-Managed Files" for Storage Locations (see Figure 3-7), then you need to rename the three Cloud Control datafiles created by DBCA to those that the CC Installer expects. The reason is that the CC Installer does not allow you to change the datafile names (see Figure 4-9 in Chapter 4). The following code shows the details of the renaming process (using an example OMF filename):

```
SQL> select tablespace_name, file_name from dba_data_files order by 1;
SQL> alter tablespace MGMT_AD4J_TS offline;
SQL> !mv o1_mf_mgmt_ad4_8gmfqckg_.dbf mgmt_ad4j.dbf
SQL> alter database rename file '/orahome/app/oraoem/oradata/EMREP/
datafile/o1_mf_mgmt_ad4_8gmfqckg_.dbf'
to '/orahome/app/oraoem/oradata/EMREP/datafile/mgmt_ad4j.dbf';
SQL> alter tablespace MGMT_AD4J_TS online;
```

Disable Auto Optimizer Statistics Collection

The only Repository requirement that cannot be satisfied in the DBCA user interface when creating the database, at least without the undesirable consequences noted next, is to disable the automatic optimizer statistics collection. This was one of the maintenance tasks implicitly enabled when you checked "Enable automatic maintenance tasks" in DBCA on the Management Options screen (see Figure 3-4).

We chose this option because it also enabled two additional jobs that should remain enabled, "auto space advisor" and "sql tuning advisor," as shown by the following query:

```
SELECT CLIENT_NAME, STATUS FROM DBA_AUTOTASK_CLIENT order by 1;
CLIENT_NAME                        STATUS
------------------------------     -------
auto optimizer stats collection    ENABLED
auto space advisor                 ENABLED
sql tuning advisor                 ENABLED
```

This query is on the same view, DBA_AUTOTASK_CLIENT, that the EM Prerequisite Kit runs to validate whether "auto optimizer stats collection" is enabled.

To disable automatic optimizer statistics collection, run the following SQL to call the DISABLE procedure in the DBMS_AUTO_TASK_ADMIN package (the command is shown on separate lines for clarity, but you must enter it entirely on one line):

```
exec DBMS_AUTO_TASK_ADMIN.DISABLE(
client_name => 'auto optimizer stats collection',
operation => NULL,
window_name => NULL);
```

Then, rerun the same query above to ensure that auto optimizer statistics collection has been disabled. You should re-enable this job after running the CC Installer, which we will remind you to do in Chapter 4.

Set the COMPATIBLE Initialization Parameter

As you may recall from the previous section, DBCA requires that the COMPATIBLE parameter remain set to the default value of the base release, which is 11.2.0.0.0. Now that you have created the database and exited DBCA, you should change the COMPATIBLE initialization parameter setting to the actual database version (for example, 11.2.0.3.6) or "point release" to take advantages of the new features, maintenance improvements, and bug fixes in this later release. This parameter cannot be dynamically changed, so it requires bouncing the database to put it into effect. If using a PFILE, simply change the COMPATIBLE parameter setting in the initialization parameter file. If using an SPFILE, set the COMPATIBLE parameter only in the SPFILE to the database release you're running, as follows:

```
ALTER SYSTEM SET COMPATIBLE='11.2.0.3.3' SCOPE=SPFILE;
```

Whether using a PFILE or SPFILE, you must bounce the database to effect this change.

Create Additional Redo Log Groups If Using OMF

As mentioned previously when covering creation of the database, DBCA creates only three redo log groups when using the EM template for the Management Repository (and other templates for that matter). This is the minimum number of redo log groups required for Oracle database operations, but it is a database best practice to make at least four redo log groups available (for each thread, if RAC). As instructed earlier in coverage of the Redo Log Groups screen in DBCA, we recommend waiting to create additional redo log groups until after DBCA finished, due to a DBCA bug that does not allow OMF to correctly name members of redo log groups. To manually create one or more additional redo log groups when using OMF, execute the following in SQL*Plus as the SYS user:

```
ALTER DATABASE ADD LOGFILE GROUP <group_number> SIZE <size>;
```

Outside of DBCA, with the above command, Oracle will assign OMF-compliant names to redo log group members. Take the time now to determine whether the redo log configuration complies with other best practices; namely, that you created each redo log group with at least two members (which DBCA should have done for you automatically, if you chose to manage datafiles with OMF), and that each member is stored on a separate device and controller, if possible. Mirroring the redo logs at the Oracle level is a sound idea even if they are also mirrored at the hardware level to protect against OS-level failure, such as inadvertent removal of a redo log member on the file system. For additional protection, physically separate redo logs from datafiles. Redo logs store database transactions, so losing all members of a current online redo log can result in unrecoverable data loss.

Confirm Listeners Load Balance Across RAC Nodes

(The following applies only to those who created a RAC database, and therefore could not use the EM template, and now need to configure the RAC database for a Management Repository.) The Management Services rely on server-side connect-time load balancing on a RAC OMR database to evenly distribute connections between RAC nodes. To distribute the load optimally for a RAC Management Repository, ensure that the PREFER_LEAST_LOADED_NODE_*<listener_name>* property is set to ON (the default value) in the listener.ora file on each RAC database node. (We recommend setting this property explicitly as a reminder not to set it differently.) With this property setting, a listener selects an instance in the order of least loaded node, then least loaded instance. In the case of dedicated OMR nodes, this setting will likely not change anything, given that the least loaded node will probably be running the least loaded instance. However, if you share OMR node(s) with other applications or databases, this property setting will maximize overall OMR database performance by taking into account loads from applications other than Cloud Control and directing CC traffic to the least loaded RAC node.[18]

[18] See MOS Note 226880.1 for more background on server-side connect-time load balancing and on testing it with client-side connect-time load balancing (for which the OMS is already configured).

Check OS Default Locale vs. Database NLS Settings

It is not mandatory, but recommended that the operating system default locale setting be consistent with the Repository database NLS character set, language, and territory.

NOTE
The NLS_LANG environment variable does not need to be set for the oracle *OS user for Cloud Control to function properly. However, if you would like to set NLS_LANG for other reasons, such as to display timestamps when running the RMAN client, make NLS_LANG consistent with the OS default locale and database character set.*

To show the OS current default locale on UNIX, enter the following OS command:

```
locale
```

Here is typical command output for the United States:

```
LANG=en_US.UTF-8
LC_CTYPE="en_US.UTF-8"
LC_NUMERIC="en_US.UTF-8"
LC_TIME="en_US.UTF-8"
LC_COLLATE="en_US.UTF-8"
LC_MONETARY="en_US.UTF-8"
LC_MESSAGES="en_US.UTF-8"
LC_PAPER="en_US.UTF-8"
LC_NAME="en_US.UTF-8"
LC_ADDRESS="en_US.UTF-8"
LC_TELEPHONE="en_US.UTF-8"
LC_MEASUREMENT="en_US.UTF-8"
LC_IDENTIFICATION="en_US.UTF-8"
LC_ALL=
```

These locale environment variables may also be set at the system or session level, and will override default locale values as reflected in the `locale` command output. The value for the variable LANG is the one to compare to the database NLS parameter settings, unless LC_ALL is set, as LC_ALL takes precedence over LANG.

To list the OS default locale on Windows, enter the following at the command line:

```
systeminfo | findstr /C:"System Locale"
```

The following is example output:

```
System Locale:              en-us;English (United States)
```

To list the database character set, language, and territory, execute the following command in SQL*Plus:

```
SELECT * FROM V$NLS_PARAMETERS
  WHERE PARAMETER IN ('NLS_CHARACTERSET',
'NLS_LANGUAGE', 'NLS_TERRITORY');
PARAMETER            VALUE
---------------- ---------
NLS_LANGUAGE       AMERICAN
NLS_TERRITORY      AMERICA
NLS_CHARACTERSET   AL32UTF8
```

NOTE
The preceding output for the OS locale variable LANG, en_US.UTF-8, is consistent with the language, territory, and database character set, AMERICAN, AMERICA, and AL32UTF8, respectively. If your output is not consistent, log in as root *and change the OS locale to match the database NLS settings.*

Ensure Database Time Zone Matches OS Time Zone

It is not mandatory, but recommended that the database time zone match that of the operating system on the database server.[19] To determine the current database time zone, execute the following in SQL*Plus (sample output is provided):

```
SELECT DBTIMEZONE FROM DUAL;
DBTIME
------
+00:00
```

Compare this database time zone to the OS time zone on UNIX and Windows, shown when executing the `date` command.

If you need to change the database time zone because it is not consistent with the OS time zone, execute the following in SQL*Plus:

```
ALTER DATABASE SET TIME_ZONE = '<timezone>';
```

where <*timezone*> is the offset from GMT in the form +|- ##:##

For example, *+00:00* is GMT and *-05:00* is EST.
You must restart the database for the time zone change to take effect.[20]

---

[19] The database time zone should also match the OS time zone you plan to use on target hosts for Agents, and the Agent time zone, as set by agentTZRegion in the $AGENT_INSTANCE_HOME/sysman/config/emd.properties file.

[20] You can only change the database time zone this way if no TIMESTAMP WITH LOCAL TIMEZONE columns exist in the database, which is the case with an Oracle 11*g* database.

Implement HugePages (Conditional)

On many UNIX operating systems (including Linux and AIX) and on Windows,[21] it is recommended that you configure HugePages for databases with a large SGA (such as greater than 2GB), and accompanying ASM instances. HugePages is also known as "Large Pages" for AIX and Windows. As the focus of this book is on installing and using Cloud Control, we need to confine the HugePages discussion—and the steps to enable it—to Linux, as this is the most popular OS for an Oracle database. If you are using another platform, please consult your operating system documentation for the equivalent steps to set up HugePages (or Large Pages).

HugePages is a feature integrated into the Linux kernel from Release 2.6 that allows large SGA memory to be utilized with reduced overhead by ensuring that the memory is not paged to disk. HugePages allows you to use much larger page sizes (for example, 2MB or 4MB) than the default 4K page size, which can be crucial for faster Oracle database performance on Linux, and increasingly so for systems with large RAM and database SGA sizes, as is the case even for small CC deployments (if built according to the specifications presented in this chapter).

One possible drawback of using HugePages is that you cannot use it in conjunction with Automatic Memory Management (AMM); you must use Automatic Shared Memory Management (ASMM) instead. Therefore, before you decide to implement HugePages, you may want to weigh its advantages against any disadvantages of not being able to enable AMM.

For those unfamiliar with AMM and ASMM, ASMM was introduced in Oracle 10*g* with the SGA_TARGET and SGA_MAX_SIZE parameters that dynamically resize many SGA components on demand. With Oracle 11*g*, Oracle developed this feature further to include the PGA as well, and called it Automatic Memory Management (AMM), which is enabled by setting the parameter MEMORY_TARGET. AMM makes use of the SHMF—a pseudo file system like /proc. Every file created in the SHMFS is also created in memory.

In our experience, ASMM works well and has been extensively tested in the field. By contrast, AMM has several bugs that you may encounter, including non-public Bug 6325878, which affects 11.1 databases, and whose fix is to disable native compilation by setting JAVA_JIT_ENABLED=FALSE. That said, both AMM and ASMM are supported for the Cloud Control Repository database.

While there are several MOS bulletins on HugePages (notably MOS ID 361323.1) and how to configure it (MOS ID 361468.1), we have not found a bulletin that covers all steps to our satisfaction. So in the following steps, we provide a detailed procedure on how to configure HugePages for an Oracle 11*g* database on Linux. All steps should

---

[21] Solaris automatically uses 4M large pages for the SGA segments.

be performed as the owner of the Oracle Database software (for example, the *oracle* user), unless otherwise indicated as needing to be run as the *root* user.

1. If you're not sure whether HugePages has already been configured, you can check the HugePages state in /proc/meminfo:

   ```
   grep Huge /proc/meminfo
   ```

   All HugePages states except AnonHugePages and Hugepagesize will be 0 when HugePages is not configured:

   ```
   AnonHugePages:        53248 kB
   HugePages_Total:          0
   HugePages_Free:           0
   HugePages_Rsvd:           0
   HugePages_Surp:           0
   Hugepagesize:          2048 kB
   ```

2. Determine the current value for memlock (reported in KB) for the *oracle* user:

   ```
   ulimit -l
   ```

   The memlock value should be slightly smaller than the amount of RAM installed on the database server. On UNIX, you can determine the RAM on your system with the following command:

   ```
   cat /proc/meminfo | grep MemTotal
   ```

3. If the current value for memlock is not set as required, log in as *root* to set the memlock user limit, which must be expressed in KB (enter only the number of KB for <memlock_value>, not the units themselves), in /etc/security/limits.conf:

   ```
   * soft memlock <memlock_value>
   * hard memlock <memlock_value>
   ```

   For guidance on what would be considered a slightly smaller *<memlock_value>* than the amount of RAM installed, see the following table, which lists memlock values appropriate for the more common amounts of RAM found on database servers:

RAM (GB) on Database Server	Memlock Value (KB) to Use
64	60397977
32	30198988
16	15099494
8	7549748

   You can also set memlock to "unlimited," though this is not recommended.

4. Exit the *oracle* account, log in again, and confirm that the new memlock limit has been set as intended:

   ```
   ulimit -l
   ```

5. Ensure that the Automatic Memory Management (AMM) feature is disabled, because AMM is incompatible with HugePages. AMM is set by default for 11*g* Database, but can be disabled by unsetting (setting to "0") the following initialization parameters:

   MEMORY_TARGET

   MEMORY_MAX_TARGET

   First, check the setting for these parameters with:

   ```
   SHOW PARAMETER MEMORY_TARGET;
   SHOW PARAMETER MEMORY_MAX_TARGET;
   ```

   If you're using an SPFILE, and these parameters are explicitly set to non-zero values, run the following commands to unset them (that is, set them to "0") in the SPFILE:

   ```
   ALTER SYSTEM RESET MEMORY_TARGET SCOPE=SPFILE;
   ALTER SYSTEM RESET MEMORY_MAX_TARGET SCOPE=SPFILE;
   ```

   If these parameters are not explicitly set (that is, set to 0), you do not need to unset them, and the preceding commands will accordingly error out with "ORA-32010: cannot find entry to delete in SPFILE."

6. Confirm that Automatic Shared Memory Management (ASMM) is being used instead of AMM, as evidenced by the following initialization parameters being set to nonzero values:

   SGA_TARGET

   SGA_MAX_SIZE

   If using an SPFILE, the following commands will set these parameters to 2G and 2.4GB respectively (as an example, using the recommended values for a small CC site) in the SPFILE, to take effect on database restart:

   ```
   ALTER SYSTEM SET SGA_TARGET = 4G SCOPE=SPFILE;
   ALTER SYSTEM SET SGA_MAX_SIZE = 6G SCOPE=SPFILE;
   ```

7. If the database is Oracle 11.2.0.2 or higher, set the initialization parameter USE_LARGE_PAGES=ONLY to ensure that the database instance will start only when it can get all of its memory for SGA from HugePages, and to avoid out-of-memory errors. Use this setting only for database instances; for ASM instances leave USE_LARGE_PAGES=TRUE (the default value). This ensures that HugePages are used when available, but that ASM will start when HugePages are not sufficiently configured.

   If using an SPFILE, execute the following command to set USE_LARGE_PAGES=ONLY, made effective when the database is restarted:

   ```
   ALTER SYSTEM SET USE_LARGE_PAGES=ONLY SCOPE=SPFILE;
   ```

Note that the USE_LARGE_PAGES parameter is not currently documented in the Oracle documentation and cannot be set up during database creation with DBCA. For more information on USE_LARGE_PAGES, see MOS ID 1392497.1.

8. As *root*, edit /etc/sysctl.conf and set the kernel parameter *vm.nr_hugepages* as recommended by the Oracle-supplied script hugepages_settings.sh, contained in MOS ID 401749.1:

```
vm.nr_hugepages = <hugepages_value>
```

9. As *root*, dynamically enable this new kernel parameter setting to ensure it does not error:

```
sysctl -p
```

10. Stop all databases and database listeners on the server, and as *root* reboot the server, such as with the `reboot` command.

11. Validate the HugePages Configuration. After the system is rebooted, ensure that all database instances on the host are started, then check the HugePages state from /proc/meminfo:

```
grep Huge /proc/meminfo
```

The following type of output is expected (values will vary), now that HugePages has been configured:

```
AnonHugePages:        55296 kB
HugePages_Total:       2050
HugePages_Free:        1551
HugePages_Rsvd:        1550
HugePages_Surp:           0
Hugepagesize:          2048 kB
```

To verify that the configuration is valid, ensure that HugePages_Total is set as follows, and note that the remaining values will be set as indicated:

- The value for HugePages_Total is that set for *vm.nr_hugepages* in Step 8.
- The value for HugePages_Free will be smaller than that for HugePages_Total.
- HugePages_Rsvd will be set to a nonzero value.
- The sum of HugePages_Free and HugePages_Rsvd, multiplied by the Hugepagesize, will be somewhat smaller than the total combined database SGA sizes of all databases on the system. This is expected because database instances allocate pages dynamically and proactively as needed.
- The value for HugePages_Surp will be 0 or thereabouts.

12. Restart the database listener on the database tier:

```
lsnrctl start <listener_name>
```

This concludes the configuration process for HugePages on Linux.

Enable Flashback Database

With Flashback Database, you can rewind the database to a previous point in time without media recovery (that is, without restoring backup copies of the datafiles). When the database is running, Flashback Database buffers and writes before-images of data blocks to *flashback logs*, which are generated by default for all permanent tablespaces and which reside in the fast recovery area (FRA). Flashback logs allow Flashback Database to reduce the time to correct an error proportionally to the time it takes to detect the error, rather than to media recovery time (when Flashback Database is not enabled), which depends on database size.

To enable Flashback Database, do the following:

1. Shut down the database and start up the database in mount mode in SQL*Plus:

```
SHUTDOWN IMMEDIATE;
STARTUP MOUNT;
```

2. Confirm that the database is in ARCHIVELOG mode, which is required for Flashback Database, and enable ARCHIVELOG mode if needed (it should already be enabled if you checked Enable Archiving as instructed earlier on the Recovery Configuration screen, shown in Figure 3-8):

```
ARCHIVE LOG LIST;
ALTER DATABASE ARCHIVELOG;
```

3. Set the flashback retention target to the desired value (in minutes). The following example value is for a 48-hour flashback target (as recommended earlier):

```
ALTER SYSTEM SET DB_FLASHBACK_RETENTION_TARGET=2880;
```

4. Set or change the relevant FRA parameters for Flashback Database, as noted in the following example (these commands assume the FRA disk group is named +FRA and that you are adding 20GB to the FRA size suggested earlier, which is more than enough to accommodate the flashback logs that will be generated):

```
ALTER SYSTEM SET DB_RECOVERY_FILE_DEST_SIZE=60G;
ALTER SYSTEM SET DB_RECOVERY_FILE_DEST='+FRA';
```

For a RAC database, you must locate the FRA on ASM or a clustered file system.

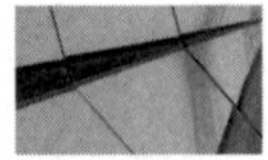

NOTE
If DB_RECOVERY_FILE_DEST is previously unset and you want to dynamically set it, you must first set DB_RECOVERY_FILE_DEST_SIZE. (This constraint makes sense if you think about it. The way to remember which parameter you must set first is to remind yourself that Oracle cannot allocate a FRA on disk until it knows how large to make the FRA.)

If these parameters are already set, increase the FRA size to allocate space for flashback logs. The volume and rate of flashback log generation is approximately the same order of magnitude as those of redo log generation.

5. Set the associated undo retention, required for certain flashback features. Here, we set a 24-hour undo retention (in seconds), equivalent to half the DB_FLASHBACK_RETENTION_TARGET, as in Step 3:

```
ALTER SYSTEM SET UNDO_RETENTION=86400;
```

6. Finally, enable Flashback Database and FORCE LOGGING while the database is mounted, then open the database:

```
ALTER DATABASE FLASHBACK ON;
ALTER DATABASE OPEN;
```

Enable FORCE LOGGING Mode

In addition to enabling Flashback Database, set FORCE LOGGING mode to ensure that all DDL operations can be recovered when doing media recovery. Some DDL statements such as CREATE TABLE allow the NOLOGGING clause, suppressing the generation of redo records for the operation, and thereby preventing its recovery. If you are planning to implement a standby Repository database for disaster recovery purposes, enabling FORCE LOGGING mode on the primary database is also required to guarantee that all database operations are logged and thereby propagated to the standby database.

To enable FORCE LOGGING mode, start up the database in mount mode and run the ALTER DATABASE FORCE LOGGING command, as follows:

```
SHUTDOWN IMMEDIATE;
STARTUP MOUNT;
ALTER DATABASE FORCE LOGGING;
ALTER DATABASE OPEN;
```

Enable Block Change Tracking

When you enable block change tracking in Oracle 11*g*, Oracle tracks the physical location of all database changes for incremental backups. RMAN automatically uses the change tracking file to determine which blocks need to be read during an incremental backup, and directly accesses those blocks to back them up. When block change tracking is not enabled, the entire datafile is read during each incremental backup to find and back up only the changed blocks, even if just a very small part of that datafile has changed since the previous backup.

The change tracking file is a binary file and resides in the fast recovery area (FRA). This file should be located in the same directory as your database files. To determine if block change tracking is already enabled, issue the following query:

```
SELECT * FROM V$BLOCK_CHANGE_TRACKING;
```

To enable block change tracking, execute the following command (the database can be mounted or open):

```
ALTER DATABASE ENABLE BLOCK CHANGE TRACKING;
```

The above command assumes you are using OMF, which will name the block change tracking file under the DB_CREATE_FILE_DEST location. If not using OMF, name the block change tracking file yourself:

```
ALTER DATABASE ENABLE BLOCK CHANGE TRACKING
USING FILE '<ORACLE_BASE>/oradata/<DB_UNIQUE_NAME> block_change_
tracking.dbf' reuse;
```

Run the EM Prerequisite Kit in Standalone Mode

The EM Prerequisite Kit is a routine that automatically validates whether the database intended for the Repository meets all prerequisites for installing or upgrading an Enterprise Manager system. The Kit can also take corrective action, to the extent possible, when a prerequisite check fails.

The CC Installer automatically runs the EM Prerequisite Kit, and you can also run it in standalone mode beforehand, whether for a database preconfigured with a Repository, as in our case, or for a database in which the CC Installer will be creating a Repository. When executed by the CC Installer, EM Prerequisite Kit routines automatically run and report their results on the Prerequisite Checks screen. You invoke the EM Prerequisite Kit in standalone mode by running the `emprereqkit` command, provided in the CC distribution software. Any issues and/or missing components can be identified and addressed prior to the installation.

TIP

Although the Cloud Control Installer runs the EM Prerequisite Kit for you, we recommend running it in standalone mode first, at this point, after you install and configure the database. It's easier to let the `emprereqkit` *verify requirements and report all results before kicking off the CC Installer, rather than having to resolve unmet requirements on the fly during CC installation.*

To run the Prerequisite Kit to list Repository prerequisites and show any corrective actions needed, execute the following commands on the host where you installed the database for the Repository:

```
cd <Software_Location>/install/requisites/bin
emprereqkit -executionType install -prerequisiteXMLLoc ../list -dbHost <db_hostname> \
-dbPort <db_port> -dbSid <instance_name> -dbUser SYS -dbPassword <db_password> \
-dbRole sysdba -runPrerequisites -showCorrectiveActions
```

The log files created when running the EM Prerequisite Kit are located under the subdirectory <*Software_Location*>/install/requisites/bin/prerequisiteResults/log/<*timestamp*>, and the latest run is also found in the LATEST subdirectory alongside the <*timestamp*> subdirectory.

For a description of all available arguments you can pass to the `emprereqkit` command, execute `emprereqkit -help`, or see Section Appendix A, Section A.3 of the *Cloud Control Basic Installation Guide*. See Section A.5 for a description of all log files created.

Note that while most of the prerequisite checks that the EM Prerequisite Kit performs will pass (a sizeable number of which confirm initialization parameter settings), a handful of checks will fail because the Kit software, which Oracle released before the EM template, does not allow for certain preconfiguration that the EM template performs. In other words, the EM Prerequisite Kit was not designed to run in standalone mode against a database preconfigured with a Repository by the EM template. For example, the EM template creates the three EM tablespaces, but one of the EM Prerequisite Kit validations is to confirm that these tablespaces do not exist, because the Kit expects the CC Installer to create them. Following is a list of the five prerequisite names listed in the emprereqkit.output file that will fail, if you've created the database using the EM template, and which you can ignore as expected behavior:

- Check if SYSMAN schema is absent for new install.
- Check the existence of public synonyms.

- Check the absence of mgmt tablespaces.
- Check the absence of EM schemas.
- Check the RCU metadata.

Interestingly enough, the EM Prerequisite Kit will report these as "false positive" failures when run in standalone mode, but not when run by the CC 12.1.0.2 Installer. Apparently, the CC 12.1.0.2 Installer can take a preconfigured Repository into account and suppresses these "failures."

Summary

This chapter provides instructions for installing and configuring an Oracle 11gR2 database to support a Management Repository for Cloud Control.

Part I on installing the database software and creating the database is divided into two main sections. The first section covers the high-level steps to install and patch an 11.2.0.3 Grid Infrastructure (GI) home, if used, and database software home, to host a Repository database. These sections are straightforward in that the GI and database software installations are generic, and you only need to make a few specific choices to ensure the installation will support a Repository database. The second section tackles the DBCA database creation procedure using the newly released DB11.2.0.3 EM seed database template (or "EM template"). The EM template is new, so accordingly, its coverage in the chapter is much more extensive. We present screen shots of the DBCA interface and detailed input instructions for navigating through it to select this template, alter some of its default settings, as required, and apply some database best practices that the template overlooks.

Part II of this chapter is devoted to completing the Repository database configuration process, picking up where DBCA left off. Only the first configuration steps are specific to Cloud Control; the remaining steps are taken from MAA database best practices and field experience with Cloud Control, such as to address possible inconsistencies in time zone or locale between the database and operating system.

The chapter concludes with directions for running the EM Prerequisite Kit, to check that you have met all database requirements for installing a Management Repository. If, as suggested in this chapter, you create the database using the EM template, and make the subsequent database configuration changes suggested, all prerequisite checks will succeed, except a handful that are expected to fail, as noted. These Prerequisite Kit failures occur because the Kit was not designed with the EM template in mind; namely, the EM template pre-creates the Repository database structures, which the Kit is expecting the CC Installer to create. Nevertheless, you can still use the EM Prerequisite Kit to check the majority of Repository requirements, and have confidence that the failed checks reported are accurate.

Let's turn now to Chapter 4 and install Cloud Control, or more accurately, the OMS and chain-installed Agent. Thanks to the EM template, we've already installed and configured the third Cloud Control component, the Repository database.

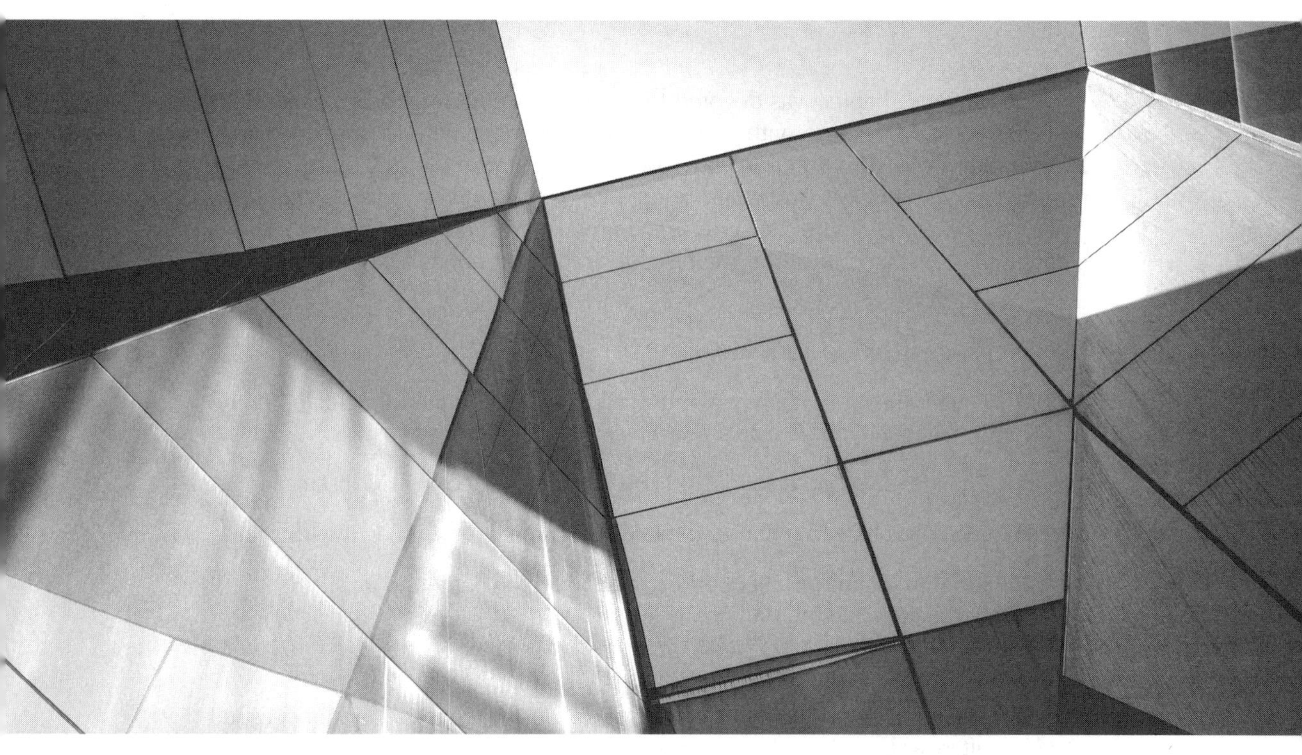

CHAPTER 4

Cloud Control Installation and Configuration

The previous chapter was devoted to creating, configuring, and tuning a new 11gR2 Database with a preconfigured Management Repository. This chapter gives you directions on how to install a new Cloud Control system, consisting of an initial OMS and chain-installed Agent to work with this preconfigured Repository, how to configure the system, then install any additional OMSs required. The chapter is organized into four main sections, broken out as follows:

- Preparation for CC Installation
    - Details the information you must gather as input to the CC Installer for the installation type "Create a new Enterprise Manager System."
    - Provides direction on addressing bugs that may affect the CC installation itself.
    - Describes how to initialize the OS environment for running the Installer.
    - Briefly explains Installer options, elaborating in particular on silent installation and the static ports feature.
- Installation of a New CC System
    - Describes key installation log files to tail during the installation, or consult afterward.
    - Supplies detailed instructions for advancing through all of the screens for the Advanced option of the installation type "Create a new Enterprise Manager System," when running the Installer interactively.
- Configuration of the New CC System
    - Takes you through the initial setup to allow you to log in to the Console via HTTPS or HTTP, and use Cloud Control to download and stage CC patches to apply as the next step in the configuration (see next bullet point).
    - Elaborates on three categories of CC patches to apply: the latest CC Bundle Patch, the latest EM Critical Patch Update (CPU), and any functionally required one-off patches.
    - Supplies the list of configuration changes to make for the initial OMS installed and OMR database nodes, some of which are optional or conditional to your installation choices.
- Installation of an Additional OMS (Conditional)
    - Provides the additional prerequisites for deploying another OMS, over and above those for installing the initial OMS.

- Introduces you to the Add Management Service Wizard, a new feature in CC 12*c* for cloning the first OMS to an additional OMS. This deployment method has the distinct advantage over that in Grid Control 11*g* (GC 11*g*) of replicating all patches and configuration changes from the first OMS to subsequent OMSs, thus avoiding the need to manually perform these changes.

Before you start readying your environment to run the CC Oracle Universal Installer (OUI), referred to herein as "Installer," let's look at the installation type we'll be choosing, "Create a new Enterprise Manager System," in the context of the three installation types offered by the Installer:

Installation Type	Options	Description
Create a new Enterprise Manager System	Simple, Advanced	Install a 12*c* OMS, Agent, and Repository (if not already preconfigured) in an existing Oracle database
Upgrade an existing Enterprise Manager System	One System Upgrade, Two System Upgrade	Upgrade GC 11*g* or GC 10*g* to CC 12*c*, either in-place with downtime (One System Upgrade), or on a different host (Two System Upgrade).
Install software only	(None)	Install 12*c* OMS and Agent software binaries only. Later you need to create a database and run a CC 12*c* configuration script to install the Repository in it and configure all CC components.

This book's focus is on installing and using rather than upgrading Cloud Control, and as such, can only delve into this first, most common installation type.

The second installation type, to upgrade to CC 12, is applicable to those who have invested in implementing an earlier OEM version that they need to upgrade to CC 12*c*. The *Cloud Control Upgrade Guide* contains comprehensive instructions on how to upgrade your earlier EM release. It is much easier to install CC from scratch than to upgrade, so if you haven't done a lot of configuration for your GC 10*g* or GC 11*g* systems, consider the time savings of installing a new CC 12*c* system and redoing the configuration, such as rediscovering targets and re-creating administrators. You can then continue your EM configuration on the more robust CC 12 platform and take advantage of its many new features.

The third option, to install only the CC software binaries, is only marginally useful, in our view. It does allow you to divide the CC installation process into two phases: (a) install the OMS, Agent binaries, and Management Plug-ins, then (b) install a database and run the script ConfigureGC.sh to create a Repository in the database and configure all CC components. This is a bit of a "cart before the horse" approach, though it could reduce the clock time of installation, for example, for a DBA who needed to get started installing CC while waiting for the Repository database server to be built. See Chapter 4 of the *Cloud Control Advanced Installation and Configuration Guide* for the procedure to install CC in this two-step manner.

Now that you have a general idea of the three installation choices, let's begin with the CC preinstallation tasks as preparation for running the Installer. While these tasks generally apply to all three CC installation options, they are comprehensive only for creating a new EM system or installing the CC software. If upgrading to CC 12*c*, consult the *Cloud Control Upgrade Guide* for its additional prerequisites.

Preparation for CC Installation

The preparation steps in this section are necessary to install a new CC environment, consisting of an Oracle Management Repository (OMR) database servicing one or more Oracle Management Services (OMSs), that in turn talk to Oracle Management Agents (OMAs) on each target host (installed in Chapter 5). These steps prepare the initial OMS host to run the Installer to lay down the Repository and OMS, either on the same host or separate hosts.

Gather Needed Installation Information

OMR, OMS

We strongly advocate determining the input you will provide to all installation questions *before* launching the CC Installer. Such a fact-finding session streamlines the installation process and prevents having to reinstall Cloud Control due to insufficient preparation. The installation information requested when choosing the first installation type, "Create a new Enterprise Manager System," is detailed in Table 4-1.

Where applicable, an input value or choice is recommended in Column 4 based on Cloud Control best practices and Database Optimal Flexible Architecture (OFA)[1] standards. The figure numbers listed in Column 6 are for the installation screen shots themselves found in this chapter, with accompanying details.

After documenting the information you'll enter when running the CC OUI to install a new EM system, we will move on to evaluating installation snags you may encounter, which may depend upon the CC platform used, as described next.

---

[1] For more information on OFA standards, see the *Oracle Database Installation Guide* for your Repository platform and release. For Database 11*g* Release 2 (11.2) for Linux, this OFA coverage is in Appendix D.

(1) Installation Screen Title	(2) Input Field(s)	(3) Field Description(s)	(4) Recommended/ Example Input	(5) Is Input Mandatory or Optional?	(6) Figure Number
My Oracle Support Details	Email	MOS e-mail address to enable installation of OCM	*<e-mail_address>*, for example, oraoem@ndbas.com	Optional	4-1
	I wish to receive security updates via My Oracle Support	Check this box to receive security updates from MOS	Check the box	Optional	
	My Oracle Support Password	If host has Internet connectivity, enter MOS password to enable OCM collections after CC installation.	Specify the password if OMS host has Internet connectivity	Optional	
Software Updates	Skip OR Search for Updates: Local Directory OR My Oracle Support	Skip OR Search for Updates to CC software (Prerequisites, Critical Patches, Interim Patches, and so on)	Select Search for Updates. Select My Oracle Support and enter MOS username and password.	Mandatory	4-2

TABLE 4-1. *CC Installation Information Needed to Create a New Enterprise Manager System* (Continued)

(1) Installation Screen Title	(2) Input Field(s)	(3) Field Description(s)	(4) Recommended/ Example Input	(5) Is Input Mandatory or Optional?	(6) Figure Number
Oracle Inventory[a]	Inventory Location	Local (nonshared) directory to contain inventory data for CC release being installed	$ORACLE_BASE/../oraInventory where ORACLE_BASE=<*mount point*>/app/<*oracle_user*>, for example, /u01/app/oraInventory	Mandatory	4-3
	Operating System Group	OS group name to own the Oracle inventory directory	*oinstall* or *dba* (site-specific)	Mandatory	
Prerequisite Checks	N/A	List of all prerequisite checks for the OMS host	Click Rerun or Ignore for each failed prerequisite, then click Next	Mandatory	4-4
Installation Types	Create a new Enterprise Manager System: Simple OR Advanced	Installs a 12*c* OMS, Agent, and Repository (if not already preconfigured) in an existing Oracle database	Select the Advanced radio button to provide greatest configurability	Mandatory	4-5

TABLE 4-1. *CC Installation Information Needed to Create a New Enterprise Manager System*

(1) Installation Screen Title	(2) Input Field(s)	(3) Field Description(s)	(4) Recommended/ Example Input	(5) Is Input Mandatory or Optional?	(6) Figure Number
	Upgrade an existing Enterprise Manager System: Two System Upgrade OR One System Upgrade	Upgrades GC 11*g* or GC 10*g* to CC 12*c*, either in-place with downtime (One System Upgrade), or on a different host (Two System Upgrade)	Site-specific		
	Install software only	Installs CC software now, to be configured later	Use this option only if you cannot first create a database to host the Repository. Otherwise, select "Create a new Enterprise Manager System"		
Installation Details	Middleware Home Location	Directory under which Oracle homes for WebLogic Server, JDK, and OMS are created	For example, $ORACLE_BASE/middleware, where ORACLE_BASE=*<mount point>*/app/*<oracle_user>*	Mandatory	4-6

TABLE 4-1. *CC Installation Information Needed to Create a New Enterprise Manager System* (Continued)

(1) Installation Screen Title	(2) Input Field(s)	(3) Field Description(s)	(4) Recommended/ Example Input	(5) Is Input Mandatory or Optional?	(6) Figure Number
	Agent Base directory	Directory under which the Oracle home for the chain-installed Agent software is created	Typically $ORACLE_BASE/agent, or other location outside the Middleware home	Mandatory	
	Host Name	Local or virtual host name on which the Installer is running and OMS and chain-installed Agent will be installed	For example, omshost.ndbas.com	Mandatory	
Plug-in Deployment	List of plug-ins	List of default and optional plug-ins to be installed	Choose any optional plug-ins (for example, Microsoft Active Directory, Oracle Cloud Application, and so on) in addition to default plug-ins installed by default	Optional	4-7

TABLE 4-1. *CC Installation Information Needed to Create a New Enterprise Manager System*

(1) Installation Screen Title	(2) Input Field(s)	(3) Field Description(s)	(4) Recommended/ Example Input	(5) Is Input Mandatory or Optional?	(6) Figure Number
WebLogic Server Configuration	WebLogic User Name	User account for administrator to create the default WebLogic domain GCDomain	*weblogic*	Mandatory	4-8
	WebLogic Password		Enter a password	Mandatory	
	Node Manager Password		Enter a password	Mandatory	
	OMS Instance Base Location	Directory where the OMS-related configuration files will be stored	*<Middleware Home Location>*/gc_inst by default, for example, $ORACLE_BASE/middleware/gc_inst	Mandatory	
Database Connection Details	Database Host Name	Host name for the Repository database	*<DB_hostname>.<domain>*, for example, dbhost.ndbas.com	Mandatory	4-9
	Port	Database listener port	For example, 1521	Mandatory	
	Service/SID	SERVICE_NAME for single-instance or RAC database	For example, EMREP	Mandatory	

TABLE 4-1. *CC Installation Information Needed to Create a New Enterprise Manager System* (Continued)

(1) Installation Screen Title	(2) Input Field(s)	(3) Field Description(s)	(4) Recommended/ Example Input	(5) Is Input Mandatory or Optional?	(6) Figure Number
	SYS Password	Password for SYS database user	Enter a password	Mandatory	
	Deployment Size	Expected size of the CC environment: SMALL, MEDIUM, or LARGE	For example, SMALL	Mandatory	
Repository Configuration Details	SYSMAN Password	Password for SYSMAN user	Enter a password	Mandatory	4-10
	Registration Password	Password for Agents to securely communicate with OMS	Enter a password	Mandatory	
	Management Tablespace	Full path of datafile for all target-related monitoring and metrics data	File system: *<mount_point>*/app/oradata/EMREP/datafile/mgmt.dbf, OMF-assigned: *<mount_point>*/app/oradata/EMREP/datafile/o1_mf_mgmt_8gmfqckg_.dbf ASM: +DATA[b]	Mandatory	

TABLE 4-1. *CC Installation Information Needed to Create a New Enterprise Manager System*

(1) Installation Screen Title	(2) Input Field(s)	(3) Field Description(s)	(4) Recommended/ Example Input	(5) Is Input Mandatory or Optional?	(6) Figure Number
	Configuration Data Tablespace	Full path of datafile for configuration data collected from monitored targets	File system: <*mount_point*>/app/oradata/EMREP/datafile/mgmt_ecm_depot1.dbf, OMF-assigned: <*mount_point*>/app/oradata/EMREP/datafile/o1_mf_mgmt_ecm_8gmhrdmf_.dbf ASM: +DATA[c]	Mandatory	
	JVM Diagnostics Data Tablespace	Full path of datafile for diagnostics data related to JVM Diagnostics and ADP	File system: <*mount_point*>/app/oradata/EMREP/datafile/mgmt_ad4j.dbf, OMF-assigned: <*mount_point*>/app/oradata/EMREP/datafile/o1_mf_mgmt_ad4_8hniseng_.dbf ASM: +DATA[d]	Mandatory	
Port Configuration Details	Port	List of Component Names and associated ports to be allocated	Use first available port in recommended port range for each component	Mandatory	4-11

TABLE 4-1. *CC Installation Information Needed to Create a New Enterprise Manager System* (Continued)

(1) Installation Screen Title	(2) Input Field(s)	(3) Field Description(s)	(4) Recommended/ Example Input	(5) Is Input Mandatory or Optional?	(6) Figure Number
Review	N/A	Installation Information provided by user	Click Install after verifying all input	Mandatory	4-12
Install Progress	N/A	Directory path for script allroot.sh	Click OK after running allroot.sh	Mandatory	(No screen shot provided)
Finish	N/A	Provides URLs to access Consoles for CC and Admin Server	Click Close	Mandatory	4-13

[a] (UNIX only) This screen appears only for UNIX hosts and if this is the first Oracle installation on that host. On Windows, the Inventory location defaults to <*SystemDrive*>:\Program Files\Oracle\Inventory.

[b] Though the *Cloud Control Basic Installation Guide* agrees that only the disk group should be entered, the Online Help in the CC Installer states that, if the database is on ASM, the path must look like +<*disk_group1*>/prod/oradata/mgmt.dbf. However, this is incorrect, as OMF must decide on the location and name of datafiles on a disk group.

[c] Ibid.

[d] Ibid.

TABLE 4-1. *CC Installation Information Needed to Create a New Enterprise Manager System*

Address Installation Bugs

OMR, OMS

This book is intended to help you navigate the CC installation and configuration process. To make this experience as painless as possible, we try to minimize the need to bounce between this book and the Oracle Cloud Control documentation, but you cannot ignore the Oracle documentation altogether. Release notes, which contain information on installation and postinstallation bugs, documentation errata, and the like, accompany each new software release for a specific OS, leaving us with a wide array of current release notes that would be too lengthy to incorporate into this book.

Release notes for the latest 12.1.0.x release on OTN are available in the Oracle Enterprise Manager Documentation Library located at http://www.oracle.com/pls/em121/homepage. In case the location of this page has changed, you can navigate to it from the OTN home page at http://oracle.com/technetwork, by hovering over the Support tab and selecting Product Documentation, clicking on Enterprise Manager at the top, then selecting Enterprise Manager 12*c* Release 1 (12.1) twice. Before installing Cloud Control, read the release notes for updated information, and particularly, the section "Critical Patches to Apply." These patches are typically for bugs discovered between releases to be folded into the upcoming release. You need to address any installation bugs now and, postinstallation, deal with bugs relating to CC operations.

If upgrading, be sure to read "Known Upgrade Issues" in the release notes.

Initialize the *oracle* User Environment

OMS

Before running the Cloud Control OUI, you need to initialize the environment from which you will launch the Installer as the *oracle* user (or other user chosen to own the software). This initialization involves setting up X Server for UNIX platforms, then setting or unsetting the appropriate environment variables.

Set Up X Server (UNIX Only)

To run the CC OUI interactively on UNIX, you need to set up X Server on the Installer host on which the OMS is to run. If you are on a UNIX platform, you can use either a PC with X Server software installed or a UNIX workstation.

NOTE

You can also run the Installer silently, in which case you don't need to install X Server libraries or run X Server. See the later section entitled "Silent Installation Method" for more information.

UNIX Shell Variations

Initializing the environment on UNIX platforms varies according to the UNIX shell you use. There are four main UNIX shells in use today. For each of these shells, the table shown here lists the shell startup script name, how to run the startup script, and the command syntax for setting environment variables.

	Bash Shell (bash)	**Bourne Shell (sh)**	**Korn Shell (ksh)**	**C Shell (csh or tcsh)**
User's Startup Script for Shell	.bash_profile	.profile	.profile	.login
How to Execute Startup Script from User's Home Directory	. ./.bash_profile	. ./.profile	. ./.profile	source ./.login
Syntax to Set x=1 (Set Environment Variable x to "1")	`x=1; export x`	`x=1; export x`	`x=1; export x`	`setenv x 1`

The Bash shell is used in examples throughout this book.

If using a workstation with X Server software, start the X Server on the workstation. If using a UNIX workstation, start a terminal session such as an X terminal (xterm) to the remote UNIX system where you want to install the software. Either way, log in directly as the *oracle* user—if you use `su` or `sudo` to log in as *oracle*, the X Server software may not work.

CAUTION
Leave the session open where you're logged in to the X terminal session directly as the oracle *user, as you will be initializing the environment and launching the Cloud Control Installer in this session.*

1. Before setting the environment variables as indicated in the section "Set/Unset OS Environment Variables," first determine the default shell for the *oracle* user:

```
echo $SHELL
```

2. Open the shell startup file for the *oracle* user in a text editor, such as *vi*. Consult the table in the sidebar "UNIX Shell Variations" for the shell startup file name. The example here assumes a Bash shell startup file is used.

```
vi .bash_profile
```

3. Allow the remote UNIX host to display X applications on the local X server by adding the following command on the remote host (use the fully qualified host name of the remote host):

```
xhost <remote_hostname>
```

4. Also, enter or edit the following line to set the default file mode creation mask to 022 in the shell startup script. This ensures that the CC installation lays down files with 755 permissions:

```
umask 022
```

5. Save the shell startup file and exit the editor. Then run the shell startup script (again, we use the Bash shell in examples throughout this book):

```
. ./.bash_profile
```

6. Enter the following command to direct X applications like the OUI to display on your local PC[2]:

```
DISPLAY=<local_system>:0.0; export DISPLAY
```

where *<local_system>* is the host name or IP address of your local PC.

Test X Windows functionality by verifying that when you run the `xclock` command on the UNIX host, a clock appears on your X Server display. You should not need to specify the directory where the `xclock` executable is located, as it is usually contained in the PATH set for all OS user accounts. However, if this is not the case, the following table lists the location of `xclock`, which varies by UNIX platform:

Platform	**xclock Command Location**
AIX	/usr/bin/X11/xclock
HP-UX	/usr/bin/X11/xclock
Linux	/usr/X11R6/bin/xclock
Solaris	/usr/openwin/bin/xclock

Set/Unset OS Environment Variables

The following environment variables should be set or unset as noted in Table 4-2.

As Table 4-2 shows, set ORACLE_BASE (not required but recommended), and set temporary directory variables only as needed. Unset all other Oracle-related variables, even those not specifically mentioned in the table, such as may be listed on UNIX by the `set | grep ORA` command or on Windows by the `set | findstr ORA` command.

---

[2] You do not need to set the DISPLAY environment variable for CC silent installations.

Variable Name	Value	Description
LANG, NLS_LANG, and other NLS variables	Unset	Might be incompatible with OS default locale and OMR database character set.[a]
ORACLE_BASE	Set	Set to /u01/app/oracle, for example. This is not required, but the OUI picks up this location to prepopulate the Middleware Home Location and oraInventory directory (/u01/app/oraInventory in this example).
ORACLE_HOME	Unset	Do not set because the OUI prompts only for the Middleware Home Location, which contains multiple Oracle homes.[b]
ORACLE_SID	Unset	OUI will prompt you to enter the OMR database name.
PATH	Do not include Oracle directories in the PATH. Include `fuser` executable in PATH (usually in /sbin or /usr/sbin).	Should not contain any paths for installed Oracle products, only standard OS paths for all users.
TMP and TMPDIR (UNIX), TEMP (Windows)	Unset (set if required)	OUI uses this directory for executables and link files. Unset if free space in temporary directory is at least 400MB. Otherwise, set to an alternate directory path that meets these specifications.
TZ	Unset	Set desired timezone at OS level instead, as reported by the `date` command on UNIX.

[a] This is a recommendation, not a requirement. In OEM 10*g* Cloud Control, the installation could fail if NLS_LANG is set on Linux x86. See MOS Note 272493.1. There are no such bugs logged against CC 12*c*, but it is safer to unset NLS variables, given this history with previous OEM releases.

[b] The multiple Oracle homes installed under this Middleware Home Location include those for OMS and WLS.

TABLE 4-2. *Variables to Set and Unset for Cloud Control Installation*

On UNIX, see the earlier table in the sidebar "UNIX Shell Variations" for the syntax to set or unset variables in the various UNIX shells. To verify that the `umask` command displays a value of 22, 022, or 0022 and that the environment variables that you set in this section have the correct values, enter the following commands as the *oracle* user:

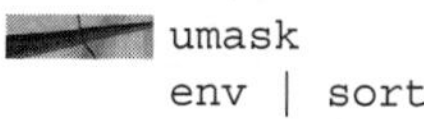

```
umask
env | sort
```

To verify whether the Windows environment is set correctly, execute the following command from a command shell:

```
set
```

Whether on UNIX or Windows, leave the command shell open to execute the CC Installer later, thereby allowing the OUI to pick up all environment variable settings.

Choose Desired Installer Options

Before kicking off the Cloud Control installation, determine what options (or "parameters"), if any, to specify for the Installer executable. Following are the available options (<*Software_Location*> indicates the directory where you downloaded the CC software or DVD location):

Syntax for Option	Description
`-silent -responseFile <Software_Location>/response/new_install.rsp`	Silent installation method
`-pluginLocation <absolute_path_to_plugin_software>`	Location for installing additional plug-ins not in software kit. Download as directed at http://www.oracle.com/technetwork/oem/extensions/index-100685.html#OEM12c.
`-invPtrLoc <absolute_path_to_oraInst.loc>`	(UNIX only) Use this option if CC is the first Oracle product to be installed on host or if the oraInst.loc file is in a nondefault location. Central Inventory location cannot be on a shared file system.
`ORACLE_HOSTNAME=<host_name>`	Specify host name to use for OMS when there are multiple host names, such as virtual hosts.

Syntax for Option	Description
`WLS_DOMAIN_NAME=<custom_domain_name>`	Custom WebLogic Domain Name (default is CCDomain). Do not use a custom value if at all possible.
`EM_STAGE_DIR=<custom_paf_staging_dir>`	Custom Provisioning Advisor Framework (PAF) staging directory (default is /tmp).
`START_OMS=TRUE | FALSE` `b_startAgent = TRUE | FALSE`	Start OMS/Agent automatically, or not, after installation completes. Buggy[a] and of little value.

[a] Sometimes, when testing these options, the Agent and host on which CC was installed did not appear as targets in the Console, after the installation completed and the OMS and/or Agent were manually started.

The first options in the preceding table, which allow for silent installation and specification of a static ports file in a response file, are useful enough to warrant additional explanation.[3] We provide details for performing a silent installation and using the static ports feature, and outline the usual reasons for utilizing these options.

Silent Installation Method

Whether you employ the silent or graphical (that is, interactive) installation methods, the resultant CC system created is the same. The silent installation method is available for the initial OMS (including chain-installed Agent), an additional OMS, and standalone Management Agents. (Unlike GC 11*g*, CC 12*c* does not offer a graphical Agent installation method.) This section covers silent installation of just the first OMS (and chain-installed Agent) laid down by the CC Installer. Silent installation of an additional OMS involves a lot of manual configuration steps,[4] whereas OMS cloning is very straightforward, as described in the section "Installation of an Additional OMS." Standalone silent Agent installation is straightforward, and covered in Chapter 5 of this book in the section, "Installing Agents Using the Silent Install."

There are several reasons why you may need or want to run the CC Installer silently rather than interactively, to deploy an initial OMS, standalone Agents, or if absolutely necessary, an additional OMS:

- **Security and audit constraints disallow graphical OUI** Your site may have security restrictions or audit requirements preventing you from using the CC interactive OUI, such as prohibit the running of X Server on the Installer host.

[3] For remaining options, please consult Section 6.4.2.1 of the Oracle *Cloud Control Basic Installation Guide*.

[4] The OMS silent installation procedure can be found in Appendix D of the *Cloud Control Advanced Installation and Configuration Guide*.

- **When installing many CC environments** The silent Installer eliminates the need to interact with the installation, and saves time and effort in that you only need to specify the required input once. This can reduce installation time appreciably when building multiple CC environments, such as at corporate satellite offices or in a training setting. The time savings of silent versus graphical installation of CC 12*c* is not as pronounced as with GC 11*g*, because the CC 12*c* OUI has far fewer screens and input fields.
- **When installing Agents on many target hosts and cannot mass deploy** The Agent Deployment method pushes Agent software in one operation from the OMS to multiple target hosts of the same platform. However, Agent Deployment may not be a viable installation option, usually for security reasons as it requires `ping` and `ssh` connectivity between OMS and target hosts.
- **To ensure installation reproducibility** Silent installation of initial OMS and standalone Agents better ensures identical production and test environments than does the graphical OUI method, especially when used with the static ports feature to explicitly assign the same OMS or Agent ports. The advantage of reproducibility is particularly relevant when multiple administrators are installing Cloud Control across the enterprise.

To perform a silent OMS (or Agent) installation, you start by editing an OMS (or Agent) response file template, supplying the same information that the OUI screens request. The response file takes the place of entering this information interactively. The OMS response file templates, including those for the installation types software-only and upgrade of an OMS, are located in the response directory below the top-level directory of the CC distribution. The response file for a new installation is aptly named new_install.rsp. To install silently, you would simply change directory to <*Software_Location*>, and launch the CC Installer executable with certain parameters. These parameters include the *-silent* parameter, the *-responseFile* parameter to specify the edited response file location, and any additional optional parameters, using the following syntax (remember, don't actually run the Installer yet):

On UNIX:

```
./runInstaller -silent -responseFile <Software_Location>/response/new_
install.rsp

[-invPtrLoc <absolute_path_to_oraInst.loc>] <other_optional_parameters>
```

On Windows:

```
.\setup.exe -silent -responseFile <Software_Location>\response\
new_install.rsp <optional_parameters>
```

Optional parameters for silent installation are covered in Section 3.4.2 of Chapter 3 in the *Cloud Control Advanced Installation and Configuration Guide*. Section 3.4.4 of Chapter 3 in the guide contains a description of all variables in the new_install.rsp file, and the response file itself is heavily commented. Note that the optional variable STATIC_PORTS_FILE in the response file can be used to specify a static ports file, discussed next.

Static Ports Feature

The static ports feature allows you to specify custom port numbers for the OMS, chain-installed Agent, and Console components, perhaps to override one or more default port numbers that the Installer otherwise assigns, or to better enforce that only default ports be used. For both silent and interactive installations, you can specify the static ports to use in a file called staticports.ini. For silent installations, the staticports.ini file location is provided as the value of the responsefile STATIC_PORTS_FILE parameter when running the Installer executable. In the interactive OUI, you can import the staticports.ini file on the Port Configuration Details screen (see Figure 4-11). This screen alternatively allows you to enter a port for each component. (The default port is the first and lowest port number in the recommended range shown for each component.)

There are two principal reasons to consider using the static ports feature:

- **When you want identical port assignments for an additional OMS** Using a static ports file is a more reliable way to ensure that the port configuration will be identical across OMS servers. Otherwise, the Installer may not assign all default ports for additional OMSs, even if these ports are available. (This behavior has been observed in GC 10*g* and GC 11*g*, but not tested in CC 12*c*.) Whether using default or custom ports, explicitly set them rather than trusting the Installer to assign them.
- **If one or more default OMS ports are not free** This is unlikely if you dedicate the OMS host to Cloud Control, as the default ports are not in the range of Internet Assigned Numbers Authority (IANA) Well Known Ports (0 to 1023), and are different than Registered Ports (1024 to 49151), except for two conflicts with ports for somewhat obscure products.[5] Oracle has Registered Ports reserved for many of their product components, including the Oracle OMS (1159) and Agent (3872).

[5] These conflicting ports are 7401/tcp registered for RTPS Data-Distribution User-Traffic, and 7201/tcp registered for DLIP. It is a bit of a mystery why Oracle chose these two ports for the OMS, when they are registered ports for other products.

Postinstallation, you can reconfigure any CC component to use a different port, but the static ports feature makes it easier to use custom ports up front. A template staticports.ini file is located in the response directory below the top-level directory of the CC distribution. (This directory is also where the OMS silent installation response file templates are found.) Example default port entries in the file are as follows:

```
Enterprise Manager Upload Http SSL port=1159
Oracle Management Agent Port=3872
```

When employing the static ports feature, the Installer uses any custom values defined in the staticports.ini file instead of the default port numbers. The EM documentation states that default port numbers are used for any components not explicitly listed in the staticports.ini file. However, our own experience with this feature suggests otherwise. We recommend explicitly specifying ports for *all* components in this file, assigning each component a default or custom port number, whichever the case may be.

Installation of a New CC System

You are now ready to start installing a new CC system. When launching the Installer, you will run it interactively or silently using either default or custom ports, whether provided as input in the OUI or in a staticports.ini file, as just discussed. Most likely, you will install Cloud Control interactively rather than with the silent Installer, and will probably not need to use the static ports feature, unless installing an additional OMS to ensure port assignments are the same as for the initial OMS. Whatever installation options you choose, remember to start the Installer in the same command shell you opened and initialized in the earlier sidebar "Set/Unset OS Environment Variables." You will execute one of the following commands, depending on the platform, with the appropriate optional parameters, such as for a silent installation, with the static ports variable set in the response file, if desired:

On UNIX:

```
<Software_Location>/runInstaller <optional_parameters>
```

On Windows:

```
<Software_Location>\setup.exe <optional_parameters>
```

Again, *<Software_Location>* is the top-level directory whether the installation software is downloaded from edelivery.oracle.com or OTN, or the DVD location if using the Cloud Control Media Pack.

Regardless of the installation method you opt for—interactive or silent—at some point the Installer will take over and the process behind the scenes will become identical. That point for interactive installations is when you click Install after completing the interview process in the OUI screens, or if running the Installer silently, after launching it.

Don't be too hasty to terminate an installation that may appear to be hung because of the limited output from the Java Installer. You can find out what's happening behind the scenes by tailing the installation log files using the command `tail -f <logfile>` on UNIX systems. For Windows, UNIX-style `tail` utilities are also available, such as BareTail from baremetalsoft.com (both a free and registered version). Here are some notable log files:

- ***<oraInventory_dir>*/logs/installActionsYYYY-MM-DD_HH-MI-SS-[A-P]M.log** The main Installer log file, echoed to `stdout`. It is useful to consult this log file to review all Installer activity. On UNIX platforms, the directory *<oraInventory_dir>* is specified by the Inventory pointer location file, oraInst.loc, if it exists. If it doesn't exist, you specify *<oraInventory_dir>* when installing Cloud Control on the Oracle Inventory screen (see Figure 4-3). On Windows platforms where no Oracle products have been installed, the inventory directory is located under *<ORACLE_BASE>\oraInventory* if ORACLE_BASE is set in the environment where the Installer was launched. If at least one Oracle product was previously installed (depending upon the product), *<oraInventory_dir>* can be *<SystemDrive>*:\Program Files\Oracle\Inventory.
- **$OMS_HOME/sysman/log/schemamanager/** Log files for the Repository Configuration-Assistant, listing creation and configuration operations.
- **$OMS_HOME/cfgtoollogs/** Log files for OMS and Plug-in Configuration Assistants. All configuration logs are appended to cfgfw/CfmLogger_YYYY-MM-DD_HH-MI-SS-[A-P]M.log.

The option "Create a new Enterprise Manager System" is the default installation type selected when you run the Installer. As already mentioned, this option creates a Management Repository in a pre-existing database (unless this database is preconfigured with a Repository using the EM template in DBCA as discussed in Chapter 3), and installs an OMS and Agent.

The following sections correspond to the screen shots presented when you choose this installation type.

My Oracle Support Details Screen

(Figure 4-1) On this screen, you choose whether to install Oracle Configuration Manager (OCM), and if so, OCM installation options and whether to receive security updates. OUI is bundled with OCM, which collects host configuration information and uploads it regularly to My Oracle Support to help improve the level of Oracle's technical support service for your Cloud Control installation.

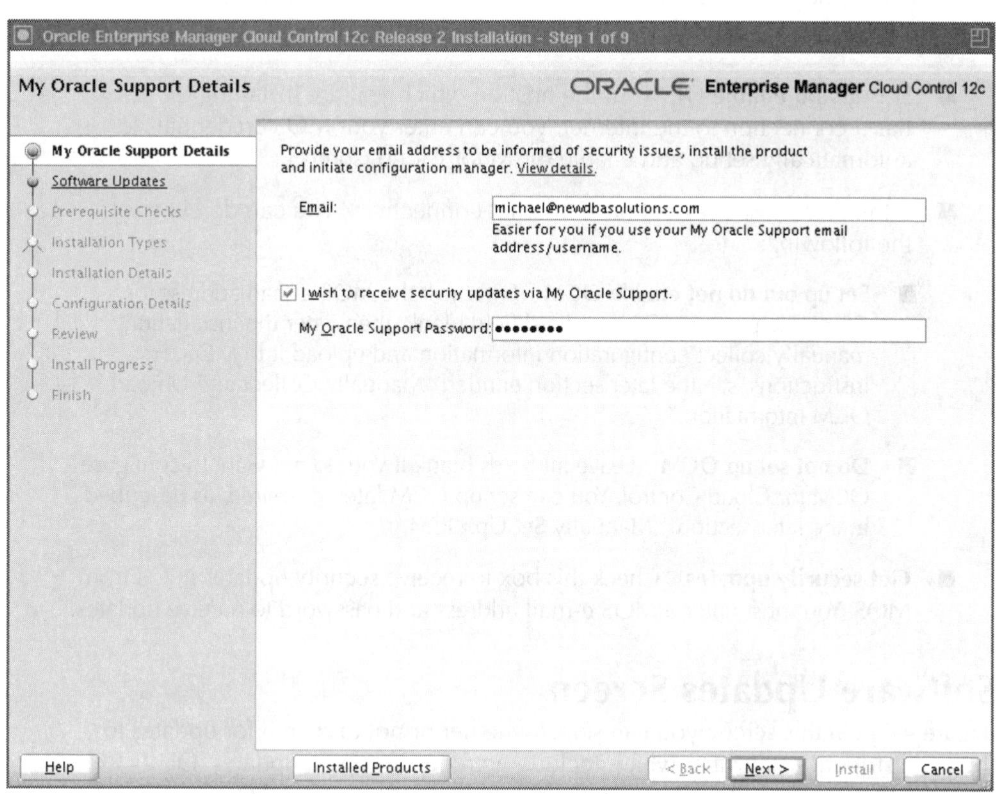

FIGURE 4-1. *My Oracle Support Details screen*

TIP

Completing this screen is more convenient than manually installing and configuring OCM later. You can enable OCM to automatically collect configuration information from your CC environment at regular intervals and upload it to My Oracle Support (MOS) under the e-mail address specified here. This is helpful when logging Service Requests (SRs), in that OCM will automatically supply CC configuration details that you would otherwise need to enter manually when creating an SR.

Do one of the following on this screen with respect to setting up OCM (your choices depend on whether the OMS host has an Internet connection):

- **Set up and enable OCM** If the host on which you are installing CC has a connection to the Internet, you can enter your MOS credentials to automatically set up and enable OCM for Cloud Control.
- If the local host does not have Internet connectivity, you can do either of the following:
  - **Set up but do not enable OCM** Enter just the MOS e-mail address for CC and leave the MOS password field blank; then, after the installation, manually collect configuration information and upload it to MOS. For instructions, see the later section entitled "Manually Collect and Upload OCM Information."
  - **Do not set up OCM** Leave all fields blank if you do not want to configure OCM for Cloud Control. You can set up OCM later, if desired, as described in the later section, "Manually Set Up OCM."
- **Get security updates** Check this box to receive security updates in CC from MOS. You must enter a MOS e-mail address and password to receive updates.

Software Updates Screen

(Figure 4-2) On this screen you can select whether or not to search for updates to the CC distribution software, which include prerequisite-check updates, OUI/Opatch updates, EM Installer updates, and interim patch updates. You can also choose the location from which to download these updates (either directly from MOS or a local directory location where you've downloaded them), or skip the search process altogether and apply any needed patches after installing CC. Following are details on the choices you can make on this screen:

- **Skip** Skipping the update process altogether would not be well-advised, as updates often contain fixes or improvements to the CC Installer itself. If you choose to search for updates and none exist, the Installer will simply return "No Updates are found." If you choose not to search for updates, any available critical or one-off patches (that is, for an individual bug) not relating to CC installation itself could be applied after the Installer completes. (Installation-related updates could also be applied to the OUI code in the OMS home, but that horse has already left the stable.)
- **Search for Updates** There are two choices for pointing the Installer to the location of these updates, depending on whether or not you have an Internet connection from the OMS host:

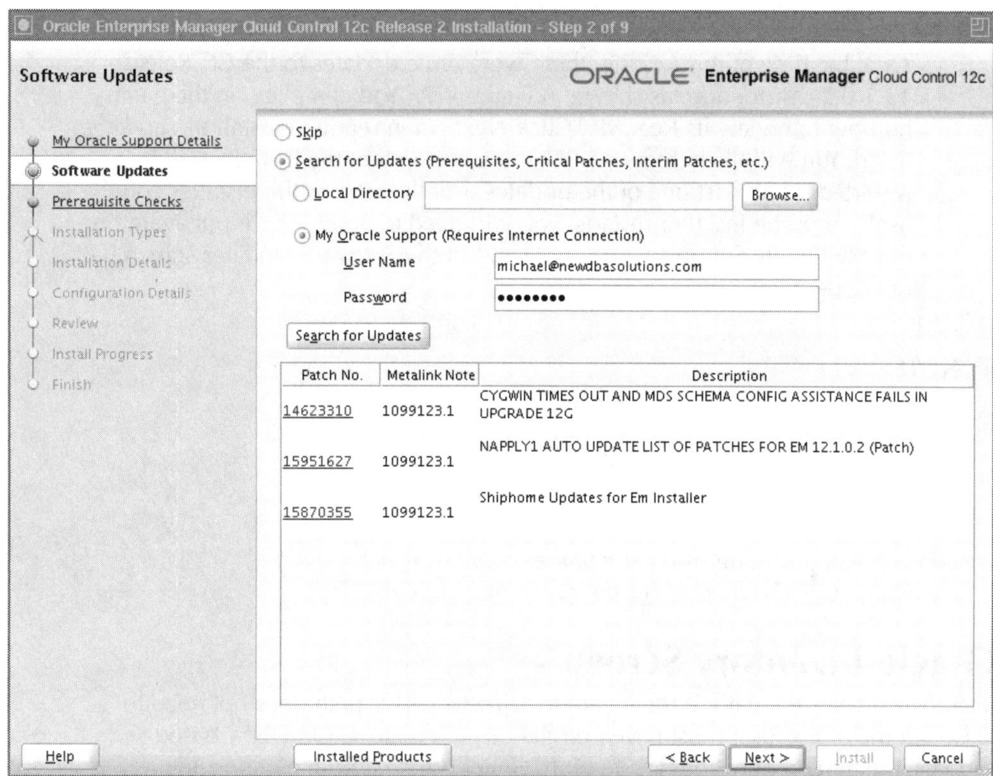

FIGURE 4-2. *Software Updates screen*

- **Local Directory** (Offline) If the OMS does not have an Internet connection to MOS, you can stage the updates in a directory accessible to the OMS and specify or browse to this directory. You would first need to search MOS, such as from your PC, and manually download the patches.
- **My Oracle Support** (Online) This option requires an Internet connection from the OMS host where you are running the Installer. It is more reliable and less cumbersome to have the CC Installer check MOS for CC software updates rather than having to download and stage them locally. After checking this option, enter valid MOS credentials to automatically search for and download all available updates. Ideally, you should set up a dedicated MOS account for Cloud Control that is not tied to a particular person.[6] This will prevent

[6] To create an Oracle.com account, go to http://support.oracle.com, click on "Register here," and complete the interview process. You need a valid Support Identifier (CSI Number) to create Service Requests under this account.

connectivity problems due to a user password change or to an account that needs to be closed when someone leaves the company.

As of the time of this writing, there were three updates to the CC Release 12.1.0.2 distribution, as shown in Figure 4-2.[7] You can click on the patch number to review its ReadMe. Click Next when ready to install the updates listed. You will likely receive a Warning popup that the Installer will be restarted, as at least one of the updates usually patches the Installer code itself. After the Installer restarts, you will need to enter your input again on the My Oracle Support Details screen, but the Software Updates screen will not appear.

NOTE
After you click OK to restart the Installer, the initial Installer screen will not reappear for at least several minutes, while the listed OUI-related patches are being applied. Do not terminate the installation prematurely (that is, do not kill the Java process), thinking that it is hung. You can tail the main installer log file to track the progress of the patching.

Oracle Inventory Screen

(Figure 4-3) Enter the path to the inventory directory. This path does not need to exist, but the *oracle* user must have permissions to create it. On UNIX-based systems, this screen only appears if you have not pre-created the oraInst.loc Inventory pointer file, and will not ever appear on Microsoft Windows platforms, because the inventory location defaults to <*SystemDrive*>:\Program Files\Oracle\Inventory. (The other Installer screen shots do not list this screen title in the left navigation pane because they are from an installation performed with a pre-created oraInst.loc file.)

The Oracle documentation recommends that the central inventory location you enter not be on a shared file system. If this is already the case, follow MOS Note 1092645.1 to move the inventory to a local disk (that is, nonshared). The reason for this recommendation is that the central inventory is supposed to be machine-specific, and if shared across machines could be corrupted by other Oracle installations on these machines.

---

[7] The details of the updates available at the inception of a new CC release are listed in Section 2.1.5 of the *Cloud Control Advanced Installation and Configuration Guide* for that release. However, the list of all updates in this guide may not be current, as with CC 12.1.0.2, which lists two updates, whereas an additional software update has since been made available, as shown in Figure 4-2.

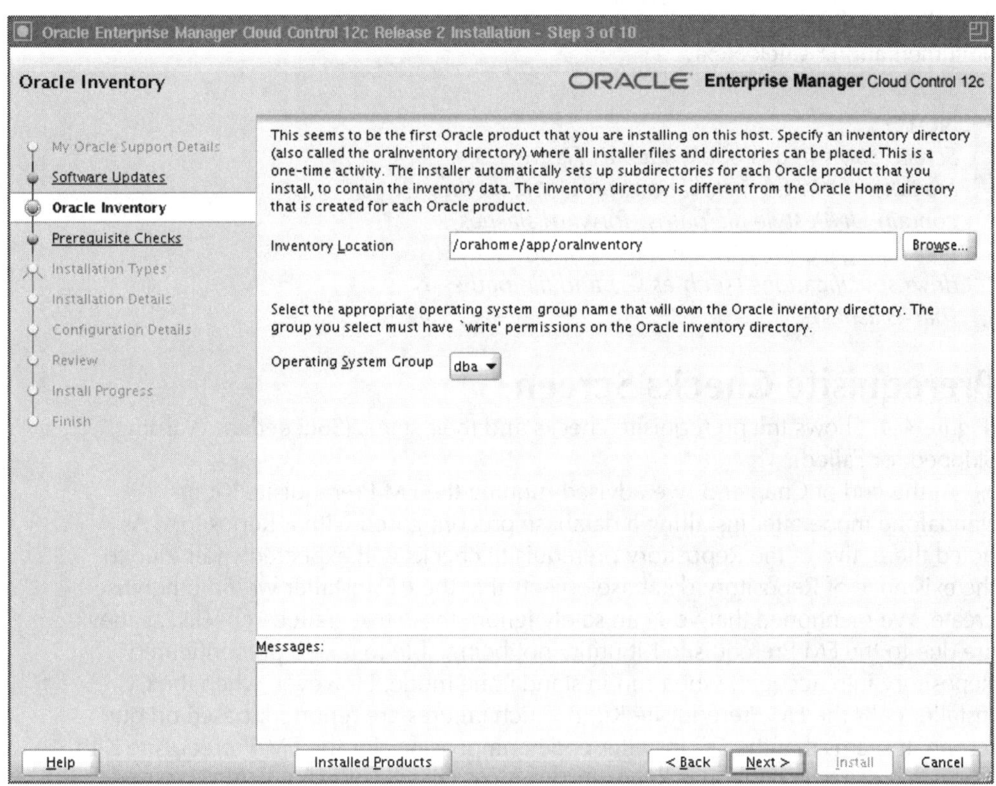

FIGURE 4-3. *Oracle Inventory screen*

CAUTION
If on the Oracle Inventory screen you receive the error, "OUI-10182: The effective user ID does not match the owner of the file, or the process is not the super-user, the system indicates that super-user privilege is required," it is probably due to insufficient privileges to create the oraInst.loc file in the default location. To resolve this error, either pre-create this file or grant the OS user running the Installer (or the OS group you specify on this screen) write permissions to the directory where oraInst.loc is created. This should enable you to continue without having to restart the installation.

In this screen shot, the *dba* group is used as the operating system group name, though *oinstall* is the standard group recommended in the Oracle CC documentation.[8] Click Next.

NOTE
Screen shots in this book, such as Figure 4-3, are taken from CC installations on UNIX, so they contain UNIX-style file paths (forward slashes). If installing CC on Windows, use Windows-style drive specifications (such as C:) and file paths (backslashes).

Prerequisite Checks Screen

(Figure 4-4) Shows the prerequisite checks and their status (Succeeded, Warning, Skipped, or Failed).

At the end of Chapter 3, we advised running the EM Prerequisite Kit in standalone mode after installing a database preconfigured with a Repository. As noted there, five of the Repository prerequisite checks will expectedly fail, due to the existence of Repository database objects that the CC Installer would otherwise create. We mentioned that you can safely ignore these five "failed" checks, as they are due to the EM Prerequisite Kit utility not being able to take a preconfigured Repository into account, when run in standalone mode. However, when the CC Installer calls the EM Prerequisite Kit, no such failures are reported, based on our testing. It seems that the CC Installer code compensates for the EM Prerequisite Kit's ignorance of a preconfigured Repository.

After the prerequisite checks finish, click each failed prerequisite check to view its corresponding details at the bottom of the screen. These details show expected versus actual results, error messages, and instructions to resolve it. Fix the failed checks manually if possible, and if fixed, click Rerun. It is best to resolve all unexpected errors before continuing. However, you can click Ignore for the remaining errors, then Next to proceed with the installation, though the Installer may not allow you to continue, depending upon the severity of the error.

Installation Types Screen

(Figure 4-5) Select "Create a new Enterprise Manager System," choose the Simple or Advanced option, and click Next.

---

[8] For more information, see "Create Oracle Inventory Group (*oinstall*)" in Chapter 2.

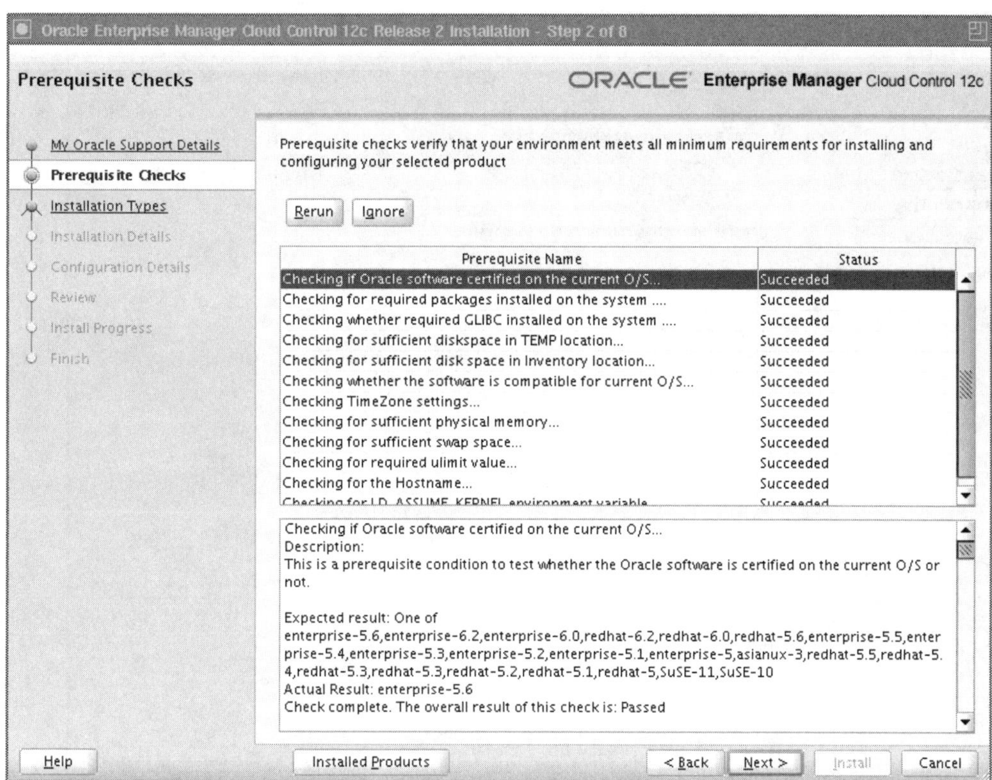

FIGURE 4-4. *Prerequisite Checks screen*

Using the Simple option is not much "simpler" than the Advanced option, so it provides little benefit. The latter has just a few more screens so that you can select individual plug-ins and passwords for CC users, and specify custom ports for components.

Installation Details Screen

(Figure 4-6) Enter details regarding the Middleware home, Agent base directory, and OMS host name.

- **Middleware Home Location** Enter a Middleware Home Location under $ORACLE_BASE, such as /*<mount_point>*/app/*<oracle_user>*/middleware. This is the location where WebLogic Server 11*g* (10.3.5), Java Development Kit (JDK) 1.6, and the OMS will be installed. Ensure that this location is

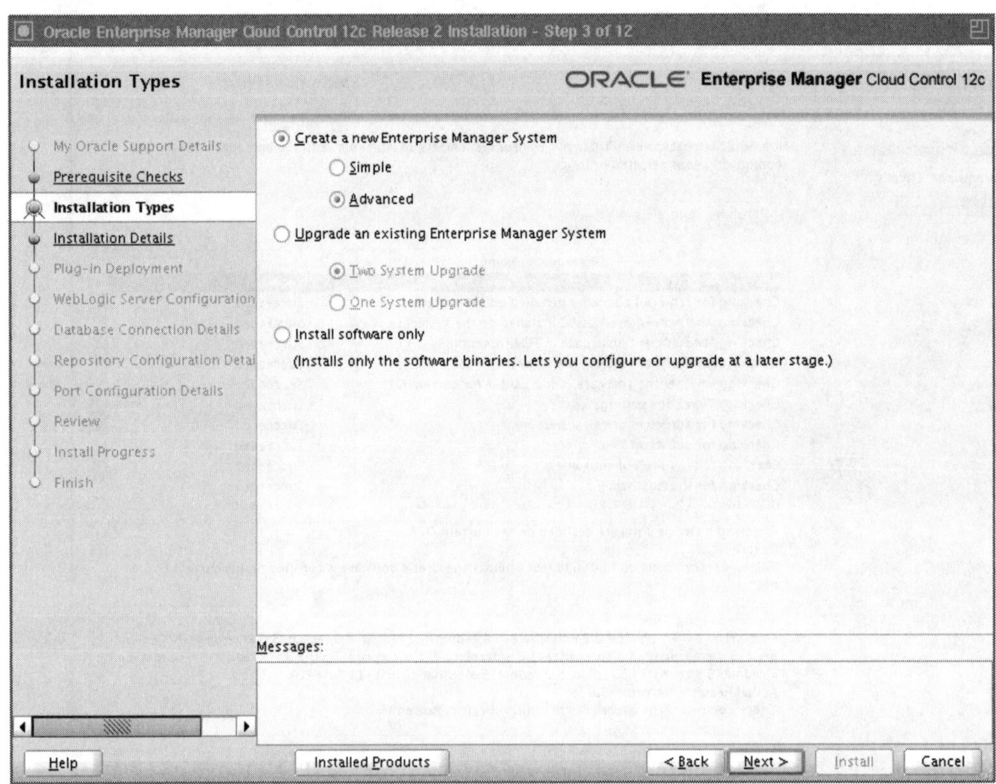

FIGURE 4-5. *Installation Types screen*

empty and that the *oracle* user has read and write permission to create it. For more information, see "Oracle Management Service" in Chapter 1.

- **Agent Base directory** This is the directory under which the Management Agent software will be installed. This directory should be outside the Middleware home.[9] Ensure that this location is empty and that the *oracle* user has read and write permission to create it. For more information, see "Management Agent Files and Directories" in Chapter 1.

[9] This is true as of CC 12.1.0.2. CC 12.1.0.1 did not prompt for the Agent base directory, but automatically installed it under the Middleware home.

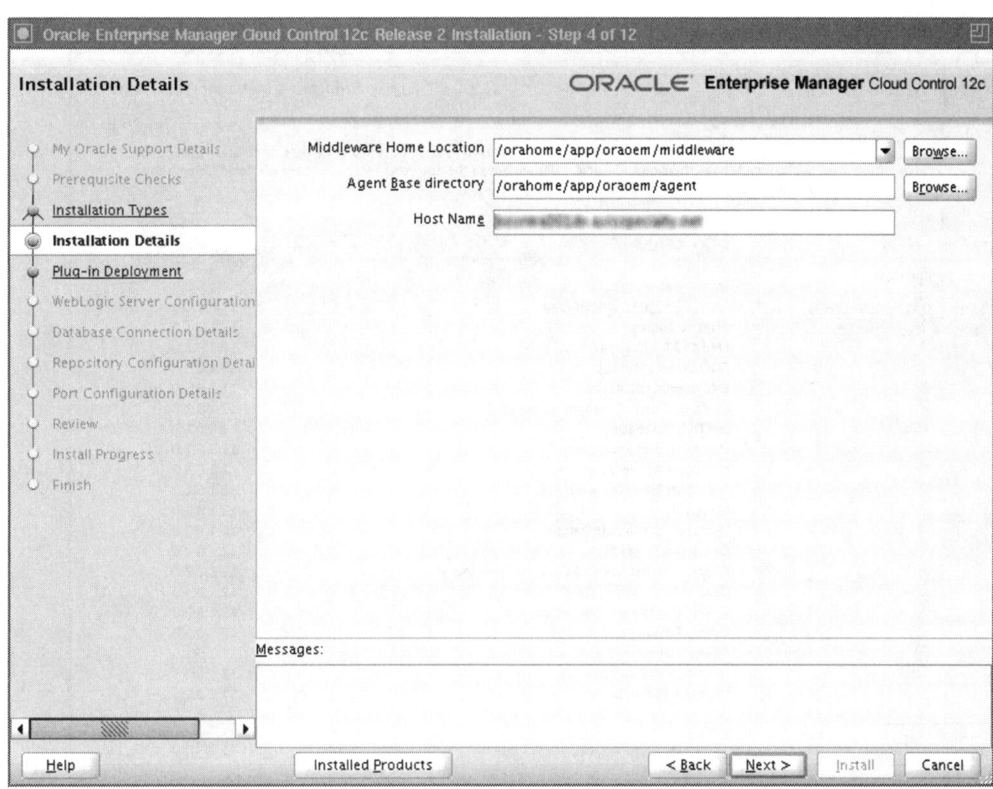

FIGURE 4-6. *Installation Details screen*

- **Host Name** Use a fully qualified host name (or short host name if a fully qualified name is not configured in the hosts file) for the OMS server on which the Installer is running. A virtual host name can also be used if the host is configured with a virtual machine.

Plug-in Deployment Screen

(Figure 4-7) This screen lists mandatory plug-ins (shown grayed-out) and optional plug-ins (some of which are shown as checked in the screen shot) available in the CC software kit.

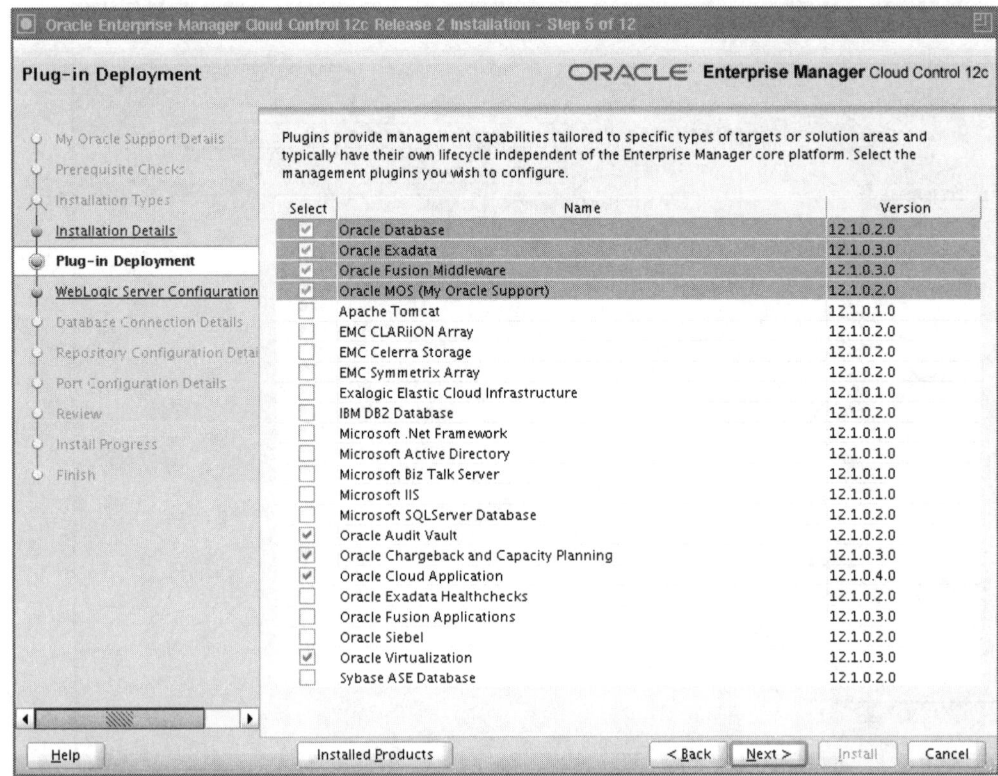

FIGURE 4-7. *Plug-in Deployment screen*

NOTE

In EM 11g, a few target types, including Oracle Database, were integrated into the core release, but in CC 12c, these target types have been isolated as plug-ins. Plug-ins are on a different lifecycle than the core CC software, so they can now be upgraded independently. With this more modular design, Oracle no longer has to "point" upgrade the entire CC platform (that is, 12.1.0.1.x) to upgrade the software that manages a particular target type, as this software is now provided as separate plug-ins.

Additional optional plug-ins also appear if you invoked the Installer with the *-pluginLocation* option specifying a custom location for additional plug-ins (see the earlier section "Choose Desired Installer Options"). Select all optional plug-ins to install, and click Next.

WebLogic Server Configuration Details Screen

(Figure 4-8) Enter credentials for the WebLogic server and Node Manager user accounts. The WebLogic user is the administrator for the default WLS domain, GCDomain. Use the default WebLogic User Name *weblogic*, unless otherwise required. The Node Manager allows you to control an Oracle WLS instance remotely and the default *nodemanager* user name is hard-coded and cannot be changed.

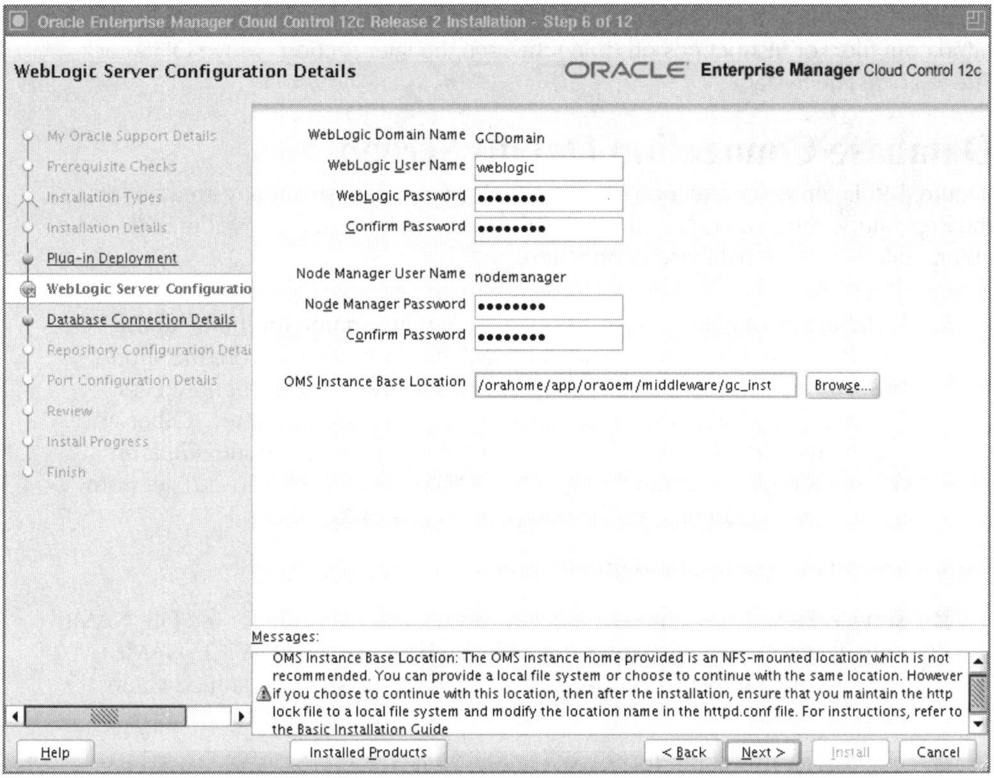

FIGURE 4-8. *WebLogic Server Configuration Details screen*

You may want to use the same password for the *weblogic* and *nodemanager* users, and for the SYSMAN user entered two screens hence, provided this does not violate any corporate security standards at your site.

NOTE
The passwords specified in the CC Installer for all users must contain at least eight characters without any spaces, begin with a letter, and contain at least one numeric value.

The OMS Instance Base Location should autopopulate to the subdirectory gc_inst (which you should let the Installer create) under the Middleware Home Location entered previously on the Installation Details screen (Figure 4-6). If you specify an NFS-mounted location, you will receive a warning message as shown in the screen shot that this is not recommended but can be done if, after the installation, you move the HTTP lock file to a local file system and change the location accordingly in the httpd.conf file. For instructions on doing this, see the later section "Move OHS Lock File to Local File System."

Database Connection Details Screen

(Figure 4-9) Enter the connection information for the database already created for the Repository. After you enter all information and click Next, the Installer will automatically test the database connection.

- **Database Host Name** Use a fully qualified host name for the database server (or if not resolvable from the OMS host for some reason, the short host name). For a RAC database, you can specify a Single Client Access Name (SCAN) listener if used, which is a Database 11.2 feature. Otherwise, specify the virtual IP (VIP) name for one of the nodes. A popup will then prompt for a Connection String for all RAC nodes, which you can get from the tnsnames.ora entry for the database on one of the nodes.
- **Port** Enter the database listener port.
- **Service/SID** For a single-instance database, use the value for the DB_NAME initialization parameter, and for a RAC database use the SERVICE_NAME (customarily for the first node, such as EMREP1). Use nonqualified values for Service/SID.
- **SYS Password** Enter the SYS password for the database. If the database connection fails with ORA-01017 invalid user name/password, check that the SYS password is correct when connecting locally on the database server itself, using the *tnsnames* alias (that is, sqlplus sys/<*sys_pwd*>@EMREP

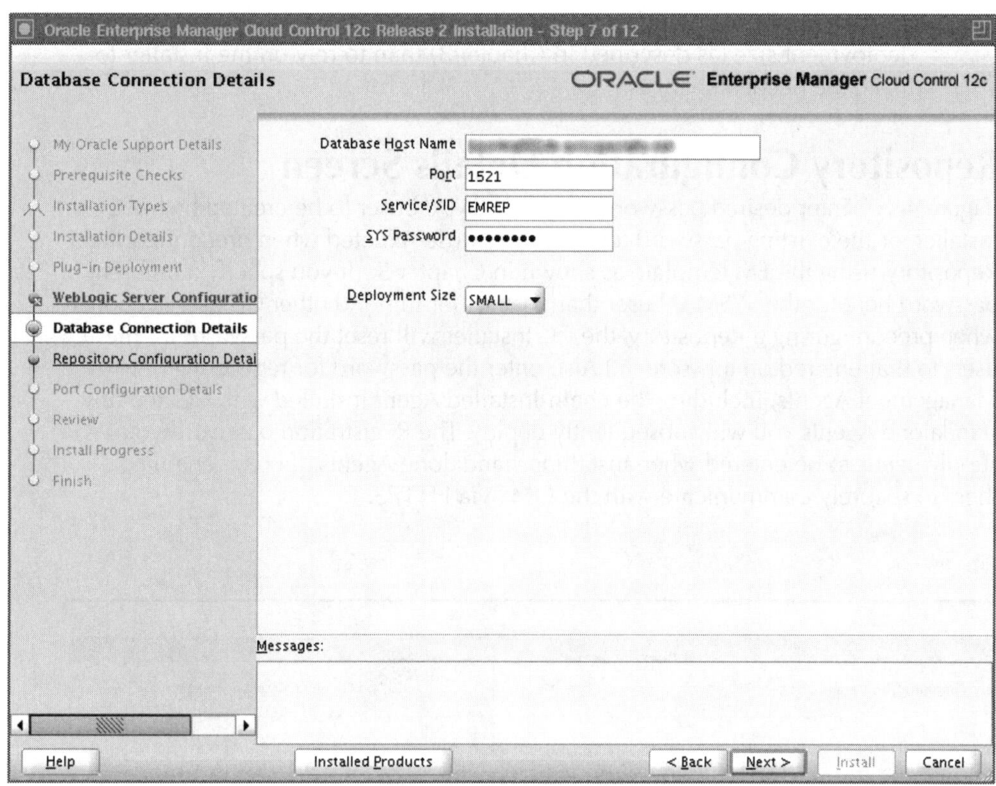

FIGURE 4-9. *Database Connection Details screen*

as sysdba), that the initialization parameter REMOTE_LOGIN_PASSWORDFILE is set to EXCLUSIVE or SHARED, and that a password file $ORACLE_HOME/dbs/orapw<*SID*> exists on the database server(s).

- **Deployment Size** Choose a SMALL, MEDIUM, or LARGE deployment size to indicate your plans for the number of targets, Agents, and CC administrator concurrent sessions your system will have. See Table 2-5 in Chapter 2 for the exact definition of these deployment sizes. The EM Prerequisite Kit checks for a Repository database will be run after you click Next, using the requirements for a SMALL deployment size, regardless of your choice here. (For details, see "Run the EM Prerequisite Kit in Standalone Mode" at the end of Chapter 3.) The CC documentation states that the Installer will make all changes to parameter settings necessary to meet the deployment size you select. We have not tested this functionality, because we think it is safer to set parameter values manually for your chosen deployment size (as described in Chapter 3) than to rely on the Installer to make the needed changes.

Repository Configuration Details Screen

(Figure 4-10) Enter desired password for the SYSMAN user to be created by the CC Installer, or the existing password for a SYSMAN user created when preconfiguring a Repository using the EM template as shown in Chapter 3. (If you specify a different password here for the SYSMAN user than that set for this and other CC user accounts when preconfiguring a Repository, the CC Installer will reset the password for these users to that entered on this screen.) Also enter the password for registering new Management Agents, including the chain-installed Agent installed with CC and any standalone Agents you will subsequently deploy. The Registration password you supply needs to be entered when installing standalone Agents, thereby enabling them to securely communicate with the OMS via HTTPS.

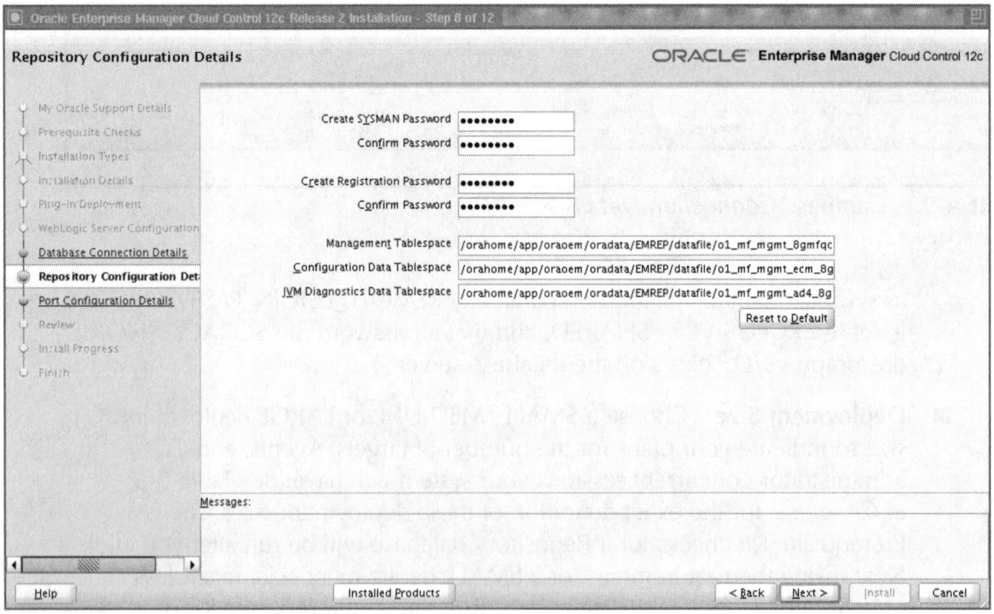

FIGURE 4-10. *Repository Configuration Details screen*

Also enter datafile names for the CC tablespaces to be created. (For a description of these three tablespaces, see the section "Oracle Management Repository" in Chapter 1.) Make sure the CC software owner has permissions to create all datafiles specified.

If you have preconfigured a Repository and the database files are located on a flat file system, enter the full path to all datafiles, whether they are the default names or OMF-assigned as depicted in Figure 4-10. However, if the Repository does not exist yet and is in a database configured with Automatic Storage Management (ASM), enter the disk group name, such as *+DATA*, for all three datafile locations. Datafiles will be created on ASM in the *+DATA* disk group in a location determined by OMF under +DATA/<DB_NAME>/datafile/*<OMF_datafile_name>*.

NOTE
Though the Cloud Control Basic Installation Guide *agrees that only the disk group name should be entered, the Online Help in the CC Installer states that, if the database is on ASM, the path must look like* +<disk_group1>*/prod/oradata/mgmt.dbf. However, this is incorrect, as ASM must use OMF, which in turn must decide on the location and name of datafiles on a disk group.*

The CC Installer does not allow you to set the size of tablespaces that will be created for the Management Repository. The default initial datafile extents assigned may not be sufficient for a production environment, so the Installer sets AUTOEXTEND ON to allow these datafiles to grow. However, the default extent sizes become a problem when storage for the database (usually a RAC database) is on a raw device, because the AUTOEXTEND ON feature does not work for raw devices. If the database used for the Management Repository is configured with raw devices, there are two options for increasing the size of the CC tablespaces.

- Pre-create two raw partitions, with sizes as shown in the following table. Set the first raw partition size equal to the datafile sizes for each tablespace as created by the Installer. Create the second raw partition to allow for growth.

Tablespace	Datafile Name	First Raw Partition Size (MB) to Match Installation Size	Second Raw Partition Size to Allow for Growth (MB)
MGMT_ TABLESPACE	mgmt.dbf	1950	51200 (small), 204800 (medium), 307200 (large)[a]

Tablespace	Datafile Name	First Raw Partition Size (MB) to Match Installation Size	Second Raw Partition Size to Allow for Growth (MB)
MGMT_AD4J_TS	mgmt_ad4j.dbf	200	2048
MGMT_ECM_ DEPOT_TS	mgmt_ecm_ depot1.dbf	40	10240

[a] The partition sizes are based on whether your CC site is small, medium, or large, as defined in Chapter 2 in the section "Make Required CC Architectural Choices." Required partition sizes for the other two datafiles are much smaller, and suffice for any size CC site.

- Alternatively, pre-create a large raw partition sized to allow for CC growth (equal to the sum of the first and second partition sizes in the preceding table), create a tablespace using the default size, create a dummy object that will increase the size of the tablespace to the end of the raw partition, then drop the dummy object.

Regardless of which option you choose, when using raw devices, disable the default AUTOEXTEND ON space management for all datafiles to avoid confusion, as this feature is disabled on raw devices.

When using flat-file system or ASM managed storage for the Repository database, leave AUTOEXTEND enabled for all datafiles, including those for CC.

Port Configuration Details Screen

(Figure 4-11) Specify the ports to be used for CC components.

The first available port, or default port, from the recommended range is supposed to be chosen by the Installer for each component. However, we have found that the first available port for some components is not chosen, even though it is free. Typically, you should use the first available port, or one within the recommended range. However, you could also use a port outside this range, if no ports within the range were available.

To determine whether a port is free, run the following command:

On UNIX:

```
netstat -an | grep <port_no>
```

On Windows:

```
netstat -an | findstr <port_no>
```

If the specified port is free, the command will not return any output. Ports chosen must be greater than 1024 and less than 65535. You can enter ports manually or specify them in a staticports.ini file as described earlier in the section "Static Ports

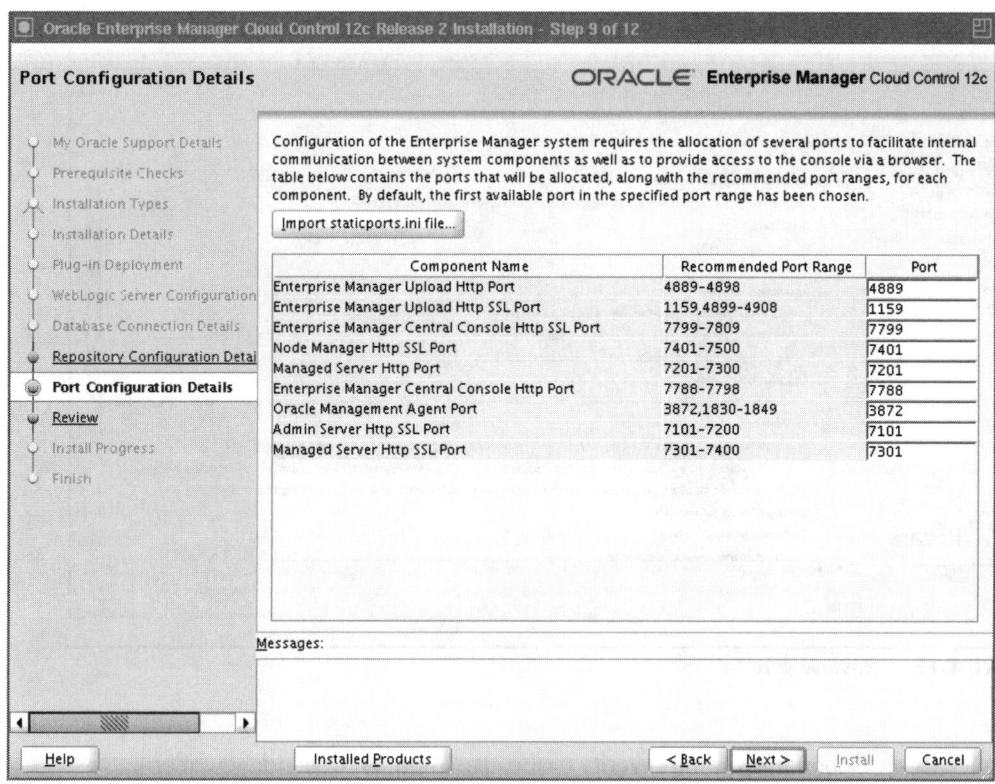

FIGURE 4-11. *Port Configuration Details screen*

Feature." In this case, the ports defined in the staticports.ini file will be displayed. Choose the desired ports and click Next.

Review Screen

(Figure 4-12) Verify the information you provided for the installation, and click Back to return to previous screens to correct anything. When you're satisfied with all input, click Install to start the installation process.

Install Progress Screen

(not shown) The Install Progress screen has a Progress bar showing the overall installation percentage completed and the status of each of the Configuration Assistants. If an assistant fails, you can select that assistant, fix the problem, then

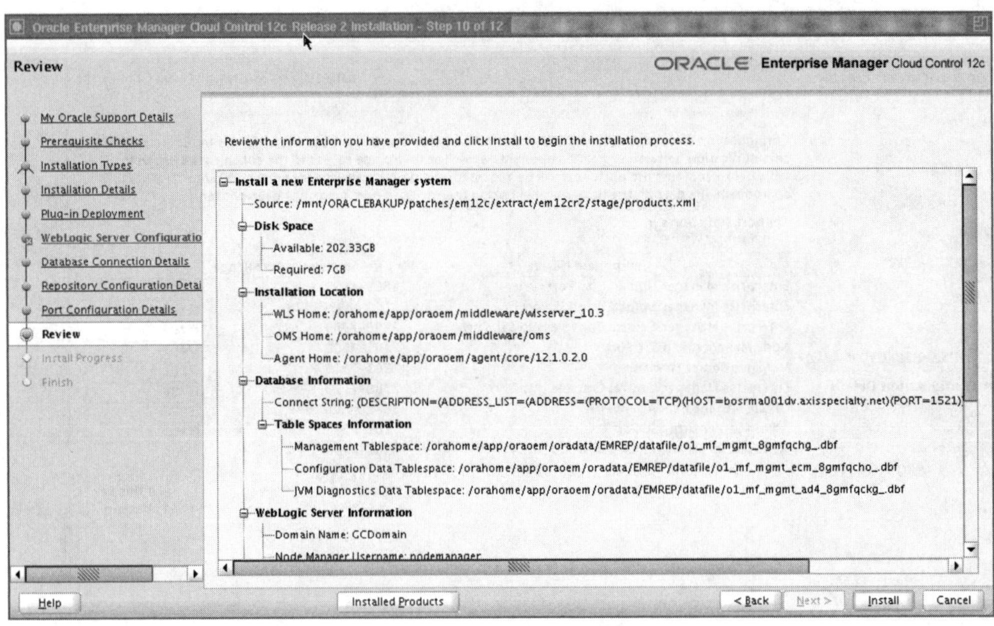

FIGURE 4-12. *Review screen*

click Retry. Depending on the severity of the error, and the dependency of one assistant on another, the Installer may not give you the chance to continue to the next assistant. In this case, you must either click Cancel, or manually kill the Installer. Regardless of how many configuration assistants fail, if the Installer gets through all of them, it may not report the installation as having failed at the end. This is misleading, as failure of any of the assistants leaves the installation in a questionable state. You should seriously think about uninstalling Cloud Control even if only one assistant fails. It is better to address the problem and reinstall cleanly, or CC may not function properly, either immediately or down the road after much postconfiguration effort. It's a painful sight to spy an otherwise cool-headed IT professional spewing invectives at their monitor.

NOTE

You can also run a failed configuration assistant in standalone mode. However, it is definitely a more reliable installation if you can uninstall Cloud Control entirely, resolve the problem that caused the failure, and rerun the Installer from the beginning to completion without error.

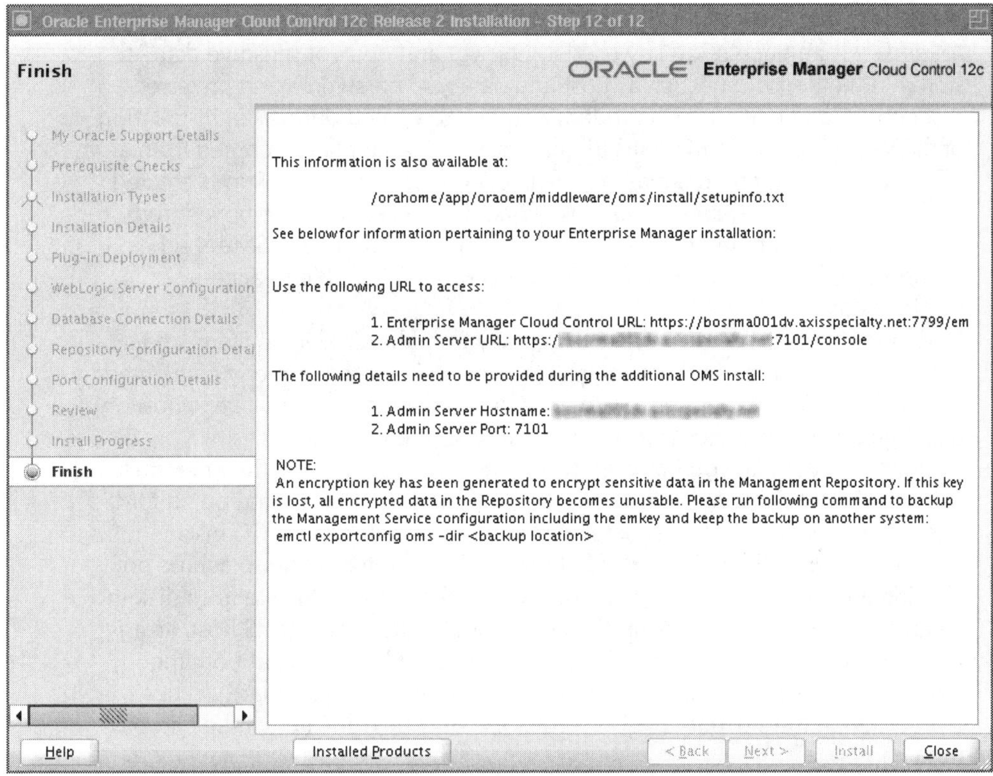

FIGURE 4-13. *Finish screen*

Approximately 30 minutes into the installation, after the software binaries are laid down, the Execute Configuration Scripts dialog box pops up for UNIX platforms (it does not appear on Windows platforms). You are prompted to log in as *root* and run orainstRoot.sh under the Inventory directory, if this is the first Oracle installation on the server. The Installer then prompts you to execute allroot.sh under $OMS_HOME. After running the specified script(s), return to the dialog box and click OK to continue.

Finish Screen

(Figure 4-13) Shortly after you click OK in the Execute Configuration Scripts dialog box, the Finish screen appears with information about the EM installation, including the URL to log in to the CC Console.

Click Close. A dialog box asks you to confirm if you really want to exit. Click Yes.

Back Up the emkey

An *emkey* is an encryption key used to encrypt and decrypt sensitive data stored in the Repository such as host and database passwords and preferred credentials, and consists of a random number generated during the installation of the Repository. When you install the first OMS, an emkey is copied from a table in the Repository database to the Credential Store,[10] a backup is created in $OMS_HOME/sysman/config/emkey.ora, and the emkey is removed from the Repository.[11] Storing the key separately from the CC 12*c* SYSMAN schema keeps the schema owner and SYSDBA users from being able to access sensitive data.

During startup, the OMS reads the emkey from the Credential Store, and if not found there, from the Repository. If the emkey has been properly configured, the OMS uses it as the master key to encrypt and decrypt any sensitive Repository data that an administrator stores and requests in the Console.

It is essential that you back up the emkey.ora file, given that all encrypted data would become unusable were this file to be lost or corrupted on all OMS host(s), and that the emkey is deleted from the Repository after CC installation. For now, back up the emkey.ora file to local disk and to another machine not running a CC component, so that you can quickly restore this file from disk in an emergency. You can back up the emkey.ora file from any OMS host, as it is identical across all OMS hosts. This file will also be backed up at both the OS level and using the `emctl` command, when instituting regular backups as outlined in the sidebar "Begin Regular CC Backups" located at the end of this chapter.

---

[10] A Credential Store is a logical store or repository for all named credentials of an EM administrator. It is not located in the Management Repository, but managed by WLS on which CC 12*c* relies for external authentication.

[11] In contrast to the GC 11*g* Installer, the CC 12*c* Installer automatically removes the emkey from the OMR database after installation of the first OMS.

Configuration of the New CC System

After installing a new CC system, there are configuration steps to perform before using Cloud Control to manage your Oracle environment. You should complete this postinstallation configuration on the initial OMS *before* installing any additional OMSs (covered in the last section of this chapter), so that these configuration changes will be cloned to these additional OMSs.

The specific configuration tasks presented here are divided into three parts:

- Initial Console setup
- Patch Cloud Control
- Configure OMS and OMR database nodes

Initial Console Setup

Initial setup of the Console involves dispensing with a few steps needed to allow you to log in to the Console and prepare to patch Cloud Control using the patching features available in the Console itself, if desired (you can also patch outside of CC). Here are these steps:

- Install Security Certificate in Browser for HTTPS Console Access
- Unsecure OMS for HTTP Console/Agent Access (Optional)
- Configure a Software Library Storage Location

Following is a brief description of these steps. The configuration related to the Console begins by opening a browser on your workstation and logging in for the first time. Login via HTTPS will probably require installing a Security Certificate for HTTPS browser communications, depending on your browser settings. Once logged in, you can do a brief smoke test to ensure that the CC Console menus are accessible and responsive. Then, optionally, if HTTPS Console or Agent access to the OMS is not possible at your site, perhaps due to client workstation or network (for example, firewall) constraints, or you need to provide HTTP access for some other reason, you can unsecure the OMS to allow for HTTP Console and/or Agent communications. Finally, you need to set up a Software Library storage location to allow for patching through Cloud Control and to enable other functionality.

Install Security Certificate in Browser for HTTPS Console Access

Now that you've installed Cloud Control, log in to the Console before proceeding further, both to install a security certificate and as a brief smoke test that the installation was successful. When logging in with your browser via the HTTPS URL, you will likely be prompted to install a Security Certificate in your browser. By default, the CC installation ends with all OMS processes started, which should allow you immediate access to the Console as the built-in SYSMAN administrator, using the password specified during the installation.

You should be able to get to the Console login page with the following URL, assuming you installed CC with the default Enterprise Manager Central Console Http

SSL Port as entered on the Port Configuration Details screen shown in Figure 4-11 or in a staticports.ini file, if using the static ports feature:

```
https://<OMShost>:7799/em
```

After you've entered this URL, a security alert dialog box will likely appear in your browser, informing you that the certificate of the Cloud Control site is not trusted. You can dispense with this security alert by installing the Security Certificate. In Internet Explorer, the alert message is, "There is a problem with your website's security certificate." Your browser is simply letting you know that it does not accept the CC certificate for the purposes of identifying the Console Web site itself. In other words, your browser does not assume on your behalf that the CC application certificate authority (CA) root certificate is trustworthy. This root certificate is a trusted certificate included in the Oracle HTTP Server (OHS), which also contains the server's certificate and private key. Your browser prompts you to set up a trusted relationship with this CA root certificate as required by Secure Sockets Layer (SSL) to encrypt browser-to-OHS communication.

The procedure to install the Cloud Control certificate in Internet Explorer, Mozilla Firefox, and Google Chrome, as well as to suppress the Security Information dialog box, is detailed in "Responding to Browser-Specific Security Certificate Alerts" in Section 13.8.2 of the *Cloud Control Administrator's Guide*. Safari does not support the option to install a certificate individually. You have to obtain a trusted certificate from a certificate provider.[12] After installing the certificate for your browser, you should not receive any further security alerts when logging in to the Console on your client workstation using this browser.

NOTE

On Windows 7 with Internet Explorer IE9, following this procedure did not suppress the alert. However, it worked on Windows XP with Internet Explorer 8 (IE8) and on Windows 7 and XP with Firefox. We did not test any other combinations of OS, browser, and browser version.

Once logged in to the Console, accept the License Agreement and choose an EM Home page. A simple smoke test of Console functionality will suffice at this point. For example, check that all OMS subcomponents appear on the Targets tab under the All Targets sub-tab, that all or most of these targets that are started display

---

[12] The procedure to install the certificate for Netscape Navigator is not provided in the EM documentation. Consult this vendor's documentation for how to install and permanently accept a certificate.

the correct UP status (a green arrow pointing up),[13] and that screens are responsive. We suggest reserving more in-depth testing until after patching the CC infrastructure, as described in the section "Patch Cloud Control." Also, the act of configuring and using CC as covered in this and later chapters will serve as passive testing.

Unsecure OMS for HTTP Console/Agent Access (Optional)

Out-of-box, only secure (that is, HTTPS) Console connections and Agent Uploads to the OMS are allowed. However, in some cases, you may be prevented from logging in to the Console via HTTPS and need to log in unsecured via HTTP, perhaps because you cannot install a Security Certificate in the browser of the workstation you're using. Or you may want to allow administrators to log in either via HTTPS or HTTP. Also, at some CC sites, Agents may not have network access to upload to the OMS via HTTPS, only via HTTP. In either case, you would need to unlock the OMS to allow for unsecure Console and/or Agent connections.

You can easily unlock the OMS to allow for HTTP communications with Consoles or Agents by stopping, unsecuring, and restarting the OMS, as follows:

```
cd $OMS_HOME/bin
emctl stop oms
emctl secure unlock [-sysman_pwd <pwd>] -console [-upload]
emctl start oms
```

Use the *-console* parameter to unlock the Console, and optionally, the *-upload* parameter as well to allow the OMS to accept uploads from unsecure Management Agents.

Once the OMS is unlocked, you should then be able to log in to the Console via HTTP with the following URL, assuming you specified a default Enterprise Manager Central Console Http Port on the Port Configuration Details screen shown in Figure 4-11 or in a staticports.ini file if using the static ports feature:

```
http://<OMShost>:7788/em
```

Configure a Software Library Storage Location

Before you can patch CC, which is recommended as the next configuration step, you must first configure an Oracle Software Library storage location. This is only the first step in setting up a Software Library, but the remaining steps can be deferred until you need to use some of its more advanced features, such as to create and manage entities.

The Software Library is a repository that stores software patches, reference gold and virtual appliance images, and application software. The principal building

[13] Don't be surprised if any running database and ASM targets (except a new Management Repository database) show a DOWN status. You must configure them in Cloud Control by entering the password for the DBSNMP and SYS users, respectively.

blocks of the Software Library are called "entities," which can be automatically mass-deployed in the CC Console to provision software and servers. Entities include Components, Directives, Bare Metal Provisioning, and Virtualization. For more details on entities, see "Understanding Entities and Their Privileges" in the Enterprise Manager Online Help. For more in-depth coverage on setting up the Software Library, see Chapter 11 of the *Cloud Control Administrator's Guide*.

For instructions on configuring the Software Library storage location, see the introductory section "Configuring the Software Library" at the beginning of Chapter 14 of this book. Then return to the next section in these configuration procedures to patch Cloud Control, as discussed next.

Patch Cloud Control

One of the advancements of CC 12*c* over GC 11*g* is the method of deploying additional OMSs. In CC 12*c* you clone an OMS, whereas in GC 11*g* you must rerun the Installer and select the Additional Management Service installation type. Cloning has the major advantage that configuration changes and patches applied on the source OMS are automatically carried over to a cloned OMS instance.

This is why this CC configuration section, which includes patching CC, comes before the later section, "Installation of an Additional OMS." Patching the OMS *before* deploying one or more additional OMSs will avoid your having to patch them individually.

Following are the three categories of CC patches presented in this section, some of which you may already have applied:

- Apply the latest CC Bundle Patch.
- Apply the latest EM Critical Patch Update (CPU).
- Apply any functionally required CC one-off patches.

CAUTION
It is not supported to change the WebLogic Server configuration forming the Cloud Control middle tier outside of applying Cloud Control patches to it.

The Console provides patching features to allow it to download and stage patches for itself, and in some cases actually patch itself. The limitations to "CC patching CC" are that CC can only apply patches that are part of its provisioning features, and the Repository and OMS must generally remain running but typically need to be shut down if being patched themselves. The same constraints on manual patching apply to patching through CC. For example, you may be able to patch the Grid Infrastructure for the Repository Database in a rolling fashion, but will likely not be able to be patch a single-instance Repository database; likewise for CC environments with multiple OMSs versus a single OMS.

As for the three types of patches we mentioned, it's efficient to download and stage almost all of them in the Console. This way, you also learn how to *use* Cloud Control *while configuring* it. (See the "Patching" section in Chapter 13 of the *Cloud Control Administrators Guide* for how to use CC patch functionality.) However, you cannot use the Console to *apply* the three types of patches to the OMS at this point, with only one OMS installed. You must be running multiple OMSs to allow at least one OMS to remain operational to apply the patch, assuming it does not require shutdown of all OMSs at once.

It gets a little reflexive here, but think of it this way: Cloud Control can patch itself to the same extent that a doctor can patch (or "operate" on) himself/herself. A doctor can stitch his or her own leg and even perform minor surgery under local anesthesia, but certainly can't operate on himself/herself under general anesthesia. For Cloud Control, local anesthesia to self-patch is provided by multiple OMSs. You keep one OMS running while patching another (check first that the patch Readme allows for this). Similarly, patching the Repository database with Cloud Control is only possible when it is a RAC database and the patch can be applied in a rolling fashion. The upshot is that at least one OMR database instance and one OMS must remain running when applying a patch to CC through the Console.

Let's begin the CC patching process now. It's always best to test these patches in a nonproduction environment before putting them into production. However, that ship sailed at the beginning of Chapter 2 when you decided how many CC environments to build:

- If you built a production CC environment to manage both production and nonproduction targets, then take a good backup (as noted in the later sidebar "Begin Regular CC Backups") and hope for the best, because you're patching production.

TIP

If it eases your mind, dub this CC site "nonproduction" until you patch and configure it, at which time it becomes "production." It's easier to pull this off if no one knows you already installed Cloud Control. Please forgive my geek humor, but if a tree falls in the IT forest, no one hears it unless it's a production tree.

- If you opted to build both nonproduction and production CC environments, apply these patches first on your nonproduction system, before applying them to production.

Apply the Latest CC Bundle Patch

Cloud Control Bundle Patches (BPs) are composed of many integration-tested bug fixes for the initial and subsequent CC 12.1.0.x releases, some of which provide functionality critical to CC. Bundle Patches have both OMS and Agent components, update the Repository, and are cumulative (that is, you can directly apply BP2 without first applying BP1). Bundle Patches can include new Agent Plug-in versions that can also be separately installed; Oracle strongly recommends installing the latest Plug-ins. At the time of this writing, the latest CC full Installer release was 12.1.0.2, for which no Bundle Patch had yet been released. EM 12.1.0.2 is built on top of EM 12.1.0.1 BP1 and includes additional new features and bug fixes.

You will find yourself in one of two situations with respect to Bundle Patches. Ideally, you will have installed the latest CC Full Installer release for which no Bundle Patch has yet been made available. However, you may be less lucky, having installed CC just before a new Bundle Patch came out, in which case you would need to apply this BP to be on the latest and greatest. Also, because Agent Plug-ins follow an independent patch level, you may need to install the latest Plug-ins too. If this is the case, consult the Bundle Patch documentation and related MOS Bulletins.[14]

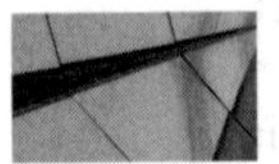

TIP

You can apply a CC Bundle Patch to many Agents at one time through the Cloud Control Console. By contrast, you cannot apply a Bundle Patch to OMS hosts through the Console, as it requires shutting down all *OMS instances to patch any one of them.*

Apply the Latest EM Critical Patch Update

Oracle highly recommends that customers apply the latest Critical Patch Update (CPU) for all Oracle products used, including Enterprise Manager Cloud Control. A CPU is a cumulative set of patches that address both critical security vulnerabilities and nonsecurity bugs on which these security fixes depend. CPUs are put out every quarter, on the 17th day of the months of January, April, July, and October. Like Patch Sets, CPUs are rigorously tested as a collection, and thus are more reliable than one-off patches.

To determine the CPU requirements and patch number to apply, see the Critical Patch Update <*Month Year*> Documentation Map on the MOS Web site. This document contains a link to a document called the Patch Set Update and Critical

[14] The first such Bulletin for 12.1.0.1 BP1 (now superseded by CC 12.1.0.2) was named "Announcing Enterprise Manager Cloud Control 12*c* Release 12.1.0.1 Bundle Patch 1 (BP1) and 12.1.0.2 Plug-ins [ID 1395505.1]." Future Bundle Patches will likely have a similar name.

Patch Update <*Month Year*> Availability Document, which contains a section called "Patch Availability for Oracle Enterprise Manager Cloud Control 12*c* (12.1.0.x)." A table in this section has links to other sections in the document listing CPU patch numbers based on CC release and platform (UNIX or Windows) for all CC components, as follows:

- Base Platform Repository home (Oracle Database)
- Base Platform OMS home
- Base Platform Agent home
- Base Platform Fusion Middleware home
- Oracle Database Management Plug-in (12.1.0.x) home
- Patch Availability for Oracle Database Management Plug-in (12.1.0.x)

Follow the instructions for applying the CPU to each of the CC components in the preceding list. The CC component being patched almost always needs to be shut down first.

Apply Required CC One-Off Patches

One CC patching step that is often overlooked is to apply any one-off patches that are functionally required. As already mentioned, one-offs are patches that address individual bugs, some of which resolve significant functional deficiencies. Some Oracle-recommended one-offs may have already been applied as part of the initial CC Installation, if you selected Search for Updates on the Software Updates screen (see Figure 4-2). However, you may need to apply additional one-offs to fix other (perhaps more tangential) issues with features you expect to use at your site. If a one-off is not available for a critical bug, the CC release notes for your platform may spell out how to implement a workaround for the bug, as mentioned earlier in the section, "Address Installation Bugs."

Oracle creates one-offs as interim patches to apply on top of a specific CC release and Bundle Patch, and rolls these one-offs into the next CC release or Bundle Patch. Many one-offs are intended for the OMR database. The proactive way to determine which one-offs you functionally require is to scan their descriptions (and ReadMes if needed), then choose those one-offs that provide fixes you cannot live without. A more reactive way to choose needed one-offs is to wait until Cloud Control fails in some unacceptable way, then look for a one-off that fixes that particular failure.

TIP

If you are not sure whether a one-off is needed, take the conservative approach and do not apply it until proven otherwise. War stories abound among DBAs of patches that broke something else that was working. It seems that Oracle agrees with this conservative stance; nearly every database one-off ReadMe says: "You must have NO OTHER PATCHES installed on your Oracle Server since the latest Patch Set (or base release x.y.z if you have no Patch Sets installed)." This leaves you in a quandary if needing to apply more than a single one-off; such a decision must be left to your good judgment.

Identify an up-to-date list of one-off patches applicable to your site, for your specific CC release and Bundle Patch, and then download, stage, and apply these patches. Providing a list of recommended one-offs in this book is likely not going to be very timely, as many or all of them may be rolled into a Bundle Patch or new release that will be made available after the time of this writing.

Configure OMS and OMR Database Nodes

This section identifies the configuration changes to make on the first OMS host and Repository database nodes. You should consider the changes mentioned as being highly recommended, unless labeled "Conditional" or "Optional." "Conditional" changes depend on CC installation choices, such as whether you let the Installer configure OCM. "Optional" changes depend on your site's CC requirements, such as which operations to audit. Reasons for these classifications are cited in the text.

The configuration changes for OMS and OMR database nodes are as follows:

- Move OHS lock file to local file system (conditional).
- Enable auto optimizer statistics collection.
- Set up the *oracle* user environment on OMS hosts.
- Schedule periodic purging of rotated CC logs.
- Modify the default Console timeout (optional).
- Add an OMR connect string to the OMS tnsnames.ora file.
- Manually configure OCM (conditional).
- Set up the *oracle* user environment on OMR nodes.
- Specify CC Audit settings (optional).

UNIX Shell Scripting Technique to Programmatically Modify Configuration Files

Some of the following configuration steps, and others in later chapters, call for you to change OS configuration files. You can certainly make these changes manually in a text editor such as *vi* in UNIX or Notepad in Windows. To make the same change to a file on multiple hosts, consider leveraging UNIX shell techniques to programmatically change files, such as those described in this sidebar to make substitutions in a file or append lines to it. You can even do this on Windows if running a UNIX shell such as Cygwin, or other shells available as freeware.

For example, to append lines to the file called *filename*, use the following inline scripting technique:

```
cat >> filename <<EOF
<insert text to append>
EOF
```

To make substitutions in a file, use the UNIX command, `sed`, in conjunction with the *vi* substitute command, `s`. For instance, to change all occurrences of PROD to TEST in *filename* and to save these changes in *newfilename*, issue the following command (file entries changed are case sensitive):

```
sed 's/PROD/TEST/g' filename > newfilename
```

The more files you need to change, the more time you will save using these techniques. As described in later chapters, you may need to make changes to certain configuration files, such as the Agent emd.properties file. If you are monitoring scores of target hosts, rather than manually changing each file, you can save a lot of time by writing an OS script to make the required changes and executing this script in one operation on all target hosts by running a CC OS job.

Move OHS Lock File to Local File System (Conditional)

As mentioned in Chapter 2 under the section "Hardware Requirements," if you install the OMS on an NFS-mounted drive, you need to make changes to the Oracle HTTP Server configuration file httpd.conf, which are specific to the operating system on which the OMS is running. Not doing so can cause frequent OMS restarts as often as every few minutes, startup failures, and delays. See MOS Note 1474015.1 for how to confirm whether the OMS is experiencing symptoms of this problem. However, do not follow the Solution proposed in this Note, as it does not apply to OMS installations on Linux or Solaris, and omits mention of a third LockFile location. Instead, if you're feeling lucky,[15] follow instructions in the *Oracle Fusion Middleware Administrator's Guide*, Section 4.4.7, "Updating the Configuration for Oracle HTTP Server Instance on a Shared Filesystem," to modify the lock file location in the <*Middleware_home*>/gc_inst/WebTierIH1/config/OHS/ohs1/httpd.conf file. Moving the lock file requires bouncing the OMS, so do this up front, before proceeding further in configuring Cloud Control.

Enable Auto Optimizer Statistics Collection

In Chapter 3, after running DBCA to create a database with a preconfigured Repository, one of the finishing tasks to prepare the Repository database for CC installation was to disable automatic optimizer statistics collection, one of the three automated maintenance jobs enabled by DBCA. Now that CC is installed, it is important to maintain accurate Repository database statistics to optimize SQL execution plans, so you should re-enable this automated statistics collection. To do so, run the following SQL to call the ENABLE procedure in the DBMS_AUTO_TASK_ADMIN package:

```
exec DBMS_AUTO_TASK_ADMIN.ENABLE(
client_name => 'auto optimizer stats collection',
operation => NULL,
window_name => NULL);
```

Execute the following query to ensure that auto optimizer statistics collection has been re-enabled and that the other two jobs are still enabled:

```
SELECT CLIENT_NAME, STATUS FROM DBA_AUTOTASK_CLIENT order by 1;

CLIENT_NAME                          STATUS
-------------------------------      -------
auto optimizer stats collection      ENABLED
auto space advisor                   ENABLED
sql tuning advisor                   ENABLED
```

---

[15] We tested this solution on an OMS system running Oracle Linux 5 on a NetApp filer, but it actually seemed to worsen the frequency of the problem, causing repeated "Oracle HTTP Server instance is down" alerts on the EMGC_GCDomain/instance1/ohs1 target. The stopgap solution was to suppress this alert using an Incident Rule that excluded this target.

The STATUS column should be "ENABLED" for these three maintenance jobs listed in the output from the preceding query.

Set Up *oracle* User Environment on OMS Hosts

As with most IT products, Cloud Control is easier to administer when you can specify environment variables rather than directory paths, and when executables do not need to be qualified. CC administrators find it convenient to use environment variables such as $OMS_HOME in scripts or when changing to a particular CC home directory on the fly. Admins must also frequently run certain executables in these homes to control CC components, such as `emctl` under $OMS_HOME/bin, which is used to start and stop all OMS processes. It is convenient to be able to call such executables without having to qualify them with their full path, and adding executable paths to the PATH environment variable provides this convenience.

The following listing in UNIX format shows suggested environment variables to define and executable directory paths to add to the PATH for the *oracle* user on OMS hosts.

```
export ORACLE_BASE=/u01/app/oracle #example value
#
#OMS environment variables
export MIDDLEWARE_HOME=$ORACLE_BASE/middleware
export OMS_HOME=$MIDDLEWARE_HOME/oms
export OMS_INSTANCE_HOME=$MIDDLEWARE_HOME/gc_inst
export ORACLE_HOME=$OMS_HOME
export ORACLE_CONFIG_HOME=$MIDDLEWARE_HOME/gc_inst
export PATH=$PATH:OMS_HOME/bin:$ORACLE_HOME/OPatch
#
#Agent environment variables
export AGENT_BASE=$ORACLE_BASE/agent
export AGENT_HOME=$AGENT_BASE/core/12.1.0.2.0 #example value
export AGENT_INSTANCE_HOME=$AGENT_BASE/agent_inst
#
#Add emctl path below to PATH on target hosts only, not on OMS host
#export PATH=$PATH:$AGENT_HOME/bin
#
export NLS_LANG=AMERICAN_AMERICA.AL32UTF8 #example value
export NLS_DATE_FORMAT='DD-MON-RR HH24:MI:SS' #example value
```

Note the following points regarding this initialization listing:

- Replace the example values with your site's actual values.
- ORACLE_HOME is defined as the OMS home, as needed when running `opatch` or OUI to apply OMS patches.

- Some CC executables are located in two Oracle homes, such as `emctl`, which occurs in both the OMS and Agent homes. If you run `emctl` without qualification, the PATH ordering executes it from the OMS home, not the Agent home. This makes more sense, given that the environment is for the OMS host. $AGENT_HOME/bin is omitted from the PATH on OMS hosts to eliminate this confusion. To control the Agent on an OMS host, change directory to $AGENT_HOME/bin/, and run `./emctl`.

NOTE
No harm will result if you accidentally execute `emctl` *from the Agent home to control the OMS, or vice versa; the command will simply return an Agent or OMS usage error, respectively.*

- If the Repository database is on the same host as the OMS, also add the environment variable settings listed in the section "Set Up *oracle* User Environment on OMR Nodes."

Later steps in this chapter reference the variables shown in the preceding listing. Therefore, on each OMS host, after adding the appropriate lines to the *oracle* user login script on UNIX, initialize the environment again with these new variables (on UNIX, log out and log in again as *oracle*, and on Windows, open a new command window).

Following are procedures to set the environment variables and PATH specifications in the *oracle* user environment on UNIX and the various Windows operating systems:

- On UNIX systems, add these lines now to the login script for your selected UNIX shell (see Table 4-3 for login script names for the most popular UNIX shells).
- On Windows platforms, you can also create a logon script (see the following Note), but in our experience it is more reliable to set *oracle* user environment variables as follows:
    - Log in as the *oracle* user and navigate to the Environment Variables screen. The navigation method varies by Windows OS:
        - On Windows XP, click the Start button, select Control Panel, and then System. In the System Properties window, click the Advanced tab, and click the Environment Variables button.

    - On Windows Server 2003, open Computer Management. In the console tree, right-click Computer Management (local), and then click Properties. On the Advanced tab, under Environment Variables, click Settings and select a user in the "User variables for" list.
    - On Windows 7, click the Start button, select Control Panel, and then System. In the System Properties window, click "Advanced system settings," then Environment Variables.
- Under User variables for the *oracle* user, click New, then enter the variable name and variable value and click OK. Repeat this procedure for all variables to be defined. Add the PATH variable, defining all values separated by a semicolon (rather than a colon in UNIX).
- Click OK as required to close all popups.

NOTE
To create a Logon script in Windows XP, navigate to System Tools, Local Users and Groups, Users. Right-click on the oracle *user and select Properties. Click the Profile tab. In the User Profile section, fill in values for Profile path (such as C:\app\oracle) and Logon script (such as profile_oracle.bat). Create this Logon script under the Profile path specified, in which you define all environment variables and the PATH as listed earlier. Log out and log in again for variable settings to take effect, or execute the script manually. To create a Logon script in Windows Server 2003, see http://technet.microsoft.com/en-us/library/cc784088%28v=ws.10%29.aspx, and in Windows 7 see http://technet.microsoft.com/en-us/library/cc770908.aspx.*

Table 4-3 offers a summary of the syntax differences between UNIX and Windows platforms for elements used in shell scripts for each platform.

Schedule Periodic Purging of Rotated CC Logs

Cloud Control server-side logging can be useful in debugging OMS process startup and runtime errors, Console access issues, and Agent upload problems. All OMS and WLS logs are automatically rotated after reaching a certain size (typically 5MB), and most are automatically purged after rotation. The remainder of these log files must be manually removed at regular intervals to reduce their footprint on the OMS

Script Element	UNIX	Windows	Example for Windows
Comment line	#	REM (must be the first characters)	REM This is a comment.
Define environment variable	`<variable name>=<value>`	`set <variable name>=<value>`	`set ORACLE_BASE=C:\app\oracle`
Use a defined variable in a value	`$<variable_name>`	`%<variable name>%`	`OMS_HOME=%MIDDLEWARE_HOME%\oms`
PATH separator	: (colon)	; (semicolon)	`PATH=%PATH%;%OMS_HOME%\bin`
Export a variable	`export <variable_name>`	Not applicable.	Not applicable.
Unset a variable	`unset <variable name>`	`set <variable name>=`	`set ORACLE_HOME=`

TABLE 4-3. *Syntax Differences Between UNIX and Windows Shell Scripting*

file system. Without such measures, an OMS disk could eventually fill up, which would halt most CC operations, notably uploads of Agent metric alerts and data.

See MOS Bulletin 1445743.1 for a list of CC log files that need to be periodically removed. You can schedule an operating system job to regularly purge the older rotated logs identified in this note. For example, on UNIX, add the following entries to the crontab file for the *oracle* user on the OMS host:

```
0 4 * * * find <fully_qualified_logfile_name>.* -ctime +5 -exec rm {} \;
```

The ".*" is to match the timestamp appended to the log file name. The command in the preceding entry runs every day at 4 A.M. to remove all rotated logs older than five days matching the specified log file name. Change the scheduled time and rotation period as desired.

Also see MOS Bulletin 1450535.1 for how to enable a log rotation policy in the WLS Admin Server Console to automatically delete older Domain logs and EMGC_ADMINSERVER logs on the primary OMS server. The Admin Server only runs on the initial OMS host, so these logs will only exist there.

For a detailed description of all OMS log/trace files, logging/tracing parameters, and how to modify trace levels, see MOS Bulletin 1448308.1.

Modify the Default Console Timeout (Optional)

By default, CC logs out sessions that have been inactive for 45 minutes. To change this timeout according to administrator preference and your company's security policy, perform the following procedure:

1. Set ORACLE_HOME to the OMS home, as recommended in the previous section, and change to this directory:

```
export ORACLE_HOME=$OMS_HOME
cd $ORACLE_HOME/bin
```

2. Update the OMS property *oracle.sysman.eml.maxInactiveTime* for the default login timeout using the OMS `emctl set property` command:

```
./emctl set property -name oracle.sysman.eml.maxInactiveTime
-value\
<timeout_in_minutes> -sysman_pwd <sysman_password>
```

3. Finally, bounce the OMS as follows to put this change into effect:

```
$OMS_HOME/bin/emctl stop oms
$OMS_HOME/bin/emctl start oms
```

For procedures on how to view and set, update, and delete OMS and Repository configuration properties using the `emctl` utility, see MOS Bulletin 1399896.1.

Add OMR Connect String to OMS tnsnames.ora File

To apply many of the Cloud Control one-off patches from the Console (as referenced in their ReadMes), you need to create a new $OMS_HOME/network/admin/tnsnames.ora file on all OMS hosts to contain a connect string for the Repository database. Use the same connect string found in the tnsnames.ora file on the OMR database node(s), which should match the DB_NAME (for example, EMREP). This alias can also be used for connecting in SQL*Plus from the OMS host to the OMR database with "sqlplus <username>/<password>@EMREP" to perform ad hoc queries (if on separate tiers or if on the same tier but the environment is set for the OMS).

TIP
If you plan to configure RMAN in Cloud Control, also add a Recovery Catalog database connect string to the tnsnames.ora file on the OMS host.

Note that the OMS does not need this tnsnames.ora connect string to connect to the Repository database for normal operations. Instead, the OMS communicates with the Repository database via a thin JDBC connection, which is defined in the Repository database itself during CC installation.

Manually Configure OCM (Conditional)

On the My Oracle Support Details screen, which was the first CC installation screen as shown earlier in Figure 4-1, if you did not enter a MOS username or password, or just entered a username but no password, and you would like to use Oracle Configuration Manager (OCM) with Cloud Control, then you will need to manually set up or configure OCM to collect and upload OCM information to MOS.

Manually Set Up OCM If you did not enter either a MOS username *or* password on the My Oracle Support Details screen, you can manually set up OCM for the OMS and chain-installed Agent after CC installation by doing the following:

1. To configure OCM for the OMS, set the environment variable ORACLE_CONFIG_HOME to the OMS Instance Base directory $ORACLE_BASE/Middleware/gc_inst, where the OCM configuration files are to be created.

   ```
   export ORACLE_CONFIG_HOME=$ORACLE_BASE/middleware/gc_inst
   ```

2. Set up OCM for the OMS by executing

   ```
   $OMS_HOME/ccr/bin/setupCCR
   ```

3. Set up OCM for the chain-installed Agent by running

   ```
   $AGENT_HOME/ccr/bin/setupCCR
   ```

Manually Collect and Upload OCM Information If you entered only the MOS username (e-mail address), but *not* the password, on the My Oracle Support Details screen, then OCM has not been automatically enabled. However, you can still *manually* collect and upload OCM information to MOS for the OMS and chain-installed Agent, as follows:

1. Collect configuration information for the OMS and Agent by running the following command from the respective OMS and Agent homes:

   ```
   <OMS_HOME or AGENT_HOME>/ccr/bin/emCCR collect
   ```

2. Upload the resultant file, *<OMS_HOME or AGENT_HOME>*/ccr/hosts/state/upload/ocmconfig.jar, to a Service Request on MOS. Note that this file is overwritten each time `emCCR collect` is run.

Set Up *oracle* User Environment on OMR Nodes

The following listing in UNIX format shows suggested *oracle* user environment variables to define on OMR nodes for the Repository database (including Grid Infrastructure, if present) and Agent, and executable directory paths to add to the PATH.

```
export ORACLE_BASE=/u01/app/oracle #example value
#
#Grid Infrastructure environment variables
export CV_NODE_ALL=node1,node2 #example value
export GRID_HOME=/u01/grid #example value
export PATH=$PATH:$GRID_HOME/bin
#

#Agent environment variables
export AGENT_BASE=$ORACLE_BASE/product/agent #example value, if
#OMR is on dedicated host
export AGENT_HOME=$AGENT_BASE/core/12.1.0.2.0 #example value
export AGENT_INSTANCE_HOME=$AGENT_BASE/agent_inst
export PATH=$PATH:$AGENT_HOME/bin
#
#Database environment variables
export ORACLE_SID=emrep #example value. For RAC OMR, set to
#SID of instance, i.e. emrep1
export ORACLE_HOME=$ORACLE_BASE/product/11.2.0/db #example value
#
export LD_LIBRARY_PATH=$ORACLE_HOME/lib
export SHLIB_PATH=$ORACLE_HOME/lib #On HP-UX
export LIBPATH=$ORACLE_HOME/lib #On AIX
#
# General environment variables
export NLS_LANG=AMERICAN_AMERICA.AL32UTF8 #example value
export NLS_DATE_FORMAT='DD-MON-RR HH24:MI:SS' #example value
PATH=$PATH:$ORACLE_HOME/bin:$ORACLE_HOME/OPatch
```

Note the following points regarding the preceding initialization listing:

- Replace the example values with your site's actual values.
- Naturally, shared library variables for HP-UX and AIX should only be defined on a host running on the respective platform.
- ORACLE_HOME is defined as the Repository database home, as needed when running `opatch` or OUI to apply database patches.
- Define ORACLE_SID as follows:
    - For a single-instance Repository, set ORACLE_SID to the database name (equal to the DB_NAME initialization parameter).
    - For a RAC Repository, set ORACLE_SID to the specific INSTANCE_NAME running on that node. As an example, for a two-node RAC OMR database named `emrep`, set ORACLE_SID to **emrep1** on *node1* and to **emrep2** on *node2*.
- If the OMS is on the same host as the Repository database, the Agent is chain-installed with the OMS, so AGENT_BASE=$ORACLE_BASE/agent.

In this case, also set the environment for the OMS as listed in the earlier section "Set Up *oracle* User Environment on OMS Hosts."

- If the OMS is on the same host as the Repository database, decide whether you prefer to set ORACLE_HOME to the database home or OMS home.

When finished making changes, reinitialize your OS environment by logging out and logging in to the OMR node(s) again as *oracle*.

Specify CC Audit Settings (Optional)

In contrast to GC 11*g* where no auditing was enabled by default, in CC 12*c* basic auditing is enabled out-of-box, including all operations related to credentials (for example, creating, editing, and deleting) to track the privileges assigned/revoked to/from them.

The best time to set up any additional CC auditing you need is before handing off the system to administrators, not after you've experienced a security breach. You can't prevent or track down a suspicious operation unless auditing procedures are in place to capture information about that operation. Auditing allows you to capture all changes in CC or a subset of changes for certain operations you specify. CC security features, including those for auditing, are compliant with standards set in the Sarbanes-Oxley (SOX) Act of 2002 (SAS 70).

In GC 10*g* and GC 11*g*, the Oracle documentation provided both the PL/SQL (using audit APIs that call the MGMT_AUDIT_ADMIN package) and the EM Command Line Interface (EM CLI) commands for setting up auditing. In CC 12*c*, only EM CLI audit commands are cited. In EM CLI, you can choose the audit level—all operations, no operations, or selected operations. EM CLI commands also let you specify which operations to audit and how often to purge audit data (the default is 365 days). You can audit logon, logoff, changes in users, passwords, privileges, roles, or jobs, and many other operations. Cloud Control audits basic information for each operation chosen, such as administrator name, operation performed, and whether or not the operation succeeded.

The following list of all `emcli` commands related to auditing is surprisingly small, and their functionality proportionally somewhat limited:[16]

- `enable_audit`
- `disable_audit`

[16] In GC 10*g*, `emcli show_audit_actions_list` displayed the list of user operations being audited. However, this `emcli` command does not appear to be available in GC 11*g* or CC 12*c*. You can use the procedure MGMT_AUDIT_ADMIN.GET_AUDIT_OPERATION_LIST to extract a list of audit operations currently enabled.

- `show_operations_list`
- `show_audit_settings`
- `update_audit_settings`

A description of each command follows, presented in the order in which you will likely use them. You can invoke `emcli` either on an OMS host at the command line as the CC software owner, or from a client PC if EM CLI is installed there. First, log in to EM CLI as follows:

```
$ emcli login -username=<EM Console username> -password=<EM Console
password>
```

You should see a "Login successful" message.

To enable auditing for all operations, not just the default ones, enter:

```
emcli enable_audit
```

The system overhead should be negligible from enabling auditing of all operations, but you'd do well to test this on a nonproduction system first to measure the overhead for your particular CC environment.

To disable auditing for all operations, enter:

```
emcli disable_audit
```

To see a list of all available audit operations, not those currently enabled, enter:

```
emcli show_operations_list
```

To show the current audit settings, enter the following command (the following output is from the default settings):

```
emcli show_audit_settings
Audit Switch            : Enabled
Externalization Switch : Disabled
Directory               : Not configured
File Prefix             : em_audit
File Size               : 5000000 Bytes
Data Retention Period   : 365 Days
```

Use the `emcli update_audit_settings` command to change audit settings, using the following syntax:

```
emcli update_audit_settings
-audit_switch="ENABLE/DISABLE"
-operations_to_enable="name of the operations to enable, for all operations
use ALL"
-operations_to_disable="name of the operations to disable, for all
```

```
operations use ALL"
-externalization_switch="ENABLE/DISABLE"
-directory_name="directory_name (DB Directory)"
-file_prefix="file_prefix"
-file_size="file_size (Bytes)"
-data_retention_period="data_retention_period (Days)"
```

Most of these arguments to the `emcli update_audit_settings` command are self-explanatory,[17] but the following arguments deserve special mention:

- *-operations_to_enable, -operations_to_disable* As already mentioned, a complete list of operations you can specify with these arguments is given in the output to `emcli show_operations_list`.
- *-externalization_switch* This argument enables the CC audit externalization service to export audit data at regular intervals to the file system in XML format in compliance with the Oracle Diagnostic Logging (ODL) format. As already stated, the default audit retention period is one year, but SOX requirements dictate that audit data be protected and maintained for several years. It is not recommended to store more than the default 365 days of audit data online, as the volume can quickly grow very large and reduce CC system performance. Therefore, rather than changing the default retention period, use this argument to regularly export audit data older than one year.
- *-directory_name* This argument requires that you first create a directory in the Repository database using SQL*Plus, while logged in as SYSMAN (or any user with the CREATE ANY DIRECTORY system privilege):

  ```
  SQL> CREATE DIRECTORY <audit_dir_name> AS '<path>';
  ```

  Be sure to create the directory at the OS level too, while logged in as the OMS software owner.

You can examine audit operations data in the CC Console under Setup | Security | Audit Data. See "Audit Data" in Chapter 7 for more on Cloud Control's audit search capabilities.

TIP
IT shops with stringent security policies may also want to jump directly to Chapter 7 now to institute other best-practice security measures covered there, in addition to auditing.

---

[17] Section 13.7.3 of the *Cloud Control Administrator's Guide* contains a description of all arguments to `emcli update_audit_settings`.

Installation of an Additional OMS (Conditional)

Now that you have installed, patched, and configured the Repository and first OMS and chain-installed Agent, you are in a great position to deploy any additional OMSs required. As explored in the section "Deciding on OMS Architecture" in Chapter 2, the installation of one OMS may meet the requirements of smaller CC sites, but larger production environments may need at least one more OMS for scalability or geographical coverage. Still other sites require multiple OMSs for high availability.

Unlike in GC 11*g* where you must use the CC Installer to deploy an additional OMS, in CC 12*c*, no such Installer option exists, but better yet, there is a wizard in the Console to clone the first OMS to an additional OMS. The major advantage in being able to clone the OMS in CC 12*c* over having to rerun the installer in GC 11*g* to install another OMS is that, unlike in GC 11*g*, all patches applied and configuration changes made on the source OMS in CC 12 will be cloned to additional OMS instances. You can clone only one CC 12 OMS at a time to only one destination host. In other words, you can't install two additional OMSs in one operation; you'd have to repeat the cloning procedure for each additional OMS. However, the same applies to GC 11*g*—you'd have to rerun the Installer to deploy each additional OMS.

Before you can clone an OMS in CC 12*c*, you must perform all OMS preinstallation tasks described in Chapter 2 that apply to any OMS host, whether the first or an additional one. Circle back now to Chapter 2 and perform all OMS (and Agent) preinstallation tasks on the additional host where you plan to install a second or subsequent OMS.

After you've taken care of the preinstallation tasks from Chapter 2 that apply to any OMS, complete the following additional prerequisites now, which are unique to installing a subsequent OMS host:[18]

1. The source and destination hosts must run on the same operating system and architecture, such as Linux 64-bit.

2. Configure an upload file location in the Software Library, as described in the earlier section, "Configure a Software Library Storage Location." If you chose a local file system for the OMS Shared Storage location, you must migrate it to shared storage among all designated OMS hosts. To do so, in the Console under Setup, select Provisioning and Patching, then Software Library. Add a new OMS Shared storage location, then select the nonshared location and click Migrate and Remove.

---

[18] Many of these additional preinstallation steps are listed in the *Cloud Control Basic Installation Guide*, Section 8.3, Table 8-1. However, this eight-page table is rather unwieldy because it also contains preinstallation steps in common between the first and additional OMSs, whereas the preceding steps are just for an additional OMS.

3. As required for multiple OMS environments, set Normal preferred credentials for all OMS hosts. To do so, click Setup, Security, then Preferred Credentials. Click the Manage Preferred Credentials button and select the first OMS host name under Target Preferred Credentials. Click Set, select New, enter the user name (owner of the OMS software) and password. Optionally, click Save As and enter a Credential Name. You will need to set these preferred credentials for the additional OMS hosts, once installed.
4. Deploy an Agent on the destination host where the additional OMS is to be installed, as described in the previous section. See Chapter 2 for Agent preinstallation requirements, and Chapter 5 for instructions on all standalone Agent installation methods. The Agent Deployment "push" method is generally the easiest method, and the only method where you can deploy multiple Agents in one operation, which is useful if you are planning to install more than one additional OMS (i.e., two or more).

TIP

While installing Agents on additional OMS hosts to-be, consider using the Agent Deployment method to install standalone Agents at the same time on any dedicated Repository database node(s) lacking an Agent. You need to manually install a standalone (not chain-installed) Agent on dedicated Repository database nodes, as the CC installation deploys a chain-installed Agent only with the first OMS when choosing to create a new EM system. You can wait until Chapter 5 to install Agents on Repository database nodes. But if you do, include OMR nodes in your first batch of standalone Agent deployments. Monitoring the OMR database and node(s) is paramount, because all other target monitoring relies on the OMR database remaining operational.

5. An optional but highly recommended step[19] is to configure a Server Load Balancer (SLB) to work with the first OMS, so that all Agents upload data only via the SLB. Less configuration is required to set up the SLB for CC 12 before installing an additional OMS. An SLB is needed if you want to virtualize or "front-end" multiple OMS hosts and distribute Console and

---

[19] Without an SLB, users would need to log in (and Agents to upload) to each OMS with a distinct URL, which includes (and is distinguished by) the OMS host name. This would require manually configuring each Agent to upload to a particular OMS, and to supply CC admins with just one or all Console URLs.

Agent traffic to each OMS. See the following reference material for step-by-step instructions on configuring two of the most widely used SLBs:

a. **F5 Networks BIG-IP Local Traffic Manager (LTM)** See the following documentation available from Oracle and F5 Networks:

   i. Oracle White Paper: "Enterprise Manager 12*c* Cloud Control: Configuring OMS High Availability with F5 BIG-IP Local Traffic Manager," March 2012 (http://www.oracle.com/technetwork/oem/framework-infra/wp-em12c-config-oms-ha-bigip-1552459.pdf).

   ii. F5 Networks Deployment Guide: "Deploying the BIG-IP LTM with Oracle Enterprise Manager 12c Cloud Control" (http://www.f5.com/http://www.f5.com/pdf/deployment-guides/oracle-enterprise-manager-12c-dg.pdf).

b. **Cisco ACE Application Delivery Switch** See the white paper published jointly by Oracle and Cisco, called "Configuring Oracle Enterprise Manager Grid Control 11*g* for Maximum Availability Architecture with Cisco Application Control Engine (ACE) Application Delivery Switch," October 2010 (http://www.cisco.com/en/US/solutions/collateral/ns340/ns517/ns224/ns955/ns967/Oracle_ACE_wp.pdf). This white paper is for GC 11*g* but applies equally to CC 12c. Check the Cisco Web site to see if an updated white paper for CC 12c and the Cisco ACE has since been made available.

6. If you are on a Windows platform and Oracle Configuration Manager (OCM) is configured, stop OCM from the OMS and Web Tier homes as follows:

```
set ORACLE_CONFIG_HOME=$MIDDLEWARE_HOME\gc_inst\em\EMGC_OMS1
$MIDDLEWARE_HOME\oms\ccr\bin\emCCR.bat stop
set ORACLE_CONFIG_HOME=$MIDDLEWARE_HOME\gc_inst\WebTierIH1
$MIDDLEWARE_HOME\Oracle_WT\ccr\bin\emCCR.bat stop
```

   where, for example, MIDDLEWARE_HOME=C:\app\oracle\middleware.

7. Ensure that the middleware home does not already exist on the destination host, and can be created by the CC software owner.

NOTE
Before installing an additional OMS, be sure to take a cold backup of all Cloud Control components. For details, see the sidebar entitled "Begin Regular CC Backups."

In the CC 12 Console, you launch the wizard to add an OMS by selecting Provisioning and Patching in the Enterprise menu, then Procedure Library. On the Deployment Procedure Manager page, in the Procedure Library tab, select Add Management Service near the bottom of the table, and click Launch.

Begin Regular CC Backups

Now that you've completed the Cloud Control installation and configuration process, it would be a shame to suffer a hardware or software failure, or a human error that sent you reeling back to the beginning of this great adventure.[20] If you haven't already done so, now is certainly the time to begin a regular schedule of complete CC environment online backups, and cold backups at select times such as now to capture the CC configuration at a particular point in time. For instructions on how to back up all CC components, see Chapter 28 of the *Cloud Control Administrator's Guide*. Following is a summary of the regular CC component backup strategy recommended in this guide (back up all components to disk and tape if possible):

- **Management Repository** Regularly back up the OMR Database and database server software using Oracle Database backup and recovery best practices recommended in the *Oracle Database High Availability Best Practices Guide* for your database Release, which can be summarized as follows:
  - Back up the Database server Oracle homes for Grid Infrastructure (if used) and Oracle Database, and the Oracle Inventory, all as part of a server-wide operating system backup.
  - Back up the Oracle database containing the Repository using Oracle Recovery Manager (RMAN), either with RMAN command-line scripts or by accessing RMAN via the CC Console and using the *Recommended Backup Strategy* option shown there.
- **OMS** Schedule regular backups of the OMS as follows:
  - Back up the OMS Oracle home and Oracle Inventory as part of a server-wide file system operating system backup.
  - Take a snapshot backup of the OMS configuration using the `emctl` utility, as follows:

    ```
    emctl exportconfig oms -dir <backup_dir> -sysman_pwd <pwd>
    ```

---

[20] Lou Reed, loosely quoted.

A backup file in zip archive format will be created with the name opf_ADMIN_<*timestamp*>.bka, and will be on the order of hundreds of MB in size. You can specify a backup directory on the local OMS file system, and you can also copy the OMS backup to a remote system for safekeeping, in addition to archiving the local backup to tape.

- **Management Agent** Agent backups are generally not necessary, as you can simply reinstall an Agent by cloning it from a "reference" Agent (that is, kept up-to-date as to patches applied) in your environment running on the same platform as that where the Agent software needs to be restored.

The Getting Started page, the first of five pages, will guide you through three of the preinstallation tasks in the preceding list, which you should have already taken care of. Click Next. You can then follow the well-heeled instructions in the *Cloud Control Basic Installation Guide*, Section 8.4 to get through the rest of the wizard, and the postinstallation procedures in Section 8.

Summary

This chapter focuses on installing the Cloud Control infrastructure using the "Create a new Enterprise Manager System" installation type, and is organized into four main sections:

- Preparation for CC Installation
- Installation of a New CC System
- Configuration of the New CC System
- Installation of an Additional OMS

The "Preparation for CC Installation" section summarizes installation information to gather, directs where to look for installation-related bugs, tells how to initialize the OS environment for the CC Installer, and takes you through the Installer options, delving into the two most commonly used ones, silent installation and the static ports feature.

The "Installation of a New CC System" section, which is the focus of the chapter, lists the main installation log files you can consult in case of issues, then presents the Installer screens when selecting the Advanced option of "Create a new

Enterprise Manager System," providing guidance on what to input to achieve the desired CC system configuration.

The section "Configuration of the New CC System" leads you through the minimal setup needed to log in to the CC Console via HTTPS and HTTP and configure a Software Library storage directory. We recommend how to patch CC to ensure that you are on the latest point release and CPU and have applied any required one-offs. Finally, we provide specific instructions for configuring the OMS and Repository database to ensure smooth CC operations.

In the final section, "Installation of an Additional OMS," for CC sites that need more than one OMS, we delineate its unique prerequisites, over and above those for installing the initial OMS (presented in Chapter 2), then tell you how to use Console functionality to clone the first OMS to an additional OMS. The ability to clone an OMS in CC 12*c* versus having to rerun the Installer in GC 11*g* and select the additional OMS option, has the key benefit of allowing patches and configuration changes to the first OMS to be replicated to additional OMSs without having to redo these changes.

Now that you have completed the CC installation and configuration tasks in this chapter, you are ready to install standalone Agents on target hosts, as covered in the next chapter.

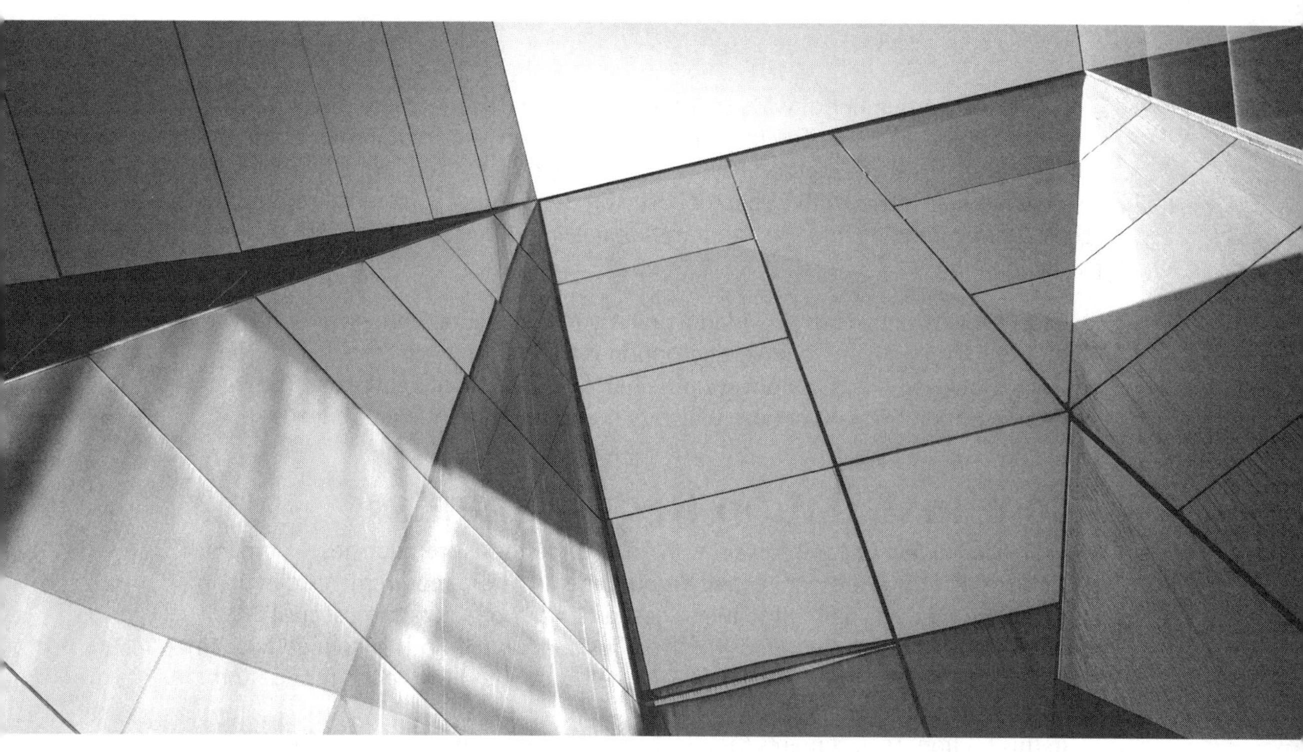

CHAPTER 5

Installing and Configuring Management Agents

There are a number of ways to install the Oracle Management Agent (OMA) on a host machine. The method varies based on your requirements and restrictions. Each method has its own characteristics and requirements. We have intentionally ordered this chapter based on our order of preference for installing Agents. Before jumping into the Agent install, it is important to understand what the installation requires.

OEM Cloud Control has provided many Agent installation enhancements over OEM Grid Control. The recommended option is to perform mass installation from the OMS; however, this is not always possible, so other options still exist. The Agent installation option that you choose will vary based on your individual needs.

Agent Installation Requirements

There are only a few OS prerequisites. In addition to these prerequisites, in order to install the Agent there are connectivity requirements. These requirements can be either easy to meet, or difficult to meet, based on your organization's security policies. The biggest hurdle to most of these installation methods is connectivity. In order to install the Agent via some of these methods, both ICMP echo (`ping`) and `ssh` access is required.

In this section, requirements for all Agent deployment methods and specific methods will be presented. This will give you a better idea of which methods will work for you and/or which ports must be opened for the installation and configuration of the Agents.

General Agent Requirements

In order for the Agent to communicate to the OMS and for the OMS to communicate with the Agent, both the Agent listener port and Agent Upload ports must be opened. The value of these ports will vary based on your configuration. The default Management Agent port is 3872 and the default OMS Agent Upload port is 1159. These two ports are sufficient for communication between the OMS and Agent. Firewalls can be opened unidirectionally between the OMS and Agent on the Management Agent port and between the Agent and OMS on the OMS Agent Upload port.

In addition to these ports, additional ports will be required for management of specific components such as databases, application servers, E-Business Suite, and so on. These additional requirements will be covered in the appropriate chapters within this book.

Agent Deployment Requirements

Several of the specific Agent deployment methods have additional requirements. These requirements are shown here in tabular form.

Deployment Method	ICMP Echo (`ping`)	`ssh`	NFS	Notes
Agent Deployment Wizard	Yes	Yes		Must establish communication and push software to the target host.
Silent Install				No additional requirements.
Agent Download Script	Yes	Yes		
Agent Cloning Wizard	Yes	Yes	Yes	
Shared Oracle Home	Yes	Yes	Yes	This requires all systems to have the same mount point for the Agent.
ZIP File	Yes		Yes	

These requirements must be met or the installation will fail. An issue of an unreachable port will usually show up in the validation phase of the Agent deployment; however, some issues might show up later.

Agent Deployment Requirements Summary

The following table describes the Management Agent and OMS Agent Upload ports as well as other system ports.

Component	HTTP Port	HTTPS Port
OMS Agent Upload port	4889. If port 4889 is not available, the first available port within the range 4889–4898 is used.	1159. If port 1159 is not available, the first available port within the range 4889–4908 is used. It is not uncommon to have the initial installation use a port other than 1159.
Management Agent port	3872. If port 3872 is not available, the first available port within the range 1830–1849 is used.	3872. If port 3872 is not available, the first available port within the range 1830–1849 is used.
ICMP Echo (`ping`)	Not a port, but a service that must be enabled through firewalls.	NA

Component	HTTP Port	HTTPS Port
ssh	Secure shell is a protocol that runs on port 22 for secure system access and is used for ssh, scp, and sftp.	NA
NFS	Network File System. Uses the UDP protocol for file sharing.	NA

In order for your installation and configuration to be successful, these ports and services must be available between the OMS and Agent system.

Downloading Agent Software to Cloud Control

In order to prepare for the Agent installation, you must have Cloud Control Agent software to deploy. Depending on the type of installation being done, the Agent software can be downloaded directly to the target, or to the Cloud Control server. The software can be downloaded to the Cloud Control server within Cloud Control itself. There are a few prerequisites necessary to update Cloud Control:

1. The My Oracle Support Credentials must be set up.
2. The Software Library must be set up.
3. Self Update must be configured.
4. Agent software is downloaded.

Setting My Oracle Support Credentials

Before setting up software updates, you must make sure that the My Oracle Support credentials are properly configured. From the main toolbar, select Setup | My Oracle Support | Set Credentials. This will invoke the My Oracle Support Preferred Credentials screen. Put in your preferred credentials and password. Click the Apply button to enter these credentials. A confirmation screen will verify that you were successful.

Setting Up the Software Library

By default, the Agent associated with the OMS platform will be available for installation; however, to add Agents for other targets, the Software Library must be configured. From the main toolbar, select Setup | Provisioning and Patching | Software Library. This will invoke the Software Library: Administration screen as shown in Figure 5-1.

Click the Add button. A pop-up will prompt you for a name and path for the initial software library location. Choose a location that is available from all OMS locations. A name might be something like SoftwareLib1 and the location could be an NFS mount point or a local directory such as /u01/app/OracleHomes/softwarelib1.

Once the software library location has been entered, you will see it in the Software Library: Administration screen.

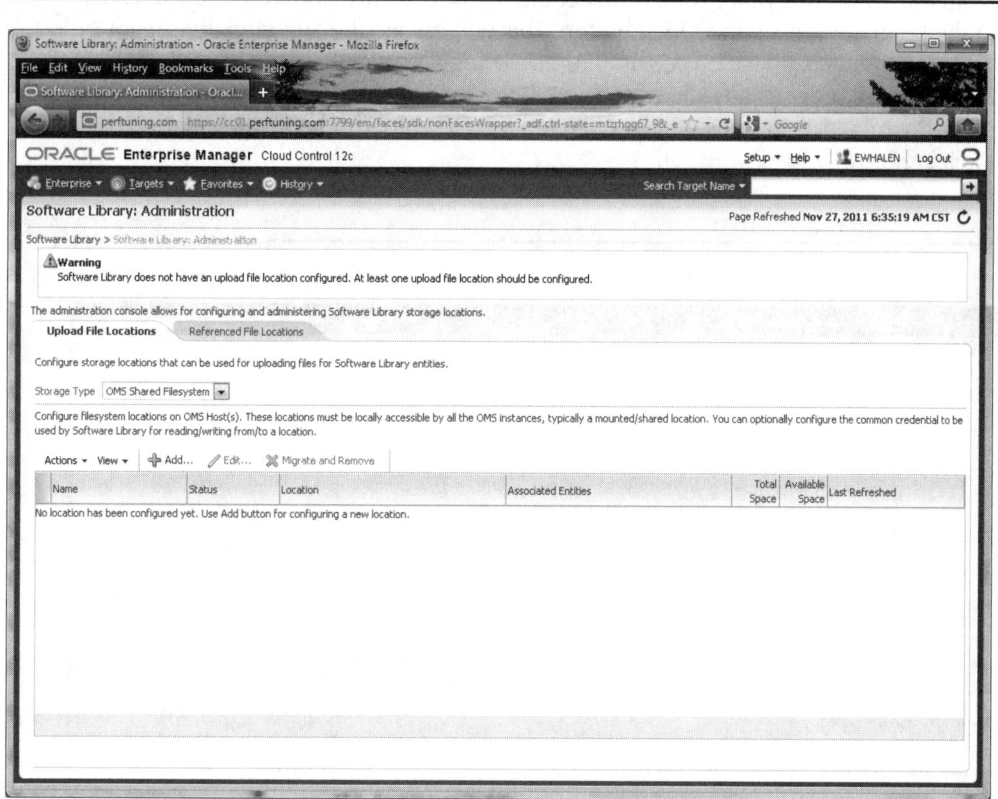

FIGURE 5-1. *The Software Library: Administration screen*

Configuring Self-Update

Finally, Self Update must be configured. In order to configure Self Update, select Setup | Extensibility | Self Update. This will invoke the Self Update screen as shown in Figure 5-2.

From here you can manage the updates to Cloud Control itself. There are options for Check Updates and Agent Software. Selecting Check Updates will submit a job to check My Oracle Support for updated software. The Agent Software button will allow you to provision an Agent on a host. You will see this later.

Downloading Agent Software

From the Software Library screen, select the Agent Software line from the list shown in the library and click the Open button. This will invoke the Self Update | Agent Software screen. Choose an Agent that is showing a status of available, and click Download in order to download and configure that Agent for installation. Once you click Download, the status will be changed to "Download scheduled," as shown in Figure 5-3.

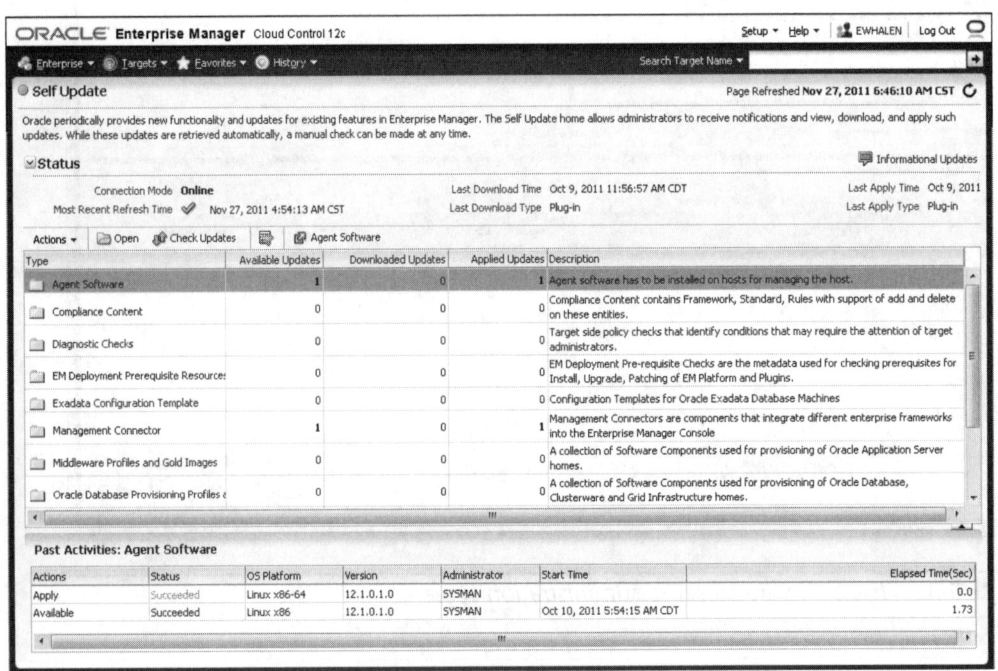

FIGURE 5-2. *The Self Update screen*

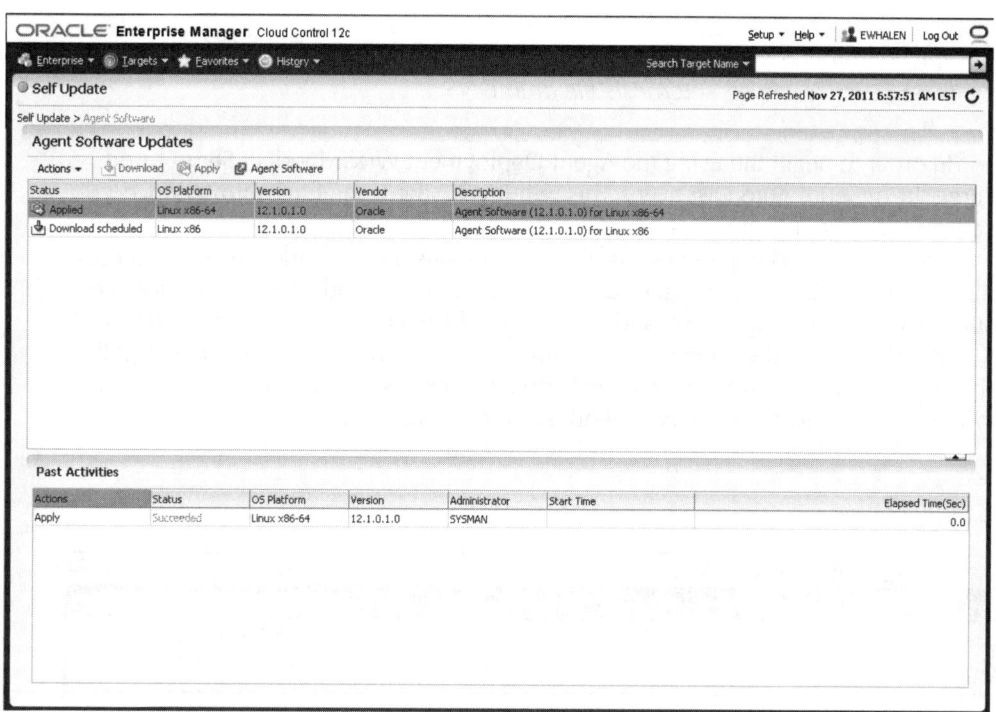

FIGURE 5-3. *The Self Update | Agent Software screen*

Once the download has completed, the status will change to "Download in progress" and finally to Downloaded. At this point, each of the platforms is available for installing on a client system using the various methods described in this chapter.

Installing Agents Using the Agent Deployment Wizard

The Agent Deployment Wizard is this author's preferred method of deploying Agents, since it is all done from the OMS, pushing out the Agent to the target system. This method requires not only the Agent ports and `ssh` but also requires ICMP echo (`ping`) in order to install successfully. The Agent Deployment Wizard can be invoked from a number of different locations within Cloud Control, including the Agent Software screen. If all prerequisites are met, this deployment method is very straightforward and can quickly be implemented.

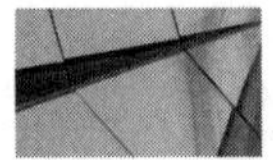

NOTE
In order for the Agent Deployment Wizard to function properly, the IP address of the OMS server must be in the targets /etc/hosts file or in DNS.

In order to begin the using the Agent Deployment Wizard, select Setup | Add Target | Configure Auto Discovery. This will invoke the Configure Auto Discovery screen as shown in Figure 5-4.

Here you can configure how to discover hosts using an IP address scan. You can also configure discovery modules that are used to provide additional auto discovery such as Cluster and HA services, databases and listeners, Oracle homes, and so on.

In order to start the process of installing the Agent on a host or set of hosts, click the configure icon next to "Hosts and Virtual Server Discovery Using IP Scan." This will invoke the Host Discovery (Agentless) screen, which is shown in Figure 5-5.

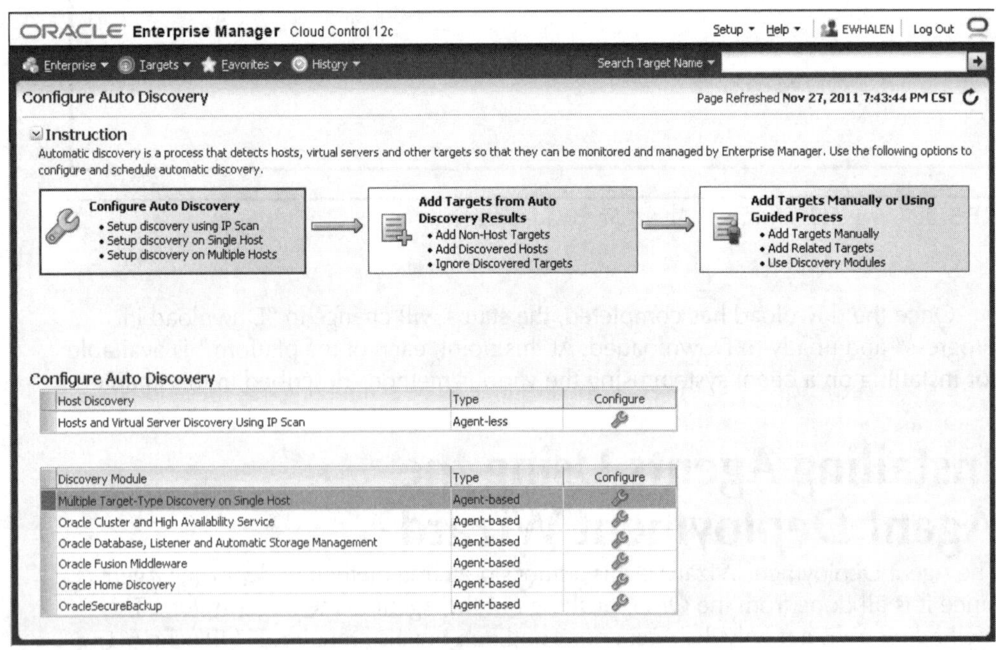

FIGURE 5-4. *The Configure Auto Discovery screen*

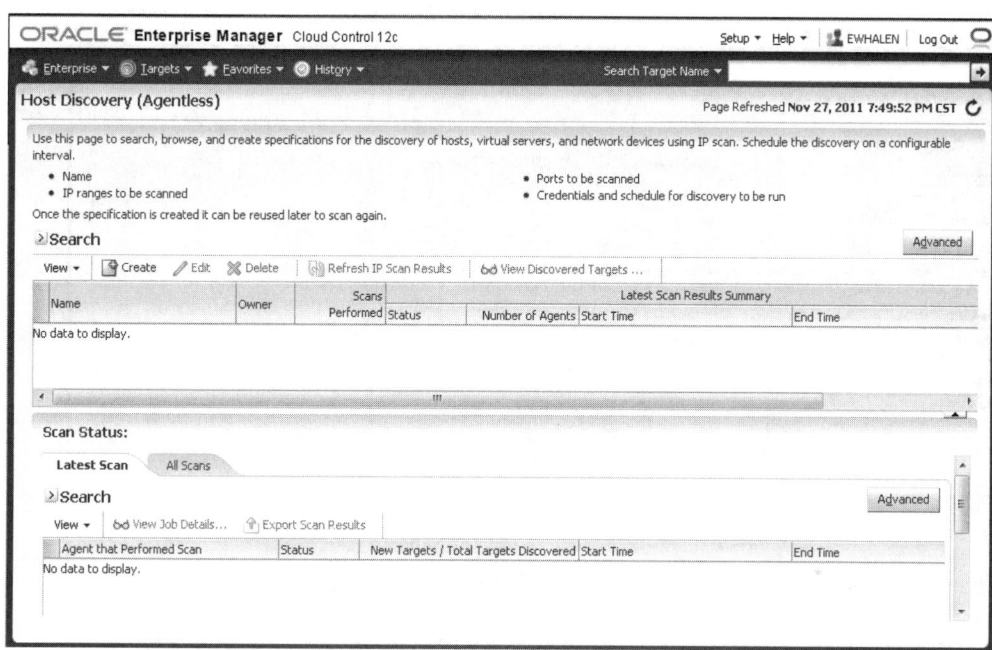

FIGURE 5-5. *The Host Discovery (Agentless) screen*

Here you can create a new search that will be used to search for hosts that are good candidates to add Agents. Click the Create button to create a search criteria that will be used for the Agent search. Clicking this button invokes the Host Discovery Specification: Create screen as shown in Figure 5-6.

This screen allows you to set up the IP range to be scanned. Click the Add button to configure an existing Agent to perform the scan. This Agent can be any Agent, but Sudo or PowerBroker must be enabled and privilege delegation must be configured for this host.

NOTE

Both Sudo and PowerBroker are utilities that allow users to run specific operations at a higher security level than they are normally authorized for. They are standard utilities and Sudo is built into Linux and Unix. PowerBroker is an add-on utility. Both are typically used to allow users other than root to run programs with root privileges.

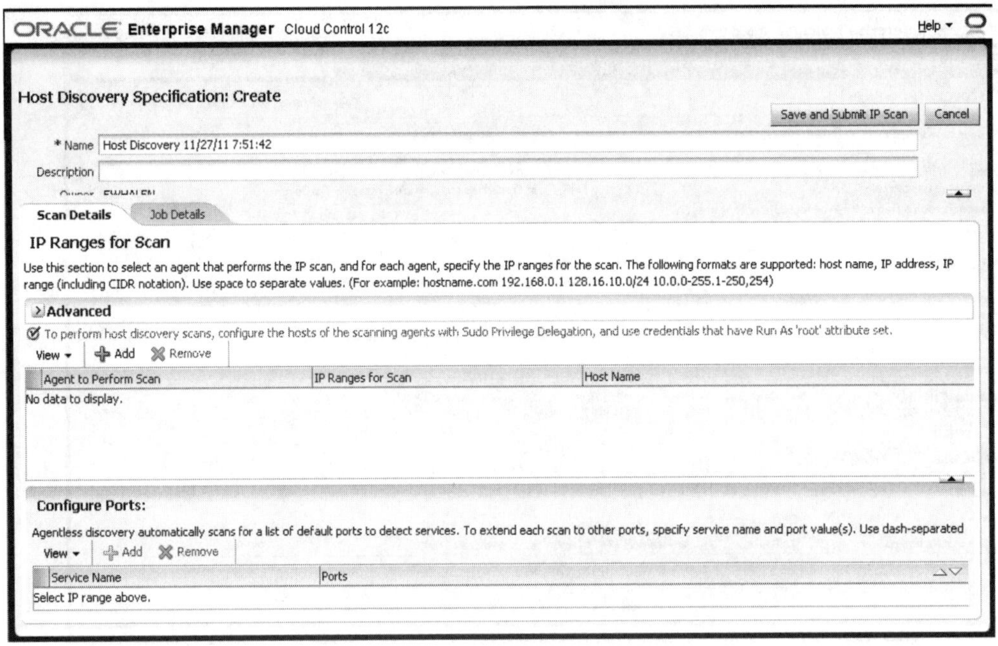

FIGURE 5-6. *The Host Discovery Specification: Create screen*

Privilege Delegation is configured from the Setup | Security | Privilege Delegation drop-down, as covered in Chapter 7. The available Agents will be displayed and one should be selected. The OMS Agent can be used as well. Once the Agent has been selected, the Host Discovery Specifications Create screen will be displayed again, this time with the Agent displayed and a place to put in an IP address range.

Options for this format are

- hostname
- IP Address, such as 192.168.0.1
- Subnet range, like 128.16.10.0/24
- Or IP address range, like this: 10.0.0-255.1–250,254

For this example, we are using the IP address range 192.168.60.30–192.168.60.38. This is shown in Figure 5-7.

Once you have completed the Host Discovery Specification: Create screen, click the Job Details tab and select the credentials to be used. If there are no predefined credentials and the preferred credentials are insufficient, click the New button. This will allow you to provide a username and password to be used.

Included on this screen is a Test button. Once you have selected the credentials to be used, click Test and make sure that they work. Once you are satisfied, click the Save and Submit IP Scan button. This will submit a job to search for candidate targets.

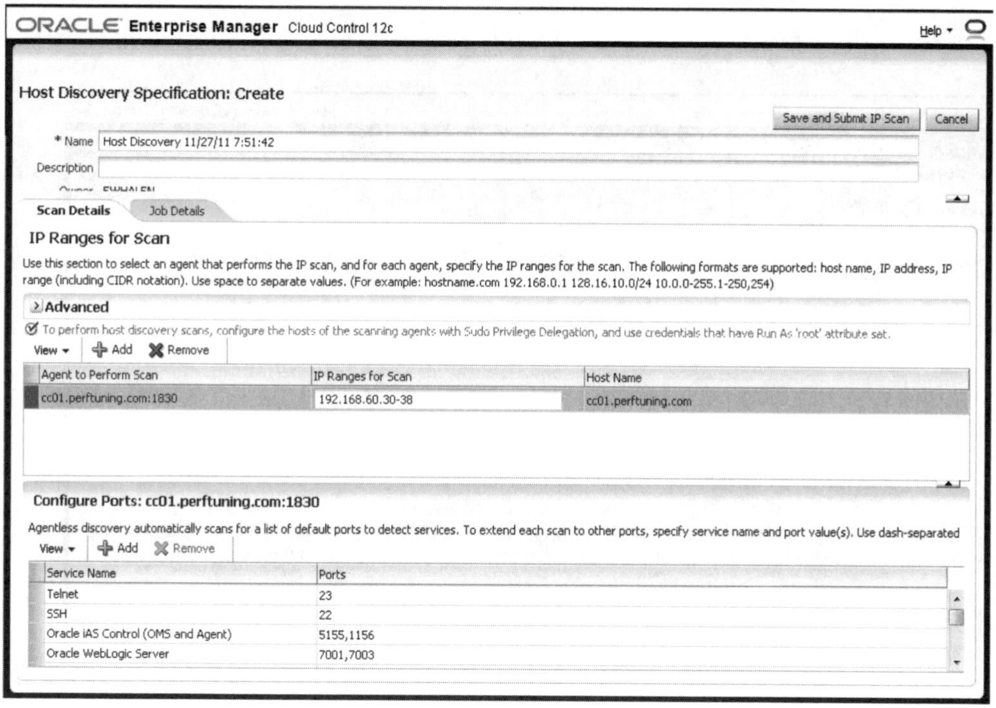

FIGURE 5-7. *The Host Discovery Specification: Create screen with IP address range*

Once you have submitted the search, the screen will show you when it is scheduled to run. After that run time you can check the results of the scan and proceed from there. In order to view the results of the scan, select Setup | Add Target | Auto Discovery Results. This will display the Auto Discovery Results screen as shown in Figure 5-8.

The automatic discovery process will scan the IP range looking for hosts with the credentials supplied and suitable for installation of an Oracle Agent. Once this process has completed, the Agent can be installed, either by following the link from the Auto Discovery Results screen or by selecting Setup | Add Target | Add Target Manually from the toolbar. This will bring you to where you can start the Agent installation process.

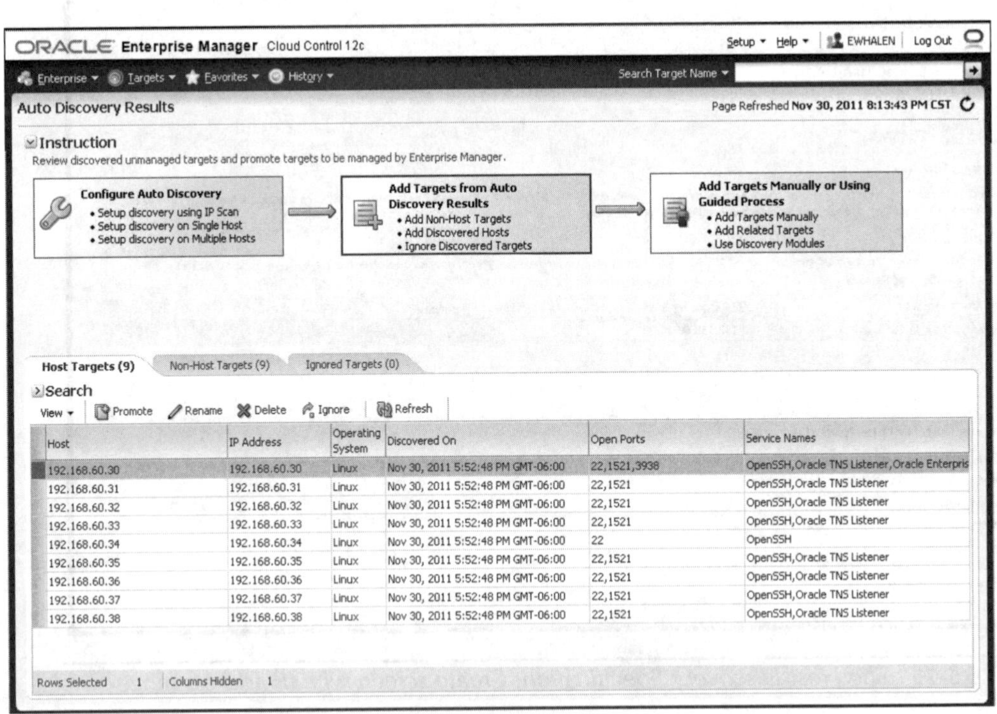

FIGURE 5-8. *The Auto Discovery Results screen*

In order to install from the Auto Discovery Results screen, select one or more of the hosts displayed and click the Promote button. This will invoke the Add Host Targets: Host and Platform screen as shown in Figure 5-9.

Here you can add hosts, change the host platform, or remove a host. Click Next to continue. This will take you to the Add Host Targets: Installation Details screen as shown in Figure 5-10.

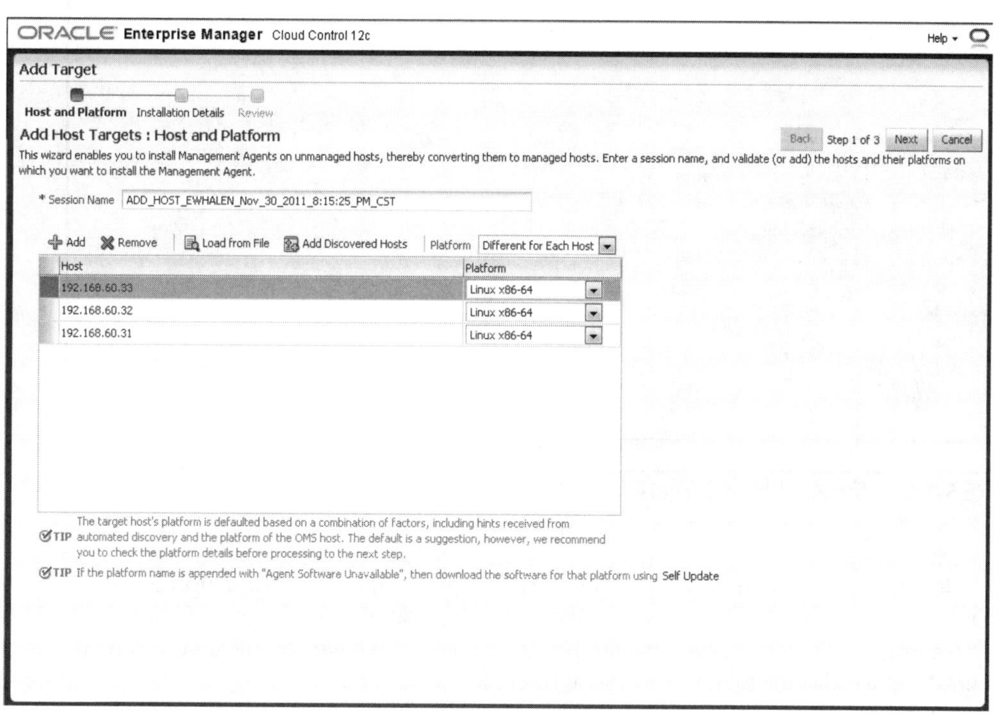

FIGURE 5-9. *The Add Host Targets: Host and Platform screen*

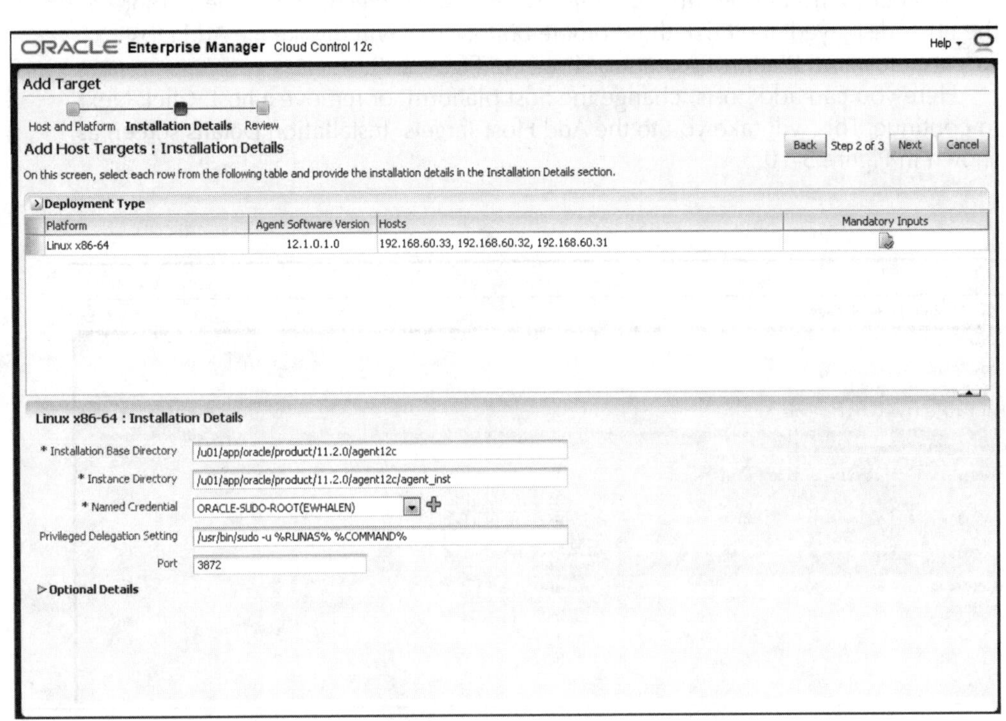

FIGURE 5-10. *The Add Host Targets: Installation Details screen*

It is necessary to fill in some mandatory details, such as the Installation Base Directory, the Instance Directory, and the Named Credential, as shown in Figure 5-11. These must be filled in before you can proceed. Once you have completed this screen, click Next to advance to the Add Host Targets : Review screen.

Once you have completed this screen, click the Deploy Agent button for the Agent installation process to proceed. This will then advance you to the Add Host

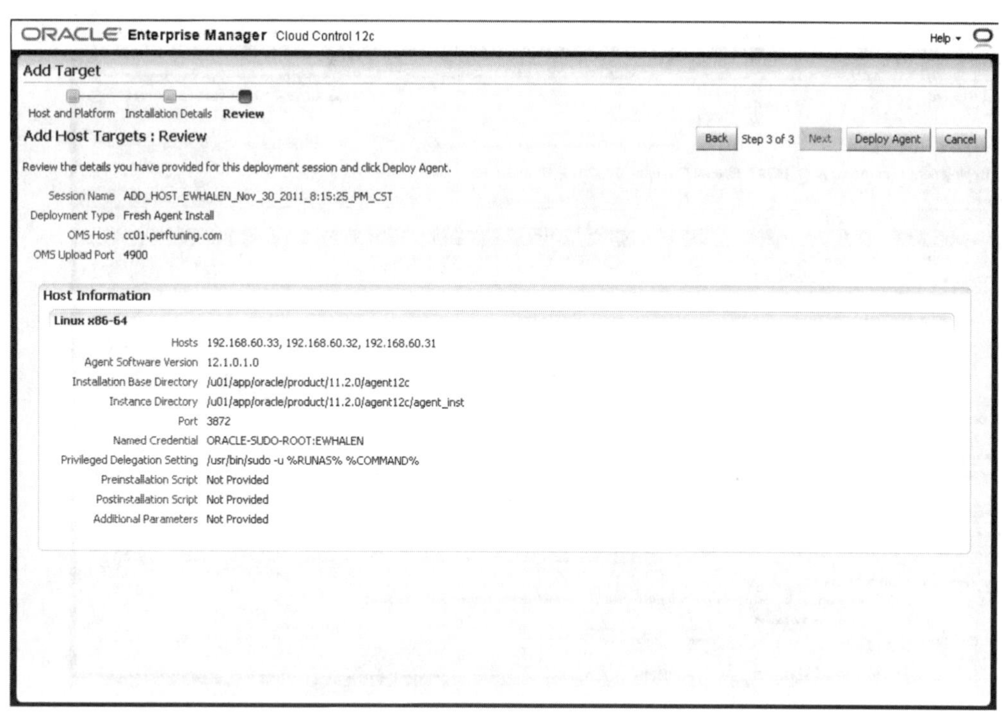

FIGURE 5-11. *The Agent Add Host Targets: Review screen*

Status screen, where you can see the progress of the installation on these hosts. This screen is shown in Figure 5-12.

You can watch the Agent installation proceed from here. It will take a while to complete, but the progress will be updated regularly. Once the installation has completed, the new hosts should show up in the hosts monitoring screen.

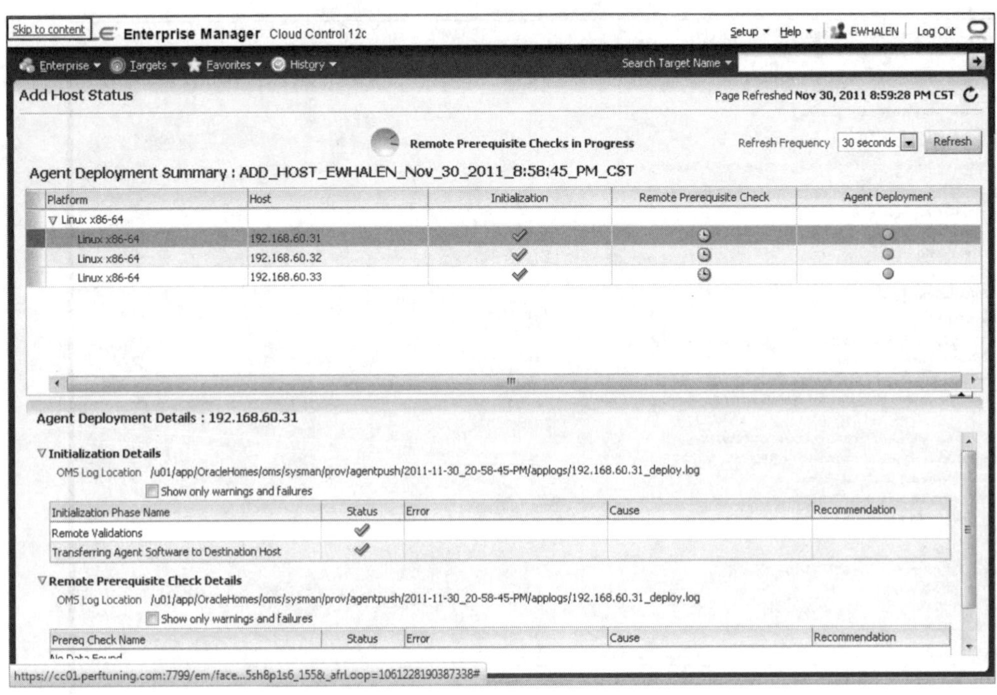

FIGURE 5-12. *The Add Host Status screen*

Installing Agents Using the Silent Install

In many cases the ability to push an Agent out to the target is restricted by security rules. Unlike previous releases of the OEM Grid Control Agent, Cloud Control 12c does not have an interactive installation. In order to install manually you must use the silent installation method. This method is quite straightforward and easy to use. It involves a few basic steps:

1. Synchronize EMCLI.
2. Download the Installer to the target host.
3. Edit the response file.
4. Run the Installer.

Synchronize EMCLI with the OMS

On the OMS server, log in to the OMS using `emcli` and synchronize EMCLI as shown here:

```
[oracle@cc01 ~]$ emcli login -username=sysman -password=cloud123
Login successful
[oracle@cc01 ~]$ emcli sync
Synchronized successfully
```

Once EMCLI is synchronized, you can download the Agent software to the target system.

Download the Installer to the Target Host

The download to the target system is done via the OMS. The first step is to find the supported platforms that are currently in the OEM Software Library. This is done via the `emcli get_supported_platforms` command. This command is shown here:

```
[oracle@cc01 tmp]$ emcli get_supported_platforms
Getting list of platforms ...
Check the logs at /tmp/agent.log
About to access self-update code path to retrieve the platforms list..
Getting Platforms list  ...
-----------------------------------------------
Version = 12.1.0.1.0
 Platform = Linux x86-64
-----------------------------------------------
Version = 12.1.0.1.0
 Platform = Linux x86
-----------------------------------------------
Platforms list displayed successfully.
```

From the platform list you can download the software that you desire to the OMS system, so that it can be copied to the target host using the `emcli get_agentimage` command as shown here.

```
 [oracle@cc01 ~]$ emcli get_agentimage -destination=/tmp -platform="Linux x86-64"
-version=12.1.0.1.0
Platform:Linux x86-64
Destination:/tmp
 === Partition Detail ===
Space free : 1 GB
Space required : 1 GB
Check the logs at /tmp/get_agentimage_2011-12-01_15-02-28-PM.log
Setting property ORACLE_HOME to:/u01/app/OracleHomes/oms
calling pulloneoffs with
arguments:/u01/app/OracleHomes/oms/u01/app/OracleHomes/oms/sysman/agent/12.1.0.1.0
_AgentCore_226.zip12.1.0.1.0linux_x64
Check this logs for more information:
/u01/app/OracleHomes/oms/sysman/prov/agentpush/logs
```

Now the final step is to copy this Agent zip file to the target host system. This can be done via scp or other network copy program.

```
[oracle@cc01 tmp]$ scp 12.1.0.1.0_AgentCore_226.zip rac01a:/tmp
```

Once the Agent software file has been copied, the work shifts from the OMS system to the target host itself, where you unzip and configure the Agent software.

On the target host, change to the directory where the software has been installed and unzip it using the unzip command as shown here:

```
[oracle@rac01a tmp]$ unzip 12.1.0.1.0_AgentCore_226.zip
Archive:  12.1.0.1.0_AgentCore_226.zip
  inflating: unzip
  inflating: agentDeploy.sh
  inflating: agentimage.properties
  inflating: agent.rsp
 extracting: agentcoreimage.zip
 extracting: 12.1.0.1.0_PluginsOneoffs_226.zip
```

In the list of files that have been unzipped, you will see the Agent response file. This file must be edited in order to allow the silent installation to proceed properly.

Edit the Response File

The next step is to edit the copy of the response file. There are a few things that need to be edited in this file. The items to be edited are OMS_HOST, EM_UPLOAD_PORT, AGENT_REGISTRATION_PASSWORD, AGENT_INSTANCE_HOME, AGENT_PORT, ORACLE_HOSTNAME, and s_agentHomeName. For the example in this book, these values are set as follows. Your values might be slightly different, depending on your configuration.

```
OMS_HOST=cc01.perftuning.com
EM_UPLOAD_PORT=4900
AGENT_REGISTRATION_PASSWORD=cloud123
AGENT_INSTANCE_HOME=/u01/app/oracle/product/11.2.0/agent12c
AGENT_PORT=3872
ORACLE_HOSTNAME=rac01a.perftuning.com
s_agentHomeName="agent12gR1"
```

Once the response file has been modified, you are ready for the installation.

Install the Agent Using the Silent Install

Once the response has been modified, you can install the Agent using the agentDeploy.sh script that is found in the same directory where you unzipped the Agent software. You must pass it the response file location as shown here.

```
./agentDeploy.sh AGENT_BASE_DIR=/u01/app/oracle/product/11.2.0/agent12c
RESPONSE_FILE=/tmp/agent.rsp
```

NOTE
If you do not have Sudo enabled, you must run the root.sh script as root manually.

At this point, the newly added Agent should show up in the OEM Console.

Installing Agents Using the RPM Method

Installing the OEM Agent using an RPM file is similar to using the Silent Install method, in that the package is downloaded from the OMS server to the client. In this case, a Red Hat Package Manager file is used for the installation. This method is quite straightforward and easy to use. It involves a few basic steps:

1. Synchronize EMCLI.
2. Download the Installer to the target host.
3. Edit the response file.
4. Run the Installer.

Synchronize EMCLI with the OMS

On the OMS server, log in to the OMS using `emcli` and synchronize EMCLI as shown here:

```
[oracle@cc01 ~]$ emcli login -username=sysman -password=cloud123
Login successful
[oracle@cc01 ~]$ emcli sync
Synchronized successfully
```

Once EMCLI is synchronized, you can download the Agent software to the target system.

Download the Installer to the Target Host

The download to the target system is done via the OMS. The first step is to find the supported platforms that are currently in the OEM Software Library. This is done via the `emcli get_supported_platforms` command. This command is shown here:

```
[oracle@cc01 tmp]$ emcli get_supported_platforms
Getting list of platforms ...
Check the logs at /tmp/agent.log
About to access self-update code path to retrieve the platforms list..
Getting Platforms list  ...
```

```
----------------------------------------------
Version = 12.1.0.1.0
 Platform = Linux x86-64
----------------------------------------------
Version = 12.1.0.1.0
 Platform = Linux x86
----------------------------------------------
Platforms list displayed successfully.
```

From the platform list you can download the software that you desire to the OMS system, so that it can be copied to the target host using the `emcli get_agentimage_rpm` command.

NOTE
In order for the `emcli get_agentimage_rpm` command to work properly, the `rpmbuild` program must be installed on the OMS Server. This program is part of the Linux OS `rpm-build` package that must be installed. Without this package, the next step will fail.

The RPM package is built using the `emcli get_agentimage_rpm` command as shown here.

```
[oracle@cc01 ~]$ emcli get_agentimage_rpm -destination=/u02/app/download -
platform="Linux x86-64" -version=12.1.0.1.0
Platform:Linux x86-64
Destination:/u02/app/download
 Checking for disk space requirements...
 === Partition Detail ===
Space free : 4 GB
Space required : 1 GB
RPM creation in progress ...
Check the logs at /u02/app/download/get_agentimage_rpm_2011-12-05_20-24-36-PM.log
Copying agent image from software library to /u02/app/download
Setting property ORACLE_HOME to:/u01/app/OracleHomes/oms
calling pulloneoffs with
arguments:/u01/app/OracleHomes/oms/u01/app/OracleHomes/oms/sysman/agent/12.1.0.1.0
_AgentCore_226.zip12.1.0.1.0Linux x86-64/u02/app/downloadtrue
Agent Image copied successfully...
Creation of RPM started...
RPM creation successful.
Agent image to rpm conversion completed successfully
```

Now the final step is to copy this Agent RPM file to the target host system. This can be done via `scp` or other network copy program.

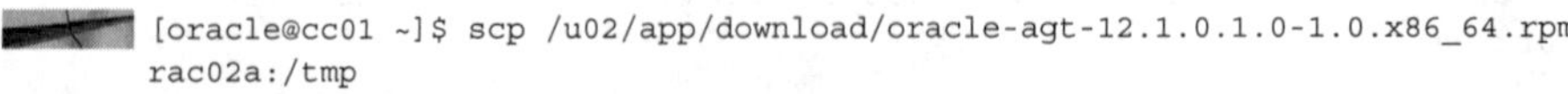

```
[oracle@cc01 ~]$ scp /u02/app/download/oracle-agt-12.1.0.1.0-1.0.x86_64.rpm
rac02a:/tmp
```

Once the Agent software file has been copied, the work shifts from the OMS system to the target host itself, where you install and configure the Agent software. On the target host, change to the directory where the software has been installed and install it using the `rpm` command as shown here:

```
[root@rac02a ~]# rpm -ivh /tmp/oracle-agt-12.1.0.1.0-1.0.x86_64.rpm
Preparing...                ########################################### [100%]
        package oracle-agt-12.1.0.1.0-1.0.x86_64 is already installed
[root@rac02a ~]# rpm -e oracle-agt-12.1.0.1.0-1.0
[root@rac02a ~]# rpm -ivh /tmp/oracle-agt-12.1.0.1.0-1.0.x86_64.rpm
Preparing...                ########################################### [100%]
Running the prereq
   1:oracle-agt             ########################################### [100%]
Follow the below steps to complete the agent rpm installation:
1. Edit the properties file: /usr/lib/oracle/agent/agent.properties with the
correct values
2. Execute the command /etc/init.d/config.pl
```

The installation of the RPM prompts you to edit the agent.properties file and execute the configuration script.

Edit the agent.properties File

The next step is to edit the copy of the agent.properties file. The agent.properties file is found in /usr/lib/oracle/agent. There are a few things that need to be edited in this file. The items to be edited are s_OMSHost, s_OMSPort, AGENT_REGISTRATION_PASSWORD, agentUserName, agentUserGroup, OraInvLoc, BASEDIR, and ORACLE_HOSTNAME. For the example in this book, these values are set as follows. Your values might be slightly different, depending on your configuration.

```
#-------------------------------------------------------------------------------
#s_OMSHost:<String> OMS host info required to connect to OMS
#s_OMSPort:<String> OMS port info required to connect to OMS
#AGENT_REGISTRATION_PASSWORD:<String> Agent Registration Password needed to
#     establish a secure connection to the OMS.
#-------------------------------------------------------------------------------
s_OMSHost=cc01.perftuning.com
s_OMSPort=4900
AGENT_REGISTRATION_PASSWORD=cloud123
#-------------------------------------------------------------------------------
#agentUserName:<String> User name with which the agent should be installed.
#agentUserGroup:<String> Group to which the agent user belogs.
#-------------------------------------------------------------------------------
agentUserName=oracle
agentUserGroup=dba
#-------------------------------------------------------------------------------
#OraInvLoc:<String> Absolute path of the inventory location where the agent user
#   has write permissions.
#Example : OraInvLoc=/usr/lib/oraInventory
#-------------------------------------------------------------------------------
OraInvLoc=/u01/app/oraInventory
#-------------------------------------------------------------------------------
#BASEDIR:<String> Location of the agent base directory.
#Example: BASEDIR=/tmp/agentNG
```

```
#-------------------------------------------------------------------------------
BASEDIR=/u01/app/oracle/product/11.2.0/agent12c
#-------------------------------------------------------------------------------
#ORACLE_HOSTNAME:<String> Virtual hostname where the agent is deployed.
#Example: ORACLE_HOSTNAME=hostname.domain
#-------------------------------------------------------------------------------
ORACLE_HOSTNAME=rac02a.perftuning.com
```

Once the response file has been modified, you are ready for the installation.

Install the Agent

Once the agent.properties file has been modified, you can install the Agent using the config.pl script that is found in the same directory where the RPM deposited the other files (/usr/lib/oracle). Run the perl script as shown here.

```
[root@rac02a tmp]# /etc/init.d/config.pl
```

NOTE
Running the config.pl script will result in a large amount of feedback being displayed. Look for the successful message at the end.

At this point, you should see a large amount of feedback ending with something like this:

```
Agent Configuration completed successfully

The following configuration scripts need to be executed as the "root" user.
#!/bin/sh
#Root script to run
 /u01/app/oracle/product/11.2.0/agent12c/core/12.1.0.1.0/root.sh
To execute the configuration scripts:
1. Open a terminal window
2. Log in as "root"
3. Run the scripts
Agent Deployment Successful.
Agent deployment log location:
/u01/app/oracle/product/11.2.0/agent12c/core/12.1.0.1.0/cfgtoollogs/agentDeploy/
agentDeploy_<timestamp>.log
Agent deployment completed successfully.
The Agent is configured successful
```

Once you have seen this message, run the root.sh script as the root user as shown here:

```
[root@rac02a tmp]# /u01/app/oracle/product/11.2.0/agent12c/core/12.1.0.1.0/root.sh
Finished product-specific root actions.
/etc exist
Finished product-specific root actions.
```

The new system should show up in the Cloud Control system soon.

Installing Agents Using the Agent Cloning Wizard

The Agent Cloning Wizard will easily and quickly clone a working Agent deployment from one system to another. In order for it to be successful, the source Agent must be functioning properly. This method requires not only the Agent ports and `ssh` but also requires ICMP echo (`ping`) in order to install successfully. The Agent Cloning Wizard is invoked from either the Setup | Add Target | Auto Discovery Results drop-down or the Setup | Add Target | Add Targets Manually drop-down. If all prerequisites are met, this deployment method is very straightforward and can quickly be implemented.

Prerequisites

There are several prerequisites that must be met before you can install the Agent using the Agent Cloning Wizard. Since the Agent Cloning Wizard takes the Agent from either the OMS server (if the same platform) or another system, there must be connectivity between all systems involved in this cloning. Thus, NFS access must be enabled from the source system and mounted on the target system and firewall access must be allowed for NFS.

In addition, in order to use the Agent Cloning Wizard, the *PubkeyAuthentication* variable must be set to yes on the OMS server that will be used as the source of the cloning. In Linux, this variable is found in the /etc/ssh/sshd_config file.

Installation Using the Agent Cloning Wizard

In order to begin the using the Agent Deployment Wizard, use either the Setup | Add Target | Auto Discovery Results drop-down or the Setup | Add Target | Add Targets Manually drop-down. For this example, the Add Targets Manually drop-down is used.

The first screen is the Add Host Targets: Host and Platform screen as shown in Figure 5-13. This is where you input the host name and select the platform.

Click Next to continue to the Add Host Targets: Installation Details screen as shown in Figure 5-14. In order to choose a cloning, rather than a fresh Agent install, expand the Deployment Type option by clicking the downward-facing arrow next to Deployment Type. This will expose the Deployment Type radio buttons where you can select Clone Existing Agent and select which Agent to clone, as shown in Figure 5-14.

In this screen you will also fill in the needed variables for Installation Base Directory, Instance Directory, and Named Credential.

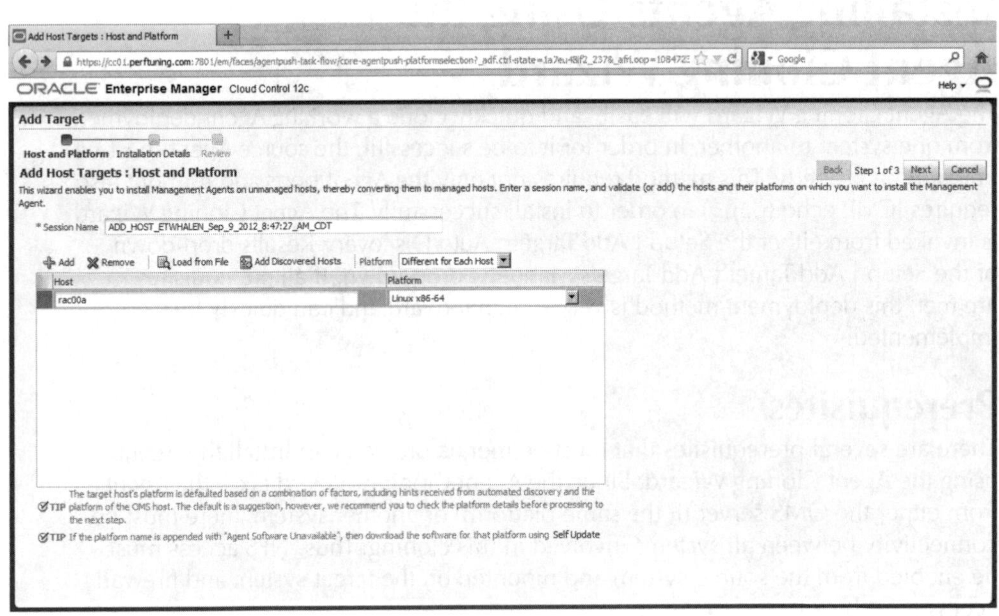

FIGURE 5-13. *The Add Host Targets: Host and Platform screen*

Add Host Targets : Installation Details
ORACLE Enterprise Manager Cloud Control 12c
Help
Add Target
Host and Platform
Installation Details
Review
Add Host Targets : Installation Details
Back
Step 2 of 3
Next
Cancel
On this screen, select each row from the following table and provide the installation details in the Installation Details section.
Deployment Type
Select the type of deployment you want to perform.
Fresh Agent Install
Clone Existing Agent
Select Target ptc:3872
Add Host to Shared Agent
Platform
Agent Software Version
Hosts
Mandatory Inputs
Linux x86-64
12.1.0.1.0
rac00a
Linux x86-64 : Installation Details
* Installation Base Directory /u01/app/oracle/agent12c
* Instance Directory /u01/app/oracle/agent12c/agent_inst
* Named Credential RAC-ORACLE(ETWHALEN)
Privileged Delegation Setting /usr/bin/sudo -u %RUNAS% %COMMAND%
Port 3872
Optional Details

FIGURE 5-14. *The Add Host Targets: Installation Details screen*

NOTE

The default provided in the Privileged Delegation Setting screen is incorrect for Oracle Enterprise Linux. The default value is /usr/local/bin/sudo and the correct value for OEL 5.x is /usr/bin/sudo.

Clicking Next will take you to the Add Host Targets: Review screen as shown in Figure 5-15. Here you can review all of your settings and go back if you have any errors to fix.

This concludes the Agent cloning installation. Click Deploy Agent to continue with the installation, which will then proceed to the Agent Deployment Summary screen, as shown in Figure 5-16.

Once the deployment has concluded, the system should be visible in the OEM Cloud Control Console.

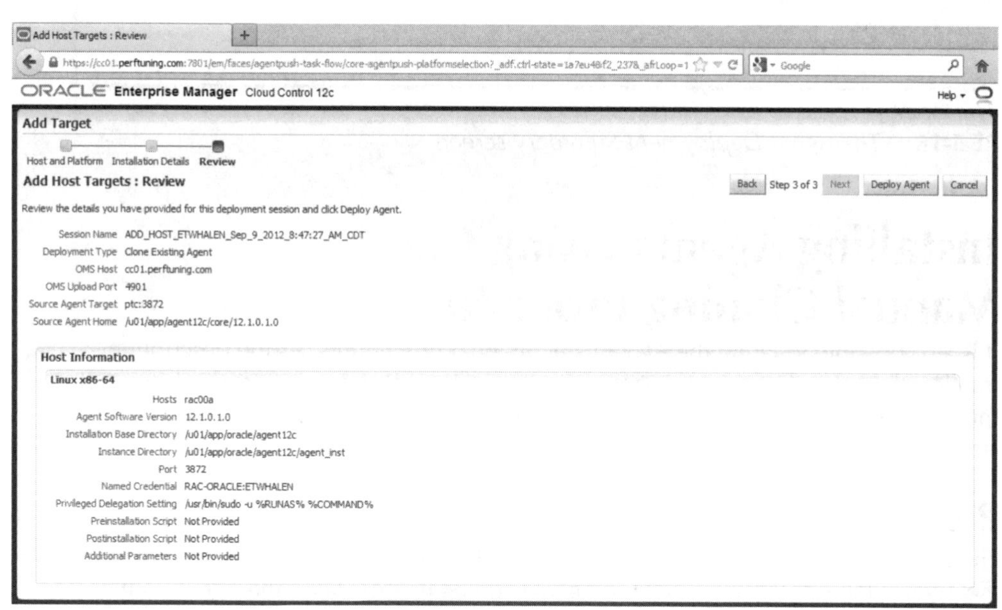

FIGURE 5-15. *The Add Host Targets: Review screen*

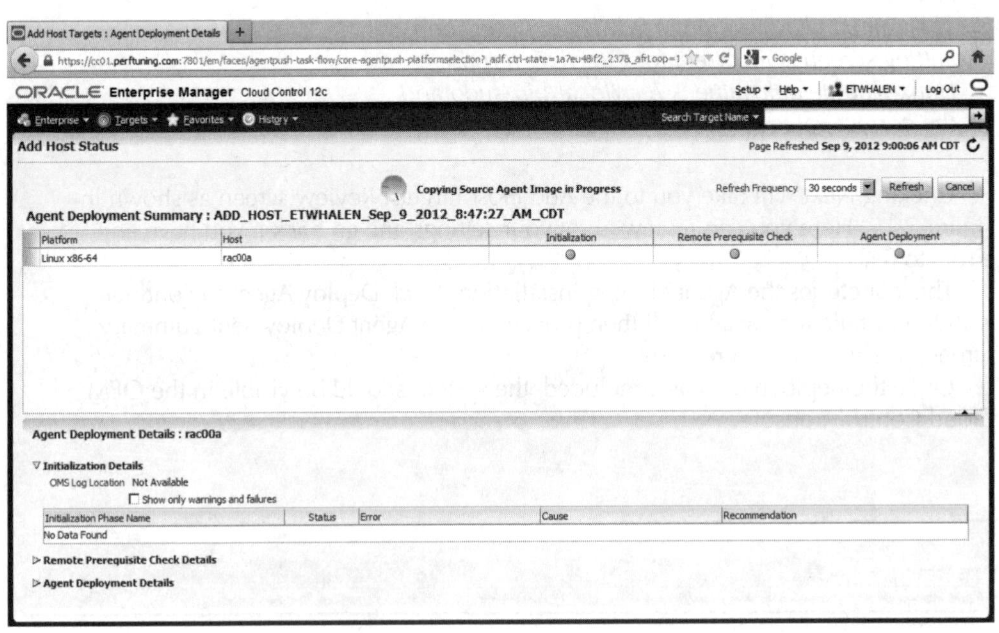

FIGURE 5-16. *The Agent Deployment Summary screen*

Installing Agents Using the Manual Cloning Procedure

It is also possible to clone the Agent using manual procedures. As the description implies, the procedure is very manual. There are several steps and prerequisites that must be followed in order for the manually cloning process to be successful. These steps are outlined in the next sections.

Prerequisites

There are several prerequisites that must be met before you can install the Agent using the Agent Cloning Wizard. Since the Agent Cloning process takes the Agent from a system that currently has an Agent to another system, there must be connectivity between all systems involved in this cloning.

Before the cloning process can proceed, the following environment variables must be set:

AGENT_BASE_DIR	The base directory of the current Agent on the system to be used as the target of the clone.
AGENT_HOME	The Oracle Home of the Management Agent to be used as the target of the cloning.
T_WORK	This should be set to /tmp/clone_work.

Once the environment variables have been set and the connectivity tested, you are ready to proceed with the manual cloning procedure.

Installation Using the Manual Cloning Procedure

In order to clone manually, follow these steps. First, on the source system, perform the following steps:

1. Set the environment variables described in the prerequisites section.

```
[root@rac01a ~]# export AGENT_BASE_DIR=/u01/app/oracle/product/11.2.0/agent12c
[root@rac01a ~]# export AGENT_HOME=/u01/app/oracle/product/11.2.0/agent12c/
/core/12.1.0.1.0
[root@rac01a ~]# export T_WORK=/tmp/clone_work
```

2. Change directory to the Agent base directory.

```
[root@rac01a ~]# cd $AGENT_BASE_DIR
[root@rac01a 11.2.0]# pwd
/u01/app/oracle/product/11.2.0/agent12c
```

3. Compress the needed directories and files into a zip file (core, sbin, plugins, plugins.txt, agentimage.properties).

```
[root@rac01a agent12c]# zip -r $T_WORK/agentcoreimage.zip core sbin plugins
plugins.txt agentimage.properties
```

4. Copy the agentDeploy.sh script to the $T_WORK directory.

```
[root@rac01a agent12c]# cp $AGENT_HOME/sysman/install/agentDeploy.sh $T_WORK
```

5. Copy the agentimage.properties file to the $T_WORK directory.

```
[root@rac01a agent12c]# cp $AGENT_BASE_DIR/agentimage.properties $T_WORK
```

6. Zip up the entire T_WORK directory.

```
[root@rac01a agent12c]# zip -r /tmp/agent.zip $T_WORK/*
```

7. Copy the agent.zip file to the target system.

```
[root@rac01a agent12c]# scp /tmp/agent.zip rac01b:/tmp
```

Then, on the target system, perform the following steps:

8. Unzip the agent.zip file using the `unzip` command (`unzip agent.zip`).

NOTE
The Agent deploy program is expecting `unzip` to be in /tmp/clone_work/unzip. Create a symbolic link to /usr/bin/unzip using `ln -s`.

```
ln -s /usr/bin/unzip /tmp/clone_work/unzip
```

9. Either create a response file or install the Agent providing the necessary installation parameters shown here:

```
./agentDeploy.sh AGENT_BASE_DIR=/u01/app/oracle/product/11.2.0/
agent12c
OMS_HOST=cc01.perftuning.com EM_UPLOAD_PORT=4900
AGENT_REGISTRATION_PASSWORD=cloud123
. . .
Configuration Log
Location:/u01/app/oracle/product/11.2.0/agent12c/
core/12.1.0.1.0/cfgtoollogs/cfgfw
/CfmLogger<timestamp>.log
Agent Configuration completed successfully

The following configuration scripts need to be executed as the
"root" user.
#!/bin/sh
#Root script to run
 /u01/app/oracle/product/11.2.0/agent12c/core/12.1.0.1.0/root.sh
To execute the configuration scripts:
1. Open a terminal window
2. Log in as "root"
3. Run the scripts
Agent Deployment Successful.
Agent deployment log location:
/u01/app/oracle/product/11.2.0/agent12c/core/12.1.0.1.0/cfgtool-
logs/agentDeploy/
agentDeploy_<timestamp>.log
Agent deployment completed successfully.
```

10. Run the root.sh script that was indicated at the end of the output of the agentDeploy script.

```
[root@rac01b ~]# /u01/app/oracle/product/11.2.0/agent12c/
core/12.1.0.1.0/root.sh
```

```
Finished product-specific root actions.
/etc exist

Creating /etc/oragchomelist file...
Finished product-specific root actions.
```

At this point the Agent installation is complete, and the Agent should show up in the Cloud Control Console.

Installing Shared Oracle Home Agents Using the Wizard

The shared Oracle Home installation takes an existing Oracle Agent that is installed on an NFS mount point (NAS) and extends this Agent to allow other systems to use it. This method can save space, but it also creates a single point of failure, since the loss of this one directory will cause all Agents using it to fail. The Shared Oracle Home installation can be done either via graphical mode or via the AgentNFS.pl script. The manual method will be covered in the next section. The prerequisites are the same.

Prerequisites

There are a few things that should be set up properly prior to attempting the installation. Because the shared Agent installation uses an NFS mounted filesystem for the Agent binaries, it is necessary to mount that partition. This should be done carefully and with some planning. A nonshared Oracle inventory directory is required, so don't mount the filesystem over where you want to have the inventory. In the previous examples the ORACLE_BASE is set to /u01/app/oracle/product/11.2.0/agent12c. This is fine. In order to make this work, there are several steps that should be done.

- Mount the Oracle Agent in the ORACLE_BASE, that is, mount the filesystem on /u01/app/oracle/product/11.2.0/agent12c.

  ```
  mount -t nfs rac03a:/u01/app/oracle/product/11.2.0/agent12c
  /u01/app/oracle/product/11.2.0/agent12c
  ```

- Create an oraInst.loc file that points to the inventory location as /u01/app/oraInventory (if not already there). This would be created as the default inventory location; however, we like to explicitly state this so that it is completely clear.

  This is an example of the /etc/oraInst.loc file from a Linux system.

  ```
  inventory_loc=/u01/app/oraInventory
  inst_group=oinstall
  ```

- Of course, NFS must be operating properly and firewall access set up correctly so that NFS works properly.
- There must be a state directory available on the NFS mount point for each host sharing the Agent software. This should not be in the Agent home directory. For example, if the Agent home directory is /u01/app/oracle/agent12c, an appropriate state directory would be /u01/app/oracle/emstate/<*host*>. Since each system using the shared home needs its own state directory, the host name should be included for uniqueness.

As with the other examples, it is also necessary to make sure that all systems involved in this installation are defined within the /etc/hosts file. Even though DNS is set up correctly, it is necessary to do this.

In addition, in order to use the Shared Oracle Home installation, the *PubkeyAuthentication* variable must be set to yes on the OMS server that will be used as the source of the Agent software. In Linux, this variable is found in the /etc/ssh/sshd_config file.

Installing the Shared Oracle Home Agent Using the Wizard

In order to use the Shared Oracle Home method, using the wizard, the Oracle Home for an existing Oracle 12*c* Agent (Master Agent) must be mounted and available in the same directory that you wish to deploy it to.

As in the previous example, in the OEM 12*c* Cloud Control Console select Setup | Add Target | Add Targets Manually, or Setup | Add Target | Auto Discovery Results. In this example I'm using the Add Targets Manually method. From the Add Targets Manually screen, select Add Host Targets and click the Add Host button. This will bring up the Add Host Targets: Host and Platform screen as shown earlier in Figure 5-13. Enter the Host name and Platform type and click Next.

This will invoke the Add Target screen. Unlike earlier examples, expand the Deployment Type section and choose Add Host to Shared Agent. You will be prompted to select the Master Agent. Configure the other installation details such as Oracle Home (filled in for you), Instance Directory, and Named Credential.

The Instance Directory should be set to the state directory that you created earlier. In this case it is /u01/app/oracle/emstate/rac03b.

NOTE

The Privileged Delegation Setting default is incorrect for Oracle Enterprise Linux. It should be changed to /usr/bin/sudo from /usr/local/bin/sudo.

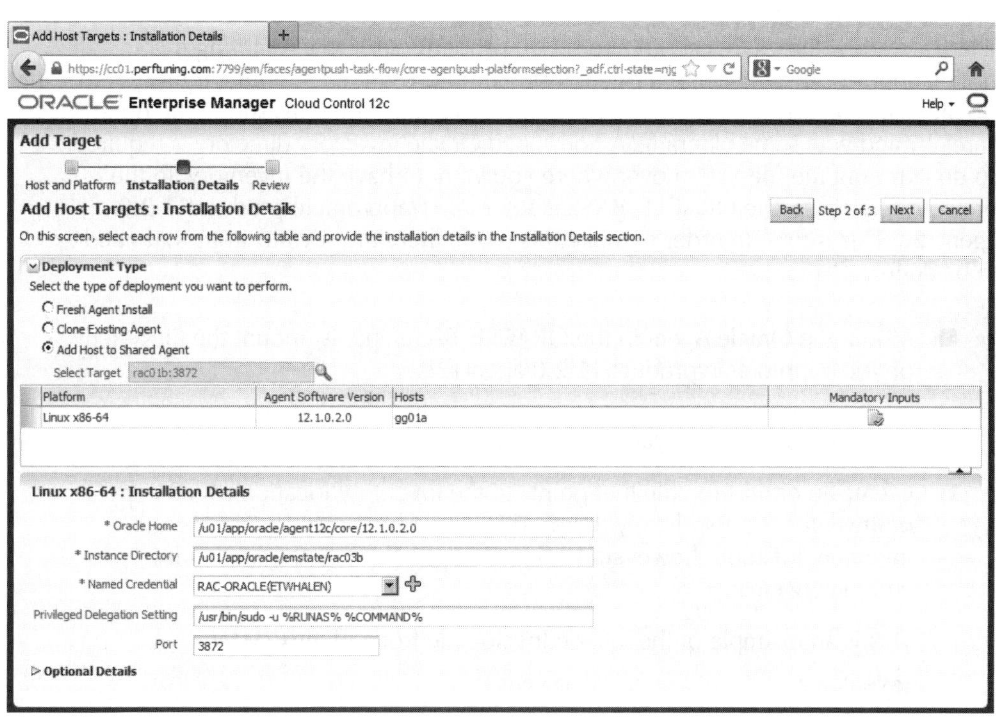

FIGURE 5-17. *The Add Target screen for Shared Agent Deployment*

The filled-in screen is shown in Figure 5-17.

Click Next to continue, followed by Deploy Agent. When this has completed, you will see the Agent Deployment Summary screen. If everything is successful, you will see all green checks and the Agent will show up in the hosts monitoring screen.

Installing Shared Oracle Home Agents Using AgentNFS.pl

The shared Oracle Home installation takes an existing Oracle Agent that is installed on an NFS mount point (NAS) and extends this Agent to allow other systems to use it. This method can save space, but it also creates a single point of failure, since the loss of this one directory will cause all Agents using it to fail. The Shared Oracle Home installation can be done either via graphical mode or via the AgentNFS.pl script. The GUI method was described in the previous section. The prerequisites are the same.

Prerequisites

There are a few things that should be set up properly prior to attempting the installation. Because the shared Agent installation uses an NFS mounted filesystem for the Agent binaries, it is necessary to mount that partition. This should be done carefully and with some planning. A nonshared Oracle inventory directory is required, so don't mount the filesystem over where you want to have the inventory. In the previous examples, the ORACLE_BASE is set to /u01/app/oracle/product/11.2.0/agent12c. This is fine. In order to make this work, there are several steps that need to be done.

- Mount the Oracle Agent in the ORACLE_BASE, that is, mount the filesystem on /u01/app/oracle/product/11.2.0/agent12c.

  ```
  mount -t nfs rac03a:/u01/app/oracle/product/11.2.0/agent12c
  /u01/app/oracle/product/11.2.0/agent12c
  ```

- Create an oraInst.loc file that points to the inventory location as /u01/app/oraInventory (if not already there). This would be created as the default inventory location; however, we like to explicitly state this so that it is completely clear.

  This is an example of the /etc/oraInst.loc file from a Linux system.

  ```
  inventory_loc=/u01/app/oraInventory
  inst_group=oinstall
  ```

- Of course, NFS must be operating properly and firewall access set up correctly so that NFS works properly.

- There must be a state directory available on the NFS mount point for each host sharing the Agent software. This should not be in the Agent home directory. For example, if the Agent home directory is /u01/app/oracle/agent12c, an appropriate state directory would be /u01/app/oracle/emstate/<*host*>. Since each system using the shared home needs its own state directory, the host name should be included for uniqueness.

As with the other examples, it is also necessary to make sure that all systems involved in this installation are defined within the /etc/hosts file. Even though DNS is set up correctly, it is necessary to do this.

In addition, in order to use the Shared Oracle Home installation the *PubkeyAuthentication* variable must be set to *yes* on the OMS server that will be used as the source of the Agent software. In Linux, this variable is found in the /etc/ssh/sshd_config file.

Installing the Shared Oracle Home Agent Using AgentNFS.pl

In order to use the Shared Oracle Home method, using AgentNFS.pl, the Oracle Home for an existing Oracle 12*c* Agent (Master Agent) must be mounted and available in the same directory that you wish to deploy it to.

There are two options: create a response file and use that as the input to the AgentNFS.pl script, or run the AgentNFS.pl script, providing it with all the data. Both options do the same thing, so it is your choice. The needed information consists of the Oracle Home, the Agent Port number, the Agent Instance Home, the Hostname, the Agent Registration Password, and whether or not to start the Agent whenever it has been configured.

If you are using the AgentNFS.rsp file, the contents should look like this example.

```
ORACLE_HOME=/u01/app/oracle/product/11.2.0/agent12c/core/12.1.0.1
AGENT_PORT=1832
AGENT_INSTANCE_HOME=/u01/app/oracle/emstate/rac04b
b_startAgent=TRUE
ORACLE_HOSTNAME=rac04b.perftuning.com
AGENT_REGISTRATION_PASSWORD=cloud123
```

Next, call the AgentNFS.pl script by passing it the location of the response file as shown here:

```
<AGENT_HOME>/perl/bin/perl <AGENT_HOME>/sysman/install/AgentNFS.pl
-responseFile=<response file (including path)>
[oracle@rac04b ~]$ $AGENT_HOME/perl/bin/perl
$AGENT_HOME/sysman/install/AgentNFS.pl
AGENT_INSTANCE_HOME=/u01/app/oracle/product/11.2.0/agent12c/rac04b
ORACLE_HOME=/u01/app/oracle/product/11.2.0/agent12c/core/12.1.0.1.0
AGENT_PORT=1832 AGENT_REGISTRATION_PASSWORD=cloud123 b_startAgent=TRUE
-invPtrLoc
 /etc/oraInst.loc
```

You will see a lot of text feedback, which should end with something like this.

```
The inventory is located at /u01/app/oraInventory
'UpdateHomeDeps' was successful.

Configuring the Agent Instance Home
Copying install related scripts
Generating root.sh
Completed the Shared Agent Installation

NOTE: Post install steps to follow :
Please execute /u01/app/oracle/product/11.2.0/agent12c/rac04b/root.sh
script as root
```

Once these steps have completed, and the root.sh script has been run, the Agent should be visible in the hosts monitoring section of the Cloud Control Console as well as in the Setup | Agents drop-down.

Agent Configuration Issues

You might run into various issues when installing and configuring Management Agents. Among the most common are issues with firewall ports and port configuration.

In order to view or change the port being used by the Management Agent, the port used to connect to the OMS or the OMS name, look in the *<agent home>*/sysman/config directory in the emd.properties file. Here you can modify and change these values.

NOTE

Before changing any Agent configuration parameters, be sure to stop the Agent. Both starting and stopping the Agent depends on the emd.properties file. If you change the port number while the Agent is running, you cannot stop it with `emctl` until you change the emd.properties file back to its original settings.

Firewall Issues

If you think that a firewall has blocked connectivity to the OMS server, try using telnet to test the port. You can pass telnet the port number as well as the target system using this syntax: `telnet <target> port`. For example:

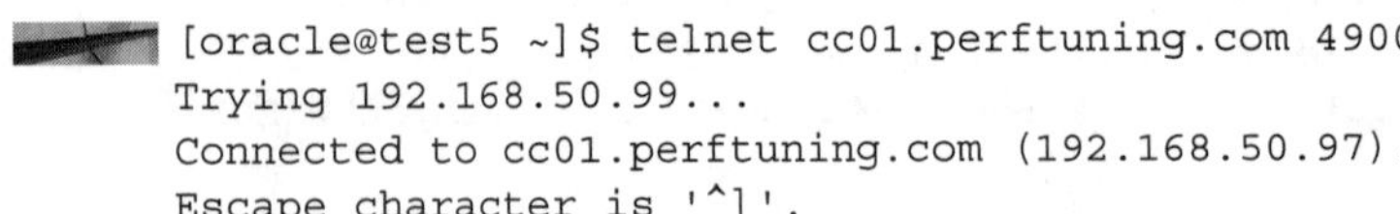

```
[oracle@test5 ~]$ telnet cc01.perftuning.com 4900
Trying 192.168.50.99...
Connected to cc01.perftuning.com (192.168.50.97).
Escape character is '^]'.
```

If you see something similar to this, the port is open. If you get a response of `connection refused`, the port is blocked and must be opened.

Agent Issues

Another common problem is a nonsecure Agent trying to talk to an OMS that only accepts secure connections. This is easily seen in the output of `emctl status agent`. The output of this command shows both the Agent and OMS ports:

```
Agent URL          : https://rac04b.perftuning.com:1832/emd/main/
Repository URL     : https://cc01.perftuning.com:4900/empbs/upload
```

If the Repository is showing as an HTTPS connection and the Agent as an HTTP connection, then you probably have a mismatch. Conclusive proof is in the heartbeat, as shown here:

```
Last attempted heartbeat to OMS              : 2011-12-09 14:29:16
Last successful heartbeat to OMS             : unknown
```

If you see an attempted heartbeat and a last successful heartbeat to OMS as unknown or far apart (and both are shown), then there is a connectivity problem of some sort. You should see the following as the only heartbeat message to the OMS.

```
Last attempted heartbeat to OMS              : 2011-12-09 14:29:16
Last successful heartbeat to OMS             : 2011-12-09 14:29:16
```

The Oracle documentation, My Oracle Support, and Oracle forums can be good places to debug connectivity issues.

Summary

This chapter has covered multiple ways of installing the Oracle Cloud Control 12*c* Agent. Depending on the method of installation, there are different requirements and different methods. Find one that you are comfortable with and you will do fine. As you have seen in this chapter, some might be more appropriate than others for each system, but the end result is the same.

In the next chapter you will learn about the Cloud Control Console configuration. By configuring and customizing the Console, you will be able to create a tool that meets your specific needs.

CHAPTER 6

Cloud Control Console Configuration

Finally! After completing the time-consuming installation steps, we are now ready to reap a little reward. The initial selection and configuration of the OEM Cloud Control Console provides the first opportunity to obtain some return on our investment. With a few steps, we can quickly implement monitoring for many if not all of our targets.

Most, if not all, Cloud Control configuration takes place through the Console. We begin this chapter by first laying the groundwork for the general Console features. Then, after we cover this material, we perform the steps to ensure basic (e-mail-based) notification.

Selecting the Home Page

Even if you've never accessed the system before, after your initial login to Cloud Control you are immediately asked to determine which screen should be your Home Page. Oracle refers to this functionality as "login customization." Fortunately, there are several good choices and you can always change your selection later. Users familiar with earlier versions of Enterprise Manager will note that this choice and available selections—in general, the entire framework—are significantly different. Oracle's desire is to make this utility the central control for all the enterprise-related services. Consequently, different options, functions, and features need to be provided based on the end user.

The initial choices for a Home Page are as follows:

- **Summary** A complete, although abbreviated, view of all Cloud Control–monitored targets and a filtered listing of critical alarms.
- **Databases** All monitored single and RAC-based instances and pertinent alarms.
- **Incidents** A central Console for tracking, debugging, and otherwise managing raised events. Key features of this functionality include packaged and user-defined views for researching incidents of interest. Incidents can also trigger Knowledge Base article retrieval or SR creation. Incident functionality also provides for integration with external ticketing systems.
- **SOA** Services Oriented Architecture (SOA) designated targets along with related alerts, policy violations, and critical metrics.
- **Middleware** Monitoring and managing both Oracle and non-Oracle middleware targets, for example, Fusion Middleware.
- **Composite Application** These are user-defined complex applications with multiple tiers and multiple application deployments. This home page

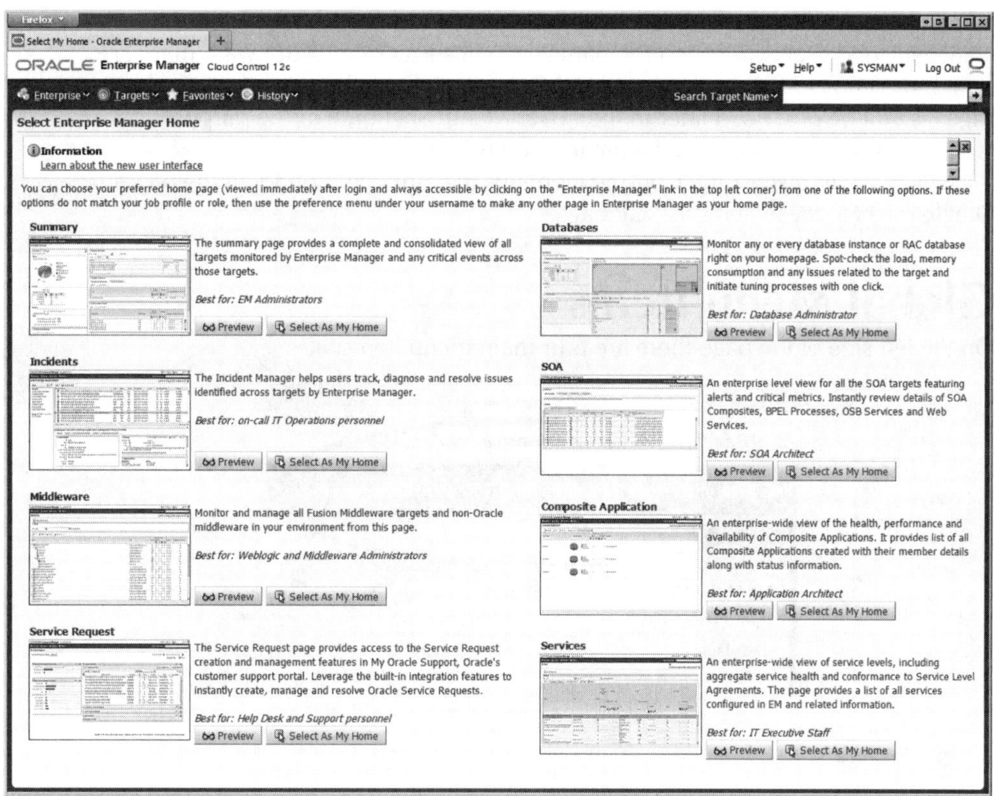

FIGURE 6-1. *The Home Page Selection screen*

provides a single point of reference for monitoring these targets. As noted by Oracle, "The Composite Application dashboard provides full visibility across the composite application with access to key monitoring and diagnostics regions, which can be easily customized and personalized. The overall result of this enhancement is a single dashboard view providing not only health information about the application, but also deeper visibility into component health and incidents at a glance."

- **Service Request** The service request page is a direct interface to My Oracle Support (MOS)–submitted Service Requests (SRs).
- **Services** A global view of service levels, including aggregate service health and conformance to service level agreements.

As you can see, there are numerous and varied choices with respect to the Home Page. While technical personnel will gravitate toward certain choices, managers, end users, and account managers will select others. But wait, there are even more choices. Basically any Cloud Control page can become a user's Home Page, as will be described later in the "User Menu" section. For the purposes of our description, we will select the Summary Home Page.

Next we will discuss the Console elements that are common to all the pages. Oracle refers to these items as "Global."

Global Menu Items

On the left side of the page there are four main menu items:

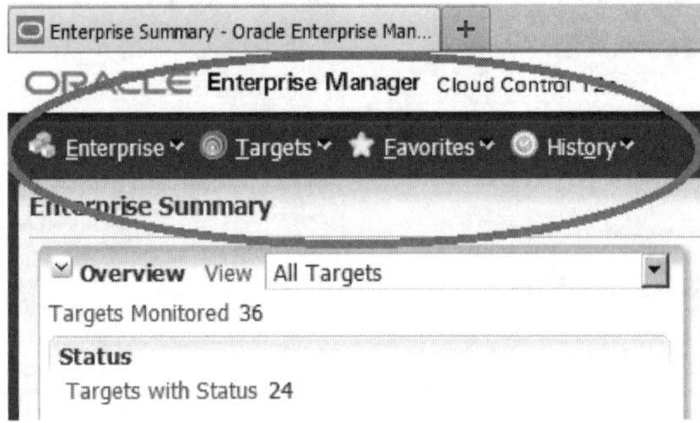

- Enterprise
- Targets
- Favorites
- History

The following sections provide a description of the functions within these menus.

The Enterprise Menu

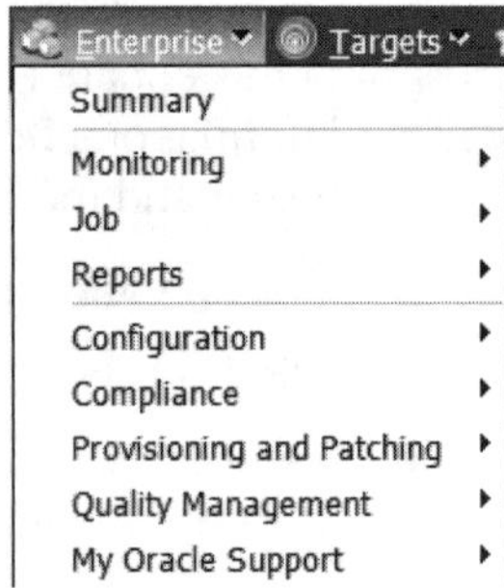

The Enterprise Global menu offers the selections described in the following list. These choices are considered the key functionality offerings of the Cloud Control product.

- **Summary** This choice provides a quick means to access the enterprise-wide monitoring page.
- **Monitoring** This item and its related submenus provide functionality for managing the monitoring

features, for example, modifying thresholds, adjusting templates, configuring corrective actions for alerts, or creating blackouts. Blackouts permit administrators to suppress data collection and DOWN notifications (indeed all notifications) for selected targets when purposefully brought down, such as for scheduled maintenance. Blackouts prevent off-duty DBAs from being paged unnecessarily, and allow Cloud Control to more accurately report on a target's performance, such as in meeting service level agreements (SLAs). Although there are other means to circumvent the distribution of unwanted notifications, blackouts should still be implemented in order to maintain the integrity of the reporting data, for example, unplanned versus planned downtime (Cloud Control interprets blackouts as planned downtime). Monitoring templates let you standardize target monitoring by specifying monitoring settings once for a target, then applying them to multiple targets of that target type. Templates define metrics (including user-defined metrics), thresholds, collection schedules, corrective actions, and policies you can propagate to specified targets. You can later edit templates and reapply them. You can elect to prevent a target's settings from being changed when a monitoring template is applied. This allows you to use templates and still customize target monitoring. The Corrective Action Library allows you to automate and reuse responses to alerts or policy violations. Corrective actions automatically execute to save administrators time and improve the execution time of responses. A corrective action can run on the target where an alert or policy violation triggers, or can contain multiple tasks, each running on a different target. You can configure both critical and warning corrective actions and send notifications when they succeed or fail.

- **Job** Direct access to the Job library and activity status. The Enterprise Manager Job System automates routine administrative tasks and synchronizes components in your environment so you can manage them more efficiently.

- **Reports** Configuration and monitoring the Information Publisher utility, which controls all Cloud Control reporting. For example, using the Information Publisher feature, you can view reports of any compliance violations and compliance framework reports.

- **Configuration** Access to the Configuration subsystem including saved configurations, reports, and comparisons. Configuration provides three distinct areas of functionality: Configuration Search, Configuration History, and Configuration Browser. Configuration Search allows for the enterprise-wide search of various tailored criteria (platform, version, target, and so on). Configuration History is used to monitor change activity across the enterprise. This facility allows the DBA to identify where changes have impacted availability or performance. The Configuration Browser feature allows the DBA to view configuration data in the "context of single managed entity." The Configuration suite includes utilities for developing Configuration Templates and Configuration Comparisons.

- **Compliance** Reporting and control of Compliance functionality. This feature provides the ability to evaluate the compliance of targets as they relate to business best practices or certifications.
- **Provisioning and Patching** Access to the full suite of Provisioning and Patching utilities for various targets. Patching Setup permits you to configure Cloud Control's patching features, including the ability to stage and apply Oracle patches, patch sets, and critical patch advisories, for targets on any available host.
- **Quality Management** Submenus provide access to Database and Application Replay functionality and utilities for Data Sub-setting and Masking. Database and Application Replay allows you to capture real application-level workload from a production system for a specific time segment and rerun it in a test environment. This feature enables changes in application infrastructure including mid-tier, database, operating system, and hardware to be tested and analyzed using real production application workloads.
- **My Oracle Support** Standard web-based functionality including Service Requests, Knowledge Base, Certify, and Community.

The Targets Menu

Users familiar with the previous versions of OEM will recognize many of the functional offerings within this menu. Each of the menu items described in the following list provides the capability to drill down to individual targets. The Targets Global menu offers the following selections:

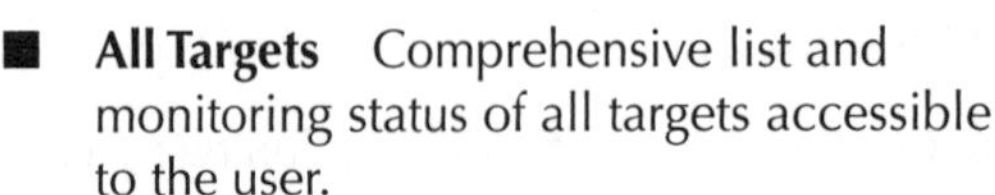

- **All Targets** Comprehensive list and monitoring status of all targets accessible to the user.
- **Groups** The status of targets in user-defined Groups or Redundancy Groups is displayed, and the user can modify Groups as desired.
- **Systems** System status and management.
- **Services** Displays the status and provides management functionality for all accessible Services.

- **Hosts** Management and monitoring functionality for hosts that are being managed by Cloud Control.
- **Databases** Displays status of monitored databases and allows direct access to underlying instances.
- **Middleware** Displays status of all user-accessible middleware targets.
- **Composite Applications** Drill-down functionality for monitoring and managing Composite Applications.

The Favorites Menu

The Favorites Global menu provides the standard browser functionality. This menu offers the following selections.

- **Add Page to Favorites** Any Cloud Control Console page can be added to the Favorites in order to provide a direct access mechanism.
- **Manage Favorites** Provides standard functionality for removing, sorting, and otherwise managing favorite Console pages.

The History Menu

As one might expect, the History menu is very similar to a standard browser's history functionality, providing a listing of the most recently navigated Console pages.

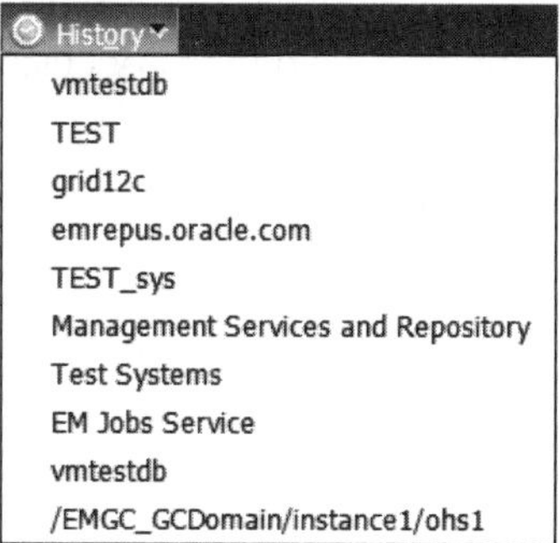

The Setup Menu

On the right-hand side of the page next to the Help menu is the Setup menu. In contrast to the menu options discussed earlier, which provide Cloud Control function, Setup is primarily oriented toward tailoring the environment. The Setup menu provides the following submenus:

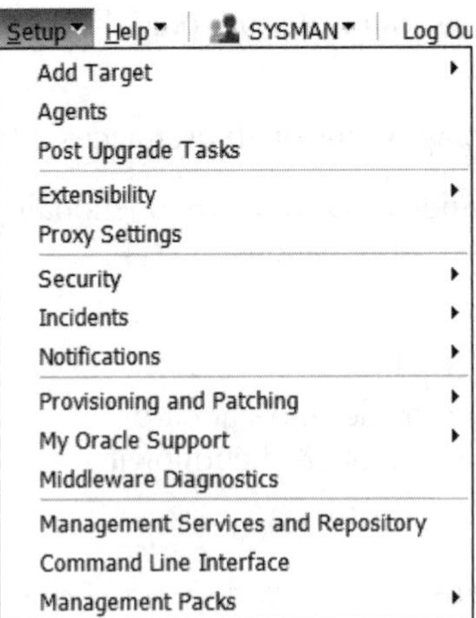

- **Add Target** Access utility for staging a new target into the Cloud Control system.
- **Agents** Provides reporting and management functionality for all accessible Agents.
- **Post Upgrade Tasks** During the installation process of Cloud Control, this feature reports on the remaining tasks.
- **Extensibility** Provides information regarding the Extensibility Development Kit. This utility is to support development of custom plug-ins for managing target types with no out-of-box support.
- **Proxy Settings** If necessary, proxy settings can be configured for Console access.
- **Security** Provides access to utilities for managing Named and Preferred credentials. Preferred Credentials simplify an administrator's Console access to targets by storing his or her login credentials in the Repository. With credentials set, an administrator can access targets without being prompted to log in. Credentials are organized and summarized by target type. An administrator can set default credentials for all targets of a particular type, can enter individual target credentials, or a combination of both, with individual credentials overriding default ones. An administrator's preferred credentials simplify Console access to targets by storing target login credentials in the Repository. Grid Control uses these credentials so that administrators can access targets in the UI without being prompted to

log in every time. Many Console functions rely on preferred credentials, particularly the Related Links at the bottom of a target's home page. As with other preferences, administrators set their own preferred credentials, allowing them to meet the most stringent corporate security standards, which require separate user accounts for each admin. However, there is nothing to prevent administrators who share credentials on targets from entering the same credentials for those targets.

- **Incidents** Incident management and configuration, including rules.
- **Notifications** This link provides functionality for both managing the Cloud Control system's access to e-mail and related services (SNMP Traps)—Notification Methods—and for configuring the user's Notification Schedule. Notification methods are global mechanisms defined to send notifications. Methods include SMTP Servers, custom OS scripts, PL/SQL procedures, and SNMP traps. Notification rules, defined per administrator, use selected notification methods to send administrators metric alerts, policy violations, or job status changes. A notification schedule determines when an administrator receives notifications, and at which e-mail address(es). An administrator can set up different notification e-mail addresses for every hour of every day. Schedules are based on a selected rotation frequency (or repeatable pattern) of one to eight weeks, and you can suspend notifications for a certain period as needed. This atomic level of configuration allows you to model almost any conceivable DBA schedule, however complex (such as when different DBAs are on call to handle a launch or maintenance period). Administrator schedules can dovetail or overlap as desired, because each schedule is independent of the other.
- **Provisioning and Patching** Setup configuration for patching and provisioning.
- **My Oracle Support** Configure credentials for MOS access.
- **Middleware Diagnostics** Configuration utilities for middleware targets.
- **Management Services and Repository** Credential management for the data Repository.
- **Command Line Interface** Provides information on how to set up the EM Command Line Interface (CLI) on target machines.
- **Management Packs** Licensing and access controls for the various Management Packs. Management Packs are licensed add-ons to Cloud Control that considerably extend its functionality. On this page, you enable access to each pack on a target-by-target basis by acknowledging that

you've licensed a pack for that target. Example key packs are the Database Diagnostics Pack, which supplies many advanced database metrics, and the Database Tuning Pack, which affords many of the performance features accessible as links on the Performance page for a database target.

The Help Menu

The Help Menu is next to the Setup menu. The menu contains links to both local and web-based documentation. The final entry is an "About" page, which provides the specific Cloud Control version.

The "User" Menu

The final global menu is found on the upper right-hand corner under the Cloud Control user's name. In our example, we are logged in as SYSMAN; consequently, the menu item is listed as SYSMAN. As one might expect, the functions available on this menu are user customizations or preferences. The User menu provides the following submenus:

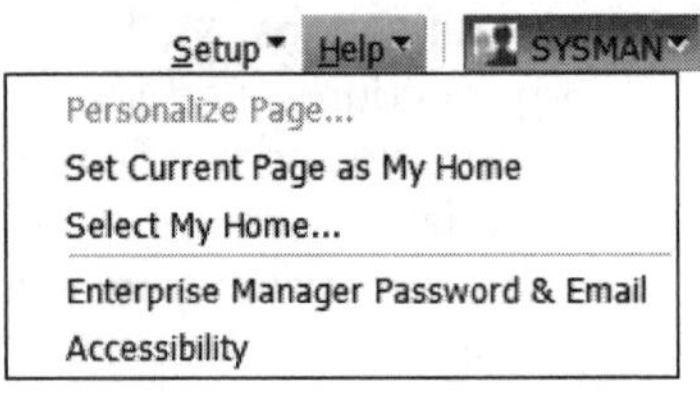

- **Personalize Page** When applicable, this option allows the Administrator to modify the contents of the current page.
- **Set Current Page as My Home** From virtually any page, the Administrator can execute this function and set the current page as the default login page.
- **Select My Home** This option navigates the user to the Select Enterprise Manager Home screen. This is the page the user encounters upon the first login.
- **Enterprise Manager Password & Email** From this page the Administrator can change their login password and applicable e-mail addresses. An Administrator can enter multiple addresses. The use of the different e-mail addresses will be described in the next section. As the SYSMAN account is the Enterprise Manager owner, special steps need to be taken in order to modify this account's password.[1] However, ordinary Cloud Control administrators can change their passwords from within this form.
- **Accessibility** This page allows the user to modify the contrast and font of the user interface.

---

[1] In the case of the SYSMAN account, the user is directed to the documentation, which describes the steps that are needed for changing this account's password.

Notification Requirements

Now that we've established the basic Cloud Control Console tools, we can identify those that are required to implement notification. In order to begin receiving e-mail notifications of stock (noncustomized) alerts, we need to complete the following steps:

1. Define access to an available SMTP server. This functionality is obtained through the Setup Notification Methods sub-menu.
2. Define an e-mail address for general user distribution. We perform this step in the User menu Enterprise Manager Password & Email screen, as noted earlier.
3. Finally, we need to tell Cloud Control when we wish to receive these notifications. This step is performed in the Setup | Notifications | My Notification Schedule sub-menu.

In the following sections we will describe each of these steps in greater detail.

Define Notification Methods

Notification methods define global means or mechanisms (such as e-mail) to contact administrators when events (metric alerts, policy violations, or job status changes) occur. At most CC sites, e-mail is a sufficient notification method. However, you can also define other notification methods, including SNMP traps for other System Management Products (SMPs), OS scripts, PL/SQL procedures, and Remedy built-in Java callbacks. A super administrator only needs to set up a particular notification method one time. Administrators then subscribe to *notification rules* (discussed later) that define, among other things, one or more of these notification method(s) to employ when sending event notices. At least one notification method must exist before you can define any notification rules. Notification methods are managed independently of notification rules, so you can apply the same method to multiple rules. The Notification Methods screen is shown in Figure 6-2.

This page is divided into three sections: one for the Mail Server, another for Scripts and SNMP Traps, and, finally, Repeat Notifications. At this stage, we will only concern ourselves with the Mail Server and other notification methods (Scripts and SNMP Traps).

Mail Server

E-mail is the predominant notification method used at Cloud Control sites to send alerts to administrators. A super administrator must specify one or more mail servers through which Cloud Control can send such notifications. The Outgoing Mail (SMTP) Server field on this page will already contain an entry if you specified

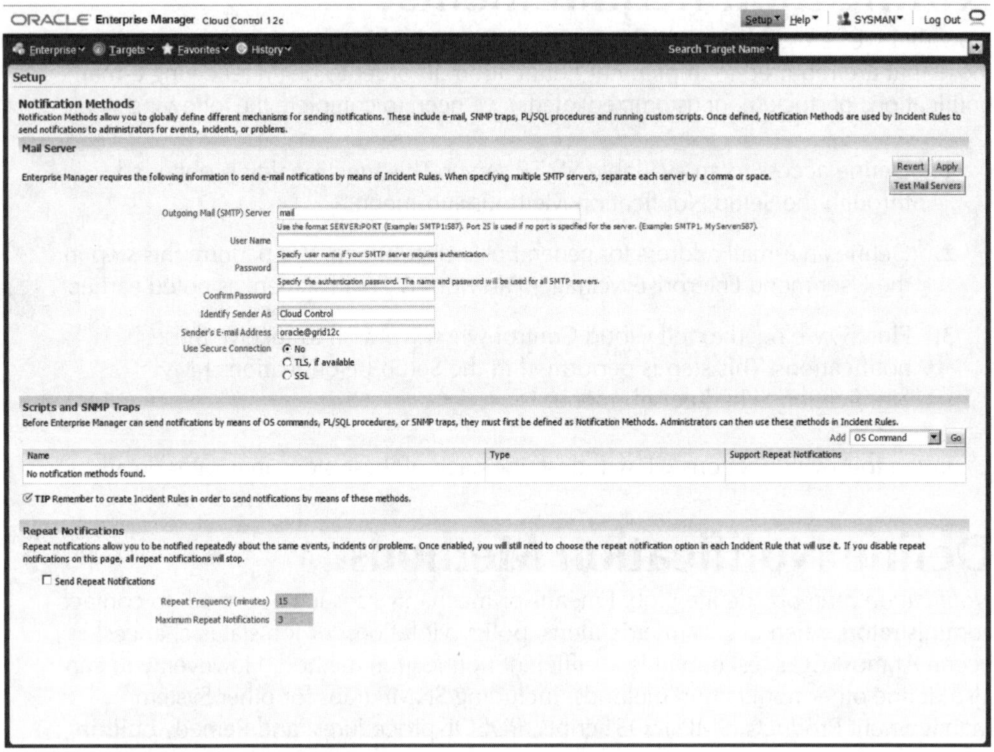

FIGURE 6-2. *Notification Methods screen*

an SMTP server when installing Cloud Control. To provide high availability for notification delivery, you can enter additional mail gateways, if your company uses them. Cloud Control will attempt to deliver mail using the first listed mail server, and if unsuccessful, will use the next mail server listed. (Ask your network administrator whether your mail gateway is configured externally for high availability. If so, you may only need to enter a single virtual mail server name, which would forward the notification to a running mail server.)

Do the following to specify mail servers for all administrators to use:

1. Log in to the Console as a super administrator and note which OMS host is used. If employing an SLB as a front end for multiple OMSs, log in directly through a particular OMS.

2. Click the Setup link at the top right and select the Notification Methods link (Setup | Notification | Notification Methods).

3. In the Mail Server section of the Notification Methods page, complete the following fields, which apply to all OMS hosts:

   - **Outgoing Mail (SMTP) Server** Enter one or more mail servers in this field. Use the format "*<SMTPServer>*:*<port>*"and specify the port only if the mail server doesn't listen on default SMTP port 25. Separate mail server entries by commas or spaces. (This example shows two mail servers, where the second one uses nondefault port 587.)

   - **User Name and Password** Enter a username and password if the SMTP servers require authentication. These credentials will be used for all SMTP servers.

   - **Identify Sender As** Enter the name of the e-mail account you want to appear as the sender of notification messages as shown in the From: field of the e-mails.

   - **Sender's E-mail Address** Specify the e-mail address through which to send e-mail notifications and to receive notification delivery problems. (This is not the address where Cloud Control sends notifications.) This must be a valid address from which the specified SMTP server(s) can send e-mail.

4. Click Test Mail Servers to verify that the OMS rendering the Console can use all specified mail servers to relay test messages to the sender's e-mail address. Test results are returned in the Console reporting on each SMTP server (see Figure 6-3), and a test e-mail is sent through each SMTP server to the sender's e-mail address. If the test succeeds, click Apply to save all changes.

5. Test that each additional OMS host can send test e-mails through the configured SMTP server(s), as shown in Figure 6-4. To do so, log in to the Console through each additional OMS (Step 1) and repeat Steps 2 and 4.

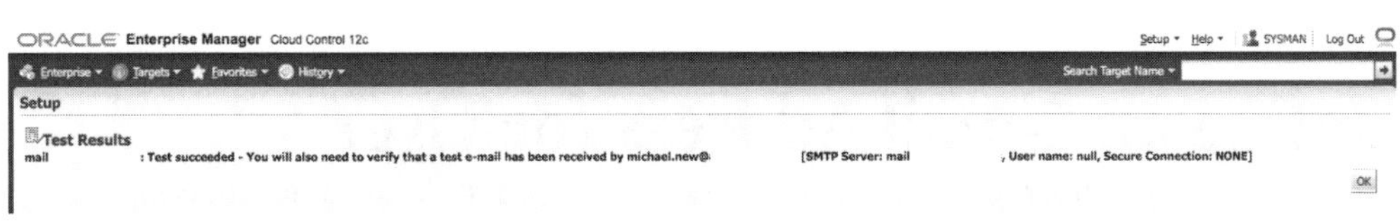

FIGURE 6-3. *Successful Notifications Methods test*

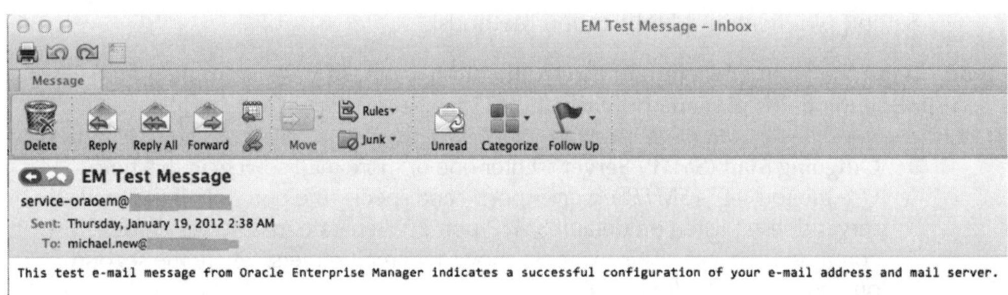

FIGURE 6-4. *Successful reception of Notification Methods test*

Other Notification Methods

In addition to the e-mail server notification method, you can define other methods to automate responses to target events, where both the targets and events are defined in a notification rule employing the method. Following are the additional notification methods available over and above e-mail notification:

- **OS scripts** You can create OS scripts to automate event responses. OS scripts must exist in the same specified location on all OMS hosts. For example, you can automatically open an in-house trouble-ticket using an OS script.
- **PL/SQL procedures** You can create PL/SQL procedures in the Repository database to perform actions in response to events. For instance, you can notify a third-party application using a custom PL/SQL procedure.
- **SNMP traps** SNMP traps can invoke and pass event data to SNMP-enabled third-party applications, such as HP OpenView.
- **Built-in Java callbacks** You can also select in the UI from built-in Java callbacks to the BMC Remedy Help Desk to prioritize the urgency of notifications.

Define an E-mail Address for User

Now that we've configured a notification service, we need to define a destination address. Figure 6-5 shows the user's Enterprise Manager Password & Email submenu. On this screen you enter the e-mail address at which you would like to

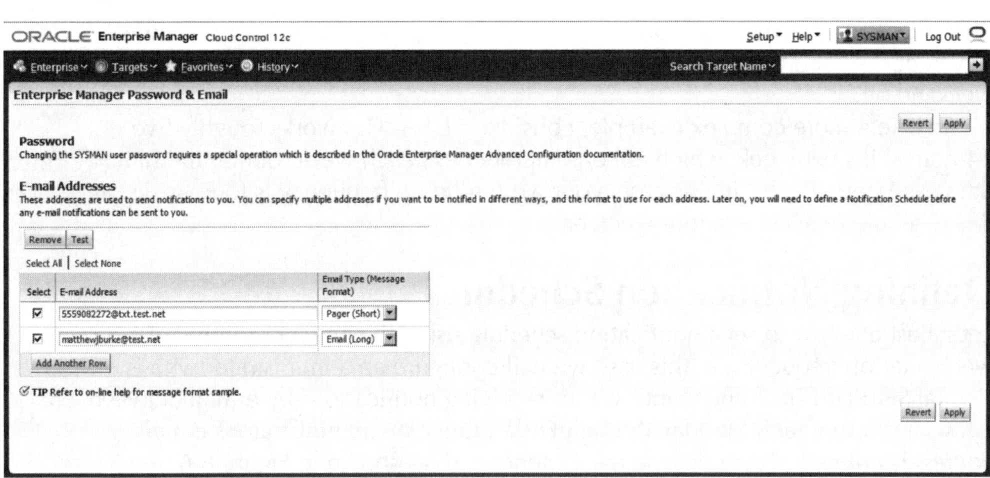

FIGURE 6-5. *Configuring the user's e-mail address*

receive notifications. The Test functionality should be exercised to ensure the integrity of the address. If desired, the Message Format can be tailored to the target address (Outlook e-mail, Phone, and so on).

Set Notification Schedules

A notification schedule defined for each administrator determines when and at what e-mail address(es) they will receive Cloud Control notifications. Schedules are very configurable—you can specify a different notification e-mail address (or addresses) for every hour of every day, if desired. You can also suspend notifications as needed, such as when an administrator is on vacation. A super administrator can set the notification schedule for any other administrator, including another super administrator, but super administrators cannot change SYSMAN's schedule—only SYSMAN can. (SYSMAN's schedule is no different from a notification schedule for any other administrator; it dictates when the e-mail addresses for SYSMAN—if any are specified—will be sent alerts.)

The mechanics of specifying a notification schedule in the Console are straightforward enough and are similar to those in earlier Grid Control versions. The schedule hinges on a *rotation frequency*, a concept not intuitively obvious to everyone. A rotation frequency is a repeatable pattern of the smallest time period you can define to model your desired notification schedule. Cloud Control allows for a one- to eight-week rotation schedule. Many IT professionals work a one-week (seven-day) rotation frequency, made up of a five-day work week and a two-day weekend off.

To take a more complex example, consider a DBA who works roughly two 24-hour shifts per week, which fall on different days each week, but on the same days every four weeks. In this case, your work rotation frequency is four weeks, as this schedule repeats on a four-week basis.

Defining Notification Schedules

Let's illustrate how to set a notification schedule using the typical example of a one-week rotation frequency. In this case we will configure an administrator who is on Central Standard Time and wants to start receiving notifications by e-mail between 8 A.M. and 5 P.M. each Monday through Friday. Once an administrator's e-mail address is entered, a default schedule is generated, as shown in Figure 6-6.

1. Define (or edit) the time period of the schedule, including the rotation frequency, by clicking the Define Schedule button (if you're editing, the button is named Edit Schedule Definition). The page shown in Figure 6-7 appears.
2. Enter the desired Rotation Frequency.
3. Click Edit Existing Schedule or Replace Existing Schedule, as appropriate.
4. Enter a Start Date of Monday of the current week, as this allows you to specify a schedule for the entire week.
5. Choose the Time Zone in which this administrator is located.
6. Click Continue, and you navigate to the E-mail Addresses form (Figure 6-8).
7. Enter or edit the notification schedule on the page that appears. The schedule defaults to 24×7 notifications for the e-mail address(es) you specified when creating the administrator.

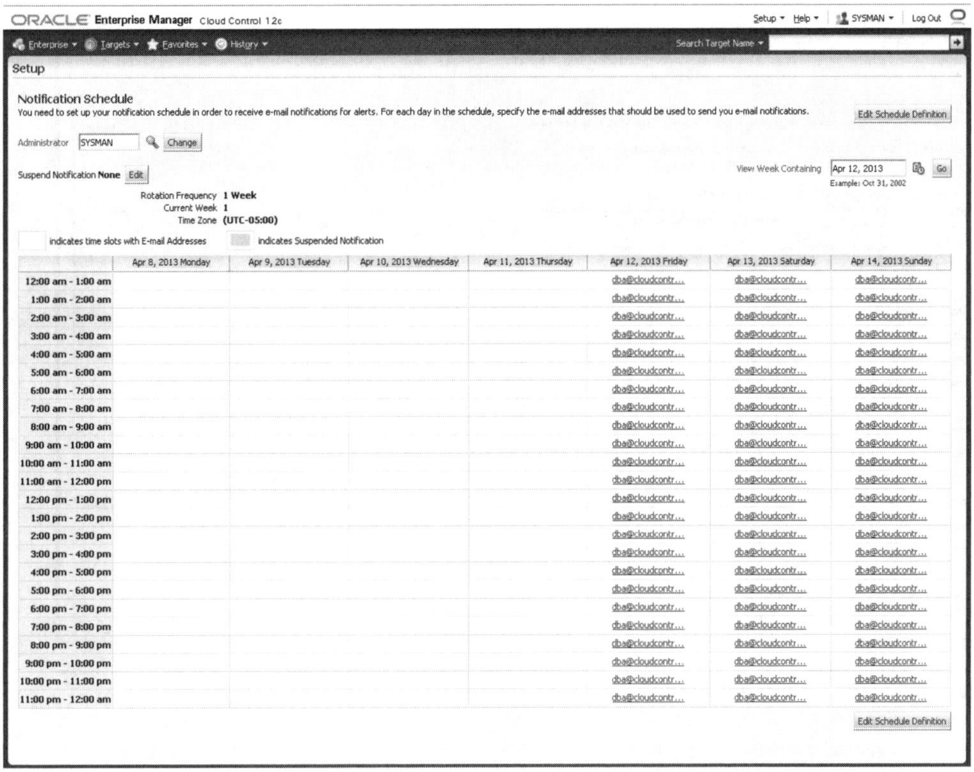

FIGURE 6-6. *The Notification Schedule page under the Setup | Notifications | My Notification Schedule menu*

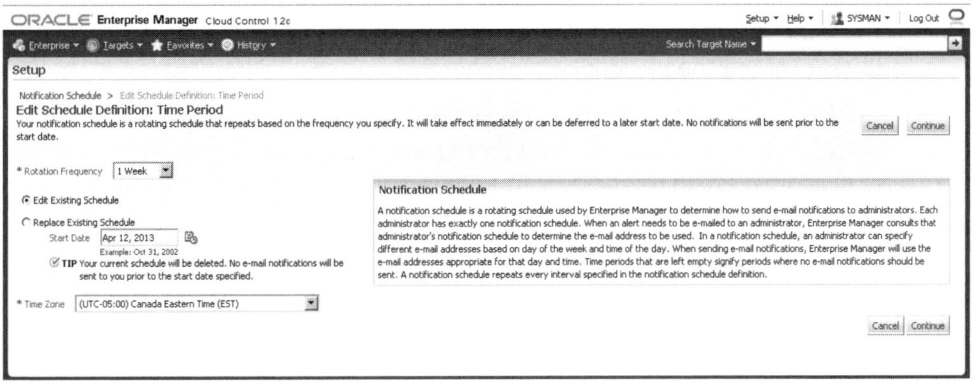

FIGURE 6-7. *Edit Schedule Definition: Time Period*

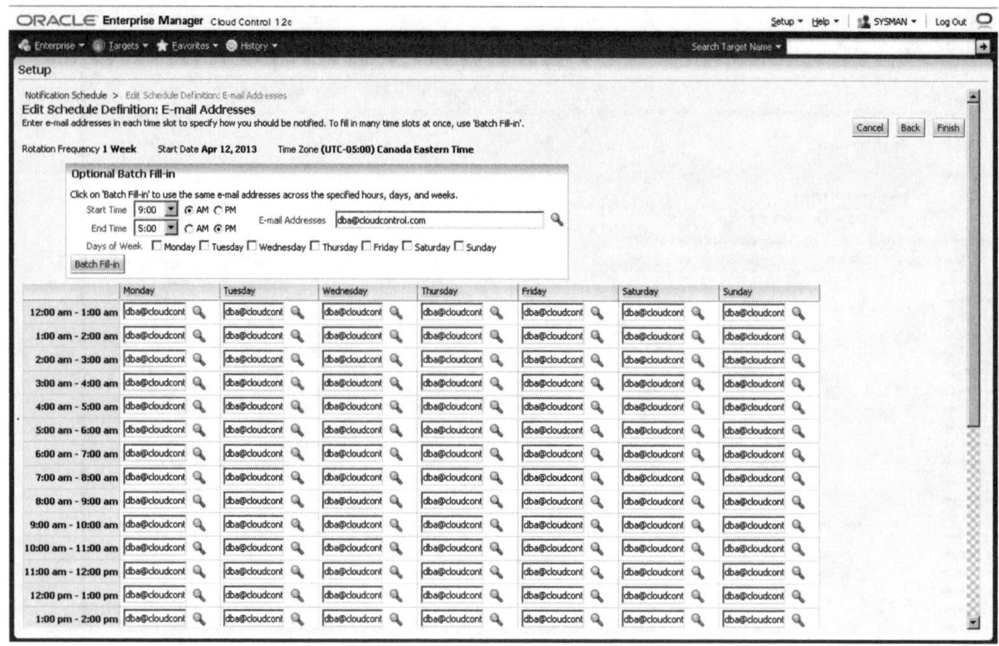

FIGURE 6-8. *Edit Schedule Definition: E-mail Addresses*

You can take advantage of the Batch Fill-in functionality by filling in a block of time on given days to be notified at the same e-mail address(es). To do this, follow these steps:

1. Click the magnifier icon next to the E-mail Addresses field and select one or more addresses you'd like to use for a particular block of time. Following is the result of all steps to set the example schedule. Here, the first e-mail address chosen is dba@cloudcontrol.com.

2. Complete the Start Time, End Time, and Days of Week fields for the first block of time where Cloud Control should send notifications to the specified e-mail address(es). In this case, Start Time is 8 A.M., End Time is 5 P.M., and Days of Week are Monday through Friday. See Figure 6-9.

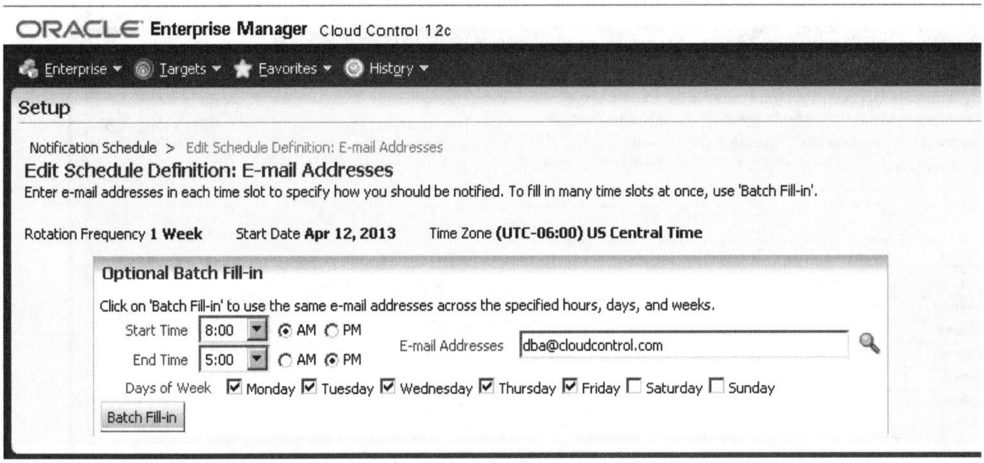

FIGURE 6-9. *Edit Schedule Definition: Batch fill-in parameters*

3. Click the Batch Fill-in button. The desired schedule is populated as shown in Figure 6-10.
4. Repeat Steps 1 and 2 for any other blocks of time desired. If, as in this example, one of these blocks of time crosses the midnight hour (from 5 P.M. to 8 A.M.), use two different Batch Fill-in operations for that block of time. In the first operation, start and end times are both before midnight (from 5 P.M. to 12 A.M.). In the second operation, start and end times are both after midnight (from 12 A.M. to 8 A.M.).
5. Click Finish to save your changes.

Suspending notifications is easy. To suspend notifications for a time period, click the Suspend Notification Edit button on the Preferences Schedule page. On the Edit Suspended Notification page that appears, enter or choose from the Calendar icon a Start Date and an End Date for the period during which to suspend notifications for this admin, and click OK.

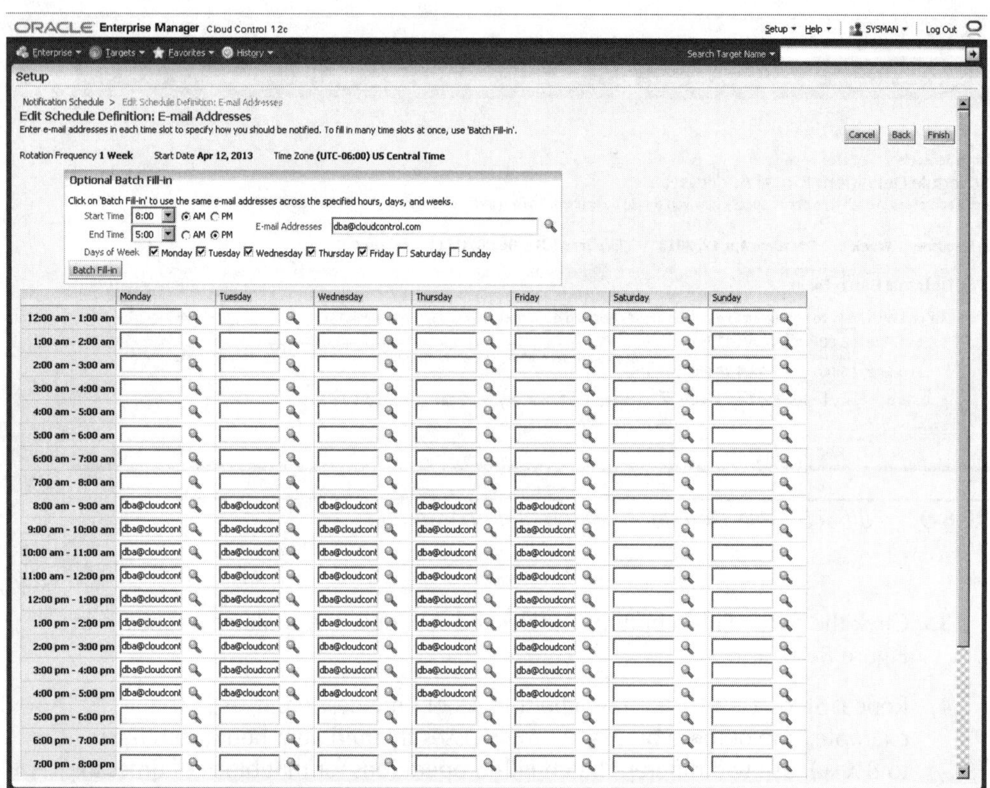

FIGURE 6-10. *Edit Schedule Definition: Desired schedule*

Summary

This chapter described the basic functionality of the Cloud Control Console. The 12c Console differs substantially from earlier versions and the changes represent the goal of OEM Cloud Control to provide enterprise-wide management.

In the next few chapters we will investigate additional Cloud Control Console functionality particularly as it pertains to managing complex environments with a significant number of targets. However, first we need to consider securing the Cloud Control environment and reaching targets behind firewalls.

CHAPTER 7

Cloud Control Security and User Management

Security is an important part of administering Oracle Enterprise Manager Cloud Control 12*c*. Security within OEM Cloud Control 12*c* is greatly enhanced over OEM 11*g* via the introduction of credential sharing. This allows privileges that an administrator has established to be propagated to another administrator, thus allowing for access, while at the same time reducing the number of people who share the same password. This and other security topics, such as the enhanced use of Sudo and PowerBroker, will be covered in this chapter.

Administrators

Each OEM Cloud Control user is called an administrator. There are two types of OEM users: administrator and super administrator. There is actually a third type of administrator, the Repository owner. There is only one Repository owner, SYSMAN. A super administrator has all of the privileges available to the administrator as well as the permissions available to manage administrators within the OEM Cloud Control environment.

Administrator

An administrator is an OEM Cloud Control 12*c* user. Each user of OEM Cloud Control should be given their own account with their own password. It is not recommended that accounts and passwords are shared among staff that utilizes OEM Cloud Control. New with Cloud Control is the ability to share credentials among administrators with credential sharing. With Cloud Control there are several types of roles available for specific types of OEM users: super administrator, designer, and operator.

Super Administrator Accounts

The Super Administrator account is similar to the Administrator account, but has additional capabilities to manage administrators within the Cloud Control environment. The super administrator has full access to all targets within the Cloud Control environment. In addition, the super administrator has privileges for creating and maintaining other administrators within Cloud Control.

Designer Accounts

A designer is a Cloud Control administrator with enhanced deployment procedure and software library permissions. The designer can create deployment procedure templates as well as patch plans and patch templates. The designer administrator is given the EM_ALL_DESIGNER role, which includes several other designer roles.

Operator Accounts

An operator is essentially an OEM administrator with reduced privileges on deployment procedures and the software library. An operator is intended to deploy and use procedures, patch plans, and patch templates, but not create or modify them. The Operator account is created with the EM_ALL_OPERATOR account.

Repository Owner

The last class of administrator is the Repository owner. The Repository owner is a super administrator who has additional privileges for maintaining and managing the OEM Repository. The Repository owner is SYSMAN by default. The SYSMAN account only needs to be used when upgrading or maintaining the Repository and should not be used for day-to-day operations.

Creating Administrators

As with most administrative tasks within OEM Cloud Control, administrators are created and maintained using the Setup menu. From the Setup menu, select Security | Administrators. This invokes the Security: Administrators screen as shown in Figure 7-1.

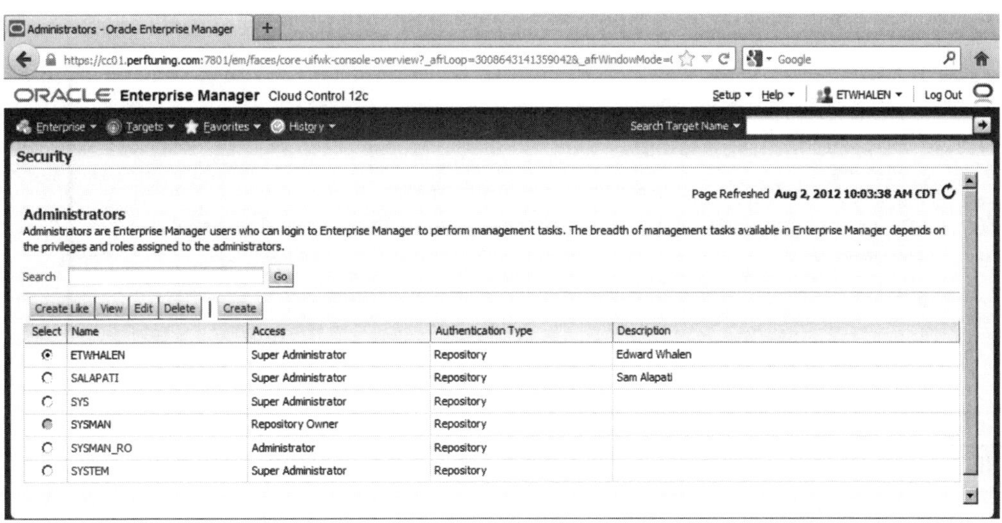

FIGURE 7-1. *The Security: Administrators screen*

From this screen you can either select an existing administrator and click the Create Like button to create an administrator like the existing administrator, or click the Create button to create an administrator from scratch. For this example, click Create in order to create the new administrator. This will invoke the Create Administrator: Properties screen as shown in Figure 7-2.

This is where you will provide the administrator name and password in addition to setting the password profile. Here you can manage the passwords and password profiles as well as providing a description of the administrator. It is very important that the administrator's e-mail address is provided for setting up and configuring alerting as covered in Chapter 6.

Click Next to continue to the Create Administrator <*administrator*>: Roles screen as shown in Figure 7-3. This screen is where the administrator roles are selected. OEM Cloud Control roles are covered in the next section.

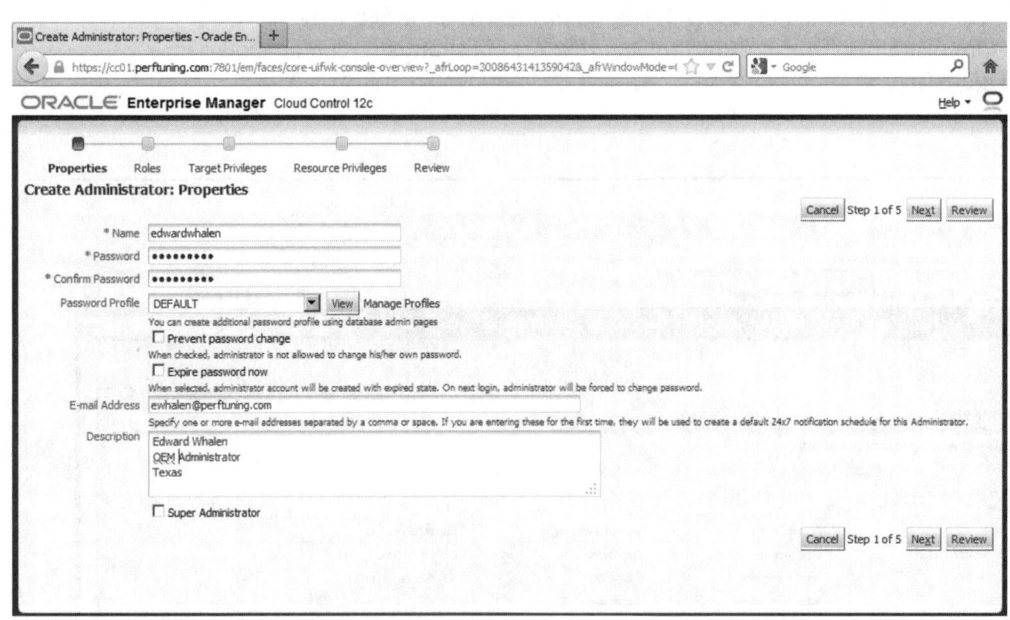

FIGURE 7-2. *The Create Administrator: Properties screen*

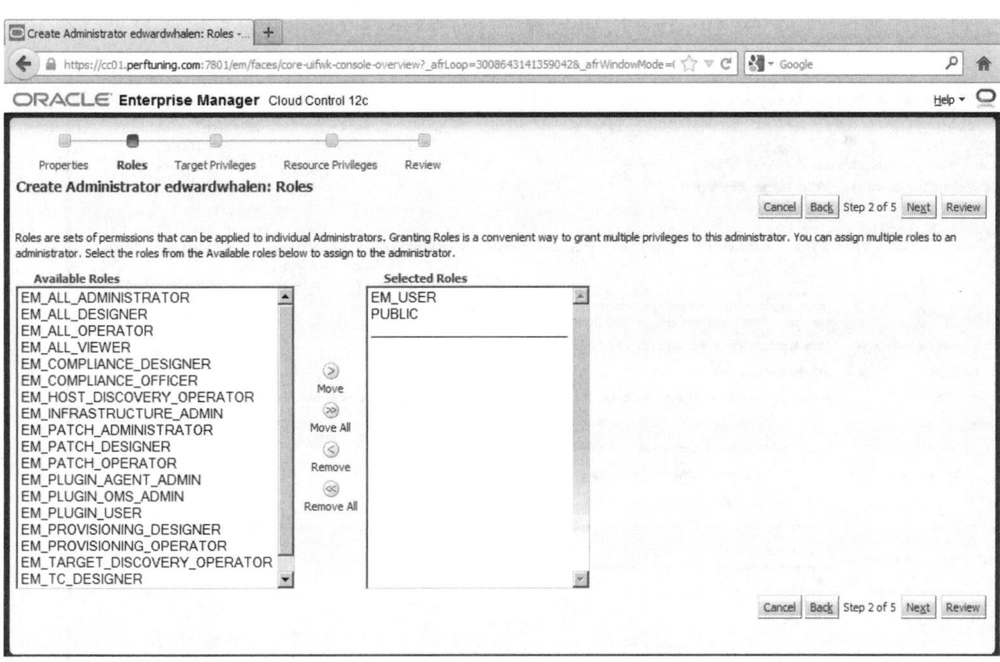

FIGURE 7-3. *The Create Administrator* <administrator>*: Roles screen*

Select the roles that are desired for this user and click Next to proceed to the Target Privileges screen. The Create Administrator *<administrator>*: Target Privileges screen is used to select the specific target privileges desired for this user as shown in Figure 7-4.

In this screen you can select privileges globally for all targets, or you can select specific targets and specific privileges on those targets. Once you have selected the desired privileges, click Next to proceed to the Create Administrator *<administrator>*: Resource Privileges screen. This screen is shown in Figure 7-5.

In this screen you will be able to manage resource privileges for each resource type. Click on the Edit icon and select the individual resource privilege that you want to allocate to this administrator. When you have set up the specific resource privilege, the column shown in the resource privilege column will move from "-" to

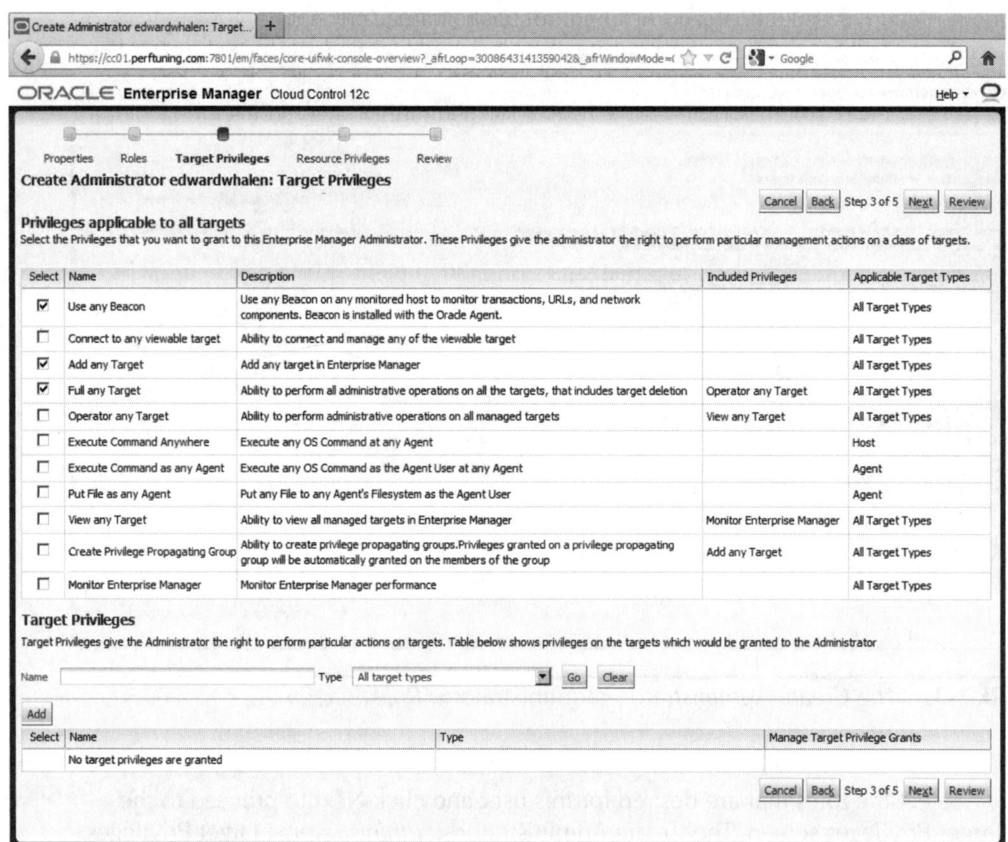

FIGURE 7-4. *The Create Administrator* <administrator>*: Target Privileges screen*

the specific privilege. Once you have added resource privileges to your satisfaction, click Next to continue.

Clicking Next takes you to the Review screen. Once you are satisfied with all of your settings, click Finish to create the administrator. You can also click Back in order to change settings. The Create Administrator <*administrator*>: Review screen is shown in Figure 7-6.

Create Administrator edwardwhalen: Resour...

https://cc01.perftuning.com:7801/em/faces/core-uifwk-console-overview?_afrLoop=3008643141359042&_afrWindowMode=(

ORACLE Enterprise Manager Cloud Control 12c

Setup ▾ Help ▾ ETWHALEN ▾ Log Out

Enterprise ▾ Targets ▾ Favorites ▾ History ▾ Search Target Name ▾

Security

Properties Roles Target Privileges **Resource Privileges** Review

Create Administrator edwardwhalen: Resource Privileges

Cancel Back Step 4 of 5 Next Review

For each of the resource types in the list below, identify specific privileges to be explicitly granted on "all resources" level or individual resources to grant

Resource Type	Description	Privilege Grants Applicable to all Resources	Number of Resources with Privilege Grants	Manage Privilege Grants
Access	Defines the access to different application in Enterprise Manager Cloud Control	-	NA	
Application Replay Entities	Application Replay Entities include captures, replay tasks, and replays.	-	NA	
Backup Configurations	Security Class for System Backup/Recovery Manager.	-	-	
Change Plan Security Class	Security behavior for Change Plans	-	-	
Cloud Policy	Defines access privileges for Cloud Policies	Create any Policy, View any Policy	-	
Cloud Policy Group	Defines access privileges for Cloud Policy Groups	-	-	
Compliance Framework	Compliance Framework provides capability to define/customize/manage compliance frameworks, and compliance standards/rules and evaluate compliance of targets/systems with regards to business best practices for configuration/security/storage etc.	-	NA	
Custom Configurations	Custom Configurations allow extending target configuration collections	-	NA	
Deployment Procedure	Deployment procedures are customizable orchestration routines for various Provisioning and Patching tasks	-	-	
Discovery Security Class	Discovery Security Class	-	NA	
EM Plug-in	Manage the access control for Enterprise Manager plug-ins	Plug-in Agent Administrator, Plug-in OMS Administrator, Plug-in view privilege	NA	
Enterprise Manager High Availability	Enterprise Manager High Availability Administration allows to add additional management service through deployment procedure.	-	NA	
	Collection of rules that apply to Enterprise Manager			

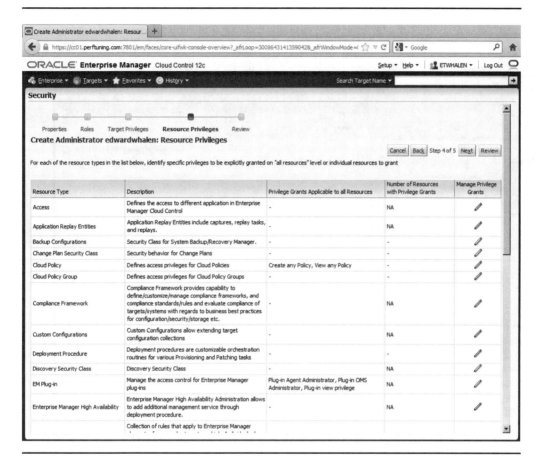

FIGURE 7-5. *The Create Administrator* <administrator>*: Resource Privileges screen*

When you click the Finish button, the administrator will be created and you will be returned to the Security screen. As soon as the administrator has been created, that account can be accessed immediately.

NOTE
When you're creating a super administrator, the Target Privileges screen is skipped and the Resource Privileges screen is reduced.

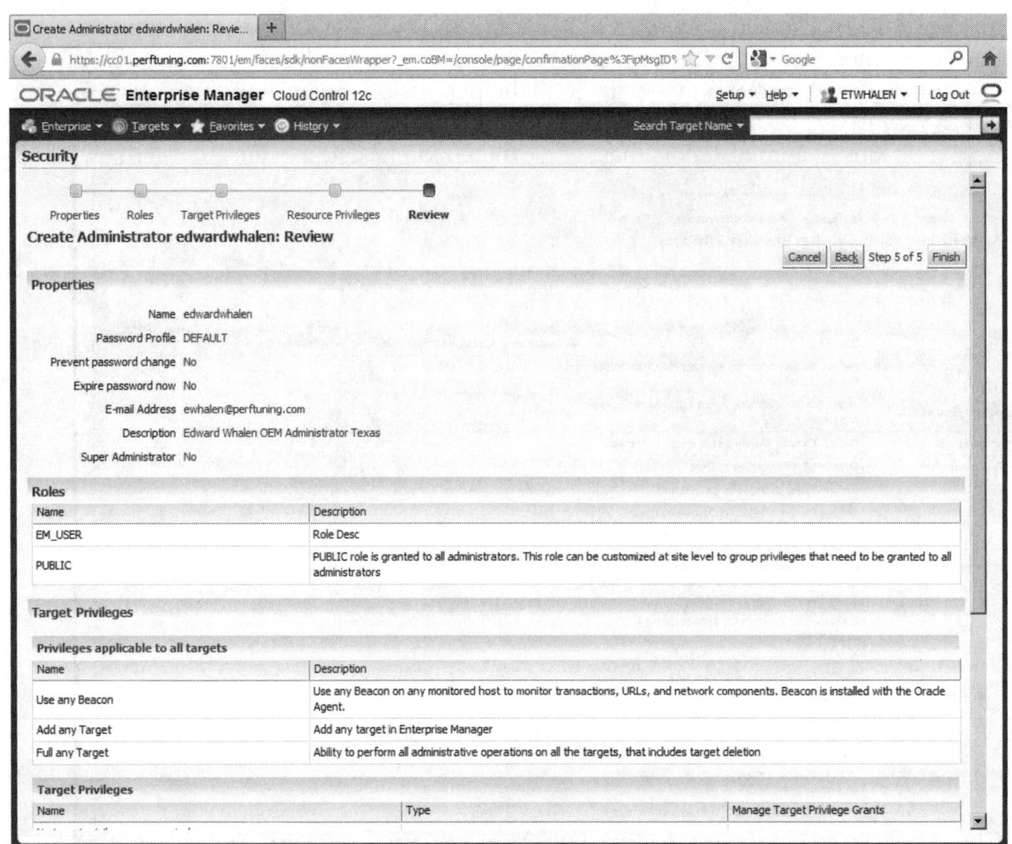

FIGURE 7-6. *The Create Administrator* <administrator>*: Review screen*

Roles

Roles assist with the creating of administrators by allowing you to create a predefined set of permissions by assigning them to a role. The role can then be applied to the administrator. Applying the role to an administrator will assign all of the privileges assigned to the role to the administrator that has been granted that role.

Viewing or modifying a role is done from the Security Roles screen as shown in Figure 7-7. This screen is invoked by selecting Security | Roles from the Setup drop-down menu.

From this screen you can view and edit the permissions associated with each role. Typically you do not have to modify roles. However, if you want to create specific groups of administrators that are permitted to manage specific targets, roles can be quite useful.

From the Roles screen, you can select an existing role and choose Create Like in order to create a role like the one that you have selected. You can manage administrator grants in order to allow an administrator to administer other users. In addition, you can view and edit roles or create a new role.

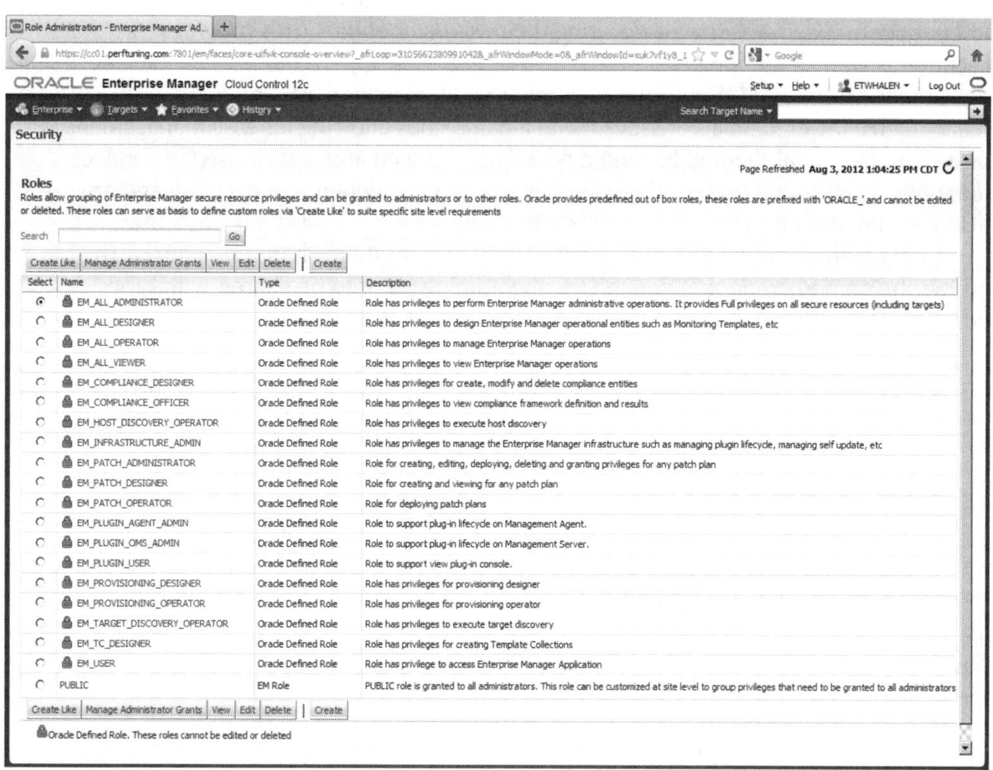

FIGURE 7-7. *The Security: Roles screen*

NOTE
Roles that are prefixed with EM_ are OEM-supplied fixed roles and cannot be deleted or modified.

When modifying and creating roles, simply follow the same steps as you did previously to assign privileges to administrators. This role can then be applied to any new administrators that are created.

Credentials

Credentials are the heart of OEM Cloud Control security. When an administrator logs into OEM Cloud Control, they are only allowed to view basic monitoring information that is collected by the Agent. Additional information that is obtained by connecting to the Oracle database instance is done through individual credentials for each user. This allows database developers, managers, and database administrators to connect to the Oracle database using their own credentials. This provides for security as well as auditing.

Credentials within OEM Cloud Control are now managed as named credentials, meaning that the credentials are saved with a name, thus allowing for easy management as well as credential sharing. Named credentials are saved and can be used to connect to targets. In addition, preferred credentials are used for default connectivity and are also saved in the OEM Repository. This allows for easy access as well as security.

A new feature of OEM Cloud Control 12*c* is the ability to share credentials. This allows the named credential created by one administrator to be shared with other administrators. There are several advantages and uses of credential sharing.

- **Reduce password sharing** The lead DBA is now the only person who needs to know the sys or system account passwords for an Oracle database. That information can be shared with other DBAs via credential sharing.
- **Provide group permissions** For example, a read-only database account can be created that is shared with developers and/or designers to allow them to have access to the database. This account can be given special privileges for monitoring SQL executions, and so on, as needed.

This is a significant new feature of OEM Cloud Control and is very useful for maintaining and enhancing OEM security.

Named Credentials

Named Credentials are saved in the Repository database and associated with each administrator. These credentials can be database credentials, host credentials, and application credentials. Within these credentials is a username and password associated with the type of target that the credentials are designated for. A named credential can be used for both a single target or multiple targets, if they use the same username and password. In addition, in OEM Cloud Control 12*c*, the credentials can now be shared with other users by granting them access. This is discussed later in this chapter.

Named credentials are managed within OEM Cloud Control via the Security Named Credentials screen. This screen is accessed via the Setup menu by selecting Security | Named Credentials and is shown in Figure 7-8.

Here you can create new named credentials or edit existing named credentials. In order to delegate these named credentials to other administrators, you can use the Manage Access button to share access to this named credential. You can also delete and test named credentials from this screen.

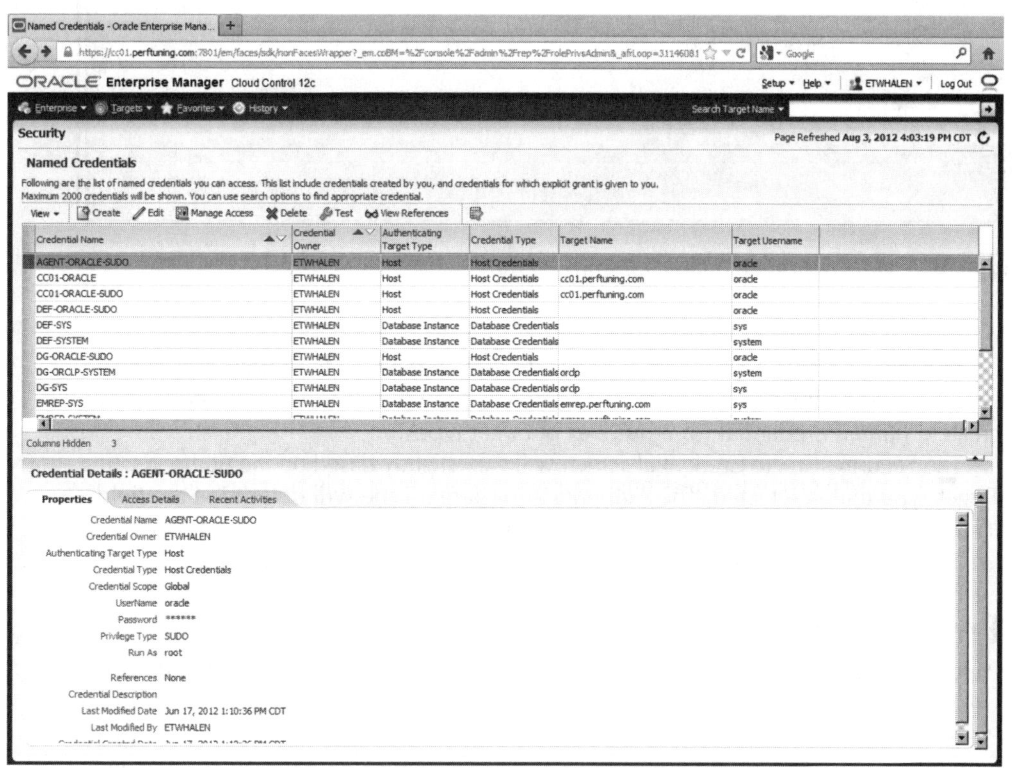

FIGURE 7-8. *The Security: Named Credentials screen*

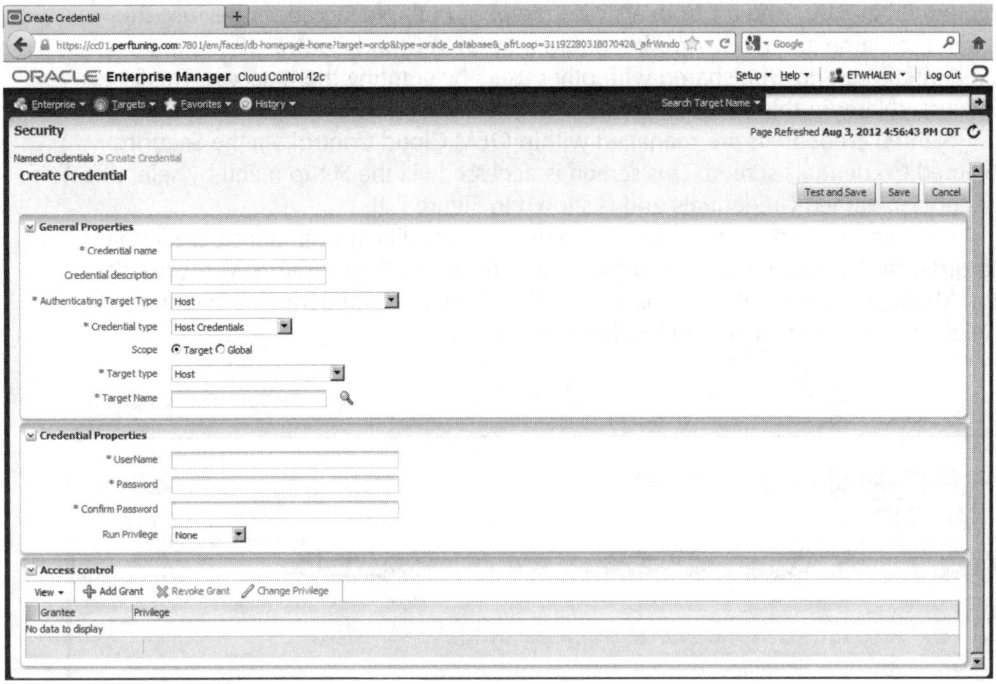

FIGURE 7-9. *The Security: Create Credential screen*

In order to create a new named credential, click the Create button. This will invoke the Security: Create Credential screen as shown in Figure 7-9. Here you can create a named credential for a number of target types.

The Security: Create Credential screen will vary slightly based on the Authenticating Target Type that is selected. The Authenticating Target Type will determine the fields displayed in the Credential Properties section. The Access control section can be used to delegate this credential to others.

Preferred Credentials

Preferred credentials are stored credentials that are assigned to specific targets. Preferred credentials can be set for specific targets and for general target types from within the Preferred Credentials tool. If preferred credentials are not set, you will be prompted for credentials when you try to access a target that requires credentials. To manage preferred credentials, select Security | Preferred Credentials from the Setup menu as shown in Figure 7-10. From this screen you can also set the MOS (My Oracle Support) Credentials.

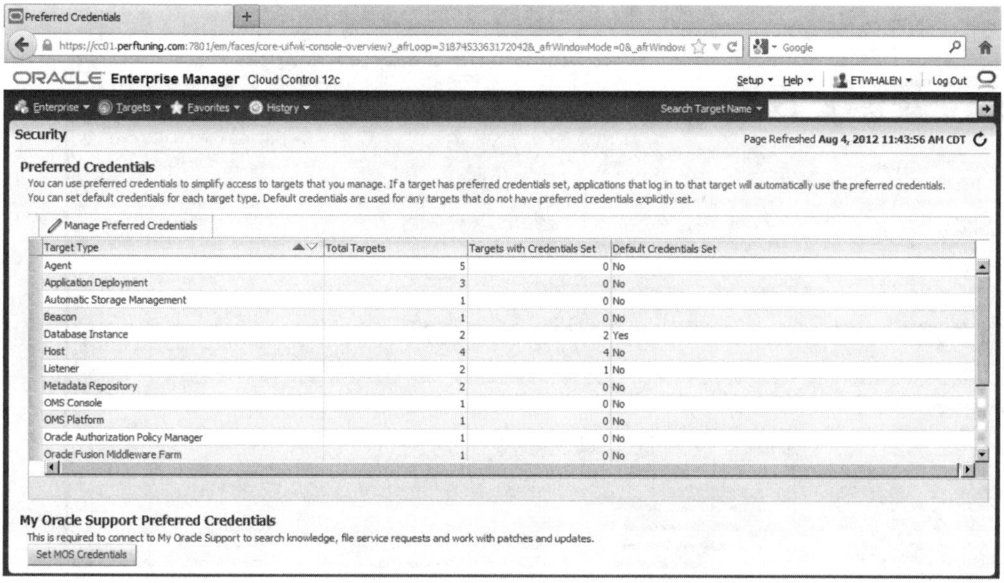

Preferred Credentials

ORACLE Enterprise Manager Cloud Control 12c

Setup ▾ Help ▾ ETWHALEN ▾ Log Out

Enterprise ▾ Targets ▾ Favorites ▾ History ▾ Search Target Name ▾

Security

Page Refreshed Aug 4, 2012 11:43:56 AM CDT

Preferred Credentials

You can use preferred credentials to simplify access to targets that you manage. If a target has preferred credentials set, applications that log in to that target will automatically use the preferred credentials. You can set default credentials for each target type. Default credentials are used for any targets that do not have preferred credentials explicitly set.

Manage Preferred Credentials

Target Type	Total Targets	Targets with Credentials Set	Default Credentials Set
Agent	5	0	No
Application Deployment	3	0	No
Automatic Storage Management	1	0	No
Beacon	1	0	No
Database Instance	2	2	Yes
Host	4	4	No
Listener	2	1	No
Metadata Repository	2	0	No
OMS Console	1	0	No
OMS Platform	1	0	No
Oracle Authorization Policy Manager	1	0	No
Oracle Fusion Middleware Farm	1	0	No

My Oracle Support Preferred Credentials

This is required to connect to My Oracle Support to search knowledge, file service requests and work with patches and updates.

Set MOS Credentials

FIGURE 7-10. *The Security: Preferred Credentials screen*

As you can see, the different credential types are listed along with the total number of targets, the number of targets with credentials set, and the number of target types with default credentials. Highlight a Target Type and click the Manage Preferred Credentials button as shown in Figure 7-10.

From the Security: Database Instance Preferred Credentials screen, shown in Figure 7-11, you can see the default and target specific preferred credentials. From this screen you can set, clear, test and view references for the preferred credentials. All of the credentials are set up as named credentials. When setting a preferred credential, you can either choose to use an existing named credential or to create a new named credential. If a named credential has been delegated to your Administrator account, you can select that as a preferred credential as well.

If a preferred credential has been set for a specific target, that credential will be used. If there is not a preferred credential for the specific target, then the default preferred credential for that target type will be used. If there is no default preferred credential for that target type, then you will be prompted for credentials. In the prompt, there is usually a check box that allows you to save the credential as the preferred credential for that target.

Preferred credentials are essential for increasing the usability and security of the OEM Cloud Control environment. Preferred credentials should always be used for your administrator account.

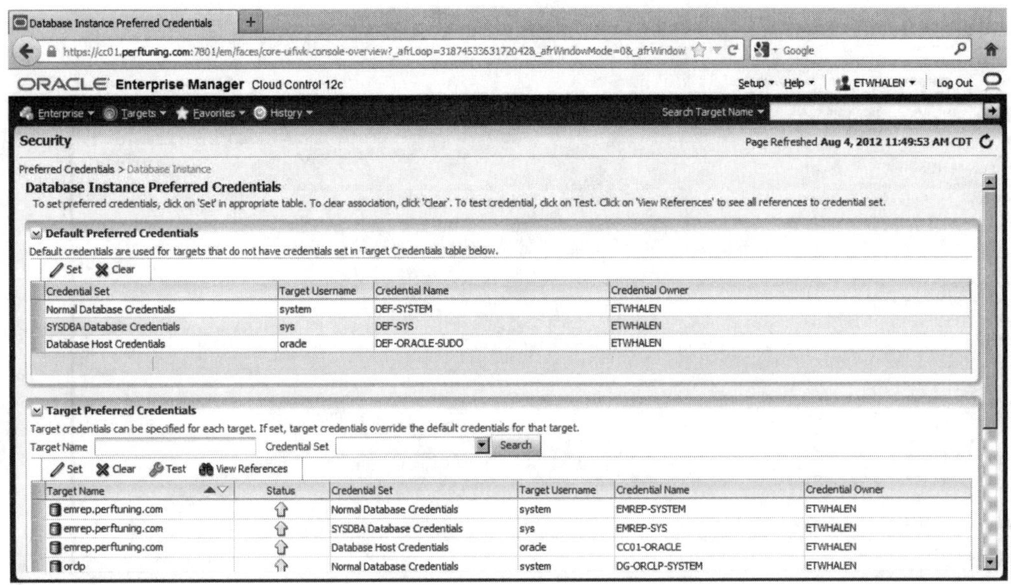

FIGURE 7-11. *The Security: Database Instance Preferred Credentials screen*

Monitoring Credentials

Monitoring credentials are the credentials used for the Agent to monitor specific targets in the OEM Cloud Control environment. These credentials can be set by super administrators and work for each Agent. It is not necessary to set up monitoring credentials for each individual administrator account. To configure monitoring credentials, select Security | Monitoring Credentials from the Setup menu.

This will invoke the Security: Monitoring Credentials screen as shown in Figure 7-12. Here you will see the various Target Types that are being monitored as well as the total number of those targets. In order to set monitoring credentials, highlight the Target Type and click the Manage Monitoring Credentials button.

When you click the Manage Monitoring Credentials button, you will be taken to a screen that has the various targets for that target type listed. Select the specific target and click either Set Credentials, Clear, or Test. This will allow you to set up the monitoring credentials for that specific target. This is a much easier method of setting up and managing monitoring credentials than we had in Cloud Control.

The monitoring credentials are key to a well-functioning Cloud Control system and are easy to maintain. Be sure to coordinate changing the monitoring password

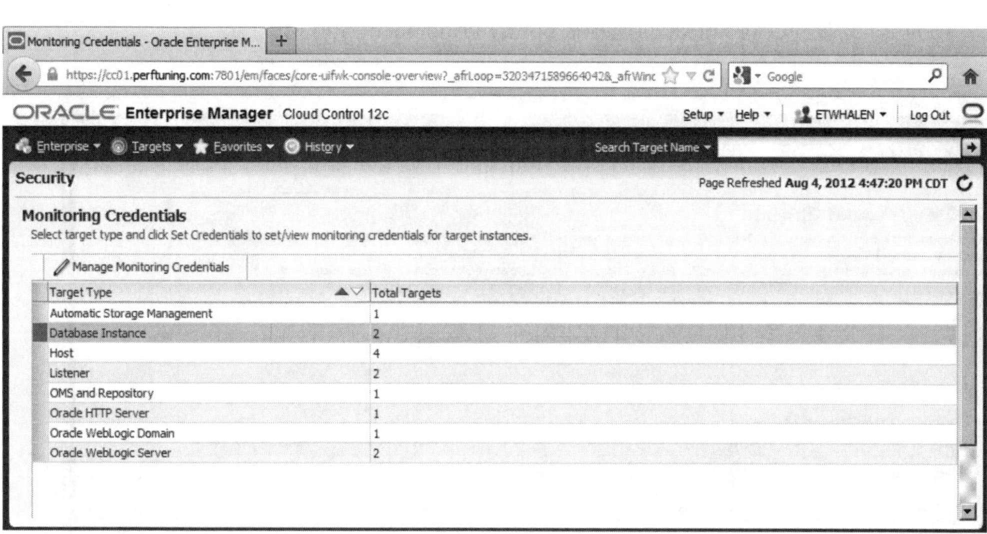

FIGURE 7-12. *The Security: Monitoring Credentials screen*

in Cloud Control whenever you change passwords at the OS and database level. It is important to change passwords occasionally as part of a regular security regime.

Privilege Delegation

Privilege delegation allows OS users on a host target to run as a user with higher privileges via either Sudo or PowerBroker. These privileges are used during the Agent configuration process based on how the Agent installation is specified; however, in order to use privilege delegation after the installation has completed, it is necessary to configure privilege delegation.

In order to configure privilege delegation, select Security | Privilege Delegation from the Setup menu. This will invoke the Security: Manage Privilege Delegation Settings screen as shown in Figure 7-13.

Here you can see the various host targets and their current settings. You can either select a target and click the Edit button, or mass apply by applying a template. We prefer using the template, since you can do many or all of the targets at the same time. At the bottom of the screen, you can see the hyperlink to the Manage Privilege Delegation Setting Templates screen where you can create and/or edit templates.

Privilege delegation is very straightforward. For each target you will set the privilege delegation to Sudo, PowerBroker, or none.

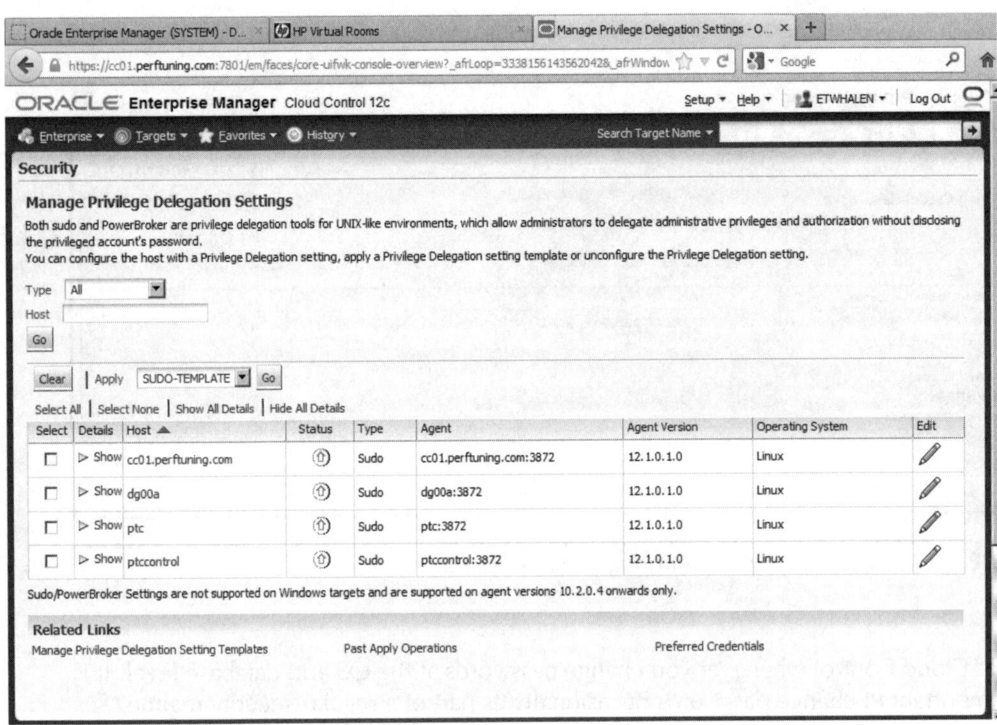

FIGURE 7-13. *The Security: Manage Privilege Delegation Settings screen*

Registration Passwords

Registration Passwords are used for OEM Intelligent Agents to connect into the OEM Management Server. The Registration Passwords can be managed by Cloud Control for either persistent passwords or one-time passwords. They are managed by using the Security: Registration Passwords screen, as shown in Figure 7-14.

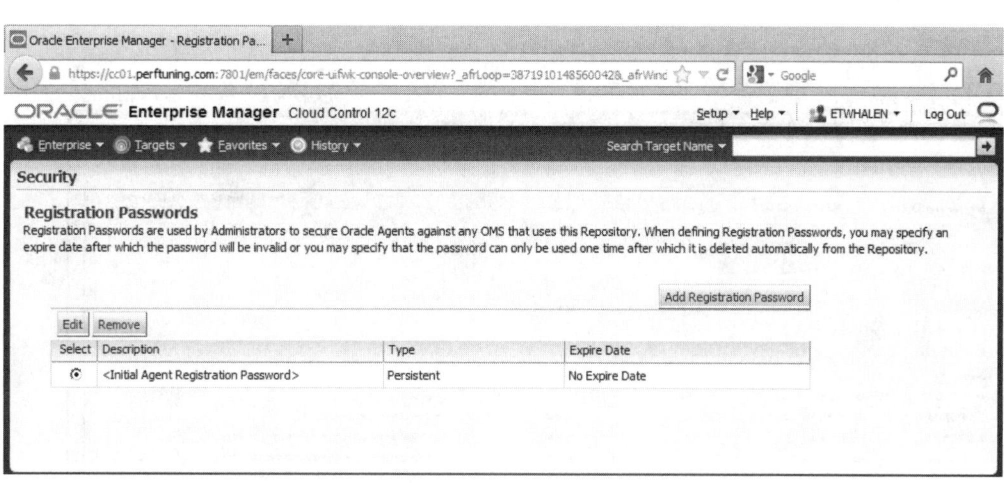

FIGURE 7-14. *The Security: Registration Passwords screen*

Here you can modify, remove, or add passwords. You cannot remove the initial registration password. When a new password is created, it can be designated a one-time password. With a one-time password, it is removed as soon as it is successfully used the first time. This is convenient, since it is unnecessary to change the password after it has been used.

Audit Data

Audit data is used to audit the use of OEM Cloud Control. Login and Logout information is audited and is viewable from the Security | Audit Data drop-down from the Setup menu. The Security: Audit Data screen is shown in Figure 7-15. You can input search criteria and browse audit data from this screen.

Audit data is useful for monitoring access to OEM Cloud Control. In order for Audit data to be effective, each user should log in with their own administrator account. This is also an OEM Cloud Control best practice.

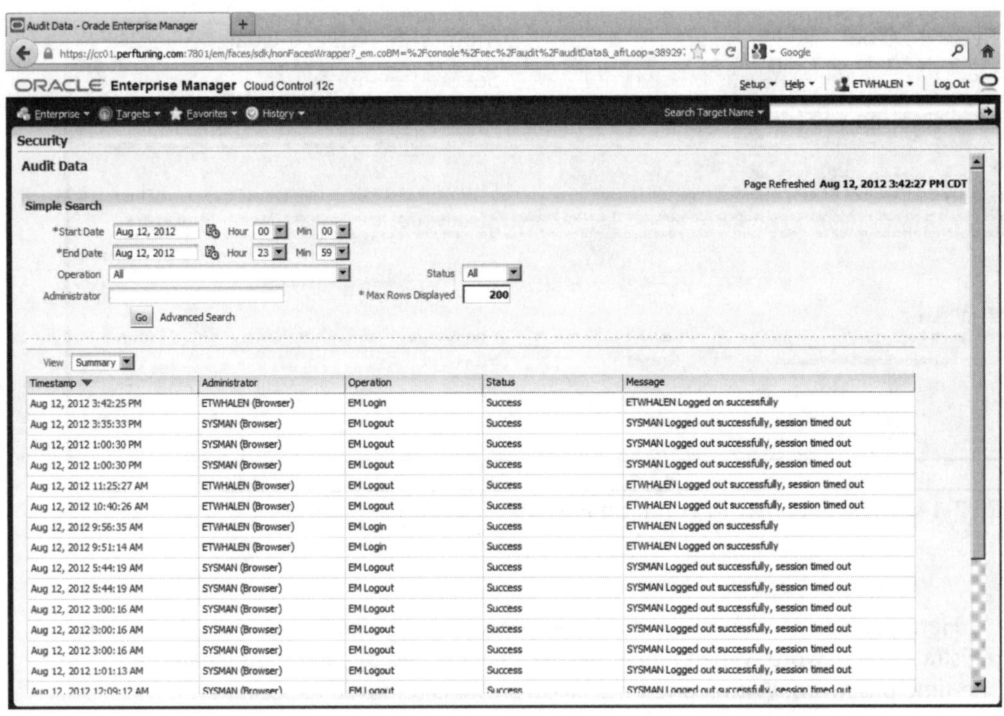

FIGURE 7-15. *The Security: Audit Data screen*

Securing Cloud Control Data Transfer

Oracle designed Cloud Control to integrate into and manage the most security-hardened data centers. Security functionality is built into the product, both at the application and underlying component levels. The Cloud Control application extends built-in features to tighten its own security. These features are available both through the Console and in executables (such as `emctl` under the OMS and Agent homes). The underlying components, the Oracle Database 11*g* and Oracle Application Server 11*g* instances (Oracle HTTP Server in particular), also provide their own built-in security services that Cloud Control co-opts to protect itself.

Consider Table 7-1 our "big board"[1] on Cloud Control security. It lists the primary Cloud Control security goals, how you achieve them, and where they are documented in this book. References include previous chapters, this present chapter

[1] A reference to the big board in the War Room in the film *Dr. Strangelove*, directed by Stanley Kubrick.

CC Security Goal	Method to Achieve Goal
Protect sensitive data such as passwords	Secure the emkey
Provide auditing capability for sites requiring it	Turn on the CC audit function
Deny unauthorized users access to the CC Console; grant privileges to authorized users	Enforce administrator access and privileges
Comply with company and industry standards for securing all CC components and hosts	Set security policies for OMR Database, other GC components, and CC hosts
Secure data transfer between Agents and OMS	Enable EM Framework Security
Transmit Repository data in encrypted form	Use Oracle Advanced Security
Safeguard data transferred between browser and Console and restrict Console clients	Leverage Oracle HTTP Server security
Integrate CC with other Oracle technologies used to authenticate users	Integrate CC with Single Sign-On (SSO) or Enterprise User Security (EUS)
Deploy CC when firewalls separate components	Set properties in CC configuration files, leverage proxy servers, and configure firewalls

TABLE 7-1. *Cloud Control Security Goals and How to Accomplish Them*

of course, and OEM Advanced Configuration 11*g*, which you must consult for the last two goals listed.

Let's run through the big board and break it down this way:

- **Cloud Control Security** This chapter addresses a particular aspect of Cloud Control security: how to secure data transmitted between CC components. (We also briefly cover how to restrict Console access to certain clients.) Security systems should implement secure connections between all critical and sensitive points of communication. For Cloud Control, the communication points are between its components: Repository, OMS, Agents, and Console, and such communication is secured by strong encryption.
- **SSO and EUS** If you use either of these products, evaluate using them in tandem with GC for authentication.

- **Firewalls** Configuring CC with firewalls is an important security matter, but a relatively straightforward process. Before installing CC, open the firewalls between CC hosts to all traffic on CC communication ports. Then, after completing the steps in this current chapter, lock down the firewalls.

Let's focus in now on securing data transfer between GC components. The major contributor to preserving the privacy and integrity of GC traffic is EM Framework Security ("Framework Security"), so named because it protects the flow of data within the CC framework (that is, between Agents, OMS, and Repository). Bringing up the rear is the Oracle HTTP Server bundled with CC, responsible for protecting browser/Console exchanges and restricting Console access based on client network characteristics. Let me introduce this dynamic duo by drawing the big picture, which you can refer back to as we delve in. Figure 7-16 shows how Framework Security and Oracle HTTP Server (OHS) together protect all GC communications.

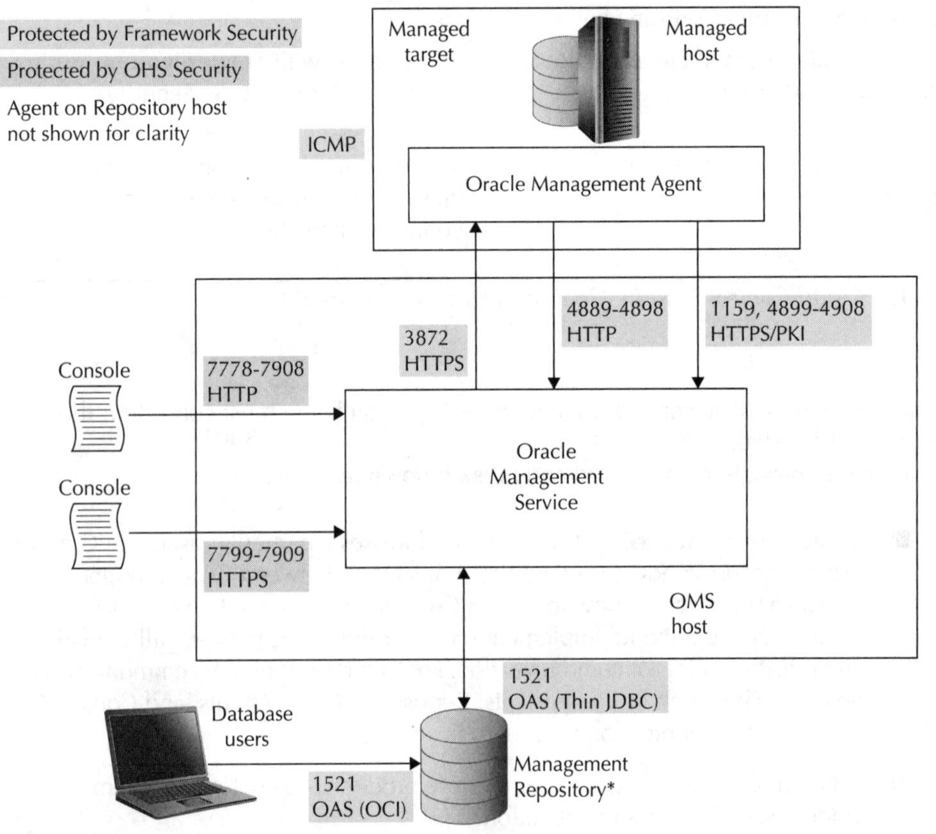

FIGURE 7-16. *Framework Security and OHS together secure GC communications.*

As you can see, Framework Security and OHS are tightly integrated and complement one another to secure all data channels between GC components. Table 7-2 presents this same information in tabular form for those of you who find tables more palatable than figures.

Both Figure 7-16 and Table 7-2 detail the security method employed to protect data flow, whether the method is considered part of Framework Security or OHS security, and the ports where communications take place. HTTPS signifies that Secure Sockets Layer (SSL) is used, which is an industry-standard technology for encrypting data.

Method	Port
Enterprise Manager Upload HTTP Port	4889 – 4898
Enterprise Manager Upload HTTPS (SSL) Port	1159, 4899 – 4908
Management Agent Port	3872
Management Repository Database Port	1521
Cloud Control Console HTTP Port	7788 – 7798
Cloud Control Console HTTPS (SSL) Port	7799 – 7809
EM Domain WebLogic Admin Server HTTP Port	7001
EM Domain WebLogic Admin Server HTTPS (SSL) Port	7101 – 7200
Cloud Control Managed Server HTTP Port	7201 – 7300
Cloud Control Managed Server HTTPS (SSL) Port	7301 – 7400
WebLogic Node Manager HTTPS (SSL) Port	7401 – 7500
JVM Diagnostics Managed Server	3800
JVM Diagnostics Managed Server (SSL)	3801
Application Dependency and Performance RMI Registry Port	51099
Application Dependency and Performance Java Provider Port	5503
Application Dependency and Performance Remote Service Controller Port	55000

TABLE 7-2. *Methods and Ports Involved in Securing GC Traffic*

What Is Secure Sockets Layer?

Earlier, and throughout this chapter, we refer to SSL as the encryption method. Therefore, let me give you an overview[2] of SSL, for those not completely familiar with it. SSL is an encrypted communication protocol that securely sends messages across the Internet. The mod_ossl plug-in to Oracle HTTP enables SSL capability. SSL resides between Oracle HTTP Server on the application layer and the TCP/IP layer and transparently handles data encryption and decryption between client and server.

A typical application of SSL is to secure HTTP traffic (that is, to use HTTPS) between a browser and a Web server. You learn later in this chapter that the Oracle HTTP Server supplied with Cloud Control employs SSL to secure browser/Console connections. However, as you also learn later, configuring SSL does not restrict unsecured (that is, HTTP) access. It simply provides an additional secure channel of HTTP access over SSL (called HTTPS). (Throughout this chapter, we use the terms "SSL" and "HTTPS" interchangeably.) SSL thereby allows URLs beginning with *https://* without disturbing working URLs that start with *http://*. In addition to the http/https difference in URL specification, you must dedicate different ports for HTTP and HTTPS traffic for a given Web application. The default ports used vary by Web application. This is why you can access the GC Console out-of-box via Oracle HTTP Server on both http://<*OMShost*>:4889 and https://<*OMShost*>:1159.

---

[2] Source: *Oracle HTTP Server Administrator's Guide* 12*c*.

EM Framework Security

So what does Framework Security encompass, as defined by the Oracle EM documentation? A quick scan of the Table 7-2 shows that Framework Security safeguards data sent between Agents, OMS, and Repository, as well as between database users and the OMR Database. (OHS protects browser/Console connections.)

Framework Security for Agent/OMS traffic is enabled when you install Cloud Control. This piece of Framework Security also affords out-of-box HTTPS browser access to the Console via OHS over the same port used for secure Agent uploads. But such access is not considered part of Framework Security, as reflected by Figure 7-16 and Table 7-2. As the EM documentation puts it, "Framework Security works in concert with—but does not replace—the security features you should enable for your Oracle HTTP Server."[3] This classification of what is and isn't part of Framework Security is somewhat arbitrary, in our opinion. To wit, the security model called "Framework Security" secures Agent/OMS traffic and browser/Console traffic using the same OHS security mechanism (HTTPS and PKI), in the same installation process, and over the same port to boot. Yet, Framework Security is credited with protecting Agent/OMS traffic, and OHS is credited with safeguarding browser/Console traffic.

In deference to the EM documentation, we also characterize the Repository security that the WebLogic server provides as part of "Framework Security." In actuality, the WebLogic configuration is no different from a generic WebLogic implementation between database client and server. The only crossover into Cloud Control is that you set up WebLogic for the OMS and the Agents using their respective Cloud Control configuration files, emoms.properties and emd.properties.

In the end, it doesn't matter what elements of CC security you draw a box around and call "Framework Security." We'll adopt Oracle's definition of the term. Our rationale for not redefining Framework Security is twofold: to explain exactly what Oracle means by the term so that you can decipher the Oracle EM documentation relating to security, and to avoid confusing you further over such a frivolously logical construct, in our humble view.

NOTE
Framework Security encompasses all OMS hosts at a particular CC site. OMS hosts at different sites must use distinct Framework Security. Therefore, in this section, when we refer to the OMS, it signifies each OMS host at your site.

With Oracle Enterprise Manager Cloud Control 12*c*, the default behavior of the components is to be secured. This is done via the Agent installation procedure. One of the biggest challenges in setting up OEM Cloud Control is preparing for the installation by opening ports through firewalls. The information in this chapter and the excellent information in the Cloud Control documentation will assist with that.

Summary

In this chapter you learned the basics of setting up and configuring security within OEM Cloud Control. This includes setting up administrators, privilege delegation, credentials, and auditing. It is a best practice for OEM Cloud Control that each user has their own administrator account and that they do not share passwords.

---

[3] *OEM Advanced Configuration* 12*c*.

With shared credentials, this is easier than previous releases. Security is an important topic and should not be taken lightly. Security is one of the most important tasks that the DBA or system administrator has.

In addition, some basic information about ports used for OEM administration and communication was presented. This information can assist you with the installation and configuration of the Cloud Control system.

CHAPTER 8

Cloud Control Maintenance and Tuning

At this point the reader has hopefully obtained a basic understanding of the various modules that comprise Cloud Control. In earlier chapters we covered installation of the primary components: the Oracle Management Server (OMS), the supporting Oracle Management Repository (OMR) database, and the Oracle Management Agents (OMA) on the targets. In addition, the basic Console configuration and the implementation of notifications were outlined. Finally, Cloud Control Security and User Management were also covered. As this is the final chapter of Part I, the goal is to construct an effective monitoring and control system.

In this chapter both maintenance and tuning are covered. Maintenance will be addressed from two different perspectives, which are labeled operational and physical. *Operational* maintenance is considered the steps or procedures that need to be followed to effectively implement Cloud Control within the enterprise. *Physical* maintenance is the more commonly accepted definition where the interest is maintaining the resources for the supporting services.

Maintaining Cloud Control

The topic of Cloud Control maintenance is divided into two categories: operational and physical. Operational maintenance consists of the functions that need to be implemented in order to effectively manage an Oracle enterprise. A small Cloud Control environment can quickly attain hundreds of targets including databases, systems, and supporting resources (listeners and agents, for example). Without suitable operational controls, the task of managing the targets can be overwhelming and the monitoring tools themselves will begin to lose their effectiveness. False, redundant, or misleading alarms lead the DBA to question the integrity of the product. A continuously blinking red beacon begins to lose its effectiveness when the DBA can no longer distinguish between true and worthless alarms. Fire trucks are equipment with numerous sirens, specifically for this purpose. Eventually drivers become accustomed to the standard siren, so different sirens can be triggered either automatically or manually in order to garner the attention of lulled drivers. Unfortunately, Cloud Control notifications are relatively standard (for example, e-mail or text messaging). Neither the Signal Flare nor the Bat Light has been incorporated into the notification rules, so it is important that we ensure that all notifications are true and warranted by the target. For example, blocked sessions in a test environment are significantly different than blocked users in production. Without operationally effective monitoring, we risk DBA complacency.

Physical maintenance consists of those tasks that need to be performed in order to keep your Cloud Control system working efficiently and productively. These are relatively common steps in any database system.

One additional note: Cloud Control 12*c* provides many features to address scalability within the enterprise. Many functions addressed earlier in this book and in this chapter specifically deal with the tremendous growth in managed targets. Scalability from the Oracle perspective, however, also includes the resources used to manage these targets. That is, Cloud Control has implemented numerous features that allow for a greater range of personnel and responsibilities. These features are exemplified by the large number of roles and privileges engineered into the system. These capabilities are a significant advancement over earlier versions and reflect the product's growth from a database monitoring tool to an enterprise-wide management system.

The new version allows for multiple layers of management and control including super administrators, development DBAs, developers, and support engineers, to name only a few. It has been my limited experience, however, that most DBAs wear multiple hats and are expected to handle a wide range of responsibilities. The need to segment, control, and distribute the workload between multiple resources is no doubt present in some environments, but not in the majority. These new features are beneficial but do increase the complexity of the product. For our purposes, we will concentrate on scalability functionality that addresses the large number of targets, rather than a wide range of support personnel.

Although an important feature, Compliance Rules are not addressed in this chapter. The Compliance management and reporting functionality is significantly enhanced in Cloud Control compared to earlier versions. The breadth and depth of the Compliance module is beyond the scope of this guide. Further, the product is still new and in a transitory state with new features being implemented regularly.

Operational Maintenance

Operational maintenance involves implementing and managing the following:

- Groups
- Monitoring Templates
- Incident Rules
- Support Utilities

Using these features, a single DBA can manage a wide range of resources. The ordering of these features is relevant along with a degree of planning. Rules need to be established with respect to target group membership. Once groups are established, the other features can be applied. Assigning monitoring templates, incident rules, and blackouts to groups is far simpler than assigning them to individual targets.

Groups

Many Cloud Control sites manage thousands of targets, and even the smallest sites typically contain hundreds. The group target type helps you organize targets into logical sets to facilitate managing them as a unit. Following are some of the characteristics and advantages of groups:

- Once an administrator creates a group, he or she can refer to it as to an individual target. For example, an administrator can choose to grant access to, or schedule blackouts or jobs for, a group.
- Administrators can customize their Consoles to directly access their groups on the Targets subtab.
- Group charts, dashboards, out-of-box, and custom reports help you visualize or summarize the overall status of member targets, and allow you to drill down to problem areas.
- At very large sites, you can add groups as members of other groups. This "roll-up" of groups allows for a hierarchical modeling of targets in your Cloud Control environment.
- From a group console, a user can drill down to individual targets.
- Monitoring templates can be applied to a group.
- When activated, the group can be used to propagate privileges to the members of a group. Once a privilege is granted to an administrator or role, the same privilege is automatically propagated to new members of the group.

Members of groups can be of the same target type, such as Hosts, or of different types, like a System, Service, and Web Application. The latter type of group contains aggregate target types and potentially has multiple components. Aggregate targets are top-level, composite targets made up of multiple member targets. With groups you can model certain complex aggregate targets as a single entity. You may not always be overly concerned about the status of any single component in the group, only that the group as a whole remains available to provide the intended function. For instance, groups can cut across target types to contain all targets for a particular data center or application (for example, "Customer Retail Systems").

Cloud Control also provides for groups with enhanced functionality. These are groups that possess features beyond managing multiple targets. One of these groups is the Redundancy Group. This is a group that contains members of the same type that function collectively as a unit. Redundancy Groups provide all the features of regular groups, with the additional feature of allowing you to monitor the availability of target members as a single logical target. A Redundancy Group functions like a single logical target that supports a status (availability) metric. A Redundancy Group is considered up (available) if at least one of the member targets is up. Although logically considered a "group," redundant members are classified as a "system" in Cloud Control. Consequently, redundancy systems and other special high availability groups are not accessed from the Groups page. You can access, create, and manage these systems from the All Target pages or from the Systems page. As they represent an extension of standard group functionality, we will not delve into the details of these groups since the basic group functionality satisfies our primary objective: operational maintainability.

A feature new to Cloud Control is Dynamic Groups. These groups are automatically determined by the characteristics of the underlying targets. In this case, new targets or targets whose properties are changed are automatically added to the group. Membership criteria can take various forms. Naturally, supported properties are limited to global properties, but can also include attributes such as version, platform, target name, and type.

Administrative Groups are another new feature of Cloud Control. Administrative Groups are a special type of group used to fully automate application of monitoring settings to targets upon joining the group. These groups simplify the management effort by automatically applying management settings to the members. Settings can include monitoring thresholds or compliance standards. Similar to Dynamic Groups, targets are automatically assigned to Administrative Groups based on specific target properties. Once a target is a member of the group, any applicable Template Collections are automatically applied to the target. Template Collections consist of Monitoring Templates, compliance standards, and cloud policies. Administrative Groups eliminate the need to perform many administrative tasks and standardize the introduction of new targets to the enterprise.

Dynamic and Administrative Groups are new features in Cloud Control and consequently can have aberrant and undocumented "functionality." These two new features do provide a significant advantage to enterprise management, but we do need to wait for the functionality to be fully vetted. Further, the expanded capabilities of these new features require a degree of advance planning. Administrative Groups can be configured in multiple layers of hierarchy including covering lifecycle status (production, test, QA, and so on), physical location, SLA requirements, and lines of business. The functionality is rich and Oracle is releasing new documentation to fully address the complexity of the product. A thorough examination of these products requires greater attention than can be provided in this guide.

In the meantime, standard Groups offer an excellent tool for managing numerous and varied targets.

Creating Groups Figure 8-1 shows the Create Group form. The Create Group form can be accessed from the main Console through the Setup menu, and then choose Add Target and then Group. This form is also accessible from the main menu Targets

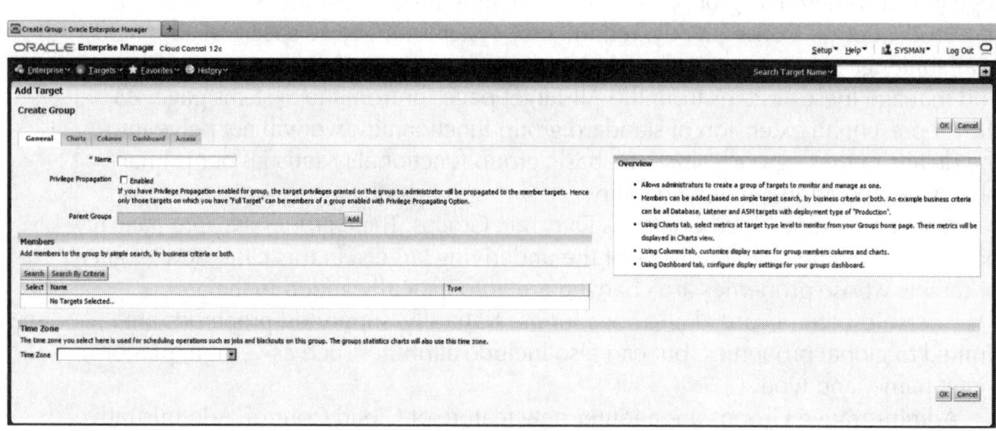

FIGURE 8-1. *Create Group*

and then choose Groups and then click Create. Creating a group is a straightforward process:

1. On the General tab, enter a unique name and determine whether you will take advantage of the Privilege Propagation functionality. This is a nice feature that allows administrator or role privileges granted to a Group to be propagated to the member targets.

2. Select the Members of the new Group. Members can be of any type: Agent, Group, Host, Listener, and so on. Member selection allows for querying by name or other criteria.

3. Carefully consider the time zone you choose for the group, as the statistics charts on the Charts page use this time zone and you cannot change it once the group is created. This time zone is also used as the default time zone for certain operations pertaining to the group, such as when setting blackouts.

Before clicking OK, review the remaining tabs on the Create Group page. These features allow for the customization of the Group displays within Cloud Control.

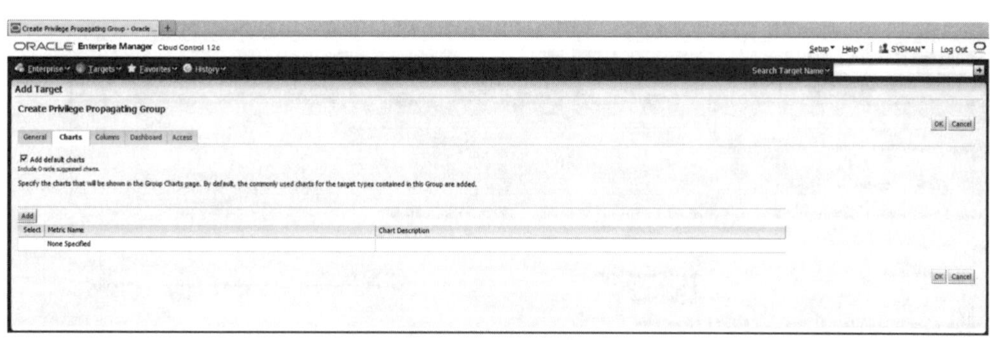

FIGURE 8-2. *Create Group – Charts*

The Create Group Charts tab (Figure 8-2) allows the administrator to specify the charts that are displayed when the Group Target is selected in Cloud Control. By default the commonly used charts are automatically displayed.

The Create Group Columns tab (Figure 8-3) allows the administrator to override the default names used in the Groups display. Names (referred to as Abbreviations) can be customized to the Group targets.

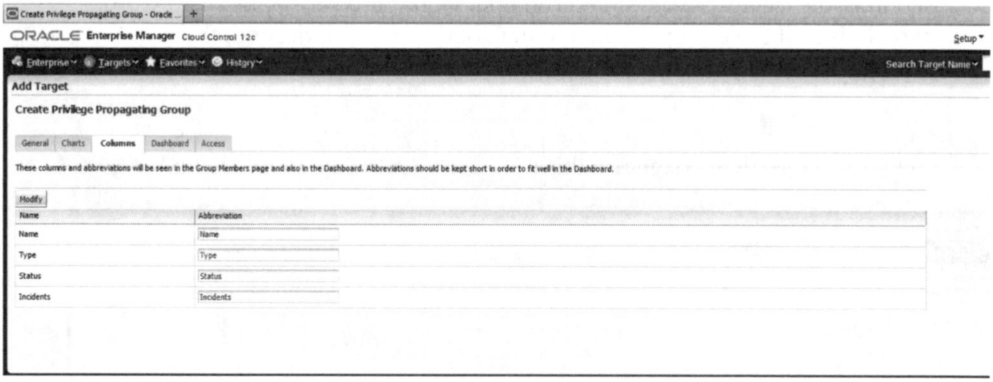

FIGURE 8-3. *Create Group – Columns*

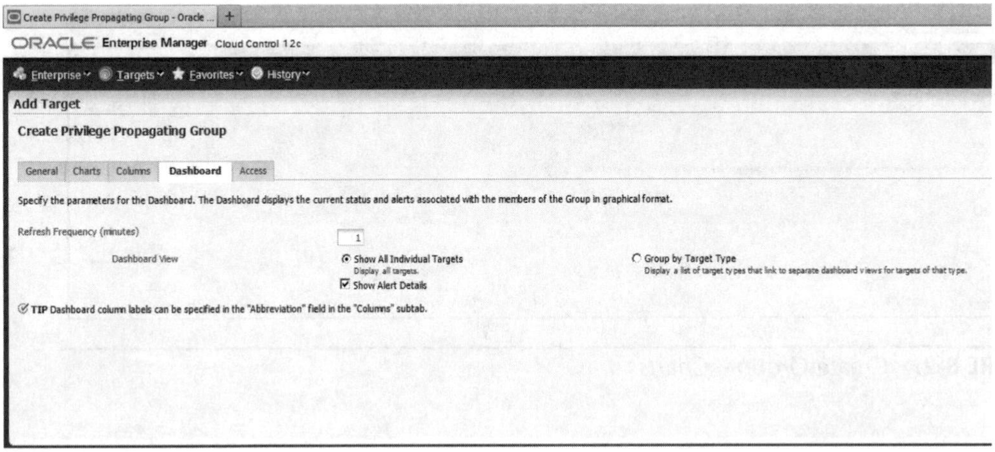

FIGURE 8-4. *Create Group – Dashboard*

The Create Group Dashboard tab (Figure 8-4) allows the administrator to configure the dashboard view when the target Group is selected, for example, refresh frequency and the sorting of targets.

The Access tab (Figure 8-5) allows the administrator to grant privileges on the group directly to other administrators or to roles.

Once created, the group can be managed from the Groups page, which is accessed from the main console's Targets menu. Figure 8-6 shows the main Groups page, which lists all the Groups available in Cloud Control. If desired, the listed Groups can be filtered by search criteria.

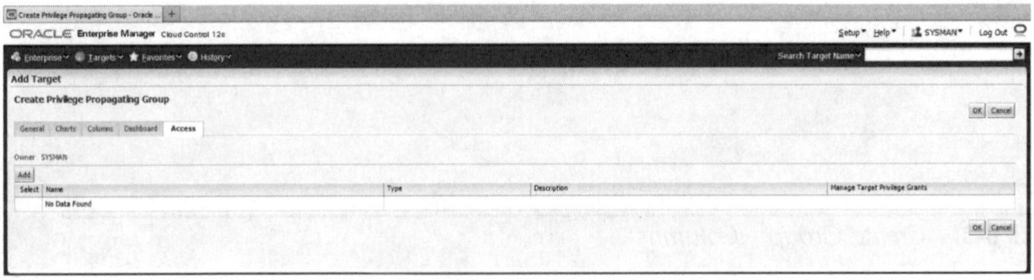

FIGURE 8-5. *Create Group – Access*

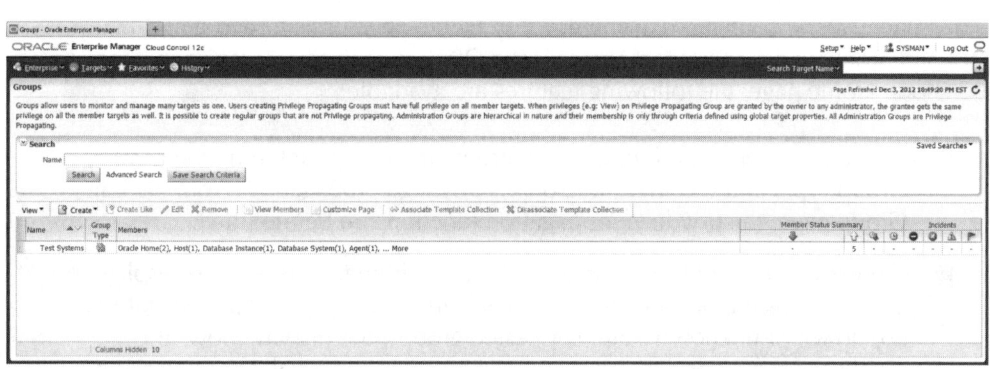

FIGURE 8-6. *Groups*

The main Groups page gives a brief overview of the status of the targets and any related incidents. When you click on a Group name, the corresponding Group Home page is displayed. Figure 8-7 displays the customizations described earlier.

Now that we have one, the Group becomes our fundamental target within Cloud Control. We can work with individual targets as needed, but the Group

FIGURE 8-7. *Test Systems Group Home page*

greatly simplifies the management, monitoring, and configuration effort. The Group Home page can be configured as the new My Home page or as a Favorite. At many sites, the production Group Home page is the DBA's default My Home page. From the Group Home page, the following features are available:

- A display of general information regarding the group including the Owner, Group Type, and whether the group is privilege propagating. From the Edit Group page, the privilege propagation function can be modified.
- View a summary of the status of the targets within the group. This display includes a listing of how many members are in the group and their status: up, down, or unknown state. For nested groups, the display shows the number of targets and their corresponding status across all the related sub-groups. The status roll-up count is based on the unique member targets across all sub-groups. Therefore, even if a target appears more than once in sub-groups, it is counted only once in the status roll-up.
- Monitor incidents or events related to the group. This section displays a summary of the member incidents that have recently been updated. It also shows a count of open problems and recently updated problems. The rolled-up information is shown for all the member targets regardless of their status. Clicking on the incident, event, or problem number takes the user to the Incident Manager page.
- Group administration including adding or removing targets.
- Group-wide blackouts can be configured and managed for maintenance periods. The display also shows information regarding current or pending blackouts.
- Job scheduling for the group as a whole. The page displays a summary of the jobs whose start date is within the last seven days. You can click Show to see the latest run or all runs. Click View to select and reorder the columns that appear in the table or adjust scrolling and expanding the table.
- A Patch section that displays the Oracle patch recommendations that are applicable to the group targets. You can view patch recommendations by classification (for example, "security") or target type.
- Modify access privileges on the group or the individual targets.
- An Inventory section, which displays inventory summaries for deployments such as hosts, database installations, and fusion middleware installations on a system-wide basis or for individual targets. By clicking on See Details, the user is directed to the Inventory and Usage page.

- A Configuration Changes display, which shows the number of configuration changes to the group in the previous seven days. Cloud Control automatically collects configuration information for group targets and changes to configurations are recorded. The user can click on the number of configuration changes to view detailed information concerning the changes.
- As with many of the pages in Cloud Control, the regions of the Group Home page can be customized by clicking on the Actions icon in the upper-right corner of each region.
- The group charts are available from the Monitoring submenu. This page displays the performance charts configured during the group setup. Out-of-box performance charts are provided based on the type of members in the group. You can view performance information over the last 24 hours, 7 days, or 31 days. Custom charts can also be added to the page.

The Group Dashboard is accessible from the Group menu. This page provides real-time monitoring of the overall health of targets in a group. The Dashboard presents information using graphics and icons that permit you to spot recent changes and quickly respond to problems. The interface, shown in Figure 8-8, displays up and down target states as green and red arrows, respectively, and metrics in critical, warning, and normal states as red, yellow, and green dots. These colors highlight problem areas and allow for drill-down as needed. An incident table lists all the open incidents in the group. The incidents in the table are listed in reverse chronological order to show the most recent incidents first, but you can also click any column in the table to change to sort order. The colors in the top bar of the Member Targets table change based on the group's incident critical level. The priority progresses from warning to critical to fatal. If the group has at least one fatal incident, the top bar becomes dark red. If the group has at least one critical incident, the top bar becomes faint red. If the group has only warning incidents, the top bar turns yellow. If the

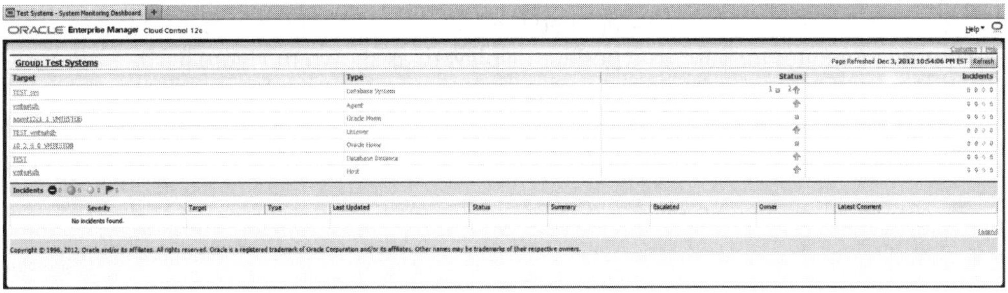

FIGURE 8-8. *Test Group Dashboard*

group has no incidents, the top bar remains colorless. The Dashboard allows you to drill down for more details on a particular target, target status, and incidents.

Now that we have a group and the ability to manage its members, our next objective is monitoring the targets within the group.

Monitoring Templates

Monitoring templates let you standardize target monitoring by specifying monitoring settings once and then applying them to multiple targets. Monitoring templates have been a feature of Enterprise Manager since version 10 and they are a very helpful tool. Rather than painstakingly configuring the monitoring thresholds on each and every target, we can use development templates for each target type. Further, if desired, we can create templates based on the logical relationship between targets; for example, one template for production databases and another for test databases. Each monitoring template is only applicable to one type of target. However, a template can be applied to a group that is composed of multiple types, and the targets corresponding to the template will have the metrics applied.

Templates define metric, metric extensions, thresholds, collection schedules, and corrective actions. You can later edit templates and reapply them. If you change a template, you must reapply it to propagate the changes; but you can change and reapply the template as often as you like. (As noted earlier, Administrative Groups automate application of monitoring templates.)

NOTE

Metric Extensions are an enhanced version of User-Defined Metrics (UDM) introduced in previous versions of Enterprise Manager. Unlike UDMs, metric extensions allow you to create full-fledged metrics for a multitude of target types.

The Monitoring Templates form can be reached from the main Console, Enterprise menu, and then the Monitoring submenu. As displayed in Figure 8-9, only custom templates are displayed by default on this form.

However, by enabling Oracle-supplied templates and clicking Go, a full set of monitoring templates for various types are displayed, as shown in Figure 8-10. Oracle provides templates for the following target types:

- Hosts
- Application deployment

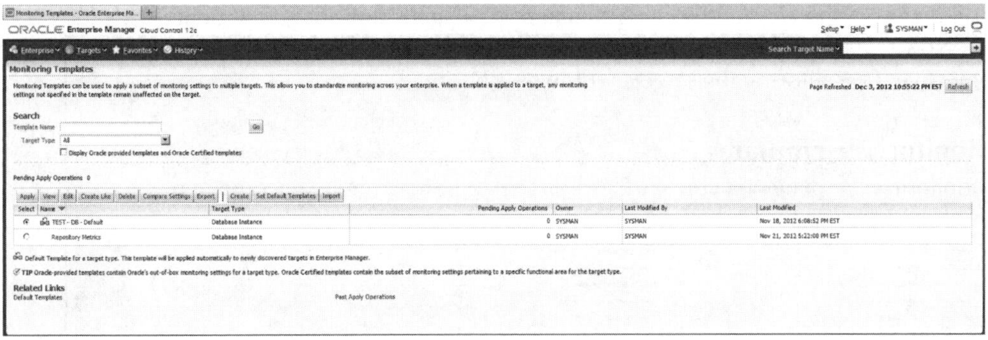

FIGURE 8-9. *Monitoring Templates form*

- Clustered application deployment
- Metadata Repository
- Oracle HTTP server
- Database instance
- Agent
- Oracle Home
- Oracle Fusion Middleware Farm
- Listener
- SOA Composite[1]
- SOA Infrastructure
- Cluster Database
- Oracle WebLogic Cluster
- Oracle WebLogic Domain
- Oracle WebLogic Server

[1] Oracle's Service-Oriented Architecture (SOA) is a software suite used to quickly build and manage applications.

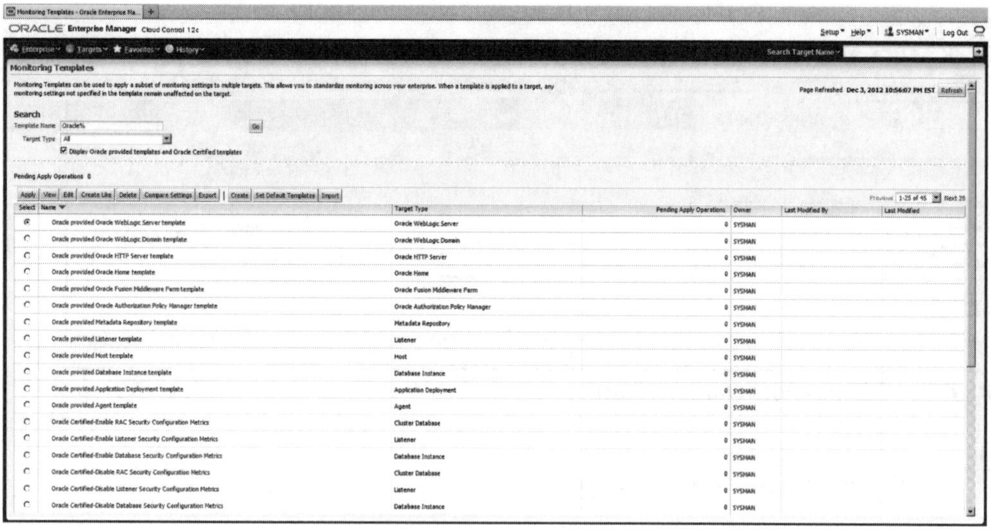

FIGURE 8-10. *Monitoring Templates form with Oracle-supplied templates*

Oracle provides several templates for each target type. Some templates include security metrics; others are configured for various functional extensions in the target itself. For example, the Oracle-provided database instance templates include templates for databases using Asynchronous Queues (AQs) and others for databases that use Streams. The Oracle-supplied templates cannot be modified, but they can be applied to targets like custom templates. Perhaps more importantly, the Oracle-supplied templates can be used as the starting point for custom templates.

Creating Monitoring Templates Monitoring templates can be created with three methods. The first involves building a template from scratch. In this case the DBA chooses which of the standard or extension metrics should be included in the template and modifies the thresholds. Due to the large number of metrics, this can be a time-consuming task. The second approach involves using a currently existing template or an Oracle-provided template as the basis for a new template. In this case you select a template and click the Create Like button. The final method builds a template from a currently configured target. This is often a preferred method because over a period of time we have tweaked a target's thresholds to a desired, comfortable setting. Alarms in these cases are valid and provide the DBA with proactive notification.

FIGURE 8-11. *Create Monitoring Template: Copy Target Settings*

Once the base metrics are determined, the steps are the same for finalizing the template. In this case we will build a template from an existing target. Start the template creation process by clicking the Create button on the main Monitoring Templates form (see Figure 8-11).

In this case, we will choose the Cloud Control Repository database as the source of our settings, as shown here:

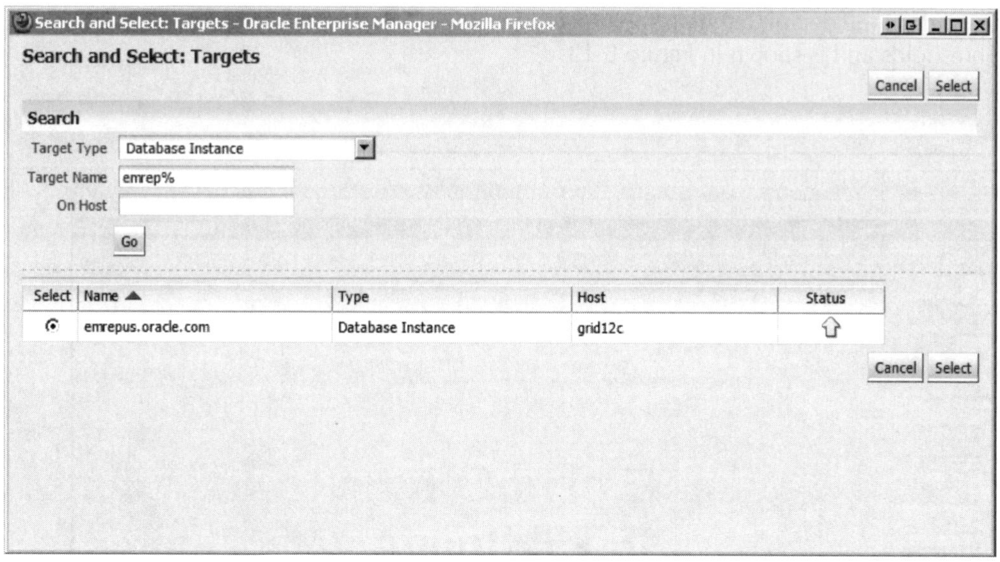

When you click Continue, the system produces a copy of the target's metrics and thresholds for the new template. Next we need to give the new template a unique name, "Repository Metrics," as shown in Figure 8-12.

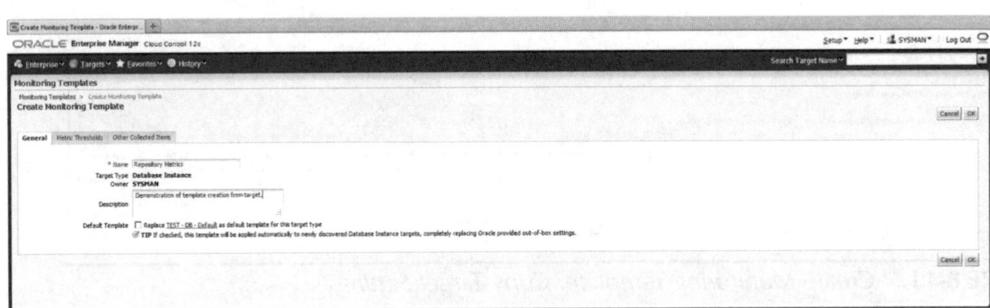

FIGURE 8-12. *Create Monitoring Template – General tab*

Note that on the General tab the template can be configured as a Default Template. If this option is selected, the metrics will automatically be applied to the target type rather than the stock metrics ("out of the box") provided by Oracle. Once we finish the template creation process, we will examine the mechanism available to manage the default templates for each target type. The next tab is Metric Thresholds and is shown in Figure 8-13.

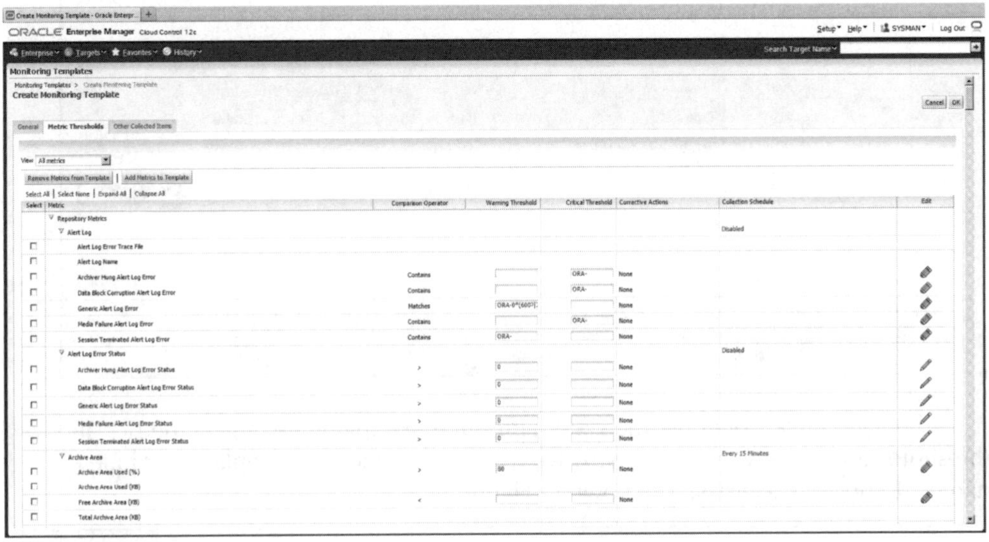

FIGURE 8-13. *Create Monitoring Template – Metric Thresholds tab*

The Metric Thresholds tab is, of course, the heart of the monitoring template. From this form, we determine when alarms are raised and whether they will be considered Critical or Warning. We also determine whether desired new metrics can be added to the template, even if they did not exist in the original source. However, please note that you can only add metrics from the currently available applicable targets. You cannot retrieve metrics at this point from another template (for some reason). In addition, metrics can be removed from the template. From this page, clicking the Pencil(s) icon for any metric leads to the Edit Advanced Settings form (see Figure 8-14).

As you may have noticed, the Edit Advanced Settings icon may be represented by a single pencil or several. This indicates whether or not the metric can monitor objects at different threshold settings: A group of pencils indicate that the metric can monitor multiple objects using different threshold values for each object. For example, the Tablespace Space Used (%) metric can monitor multiple tablespaces each with its own threshold setting; see Figure 8-15.

Of course, since we are creating a template, it is important to note that some targets may not have the corresponding object, or it may be defined differently. The template will still apply even though some individual objects may not exist.

The Advanced Settings form offers several notable features:

- Configure Corrective Actions in the event the thresholds are exceeded. This option provides for a job to be automatically executed if either a warning or critical metric is reached. Corrective Actions are configured and managed in a separate Cloud Control module. Please note that since we are configuring a template, it is important that the selected Correction Action be compatible with all targets of the applicable type. That is, the correction action should not be tailored to a specific target.

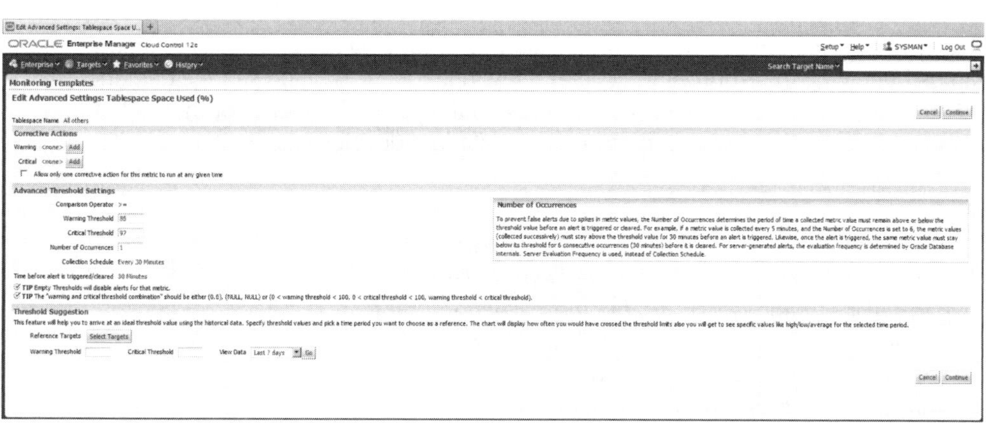

FIGURE 8-14. *Monitoring Templates – Edit Advanced Settings: Tablespace Space Used*

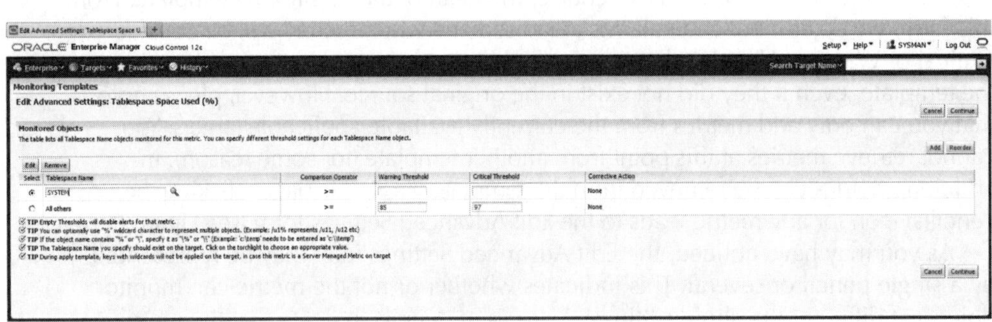

FIGURE 8-15. *Monitoring Templates – Edit Advanced Settings: Monitored Objects*

- Advanced Threshold Settings can be configured. The parameter of interest in this case is Number of Occurrences. If desired, the threshold can be configured to only trigger after a specified number of occurrences.
- The Threshold Suggestion feature, shown in Figure 8-16, is only applicable for collected metrics. The system will compare potential thresholds with historical data from a user-specified target. In the case of Tablespace Space Used (%), we can select a corresponding target and see how proposed thresholds would respond to recent data collections (the last 24 hours, 7 days, and 31 days). (Unfortunately, the Threshold Suggestion functionality does not appear to be working correctly in some versions.)

From the Metric Thresholds tab we can also configure the Collection Schedule for the various metric sets. For example, Figure 8-17 displays the collection configuration for the archive area. There are several items to note on this form. First, if desired the metric data collection can be disabled. Naturally, reducing the collection of metrics can be beneficial to resources in general – less network, CPU, and storage demand. In some cases, the DBA may have no interest in the particular metric or the associated target, for example, performance data in a development system.

NOTE

There is a difference between disabling metric monitoring and disabling metric collection. From this particular screen we can disable the collection of the metric data, which will also disable any monitoring. Or, we can continue to collect the metric for statistical purposes, but disable alarms by entering null values for the critical and warning thresholds.

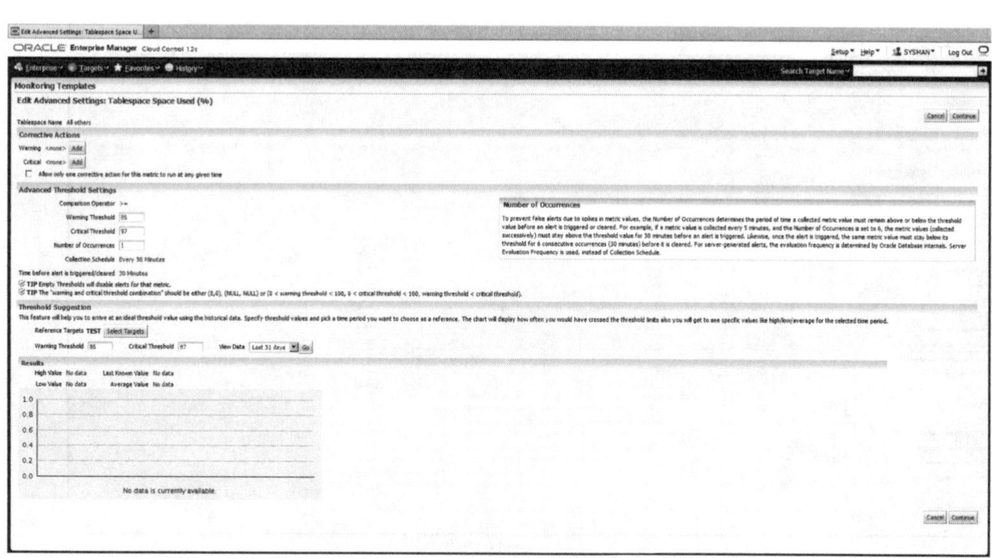

FIGURE 8-16. *Monitoring Templates – Edit Advanced Settings: Threshold Suggestion*

From the Collection Schedule page we can also modify the collection schedule and the upload frequency. For example, in the case of the Archive Area we can collect space data every 15 minutes and then either upload this data to the OMS on a regular schedule or only when an threshold is reached ("Alerting Only"). If we elect to only update the data to the OMS once an hour, the Cloud Control statistics for this metric will only be current to the last hour and each update will include four sets of metric data (one collection every 15 minutes for each hour). Note, however,

FIGURE 8-17. *Monitoring Templates – Metric Thresholds tab: Collection Schedule*

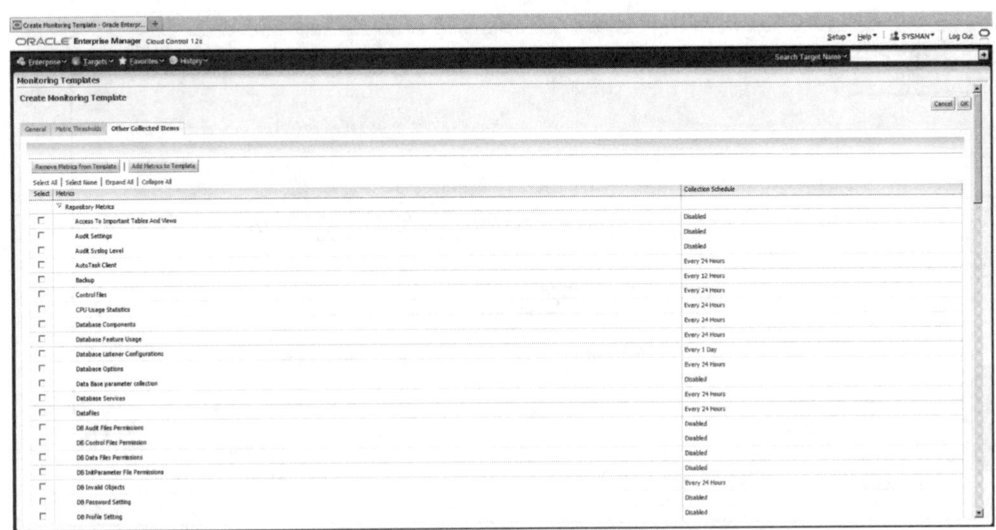

FIGURE 8-18. *Monitoring Templates – Other Collected Items*

that in the event the Agent detects a threshold violation, the collected metric data is uploaded immediately. Finally, the Affected Metrics section indicates which specific metric values are impacted by changes in the collection schedule.

The next tab, shown in Figure 8-18, of the Edit Monitoring Templates page is Other Collected Items. This tab specifies the collection of nonmetric information that is related to the target. As with the metric data, on this form you can control what information is collected and the collection schedule.

Finally, as with the numerous other constructs within Cloud Control, you can denote the access to the monitoring template (Figure 8-19). Grants can be made

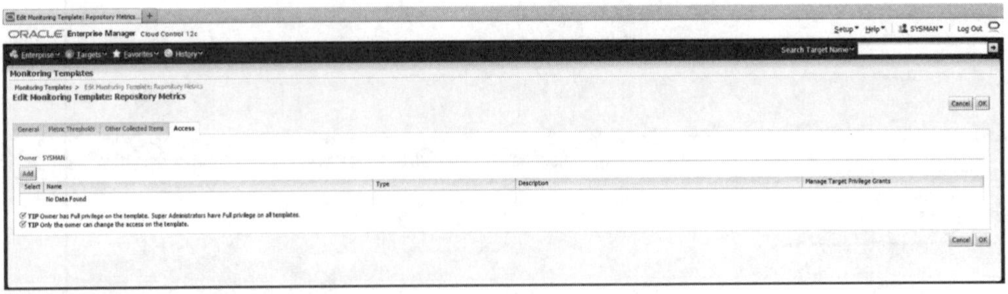

FIGURE 8-19. *Monitoring Templates – Access tab*

directly to other administrators or to roles. Once the information in the various tabs has been completed, clicking OK will complete the creation of the template.

Applying Monitoring Templates to Targets As addressed earlier, a monitoring template can be applied to one or more applicable targets, or to composite targets such as groups. For composite targets, the template is applied to all the member targets that are of the appropriate type. If you later add an applicable target to a group, however, the template will need to be reapplied. You apply a monitoring template to a group by first selecting the template and then clicking the OK button (Figure 8-20).

By clicking the Add button we can specify one or more targets of the same type or composite targets for application of the template. In this case we are applying a template to our Test Systems group created earlier. When the template is applied, the metric settings such as thresholds, comparison operators, and corrective actions are copied to the applicable destination target(s). In addition, metric collection schedules including collection frequency and upload interval are also copied to the target(s). In many cases metrics will already exist on the targets. How the template metrics affect the currently existing metrics is determined by two Apply Options, shown in Figure 8-21:

- **Template will completely replace all metric settings in the target** When this option is selected, all the currently existing metrics are removed and only the template metrics are applied. This is generally the preferred approach as this effectively eliminates and/or clears alerts from the pre-existing metrics.
- **Template will only override metrics that are common to both template and target** This option maintains any pre-existing metrics on the target,

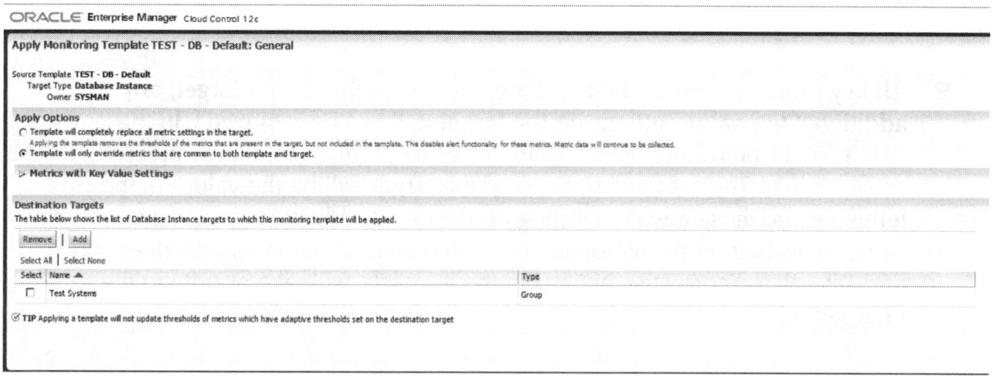

FIGURE 8-20. *Monitoring Templates – Apply Options*

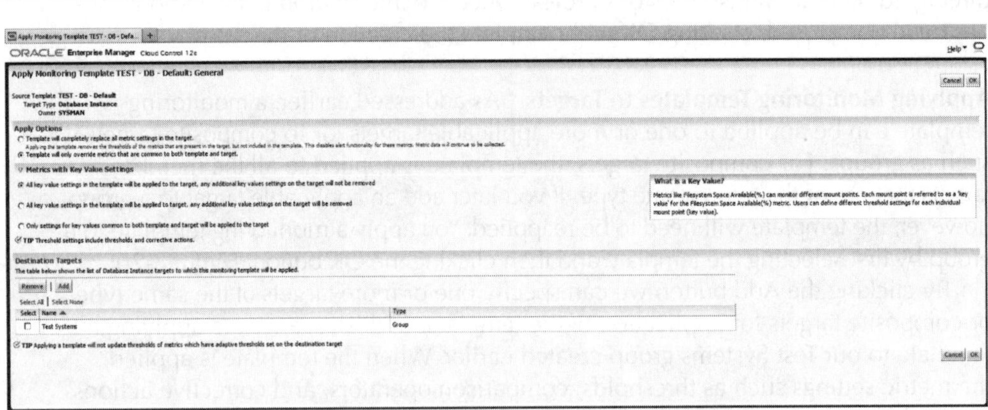

FIGURE 8-21. *Monitoring Templates – Apply: Key Value Settings*

but updates any common metrics with the new values from the template. Existing target metrics that do not exist in the template will remain unaffected. When this option is selected, additional template apply operations are made available for metrics with multiple objects (or key value settings).

As discussed earlier, some metrics provide for multiple objects, for example the Tablespace Space Used (%) metric. We may have added additional tablespaces to the metric in addition to the default classification "All others." In turn, the target itself may also have multiple objects (tablespaces) defined for this metric. Cloud Control refers to metrics with multiple defined objects as Metrics with Key Value Settings. How the template applies override metrics in this case is determined by one of the following options:

- **All key value settings in the template will be applied to the target, any additional key value settings on the target will not be removed** In this case Cloud Control performs a union of all the defined multiple objects or key values. The resulting settings on the target will be the values in the template and those already existing on the client. When the same key value exists both in the template and on the target, the threshold value and any related corrective actions in the template will take priority in the final settings.

- **All key value settings in the template will be applied to the target, any additional key value settings on the target will be removed** This approach is relatively self-explanatory; the template takes precedence and any prior multiple object values are removed.
- **Only settings for key values common to both template and target will be applied** In this case only the intersection of the set of template key values and existing key values will be applied to the target. For example, if the same tablespace name or the generic value "All others" exists in both the template and the target, then this key value will be included in the resulting set. Any existing target key values that do not have matching template values will also remain in the resulting set with their original settings.

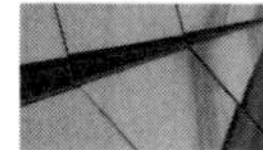

NOTE
How key value settings are applied to the target is only applicable if the template is configured to override the target settings. If the template replace option is selected, any earlier metric values on the target are discarded.

Template application is performed in the background as an asynchronous job. After you apply a template, the Pending Apply Operations column on the Monitoring Templates page displays the status of the job. If there are Pending Apply Operations, you can click on the number and see the status of each of the apply operations on the applicable targets. If desired, the application process can be stopped at this point. However, once the template is applied the procedure cannot be reversed.

Monitoring Templates Utilities Although not directly related to our operational maintenance objective, there are several template utilities worthy of note.

- **Compare settings between template and targets** This feature makes it easy to see how a target's metric settings differ from those defined in a template. This feature is useful for verifying whether a monitoring template that you applied to multiple targets successfully changes all target monitoring settings (except those configured for template override) to those of the template. This same functionality is also offered through the Information Publisher interface. Information Publisher's reporting capabilities give greater flexibility for displaying and distributing metric comparison data.
- **Exporting and importing monitoring templates** For portability, monitoring templates can be exported to an XML file and then imported to another Cloud Control system.

- **Defining default templates (Figure 8-22)** As noted earlier, when a template is created the option is provided to make the template the default for targets of its applicable type. A global default templates form is also provided. This page is reached by clicking on the Default Templates link located below the Related Links section of the Monitoring Templates page (please see Figure 8-9). On this page you can implement, change, or remove default templates for each of the target types.

- **Historical monitoring of template application operations** Another link available in the Related Links section of the Monitoring Templates page is Past Apply Operations (Figure 8-23). By default Cloud Control retains the monitoring template's apply history for a period of 180 days. (The past apply retention period for monitoring templates can be changed via the Cloud Control PL/SQL API procedure: `mgmt_tempate_ui.modify_purge_policy(p_retention_days=><num_days>)`.) Past apply data can also be reported through the Information Publisher interface, but this link provides a quick status.

At this point we have grouped our targets into logical collections and we have also defined coordinated sets of monitoring templates for these groups. We have applied the templates to the groups so our targets are now being monitored. We have performed these steps at the group level rather than with individual targets.

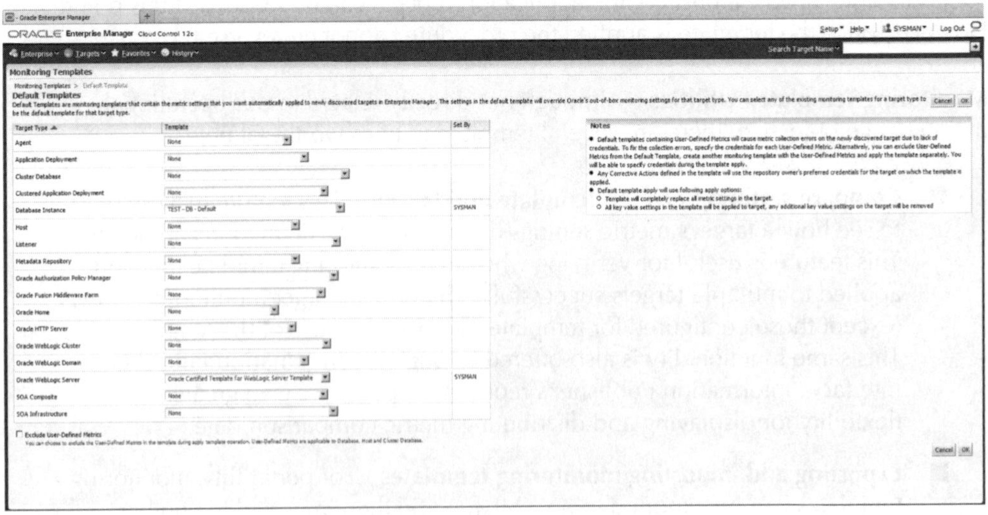

FIGURE 8-22. *Monitoring Templates – Default Templates*

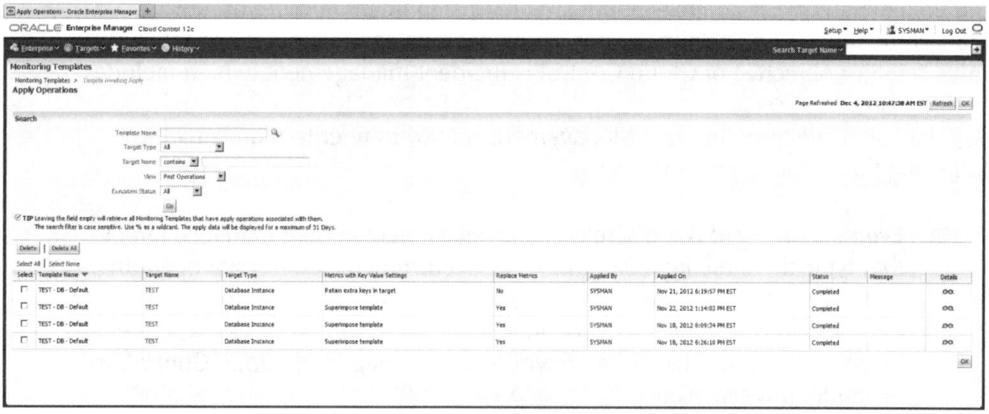

FIGURE 8-23. *Monitoring Templates – past Apply Operations*

If need be, we can modify individual target metrics, thresholds, and, corrective actions. The individual target metrics can be configured to prevent templates from overriding their settings. Specifying individual target metrics, however, generally requires a period of observation and tweaking before the preferred values are determined. However, as even small Cloud Control installations are likely to quickly accumulate dozens of targets, if not hundreds, Groups and Monitoring Templates are the only feasible means to efficiently maintain the operational environment.

Now that monitoring is implemented, we need to determine what actions should take place when thresholds are reached and events are raised. Generally events are configured to generate a notification of one type or another. In earlier versions of Enterprise Manager, notifications were the sole result of a raised event, although they did offer the ability to tag and propagate events to external systems via the Data Exchange mechanism; events could also trigger SNMP traps. In Cloud Control, however, this functionality is greatly enhanced through the Incident Rules interface. Prior versions simply provided Notification Rules for configuring event actions, but Incident Rules are more complex and offer greater functionality.

Incident Rules

Incident Rules and the associated Incident Manager are new Cloud Control functionality. Earlier versions of Enterprise Manager supported Notification Rules. As the name implies, Notification Rules dictated the notification method activated when an event was detected. In Cloud Control, however, the concept and function of notification rules has been replaced with a three-tier system consisting of Event Management, Incident Management, and Problem Management. Both the breadth and depth of the management features have expanded substantially. Along with multiple management contexts, there are also a significant number of new management functions. While the goal in earlier versions was basically notification rules, a major objective of Cloud Control is incident management (which includes notification).

The collective term Incident Management is used to refer to managing the following three categories of issues:

- **Events** An *event* is a discrete occurrence detected on a managed target that typically indicates something has occurred outside normal operating conditions. The occurrence is at a particular point in time and may indicate normal or problematic behavior. In general, an event indicates that something of interest has occurred in an environment managed by Cloud Control, for example, low tablespace free space.

- **Problems** A *problem* is defined as specifically an Oracle software error. A problem is often identified when the recommended action is to raise a Service Request with Oracle Support. For the current release, problems pertain to the diagnostic results stored in the Automatic Diagnostic Repository (ADR), which are automatically raised by Oracle software when it encounters critical errors in the software. For example, if a critical ORA-600 error is thrown by the database, it would be flagged as a problem and this would automatically trigger the corresponding ADR error. Obviously, a problem is a type of event. It constitutes something that occurs outside normal, or expected, behavior. However, Oracle distinguishes this issue from normal events based on its anticipated resolution path. In contrast to events, problems are expected to require resources that are external to the enterprise. The primary resolution path for a problem involves contact with Oracle Support, for example, a patch, upgrade, or workaround.

- **Incidents** Oracle considers *incidents* to be the logical task associated with resolving one or more events or problems. The concept is that incidents manage the response to events or problems. An incident is the product of one or more events or problems that *need to be managed.* Many events are informational, others are redundant, and some are correlated with each other. In some cases, events may be associated with problems. On the other hand, a single event by itself may require generation of an incident.

As a general example, limited available storage on a server can induce multiple events. Monitoring thresholds may be exceeded for several host and database metrics including Tablespace Free Space (%/MB), Archive Area Used (%/MB), Free Archive Area (MB), Dump Area Used (%), Free Dump Area (KB), Filesystem Space Available (%/MB), Total Disk Available (%), and Total Disk Space Available.

Although numerous alarms are raised, the solution is a single task, adding more disk space. Modifying disk space is the incident that needs to be managed, not the individual events. Adding additional disk space may require the assistance of several departments and/or individuals including storage and system administrators. Incident Management provides the utilities to manage this workflow as the task is completed and the issue resolved. The resolution of an incident can be manual or automated. If the resolution of an incident is not immediately identifiable, functions are available to assist with root-cause analysis, for example, the Incident Manager can be configured to interface with the My Oracle Support Knowledge Base.

The Incident Manager provides the ability to search, view, manage, and resolve incidents impacting the environment. Specifically, the following functions are supported:

- Prioritize, escalate, and track incidents through various states of resolution
- Assign incidents to specific personnel
- Access in-context diagnostic and resolution information
- Access My Oracle Support
- Ability to provide a manual summary
- Ability to add user comments
- Ability to manually clean the incident
- Ability to create a ticket

The Incident Management System is a significant addition to the Enterprise Manager tool set. It offers a great deal of new functionality, much of which is beyond the scope of this guide. In addition, effectively managing an environment via incidents involves planning, setup, implementation, and testing. These steps need to be customized based on the enterprise's resources, personnel, and policies. For operational purposes, we need to first concentrate on managing the monitored events and ensuring that notifications are being distributed. Fortunately, the system is flexible, and if need be, we can manually convert events in to incidents.

As noted earlier, the Incident Management system is composed of the Incident Manager and Incident Rules. Incident Rules determine what actions should be taken when events and problems occur, such as performing notifications. Beyond notifications, rules can also instruct Cloud Control to perform specific actions, such as creating or updating incidents. The actions can also be conditional in nature. For example, a rule action can be defined to page a DBA when an event severity is critical or just send e-mail if it is a warning.

Although there is a plethora of new functionality, do not lose sight of the forest from among the trees; notification is the heart of any monitoring system.

Creating Incident Rules Incident Rules can be accessed from the Setup menu. Figure 8-24 displays the default, out-of-box, rule sets provided by Oracle. These rules are intended to provide event notification, incident creation, and event clearing based on typical scenarios. As a best practice, Oracle recommends that DBAs create their own rule sets based on the out-of-box rules. Changes to out-of-box rule set definitions and the actions they perform can be made by Oracle at any time and will be applied during patching or software upgrade. In the current version there are two out-of-box rule sets:

- Incident Management Ruleset for All Targets
- Event Management Ruleset for Self Update

The first set of rules provides a nice template for building custom rules. The second set of rules basically notifies the DBA when new updates are available to the Cloud Control modules. These default rules are enterprise rules. There are two types of rule sets. Enterprise rules are used to implement global operational practices within your organization. Private rules are the second type of rule set. These rules are used when an administrator simply wants to monitor a target and be notified but not as a standard business practice. The only action a private rule can perform is to send e-mail to the rule set owner. Due to their limited functionality, private rule sets are seldom used.

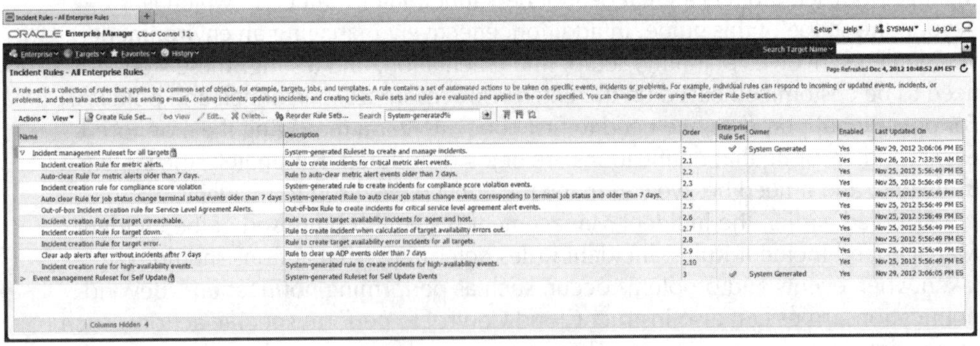

FIGURE 8-24. *Incident Rules – All Enterprise Rules*

A *rule set* is a collection of rules that generally apply to a collection of objects such as targets (hosts, databases, and groups), jobs, metric extensions, or self updates. A rule set takes configured actions to automate the processing of underlying events, problems, or incidents. Because they can be tailored to address issues from specific targets, one rule set can be created that organizes rules that will be used on production systems, and another rule set can be added for rules for development and test systems.

A rule instructs Cloud Control to take a specific action when events or other issues occur. The most common action is to send an e-mail notification; however, rules can also do other actions such as executing a script. The rules within a rule set are executed in a specified order, as are the rule sets themselves. Because rules operate on incoming issues, if you create a new rule, it will not act retroactively on events, problems, or incidents that have already occurred. Every rule is composed of two parts:

- **Criteria** The events, problems, or incidents on which the rule applies.
- **Action(s)** The ordered set of one or more operations on the specified issue. Further, each action can be executed based on additional conditions.

Each rule within a rule set is applied to an event, problem, or incident. That is, as each issue is received, it is processed through each rule of the rule set. Further, each issue is also processed through each rule set. The order of processing is dependent on the user-specified configuration.

In order to demonstrate the Incident Rule functionality, we will continue with our earlier project and create a rule set that manages events that are raised within our Test Systems group. We will need to perform the following steps to implement the desired behavior:

1. Create a new rule set tailored to the Test Systems group and based on an out-of-box rule set ("Create Like Rule Set").
2. Modify the rules within the Test Systems Rule set to meet the desired objectives.
3. Reorder the rule sets to ensure proper event evaluation.

In order to Create Like Rule Set, select the desired rule set and then from the Actions menu, select the corresponding option. Figure 8-25 is the initial page of the Edit Rule Set process. As you can see, the rule set is applied specifically to targets in the Test System. When you click the Save button in the upper right-hand corner, your new rule set is created.

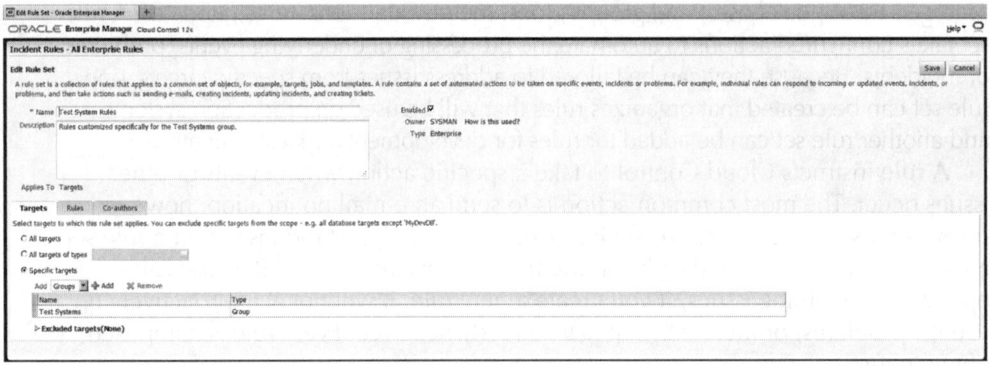

FIGURE 8-25. *Incident Rules – Edit Rule Set*

In Figure 8-26, our new rule set has been created and it contains a copy of all the rules in the out-of-box rule set Incident Management Ruleset for all Targets. Therefore, at this point, the Test System Rules set includes the following rules:

- Incident creation rule for metric alerts
- Auto-clear rule for metric alerts older than seven days
- Incident creation rule for compliance score violation
- Auto-clear rule for job status change terminal status events older than seven days
- Out-of-box incident creation rule for service level agreement alerts
- Incident creation rule for target unreachable
- Incident creation rule for target down
- Incident creation rule for target error
- Clear adp alerts after without incidents after seven days
- Incident creation rule for high-availability events

As you may have noticed, each of these rules has an associated number, and this value determines the order in which events, problems, or incidents are evaluated.

The target of our rule set is the Test Systems group. Since we are dealing with a nonproduction environment, we will concentrate at this time on notifications rather

Incident Rules - All Enterprise Rules

Page Refreshed Dec 4, 2012 10:51:10 AM EST

A rule set is a collection of rules that applies to a common set of objects, for example, targets, jobs, and templates. A rule contains a set of automated actions to be taken on specific events, incidents or problems. For example, individual rules can respond to incoming or updated events, incidents, or problems, and then take actions such as sending e-mails, creating incidents, updating incidents, and creating tickets. Rule sets and rules are evaluated and applied in the order specified. You can change the order using the Reorder Rule Sets action.

Name	Description	Order	Enterprise Rule Set	Owner	Enabled	Last Updated On
Incident management Ruleset for all targets	System-generated Ruleset to create and manage incidents.	1	✔	System Generated	Yes	Dec 4, 2012 10:51:00 AM ES
Event management Ruleset for Self Update	System-generated Ruleset for Self Update Events	2	✔	System Generated	Yes	Dec 4, 2012 10:51:08 AM ES
Test System Rules	Rules customized specifically for the Test Systems group.	3	✔	SYSMAN	Yes	Dec 4, 2012 10:50:50 AM ES
Notification Rule for All Metrics	Send email notification on all warning and critical severity alarms and also page the DBAs for critical issues.	3.1			Yes	Nov 29, 2012 2:56:21 PM ES
Incident creation Rule for metric alerts.	Rule to create incidents for critical metric alert events.	3.2			No	Nov 29, 2012 2:56:21 PM ES
Auto-clear Rule for metric alerts older than 7 days.	Rule to auto-clear metric alert events older than 7 days.	3.3			Yes	Nov 29, 2012 2:56:21 PM ES
Incident creation rule for compliance score violation	System-generated rule to create incidents for compliance score violation events.	3.4			No	Nov 29, 2012 2:56:21 PM ES
Auto clear Rule for job status change terminal status events older than 7 days	System-generated Rule to auto clear job status change events corresponding to terminal job status and older than 7 days.	3.5			Yes	Nov 29, 2012 2:56:21 PM ES
Out-of-box Incident creation rule for Service Level Agreement Alerts.	Out-of-box Rule to create incidents for critical service level agreement alert events.	3.6			No	Nov 29, 2012 2:56:21 PM ES
Incident creation Rule for target unreachable.	Rule to create target availability incidents for agent and host.	3.7			No	Nov 29, 2012 2:56:21 PM ES
Incident creation Rule for target down.	Rule to create incident when calculation of target availability errors out.	3.8			No	Nov 29, 2012 2:56:21 PM ES
Incident creation Rule for target error.	Rule to create target availability error incidents for all targets.	3.9			No	Nov 29, 2012 2:56:21 PM ES
Clear adp alerts after without incidents after 7 days	Rule to clear up ADP events older than 7 days	3.10			Yes	Nov 29, 2012 2:56:21 PM ES
Incident creation rule for high-availability events.	System-generated rule to create incidents for high-availability events.	3.11			No	Nov 29, 2012 2:56:21 PM ES

Columns Hidden 4

FIGURE 8-26. *Incident Rules – Edit Rule Set: Test System Rules*

than on incident creation and management. Therefore, the next step involves modifying several of the rules within our rule set. We will start with the very first rule, Incident creation rule for metric alerts. As already noted, we are only interested in notifications from this target group and at this time we do not want to automatically create incidents. Since we do not want to create or modify incidents with this particular rule set, we can either remove or disable the related rules. By disabling the rules at this time, we can re-enable them at a later date if desired. Rules can be disabled by simply selecting the rule and then using the Disable feature under the Actions menu.

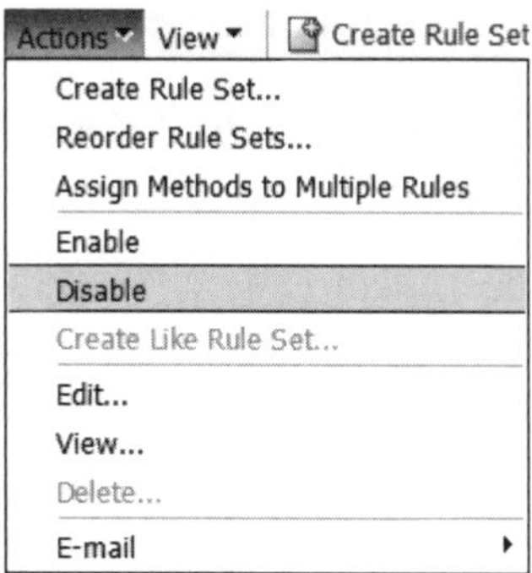

Figure 8-27 shows that the rule has been disabled within the rule set.

Finally, all the other rules associated with incident creation are also disabled. Unfortunately, the disable process cannot be executed against multiple rules, so each rule must be selected and disabled individually. The current Test System Rule set is displayed in Figure 8-28.

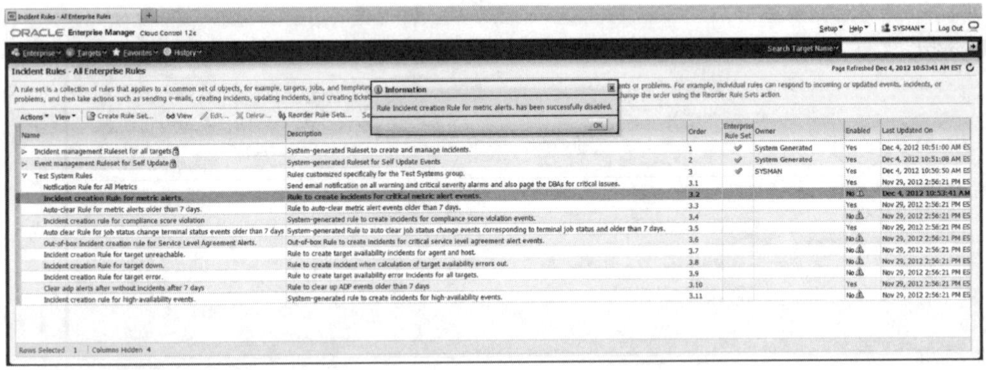

FIGURE 8-27. *Incident Rules – All Enterprise Rules – rule disabled*

Next we wish to create a rule that processes notifications for received events. In order to add a new rule to a rule set, we need to place the rule set in edit mode. Rule edit mode is reached by either selecting the rule set name—or any of the applicable rules in the set—and then clicking the Edit icon, or selecting the Edit submenu from the Actions menu. Once the Edit Rule Set page appears, click on the Rules tab to add, modify, or delete individual rules; see Figure 8-29.

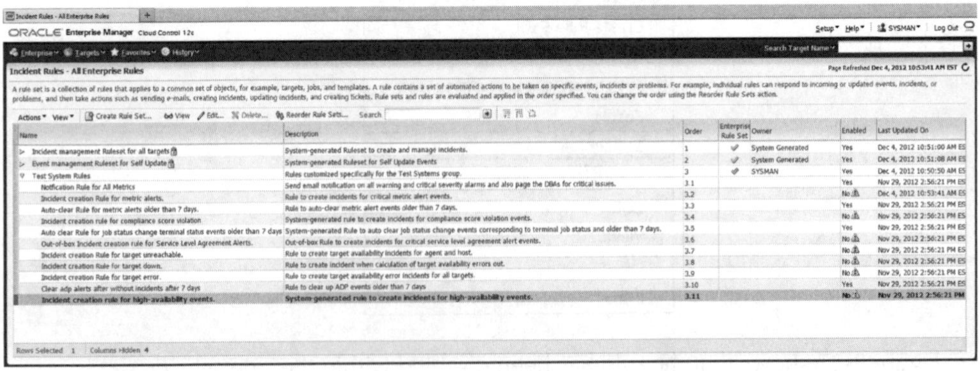

FIGURE 8-28. *Incident Rules – All Enterprise Rules – Test System Incident Rules disabled*

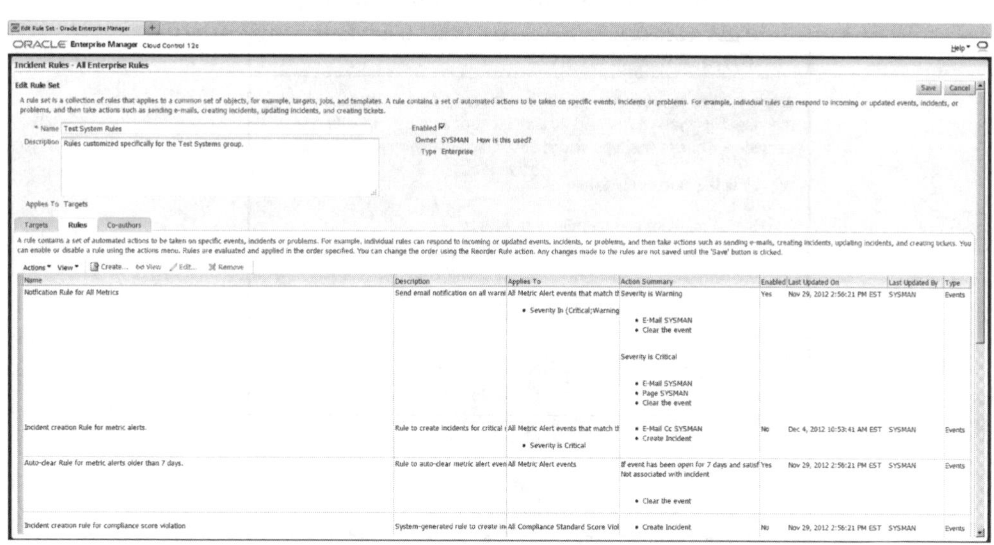

FIGURE 8-29. *Edit Rule Set – Test System Rules*

New rules can be created either from the Actions menu, as shown below, or from the Create menu icon. In either case, you are presented with a choice of three different types of rules to create:

1. Create a rule for incoming events or updates to events.
2. Create a rule for newly created incidents or updates to incidents.

3. Create a rule for newly created problems or updates to problems.

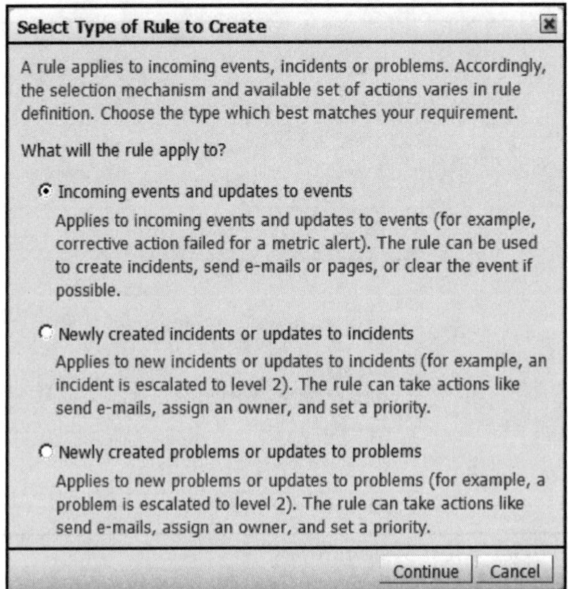

As we are interested in notifications for incoming events we will elect to build a rule for incoming events.

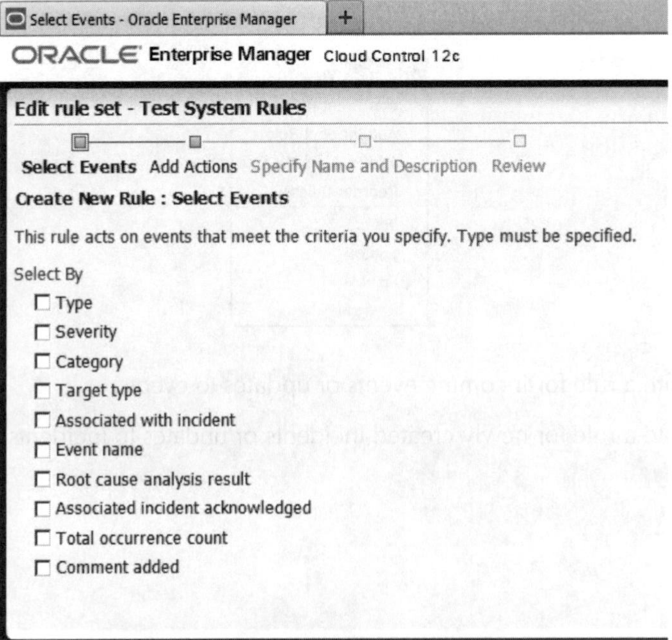

The Create New Rule function navigates us to the first of four pages. The first page is where the selection criteria are specified for the rule. At this point we determine the events that will trigger the rule. The first selection choice is event type. Cloud Control provides for the following event types:

- **Target Availability** A target's status, for example, Up, Down, Agent Unreachable, or Blackout.
- **Metric Alert** A target exceeds a configured threshold.
- **Metric Evaluation Error** A target detects an error when collecting data for a specific metric group – generally the error results in collection failure.
- **Job Status Change** Any changes to the Cloud Control jobs are treated as events.
- **Compliance Standard Rule Violation** This event is triggered for each violation of a compliance rule.
- **Compliance Standard Score Violation** Compliance scores are computed based on target attributes. Thresholds on the scoring trigger this event.
- **High Availability** These events are related to shutdown and startup operations, backups, and Data Guard functions (switchover, failover, and other state changes).
- **Service Level Agreement Alert** A service or service level objective is violated.
- **User-Reported** These are events created by end users.
- **Application Dependency and Performance Alert** These are J2EE-raised alerts indicating that some component has crossed thresholds.
- **Application Performance Management (APM) KPI Alert** A Key Performance Indicator (KPI) event is generated when an alert occurs for a metric within an APM-managed entity with a Business Application target.
- **JVM Diagnostic Threshold Violation** A metric threshold has been exceeded on a Java Virtual Machine target.

Along with type, event rules also allow selection based on the following criteria:

- **Severity** Rule applies to only the specified severity type(s): Fatal, Critical, Warning, Advisory, Informational, or Clear.

- **Category** The event rule is only applicable for one or more of the following categories: Availability, Business, Capacity, Configuration, Diagnostics, Error, Fault, Jobs, Load, Performance, and Security.
- **Target Type** The target is specific to one or more of the numerous types available within Cloud Control:
  - Agent
  - Application Deployment
  - Beacon
  - Database Instance
  - Database System
  - EM Service
  - Group
  - Host
  - Listener
  - Metadata Repository
  - OMS Console
  - OMS Platform
  - OMS and Repository
  - Oracle Authorization Policy Manager
  - Oracle Fusion Middleware Farm
  - Oracle HTTP Server
  - Oracle Home
  - Oracle Management Service
  - Oracle WebLogic Domain
  - Oracle WebLogic Server
- **Target Lifecycle Status** Event rule applies to targets with a specific lifecycle status, for example, production.
- **Associated with Incident** Event is related to a previously created incident.

- **Event Name** The selection criteria can be either the specific name or a pattern match.
- **Root Cause Analysis Result** Upon completion of a Root Cause Analysis (RCA) event, the rule applies to the event that is marked either as root cause or symptom. Alternatively, the rule can act on an RCA event when it is no longer a symptom.
- **Associated Incident Acknowledged** The rule applies when a DBA acknowledges an event that is associated with a specific incident.
- **Total Occurrence Count** This selection criterion involves duplicate events. When the total number of event occurrences reaches a specified number, the rule is applied.
- **Comment Added** Rule applies to events where an administrator adds a comment.

As we are interested in receiving notifications for all events in our previously configured monitoring template, we will select the event type Metric Alert and further specify that we are interested in all events of this type. In addition to event type, we also wish to specify that only events of severity Critical or Warning should be processed. Figure 8-30 shows that multiple selections are possible with some of the criteria.

After selecting the events to be processed by the rule, we now decide the actions to be taken. Click on the Next icon to move to the Add Actions page, as shown in Figure 8-31. Cloud Control provides for the following rule actions:

- E-mail
- Page (actually sending a shortened text message)[2]
- Advanced Notifications
  - Send SNMP Trap
  - Run OS Command
  - Run PL/SQL Procedure
- Create an Incident

---

[2] As with earlier versions of Enterprise Manager, the e-mail and page formats and contents can be site tailored.

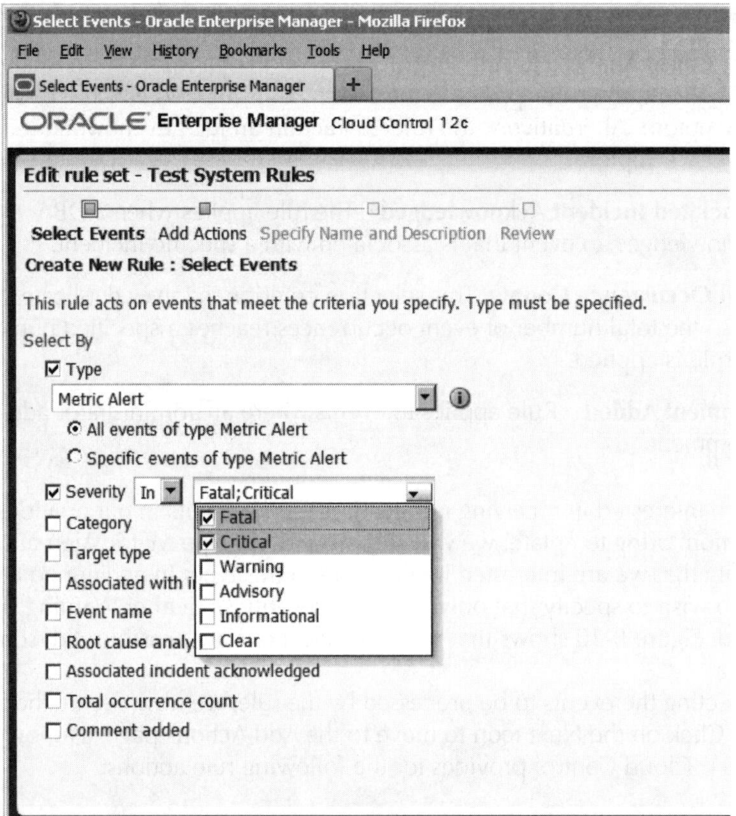

FIGURE 8-30. *Edit Rule Set – Test System Rules: Create New Rule – selection criteria*

- Set Workflow Attributes
- Create a Helpdesk Ticket
- Create/Update Service Request

Naturally, not all actions are available with each issue category: Event, Problem, or Incident. We are interested in two distinct actions to be performed when receiving events. For warning events we wish to receive an e-mail. For critical events we would like to receive both an e-mail and text message ("Page"). To create the first action, click the Add icon (see Figure 8-31).

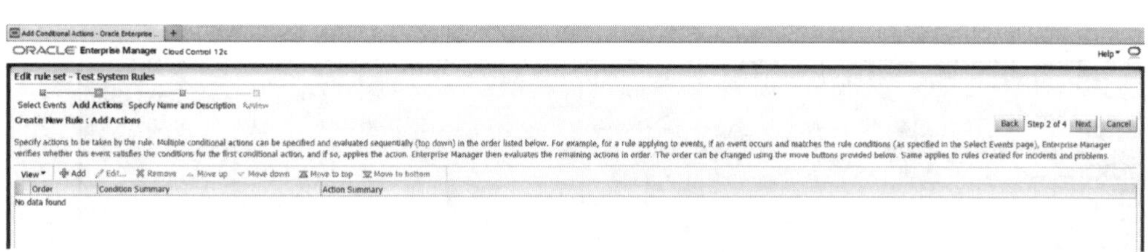

FIGURE 8-31. *Edit Rule Set – Test System Rules: Create New Rule – Add Actions*

Figure 8-32 displays the Add Conditional Actions form. In the first selection we select the option to only execute the action under specific conditions: when the severity level is Warning. We elect to not produce an incident. However, we do wish for a notification to be sent to the SYSMAN e-mail account. We do select the option to clear metric events that cannot be cleared automatically by Cloud Control. When you click Continue, this action is preserved, and you can configure a second action to address critical-level severity events – please see Figure 8-33.

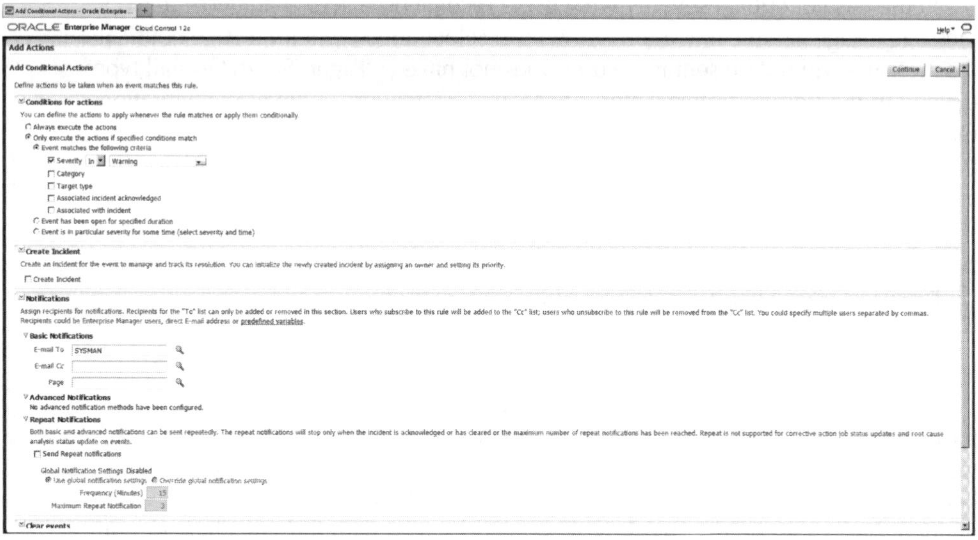

FIGURE 8-32. *Add Conditional Actions – Warning Severity*

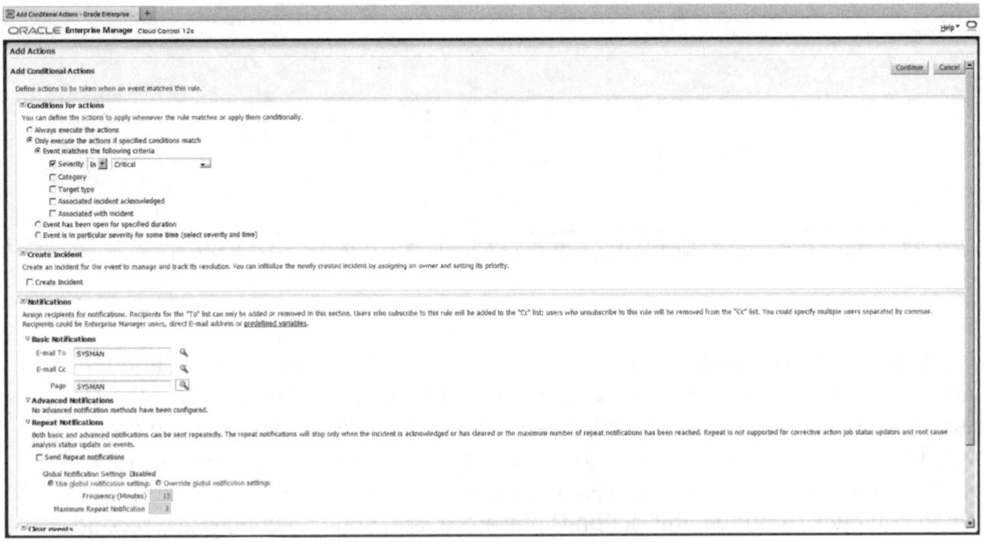

FIGURE 8-33. *Add Conditional Actions – Critical Severity*

In the case of critical severity we wish to receive both an e-mail and a text message ("Page"). Note that although we can select a recipient for a Page notification, the message will not be sent if the user does not have a "Pager (Short)" e-mail type defined in the Administrator's Enterprise Manager Password & Email configuration. Once the critical-level severity action setup is completed, click Continue to return to the Add Actions page. In Figure 8-34 the two configured actions for the metric events are displayed.

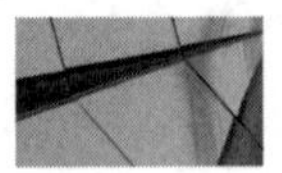

NOTE

E-mail configuration for Administrators is discussed in Chapter 6, "Cloud Control Console Configuration."

Clicking Next leads to Step 3 of the Create New Rule procedure, where we provide a name and, if desired, a description of the new rule. Clicking Next leads to the final review step, as shown in Figure 8-35. When you click Continue, the rule is finalized and the user is returned to the Edit Rule Set page. However, as the notification banner points out, the rule set is not saved with the rule changes until the Save button is clicked.

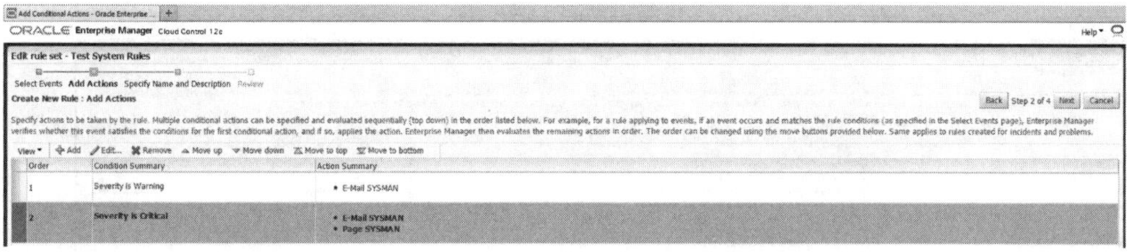

FIGURE 8-34. *Add Conditional Actions – completed*

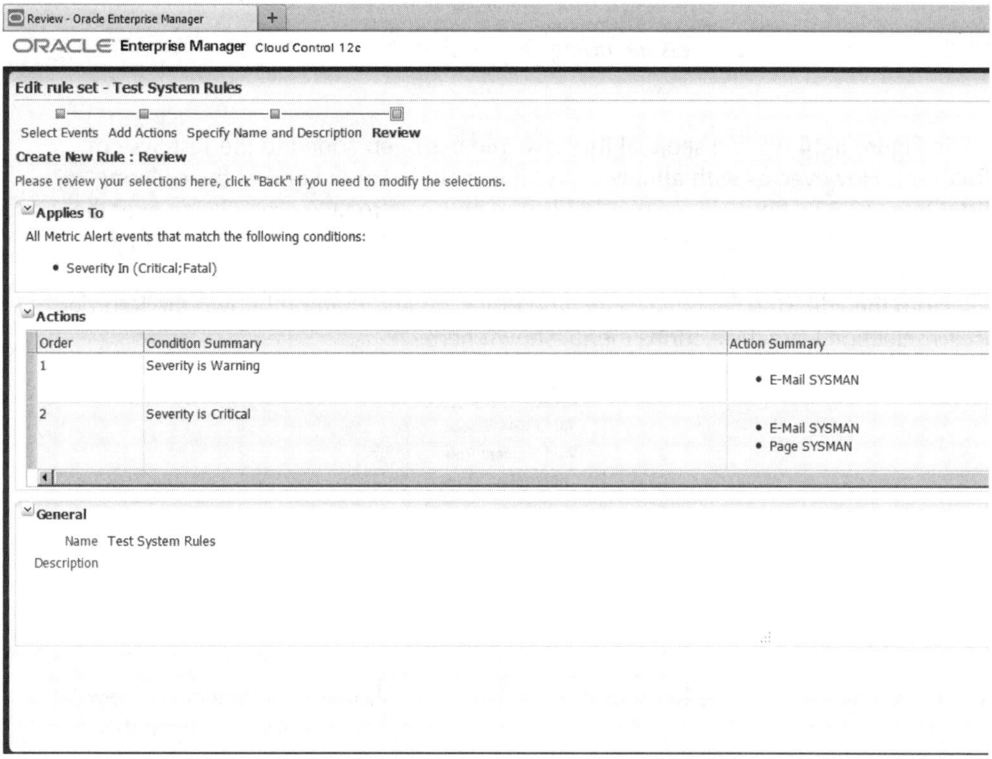

FIGURE 8-35. *Create New Rule: Review*

Incident Rules - All Enterprise Rules

ORACLE Enterprise Manager Cloud Control 12c

Setup ▾ Help ▾ SYSMAN ▾ Log Out

Enterprise ▾ Targets ▾ Favorites ▾ History ▾ Search Target Name ▾

Incident Rules - All Enterprise Rules

Page Refreshed Dec 4, 2012 11:05:29 AM EST

A rule set is a collection of rules that applies to a common set of objects, for example, targets, jobs, and templates. A rule contains a set of automated actions to be taken on specific events, incidents or problems. For example, individual rules can respond to incoming or updated events, incidents, or problems, and then take actions such as sending e-mails, creating incidents, updating incidents, and creating tickets. Rule sets and rules are evaluated and applied in the order specified. You can change the order using the Reorder Rule Sets action

Actions ▾ View ▾ Create Rule Set... View Edit... Delete... Reorder Rule Sets... Search

Name	Description	Order	Enterprise Rule Set	Owner	Enabled	Last Updated On
> Incident management Ruleset for all targets	System-generated Ruleset to create and manage incidents.	1	✓	System Generated	Yes	Dec 4, 2012 10:51:00 AM ES
> Event management Ruleset for Self Update	System-generated Ruleset for Self Update Events	2	✓	System Generated	Yes	Dec 4, 2012 10:51:08 AM ES
∨ Test System Rules	Rules customized specifically for the Test Systems group.	3	✓	SYSMAN	Yes	Dec 4, 2012 10:50:50 AM ES
Notification Rule for All Metrics	Send email notification on all warning and critical severity alarms and also page the DBAs for critical issues.	3.1			Yes	Nov 29, 2012 2:56:21 PM ES
Incident creation Rule for metric alerts.	Rule to create incidents for critical metric alert events.	3.2			No	Dec 4, 2012 10:53:41 AM ES
Auto-clear Rule for metric alerts older than 7 days.	Rule to auto-clear metric alert events older than 7 days.	3.3			Yes	Nov 29, 2012 2:56:21 PM ES
Incident creation rule for compliance score violation	System-generated rule to create incidents for compliance score violation events.	3.4			No	Nov 29, 2012 2:56:21 PM ES
Auto clear Rule for job status change terminal status events older than 7 days	System-generated Rule to auto clear job status change events corresponding to terminal job status and older than 7 days.	3.5			Yes	Nov 29, 2012 2:56:21 PM ES
Out-of-box Incident creation rule for Service Level Agreement Alerts.	Out-of-box Rule to create incidents for critical service level agreement alert events.	3.6			No	Nov 29, 2012 2:56:21 PM ES
Incident creation Rule for target unreachable.	Rule to create target availability incidents for agent and host.	3.7			No	Nov 29, 2012 2:56:21 PM ES
Incident creation Rule for target down.	Rule to create incident when calculation of target availability errors out.	3.8			No	Nov 29, 2012 2:56:21 PM ES
Incident creation Rule for target error.	Rule to create target availability error incidents for all targets.	3.9			No	Nov 29, 2012 2:56:21 PM ES
Clear adp alerts after without incidents after 7 days	Rule to clear up ADP events older than 7 days	3.10			Yes	Nov 29, 2012 2:56:21 PM ES
Incident creation rule for high-availability events.	System-generated rule to create incidents for high-availability events.	3.11			No	Nov 29, 2012 2:56:21 PM ES

Columns Hidden 4

FIGURE 8-36. *Enterprise Rule Sets including Test System Rules*

In Figure 8-36 we can see that the new rule has been added to the Test System Rules set. However, as with all new rules, it is included at the end of the ordering list (Order #3.11). Because we would like the new rule to take precedence over the other rules in the set, we need to change the ordering. This configuration change needs to be completed on the Edit Rule Set page.

From the Edit Rule Set page, select the Rules tab and then pull down the Reorder Rules selection from the Actions menu, shown here.

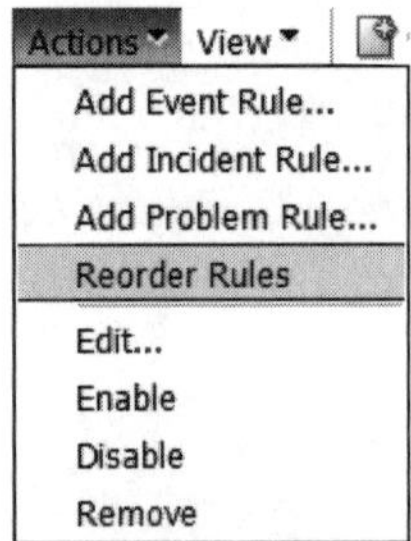

These commands open the Reorder Rules sub-form as shown next. Select our new rule, Notification Rule for All Metrics, and click the top of form icon to place this rule at the beginning of the list. Click OK to confirm the change. The Edit Rule Set

page should indicate our new rule first in the list. Click Save to complete the modifications to the rule set.

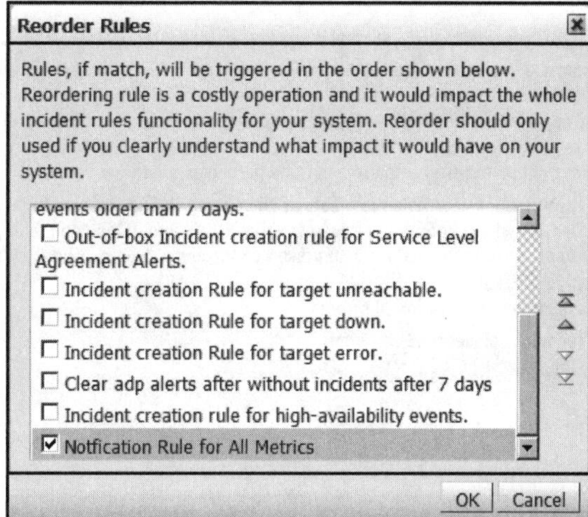

We should now be at the Incident Rules page. Our new rule, however, is listed at the end of the order of rule sets – which is the expected location for new rule sets. At this point we now need to reorder the rule sets. This operation is completed by using the Reorder Rule Sets functionality located on the Actions menu, shown here.

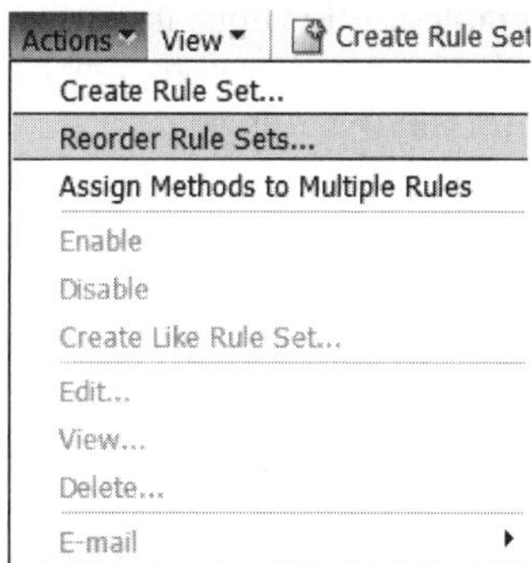

The Reorder Rule Sets sub-form is very similar to the form used to reorder individual rules. Simply select the rule set of interest, in this case our Test System Rules set, and relocate the rule set within the list. Click OK to complete the modification. The Enterprise Rules display should now show the Test System Rules at the top of the list (Order #1) as desired. You may have to re-sort the list based on the Order column.

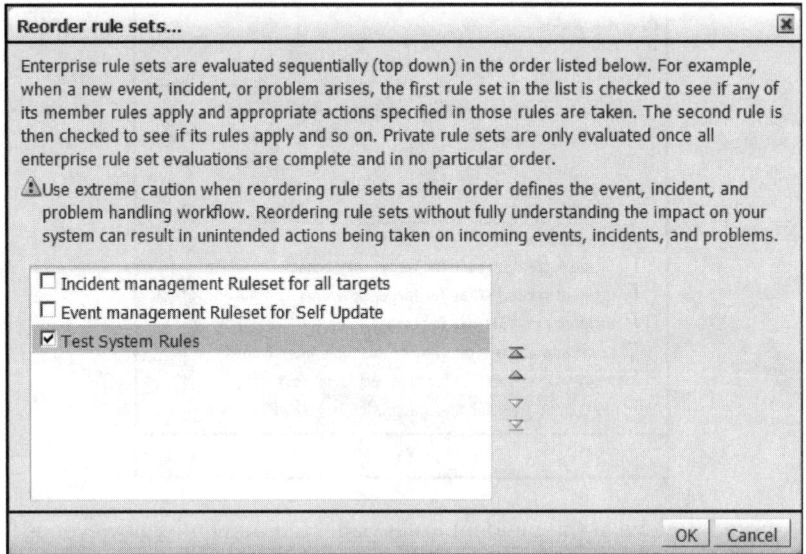

We have now completed implementation and configuration of a rule set tailored to our Test System group. Please note that the out-of-box rule set Incident Management Ruleset for all Targets is still enabled. All events, including events from the Test System group, will be processed by all rule sets; therefore, any applicable events will generate incidents as specified by the rules in this rule set.

Although we only configured Event rules in our new rule set, the process is very similar for Problem and Incident issues. All rules are made up of two pieces, selection criteria and actions. The criteria and actions differ slightly for each issue type, but the procedures, ordering, and related configuration steps are the same. We should now be able to receive notifications for events raised by objects in the Test System group. We can manage these events in the Incident Manager.

Incident Manager The Incident Manager is the companion tool to the Incident Rules. Events, Problems, or Incidents detected by the rules are collected and controlled in the Incident Manager. This tool provides a single reference point from which the user can search, view, manage, and resolve events, problems, and incidents. Incident Manager provides the following features:

- Filter incidents, problems, and events and offer custom views
- Ability to assign responsibility for an incident to a specific administrator

- Search for issues by various properties including:
    - Target Name
    - Target Type
    - Summary
    - Status
    - Lifecycle Status
- Manage incident resolution by assigning, tracking, prioritization, and escalation
- Drill down to in-context diagnostic information via action links to relevant targets

The Incident Manager page is accessible from the main Enterprise menu and the Monitoring sub-menu. In our case we are dealing specifically with events that have not generated incidents. Therefore we will use the Events without Incidents Standard view. Figure 8-37 and Figure 8-38 provide two versions of this form.

Selecting an event displays additional information and links from which the administrator can perform further analysis. When applicable, the event can be cleared from this form. This form also offers the ability to manually create an incident based upon the event. This functionality is accessed from the More menu

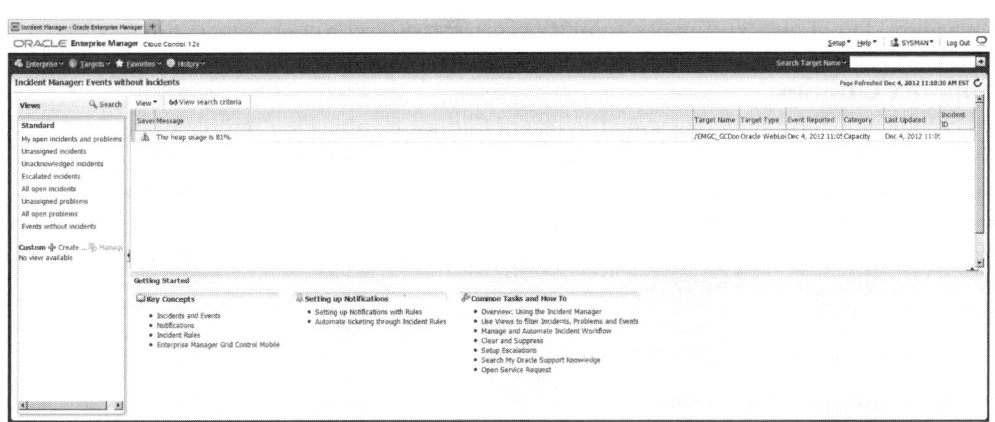

FIGURE 8-37. *Incident Manager – Standard View: Events without Incidents*

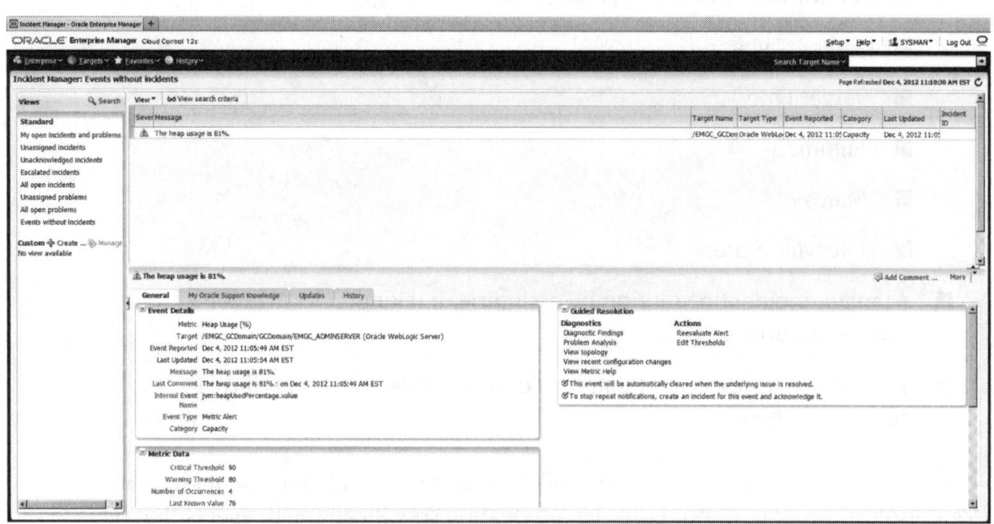

FIGURE 8-38. *Incident Manager – Standard View: Event Details*

on the lower-right portion of the screen in the event details. This menu also provides the ability to add an event to an already existing incident.

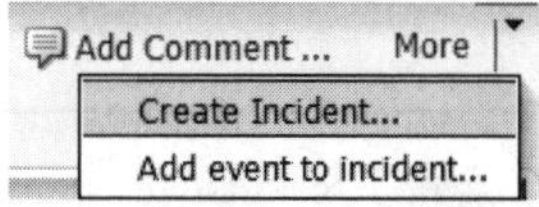

Support Utilities

Hopefully, you have now mastered the use of Groups, Monitoring Templates, and Incident Rules. These tools provide a strong basis from which more extensive functionality can be built. The following items are Cloud Control utilities that further help manage the operational needs of the enterprise. Some of these tasks and utilities are used on a routine basis, while others may only need to be performed once. We will cover the following:

- Credentials Management
- Command Line Interface

- Out Of Bound E-mail Notification[3]
- Changing the SYSMAN Passwords
- Configuring Blackouts

Credentials Management The details of the new Cloud Control credential utilities are covered in Chapter 7, "Cloud Control Security and User Management," but the importance of these new features bears repeating. Named and Preferred Credentials provide a means to handle the expansion in both targets and password complexity. Clinical studies have shown a strong correlation between passwords and psychopathology. In essence, the more passwords a DBA needs to manage, the greater the damage. Fortunately, we have a nonpharmacological treatment program available in Cloud Control. It is well worth the effort to gain an understanding of these new features.

Command Line Interface Cloud Control further extends functionality of the Enterprise Manager Command Line Interface (`emcli`). This utility incorporates many new features, especially with respect to Lifecycle Management capabilities. However, it appears that some functions that previously existed in the user interface have now been relocated to the command-line tool. One feature in particular is the ability to modify several events at the same time. In earlier versions it was possible to select multiple events and process them collectively from the user interface, but this is no longer the case in Cloud Control. Now the administrator must use the command line in order to clear events when Enterprise Manager cannot automatically detect the issue ("stateless").

As we discussed earlier, rules can be configured to address the management of these types of events, but this functionality is not implemented in the default, out-of-box rule sets. The command-line interface is very helpful for direct control of Cloud Control functionality, but it is hoped that the ability to select and manipulate several events at a time is returned to the GUI.

The command to clear one or more stateless alerts is listed following. Please note that you must first "log in" to Cloud Control via `emcli` before entering commands. In some cases it may also be necessary to synchronize the command-line interface with the Oracle Management Services (OMS), for example, `emctl sync`, as follows:

```
emcli -login -username=SYSMAN
emcli sync
emcli clear_stateless_alerts -older_than=number_in_days -target_type=target_type
-target_name=target_name [-include_members]
```

[3] These notifications are also often referred to as "Out-of-Band" communications, particularly in earlier versions of OMS.

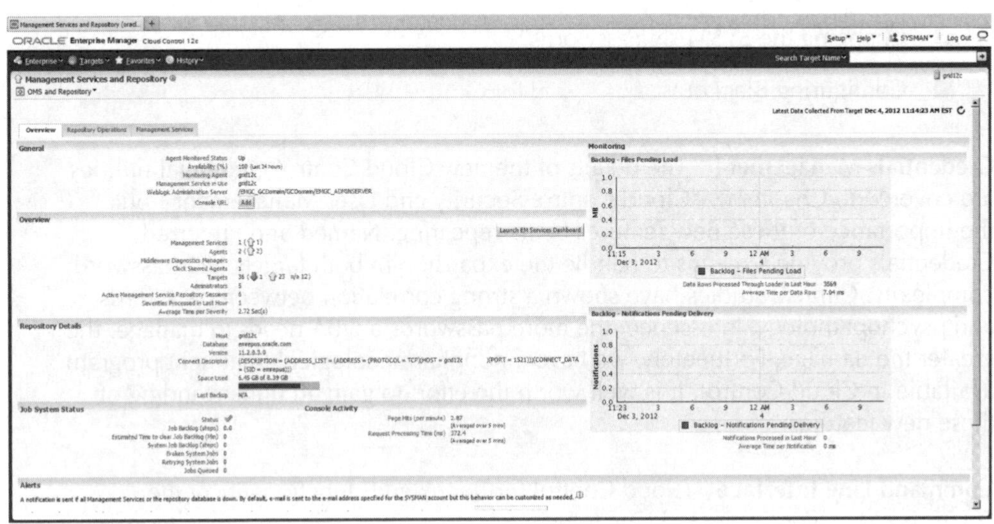

FIGURE 8-39. *Management Services and Repository – Monitoring Agent*

Out Of Bound (OOB) E-mail Notification As we become increasingly dependent on Cloud Control, it becomes more important for Enterprise Manager to monitor itself for its own availability. It performs this functionality by having the Management Agent run periodic checks for the availability of the Management Repository database and the Management Services. If the Agent detects that the Repository database is down or if the OMS services are down, then it executes a procedure to notify administrators of the problem. The notification procedure runs outside the regular mechanisms.

The Management Agent that is responsible for checking the availability of the Management Services and Repository is called the Monitoring Agent (Figure 8-39). You can determine the Monitoring Agent for your installation by displaying it in the Management Services and Repository Overview page.[4] This form can be reached by the corresponding link on the main Setup menu.

The OOB functionality is configured within the Management Agent.[5] However, the Agent is dependent on the `mailx` command on the OMS server to send an information message. Consequently, the `mailx` functionality needs to be configured and operational.

---

[4] In Cloud Control version 12.1.0.2, this page is simply labeled "Management Services."

[5] Please see MOS Bulletin 1472854.1, "How To Setup Out of Bound Email Notifications in 12c." The online help file currently directs the Administrator to nonexistent perl scripts.

The Agent relies upon e-mail settings in the emd.properties file ($AGENT_INST_HOME/sysman/config/emd.properties). Specifically, the required parameters need to be added and configured. Finally, the Management Agent needs to be restarted.

The following parameters are required for OOB notifications and example values:

```
emd_mail_address=scott.tiger@oracle.com
emd_email_gateway=smtp.grid.com
emd_from_email_address=agent@omsserver.com
```

After painstakingly configuring Cloud Control, there is nothing more disheartening than to miss a critical alarm due to service failure in the Repository or Management Services.

Changing the SYSMAN Password Changing the SYSMAN password in Cloud Control is a simple and painless task. If you inherit a system or otherwise fear the password that may be compromised, follow these steps:

1. Stop all of the OMS services:

   ```
   cd $OMS_HOME/bin
   emctl stop oms
   ```

   Please note that we do not include the `-all` option on the `stop` command. We need the Administration Server to be up in order to process the password change.

2. Modify the SYSMAN password:

   ```
   cd $OMS_HOME/bin
   emctl config oms -change_repos_pwd
   ```

   The preceding command will prompt for the current password of the SYSMAN account and for the new password. If you do not know the SYSMAN password, the command line is a little different because we need to connect to the Repository database as SYS and modify the SYSMAN password:

   ```
   emctl config oms -change_repos_pwd -use_sys_pwd -sys_pwd <sys_
   pwd> -new_pwd
   <new_sysman_pwd>
   ```

   This command does not prompt for any passwords as all the necessary information is included in the command line.

3. Stop the Administration Server on the OMS machine and restart all of the OMS services:

   ```
   cd $OMS_HOME/bin
   emctl stop oms -all
   emctl start oms
   ```

Please note the following:

- The SYSMAN password will be modified in the Repository database as well as in the WLS Credential store. The monitoring credentials for the OMS and Repository target will also be updated.
- Along with the SYSMAN password, this command will modify all the Enterprise Manager users within the Repository:
    - SYSMAN_MDS
    - BIP
    - SYSMAN_OPSS
    - SYSMAN_APM
    - SYSMAN_RO
    - MGMT_VIEW

Configuring Blackouts Blackouts permit administrators to suppress data collection and the generation of notifications for selected targets either for ad hoc or scheduled maintenance. Blackouts prevent the distribution of unnecessary alerts. As we noted at the beginning of this chapter, continuous and otherwise false or redundant alarms tend to lull the DBA into a sense of complacency. Eventually, the DBA mistrusts the monitoring configuration and ignores a valid alert. Ensuring the validity of alarms is an important part of maintaining the effectiveness of the Cloud Control environment.

Blackouts also have the important job of properly accounting for the affected period in the target statistics. This allows Cloud Control to more accurately report on a target's performance and associated metrics. Administrators are highly motivated to meet service level agreements (SLAs), and blackouts help maximize target availability calculations. For example, scheduled downtime should be configured with blackouts; otherwise, the period during which the target is unavailable will be categorized within Cloud Control as Down Time and will reduce the Overall Availability (%) results.

You can set blackouts either in the Cloud Control Console or at the command line. The Console provides more functionality than the command line. The main difference is that the Console allows you to specify targets for blackouts across multiple hosts, whereas the command line only allows you to set blackouts on a particular node or host. The Blackouts page is accessible from the main Enterprise menu and the Monitoring sub-menu. As you can see in Figure 8-40, the parameters are very similar to those in earlier versions. Clicking the Create button starts the configuration steps:

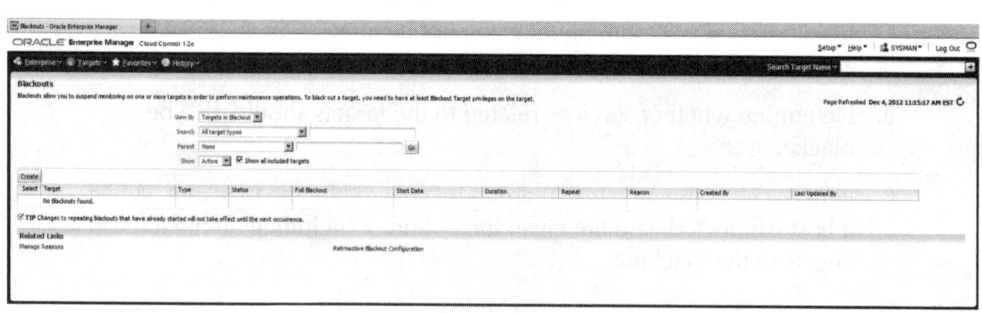

FIGURE 8-40. *Blackouts*

1. (Figure 8-41) Provide the following information:
   a. Name of the blackout.
   b. Any comments regarding the blackout, if desired.
   c. Reason for the blackout. This selection helps for later reporting and classification statistics. If needed, the selection choices can be modified.

Create Blackout: Properties - Oracle Enterpri...

ORACLE Enterprise Manager Cloud Control 12c

Properties Member Targets Targets on Host Services Schedule Review

Create Blackout: Properties

* Name Test Database Weekly Cold Backup

Comments Example of scheduled backup.

Reason DB: Database Cold Backup

Run jobs during the blackout. Jobs that are not agent-bound will continue to run during the blackout even if this option is unselected.

Detect Service that are dependent on target that will be selected in blackout.

Targets

Select the targets to be blacked out. You only see the targets for which you have Blackout Target privileges. Agents are not shown because they can only be blacked out as part of a full host blackout.

Remove | Add

Select All | Select None

Select	Name	Type ▲
☐	TEST	Database Instance

TIP The Member Targets step is only meaningful for composite targets.

TIP The Targets on Host step is only meaningful if a Host is selected.

FIGURE 8-41. *Create Blackout: Properties*

d. Decide whether normally scheduled jobs should run during the blackout, that is, assuming they will not be affected by maintenance activities.

e. Determine whether services related to the targets should also be blacked out.

f. Finally, select the targets that are to be covered by the blackout. When a host is selected, you are given the option of including all the relevant targets in the blackout.

2. (Figure 8-42) Define the Blackout schedule:

   a. Enter the Time Zone in which the blackout needs to be executed.

   b. Select the start options: Immediately or Later.

   c. Provide the duration: Indefinite, Length, or Until a specific time.

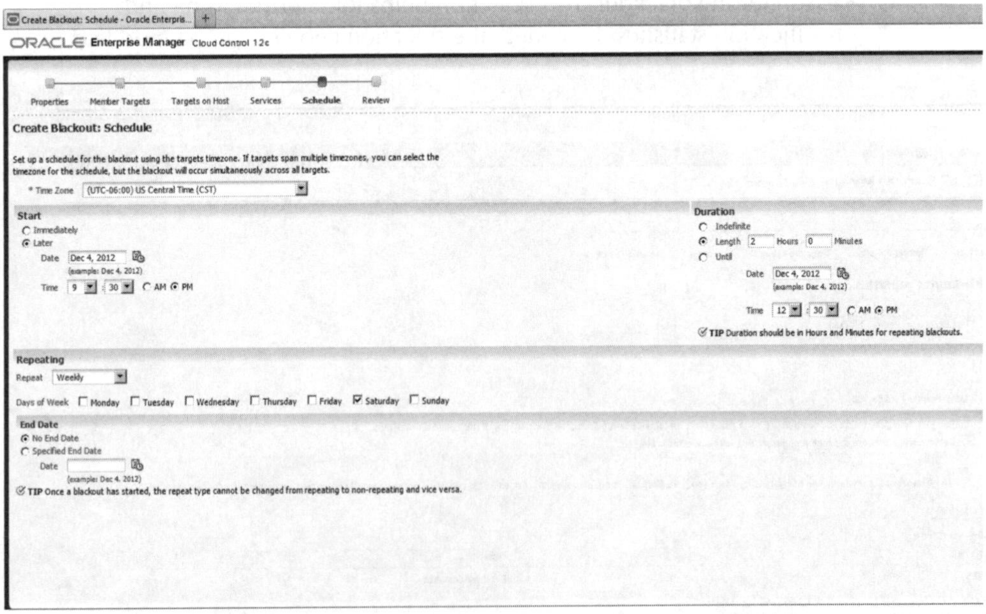

FIGURE 8-42. *Create Blackout: Schedule*

d. If desired, configure a repeatable schedule. The administrator can schedule repeatable backups based on minutes, hours, days, weeks, months, or on a yearly basis.

e. The configuration also provides for an end date to the repeatable schedule, if needed.

3. If the configuration is acceptable (Figure 8-43), click Finish.

As you may have noticed, the step counter in our blackout example skipped a few steps. This happened because we did not select any hosts with sub-targets. If we had, the additional steps would have involved further refining the blackout applicable targets. If, for example, we had selected the Test Systems Group as the target of our blackout, we would then need to be given the option to select the individual targets on hosts in the Test Systems Group; see Figure 8-44.

Another useful function provided by the Console is the ability to configure retroactive blackouts. These blackouts can be configured from the Retroactive

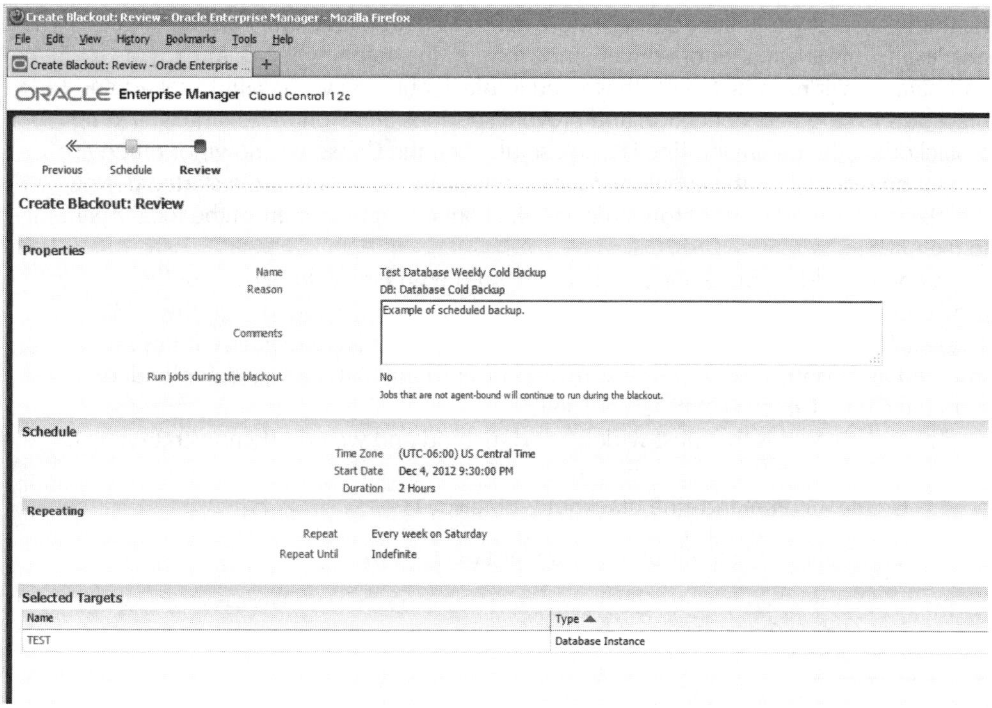

FIGURE 8-43. *Create Blackout: Review*

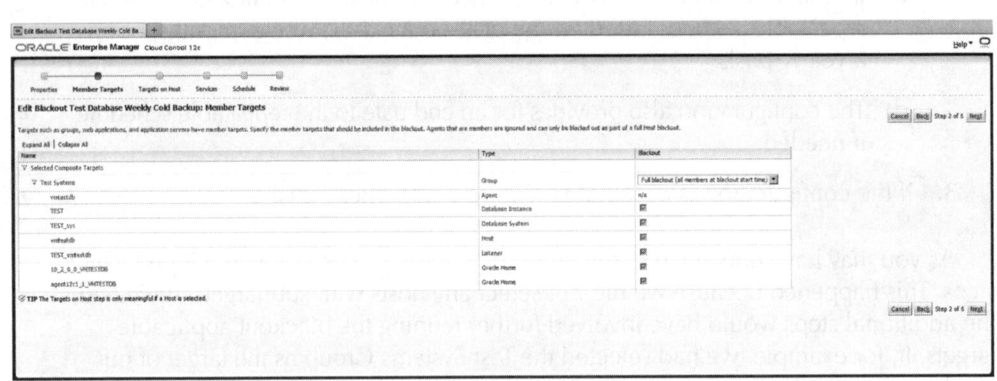

FIGURE 8-44. *Create Blackout: Member Targets*

Blackout Configuration link, which is located at the bottom right-hand side on the main Blackout page.

As noted earlier, blackouts can also be configured from the command line. This method is useful when the administrator wishes to define blackouts on the target host itself. This is a matter of convenience for administrators who are already on a particular server running targets they need to black out, and who want to set ad hoc blackouts to stop data collection and prevent spurious alerts on these targets. Setting a blackout at the command line is also useful when the Console is down or otherwise cannot be reached. In the event the OMS services are down and are restarted during the blackout, Cloud Control forwards the blackout configuration from the local Agent to the OMS.

A command-line blackout can be configured with either the `emctl` utility provided by the Agent or with the `emcli` utility, which is included with the OMS. The `emcli` utility can also be executed from any client machine where it has been installed and configured. The utility, the "EM CLI Client" kit, can be downloaded from the Cloud Control OMS server itself.[6]

The `emctl` tool is the most widely used method and we will demonstrate it first.

1. Create a command-line blackout with `emctl`:

   a. Create a blackout on a particular target:

```
${AGENT_HOME}/bin/emctl start blackout <Name of the blackout> [<Target
name>[:<Target type>]] [-d Duration]
```

[6] The EM CLI Client kit is available at the following URL: `/http(s)://`*<Omsmachine.domain>*`:`*<port>*`/em/console/emcli/download`

b. Create a node-level blackout:

```
${AGENT_HOME}/bin/emctl start blackout <Name of the blackout> -nodeLevel
[-d Duration]
```

2. Check the blackout status:

```
${AGENT_HOME}/bin/emctl status blackout [<Target name>[:<Target type>]]
```

3. Stop the blackout:

```
${AGENT_HOME}/bin/emctl stop blackout <Name of the blackout>
```

The steps needed for management of an `emcli` command-line blackout are very similar to those used by `emctl`:

1. Create a command-line blackout with `emcli`:

   a. Create a blackout on a specific target:

```
emcli create_blackout -name=<Name of the blackout> -
add_targets=<target_name>:<target_type> -schedule="
frequency:once|interval|weekly|monthly|yearly];duration:
[HH...][:mm...]" -
reason="<reason for blackout>"
```

   b. Create a node-level blackout:

```
emcli create_blackout -name=<Unique> -add_targets=<name>:host
-schedule="      frequency:;duration:[HH...][:mm...]"
-reason="<description>"]
```

2. To display a list of blackouts:

   a. Details of all blackouts:

```
emcli get_blackouts
```

   b. Details of blackout on all targets of a specific host:

```
emcli get_blackouts -hostnames=<host name>
```

   c. Details of blackout on a specific target:

```
emcli get_blackouts -target=<target name>:<target type>
```

3. Stop a blackout:

```
emcli stop_blackout -name="<name of the blackout>"
[-createdby="<blackout owner>"]
```

4. Delete a blackout:

```
emcli delete_blackout -name="name" [-createdby="<blackout
owner>" (default is current user)]
```

Physical Maintenance

In this section we examine how to maintain the physical elements in your Cloud Control environment. As we mentioned earlier, Cloud Control can scale for hundreds of users and thousands of targets, but only if you're diligent about maintenance for the life of the deployment. Such maintenance is necessary regardless of the workload or size of your site. The cornerstone of software maintenance is periodic housekeeping.

Fortunately, due to advancements in both the Enterprise Manager and the supporting database, there are some tasks that we no longer need to address. First, the Repository database runs in a version that automatically collects statistics. No additional statistics gathering is necessary for Cloud Control. Second, in earlier versions we had to schedule downtime for the Repository in order to perform partition maintenance. This task is also not required.

Another area of interest is the volume of metric data and whether it can be scaled down. The metric data that is collected and uploaded by the Agents on the target hosts and stored in the OMS Repository tables is called "raw" data. Cloud Control aggregates collected metric data by hour and by date in order to improve query performance and help reduce the size of the Repository database. One of the jobs configured in the DBMS_SCHEDULER of the Repository database is responsible for rolling up (aggregating) this raw data. Once a day the previous day's raw data is rolled up into a one-hour and a one-day table. These hourly and daily records will have hourly and daily metric data averages, minimums, maximums, and standard deviations computed. The hourly and daily tables along with the computed statistics are used for providing the historical metric information displayed in the Cloud Control Console.

After Cloud Control aggregates the data, the data is then considered eligible for purging. A certain period of time must pass for data to actually be purged. This period of time is called the *retention time*. The raw data, which has the highest insert volume, has the shortest default retention time, which is seven days. Consequently, seven days after raw data is aggregated into a one-hour record, a raw data point is eligible for purging. Hourly rollup metric data is purged after 31 days. Finally, the highest level of aggregation, the one-day rollup, is kept for 12 months.

It is possible to modify the default retention and purging policies.[7] However, Oracle strongly discourages reducing any of these values. The Cloud Control default aggregation and purging policies were designed to provide the most available data for analysis while still providing the best performance and least disk-space requirements for the Management Repository. As a result, you should not modify these policies to improve performance or decrease your disk space demand. However, Oracle does permit increasing the amount of raw or aggregate data in the Repository for those cases where users plan on extracting or reviewing the information using external analysis tools other than Cloud Control.

---

[7] The Cloud Control API procedure *gc_interval_partition_mgr.set_retention* provides this functionality.

Log File Management

Managing the size and number of Cloud Control log files is an important part of the housekeeping effort. In a Cloud Control installation, automatic log rotation is enabled by default for all OMS and WLB logs after they reach a defined size. Accordingly, the creation of large, difficult-to-manipulate log and trace files should not be a concern. However, there are certain logs that are not purged automatically after rotation, and these files have to be manually deleted (or scheduled programmatically for deletion) at regular intervals.

On the OMS server the following log files need to be managed outside of Cloud Control:

- Webtier logs in <*EM_INSTANCE_HOME*>/WebTierIH1/diagnostics/logs/OHS/ohs1:
  - em_upload_http_access_log*
  - access_log*
  - em_upload_https_access_log*
  - ohs1-*.log
  - console~OHS~1.log*
  - mod_wl_ohs.log*
- Domain logs:
  - <*EM_INSTANCE_HOME*>/user_projects/domains/GCDomain/servers/EMGC_ADMINSERVER/logs/GCDomain.log*
- EMGC_ADMINSERVER logs in <*EM_INSTANCE_HOME*>/user_projects/domains/GCDomain/servers/EMGC_ADMINSERVER/logs:
  - EMGC_ADMINSERVER.out*
  - EMGC_ADMINSERVER.log*
  - access.log*
- Managed Server logs:
  - <*EM_INSTANCE_HOME*>/users_projects/domains/GCDomain/servers/EMGC_OMS[n]/EMGC_OMS*.out*

In the preceding examples, the value of <*EM_INSTANCE_HOME*> corresponds to the location of the site-specific <*gc_inst*> directory.

The automatic purging of older domain and EMGC_ADMINSERVER logs can be enabled through the WLS Admin Server Console. This functionality can be configured with the following steps:

1. We first need to determine the proper URL to the WLS Admin server. This path can be found in the configuration file: <*OMS_HOME*>install/setupinfo.txt. Look for the parameter "Admin Server URL."
2. From a browser, log in to the WLS Admin Server Console using the URL that you determined in Step 1.

Welcome

Log in to work with the WebLogic Server domain

Username: weblogic

Password: ••••••••••

Login

3. In the upper left-hand corner of the WLS Administration Console, click on Lock & Edit in the Change Center; see Figure 8-45.

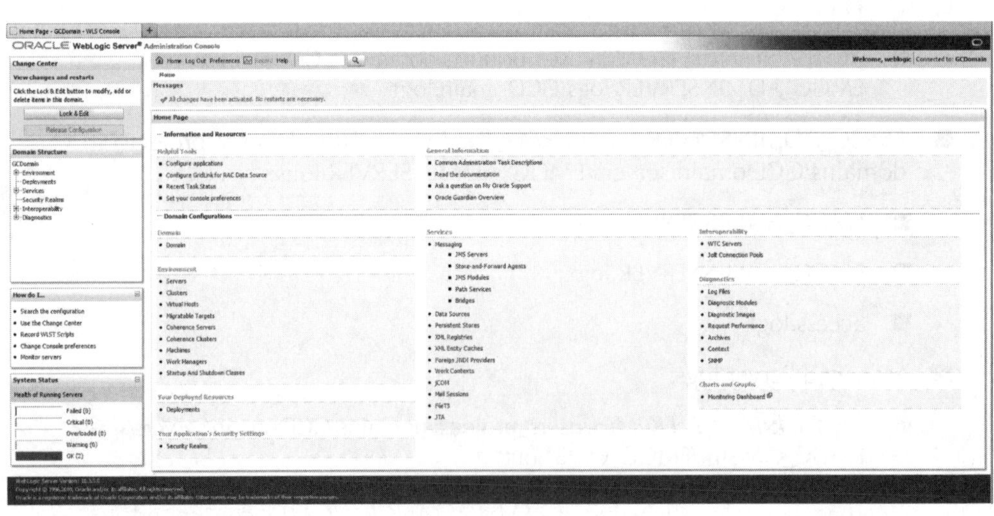

FIGURE 8-45. *WLS Administration Console*

4. In the Domain Structure box, click on the link GCDomain and then once the new screen appears, select the Logging tab (Figure 8-46).
5. In the main window, activate the function "Limit number of retained files." Finally, click the Save button in the lower section of the main window. In this configuration the number of GCDomain.log files is limited to seven, which are rotated once they reach the size of 5MB.
6. For the EMGC_ADMINSERVER logs, we need to navigate to the corresponding settings page. Again, in the Domain Structure box, expand the menu item Environment and click Servers. Once the new page appears, click on the server EMGC_ADMINSERVER(admin) (Figure 8-47).
7. In the EMGC_ADMINSERVER server settings page, select the Logging tab.
8. In the main window activate the function "Limit number of retained files" (Figure 8-48). Finally, click the Save button. In this configuration the number of EMGC_ADMINSERVER.log files is limited to 10, and they are rotated once they reach the size of 5MB.

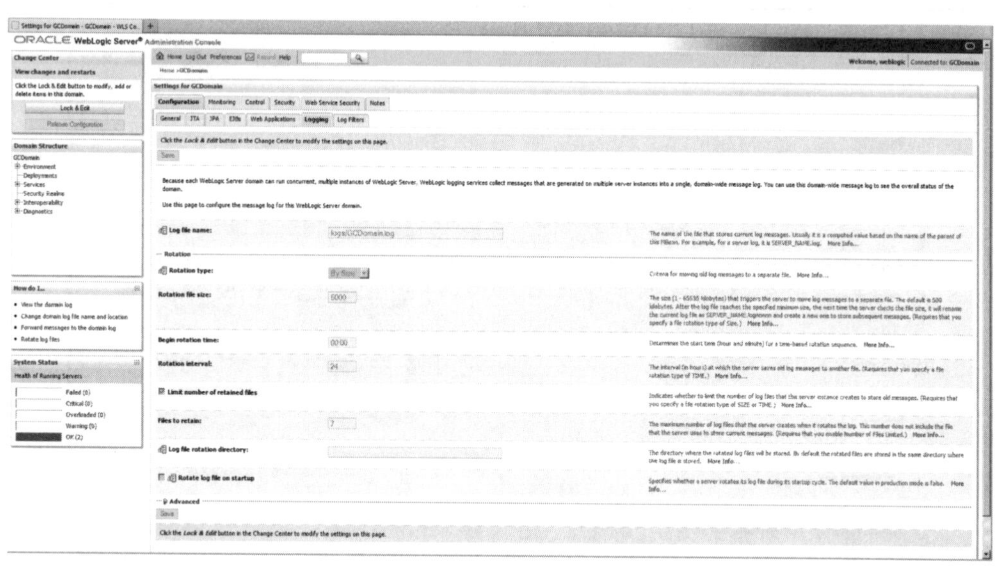

FIGURE 8-46. *Settings for GCDomain*

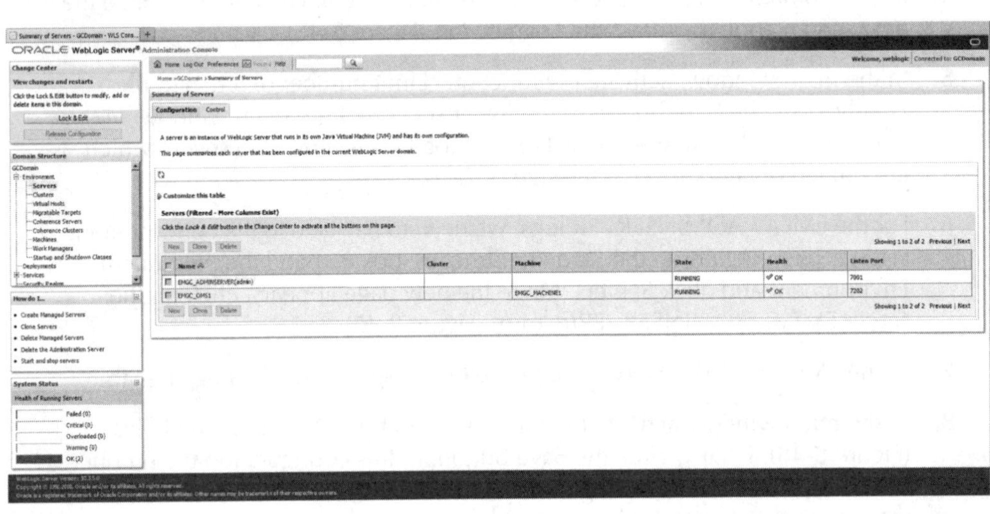

FIGURE 8-47. *Server navigation*

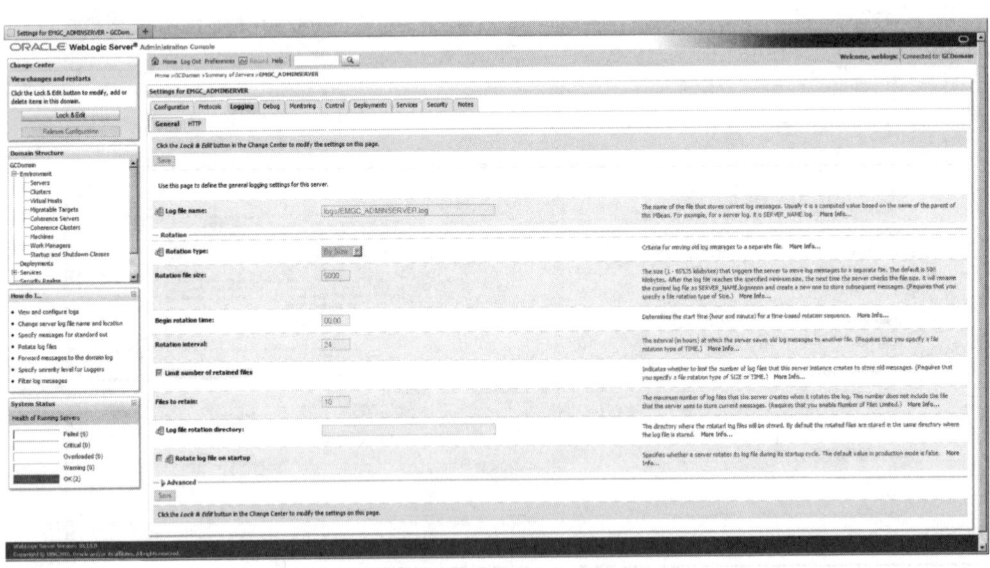

FIGURE 8-48. *Settings for EMGC_ADMINSERVER: Logging*

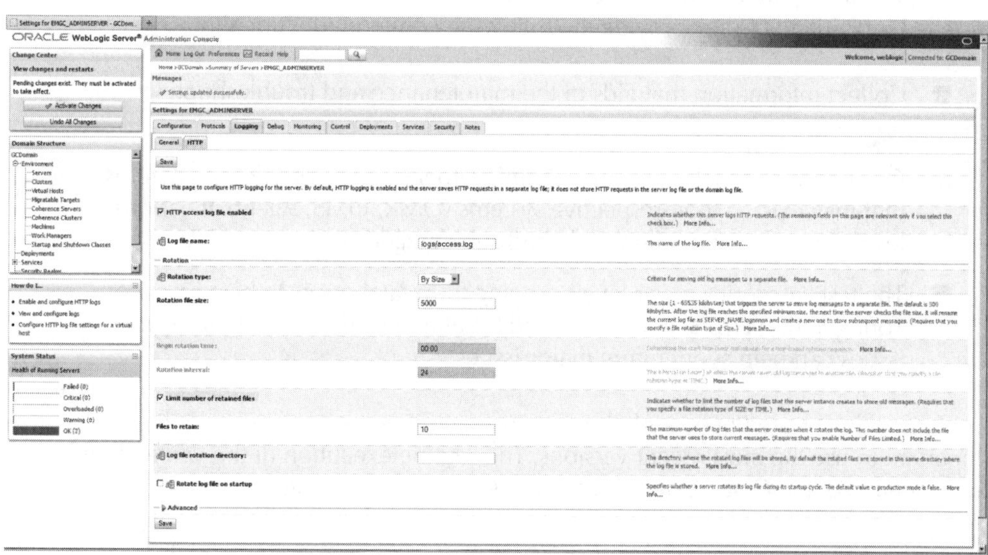

FIGURE 8-49. *Settings for EMGC_ADMINSERVER: HTTP*

9. To limit the number of Admin Server access.logs, select the HTTP tab at the top of the page. And, again, activate the "Limit number of retained files" function (Figure 8-49). Once saved, the number of access.logon files are limited to 10, and are rotated once they reach the size of 5MB.

10. Finally, it is important to activate the saved changes by clicking on the Activate Changes button in the Change Center box located in the upper left-hand corner of the page.

Diagnostic Utilities

Oracle supports Cloud Control with diagnostic utilities for each of the three major components of the system:

- **Repvfy** For researching and diagnosing issues with the Management Repository
- **Omsvfy** For managing the health of the Management Services (OMS)
- **Agtvfy** For administering the health of the Cloud Control Management Agent

These tools are separate from the main software and can be downloaded and installed individually.[8] They provide the following common functionality:

- Collect information that aids in the maintenance and troubleshooting process.
- Groups of tests that allow EM administrators to verify problem signatures that may exist in their respective systems (OMR, OMS, Agent) at various levels including the full module and sub-categories.
- The test categories cover levels ranging from fatal errors to best practices, configuration errors, and error trends. Naturally, detection of these latter issues can help avoid future major issues.

As new issues are uncovered, the diagnostic utilities are updated, so it is important to use the most recent versions. The routine execution of the verification tests for each of the Cloud Control modules is strongly encouraged.

Cloud Control Tuning

Tuning, to a degree, is similar to maintenance. In order to be effective, the effort needs to be continuous. Occasionally you'll encounter the silver bullet, but these are few and far between. Effective tuning requires routine care involving collecting baselines, removing superfluous tasks, monitoring metrics, modifying parameters or objects, and testing the results. In the following material we will examine these issues as they specifically relate to the Cloud Control environment. We will take a closer look at these topics:

- Sizing Guidelines
- OMS and OMR Systems Errors
- Target Metric Collection Errors
- Targets with Down Status
- Critical and Warning Events

---

[8] The Cloud Control diagnostic utilities are presently available at the following URLs: Repvfy - https://support.oracle.com/epmos/main/downloadattachmentprocessor?attachid=1426973.1:REPVFY12C&clickstream=no; Omsvfy - https://support.oracle.com/epmos/main/downloadattachmentprocessor?attachid=1374450.1:OMSVFY12C&clickstream=no; Agtvfy - https://support.oracle.com/epmos/main/downloadattachmentprocessor?attachid=1374441.1:EMDIAGAGTVFY12C&clickstream=no

- OMR Database Alert Log Errors
- Reorganizing Tables and Indexes
- Cloud Control Metrics

Sizing Guidelines

Before considering any other performance issues, make sure to meet or exceed the sizing guidelines addressed in Chapter 2, "Cloud Control Preinstallation." Cloud Control contains numerous functional enhancements compared to the earlier versions of Enterprise Manager. Do not assume that your old platform will satisfy the resource needs of the new version. As the product matures and new hardware is introduced (CPU, disk, and solid-state memory, for example), check back with Oracle Support for updated requirements for deployments.

OMS and OMR System Errors

Every week you should review the Errors page for the Management Services and Repository target. To access this page, click Setup and then Management Services and Repository. From the default Overview tab, you can click the Launch Incident Manager button at the bottom of the screen; see Figure 8-50.

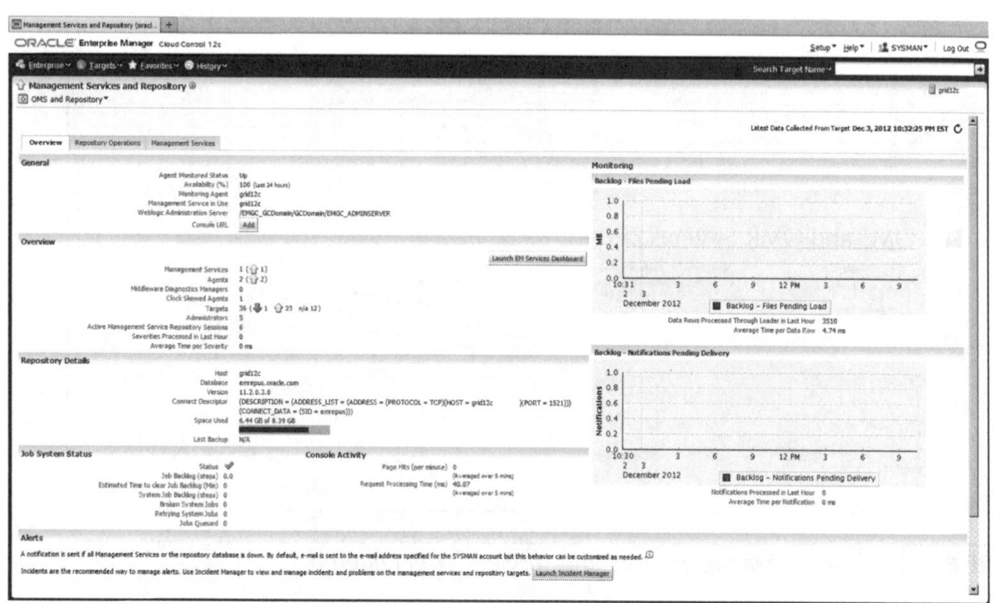

FIGURE 8-50. *Management Services and Repository – Overview*

At this point the Incident Manager page will display and the filter will default to the OMS and Services targets as shown in Figure 8-51.

This page lists the errors for each of the OMS and Repository subsystems with error text extracted from the respective OMS log files. Some errors may be due to unconfigured or misconfigured targets. Other errors may be the result of bugs. Resolve as many errors as possible by configuring targets correctly or applying applicable patches. Many of these errors will need to be cleared manually because, in many cases, the system cannot detect that the issue has been resolved.

Target Metric Collection Errors

In addition to clearing the OMS and OMR system errors, fix all metric collection errors that accrued during the last week. These errors are associated with target installation, configuration, or status issues. To display these errors, click the Metric Collection Errors count at the bottom of the Management Services and Repository overview page, as shown in Figure 8-52. Related Metric Errors should also be resolved.

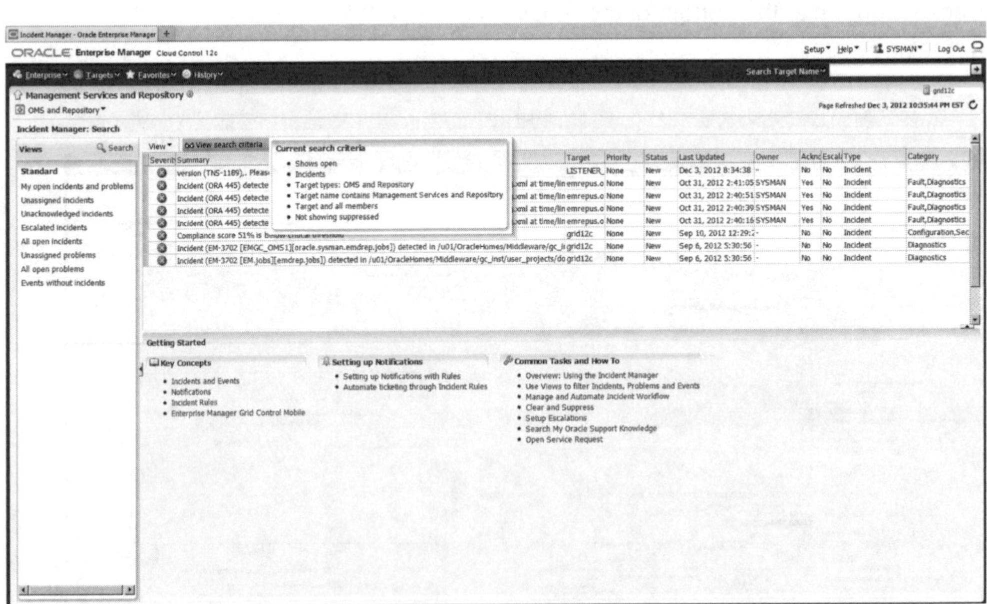

FIGURE 8-51. *Incident Manager: OMS and services target filtered*

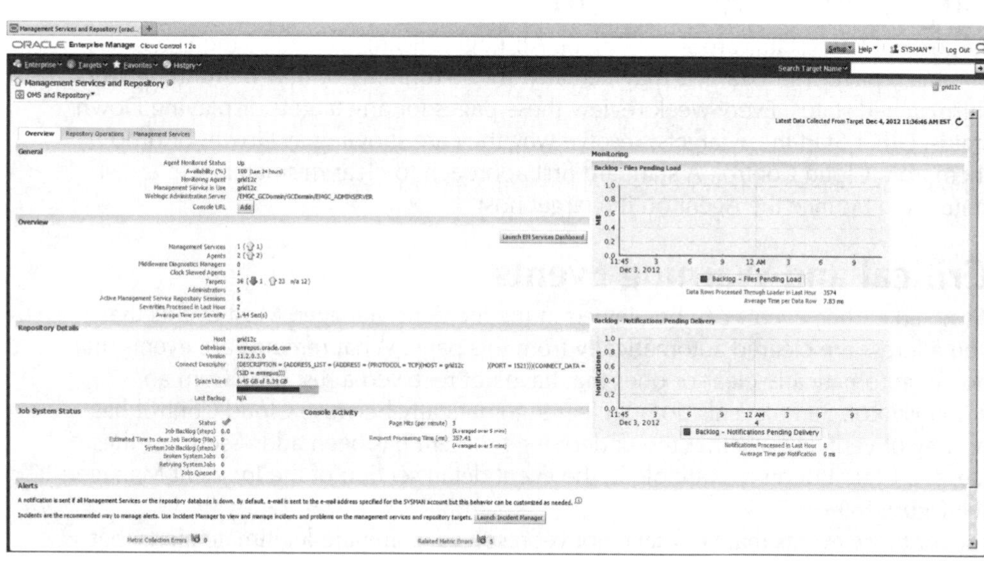

FIGURE 8-52. *Management Services and Repository: Metric Collection Errors link*

For each error, click the Message column to view the complete error message (see Figure 8-53). Consult My Oracle Support, and other sources, such as Google, for possible fixes to the problem. If you resolve the problem, the target error should automatically clear. Work your way down the error list, fixing as many errors as possible.

Related Metric Errors

These are metric errors on any of the following targets: Management Service hosts, the database containing the Repository, the Weblogic Server and Application Deployment of the Management Services, and the Management Agent that monitors the Repository.

Target	Type	Metric	Collection Timestamp	Message
EMGC_OMS1	Oracle WebLogic Server	JoltConnectionPool	Nov 2, 2012 1:34:45 PM	oracle.sysman.emSDK.agent.fetchlet.exception.FetchletException: Can't resolve a non-optional query descriptor property [SecureProtocol] (DefaultSecureProtocol)
EMGC_OMS1	Oracle WebLogic Server	JDBCDataSource	Nov 2, 2012 1:34:45 PM	oracle.sysman.emSDK.agent.fetchlet.exception.FetchletException: Can't resolve a non-optional query descriptor property [SecureProtocol] (DefaultSecureProtocol)
EMGC_OMS1	Oracle WebLogic Server	Server	Nov 2, 2012 1:34:46 PM	oracle.sysman.emSDK.agent.fetchlet.exception.FetchletException: Can't resolve a non-optional query descriptor property [SecureProtocol] (DefaultSecureProtocol)
EMGC_OMS1	Oracle WebLogic Server	JDBCMultiDataSource	Nov 2, 2012 1:34:45 PM	oracle.sysman.emSDK.agent.fetchlet.exception.FetchletException: Can't resolve a non-optional query descriptor property [SecureProtocol] (DefaultSecureProtocol)
EMGC_OMS1	Oracle WebLogic Server	StartupShutdownClasses	Nov 2, 2012 1:34:45 PM	oracle.sysman.emSDK.agent.fetchlet.exception.FetchletException: Can't resolve a non-optional query descriptor property [SecureProtocol] (DefaultSecureProtocol)

FIGURE 8-53. *Management Services and Repository: Related Metric Errors*

Targets with Down Status

Targets in Down status are shown in the All Targets listing as well as the Enterprise Summary page. These targets may actually not be running, or may be running with mismatched status. Every week review these pages for any targets displaying Down status. Either Start these targets, resolve why they are showing as Down, or drop them from Cloud Control. A standard first approach to clear mismatches in target status is to bounce the Agent on the target host.

Critical and Warning Events

As noted earlier, events can be viewed in the Incident Manager. Most events that you address are cleared automatically from this page. What remains are events that do not automatically clear or ones that have not received a response from an administrator. Some events do not clear automatically because Cloud Control has no way of verifying whether the underlying problem has been addressed. For these alerts, a Clear button is available in the event detail section of the Incident Manager; see Figure 8-54.

For those events that you have not yet resolved, some are legitimate alerts that require your attention. For these events you must remedy the underlying condition. Other events are false alarms that fire, sometimes repeatedly, due to inappropriate Critical and Warning metric threshold values. Repeated alerts for the same metric

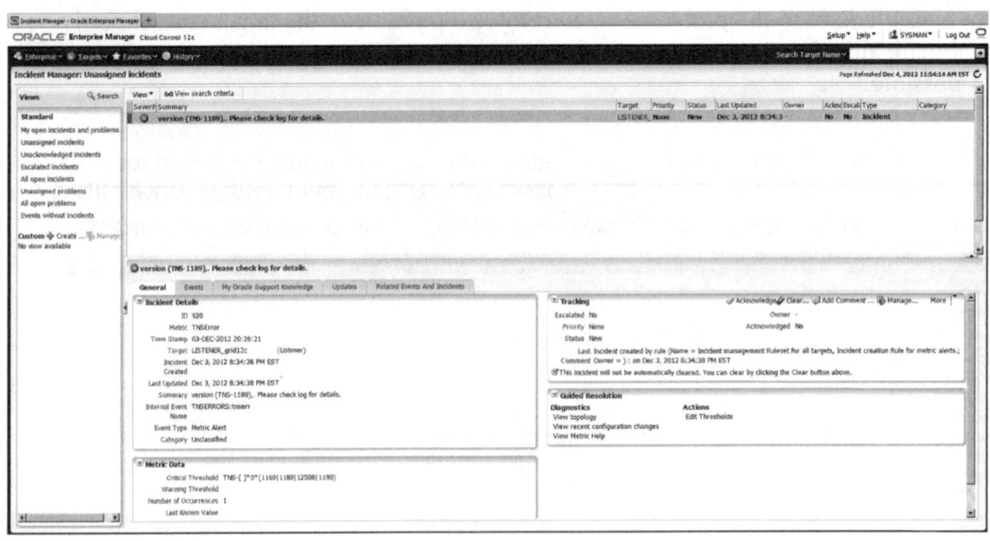

FIGURE 8-54. *Incident Manager: Clear Event button*

occur when the metric's value cycles across Critical and Warning thresholds within the collection interval, which is typically five minutes. Repeated Warning, Critical, and Clear event notifications ensue, sometimes for hours on end. These false notifications annoy administrators and can easily damage the "monitoring credibility" of a Cloud Control site. This type of rapid-fire alerting wastes OMS resources and can cause a backlog in notification delivery or metric data uploads. When this happens, relax the threshold tolerances for the offending metric. Increase the difference between the Warning and Critical threshold values, use a null value for one or the other severity, raise or lower metric values (as appropriate) for both severities, or use a combination of these methods. Adjusting thresholds is the standard way to keep an event from constantly alerting, and is the appropriate response for these situations.

OMR Database Alert Log Errors

Alerts that deserve special mention for a Cloud Control system are alert log errors for the Management Repository database. You should promptly investigate both Warning and Critical errors. For example, the default Warning threshold for the Database Instance metric called Generic Alert Log Error includes serious errors such as ORA-600 (internal errors for Oracle program exceptions) and ORA-7445 (OS exceptions that generate a trace or core file). Again, My Oracle Support is the principal source for researching such errors and for obtaining patches and workarounds.

Reorganizing Tables and Indexes

As with any Oracle database, the Repository database requires periodic upkeep of its tables and indexes. Every month you should pinpoint those tables and indexes that have undergone high inserts and deletes, causing their allocated size to balloon and actual size to become a fraction thereof. You must then shut down the Management Services and rebuild these tables and related indexes offline. Rebuilding an object re-creates its physical structure, reduces its allocated size to its actual need, and resets its high-water mark. Rebuilding all the OMR database tables and indexes is overkill and places an unnecessary burden on the Repository database. Only those tables that experience a high level of inserts and deletes need this special attention.

Cloud Control Metrics

Cloud Control offers many useful built-in metrics for monitoring performance. Many metrics can be evaluated with thresholds, but others are also available that are maintained strictly for statistical purposes. All the Management Services and Repository metrics can be viewed from the All Metrics page, which can be accessed from the OMS and Repository menu; see Figure 8-55.

As you can see on the All Metrics page (Figure 8-56), you cannot set thresholds for many of the metrics. However, historical metric values are available for all the

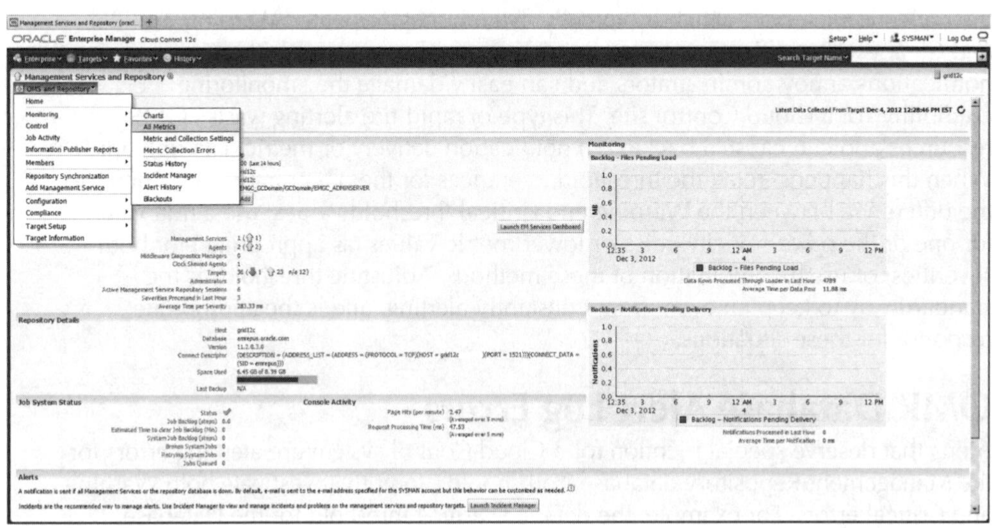

FIGURE 8-55. *Management Services and Repository: Access to All Metrics*

listed metrics on this page by drilling down as shown here by clicking on the Total Throughput Across Collection Workers metric.

As you can see, you can select historical data for different time periods, 24 hours, 7 days, 31 days, and custom ranges. To get a longer-term view of metric values, choose "Last 31 days," or step back even further by selecting Custom, which allows you to view data as far back as the retention policy provides. This page is where we collect our initial base line metrics for later comparison, review, and research.

Average weekly values for key metrics on OMS and Repository hosts are good indicators of Cloud Control resource consumption. Most host metrics of interest are regular metrics, such as Memory Utilization (%), that appear on the Metric and Collection Settings page. You will also find configuration and resource-related properties on the OMS/OMR target pages, such as the number of nodes, number and speed of CPUs, amount of RAM, and the number, speed, and configuration of network adapters. You should keep track of such properties over the long term because they can play a large role in Cloud Control performance. It is easy to overlook the tracking of host configuration changes alongside other metrics. Without such records whose datelines can be compared against other metric values, you may be left with unexplained performance changes.

It is important to periodically collect new key metrics and compare them to the original baselines. These trends help you gauge your site's relative state of health compared to the earlier period and provide a basis and direction for tuning. Potential problem errors are often identified as "bottlenecks."

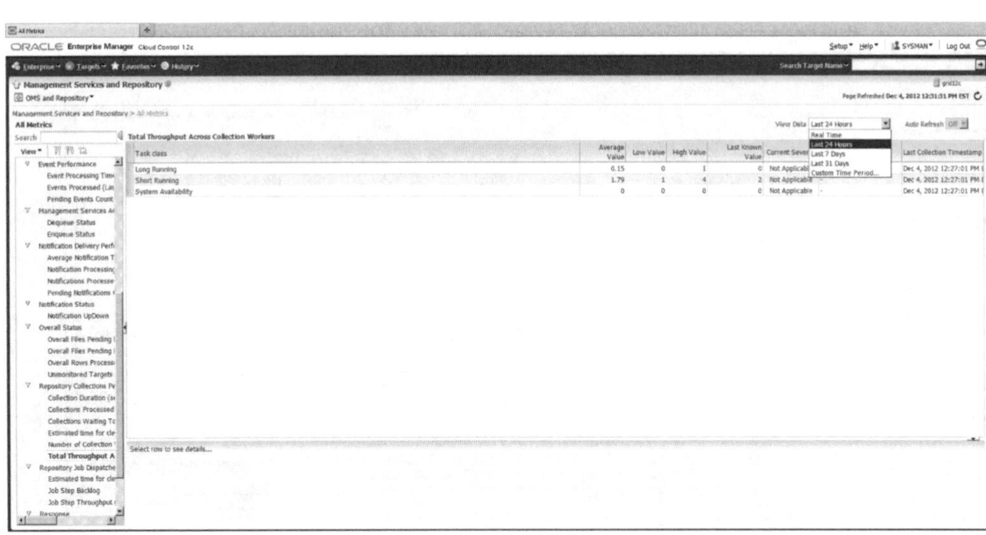

FIGURE 8-56. *Management Services and Repository: All Metrics – drill down*

The primary causes of Cloud Control bottlenecks are overlooked housekeeping or failure to meet the deployment resource requirements. However, if you've met the requirements and have been diligent about carrying out the maintenance tasks discussed in this chapter, then you may need to look elsewhere for the culprit. Likely causes include incorrectly configured resource (hardware or software) and hardware resource constraints. One example is high CPU consumption. High CPU utilization can occur on both OMS and OMS systems, but is usually a problem on the Repository nodes. OMR systems consume more CPU than the OMS because the Repository database performs most of the heavy hitting in Cloud Control. While the OMS does its own share of processing by uploading Agent files to the Repository, the other major OMS function, rendering the Console, is more of a memory-draining than a CPU-intensive operation. By contrast, the Repository must use processing power to continuously load and roll up Agent data and execute many other statistical computations. The Repository Operations tab (Figure 8-57), reached from the Management Services and Repository home page, reveals the number of these processing tasks.

The Repository Operations tab will help identify the task, or tasks, that may be consuming a disproportionate amount of CPU. With this information you can make further decisions with respect to resource configuration and allocation. As applications go, Cloud Control is a significant consumer of resources. However, in contrast to most applications, Cloud Control does provide you with the tools to investigate and identify performance issues.

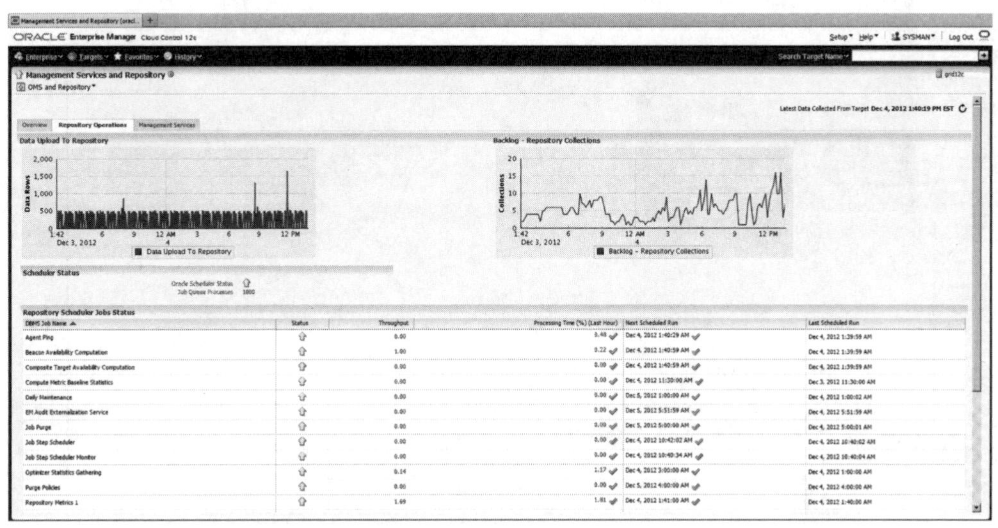

FIGURE 8-57. *Management Services and Repository: Repository Operations*

Summary

This chapter described the tasks and functions that need to be performed in order to effectively maintain and tune a Cloud Control system. The definition of maintenance was expanded to include both operational and physical considerations. Operational maintenance addressed those Cloud Control functions that are essential to any reasonable-size implementation of the monitoring system. These tools included Templates, Incident Rules, and managing Groups. These utilities provide a coordinated method to properly manage the numerous targets. Without these tools, the task would be extremely burdensome and overwhelming. Physical maintenance covered log and trace file management and utilities that can be used to diagnose problems. Finally, Cloud Control tuning was discussed along with ways to improve the efficiency of the product.

This is the final chapter in Part I, "Implementing and Maintaining Cloud Control 12c." Part II, "Cloud Control for Database, System, Storage, and Middleware Administrators," covers in greater detail many topics that received only cursory examination earlier. Databases, systems, and storage are the primary components of any Oracle implementation, and Cloud Control provides significant functions for their management.

PART II

Cloud Control for Database, System, Storage, and Middleware Administrators

CHAPTER 9

DBAs: Manage Databases with Cloud Control

Perhaps the most basic and common use of OEM Cloud Control is to manage and monitor databases. This is due to the fact that OEM Cloud Control is an Oracle product and Oracle's flagship product is the database. Oracle has built many valuable features into the database monitoring function of OEM Cloud Control, which allows for intuitive and detailed monitoring and alerting of the Oracle database server.

Within OEM Cloud Control, you can not only monitor your database and get alerts, but can also manage and deploy Oracle database servers. Cloud Control is the single tool that can provide all of your database administration and management functionality. In addition to built-in functionality, Cloud Control can be extended to provide custom monitoring and alerting as well.

In this chapter the various functions and features of database monitoring within Cloud Control will be covered. The chapter is organized by the major drop-down menus that are available within OEM Cloud Control database monitoring and includes the Oracle Database drop-down menu, and the Performance, Availability, Server, Schema, and Administration drop-down menus.

In order to access and monitor a database target within OEM Cloud Control 12*c*, start by selecting Databases from the Targets menu. The main Databases screen consists of four sections as shown in Figure 9-1: Overview of incidents and problems, Job Activities, Database Load Map, and Status.

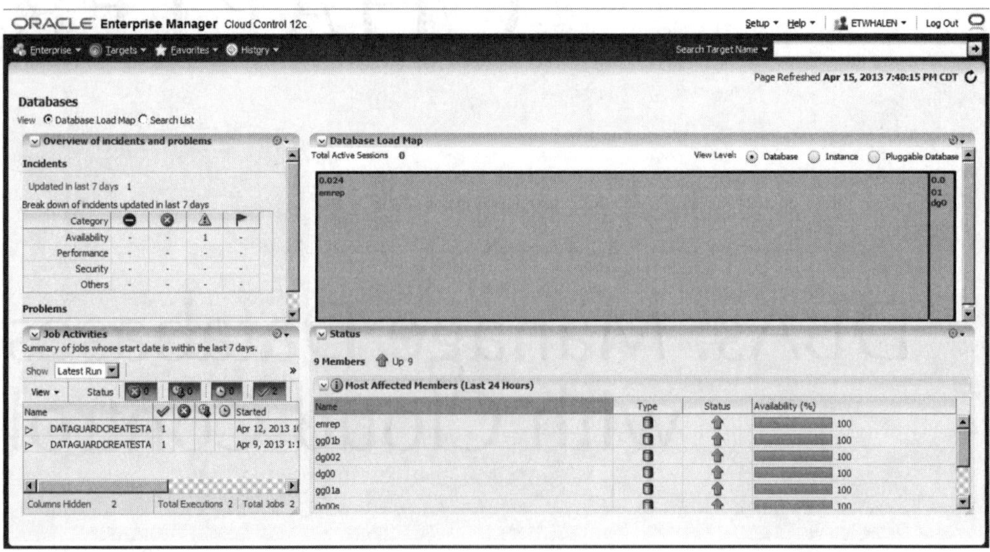

FIGURE 9-1. *The Databases Target screen*

From here you can choose one of the databases from the hyperlinks in the Status section. This will take you to the Oracle Database Home screen.

Oracle Database Home Screen

The Home page is the starting point for entering the database monitoring and managing facility within OEM Cloud Control. As with most of the screen shots in this chapter, the Home page is divided into two screen shots, shown in Figure 9-2 and later in Figure 9-3. From this screen you can access a large number of options for navigating the Oracle database. The navigation has moved from hyperlinks to the drop-down menus found at the top of the page.

The left part of the Home screen as shown in Figure 9-2 contains a summary of the state of the database server, a summary of security compliance, Performance, and Resources. The Summary section includes both Status and Diagnostics sections. Scrolling down you see the rest of this page, shown in Figure 9-3, which contains SQL Monitor and Incidents and Problems and the jobs summary (none running in this screen shot).

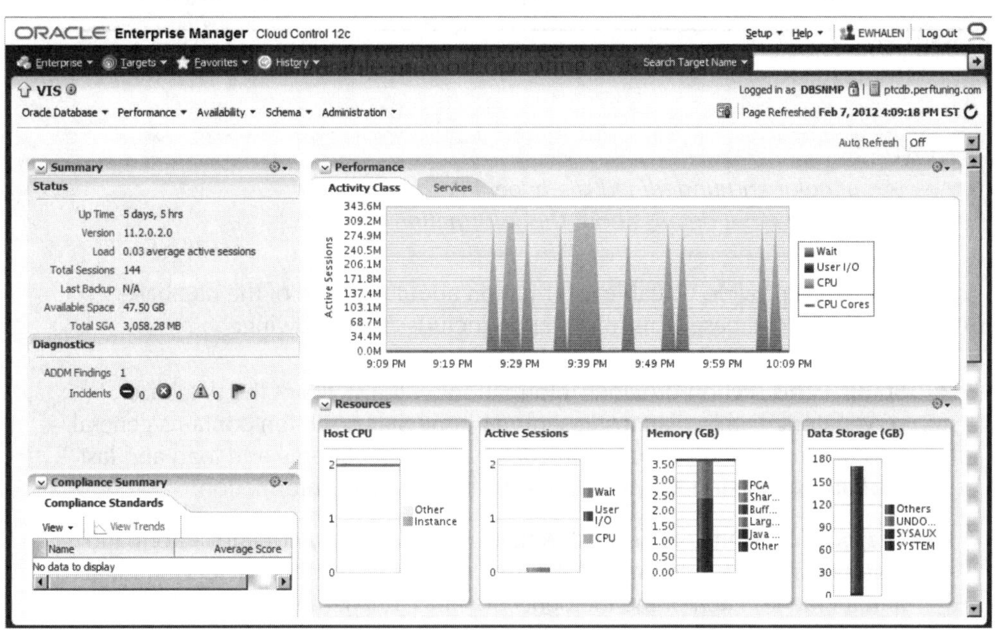

FIGURE 9-2. *The Oracle Database screen (part 1)*

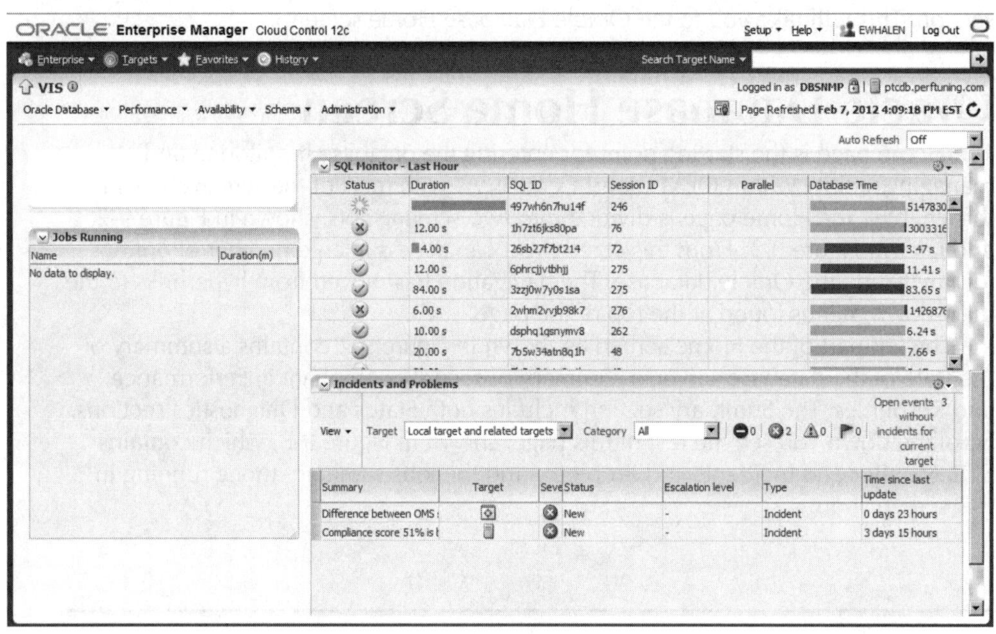

FIGURE 9-3. *The Oracle Database screen (part 2)*

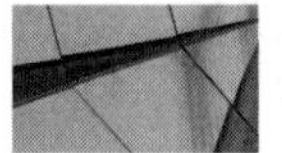

NOTE
Any text in color and underlined is a hyperlink that will take you to more details about this information.

These sections provide valuable information about the state of the database instance or cluster database. This information includes the following:

- **Status** This section provides information on the status of the database server along with a diagnostic summary. The Status section contains general information on the version of the database server, uptime and load and last backup information, as well as miscellaneous status information.
- **Diagnostics** The Diagnostics section under Summary contains information (and links) about Automatic Database Diagnostic Monitor (ADDM) findings and incidents. Each of the incidents provides a hyperlink that can be used to drill deeper into those incidences.

In the section below the Summary information is a Compliance Summary, which provides information on compliance issues found in the database. If there are issues, they will be listed here with links that can be used to drill down into those issues.

In the section below the Compliance Summary is the Jobs Running information (see Figure 9-3). Here you will see information on currently running jobs in the system. Most of the really good information is in the sections on the right side of the screen.

On the right side of the screen are the more interesting and graphical components. They include Performance, Resources, SQL Monitor, and Incidents and Problems. These sections provide valuable information about the state of the database instance or cluster database. Information includes the following:

- **Performance** Provides information at a high level about the performance of the system. Graphs are available for both activity class and services. This is a very high-level view and gives an idea of what you might see in the Performance tab.
- **Resources** Provides information on the database resource consumption. Resource consumption graphs include Host CPU, Active Sessions, Memory, and Data Storage. These graphs are useful and give you a quick view of the resource consumption of the database. The Host CPU section provides information on both Oracle and non-Oracle CPU utilization, and Active Sessions provides information on wait times. Memory displays a breakdown of Oracle database memory usage. It is broken down by components, such as buffer cache, shared pool, PGA, and so on. Data Storage provides a breakdown of Oracle data storage usage.
- **SQL Monitor** The SQL Monitor provides a list of the top SQL statements. They are listed as running or having previously run. The statements each include a hyperlink to the underlying SQL statement and execution plan.
- **Incidents and Problems** The Incidents and Problems section contains a list of incidents and problems that have occurred in the system. Each includes a hyperlink to the incident itself.

The Performance and Resource sections of the Database Home screen are shown in Figure 9-2, and the SQL Monitor and Incidents and Problems section are shown in Figure 9-3.

Additional database information is provided in the lower section of the screen as shown in Figure 9-3.

This screen provides a quick and easy dashboard that provides basic information about the state of the database. Within the Databases Target screen are a number of menus that provide additional monitoring and functionality.

Oracle Database Menu

The Oracle Database Home screen is the starting point for the Oracle Database management and monitoring. The Oracle Database drop-down menu contains a number of tools that can be accessed by selecting them from this menu, as shown here. They include the following:

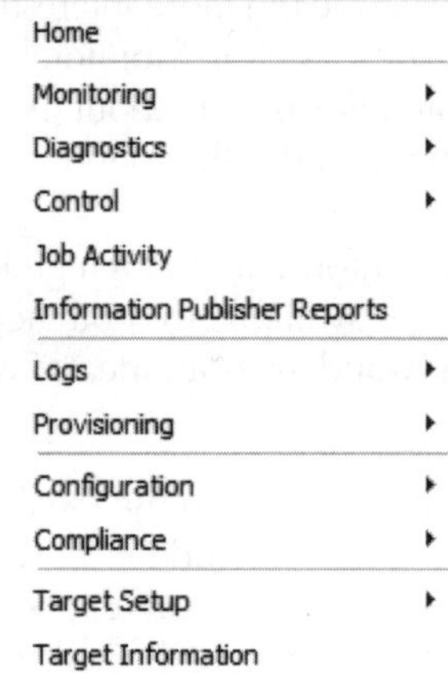

- **Home** The Oracle Database Home screen.
- **Monitoring**
  - **User-Defined Metrics** Explains the Metric Extensions that should be used instead of User-Defined Metrics and provides a hyperlink to Metric Extensions.
  - **All Metrics** Provides access to all of the database metrics and a view of the current values.
  - **Metric and Collection Settings** Provides a way to easily find and modify all of the metric thresholds for database monitoring. In the Other Collected Items tab, you can enable and disable collection schedules and other parameters.
  - **Metric Errors** Provides a list of metric errors.
  - **Status History** Provides information on the availability of the database.
  - **Incident Manager** Provides a direct link to the Incident Manager.
  - **Alert History** Provides a graphical display of the Alert History for the database.
  - **Blackouts** In this screen you can view current blackouts and create new blackouts for database objects.

- **Diagnostics**
  - **Support Workbench** Provides a link to the Oracle Database Support Workbench.
  - **Database Instance Health** Provides a graphical screen that gives an overview of the database instance health, including incident and non-incident alerts.
- **Control**
  - **Startup/Shutdown** Allows you to shut down or start up the database instance.
  - **Create Blackout** Allows you to create a blackout.
  - **End Blackout** Allows you to end a blackout.
- **Job Activity** Shows job activity for the current database instance.
- **Information Publisher Reports** Brings up all of the reports related to the database instance. Here you will find a number of reports that you can run on the state of the database as well as its configuration.
- **Logs**
  - **Text Alert Log Contents** Provides a screen where you can search the alert log or view the entire alert log.
  - **Alert Log Errors** Shows alert log entries containing errors.
  - **Archive/Purge Alert Log** Allows you to archive or purge the alert log.
  - **Trace Files** Allows you to archive or purge trace files.
- **Provisioning**
  - **Create Provisioning Profile** Creates a gold image of the selected target to be used as a source of provisioning.
  - **Create Database Template** Creates a template of the current database to be used for cloning. You can choose structure or structure and data.
  - **Clone Database Home** Invokes the Clone Database Home Wizard. This walks you through the steps of cloning an Oracle Home.
  - **Clone Database** Invokes the Clone Oracle Database Wizard. This will walk you through the steps of cloning a database.
  - **Upgrade Oracle Home & Database** Invokes a wizard that is used to upgrade the database to a new version.

    - **Upgrade Database** Invokes a wizard that is used to upgrade a database.
    - **Activity** Shows currently running deployments.
- **Configuration**
    - **Last Collected** Shows the latest collected database configuration information.
    - **Topology** Shows the current database topology.
    - **Search** Provides a list of search criteria that can be used to view specific database components, such as data files and so on.
    - **Compare** Compares different database instances and databases.
    - **Comparison Job Activity** Provides a list of currently running comparison jobs.
    - **History** Provides a list of previously run jobs.
    - **Save** Saves the current configuration of a database instance and database.
    - **Saved** Lists all saved configurations.
- **Compliance**
    - **Results** Provides a list of current compliance violations.
    - **Standard Associations** Provides a list of compliance standards that are associated with the target.
    - **Real-time Observations** Provides a list of real-time compliance standards violations.
- **Target Setup**
    - **Enterprise Manager Users** This is a link to the Administrators setup for OEM Cloud Control.
    - **Monitoring Configuration** Used to view or modify the monitoring configuration of the database target.
    - **Administrator Access** Used to grant administrator access to the database instance target.
    - **Remove Target** Used to remove the database instance target.
    - **Add to Group** Used to add the database instance target to a group.
    - **Properties** Used to view and modify the database instance target properties.

- **Metric and Collection Settings** Used to view and modify metric alert thresholds for the database instance target.

- **Target Information** Provides a quick link to basic database instance status information.

Unlike previous versions of OEM, most screens are now accessed via the drop-down menus rather than the related links, which are gone. This provides a much quicker and easier method of navigating OEM Cloud Control 12*c*.

Performance

The Performance tab of the Database Home screen is where most of us database performance tuning consultants go first, when tackling Oracle performance problems. The information shown in the Performance tab varies based on whether the database is a RAC cluster or a single-instance database and which version of Oracle you are monitoring. For this example a non-RAC database will be used. The RAC database provides cluster information such as interconnect and cache fusion information as well as aggregated performance information, but the basic information is essentially the same. The upper part of the Performance screen contains information about the runnable processes (host utilization) as well as the representation of Average Active Sessions. Both of these graphs provide valuable information about the utilization of the system. This section of the Performance screen is shown in Figure 9-4.

- **Host: Runnable Processes** This graph provides information on how busy the underlying host operating system is. The closer the number of the runnable processes is to the number of CPU cores, the busier the system is. If the number of runnable processes exceeds the number of CPU cores, then queuing is occurring and the system is in a wait state. In a RAC environment, multiple hosts will be displayed in this graph.

- **Average Active Sessions** This graph represents the running sessions in Oracle and what they are waiting for. Since I/O is typically a bottleneck, it usually is the majority of waits in this graph. Other waits that might be prominent in this graph are CPU waits and Cluster waits. This graph provides a great representation of what the Oracle sessions are waiting for over time.

Just below and to the right of to the Average Active Sessions graph is a hyperlink to Top Activity, which is one of the most important performance graphs in Cloud Control.

The lower part of the Performance tab, as shown in Figure 9-5, provides additional information on instance performance, performance of I/O, Parallel

FIGURE 9-4. *The Performance screen of the Database Target (part 1)*

Execution, and Services. As with the earlier graphs, these graphs provide valuable insight into the current utilization and performance of the Oracle database server.

- **Throughput** This graph provides information on the activity of the database and includes Logons and Transactions per second in the first graph and Physical Reads per second and Redo Size per second in the second graph. This information gives you an idea of how much activity is occurring in the database.
- **I/O** Three graphs are provided: latency in ms for single block reads, MB per second split up by I/O function, and requests per second, also split up by I/O function. Since I/O performance is critical to Oracle performance, this information is extremely valuable. There are three radio buttons, which show the I/O breakdown by I/O function, I/O type, or Consumer Group. You will also see the I/O Calibration button. This takes you to a screen where you can schedule the I/O calibrator to run.

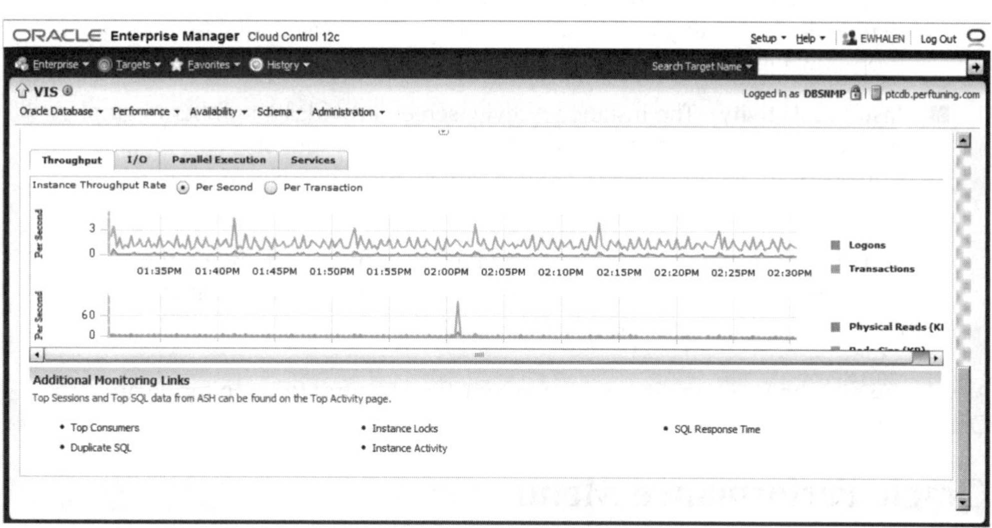

FIGURE 9-5. *The Performance screen of the Database Target (part 2)*

- **Parallel Execution** This option provides a number of graphs where parallel operations are depicted. They include sessions, parallel query slaves, statements parallelized, and statements serialized and downgraded.
- **Services** The final graph option provides information on Active sessions based on services.

These graphs provide information that lets you determine what the load on the database instance (or cluster) is.

The next section is the Additional Monitoring Links section. This provides an extensive library of additional specialized performance monitoring screens that enable you to dig in to the current activity and bottlenecks that the database is experiencing. The number and scope of the additional monitoring links is extensive, and they include the following:

- **Top Consumers** The Top Consumers screen provides a number of pie charts that show the system utilization based on Top Services, Top Modules, Top Clients, and Top Actions broken down by percentage of resources used. In addition, there are links to more details on each of these as well as Top Sessions.
- **Duplicate SQL** This is an interesting screen that shows which SQL statements would benefit from bind variables based on similarities.

- **Instance Locks** This screen provides a list of blocked sessions and objects that are locked in the database. There are several views available from the drop-down list, including blocking locks, user locks, and all locks.
- **Instance Activity** The Instance Activity screen provides a number of graphs based on several types of instance functions. The various sub-tabs include Cursors, Transaction, Session, Logical I/O, Physical I/O, Net I/O, Table activity, and All activity.
- **SQL Response Time** This screen provides a list of references and the latest collection of SQL Response times. This can be used as an indication of a potential performance problem.

As you can see, the functionality and power of Cloud Control for monitoring an Oracle database is quite extensive.

Oracle Performance Menu

The Performance Home screen is only the starting point for the Oracle Database performance. The Performance drop-down menu contains a number of tools that can be accessed by selecting them from this drop-down. Click Performance and the drop-down menu will appear. The items in the Performance drop-down menu are shown here and described in the following list. Some of them contain sub-menu items as shown in the list as well. They include the following:

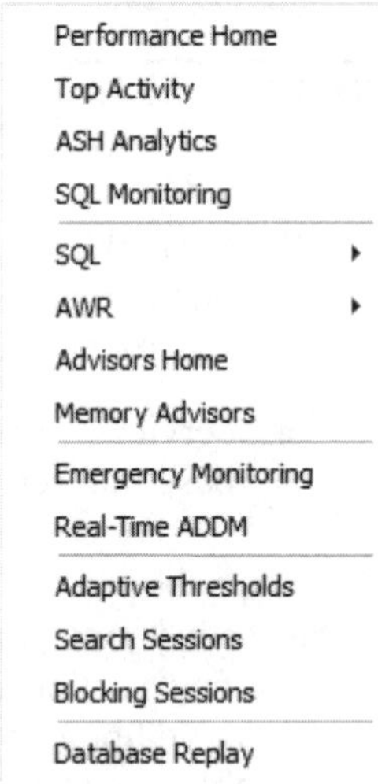

Performance Home
Top Activity
ASH Analytics
SQL Monitoring
SQL ▸
AWR ▸
Advisors Home
Memory Advisors
Emergency Monitoring
Real-Time ADDM
Adaptive Thresholds
Search Sessions
Blocking Sessions
Database Replay

- **Performance Home** The Performance Home screen.
- **Top Activity** The Top Activity screen provides valuable information on the top running sessions and SQL statements in the system.

  The Top Activity screen (Figure 9-6) provides a utility where you can view the performance of the database instance and determine which sessions, services, objects, and so on are causing the most load on the system. This is a great tool for finding specific SQL statements that are taking up system resources and then drilling into them to view the execution plan. This tool is very useful.

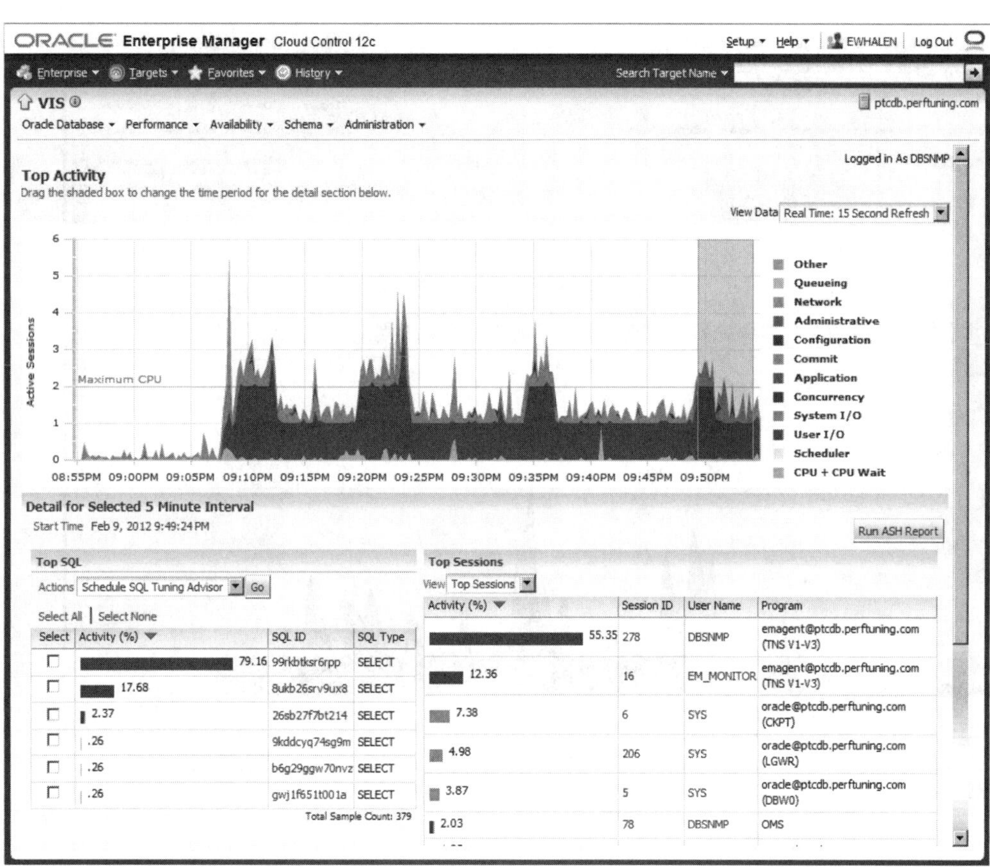

FIGURE 9-6. *The Top Activity screen*

- **ASH Analytics** ASH Analytics is a new tool in Oracle Enterprise Manager Cloud Control 12*c* that is used to analyze system activity.

  New in Oracle Cloud Control 12*c* is ASH Analytics. ASH Analytics allows you to take Active Session History (ASH) data and drill into it using various dimensions in order to determine which sessions are contributing load on the system. By using various filters and views, you can drill down and determine exactly what is going on in the database. The top part of the ASH Analytics screen is shown in Figure 9-7.

FIGURE 9-7. *The ASH Analytics Screen (part 1)*

This is a favorite database monitoring feature in Cloud Control 12*c*. The remainder of the ASH Analytics screen is shown in Figure 9-8.

- **SQL Monitoring** This utility shows the top SQL statements that are running in the system over the specified interval.

  SQL Monitoring allows you to view SQL statements running in the system and to watch their progress. With the Oracle Database 11*g* or newer, it is possible to view SQL statements in progress. The main SQL Monitoring screen is shown in Figure 9-9.

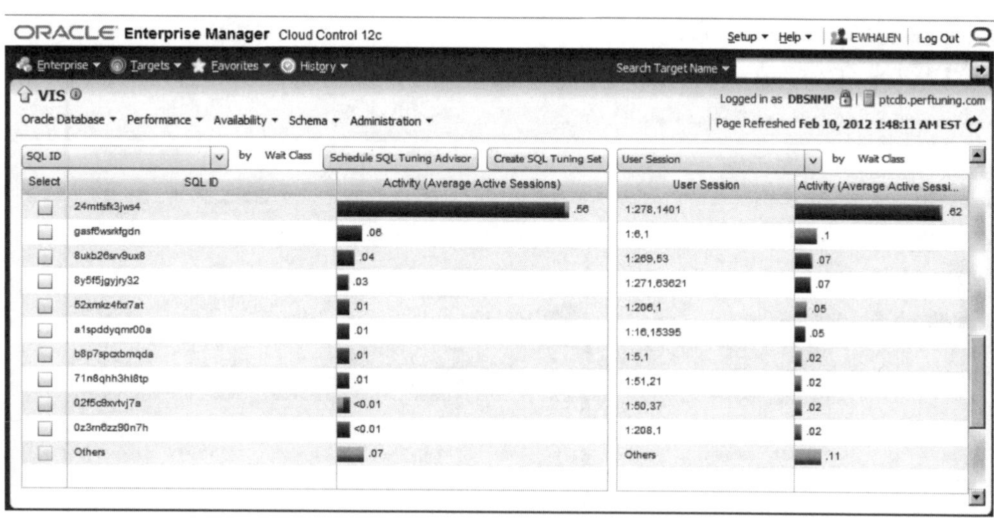

FIGURE 9-8. *The ASH Analytics screen (part 2)*

Clicking on a SQL ID allows you to drill into the SQL statement and view its progress. Notice in Figure 9-10 that in the execution plan, both estimated and actual statistics are provided.

SQL Monitoring has been available since Oracle Database 11*g*.

- **SQL**
    - **SQL Tuning Advisor** Invokes the SQL Tuning Advisor. In Oracle Grid Control 11*g* this was available from Advisor Central. The SQL Tuning Advisor screen allows you to schedule a job to run the SQL Tuning Advisor.
    - **SQL Performance Analyzer** Invokes the SQL Performance Analyzer. This tool allows you to create SQL Performance Analyzer tasks and run simulations.
    - **SQL Access Advisor** Allows you to set the SQL Access Advisor options and run the SQL Access Advisor.
    - **SQL Tuning Sets** Used to view and manage SQL Tuning Sets.

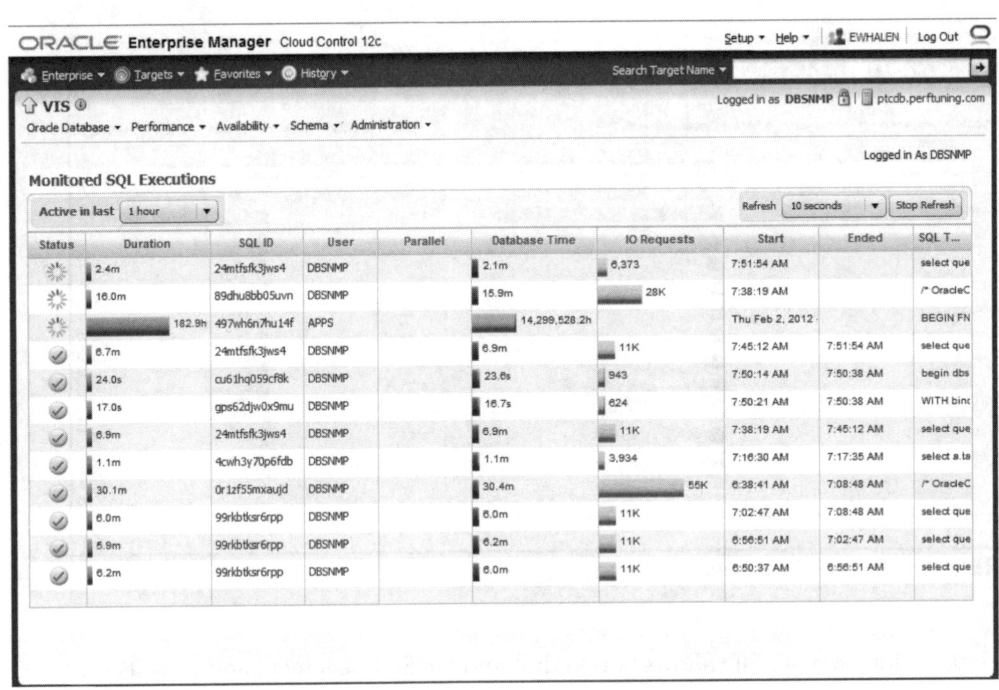

FIGURE 9-9. *The SQL Monitoring screen*

- **SQL Plan Control** Used to manage SQL Profiles, SQL Patches, and SQL Plan Baselines. These tools are used to adjust plans that the SQL Optimizer uses.
- **Optimizer Statistics** Used to manage the Optimizer Statistics. This is a top-level screen that allows you to run other utilities to gather, restore, lock, and otherwise manage optimizer statistics.
- **Cloud Control SQL History** Provides a list of SQL statements run by the Cloud Control utility, so that they can be eliminated from a tuning engagement.
- **Search SQL** Used to search for SQL statements that are available for monitoring in Cloud Control.
- **Run SQL** Used to run a SQL statement in the monitored database instance.

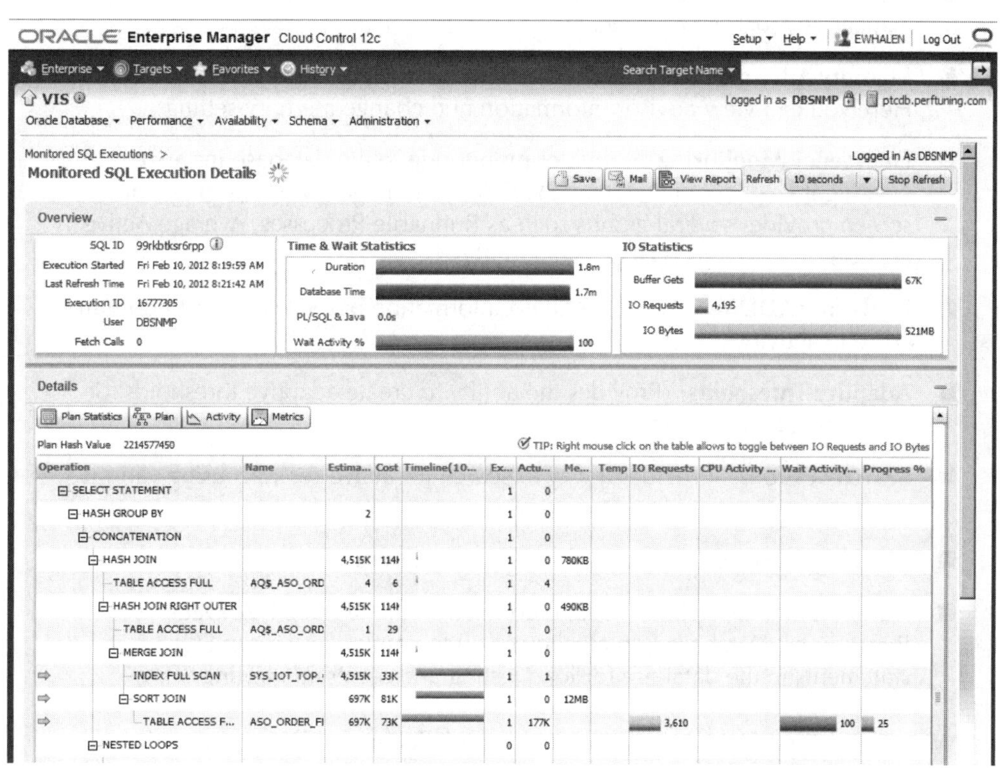

FIGURE 9-10. *The Monitored SQL Execution Details screen*

- **SQL Worksheet** Also used to run a SQL statement in the monitored database instance.

- **AWR**
  - **AWR Report** Allows you to generate an Automatic Workload Repository (AWR) report.
  - **AWR Administration** Allows you to administer AWR snapshots, frequency, retention, and so on, and to manage snapshots and baselines.
  - **Compare Period ADDM** Allows you to create an ADDM comparison report between two intervals or between an interval and a baseline.
  - **Compare Period Report** Allows you to view a previously created ADDM comparison report.

- **Advisors Home** This is a link to Advisor Central. Here you can view and manage advisors and checkers.
- **Memory Advisors** The Oracle database instance memory advisor screen. Here you can view advisor information and change memory settings.
- **Emergency Monitoring** Provides monitoring to the database instance via a lightweight connection as SYSDBA for emergency monitoring. This screen provides several graphs such as Runnable Processes, Average Active Sessions, and I/O, as well as Hang Analysis.
- **Real-Time ADDM** Provides ADDM information based on the last hour (and current) activity.
- **Adaptive Thresholds** Provides the ability to create adaptive thresholds for monitoring and alerting.
- **Search Sessions** Provides a way to search for active sessions using various criteria.
- **Blocking Sessions** Displays blocked session trees.
- **Database Replay** This is used to configure, run, and analyze Database Replay jobs. Database Replay allows you to capture and rerun SQL statements in the database for load testing and regression testing.

With Cloud Control 12*c*, the traditional hyperlinks have mainly been replaced with the drop-down menus. As you will see, some of the main components are only available from the drop-down menus. The drop-down menus are accessed by clicking on the menu, which opens up and allows you to browse into it, or drill down further into the menu.

Availability

The Availability screen of the Database Target contains summary information related to the availability of the database. This includes an Availability Summary, Backup/Recovery Summary, and a Data Guard Summary (if applicable). The main screen is shown in Figure 9-11.

The Availability Summary contains uptime information and availability details as well as links to the MAA Advisor.

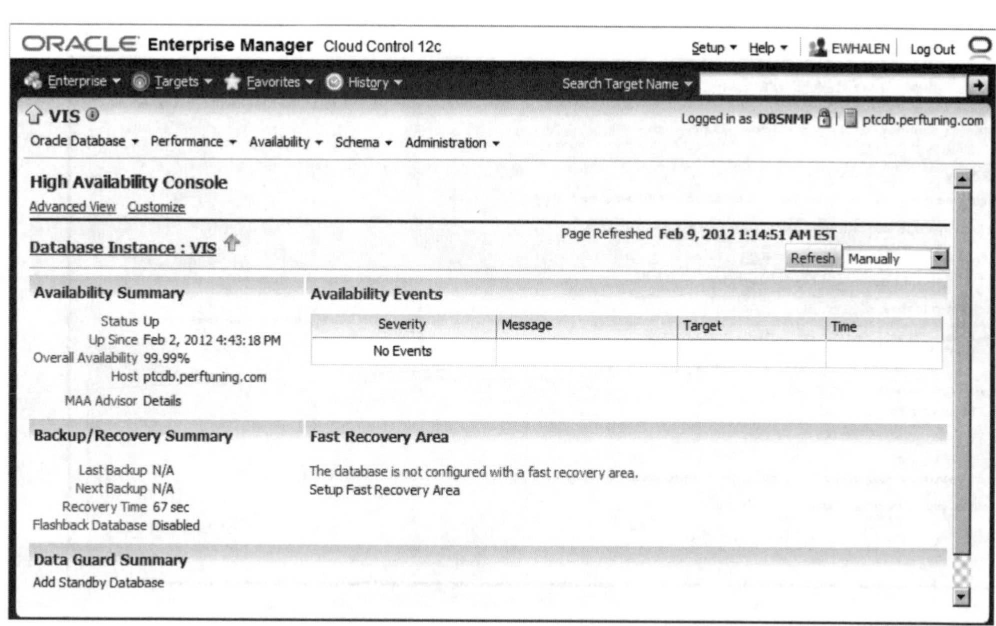

FIGURE 9-11. *The Availability screen of the Database Target*

Backup/Recovery Summary

The Backup/Recovery Summary section contains hyperlinks to the backup and recovery tools as well as backup/recovery information. The Fast Recovery Area section contains a link to set up the FRA if it is not already set up. In order to set up the FRA, click the Setup Fast Recovery Area hyperlink.

Within the Recovery Settings screen, scroll down to the Fast Recovery section and fill in the Fast Recovery Area Location path and size as shown in Figure 9-12. When you've completed filling in the information, click Apply.

Once you have completed this task, the FRA will show up in the Fast Recovery Area Usage section as shown in Figure 9-13.

At this point the FRA is configured and ready to use.

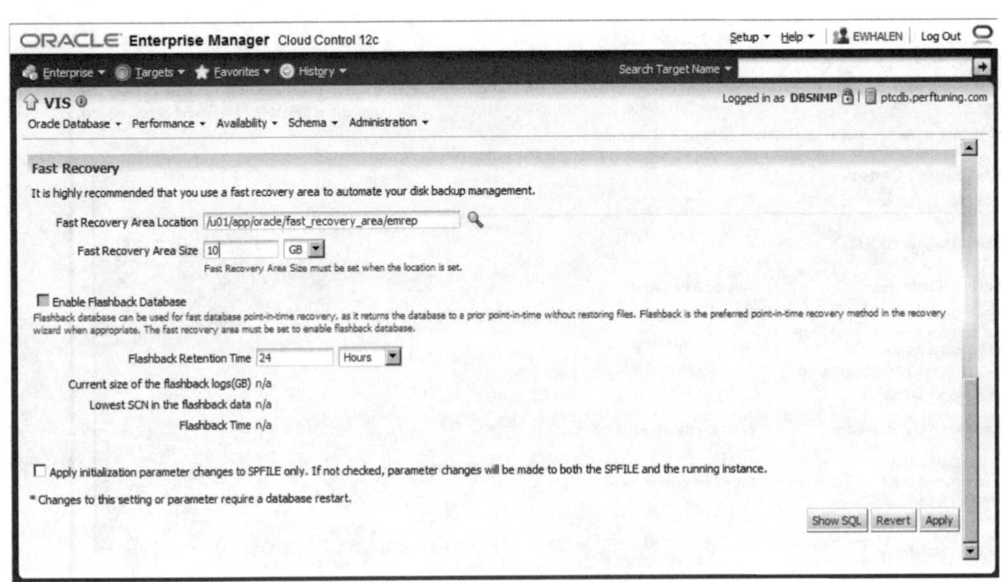

FIGURE 9-12. *The Recovery Area screen*

Data Guard Summary

The Data Guard Summary section provides the ability to create a standby system using Oracle Data Guard from Cloud Control. Since Cloud Control has the ability to clone Oracle home directories, and to control RMAN, it has all of the tools needed to create a standby database. As with most of the deployment tools, you will input all of the needed information, and then a Cloud Control job is created to set up the standby system. This can be a very convenient way of setting up a Data Guard standby without taking a lot of time to perform all of the steps by hand.

As a summary, the tasks performed by Cloud Control in order to create a Data Guard standby are as follows:

- Clone the Oracle Home directory from the primary to the secondary system.
- Create the supporting structures for the instance: Listener, ASM, directories, and so on.
- Create an RMAN backup of the primary database to a location that is accessible by both the primary and secondary systems. This step is not necessary if a duplicate with active database is used (11*g* database only).

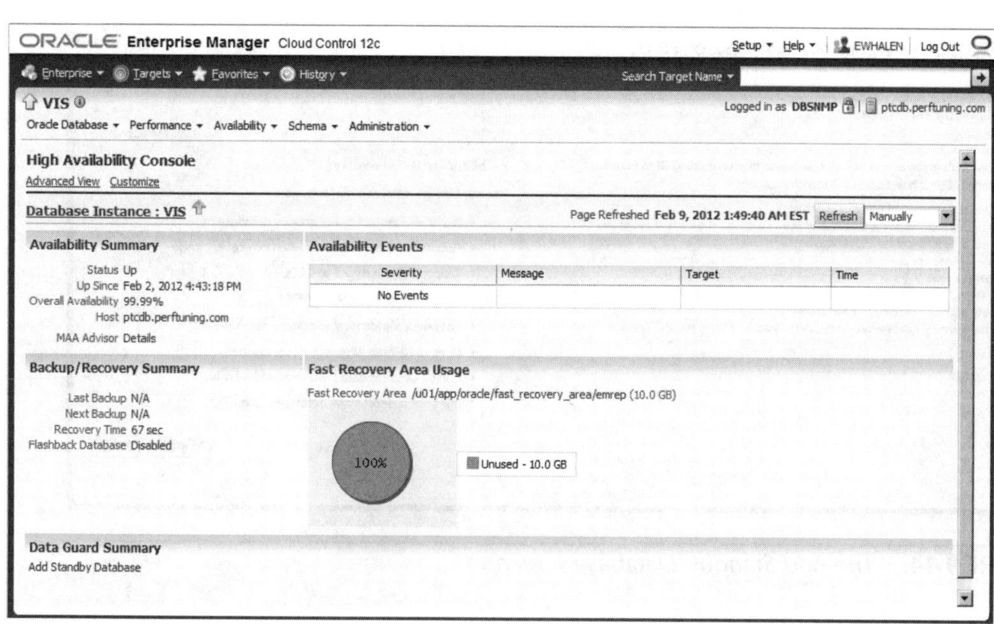

FIGURE 9-13. *The Availability tab of the Database Target screen showing the FRA Usage*

- Restore the RMAN backup of the primary database on the secondary system.
- Create a standby control file on the primary and restore it on the secondary system.
- Set parameters on primary and secondary systems.
- Start redo copy and log apply.

Once the Data Guard setup has completed, the standby should be ready to use. The following is an overview of the Data Guard configuration process:

1. Within the Add Standby Database screen (Figure 9-14), choose the type of standby—physical or logical—and whether to manage an existing standby database or create a primary database backup only. Then click Continue.
2. Within the Backup Type screen (Figure 9-15), choose Online Backup or Existing Backup and whether to copy the files via staging areas or not. Then click Continue.

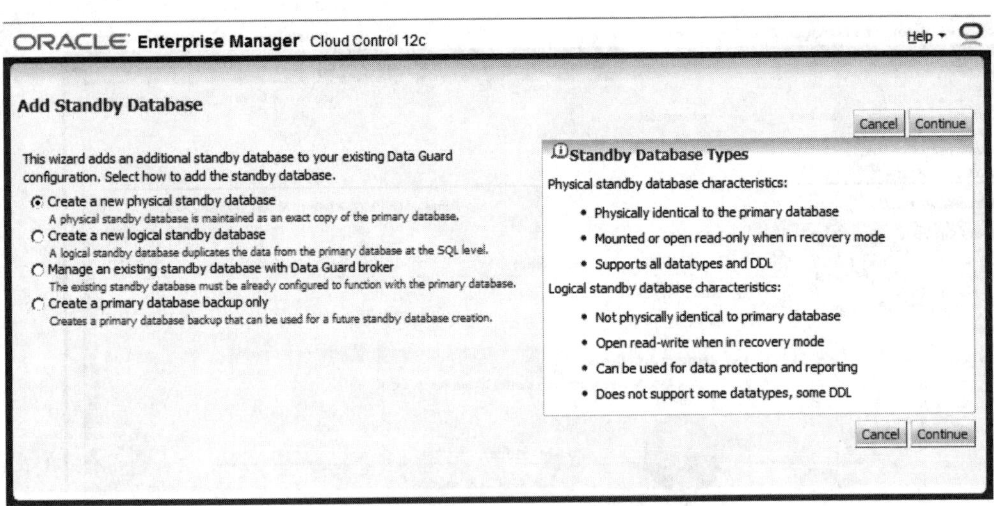

FIGURE 9-14. *The Add Standby Database screen*

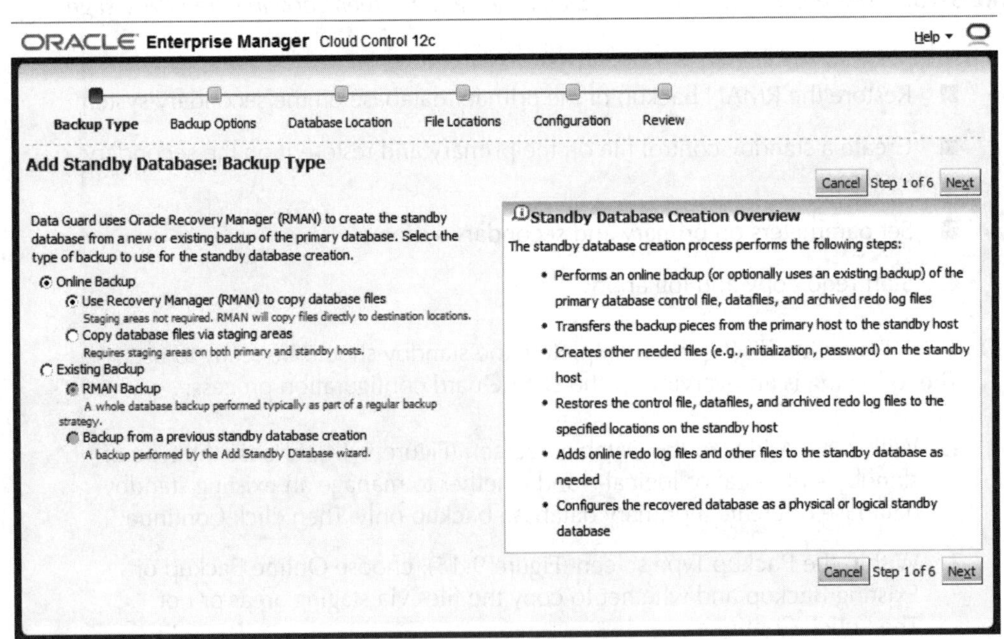

FIGURE 9-15. *The Add Standby Database: Backup Type*

3. Within the Backup Options screen (Figure 9-16), choose the Degree of Parallelism and the Primary Host Credentials.
4. Next, within the Database Location screen (Figure 9-17), choose ASM or File Systems for Database Storage. Also select the Standby Database Location for the Host and Oracle Home, as well as enter the Standby Host Credentials.
5. On the ASM Instance Login screen (Figure 9-18), enter and test credentials to log in to ASM.
6. Within the File Locations screen (Figure 9-19), specify either the database file locations (if filesystems) or the ASM diskgroups (if ASM). You also specify the Listener Configuration, either selecting the Grid Infrastructure listener or creating a new listener.

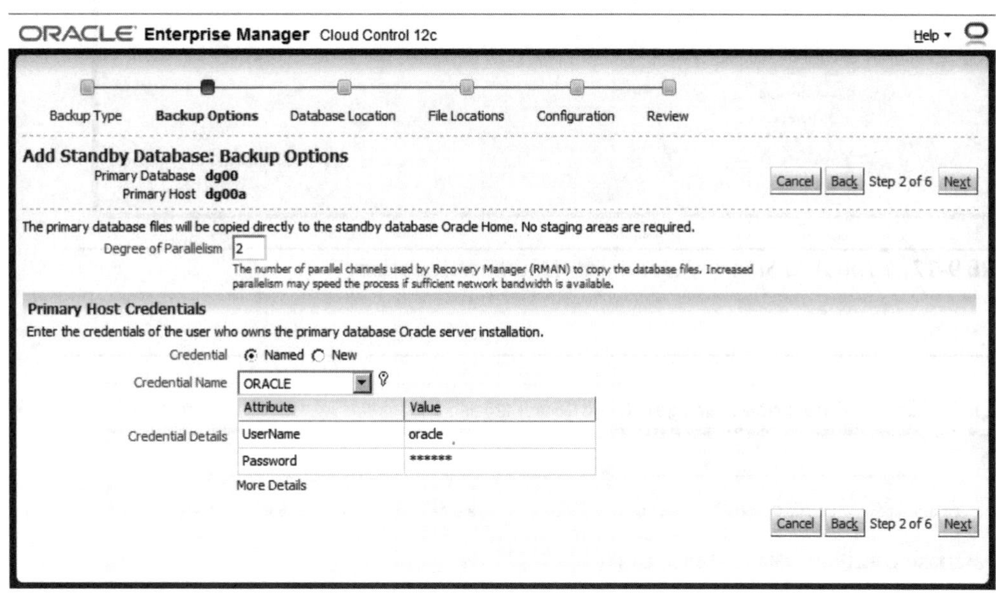

FIGURE 9-16. *The Add Standby Database: Backup Options*

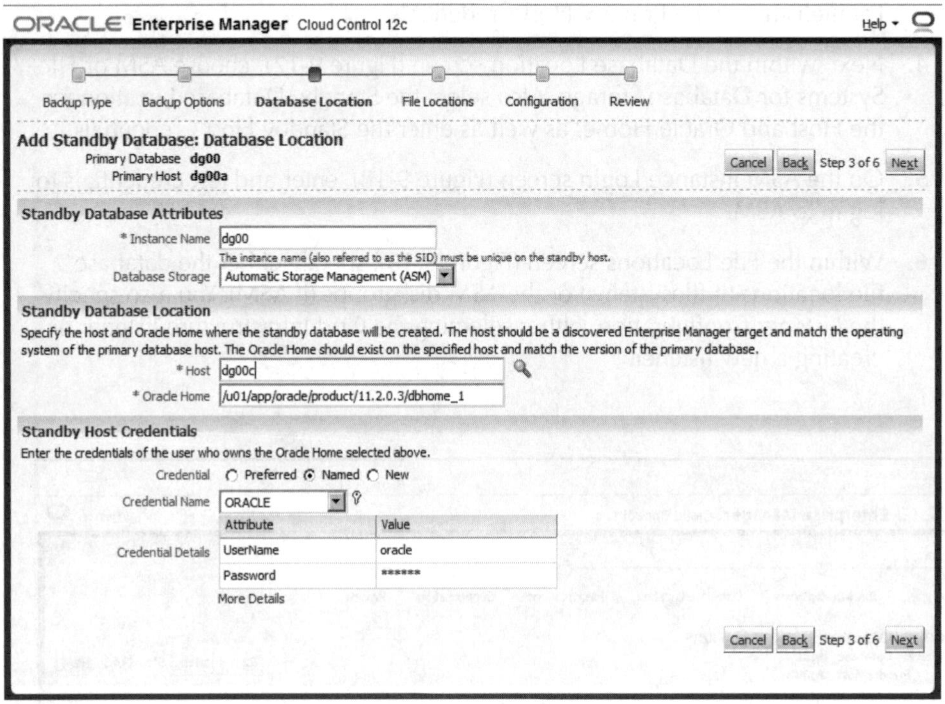

FIGURE 9-17. *The Add Standby Database: Database Location*

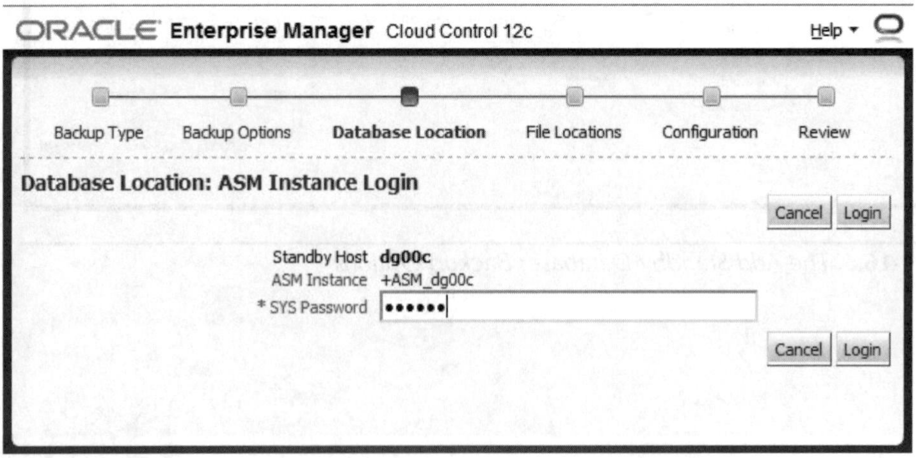

FIGURE 9-18. *The Add Standby Database: ASM Instance Login*

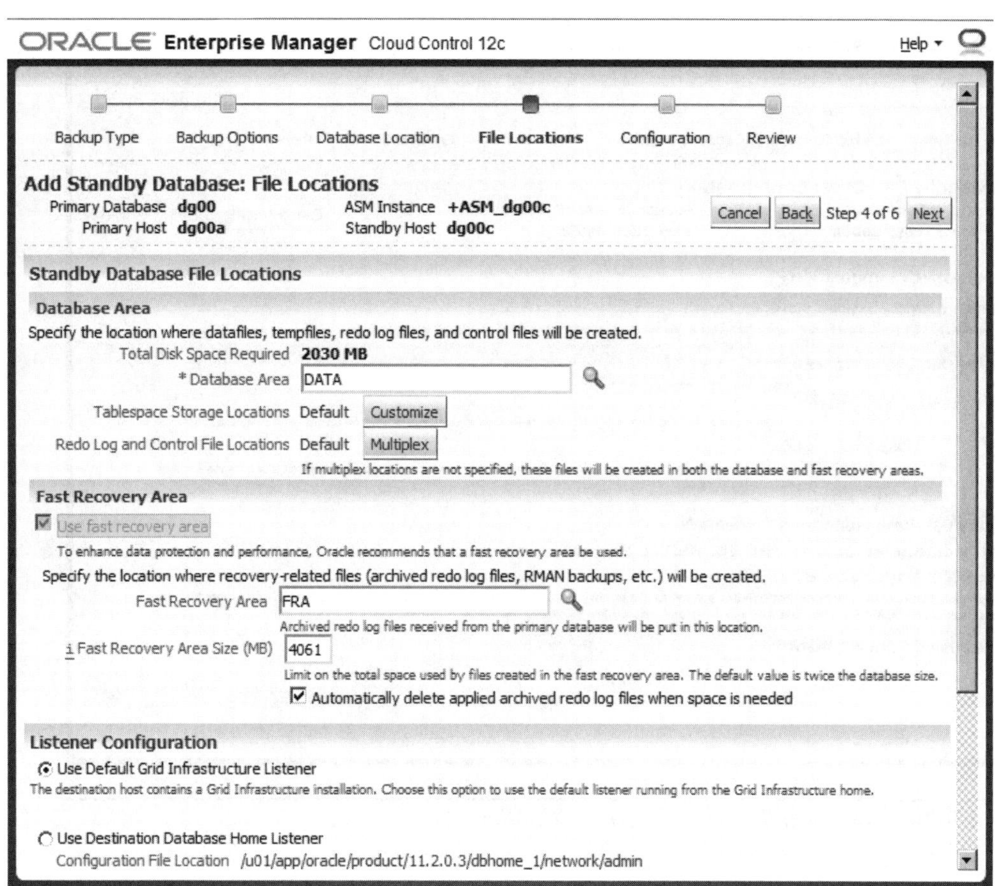

FIGURE 9-19. *The Add Standby Database: File Locations*

7. Within the Configuration screen (Figure 9-20), you can specify whether to use Oracle Restart (if applicable). Here, you also specify the Database Unique Name and Target Name. You also can specify the SYSDBA Monitoring Credentials.

8. Finally, review the configuration in the Review screen (Figure 9-21), and click Finish to begin the deployment.

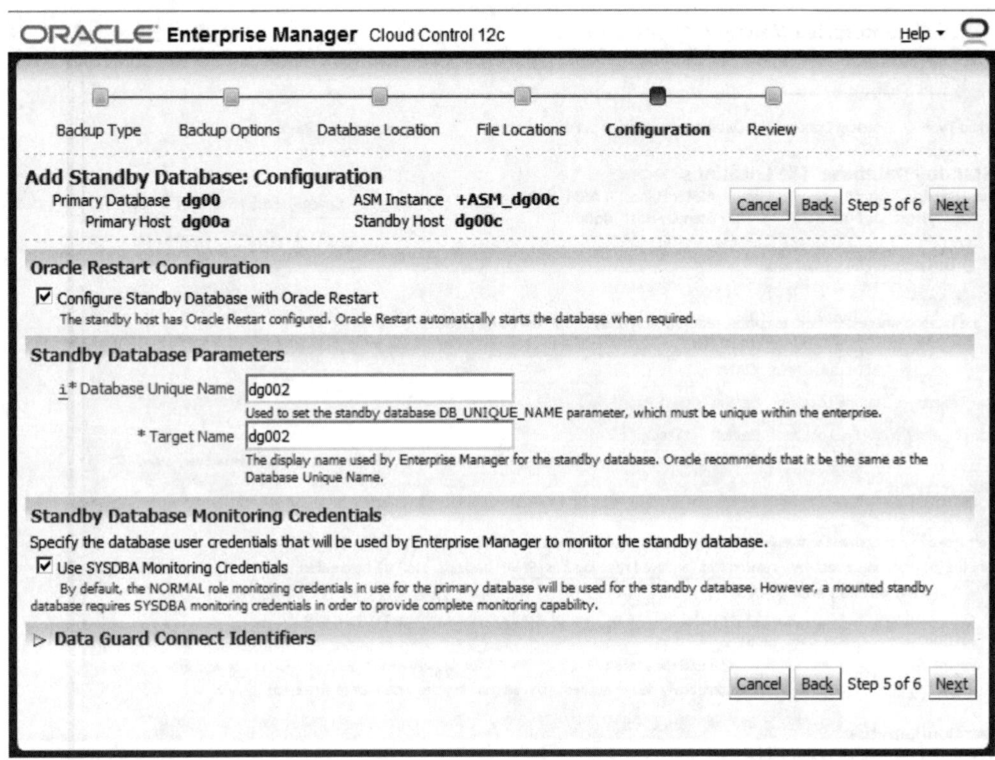

FIGURE 9-20. *The Add Standby Database: Configuration*

OEM Cloud Control 12*c* can easily and quickly create a standby database—either physical or logical—using either filesystems or ASM.

Availability Menu

The Availability Home screen is for Oracle Database availability options and monitoring and is accessible by selecting the High Availability Console screen (shown previously in Figure 9-13) from the Availability drop-down menu. The Availability drop-down menu contains a number of tools that can be accessed by selecting them from this drop down. They include the following:

- **High Availability Console** The Availability Home screen.
- **MAA Advisor** Invokes the Maximum Availability Advisor.

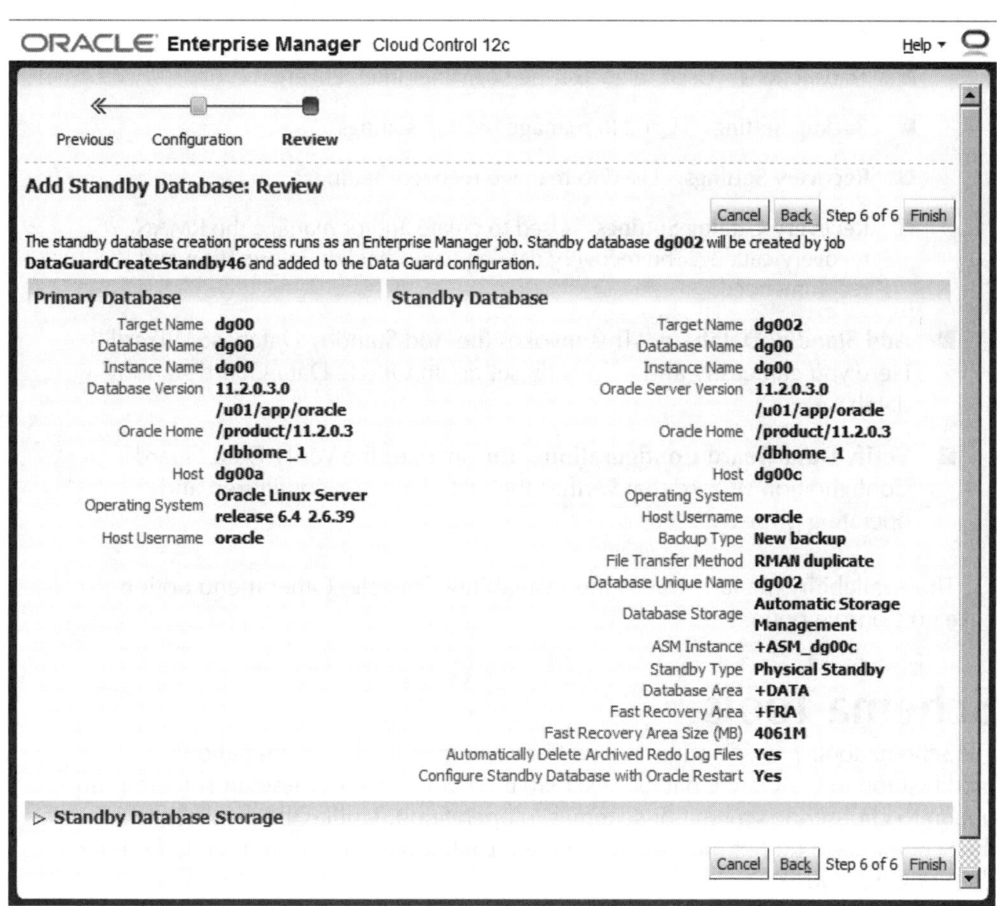

FIGURE 9-21. *The Add Standby Database: Review*

- **Backup & Recovery**
  - **Schedule Backups** Allows for the scheduling of RMAN backups.
  - **Manage Current Backups** Used to manage currently scheduled backups.
  - **Backup Reports** Used for creation of backup reports. Backup reports are very important and useful for determining the availability of the database instance.
  - **Restore Points** From this screen you can easily create one or more restore points and manage or verify current restore points.

- **Perform Recovery** Used to invoke the Recovery Wizard. This tool guides you through the recovery process.
- **Transactions** Used to access the LogMiner interactively.
- **Backup Settings** Used to manage backup settings.
- **Recovery Settings** Used to manage recovery settings.
- **Recovery Catalog Settings** Used to create and/or manage the RMAN recovery catalog. The recovery catalog tracks backup information and is recommended.

- **Add Standby Database** This invokes the Add Standby Database Wizard. Here you can easily and efficiently set up an Oracle Data Guard standby database.
- **Verify Data Guard Configuration** This invokes the Verify Data Guard Configuration Wizard that verifies the Data Guard is configured and operating properly.

The Availability menu includes the Availability Console. Other menu options have no Console option.

Schema Tools

The schema tools provide an extensive library of graphical tools that allows modification to the Oracle database schemas. Within each of these tools there is an option to choose the schema or schemas to operate on. Unlike the previous tabs, the Schema tools do not have a main screen. Each tool is accessed directly from the drop-down menu.

Schema Menu

Unlike other menu options, there is no Schema home screen. The Schema drop-down menu, shown here, contains a number of tools that can be accessed by selecting them from this menu.

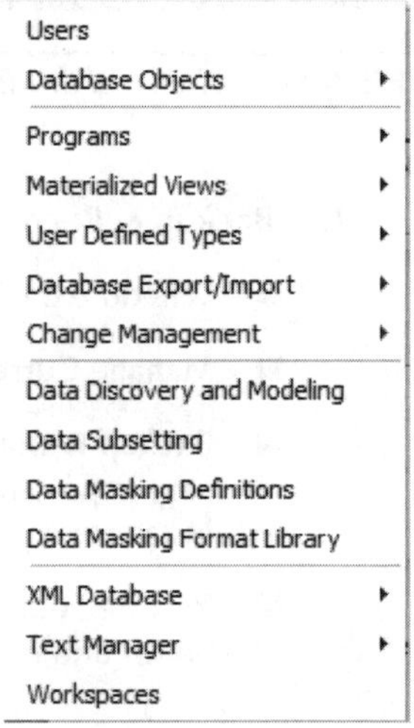

Users
Database Objects ▸
Programs ▸
Materialized Views ▸
User Defined Types ▸
Database Export/Import ▸
Change Management ▸
Data Discovery and Modeling
Data Subsetting
Data Masking Definitions
Data Masking Format Library
XML Database ▸
Text Manager ▸
Workspaces

They include the following:

- **Users** Used to view and/or manage Oracle database users.
- **Database Objects**
  - **Tables** This tool allows for the viewing and modification of tables. Searches can be done on either schemas or by object name or both.

- **Indexes** This tool allows for the viewing and modification of indexes. Searches can be done on either schemas or by object name or both.
- **Views** This tool allows for the viewing and modification of views. Searches can be done on either schemas or by object name or both.
- **Synonyms** This tool allows for the viewing and modification of synonyms. Searches can be done on either schemas or by object name or both.
- **Sequences** This tool allows for the viewing and modification of sequences. Searches can be done on either schemas or by object name or both.
- **Database Links** This tool allows for the viewing and modification of database links. Database links are global and not related to a specific schema.
- **Directory Objects** This tool allows for the viewing and modification of directory objects. Directory objects are not related to a specific schema.
- **Reorganize Objects** This tool allows for the reorganization of database objects using a graphical wizard.

- **Programs**
  - **Packages** This is a hyperlink to a tool to manage database packages.
  - **Package Bodies** This is a hyperlink to a tool to manage package bodies.
  - **Procedures** This is used to manage procedures.
  - **Functions** This is a link to a tool to manage functions.
  - **Triggers** Here you can view and manage triggers.
  - **Java Classes** This is where Java classes are managed.
  - **Java Sources** This is where Java sources are managed.
- **Materialized Views**
  - **Show All** This hyperlink invokes a tool for viewing and modifying materialized views themselves.
  - **Logs** This is where you can view and modify materialized view logs.
  - **Refresh Groups** Here you can configure the materialized views refresh groups.
  - **Dimensions** Provides a view of dimensions in the system.

- **User Defined Types**
  - **Array Types** Used for creating array types.
  - **Object Types** Used to create object types.
  - **Table Types** Used to create table types.
- **Database Export/Import**
  - **Transport Tablespaces** Used to manage and control transportable tablespaces.
  - **Export to Export Files** Used to invoke the Export Wizard. The Export Wizard guides you through the process of exporting Oracle databases, tablespaces, or tables to export files.
  - **Import from Import Files** Used to import Oracle databases from export files.
  - **Import from Database** Used to import Oracle databases, schemas, tables, or tablespaces from a database link.
  - **Load Data From User Files** Provides a graphical tool for running the Oracle SQL Loader utility.
  - **View Export and Import Jobs** This utility allows you to view currently running export and import jobs.
- **Change Management**
  - **Data Comparisons** Provides a tool to compare database objects to those in a reference database.
  - **Schema Change Plans** This is used to compare database schema definitions from those in a reference database.
  - **Schema Baselines** In this screen schema baselines can be created or imported.
  - **Schema Comparisons** Here schema comparisons can be made. Two different systems' dictionaries can be compared and viewed graphically in several different ways.
  - **Schema Synchronizations** With schema synchronizations, objects in one database can be made to be identical to objects in another database.
- **Data Discovery and Modeling** This is part of Oracle's database subsetting and data masking option and allows for the discovery and modeling of database objects for subsetting and/or masking.

- **Data Subsetting** Used for configuring data subsetting.
- **Data Masking Definitions** Used to modify data in a database for test, development, and QA purposes. The function of data masking is to remove or scramble personally identifiable information so that this information is secured. This is where data masking definitions are set up.
- **Data Masking Format Library** The format library contains formats and conversion definitions for various data types. The data masking option allows for personal information such as social security numbers, credit card numbers, and so on. This is mainly used in environments that handle personal data, where security is required.
- **XML Database** This option provides a number of tools for administering an XML database. It includes configuration tools, ACLs, and other tools for managing the XML database.
  - **Configuration** This is where the XML database is configured.
  - **Resources** These are XML resources for XML databases. They can be created, edited, and viewed here.
  - **Access Control Lists** The Access Control Lists for XML databases can be viewed and created here.
  - **XML Schemas** Here you can view and create XML schemas.
  - **XML Type Tables** This hyperlink allows for viewing and creating XML tables.
  - **XML Type Views** This hyperlink allows for viewing and creating XML types.
  - **XML Indexes** Here you can manage XML indexes.
  - **XML Repository Events** This is where XML event handlers are viewed.

Oracle Text is an add-on feature to the Oracle database server for storing, indexing, and retrieving documents stored within the database. Oracle Text allows for lexical searching and analysis and is a very powerful tool. This section has two hyperlinks to tools to assist with configuration and processing of Oracle Text data. The following Oracle Text options are available from the Schema menu by first selecting Text Manager:

- **Text Manager**
  - **Text Indexes** Used for the creation of text indexes.
  - **Query Statistics** Statistics for querying the Oracle Text database.

- **Workspaces** The Oracle Workspace Manager is used to assist the DBA and application developers in keeping separate versions of data. It is used as a virtual environment to separate and keep track of these various versions of data.

The schema tools are extensive and can be accessed only via the drop-down menu.

Administration Tools

The Administration tools enable you to manage the configuration of the database instance. These tools, like the Schema tools, are only available via the drop-down menu and there are a large number of them. These tools are very useful for administering the database and the database instance.

Administration Menu

As with the Schema menu, there is no Administration home screen. The Administration drop-down menu, shown here, contains a number of tools that can be accessed by selecting them from this drop-down.

Initialization Parameters
Security ▸
Storage ▸
Oracle Scheduler ▸
Streams and Replication ▸
Migrate to ASM
Resource Manager
Database Feature Usage

They include the following:

- **Initialization Parameters** This group has hyperlinks for configuring database parameters and so on.
- **Security**
    - **Home** The main security home screen. Provides a number of graphs showing the current state of security of the database and patch recommendations and auditing control.
    - **Reports** Security-related reports.
    - **Users** Used to view and manage user accounts.

- **Roles** Used to view and manage database roles.
- **Profiles** Used to view and manage database profiles.
- **Audit Settings** This tool is very useful for monitoring audit settings in the database. These can often be difficult to sort and view with SQL statements, whereas it is much easier on OEM Cloud Control to process these settings. The auditing can be viewed by privileges, objects, and statements.
- **Transparent Data Encryption** Oracle TDE can be configured from this utility and wallets can be created.
- **Oracle Label Security** Label security can be managed here if it is enabled on the current database.
- **Virtual Private Database Policies** Virtual Private Database policies and advanced settings are managed from this utility.
- **Application Contexts** This link provides access to the Oracle application context feature, which enables applications to be session sensitive.
- **Enterprise User Security** This is used to allow OEM to manage Oracle LDAP information.
- **Database Vault** Allows OEM to manage an Oracle database vault (if installed).

- **Storage**
  - **Control Files** This allows for configuration of the control files. Here you can see the configuration and status of the control files. Control files can be configured as well as monitored.
  - **Data Files** This is similar to the tablespaces utility but provides information and management on the datafile level.
  - **Tablespaces** Tablespace information is available from this screen. There is significant information about the configuration and the utilization of the tablespaces. You can modify tablespaces and data files from this tool. You can also drill down and actually display the contents of tablespaces.
  - **Make Tablespaces Locally Managed** This allows a dictionary-managed tablespace to be migrated to a locally managed database.
  - **Temporary Tablespace Groups** This utility provides the ability to monitor and manage the temporary tablespace groups that are configured for the current database.
  - **Rollback Segments** This is where rollback segments are managed.

- **Segment Advisor** The Segment Advisor identifies which segments can be shrunk.
- **Automatic Undo Management** This utility allows for configuration of Oracle Automatic Undo Management (UNDO tablespace).
- **Redo Log Groups** This is where redo log groups are managed and monitored.
- **Archive Logs** Archive logs are managed from this utility.

The Oracle Scheduler, also on the Administration drop-down menu, is critical to the operation of the Oracle database server. Included in Oracle 11*g* is the concept of maintenance windows when maintenance tasks are allowed to run. Maintenance windows are closely related to the Resource Manager. The Oracle Scheduler section contains links to the traditional job queues as well as the scheduler. Included in this section is a hyperlink to the automatic maintenance tasks.

NOTE
The schedulers listed here should not be confused with the Oracle Cloud Control jobs. *Those jobs are run from the OMS server and are control tasks on the target systems. These links represent connections to the schedulers within the Oracle database server itself. These schedulers can also be managed via SQL statements.*

- **The Oracle Scheduler**
  - **Home** The Oracle Scheduler home screen.
  - **Jobs** Invokes a GUI front end to the database job queue.
  - **Job Classes** The job classes are used to link jobs with resource consumer groups. This is where the resource consumer group used for jobs is defined.
  - **Chains** Chains are jobs that execute in certain steps. This link allows you to create and manage scheduler chains.
  - **Schedules** Invokes a GUI to the DBMS scheduler.
  - **Programs** The programs are stored procedures that are used within jobs. There are a number of programs that you will find that have been created during the Oracle installation.
  - **Windows** This is where you can view and configure the maintenance windows. This is a useful tool for managing and configuring the maintenance windows in a graphical fashion. The maintenance windows actually use the Resource Manager for controlling the utilization within these windows.

  - **Window Groups** This is essentially a grouping of scheduler windows for ease of use.
  - **Global Attributes** Just as the name says, this is where attributes can be set for the scheduler and its jobs.
  - **Automated Maintenance Tasks** Here you can see which Automated Maintenance tasks are enabled and can configure/disable them as desired.
- **Streams and Replication**
  - **Setup Streams** Invokes the Setup Streams Wizard. This wizard walks you through the process of setting up and configuring streams.
  - **Manage Replication** Invokes the Manage Replication Wizard. This wizard walks you through the process of setting up and configuring replication.
  - **Setup Advanced Replication** Invokes the Setup Advanced Replication Wizard. This wizard walks you through the process of setting up and configuring advanced replication.
  - **Manage Advanced Replication** Used to perform management of advanced replication.
  - **Manage Advanced Queues** Used to manage the Oracle Advanced Queues.
- **Migrate to ASM** This utility is an important utility that provides the tools for a non-ASM database to be migrated to an ASM database. This can be very useful since it automates the process.

The Resource Manager, also part of the Administration drop-down menu, is an important part of the Oracle database server and includes the ability to limit resource usage on a per session basis, group basis, or even an instance basis. It is the core of the Oracle instance caging feature introduced in 11*g*. The Resource Manager has been around for a while, but traditionally had to be managed by using SQL statements, which made it difficult to manage. Now it can be administered via Cloud Control, which has made it much easier to use.

- **Resource Manager** Used to manage and configure the Resource Manager. The Resource Manager is used for managing resources used by sessions and for the Oracle 11*g* new feature, instance caging.
- **Database Feature Usage** Provides information about what features are being used in the current database.

The Administration menu is quite extensive and provides a number of tools for administering the Oracle database instance.

Summary

This chapter provided an overview and some details on the extensive toolset available within Oracle Enterprise Manager Cloud Control 12*c* for the administration of the Oracle database. Those of you who are familiar with Oracle Enterprise Manager 11*g* Grid Control probably noticed many differences, including the introduction of ASH Analytics. These tools provide a robust monitoring, alerting, and administration console for the Oracle database server.

CHAPTER 10

System and Storage Administrators: Manage Infrastructure with Cloud Control

Although databases are, naturally, the primary target of Cloud Control functionality, the product provides a deep wealth of tools for managing both system and storage resources. In this chapter we will take a closer look at these features. Enterprise Manager comes with a comprehensive set of metrics and management tools that support the key back-end components on which databases rely: systems and storage.

Before continuing, we need to clarify the term "systems." When we refer to systems within this chapter, we are specifically addressing hosts; generally hosts where a database instance resides. Cloud Control also supports the concept of "systems." A *system* in this context is a collection of related manageable entities, which together provide one or more business functions. Members of any system can have well-defined relationships among themselves, called *associations*. A Cloud Control system is a set of infrastructure components (hosts, databases, listeners, application servers, and so on) that work together to provide an application service. For example, an e-mail application may require the services of a host, a database, a listener, and an application server. Together these services provide the e-mail functionality.

An Administrator can define a system and Cloud Control can also identify standard systems. An example of a standard system is a database system. A database relies on the functionality of the instance, host, listener, and storage. If any area of functionality is lost, the database is inoperable. Groups, which were discussed in Chapter 8, have the same features that are supported for systems, such as jobs and blackouts. Groups differ slightly from systems, however. Groups consist of any set of targets the Administrator may wish to group together for administrative purposes (including monitoring), whereas systems contain targets that work together to provide a functional service.

Our objective, however, is to take a closer look at the functionality provided by Cloud Control to manage and monitor hosts. To avoid confusion we will use the term host in the remainder of this chapter, as this is our primary interest. Without an operating host, we cannot have a functioning database system.

To access the host monitoring and management features within Cloud Control, we start by selecting Hosts from the Targets menu—see Figure 10-1.

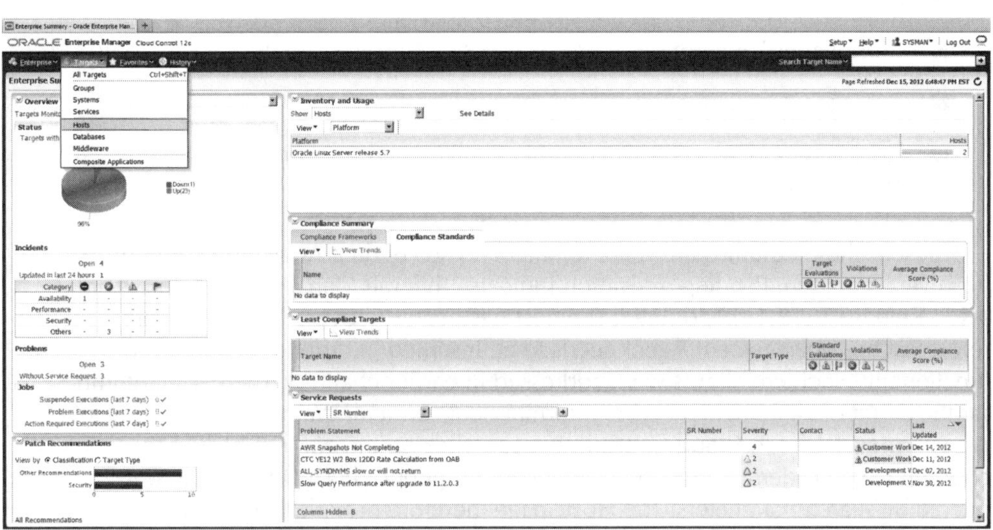

FIGURE 10-1. *Accessing hosts from the Enterprise Summary screen*

Host Administration

When you install an Agent, it automatically discovers the resident host target and provides out-of-box metrics for monitoring the host's availability and performance (unless, of course, you have configured a default monitoring template as described in Chapter 8, "Cloud Control Maintenance and Tuning"). This is the process—of converting a host from an unmanaged to a managed role. All the Managed Hosts are listed on the Hosts Targets page. Basically, a host is a machine where managed databases and other services reside. As shown in Figure 10-2, the default page displays the following information:

- Hostname
- Status (Up/Down)
- Pending Activation

- Incident Alarms
- Compliance Violations
- Average Compliance Score
- Host Summary Metrics: CPU Utilization %, Memory Utilization %, and Total I/O per Second

Most of these columns are self-explanatory. The Pending Activation column, however, is unique. Pending Activation indicates that the Management Agent is not a 12*c* Release 1 (12.1.0.1) or later. The host has been discovered, but a newer release of the Management Agent needs to be installed in order to acquire full functionality. Incident alarms were addressed in earlier chapters. There is a column for the count of each incident type: Informational, Critical, Warning, and Escalated. As with most tables in Cloud Control, you can click on the column header to choose the sort order. If there are a significant number of hosts, the list can be filtered by search parameters. The Hosts page therefore provides a quick view of the availability of the target systems and any associated alerts. A default list of metrics provides a summary of performance, and if more information is required, the metric serves as a link to detailed data.

If desired, the Administrator can modify the columns in this display by clicking on the Customize Table Columns link, to access the Customize Table Columns page—see Figure 10-3. As you can see, there are a significant number of column choices.

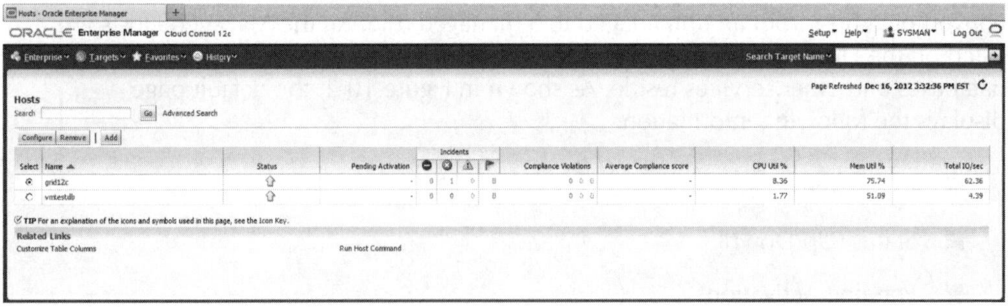

FIGURE 10-2. *Hosts Targets page*

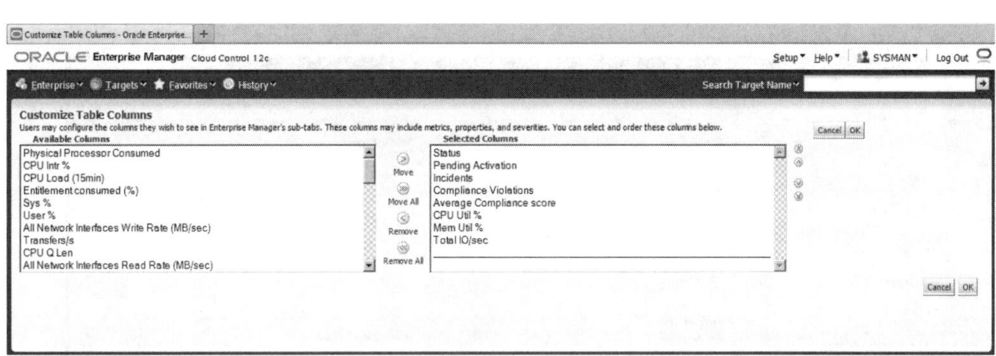

FIGURE 10-3. *Host Targets page: Customize Table Columns*

From the Host Targets page, you also have the option of executing an operating system command on one or more selected targets by clicking the Run Host Command link to access the Run Host Command page, illustrated in Figure 10-4. Additional hosts can be added to the target list for the executed command. The Administrator can select from stored Preferred or Named credentials or create new credentials.

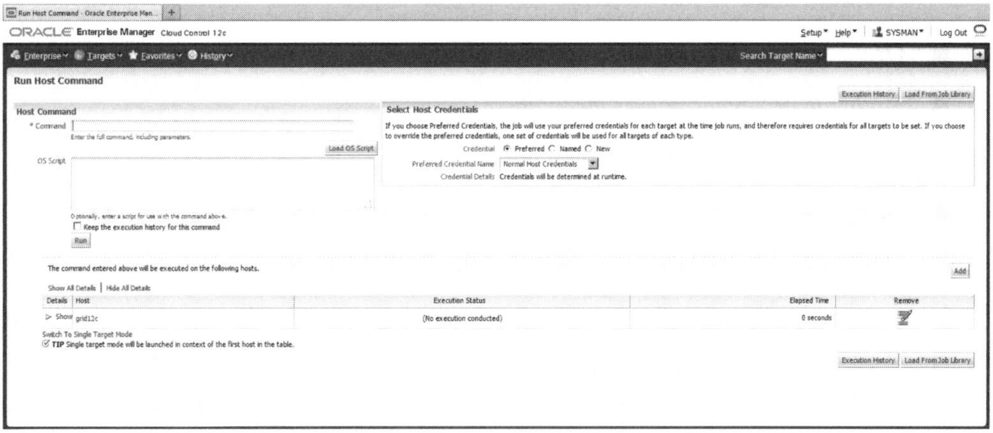

FIGURE 10-4. *Run Host Command page*

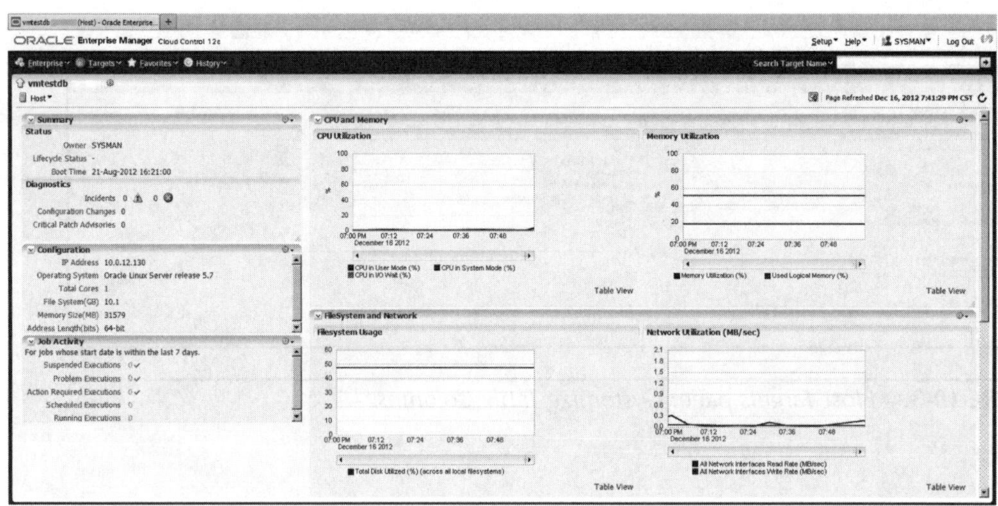

FIGURE 10-5. *Host Home page—top*

Host Home Page

The Host Home page provides a quick view of the vital statistics for the host. The top portion of the Host Home page is illustrated in Figure 10-5 and the bottom portion in Figure 10-6. Using the Host Home page, the Administrator can perform the following functions:

- Drill down to view detailed statistics about the host
- Study the policy violations for the host
- Study all the alerts associated with the host
- Analyze the job activity
- Determine whether there are outstanding patch advisories
- Determine the last security evaluation of the host
- Investigate further the health of the host

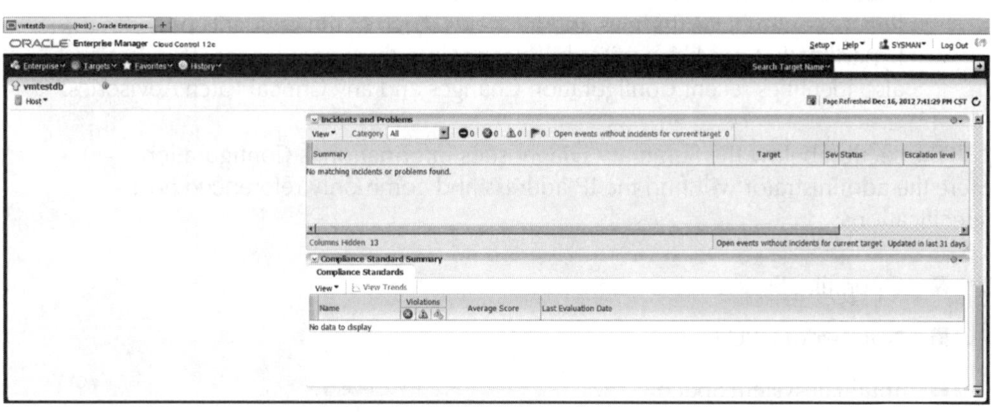

FIGURE 10-6. *Host Home page—bottom*

Once a specific host is selected from the list of targets, the Host's Home page is displayed. As is the case with many home pages in Cloud Control, the default page contains two screens of information. The default page is composed of these sections:

- Summary: Status and Diagnostics
- Configuration
- Job Activity
- CPU and Memory
- FileSystem and Network
- Incidents and Problems
- Compliance Standard Summary

Within each section you can click on hyperlinks to display detailed data. The Summary section includes the following sub-sections:

- **Status** This section provides information on the status of the host along with the last boot timestamp. If the server has been assigned a Lifecycle Status, this information will also be listed.[1]

---

[1] Lifecycle Status denotes the importance of the server in the enterprise. You can use predefined status values or create new values. Lifecycle Status is a property applied to individual targets to help categorize and manage the target within Enterprise Manager.

- **Diagnostics** The Summary Diagnostics section contains information (and links) about ADDM findings and incidents. Each of the incidents provides a hyperlink that can be used to drill deeper into those incidences. This section also identifies recent Configuration Changes and any Critical Patch Advisories.

The section below the Summary Diagnostics information is Configuration. Here the administrator will find the IP address and commonly referenced host specifications:

- Operating System
- Number of CPU Cores
- Total Filesystem Space
- Total Memory Size
- Word Address Length (32/64 bits)

The final section on the left-hand side of the display is Job Activity. This section lists the number of scheduled, running, suspended, and problem (stopped/failed) executions for all the Enterprise Manager jobs on the target. By clicking the number next to the status group, the Administrator can view a list of the associated jobs.

The CPU and FileSystem sections allow for both the graphical and table display of data. There are numerous hyperlinks in both sections that allow the Administrator to view additional data. For example, by selecting one of the CPU categories from the CPU Utilization graph, the user is presented with a choice of three additional links—see Figure 10-7:

- **Problem Analysis** Links to tools to diagnose issues and compare to related targets.
- **Metric Details** Dive down into greater detail.
- **Target Homepage** Where applicable, navigate to a different target homepage.

The Incidents and Problems display provides a summary of any issues and the related target. The Administrator can modify the viewed columns and sort order. The issues can be limited to specific categories:

- Availability
- Business

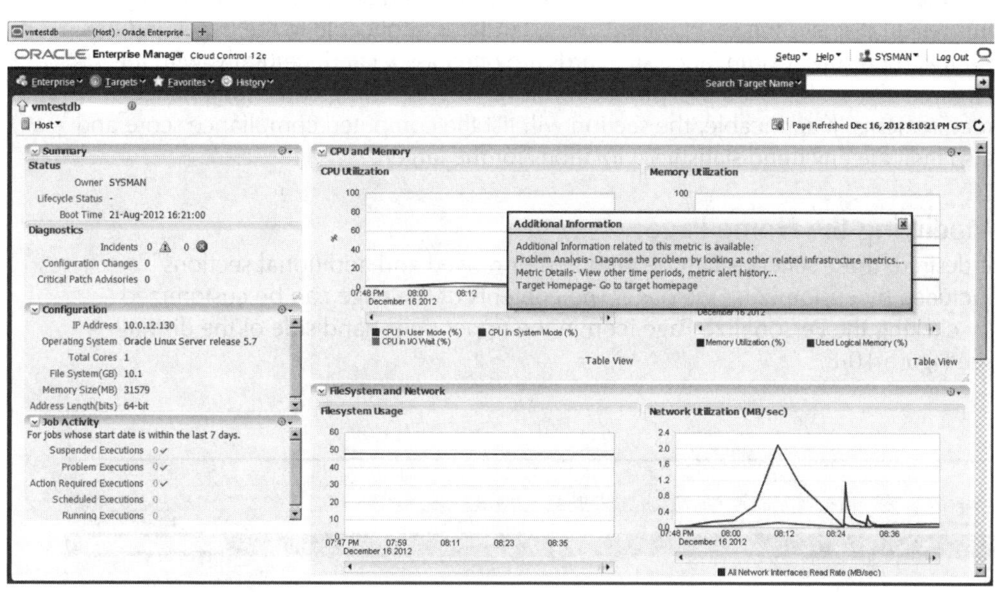

FIGURE 10-7. *Host metric data: additional information*

- Capacity
- Configuration
- Diagnostics
- Error
- Fault
- Jobs
- Load
- Performance
- Security

The bottom-most section is the Compliance Standard Summary. When configured, this region displays the set of compliance standards applicable to the target and their evaluation results. Compliance standards are often associated, naturally, with the Lifecycle Status. For example, production-level targets have greater compliance requirements. If applicable, the section will list the computed compliance score and also indicate any trend statistics (violations for the target).

Modifying the Home Page

If desired, these sections can be modified or moved and additional sections included by customizing the page. The contents of the page can be customized by clicking the Personalize Page icon in the upper right-hand side of the display—see Figure 10-8.

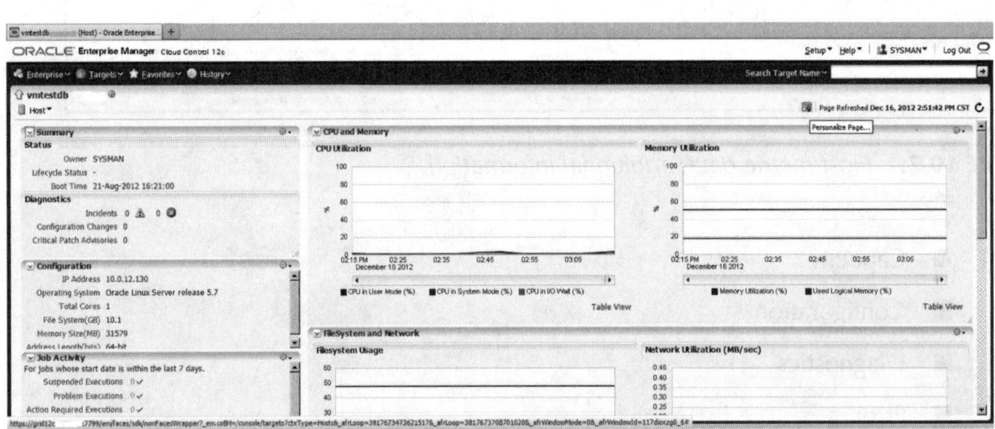

FIGURE 10-8. *Selecting the Personalize Page icon*

The Personalize Page feature allows you to add or remove content and relocate sections on the screen. The following illustration shows the Add Content window, which allows the administrator to add context-filtered data to the display.

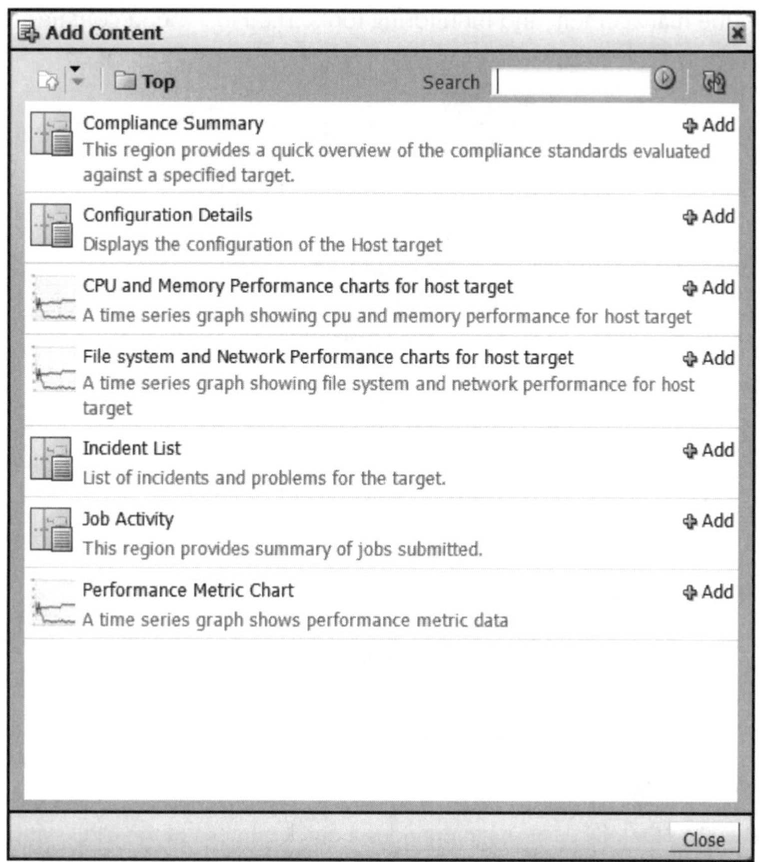

Host Menu

In contrast to the Database Home page, the Host Home only requires a single drop-down menu: Host. Of course, the Host Home page is just the starting point for accessing the management and monitoring tools. The Host menu contains numerous tools including the following:

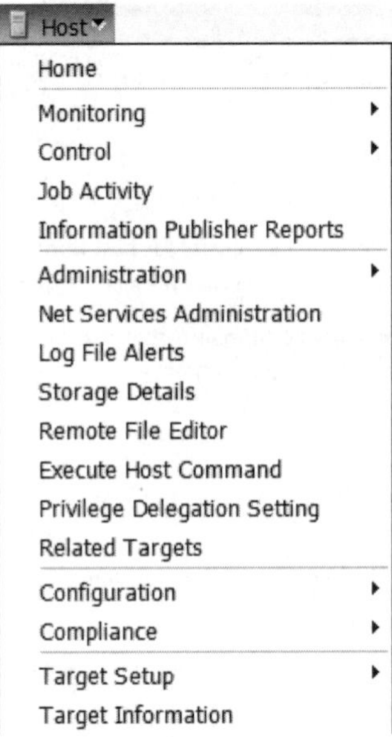

- **Home** The Host Home page.
- **Monitoring**
  - **CPU Details** This page provides a quick glimpse of the CPU statistics including utilization, I/O wait, and overall CPU load.
  - **Memory Details** Provides details with respect to the memory page scan rate, utilization, and swap utilization.
  - **Disk Details** Specific data with respect to Total I/O across all disks and the average maximum wait across all I/O resources.
  - **Program Resource Utilization** Allows the Administrator to monitor specific programs on the host.
  - **All Metrics** This is where you will find access to all of the database metrics and view the current values.

- **Metric and Collection Settings** From this page you can easily find and modify all of the metric thresholds for host monitoring. In the Other Collected Items tab, you can enable and disable collection schedules and other parameters.
- **Metric Collection Errors** Provides a list of metric errors.
- **User-Defined Metrics** A page explaining that the Metric Extensions should be used instead of User Defined Metrics and a hyperlink to Metric Extensions.
- **Status History** Provides information on the availability of the host.
- **Incident Manager** This is a link directly to the Incident Manager.
- **Alert History** This provides a graphical display of the Alert History for the host.
- **Blackouts** In this screen you can view current blackouts and create new blackouts for host objects.

- **Control**
  - **Create Blackout** Allows you to create a blackout.
  - **End Blackout** Allows you to end a blackout.
- **Job Activity** Shows job activity filtered for the current host.
- **Information Publisher Reports** This item displays reports tailored to the host target type.
- **Administration** As discussed later in the chapter, functions on the Host Administration menu require installation of the YaST ("Yet another Setup Tool") utility on the respective server.
  - **Services** View and manage operating system services.
  - **Default System Run Level** Modify the host default system run level used after reboot.
  - **Network Cards** View and configure detailed information on the host network cards.
  - **Host Lookup Table** View and modify entries in the /etc/hosts file, that is, the mapping of host names and aliases to IP addresses.
  - **NFS Client** Provides a list of all the network file system (NFS) clients mounted on the current host.
  - **User and Group Administration** View and modify user and group host configuration.

- **Net Services Administration** Utility for configuring and managing network services.
- **Log File Alerts** Display a list of alerts collected from monitored log files.
- **Storage Details** Comprehensive page that provides management and tracking of the storage resources.
- **Remote File Editor** Enables Administrator to view and edit files on the remote host.
- **Execute Host Command** Execute operating system commands against designated host and immediately view the results.
- **Privilege Delegation Setting** Configure or clear a privilege delegation setting from a host.
- **Related Targets** View summary information about the targets configured on the host target.
- **Configuration**
  - **Last Collected** Shows the latest collected host configuration information.
  - **Topology** Shows the current host topology.
  - **Search** Provides a list of search criteria that is used to view specific host components.
  - **Compare** Used to compare different host configurations.
  - **Comparison Job Activity** Provides a list of currently running comparison jobs.
  - **History** Provides a list of previously run jobs.
  - **Save** Used to save the current configuration of a database instance and database.
  - **Saved** Lists all saved configurations.
- **Compliance**
  - **Results** Provides a list of current compliance violations.
  - **Standard Associations** Provides a list of compliance standards that are associated with the target.
  - **Real-time Observations** Provides a list of real-time compliance standards violations.

- **Target Setup**
  - **Monitoring Configuration** Used to view or modify the monitoring configuration of the database target.
  - **Administrator Access** Used to grant administrator access to the database instance target.
  - **Remove Target** Used to remove the database instance target.
  - **Add to Group** Used to add the database instance target to a group.
  - **Properties** Used to view and modify the database instance target properties.
- **Target Information** Provides a quick link to basic host status information.

In the following section, we will take a closer look at each of these functions.

Host Menu – Monitoring

The Host Monitoring submenu allows you to view detailed statistics on the core resources including: CPU, Memory, and Disk. The CPU display provides the following information:

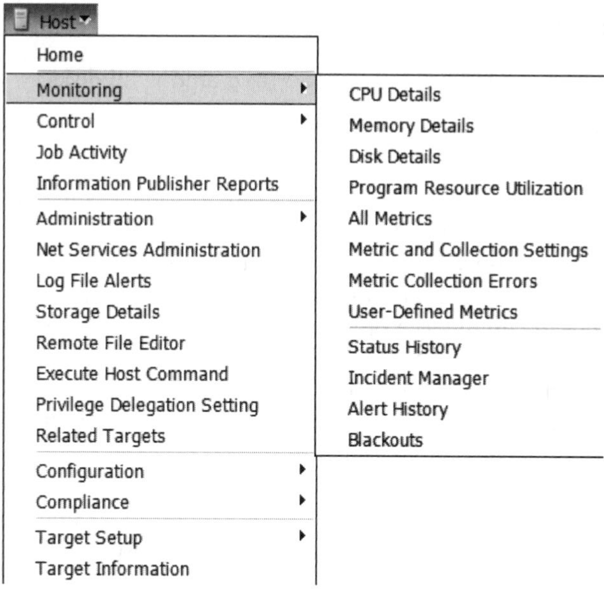

- General CPU Utilization, that is the percentage of CPU resources consumed
- CPU I/O waits over the last 90 minutes

- CPU Load—the average number of processes waiting to be scheduled for CPU resources in the previous minute
- The Top 10 Processes ordered by CPU demand

Each display provides hyperlinks that drill down to the specific historical metrics and, if applicable, the related alerting thresholds. The historical information allows the administrator to check for any trends in usage.

The Memory Details display provides a similar set of information:

- **Memory Page Scan Rate** The number of pages scanned per second
- **Memory Utilization** The percentage of memory actually in use
- **SWAP Utilization** The percentage of swap space consumed by current applications
- The Top 10 Processes ordered by Memory demand

Again, each of the displays provides hyperlinks to the detailed, historical metric data.

The Disk Details page displays the following information:

- Total Disk I/O across all disks
- Maximum Average Disk I/O Service Time among all disks
- The Top Disk Devices ordered by Percentage Busy

Another useful monitoring tool is the Program Resource Utilization page. This page displays recent Total CPU Utilization (%), Maximum CPU Utilization (%), and Maximum Resident Memory Size (MB). This data can be displayed for the current period (90 minutes) or the standard historical ranges (24 hours, 7 days, 31 days). The page also provides the ability to monitor specific programs. The programs and the owners to be monitored are configured on the Metric and Collection Settings page. You can either use the Monitoring submenu to reach the Metric and Collection Settings page, or you can click on the "Click here" link at the bottom of the Program Resource Utilization page.

Once you are on the Metric and Collection Settings page, choose the Metric tab with the All Metrics view. Navigate down to the Program Resource Utilization category and click on the pencil icon to present the corresponding Edit Advanced Settings page—see Figure 10-9.

On the Edit Advanced Settings page (see Figure 10-10), click the Add button and enter the desired program owner and program name.

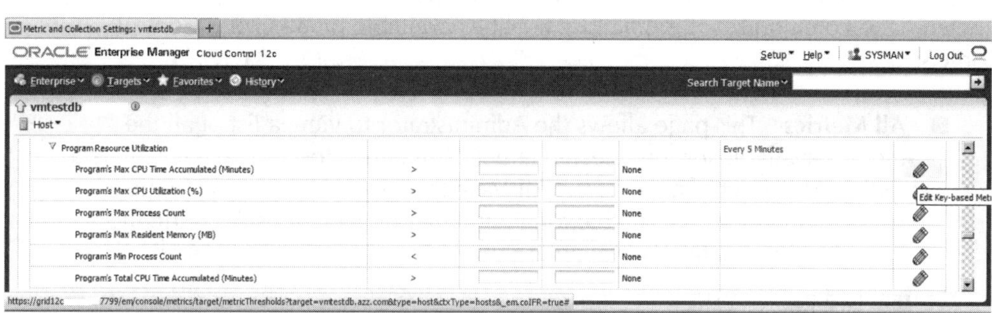

FIGURE 10-9. *Accessing Edit Advanced Settings from the Metric and Collection Settings page*

The Metric and Collection Settings page is the primary location for configuring alerting thresholds and metric collection parameters. By default, the main metrics view displays metrics with threshold values. All metrics can be viewed by adjusting the filter. Along with establishing thresholds, the page provides the following features:

- **Corrective Actions** Response actions to be performed when thresholds are exceeded
- **Collection Schedule** Enable or disable collection and adjust frequency
- **Edit Advanced Settings** Tailor metric to specific targets

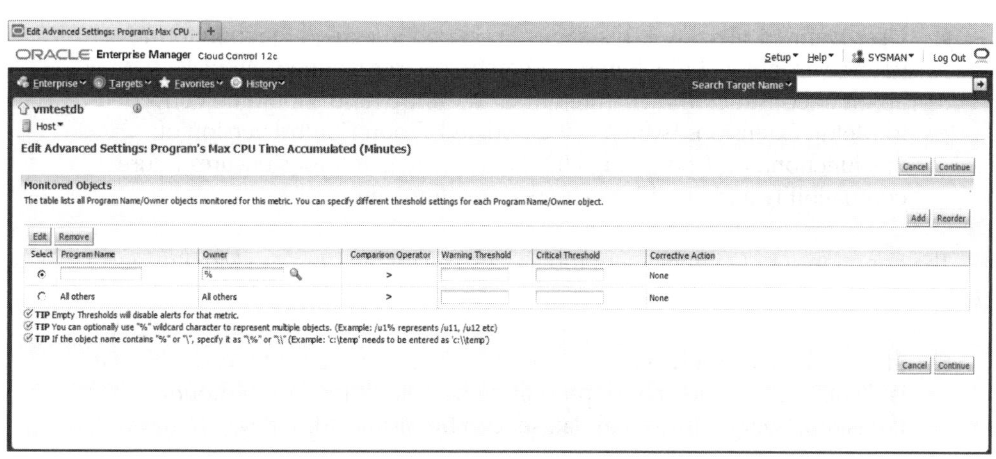

FIGURE 10-10. *Entering program monitoring specifications*

Along with the Metric and Collection Settings page, the Monitoring submenu includes the common set of monitoring facilities available for all Cloud Control targets:

- **All Metrics** This page allows the Administrator to view a list of all the metrics available for the selected target. While the Host Home page offers a more concise set of metrics, the All Metrics page provides a comprehensive list of all the metrics available for a particular target. For each metric the following information is available:
  - Last Known Value
  - Collection Timestamp
  - Average Value
  - Low Value
  - High Value
  - Warning Threshold (if defined)
  - Critical Threshold (if defined)
  - Occurrences Before Alert
  - Corrective Actions
  - Thresholds Last Modified By
- **Metric Collection Errors** This page displays problems with the collection of metrics, often due to configuration changes or related issues.
- **User-Defined Metrics** This page allows you to extend the monitoring of your environment by defining new metrics. User-Defined Metrics (UDM) is an older construct implemented in Grid Control and should be converted to Metric Extensions, which is the updated Cloud Control version of this functionality. Converting UDMs to Metric Extensions ensures future compatibility and provides extended functionality.

The common set of management tools is also available from the Monitoring submenu:

- **Status History** View the availability statistics for the host target. This data is displayed as a pie chart representing by default the last 24 hours. If desired, a larger historical dataset can be displayed: 7 days, 31 days, or a customized range.

- **Incident Manager** The Incident Manager summarizes the issues impacting the target including alerts, events, problems, and incidents.
- **Alert History** Displays a chart that reflects the alert history of the target for user-defined time periods (standard historical ranges: 24 hours, 7 days, 31 days).
- **Blackouts** The Blackouts page is multifaceted as it allows for a historical view, the current status, and the ability to create new blackouts. On the Blackouts page you can:
  - View the status of existing blackouts (whether they are active or not)
  - Define a blackout for one or more targets
  - Edit existing blackouts
  - Stop blackouts
  - Delete blackouts

Host Menu – Control

The third item on the Host Menu is the Control submenu. These menu items provide direct access to the Create Blackout Wizard and a link to quickly terminate any blackouts on the current target host. As noted in earlier chapters, blackouts are an essential mechanism both to maintain the integrity of the notification system (avoiding false alarms) and to keep accurate uptime statistics. If blackouts are not configured and targets are brought down by the Administrator, not only will critical alarm notifications be broadcasted, but the downtime will degrade the overall availability statistics.

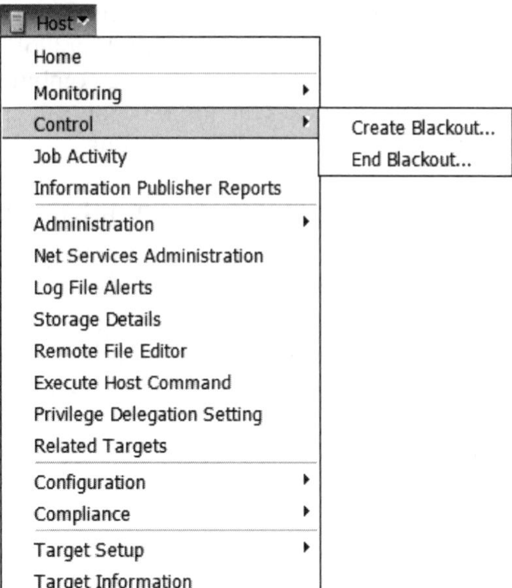

Host Menu – Job Activity

Job Activity (Figure 10-11) is the next link on the Host menu. This page allows the user to view information about all scheduled, currently running, and past jobs.

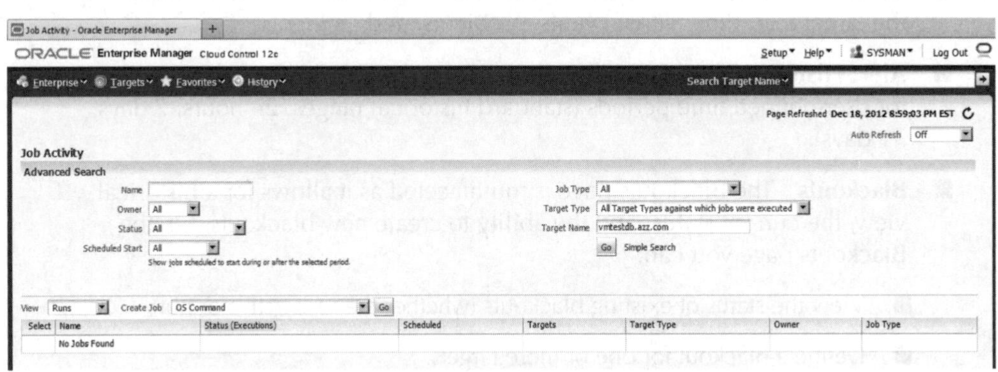

FIGURE 10-11. *Host-Specific Job Activity page*

The Administrator can search for jobs based on various criteria including: owner, job type, target name, target type, status, or scheduled start. After filtering the desired jobs, you can view job information in the Results table either by job executions or job runs. A job execution runs against its particular target. If you submit an OS Command or SQL Script job against multiple targets, multiple job executions are the result, one execution per target. The combined set of job executions at a given time for that job comprises the job run. You can choose to view job activity by individual executions or collectively by job runs.

Host Menu – Information Publisher Reports

The Information Publisher Reports link directs the user to a set of reports that are specific to the target type, in this case Hosts. The Information Publisher, shown in Figure 10-12, is a powerful reporting framework that makes information regarding the managed targets available not only to Administrators, but also to other audiences. Administrators can use reports to show activity, resource utilization, and configuration of managed targets. IT managers can use reports to show availability of sets of managed systems. Business executives can view reports on availability of applications (such as corporate e-mail or other critical business applications) over a period of time.[2]

Information Publisher is installed and ready to use with Enterprise Manager and comes with a comprehensive library of predefined report definitions, allowing you to generate reports for your managed environment with no additional setup. Information Publisher also provides you with the ability to easily create customized reports,

[2] The importance of established blackouts and their effect on availability statistics is magnified when the audience for this information is extended beyond IT.

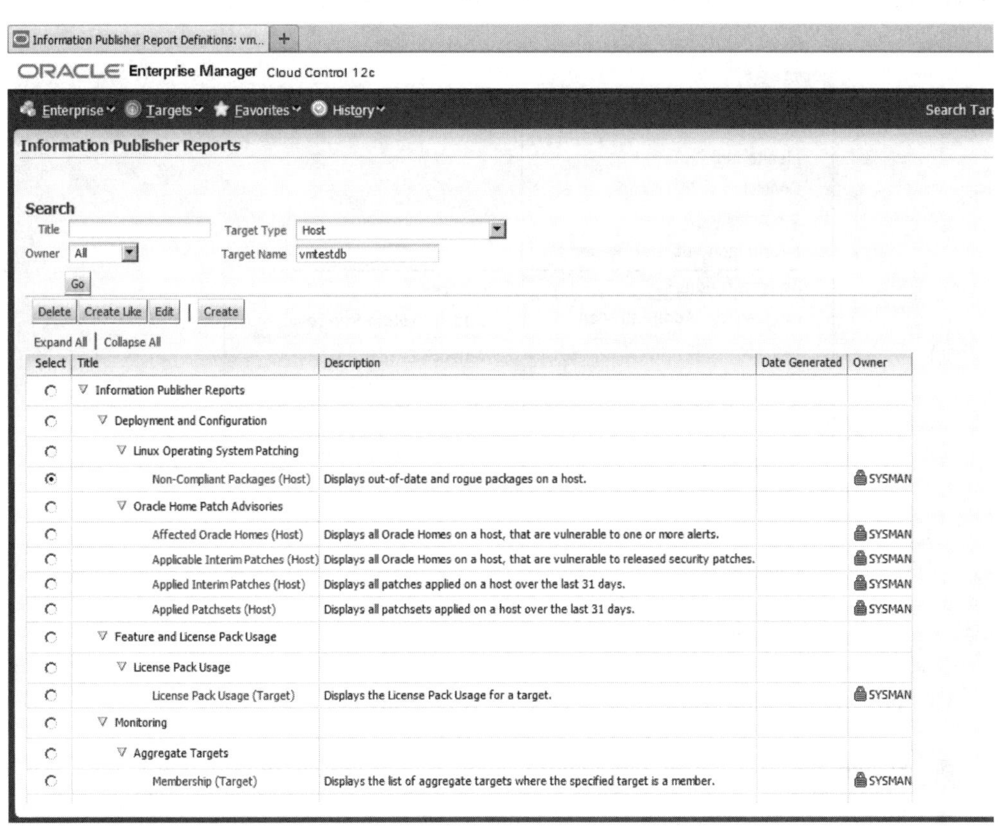

FIGURE 10-12. *Target-Specific Information Publisher Reports*

as well as create new reports using a graphical user interface that is a part of the Enterprise Manager Cloud Control Console. These HTML-based reports can be viewed interactively, generated on a schedule, and/or sent to selected recipients via e-mail. Additionally, reports can be shared among Enterprise Manager Administrators and made available to noncredentialed users via the Enterprise Manager Reporting Web site.

Host Menu – Administration

The Host Administration page gives you access to various administration functions that you can perform on the targeted host. With the submenu links, you can easily access the appropriate pages for system services, network connections, and user and group settings. The available tasks include starting services, setting users, and configuring network cards.

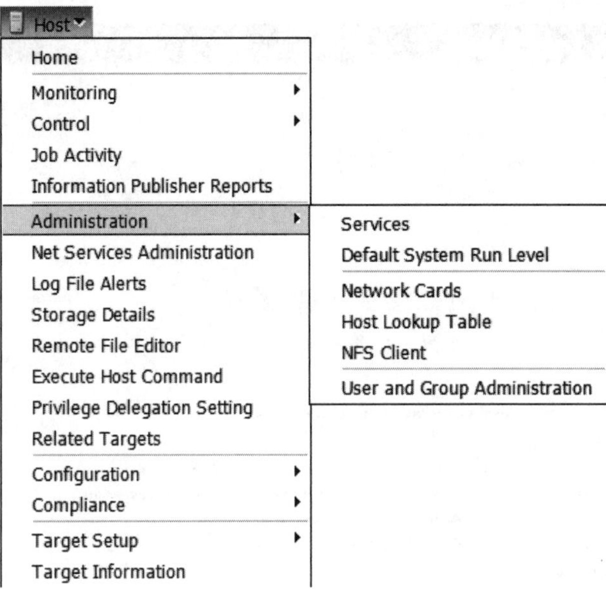

Using the Host Administration pages, you can manage:

- **System Services** Both viewing the statistics and editing the services
- **Network** Manage routing configuration, view related statistics, and view network file system (NFS) clients
- **Settings** Create, delete, and edit user and group settings

Although these are predominantly System Administrator tasks, many Database Administrators are familiar with these functions. Access to the Administration page functions, however, requires installation of the YaST (Yet another Software Tool) utility on the host—see Figure 10-13.

YaST is an operating system setup and configuration tool that comes as a standard tool as part of the SUSE Linux distribution. It features tools that can configure many aspects of the system. YaST was first released in May 1996. YaST is free software that SUSE has made available under the GNU Public License. As noted in Figure 10-13, the YaST distribution is available from Oracle at the specified URL.[3] At the present

[3] YaST is currently available at http://oss.oracle.com/projects/yast.

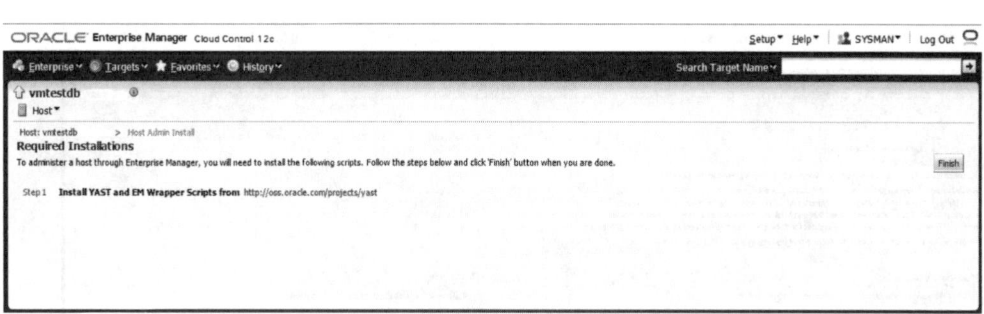

FIGURE 10-13. *YaST installation screen*

time YaST is only available for the Linux operating systems: Oracle Enterprise, Red Hat, and SUSE. Accessing the utility requires both the installation of the YaST software and the corresponding Enterprise Manager wrapper scripts. So, even though your host OS may be SUSE, you still need to obtain the wrapper scripts from Oracle.

The installation of YaST naturally requires root privileges but is otherwise relatively simple. The details of an installation, however, are outside of the purview of this book. It should be noted that there are differing opinions among both Database and System Administrators regarding the use of YaST and similar "control" utilities. The utility may conflict with established enterprise standards or the practices of the System Administrators themselves. However, if the goal is to capitalize on a centralized management interface such as Cloud Control, the YaST functionality is a significant step in that direction.

Host Menu – Net Services Administration

As you can see on the Host menu, Cloud Control now allows direct access for managing network services—you no longer need to work through a secondary utility (sweet!). From the Net Services Administration page (Figure 10-14), you can identify or select the location of your Net Services configuration files, and you can configure the listeners, directory naming methods, local naming methods, profile, and file locations used by your Oracle Net Services software. To configure your network settings, select a configuration file location from the available list and then select one of the options from the Administer drop-down menu. The Administer drop-down menu has the following edit options:

- **Listeners** Use this option to view a list of listeners associated with the selected configuration file directory, and perform listener configuration tasks.
- **Directory Naming** Use this option to manage the network configurations with Oracle Internet directory.

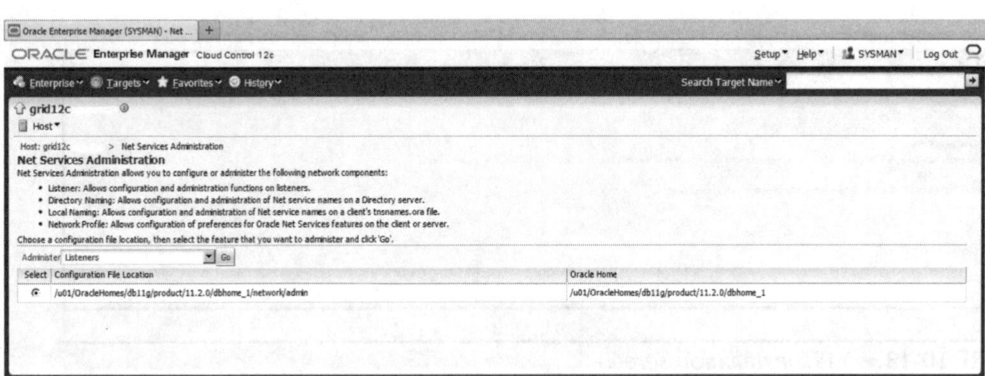

FIGURE 10-14. *Net Services Administration*

- **Local Naming** Use this option to manage the contents of the local tnsnames.ora file.
- **File Locations** This feature allows you to change the location of the network configuration files for the associated Oracle Home.

Host Menu – Log File Alerts

The next item on the Host Menu is the link to the Log File Alerts page (Figure 10-15). This page lists the alerts generated while being monitored by the Enterprise Manager.

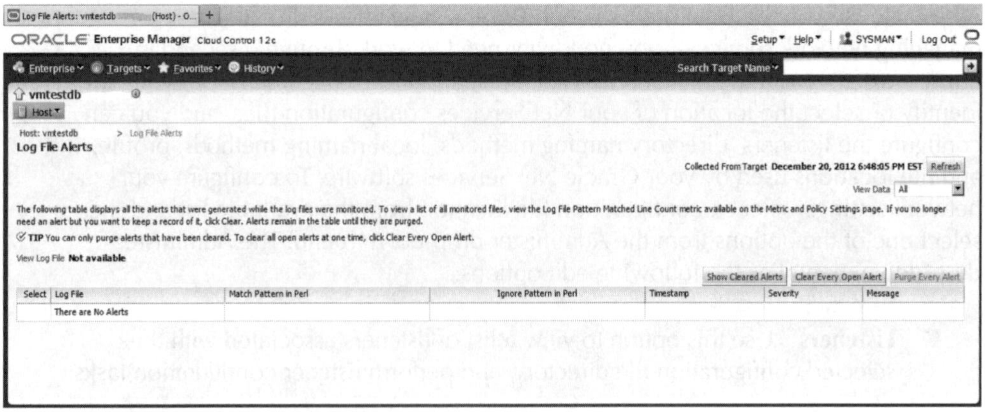

FIGURE 10-15. *Log File Alerts page*

As with the Program Monitoring facility, you specify log files for monitoring on the Metric and Collection Settings page. You select the Edit Advanced Settings option for the Log File Patterned Matched Line Count metric. In the Advanced display, click the Add button to specify files for monitoring and the corresponding ignore or match patterns along with timestamps that will trigger their display on the Log File Alerts page. If desired, you can also specify warning and critical threshold values to trigger events and/or notifications. Finally, you also have the option to specify a corrective action for threshold violations.

Host Menu – Storage Details

Tracking the storage resources of a host is a significant task. Considering its importance, the Storage Details functionality (Figure 10-16) is addressed in greater depth in the second part of this chapter.

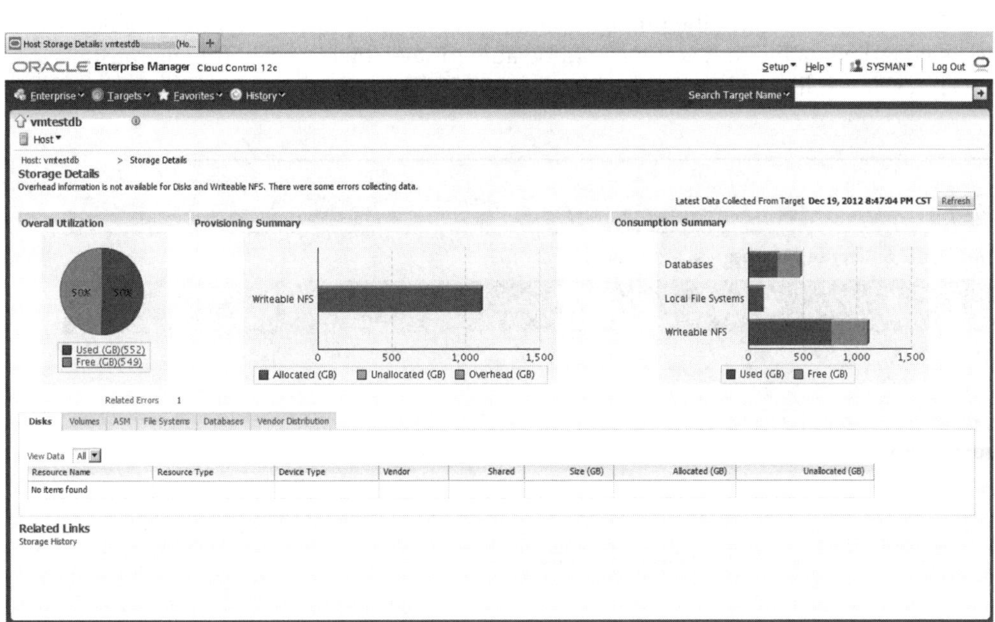

FIGURE 10-16. *Storage Details page*

Host Menu – Remote File Editor

The Remote File Editor (Figure 10-17) allows the Administrator to view and edit text files present on the remote host. From this page you can:

- With the appropriate privileges, view and edit any text file present on the remote host.
- Save a file that has been edited on the remote host by clicking Save.
- Change to another user account or use another set of Host Preferred Credentials by clicking Change next to User.
- After you have opened a file for editing, select a new file for editing by clicking Change next to File Name.
- Revert to text at the time of the last successful save operation by clicking Revert.

Of course, if you lack the proper operating system privileges, you may be able to view and edit a file, but you may not be able to save the changes. The file must be an ASCII text file and cannot be larger than 100 KB.

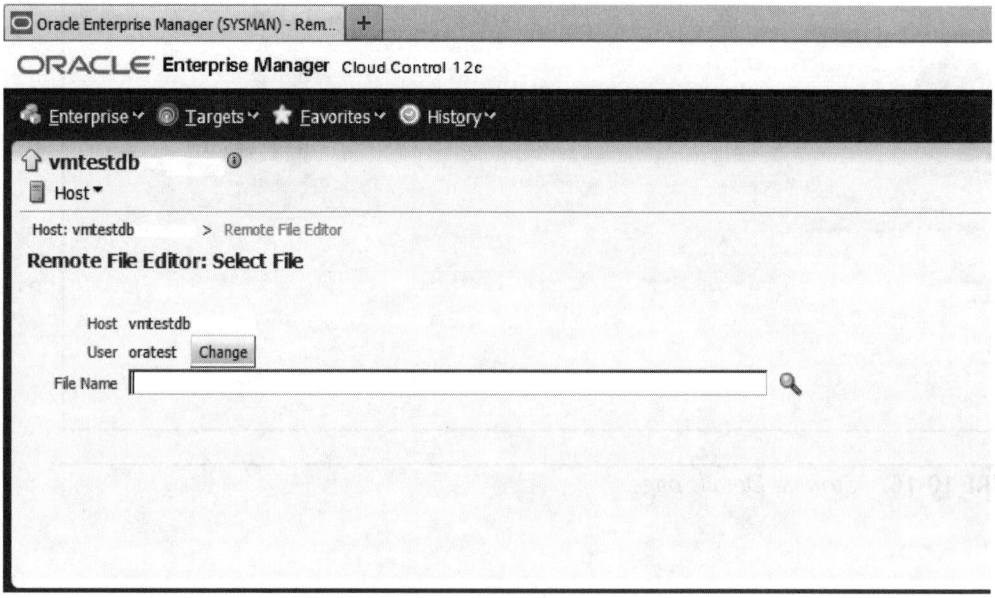

FIGURE 10-17. *Remote File Editor*

Host Menu – Execute Host Command

The Execute Host Command page (Figure 10-18) enables you to execute operating system commands against one host and immediately view the results. This gives you the opportunity to perform administrative operations on any host configured within Enterprise Manager. The link Switch To Multiple Target Mode, located at the bottom of this page, allows the Administrator to execute commands against multiple hosts at the same time. From either the single or multiple host pages, the following features are available:

- Draft and edit the command, execute the command, and view the execution results.
- Commands can be re-executed.
- A command can be one of the following types:
  - An operating system command
  - Commands from a script either on the local client, browser, or on the host
  - Commands from a job defined in the library

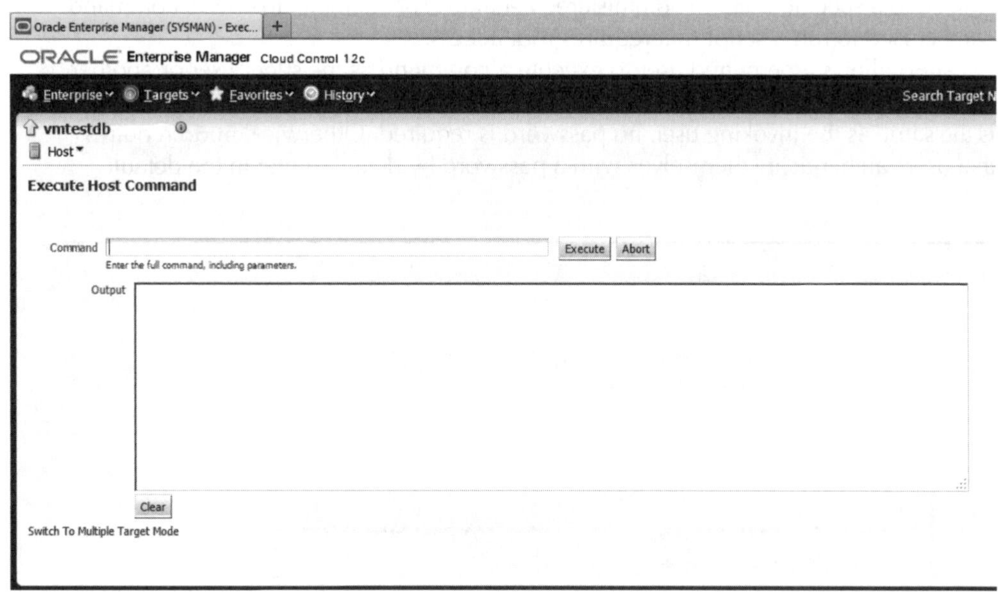

FIGURE 10-18. *Execute Host Command*

- Interactively view command execution results or hide the results to be viewed at a later time.
- Use preferred credentials or specify other credentials.
- Add, delete, and modify host target(s).
- Commands can be cancelled when the Processing: Execution Host Command page appears.
- The OS script or execution results can be saved on the local browser client.
- Commands are executed using the Enterprise Manager Job system. Consequently the set of system-specific target variables, called Target Properties, can be referenced in the command stream.

Host Menu – Privilege Delegation Setting

The next link on the Host Menu is the Privilege Delegation Setting (Figure 10-19). This page allows you to configure or clear a privilege delegation from a host. The Administrator can configure or remove Sudo or PowerBroker settings. Privilege delegation allows a logged-in user to perform an activity with the privileges of another user. Sudo and PowerBroker are privilege delegation tools that allow a logged-in user to be assigned these privileges. Typically, the privileges that are granted to a specific user are administered centrally. For example, the `sudo` command can be used to run a script that requires root access.

`Sudo` allows a permitted user to execute a command as the super user or another user, as specified in the sudoers file. If the invoking user is root or if the target user is the same as the invoking user, no password is required. Otherwise, `sudo` requires that users authenticate themselves with a password by default (note: In the default

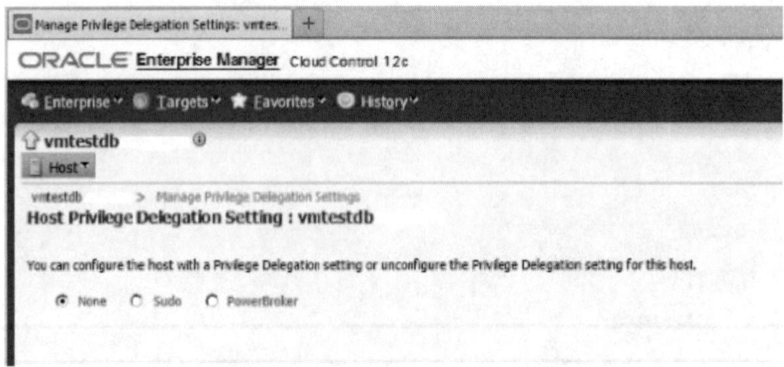

FIGURE 10-19. *Privilege Delegation Setting*

configuration this is the user's password, not the root password). Once a user has been authenticated, a timestamp is updated and the user may then use `sudo` without a password for a short period of time (five minutes unless overridden in sudoers). `Sudo` determines who is an authorized user by consulting the /etc/sudoers file.

Symark PowerBroker enables UNIX system administrators to specify the circumstances under which other people may run certain programs such as root (or other important accounts). The result is that responsibility for such actions as adding user accounts, fixing line printer queues, and so on, can be safely assigned to the appropriate people, without disclosing the root password. The full power of root is thus protected from potential misuse or abuse—for example, modifying databases or file permissions, erasing disks, or more subtle damage.

Symark PowerBroker can access existing programs as well as its own set of utilities that execute common system administration tasks. Utilities being developed to run on top of Symark PowerBroker can manage passwords, accounts, backups, line printers, file ownership or removal, rebooting, logging people out, killing their programs, deciding who can log in to where from where, and so on. They can also provide TCP/IP, Load Balancer, `cron`, NIS, NFS, FTP, `rlogin`, and accounting subsystem management. Users can work from within a restricted shell or editor to access certain programs or files as root.

The Host's Privilege Delegation Settings page functions as follows:

- Choose None and then click Update to clear a privilege delegation setting from the host.
- Choose Sudo to create a Sudo privilege delegation setting for the host. Specify the requisite Sudo Command and click Update.
- Choose PowerBroker to create a PowerBroker privilege delegation setting for the host. Specify the requisite PowerBroker Command and optionally the PowerBroker Password Prompt.

Host Menu – Related Targets

The Related Targets page (Figure 10-20) allows you to view summary information about the targets on the specified host. The Related Targets page allows you to quickly determine how the individual targets are performing by analyzing alerts and availability information. With the Related Targets page, the Administrator needs to navigate across numerous menus and links to access the different resources. The Target Name column on the Target page serves as a hyperlink to allow the user to drill down to additional details.

Host Menu – Configuration

Cloud Control Configuration is enhanced functionality that is available across all the managed targets. Configuration is an extensive module that performs numerous management and monitoring tasks with associations with Compliance and

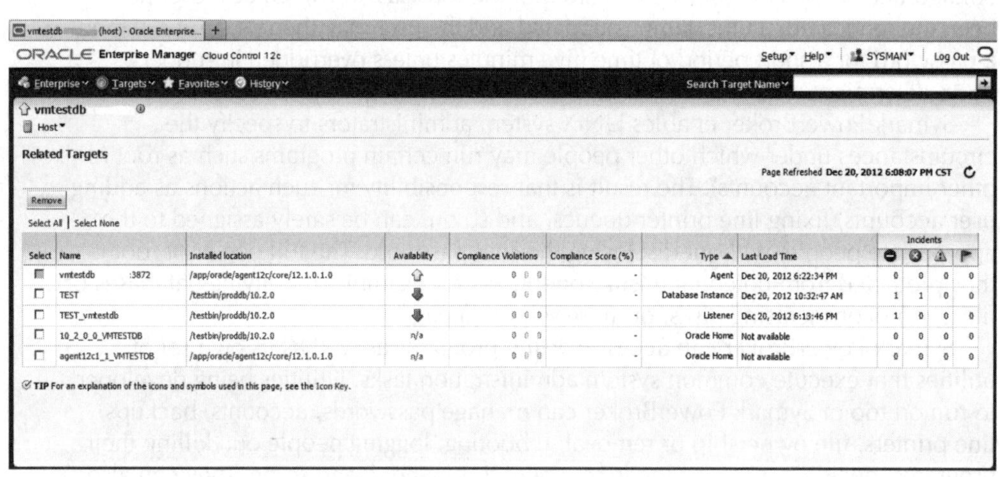

FIGURE 10-20. *Related Targets page*

Provisioning. Due to the complex nature of the functionality, we will restrict our discussion of Configuration to the host specifically. Every 24 hours, Enterprise Manager collects configuration information from the managed target. The host information includes:

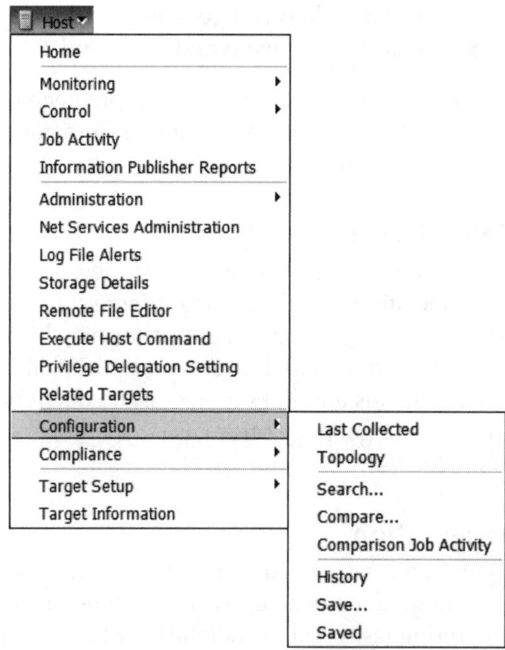

- The host's hardware.
- The operating system including properties, packages, and patches.
- Installed Oracle software including (but not limited to) installed products and their components, patch sets, and the interim patches on the host. The Agent collects this information from the Oracle Universal Installer inventories.

The Compliance utilities allow the Administrator to perform the following functions with the collected data:

- View a summary of all the categories of host configuration information for the host.
- From the summary information for any configuration category, navigate to more detailed configuration information for that category. For example, detail configuration information for each category includes history information that lists the changes that have been made to that configuration category over time.
- Determine the date and time that the host configuration was last collected.
- Manually refresh the host configuration by clicking Refresh.
- Perform other operations involving host configurations and configuration files, such as saving a host configuration to a configuration file and comparing host configurations or configuration files.
- View a list of current and past comparison jobs. The view can be filtered with search criteria.

Host Menu – Compliance

Compliance is another significant module within Cloud Control that is applicable to all the managed targets. The following illustration shows the Compliance submenu. Compliance management starts with a Compliance Framework. This is a defined set of compliance standards. The standards are hierarchical structures that serve as benchmarks by which targets are accessed or evaluated. The hierarchical functionality allows the Administrators to define successively more restrictive criteria for targets. For example, development systems will likely have fewer and less restrictive compliance requirements compared to QA or Production environments. The Compliance Framework is the entry point when looking at compliance scores from a high-level view such as the Compliance Results dashboard. Each entity of a Compliance Framework should have a user-defined importance that is assigned for reporting/ compliance score rollup. The importance can be set for all internal nodes in a compliance framework or compliance standard hierarchy. This importance at the top compliance framework is the default, but the Administrator may decide that more importance should be placed on one compliance sub-group over another. The Compliance Standard Associations page lists the compliance standards that are associated with the specified host target.

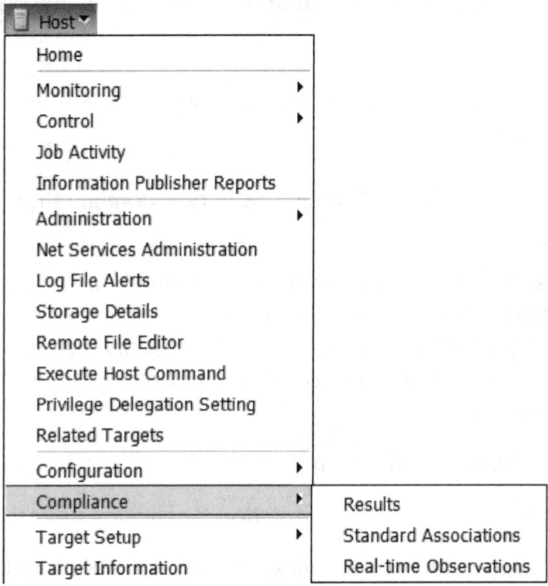

The Real-time Observations page displays compliance violations on a host that is configured to be monitored through real-time monitoring rules. Each distinct user action that results in a compliance violation results in one observation. Observations are additionally bundled if there are multiple observations of infractions in a short period of time by the same user on the same host. This degree of monitoring is, of course, resource-intensive and is primarily intended for targets that must meet high industrial, defense, or regulatory requirements.

Reasons for creating compliance frameworks include:

- Mapping underlying IT violations to the regulatory and standard compliance controls used by the company
- Compliance auditing at compliance specification level, for example, Payment Card Industry (PCI)
- Auditing, security evaluation, and trend analysis

Although it requires a comprehensive effort, Oracle highly recommends that you create a top-level compliance framework like the one provided for PCI and Oracle Generic Compliance.

Host Menu – Target Setup

The Target Setup submenu allows the Administrator to complete various functions specific to the host target. The submenu pages allow the user to perform the following tasks:

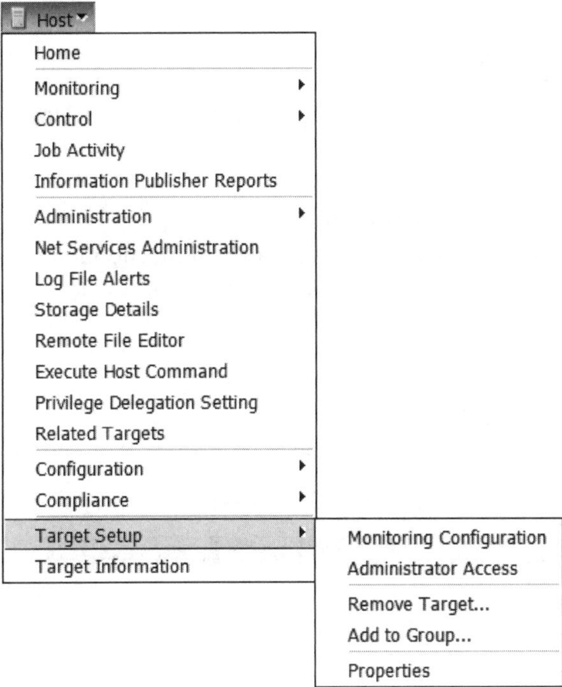

- Make modifications to host-specific monitoring parameters.
- Grant, revoke privileges, or change ownership of the host target.
- Remove the target and its related targets.
- Add the host target to a group.
- Modify the host-specific target properties. This list can be site customized, but includes at a minimum the following properties:
    - Comment
    - Contact
    - Cost Center
    - Customer Support Identifier

- Department
- Lifecycle Status
- Line of Business
- Location
- Target Version

The target properties can play an important role in other Cloud Control modules such as Compliance and Provisioning.

Host Menu – Target Information

The final link on the Host Menu is Target Information. The Target Information link opens a small display (Figure 10-21) that briefly provides availability information, key configuration data, the identity of the managing Agent, and, if applicable, the target's membership in any groups.

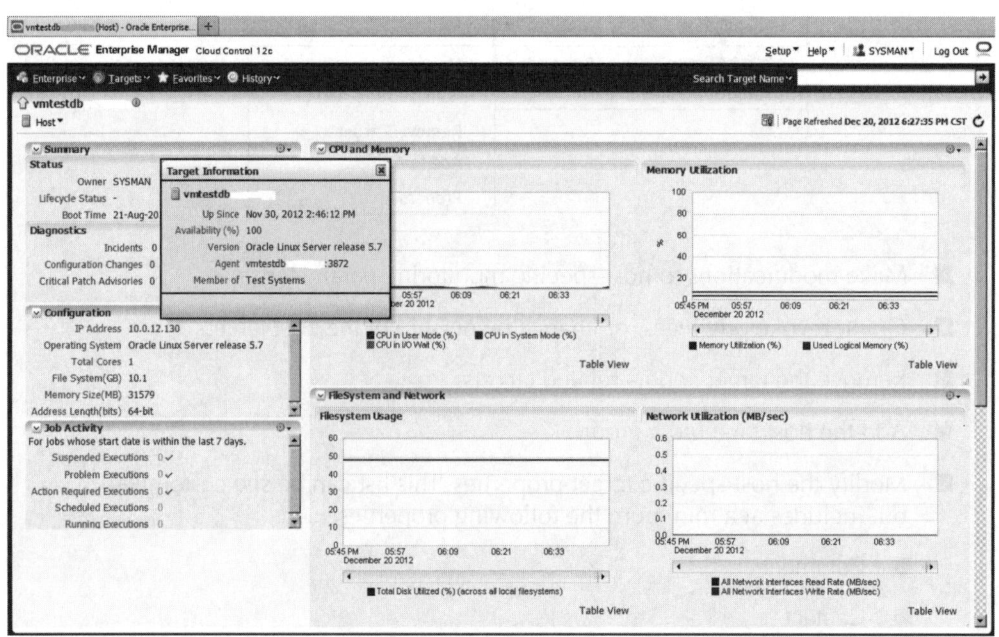

FIGURE 10-21. *Target Information*

Storage Administration

As noted earlier, Storage Administration is an important element of Database Management. The Storage Details page (Figure 10-22) is accessible from the Host menu. The graphs at the top of the Storage Details page provide statistics regarding storage utilization.

- **Overall Utilization** The pie chart provides unallocated, overhead, used, and free storage space summary at the global system level for the associated host. When applicable, the chart displays the overhead of Volume and Oracle ASM software layers.
- **Provisioning Summary** For the host, the bar chart summarizes the allocated, unallocated, and overhead for all entities present in the Disk, Volume, Oracle ASM, and Writeable Network File Systems (NFS) portions of the File System layer. If a specific layer is not deployed, the corresponding bar is omitted from the chart.
- **Consumption Summary** This bar chart shows used and free space summary information for all databases, all local file systems, and all writeable NFS partitions on the host.

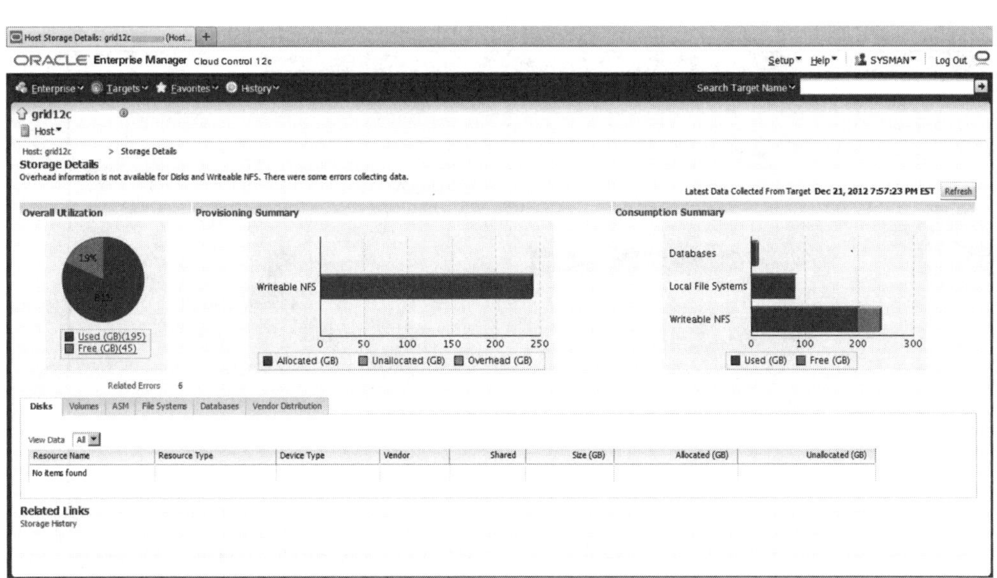

FIGURE 10-22. *Storage Details page*

Please note the following with respect to these charts:

- To see the exact allocation of space, hover the mouse over the chart. For example, though a bar in the Consumption Summary suggests that the Writeable NFS value is more than 200 GB, the exact Allocated GB is 199.41—see Figure 10-23.
- Click the Refresh button in the upper right-hand corner to update the storage data for the host.
- The display of entities in the chart is dynamic, that is, what displays in the Provisioning Summary and Consumption Summary graphs is dependent on whether the entity is actually visible on the host. For example, if the host does not have a database target that is monitored by Cloud Control, the chart will not display information related to the database.

Oracle's use of the term "layer" can be a little confusing. A stack of storage management technologies can be deployed on any host. A deployed technology layer can provide storage resources to any layer above it and consume the storage resource from any layer below. The top-level consumer of storage is the application

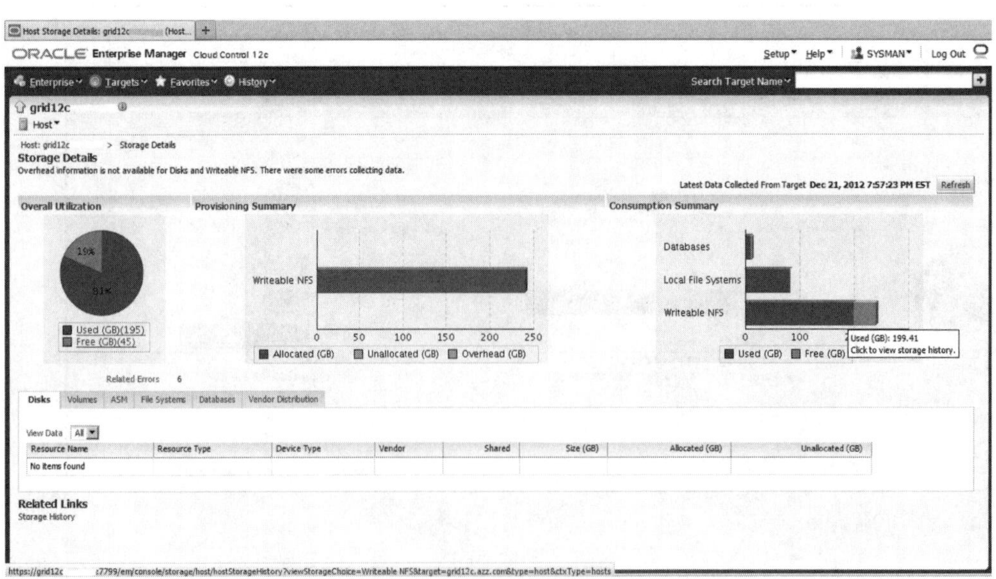

FIGURE 10-23. *Storage Details – "Hover" Details*

itself, such as a database. Starting with the lowest layers and moving up, the hierarchy looks like the following:

- **Disks** Disks are the lowest layer, and they provide storage to: Volumes, File Systems, Databases, and ASM.
- **Volumes** Volumes refers to Volume Management and Software RAID technologies. Volumes are built from Disks and can provide storage to: File Systems, Databases, and ASM.
- **ASM** ASM Disk Groups can be built from individual Disks or Volumes. ASM provides storage to databases.[4]
- **File Systems** Operating System File Systems can provide space to applications including databases.

In order to avoid misleading the Administrator and overcomputing the available storage space, Cloud Control reports statistics on the highest layer of the technology stack. For example, in the case of a File System that fully consumes a disk, Cloud Control reports the space as File System space rather than Disk.

The bottom portion of the Storage Details page contains a table with tabs corresponding to various host-based storage elements. These tabs and the data presented are as follows:

- **Disks** The Disks tab on the Storage Details page shows the allocated and unallocated storage for all the disks and disk partitions on the host. All disks are listed including virtual disks from external storage systems such as EMC Storage Array. For a disk to be deployed for usage, the disk of course must first be formatted. After formatting, the disk can be configured to have one or more partitions. A disk or disk partition can be associated with exactly one entity from one of the upper technology layers on the host (for example, volumes, Oracle ASM Disk Groups, and so on). When an association exists for a disk or disk partition to an upper layer entity, it is reported as space allocated in the advanced layer.
- **Volumes** This tab represents one of various software packages available in the industry that are either generically known as Volume Managers or as Software RAID technology. These technologies are deployed in order to improve RAS (Reliability, Availability, and Scalability) characteristics of the underlying storage. Veritas Volume Manager is one example of this product,

[4] Interestingly, the new version of ASM can also provide normal and clustered file systems from ASM storage.

which is available across numerous platforms. When this tab is selected on the Storage Details page, the display shows the allocated and unallocated storage space present in the Volume layer. The table also includes relevant attributes for the associated Volumes layer technology.

- **ASM** Oracle's Automatic Storage Management is a storage management solution that obviates the need for using Volumes layer technology. When selected, the ASM display shows size, allocated, unallocated, and overhead statistics for each of the ASM Disk Groups.
- **File Systems** The File Systems option (Figure 10-24) displays the layer of storage that contains directories and files that are accessed, managed, and updated through the use of databases, middle-tier applications, and end-user tools. In general, this layer can be broadly categorized into local file systems that are disk-based, and remote file systems like NFS.

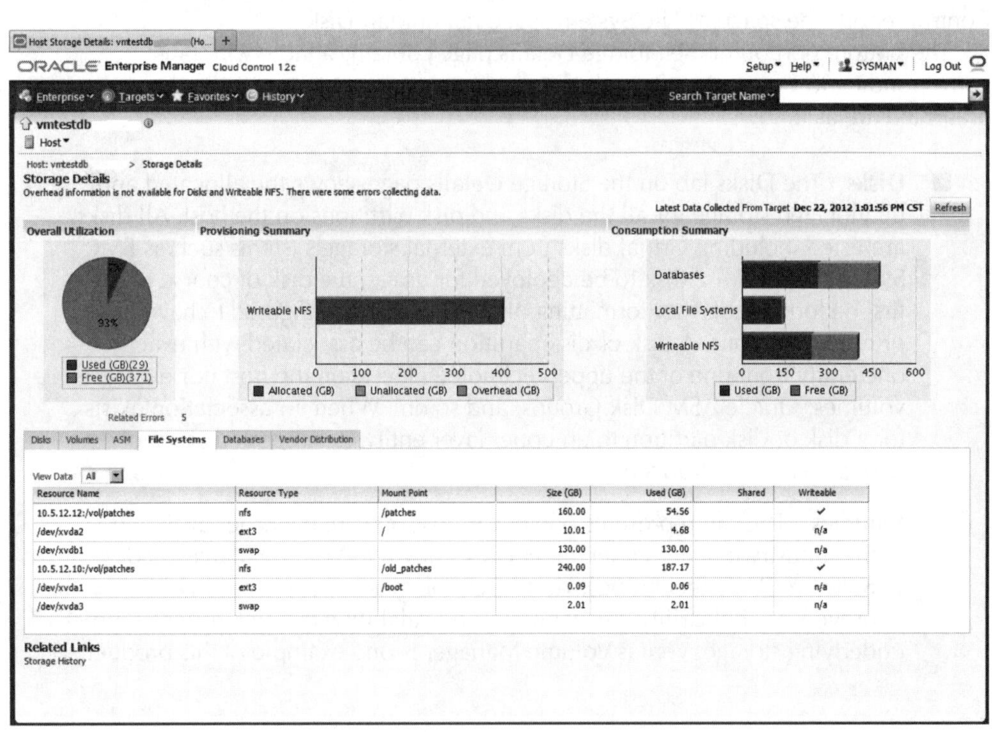

Resource Name	Resource Type	Mount Point	Size (GB)	Used (GB)	Shared	Writeable
10.5.12.12:/vol/patches	nfs	/patches	160.00	54.56		✔
/dev/xvda2	ext3	/	10.01	4.68		n/a
/dev/xvdb1	swap		130.00	130.00		n/a
10.5.12.10:/vol/patches	nfs	/old_patches	240.00	187.17		✔
/dev/xvda1	ext3	/boot	0.09	0.06		n/a
/dev/xvda3	swap		2.01	2.01		n/a

FIGURE 10-24. *Storage Details – File Systems*

The File Systems option displays standard statistics regarding size and used portions. The table also includes attributes such as the respective mount point, whether the source is shared, and if the area is writeable. The table also includes a column that identifies the type of File System, for example, ext2, ext3, zfs, vxfs, and so on.

- **Databases** The Databases tab displays the name, size, and used portion of each database on the host. The Database Name also serves as a hyperlink that allows the Administrator to quickly navigate to the respective database's home page.
- **Vendor Distribution** This tab displays statistics relevant to the underlying storage technology. In the example in Figure 10-25, the Vendor is Unknown, which is presenting an NFS mounted partition to the host.

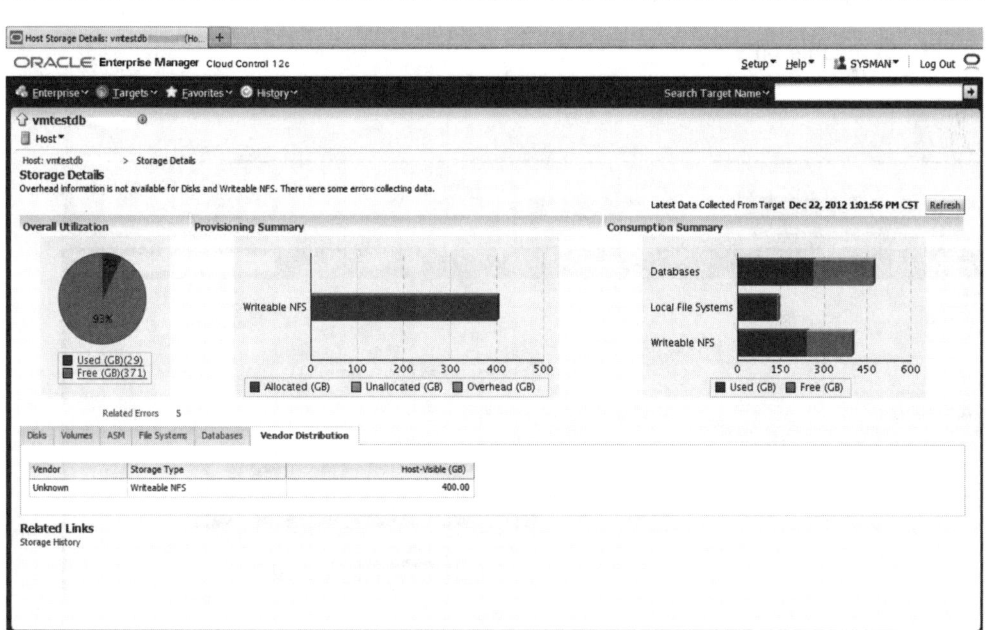

FIGURE 10-25. *Storage Details – Vendor Distribution*

Viewing Storage History

On the Storage Details page you can click on any of the links in the Overall Utilization, Provisioning Summary, or Consumption Summary charts to access the Storage History of the host. A hyperlink to Storage History (Figure 10-26) also exists at the bottom of the Storage Details page (Figure 10-25).

The Storage History page provides a quick glimpse of the history of the storage usage for the choice selected in the View list. The page provides statistical views of the following layers or elements:

- Overall Summary
- Databases
- Local File Systems
- Local Disks
- Volumes
- Writeable NFS

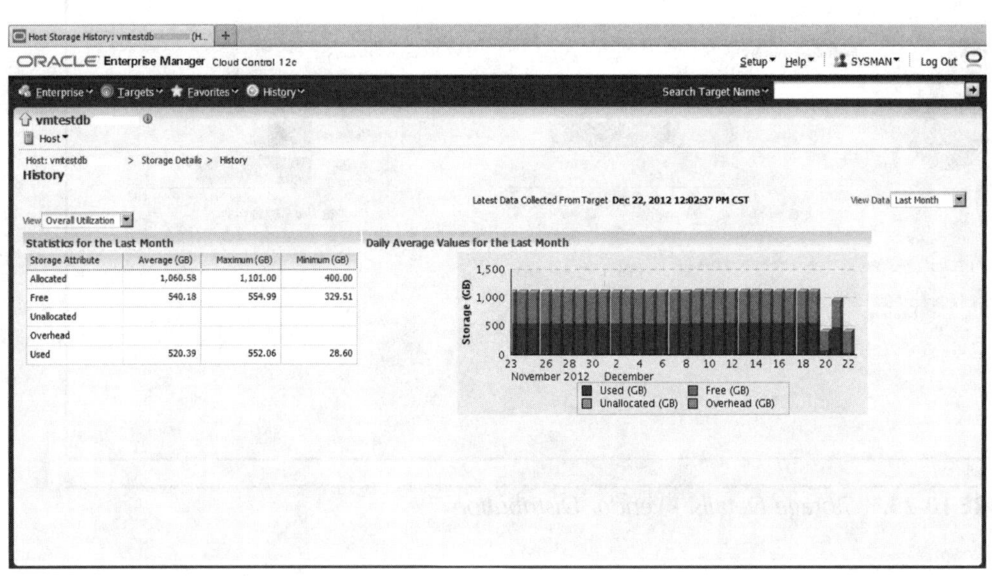

FIGURE 10-26. *Storage History*

Again, the options in the view list are dynamically generated. You are only provided options for layers or elements supported on the target host. The data selection can range from the last month, to the last three months, to the last year. For each view, the Administrator is presented with a table and a graph. The table provides Average, Maximum, and Minimum, for each of the storage attributes for the data set selected (time period). The graph provides similar information represented as daily average values. The graph helps identify trending and potential storage needs in the future.

Summary

This chapter described the various Cloud Control monitoring and management tools available for Host and Storage targets. We distinguished between host systems and Cloud Control's use of the term "system" to describe a collection of components that together provide a service. The Host Home page provides quick access to analysis tools and pertinent configuration information. The Host Home page also provides links to manage and monitor host-related storage.

With each successive release of the Enterprise Manager tool suite, more and greater functionality is provided in the user interface. Fewer steps are required on the individual targets. The ability to centralize the management of numerous and various targets greatly reduces the burden on the Administrator.

This is the third chapter in Part II, Cloud Control for Database, System, Storage, and Middleware Administrators. In Chapter 9, the database monitoring and management toolset was examined. In this chapter we covered systems (hosts) and storage. In the next chapter, we take a close look at the Cloud Control features available for managing middleware.

CHAPTER 11

Middleware Administrators: Manage Middleware with Cloud Control

Java EE applications, service-oriented architecture (SOA), and composite applications are being increasingly employed by organizations to perform various functions. While these applications provide great flexibility, the other side of the coin is that they are harder to manage efficiently. Monitoring numerous WebLogic Server domains and enterprise applications deployed across multiple tiers has become an increasingly more complex endeavor. Tracking ever-changing configurations of servers and applications and managing capacity to meet changing workloads is another major concern. Tracking multitier transactions and gaining visibility into transactions and the performance of SOA applications are big challenges as well. Oracle Enterprise Manager Cloud Control 12*c* provides a comprehensive management solution for meeting the enterprise needs that we describe in this chapter, especially for companies that depend on sophisticated applications using Oracle Fusion Middleware and its backbone, the Oracle WebLogic Server application server. OEM Cloud Control provides a comprehensive monitoring system, with built-in sophisticated performance diagnostic capabilities. It also provides automated configuration management, provisioning, and compliance features.

Managing Middleware with Cloud Control

Cloud Control comes with a set of Oracle Management plug-ins that contain management features customized for Oracle Fusion Middleware targets and designed to help you monitor and manage all the middleware targets you've deployed. Oracle also offers two additional management packs that enhance Cloud Control's capabilities to handle middleware. These are the WebLogic Server Management Pack Enterprise Edition and the SOA Management Pack Enterprise Edition, both of which are installed by default, but need additional licensing. Together, these packs provide all the ammunition you need to manage your entire middleware environment. The WLS Management Pack offers performance management, JVM diagnostics, business transaction management, and configuration features, and the SOA management pack provides these same features for SOA applications. You can monitor SOA products such as Oracle BPEL Process Manager (BPEL Process Manager), Oracle Service Bus (OSB), and Oracle SOA Suite 11*g* through Enterprise Manager Cloud Control, by enabling Oracle SOA Management Pack Enterprise Edition.

OEM Cloud Control 12*c* is a great tool for a one-stop management center for taking care of numerous Oracle Fission Middleware products such as Oracle WebLogic Server and various components of Oracle Fusion Middleware, as well as many types of middleware from other companies besides Oracle. OEM Cloud Control comes preconfigured with various performance monitoring and availability indicators, and you can, of course, configure your own levels for these indicators.

Middleware-related configuration management, performance monitoring, diagnostics, and lifecycle management are the broad areas where you can use the power of OEM Cloud Control 12*c*.

Cloud Control comes with a number of management plug-ins and connectors that enable you to manage non-Oracle software, including application servers such as IBM WebSphere Application Server and JBoss, as well as EMC storage, BMC Remedy, Check Point Firewall, and F4 BIG IP. You can use the Topology Viewer to view your middleware environment in a graphical format across multiple Oracle WebLogic domains.

It's natural for you to wonder why and how the OEM Cloud Control interface will be necessary when you already have the OEM Fusion Middleware Control (Fusion Middleware Control) at your disposal. Fusion Middleware Control, which is part of the Oracle Fusion Middleware installation, helps you manage a single Oracle Fusion Middleware farm and a single WebLogic domain. This tool is ideal for performing routine tasks such as monitoring and deploying applications and making configuration changes, for example. Cloud Control has a much wider scope and has a much more powerful set of capabilities. Cloud Control lets you monitor and manage your *entire middleware tier*—its capabilities encompass all the Oracle Fusion and other middleware running in your environment. OEM Cloud Control not only helps you monitor and manage middleware, but also fully configure and manage the entire lifecycle of all middleware components. Additionally, it helps you diagnose and tune the performance as well as troubleshoot any component in your middleware tier. Fusion Middleware Control, in addition to being limited to the management of a single domain, won't let you access and analyze historical performance metrics, whereas OEM Cloud Control provides very strong support for the analysis of historical performance data.

Following is a quick summary of the astounding number of things you can do with Cloud Control in managing your middleware tier:

- Manage Oracle Fusion Middleware components, including WebLogic Server 12*c*
- Manage other products, such as IBM WebSphere Application Server and JBoss Application Server
- Diagnose availability and performance issues relating to middleware
- Trace end-user requests from client to the service endpoint across all applications
- Analyze Java EE and SOA applications using Application Dependency and Performance (ADP)
- Use Java Diagnostics to diagnose performance problems of Java applications

Our main thrust in this chapter is to show you how to use OEM Cloud Control to monitor and manage both Oracle Fusion Middleware applications and the heart of Oracle Fusion Middleware—Oracle WebLogic Server 12*c*, the phenomenal application server that undergirds all Oracle Fusion Middleware applications.

We categorize our exploration of middleware monitoring management into the following sections:

- Discovery
- Proactive Monitoring
- Diagnostics
- Managing Oracle Exalogic Elastic Cloud

Discovering Middleware Targets

There are three main types of Cloud Control middleware targets: Oracle Fusion Middleware, Oracle Application Server, and non-Oracle middleware components. Let's summarize the individual components that could belong to one of these three types. You can manage custom Java EE applications as well as Oracle applications that are run on either Oracle Fusion Middleware or third-party middleware software. With OEM Cloud Control, you can manage multiple Oracle Fusion Middleware farms and Oracle WebLogic Server domains. You can monitor and manage the following Oracle Fusion Middleware components with OEM Cloud Control 12*c*:

- Oracle WebLogic Server farms, domains, clusters, and single-server instances
- Deployed clustered and standalone Java EE applications
- Oracle Web Tier components, including Oracle HTTP Server and Oracle Web Cache
- Service-oriented architecture (SOA) components
- Oracle Identity Management
- Oracle WebCenter
- Oracle Portal
- Oracle Forms and Reports
- Oracle Business Intelligence (BI Reporting and Publishing, OBI Discoverer, OBI Publisher)

- Oracle Universal Content Management System
- Oracle Coherence

Oracle Application Server components include Oracle Application Server 10*g* components such as Oracle Application Server Farms, Oracle Portal, and Oracle Business Intelligence.

Non-Oracle Middleware components that you can monitor include the following:

- WebSphere Application Server
- JBoss Application Server
- Apache Tomcat
- Apache HTTP Server
- Microsoft Exchange Server
- Microsoft Internet Information Services
- Microsoft Active Directory

Before you can manage any Oracle Fusion Middleware component, Enterprise Manager Cloud Control must first be aware of those applications. To do this, the tool must first discover the various components, including the Java applications that it monitors. Once a component or application is discovered, it can then be promoted to the status of a managed target. A middleware target such as an Oracle WebLogic Server domain is a managed target, just like an Oracle database. You must first install a Management Agent on the server where a middleware target is running. You can either automate the discovery of the middleware targets, or manually add them. Under an automatic discovery process, EM Cloud Control scans a host for various components it can manage. You can control the types of targets that EM Cloud Control can discover. You can then decide which of the discovered targets are to be managed by OEM Cloud Control 12*c*, by promoting them to the status of managed servers.

Automatic Discovery of Fusion Middleware Targets

Once you set up a Management Agent on a host machine, as shown in Chapter 5, Cloud Control 12*c* automatically registers all Fusion Middleware–related components running on that server. If you subsequently add Oracle Fusion Middleware targets to these registered host machines, you must either manually "discover" those targets or set up automatic discovery. Automatic discovery runs every 24 hours by default and you can modify this setting. Configuring automatic discovery does not, however, mean that Cloud Control 12*c* will automatically treat those targets as managed targets. You must formally promote any discovered new targets to the managed target status for you to be able to manage those targets through Cloud Control 12*c*.

Use the following steps to configure the automatic discovery of middleware targets:

1. Select Add Target from the Setup menu.
2. Select Configure Auto Discovery.
3. In the Discovery Module box, select Oracle Fusion Middleware, as shown in Figure 11-1.
4. Set a schedule for the auto discovery job if you want it to be different from the default schedule of every 24 hours.
5. Select the host machine by clicking Add Host.
6. Specify the Middleware homes to search for targets by clicking Edit Parameters.
7. Click OK to enable automatic discovery to run at the frequency that you've scheduled earlier.
8. To view the list of newly discovered targets, use the Setup menu and select Add Target and then select Auto Discovery Results.
9. The newly discovered Oracle Fusion Middleware targets can be viewed by clicking the Non-Host Targets tab.
10. Click Promote to promote a target. You must supply values for the port and host information, as well as the WebLogic Administration Server credentials.
11. Click Continue.
12. Click Close to automatically assign Management Agents to the targets. Click OK when you're done.

Once you configure automatic discovery of targets as shown in Figure 11-1, you can go to the Auto Discovery Results page to view the discovered middleware targets.

Discovering Targets Manually

Instead of setting up automatic discovery, you can choose to manually discover middleware targets. You can choose to discover a WebLogic 9.x or 10x domain via Cloud Control. To do this, go to Setup | Add Target | Configure Auto Discovery | Add Non-Host Targets by Specifying Target Monitoring Properties. You can then select Oracle Fusion Middleware as the target type, click Add Using Guided Discovery, and enter the necessary WebLogic-related parameter values.

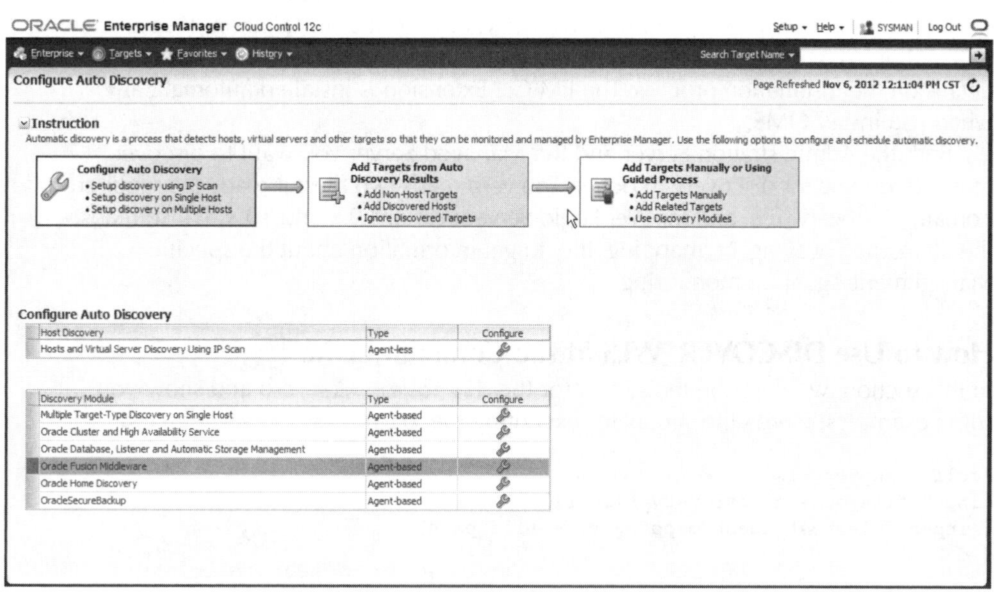

FIGURE 11-1. *The Configure Auto Discovery page*

Using the Command Line to Discover Multiple WebLogic Domains

You can use the Enterprise Manager Command Line Interface (EM CLI) `discover_wls` verb to discover multiple WebLogic domains, instead of having to discover them sequentially through the GUI screens. The file domain_discovery_file contains the domain information that will be read by the `discover_wls` verb.

The EM CLI is designed for use by admins who need to write scripts for providing business workflow for various business processes. You can also integrate Enterprise Manager with other software through the command-line scripting interface. You can also run the commands from the console, of course. The EM CLI Client uses the commands you input at the command line to identify a *verb*, which is a Java plug-in extension to the client. The verb can perform operations locally, but there's also a remote verb that can contact the EM CLI OMS Extension and send commands to the OMS through HTTP and HTTPS. The remote verb acts as the user that invokes a command from the EM CLI Client.

Use the `discover_wls` verb to discover a 7.x, 8.x, 9.x, and 10.x WebLogic domain, along with the Oracle Fusion Middleware 11*g* software deployed to the domain. You also use this verb to specify the Management Agent that should monitor managed servers from a specific host.

In order to use the command-line interface, you must install the EM CLI client (emclikit.jar) by downloading it from any 12*c* Cloud Control installation. Please refer to the Oracle Enterprise Manager Command Line Interface manual from Oracle for details on the installation process. The EM CLI Extension is installed automatically when you install OMS.

Both the Administration Server and the Managed Server you want to discover must be running for discovery to occur. The verb reads two files: it reads the required domain_discovery_file, and for WebLogic Server versions 9.x and 10.x, it also reads the file named host_agent_mapping_file, to get information about the specific Management Agent for monitoring.

How to Use DISCOVER_WLS at the Command Line

In this section, we describe the syntax for the `discover_wls` verb and show you some examples. Here's the syntax for executing the `discover_wls` command:

```
emcli discover_wls
-input_file=domain_discovery_file:file_path
[-input_file=host_agent_mapping_file:file_path]
[-debug]
```

Following is the general syntax for a domain_discovery_file for WebLogic Server 9.x and 10.x. Note that OPT denotes an optional parameter.

```
<WebLogic Server version>,<Administration Server Host>,<port>,<username>,
<password>,<External Parameters - OPT>,<JMX Protocol - OPT>,
<JMX Service URL - OPT>,<Unique Domain Identifier>,<Agent URL -OPT>
```

And here's sample data for the required input file, domain_discovery_file:

```
10,domain123.xyx.us,11990,weblogic,my\,pwd,,,farm_
demo,https://myco01.mycompany.com:3872/emd/main
```

The optional host_agent_mapping_file has the following format:

```
<Discovered_target_host_machine_name>,<Agent_URL_to_save/monitor_the_host>
```

For example:

```
myco01.mycompany.com,https://myco01.mycompany.com:3872/emd/main
myco02.mycompany.com,https://myco02.mycompany.com:3872/emd/main
myco03.mycompany.com,https://myco03.mycompany.com:3872/emd/main
```

The following example shows how the `discover_wls` command reads the two files, my_domains_info.csv and my_agent_mapping.csv, to find out which domains should be added and which management agents should monitor the managed servers.

```
emcli discover_wls
-input_file=domain_discovery_file:\emcli\my_domains_info.csv
-input_file=host_agent_mapping_file:\emcli\my_agent_mapping.csv
-debug
```

Discovering New or Modified Domain Members

Enterprise Manager Cloud Control doesn't automatically discover and enroll new members of an Oracle WebLogic domain. That is, any additions or deletions of domains, clusters, and instances or new deployments of applications are not noticed by Cloud Control out-of-box. You must either set up automatic discovery for new and modified domain members or manually check for changes in domain membership. The following sections show how to use both of these approaches to update your domain membership.

Enabling Automatic Discovery of New (or Modified) Domain Members

In order to enable the automatic discovery of new or modified domain members and to promote them to the status of managed targets, you must enable a Cloud Control job named "WebLogic Domain Refresh." You can enable this predefined job from the Middleware Home page, by selecting the WebLogic domain you want to enable the job for and using the WebLogic Domain Refresh property.

Manually Checking for New (or Modified) Domain Members

You follow the same initial procedures to manually check for a new or modified domain member(s). Once you select Refresh WebLogic Domain, let Cloud Control search the domain for new (or modified) targets. You then click Add Targets to assign a Management Agent for each new discovered domain member. If the local Agent isn't found on a host, Cloud Control will assign the Agent specified on the Targets page. Make sure the Agent is up.

Managing Middleware with Cloud Control

The starting point for all middleware monitoring and management work using Cloud Control is the Middleware Home page. You access this page by selecting Middleware from the Targets drop-down menu in the Enterprise Manager Cloud Control 12*c* Home page. At the top of the Middleware Home page, there is an icon for a menu named Middleware Features. Using this drop-down menu, you can access the following areas:

- Application Dependency and Performance
- Identity and Access
- Manage Diagnostic Snapshots
- Request Monitoring

- SOA Home
- WSM (Web Services Policy) Dashboard

On the Middleware Home page, there's a list of all the middleware targets in your environment that have been discovered by Cloud Control. These targets could be any one of the following target types:

- Oracle Fusion Middleware/WebLogic Domain
- Oracle Application Server (including OAS Farms and Clusters)
- IBM WebSphere Application Server/Server Cell
- JBoss Application Server
- Oracle Coherence

Figure 11-2 shows the home page for the default Cloud Control Oracle Fusion Middleware farm named EMGC_GCDomain. As you can see, the home page shows

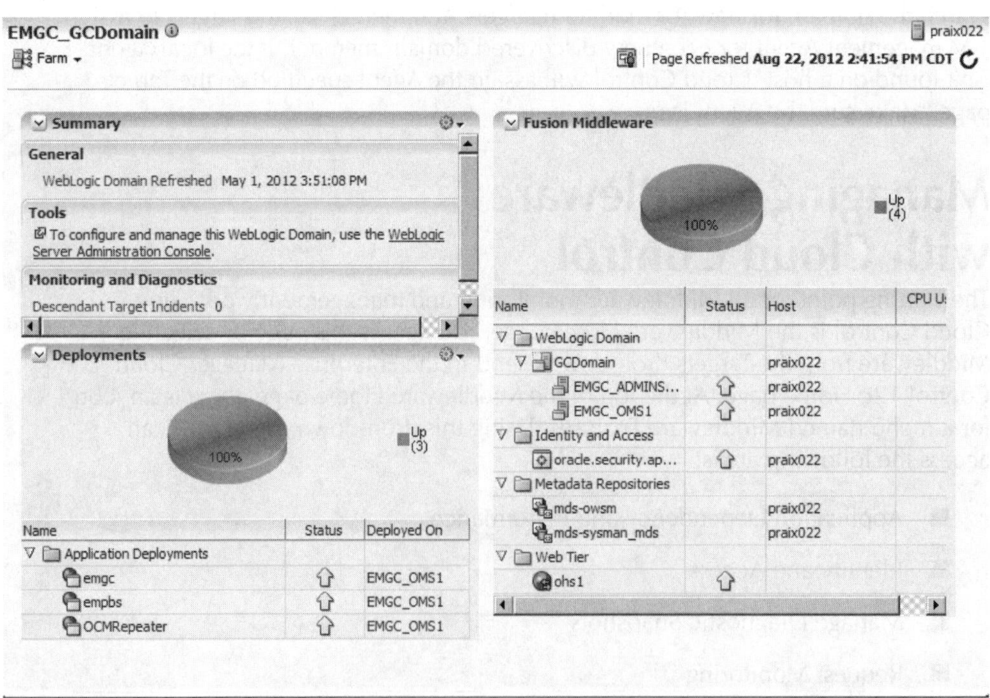

FIGURE 11-2. *Oracle Fusion Middleware Farm Home page*

all your application deployments and also a list of all your Oracle Fusion Middleware deployments, such as the WebLogic domains and the Web tier, in the Fusion Middleware section.

By default, the Middleware Home page will show the WebLogic domain for the Cloud Control application itself. The domain is named *EMGC_GCDomain*, belonging to the target type of Oracle Fusion Middleware Farm. Click on this domain link (either in the left pane after expanding the WebLogic Domain folder, or in the Fusion Middleware section in the right pane) to get to the home page for this Oracle Fusion Middleware farm.

Managing WebLogic Application Deployment

All applications that you've deployed in a WebLogic domain are listed in the Deployments section in the WebLogic Domain Home page. You can manage any deployed application from the application's home page, which you can reach by clicking the application's name in either the farm or the domain hosting the application. Figure 11-3 shows the home page of the default Enterprise Manager application, named `emgc`.

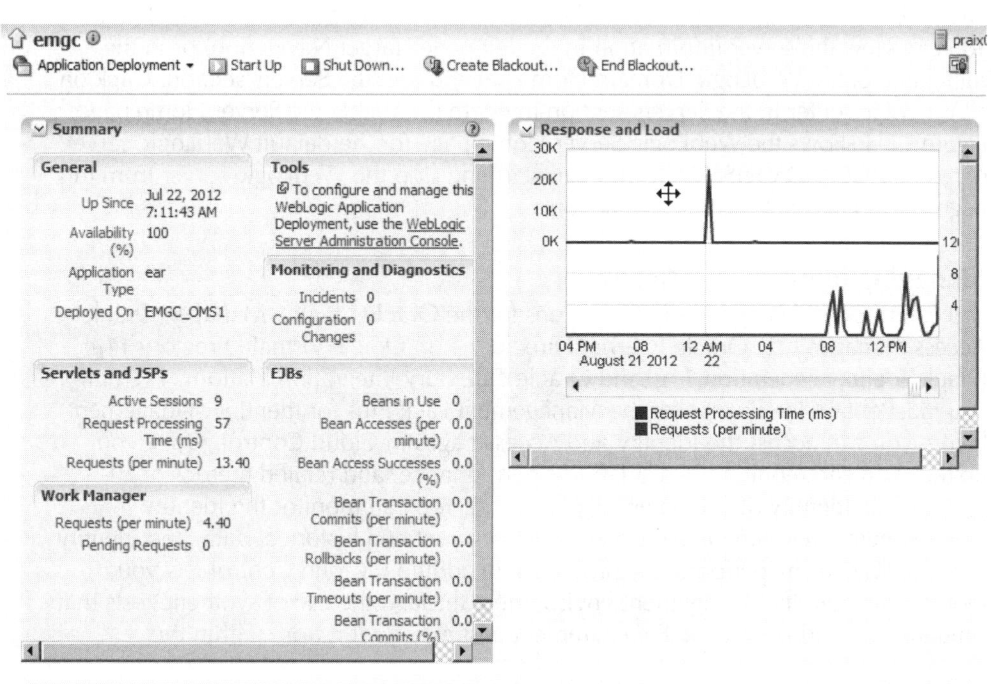

FIGURE 11-3. *Application Home page in Cloud Control*

You can check the performance of servlets, JSPs, and EJBs, including the number of requests, the average request processing time, the number of enterprise beans in use, and the number of bean accesses and bean transaction commits per minute, for example, from this page. The Response and Load section shows the number of requests per minute and the request process time (in ms) in a graphical format. The Most Requested (last 24 hours) section shows the most requested Java requests and their average execution and response times.

You can start and stop an application (except an EM system application such as the `emgc` application we're using as an example here, to which the process control command operations aren't applicable) and create and end notification blackouts for alerts for an application while it's running.

Monitoring JEE Applications

You can assess the performance of JEE applications by choosing a specific Oracle WebLogic Server Cluster in the Middleware page and clicking J2EE Applications. The Oracle WebLogic Server Cluster J2EE Applications page will show you the main performance metrics in a tabular form.

Managing WebLogic Server with Cloud Control

The WebLogic Domain Home page shows all the WebLogic servers in that domain. You can view the server information in the left pane (Target Navigation) or in the right pane of the WebLogic Domain Home page, under the Servers section. Click on a WebLogic server in the Servers section to get to the WebLogic Server Home page. Figure 11-4 shows the WebLogic Server Home page for the default WebLogic server named EMGC_ADMINSERVER. You can start and stop the WebLogic server from this page, as well as create and end blackouts.

Managing Identity and Access

You can track and compare configurations for the Oracle Identity Manager, Oracle Access Manager 11*g*, Oracle Internet Directory 11*g*, Oracle Virtual Directory 11*g*, Oracle Identity Federation 11*g*, and Oracle Directory Integration Platform 11*g* (DIP). You must obtain the license for the Management Pack Plus for Identity Management before you can access the Identity and Access pages in Cloud Control. Once you do this, you can monitor the availability, performance, and related metrics of all your Oracle Identity Management deployments. You can monitor the Identity Management environment using alerts, view current and historical data, and identify bottlenecks causing performance problems. In addition, Cloud Control lets you monitor the Identity Management environment through the use of synthetic tests that simulate real end-user work. For example, a test may be run from within the

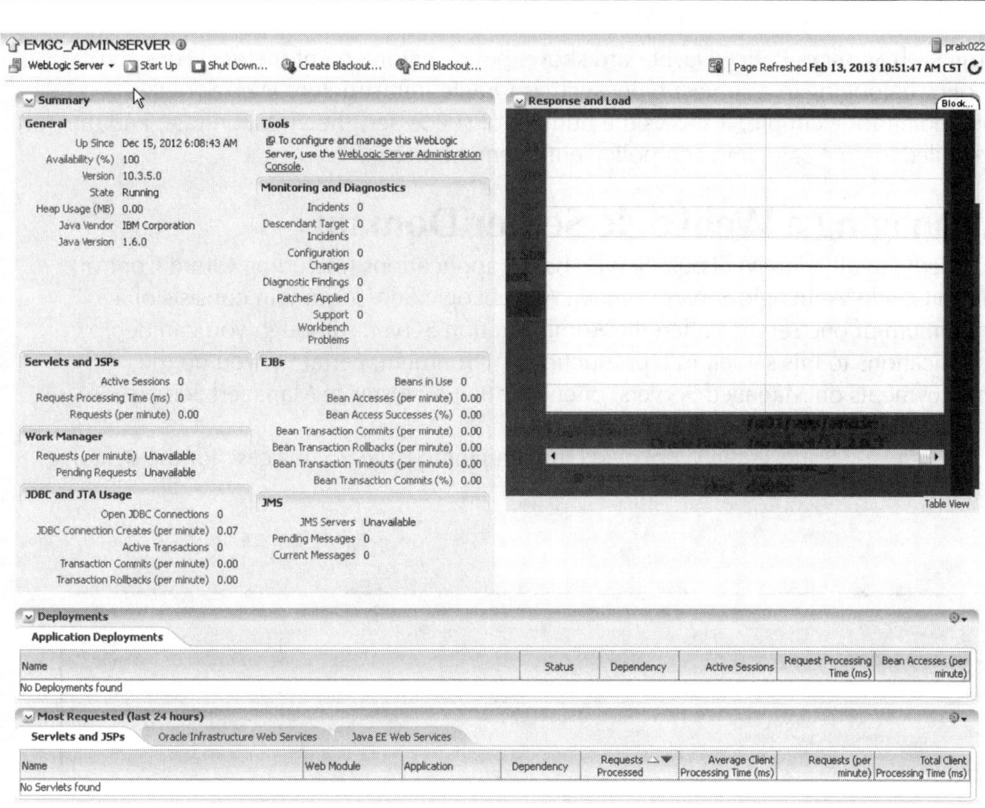

FIGURE 11-4. *The WebLogic Server Home page*

enterprise network to simulate users logging in through single sign-on. You thus can gain real insight into the end-user experience and thus learn how efficient and available your identity and access management services are in reality. You can define service levels according to your business requirements and report against your service level objectives (SLOs).

SOA Home

The SOA Home page shows all the SOA composites currently being monitored by Cloud Control. You can view critical metrics for the monitored services and compare the performance of various services.

Web Services Policy Dashboard

The Web Services Policy Dashboard shows policy enforcement metrics. For each policy belonging to a subject type, such as Oracle Infrastructure Web Services Endpoint, for example, it shows the number of successes, the violation rate, and the detailed log message for each policy enforcement metric.

Managing a WebLogic Server Domain

Underlying all your WebLogic Server–based applications (including Cloud Control) is an Oracle WebLogic Server *domain*. A WebLogic Server domain consists of a minimum of one server, called the Administration Server. Although you can deploy applications to this server, in a production environment, certainly, you do the deployments on Managed Servers, often creating a cluster of Managed Servers for high availability and performance purposes.

Figure 11-5 shows the WebLogic Domain Home page, in this case for the default Cloud Control domain—GCDomain.

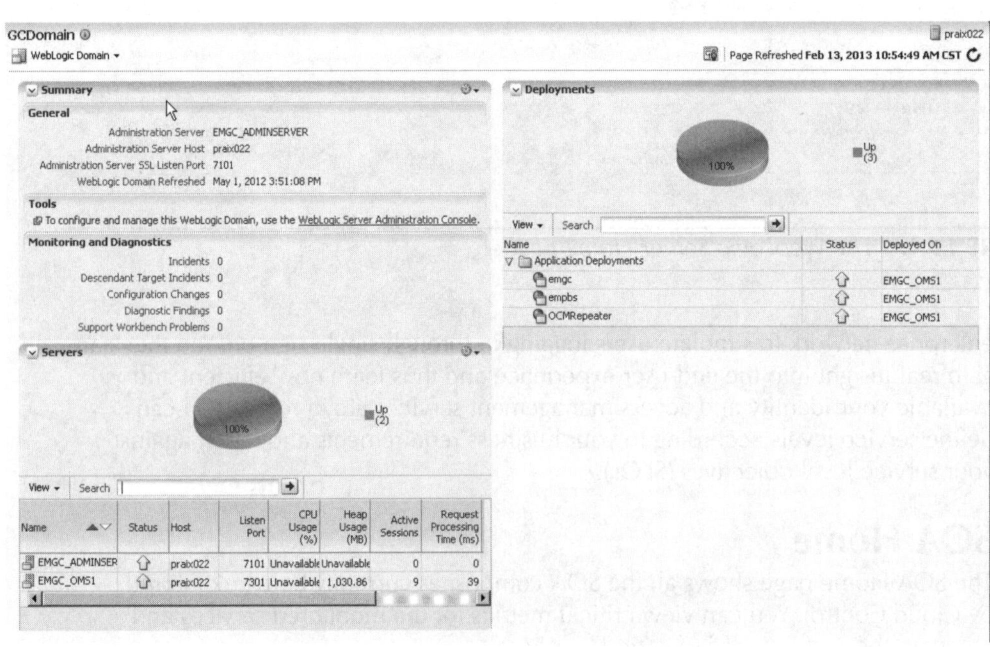

FIGURE 11-5. *The WebLogic Server Domain Home page*

Following are the main sections on the domain's home page.

- **Summary** The General section provides the port information and the last time the domain was refreshed. The Tools section provides a link to the WebLogic Server Administration Console to configure and manage the domain. The Monitoring and Diagnostics section shows any incidents or diagnostic findings.
- **Deployments** Shows the status of all your application deployments. You can click on any of the application links to get to the home page for that application deployment.
- **Servers** Shows all the WebLogic Server instances running in that domain. It provides a table summarizing the CPU usage, heap usage, number of active sessions, requests per minute, and the average request processing time (in milliseconds).

The following sections show how to perform common WebLogic Server domain–related tasks through Enterprise Manager Cloud Control.

Adding an Oracle WebLogic Server Domain

You can add an Oracle WebLogic Server domain as a target by going to Targets | Middleware and selecting Oracle WebLogic Server Domain from the Add menu in the Middleware page. Click Go to add the domain as a target to Cloud Control.

Viewing Member Targets

To view the members of your Oracle WebLogic Server Domain, go to Targets | Middleware and click the Oracle WebLogic Server domain or cluster you want to manage. Figure 11-5 shows the main page of the default WebLogic Server domain EMGC_GCDomain, which is part of every Enterprise Manager Cloud Control 12*c* installation. On the right-hand side of this domain page, you can click the name of a specific WebLogic Server instance, such as the Administration Server of the domain, for example.

Creating a WebLogic Control Job

You can employ a WebLogic Control job to start and stop an Oracle WebLogic Server domain or cluster. The following steps show how to create a WebLogic Control job.

1. Go to Targets | Middleware and click either Oracle WebLogic Server Cluster or Oracle WebLogic Server Domain.

2. Click Administration to go the Administration page. In the Job Activity section, select WebLogic Control from the Create Job list. Click Go.
3. In the Create 'WebLogic Control' Job Wizard, use the General page to set a name for the job and specify the target where you want the job to run. On the Parameters page, you can select the starting and stopping of a job. In the Credentials page, enter the credentials to run the job and schedule the job (once, repeatedly, or later) in the Schedule page. On the Access page, grant access to the job to administrators and roles.
4. Click Submit.

Viewing Cluster Metrics

You can view performance metrics for your Oracle WebLogic clusters by going to Targets | Middleware and clicking the Oracle WebLogic Server cluster you want to monitor. Click Metrics to go to the Oracle WebLogic Server Cluster Metrics page. Click Help for more information.

Proactive Middleware Monitoring

Once a middleware target such as an Oracle WebLogic domain is added to Cloud Control's list of targets, you can view the status of that target. You can view alerts generated for each managed middleware target. For both individual deployed applications, WebLogic servers and WebLogic domains, you can view the following pages by selecting Monitoring from the target's top level menu drop-down (such as the WebLogic Domain drop-down menu in the domain's home page):

- **All Metrics** Shows a list of all performance metrics you can select from for alerts, as well as the top five alerting metrics for the last seven days, with both the warning and critical alerts for each of those five alerts.
- **Metric and Collection Settings** This page shows all the metrics with threshold values. For example, a WebLogic server may have a JVM Metric such as Heap Usage (%), with a warning threshold of 80 percent and a critical threshold of 90 percent. By default, the collection schedule for this metric is every 15 minutes. For a metric such as Response, the schedule is every 1 minute.
- **Metric Collection Errors** Any metric evaluation errors, which are usually caused by installation or configuration errors.
- **Incident Manager** Shows all open incidents and problems, including escalated and unassigned incidents.

- **Alert History** Shows critical and warning alerts in a chart form.
- **Blackouts** Allows you to suspend monitoring on a target while performing maintenance operations.

In addition to these standard metrics pages, WebLogic Server also has additional metric pages such as Performance Summary and a JVM Performance page. Figure 11-6 shows the JVM Performance page for a WebLogic server. In a similar fashion, application deployment targets have specialized metrics pages, such as the Application Dependency and Performance page and the Request Monitoring page.

The JVM Performance page shows charts for the heap usage, as well as active and locked JVM threads and the performance of the garbage collection, with metrics for collections per minute and the average garbage collection time.

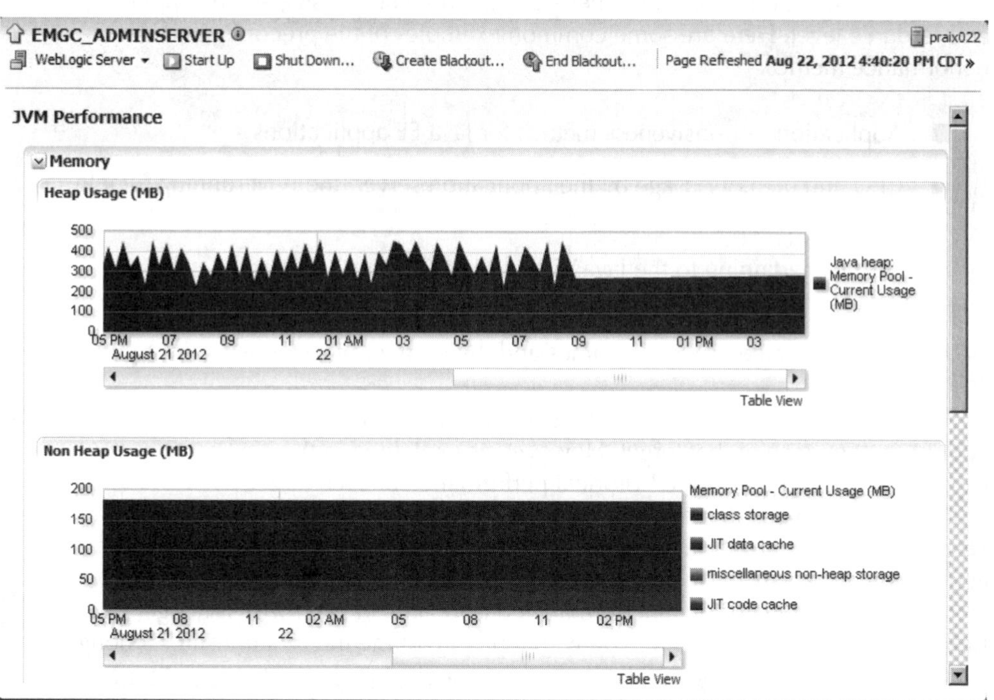

FIGURE 11-6. *The JVM Performance page for a WebLogic server*

Managing Cloud Control Metrics

OEM Cloud Control immediately starts monitoring a WebLogic Server domain and your middleware deployments with an out-of-box set of status and performance metrics, as soon as it discovers the middleware entities. You can monitor these metrics both in real time and from a historical point of view and customize the performance summary pages in the Console. As an administrator, to facilitate your monitoring, you can define a WebLogic Domain Group to monitor availability and performance in a cohesive manner.

The following sections discuss Cloud Control performance metrics and how you can create custom performance dashboards.

Performance Metrics

For each middleware target, Cloud Control has a preconfigured set of performance metrics, which are continuously captured and stored in the Management Repository. Note that there are out-of-the-box metrics at the domain, cluster, server, application, and resource level. Here are some common examples of the preconfigured performance metrics:

- Application responsiveness metrics for Java EE applications
- CPU and memory usage by the application server (the JVM running Oracle WebLogic Server)
- Metrics pertaining to the Java Virtual Machines run by Oracle WebLogic servers
- Servlet average processing times and the number of requests for each servlet

The predefined performance metrics for each target help you evaluate the current performance of that target. However, as explained in the next section, you can also gain insights into the historical performance of each target.

You can customize the display on the performance page, and in fact, you can keep a set of customized pages handy for quickly checking on various aspects of the application environment. In essence, the customizable performance pages give you the ability to create your own performance dashboards in Enterprise Manager Cloud Control 12*c*. In order to provide you with a picture of the interrelationships among multiple related targets, the Performance Summary feature lets you compute metrics for a set of targets.

Oracle recommends that you create reports to confirm that the set of performance metrics you chose is valid and useful.

Viewing Historical Metrics

Often, when you are troubleshooting performance problems, it's nice to have access to older performance data and diagnostic reports. Since Cloud Control stores all metrics in its Management Repository, you can always view historical performance data. After your system has been in production for a while, Cloud Control will be able to use the historical data it collects to make recommendations for appropriate metric thresholds to use for alerts. You can also perform a trend analysis using the historical data. Most amazing of all, you view data from as old a period as you wish—as long as you don't go past 99 years!

System Monitoring and Notifications

Cloud Control monitors a vast array of performance metrics automatically and compares them with predefined metric thresholds. You can have Cloud Control issue alerts whenever performance metric values exceed a specific threshold value, which serve as the triggers for the sending of alerts. You can specify both critical and warning alerts following the crossing of alert thresholds by monitored metrics. You can thus set up a comprehensive alert system that lets you know when performance is slow or when a target is down. For routine tasks, you can even set up the correct actions to automatically resolve certain alert conditions, during which Cloud Control won't monitor that target.

Cloud Control notifications include e-mail messaging and even the execution of scripts and the relaying of SNMP traps. You can also automate the opening of helpdesk tickets following an incident, with the help of management connectors.

For JMX-managed applications, you can extend monitoring deployed to WebLogic Server by adding performance metrics that go beyond the out-of-box metrics. You can also define new target types for monitoring via management plug-ins for more comprehensive monitoring of JMX-enabled applications. Use the command-line tool `emjmxcli` to automate the generation of metadata.

In order to increase the effectiveness of your Cloud Control deployments to manage your middleware environments, Oracle recommends that you start by creating metric thresholds and monitoring templates. Oracle further recommends that you should make the monitoring templates a part of a template collection and, finally, create administrative groups to group various target types together, so you can associate your monitoring template collections to the administrative groups. It's an Oracle recommended best practice to set up notifications by creating rules and rule sets, so you can proactively manage problems in your environment.

In the following sections, we describe these monitoring best practices in more detail.

Defining Metric Thresholds

It's extremely important to define a set of metric thresholds to guide your management and monitoring of your middleware environment. You set metric thresholds for all performance and availability–related metrics, so you are alerted when a monitored metric value crosses its threshold value. Using metric thresholds for alerts, ideally based on your service level agreements, will help you proactively monitor the availability and performance of your middleware environment instead of waiting for users to call about performance issues. As described earlier, you can set both warning and critical alerts for things such as the JVM heap usage in a production WebLogic Server.

All your Java applications, the WebLogic servers, and SOA composites will be ideal candidates for setting alert thresholds. Choose only those alerts that are really meaningful to you, and disable the rest of the metrics so you won't get unnecessary alerts. You can define acceptable performance on the basis of your existing service level agreements. You determine your performance thresholds based on your service levels. Although there are several out-of-the-box thresholds, you may need to customize them to fit your requirements.

Creating Monitoring Templates

To make it easy for you to set thresholds across your middleware environment, Cloud Control offers you monitoring templates, which help you apply uniform monitoring settings everywhere in your enterprise. By bundling templates for a set of targets into a template collection and associating that template collection with a group of targets, you can easily automate the application of monitoring settings across your middleware environment. When you add new targets, the targets automatically inherit the monitoring settings you've defined for that group through a monitoring template.

You can create monitoring templates from scratch, or better still, use Cloud Control's predefined templates for target types such as Oracle WebLogic Domain, Oracle Fusion Middleware Farm, Application Deployment, Oracle WebLogic Server, and so on. Monitoring templates help you set thresholds for various target types, which will then be automatically applied to those targets. If, for example, you want to monitor the average response time for production web services, you define a threshold for this metric, to accurately reflect your SLAs for that service. In order to apply this threshold to all Web Services, for example, create a monitoring template named Production Web Services. Any production web service that you're running on a server will be subject to the thresholds you set through this monitoring template. Since you can create thresholds at varying granularity levels, first create broad thresholds and create a template for those thresholds. You can then set fine-grained metric thresholds using the coarser-grained templates as the base.

Creating Template Collections

In order to further ease your administrative burden, you can create template collections for a set of thresholds for groups of targets that belong to a specific target type. A template collection consists of different monitoring templates, for example, one for production targets and the other for development targets. In each template collection, you can have a single monitoring template for each target type that's a part of the template collection, such as a template for WebLogic servers and another for Application Deployments and yet another for Web Services, for example.

Oracle recommends that you use template collections to apply monitoring settings and keep direct ad hoc application of monitoring templates to targets only when you have to.

Creating Administration Groups

Grouping similar targets such as WebLogic domains, SOA infrastructure, and other components into Administration Groups facilitates the application of monitoring settings across a far-flung environment with numerous components. Cloud Control offers quite a bit of flexibility in creating the Administration Groups. You can create logical groupings of targets that support key applications and associate a template collection with the Administration Groups. In fact, the main motivation behind the creation of template collections is to associate them with the Administration Groups. The association of template collections with the Administration Groups ensures the uniform application of monitoring settings to all of a group's members.

Associating template collections to Administration Groups is an Oracle recommended best practice for managing middleware. As explained earlier, doing this means that your standardized mentoring settings are quickly and automatically applied to targets of different types, including any new targets you add.

Request Monitoring

An application or a web browser invokes a request at an entry point to a server. Cloud Control lets you define key sets of requests for monitoring and performance tracking. It also provides you with default request and request groups, but you can create your own requests. Using the request monitoring feature, you can perform end-to-end monitoring of client requests and identify the source and nature of performance problems by viewing the call path of key requests. You can thus narrow down the performance issues to particular servers and reduce the time it takes to discover and identify performance problems. The important thing to note here is that request monitoring lets you correlate poor end-user performance to the specific application. You can also gain an understanding of the interaction among the servers in servicing end-user requests.

Cloud Control discovers the request call paths and provides heightened visibility into the entire infrastructure by showing you request-monitoring metrics ranging from high-level call path topology to low-level transaction tracing. You have the freedom to set your service level thresholds at various levels so as to get immediate alerts to safeguard the service level commitments of your organization.

Request monitoring provides insight into the resource utilization for a request, thus throwing light on production bottlenecks. Besides the capturing of the complete call path of key requests, request monitoring also compares the performance among the servers and lets you know which servers are contributing more to the delays and performance degradation in your system.

You can access the request monitoring feature by select Request Monitoring from the Middleware Features menu after first selecting Middleware from the Targets menu.

A web browser or an application invoking a web service can initiate a HTTP request, known as a *request instance*. Groups of request instances form a *request* and a set of requests is known as a *request group*. You monitor performance metrics for each request to evaluate its performance. You can also configure critical and warning threshold–related alerts for key requests. Cloud Control comes with a set of predefined requests and request groups, and you can create a new request group or remove existing request groups,

To define a request, go to Targets | Middleware, and select a middleware target. Select an application deployed on that target and select Monitoring | Request Monitoring. You can manage requests by clicking the Request Definitions tab and view request performance by clicking Request Performance.

Request Dashboard

How do you tell which application requests are poor performers? You can use Cloud Control's Request Dashboard to identify the worst-performing requests based on their response time. Using the dashboard, an administrator can easily compare a request's performance in two different time periods. You can identify the bottlenecks within the context of the call path for a request by making use of the topology view, which uses run-time transaction metrics. Instead of relying on ad hoc techniques, the topology code path lets you see the overall picture of request traffic among various system components.

Composite Application Dashboard

Composite applications use multitier components and are usually made up of Java EE and SOA components, and potentially other technologies such as Oracle Service Bus and Oracle Coherence. It is very useful to have a single dashboard to check the application health across the composite application. Cloud Control's Composite Application Dashboard provides you that integrated view of both service-level and component-level metrics across a composite application. The Composite Application Dashboard shows the JVM, WebLogic Server, application, and host metrics as well as providing an Incident Console to track policy violations. You can also customize the dashboard to fit your needs.

Business Transaction Management

Cloud Control's Business Transaction Management (BTM) feature offers critical insight into the transaction flow by helping you identify your application topology, key application components, and the interrelationships among those components, all of which helps you make the right management decisions. The WebLogic Server Management Pack (for Java EE applications running on WebLogic Server) and the SOA Management Pack (for SOA services running on the SOA Suite), both include BTM. BTM provides critical real-time monitoring and the ability to track cross-tier and cross-application transactions. BTM is designed to let you view transaction performance and fault conditions, by letting you understand and track the logical transaction flow, for example, by performing transaction-related diagnostic work such as capturing transaction payloads.

You must deploy a total of three BTM-related applications if you decide to extend your middleware monitoring to include BTM. These are the WebLogic Server and the SOA BTM monitors and the Central BTM servers, which manage the BTM environment and provide transaction management components. The BTM monitors collect performance data and send it to the Central BTM servers. These three services require an Oracle database for persisting their data and logs. You must deploy these three BTM-related applications to a dedicated WebLogic server. If you must, deploy BTM Observers to each WebLogic server on which the key business transactions that you wish to manage are being run.

To help you manage transactions, BTM comes with two predefined dashboards—the Top 10 Services and the Top 10 Transactions. Using a key such as a customer ID, you can search through the messages in the dashboard and review the specific transaction that's causing a performance issue, by looking it up in the *transaction inspector*. You thus have the ability to see why a certain Web Service is underperforming, and quickly fix the issue. If you've installed the optional Real User Experience Insight or RUEI, which is a separate product from Cloud Control, you can drill down from RUEI into Cloud Control and BTM to review detailed transaction data for an end user.

Oracle recommends that you monitor key transactions with BTM so you can view the operational health of those transactions as well as the systems that manage those transactions. The operational health summary dashboard provides key metrics for your enterprise and its transactions. You can quickly identify transactions that aren't running well, as well as whether all the system components (services and endpoints) are up and running.

Tracking End-to-End Performance and Service Level Management

While an after-the-fact analysis and review of performance is useful in gaining insight into application behavior, it's often even more useful to be able to view a business transaction while it's occurring, in order to zoom in on trouble spots. Cloud Control provides a snapshot of key run-time data, including throughput and response times in the content of the business transactions and the users. These snapshots of run-time data help you monitor service levels across heterogeneous environments. Cloud Control monitors all types of application services, and can instrument just about all types of distributed application services. It not only monitors the messages and application code paths to collect operational data, but it also relates that to the overall business transaction. Your visibility is extended from the primary application services such as Web applications, to the foundational components such as EJBs and JMS queue components, and even down to individual database queries.

With the help of Cloud Control's end-to-end performance-tracking features, you can define different SLAs (service level agreements) based on the various business groups and prioritize service usage according to specific business criteria, thus enabling you to focus on your key customers and partners. Cloud Control lets you see which consumers are utilizing the services, thus letting you improve the quality of service for key users based on your usage analysis.

Monitoring Performance of Oracle WebLogic Managed Servers

Cloud Control's performance charts provide a quick way to examine the status and health of your Oracle WebLogic Managed Servers. Select a Managed Server in the Middleware page and click Performance to view the Oracle WebLogic Managed Server Performance page.

Monitoring the Oracle SOA Suite

If you want to use features other than the monitoring of Oracle Service Bus (OSB), you must enable the Management Pack for SOA. To do this, select Setup | Management Packs | Management Pack Access | Oracle Service Bus and enable the SOA Management Pack for a specific Oracle Service Bus target.

Monitoring from the Incident Management Console

You can use the Incident Management Console to manage incidents. You can resolve incidents from the Console, because the Console is also integrated with My Oracle Support for your convenience. If you've created views to filter critical incidents, you can get detailed information about that incident by clicking the specific incident in the Console. Once you do this, you'll see further links to the diagnostics and resolution area to help resolve the issue quickly. You can, for example, click the View Topology link to examine the health of other targets this application depends on.

Using the Log Viewer

Instead of manually poring over the numerous logs relating to WebLogic Server and Fusion Middleware, you can simply use the Log Viewer to search across all log files. Additionally, you can correlate log messages based on time, severity, or the Execution

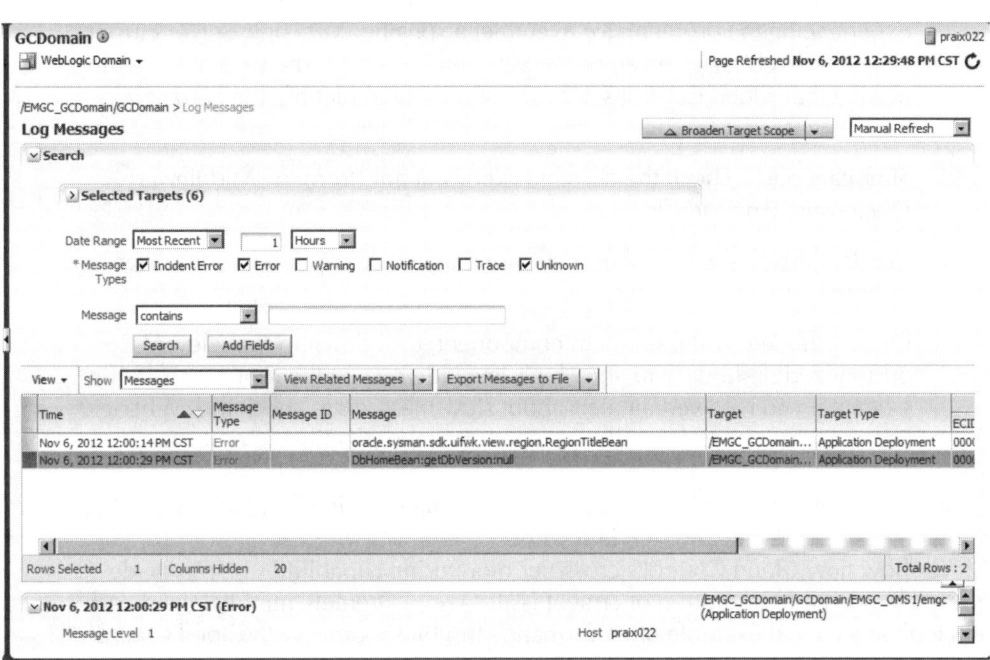

FIGURE 11-7. *The Log Messages page for a WebLogic domain*

Context ID (ECID), which enables you to unearth more comprehensive diagnostic information to help you resolve the problems.

You can view messages for a WebLogic domain by selecting Logs from the domain's drop-down menu and then selecting View Log Messages. The Log Messages page contains all log messages for all messaging types such as error, warning, and critical. The table also contains links to access the actual log associated with a log message. Figure 11-7 shows the Log Messages page for a WebLogic domain.

Middleware Diagnostics with Cloud Control

Although there's no "one size fits all" diagnostic method for all your performance issues, following is the general tuning approach recommended by Oracle to tackle complex middleware application performance problems.

1. First, rule out all non-middleware infrastructure issues causing the performance problem.

2. Narrow down the scope of the problem by ascertaining the component experiencing the problem; for example, a specific WebLogic Server cluster, a specific WebLogic server, or the SOA infrastructure. The type of notification or alert that Cloud Control sends you should help identify the correct component.
3. Simultaneously, check the current findings, if any, from the Middleware Diagnostics Advisor.
4. Create a diagnostic snapshot to ensure that you've captured useful diagnostic information for analysis later on.
5. Once you identity the problem component, drill down to the relevant customized dashboard to get a high-level idea about the root cause. If, for example, you received an alert about slow messaging, check the WebLogic Server Home page and drill down from there to identify the root cause.

It's a good practice to monitor diagnostics during peak load and at times of high resource (CPU, memory, and I/O) utilization.

To show how Cloud Control's cross-tier monitoring capabilities help provide quick diagnosis and resolution of critical issues with extremely minimal overhead, let's look at a typical example of performance troubleshooting with Cloud Control. As an example, let's say you've received an alert about a performance issue related to a composite application that consists of several SOA and Java EE components. You notice that a specific JVM is experiencing locks from viewing the threads table for that JVM. You can drill down to the JVM Diagnostics page and check the key requests. You may notice a bunch of stuck threads and several threads in the database wait state, indicating a database problem, resulting in a hung application. You can then click on the Live Thread Analysis link to understand the thread behavior. To find the actual root cause, you click on the DB wait link to get to the actual database session that's being blocked. And by clicking the Blocking ID, you can isolate the specific database session that's blocking your application. The simple example described here points to the benefits of tying in JVM diagnostics with database diagnostics by Cloud Control.

Using the Middleware Target Home Pages for Diagnostics

You can get quick summaries of the health and performance of both WebLogic and SOA targets from the middleware target home pages. For example, the Most Requested section of the WebLogic Server Home page shows you the JSPs or servlets with poor response, leading you to drill down to that servlet or JSP to identify the causes. As shown in the previous section, you can continue drilling down all the way to the database session level to identify the root cause.

Using the Middleware Performance Summary Pages

For each middleware target, there's a separate Performance Summary page showing you useful performance data. Again, you can drill down deeper in order to resolve the root causes of issues. For any metric, you can access the Problem Analysis page, which shows you what other metrics are impacting this metric. Charts such as the ones for Request/Processing Time give you information as to whether you should be looking at faster or more CPUs or memory on the server. You can go to the Relation Information pane and review the List of Related Targets for additional related information that can help you diagnose the issue. The Analyze Logs link in the Additional Information pop-up shows you relevant log messages for the target you're investigating.

The Middleware Diagnostics Advisor

The Middleware Diagnostics Advisor is a sophisticated tool that lets you go beyond traditional performance metrics and get recommendations to improve performance. The advisor performs a full stack analysis of the interrelationships among the components, their configuration patterns, and both historical and current performance metrics. The advisor takes into account the metric thresholds set by you; for example, the request processing time for a JSP or Servlet page request. When the request process time exceeds the set threshold, the advisor checks for any concurrent increase in resource usage metrics, such as the JDBC pool connection wait times. In addition to providing raw metrics, based on this correlation, the advisor may issue a recommendation to increase the size of the JDBC connection pool for a specific data source. The advisor even provides a direct link to implement the recommendations it makes. For example, a SQL execution diagnostic finding will provide a detailed analysis of the poor SQL that's slowing down an application and offers links to analyze and tune that SQL statement. The advisor makes recommendations concerning response times and other common performance issues, such as Java thread locks, to ensure that you can maintain your SLAs for key applications.

Accessing the Middleware Diagnostics Advisor

You access the Middleware Diagnostics Advisor by following these steps:

1. Go to Targets | Middleware.
2. Click on an Oracle Fusion Middleware Farm (EMGC_GCDDomain in this example).
3. In the left pane, expand WebLogic Domain and click on a domain (GCDomain in this example).
4. From the WebLogic Domain drop-down menu in the right pane, select Diagnostics and then Middleware Diagnostics Advisor. Figure 11-8 shows the Middleware Diagnostics Advisor's initial page, before you configure the advisor.

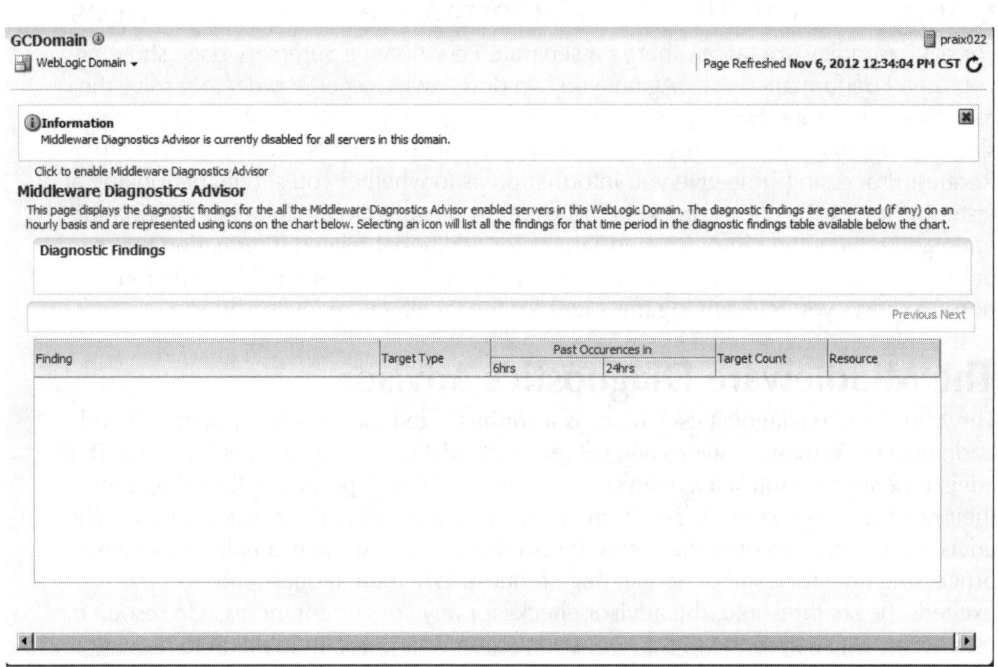

FIGURE 11-8. *The Middleware Diagnostics Advisor page before configuring the Advisor*

Enabling the Middleware Diagnostics Advisor

Initially, the Middleware Diagnostics Advisor is disabled for all servers in the domain. The Advisor's Home page displays diagnostic findings for only the Middleware Diagnostics Advisor–enabled servers in a WebLogic domain. The Advisor generates the diagnostic finds on an hourly basis.

To enable the Advisor, click the link titled "Click to enable Middleware Diagnostics Advisor." The Middleware Diagnostics Advisor – Configuration page appears when you click the link, as shown in Figure 11-9. Before you can enable a server for analysis by the Middleware Diagnostics Advisor, you must first deploy the JVMD Agent on that server. You must first set the credentials for the host and the WebLogic domain, before selecting one or more targets from the list of targets and clicking the Enable button.

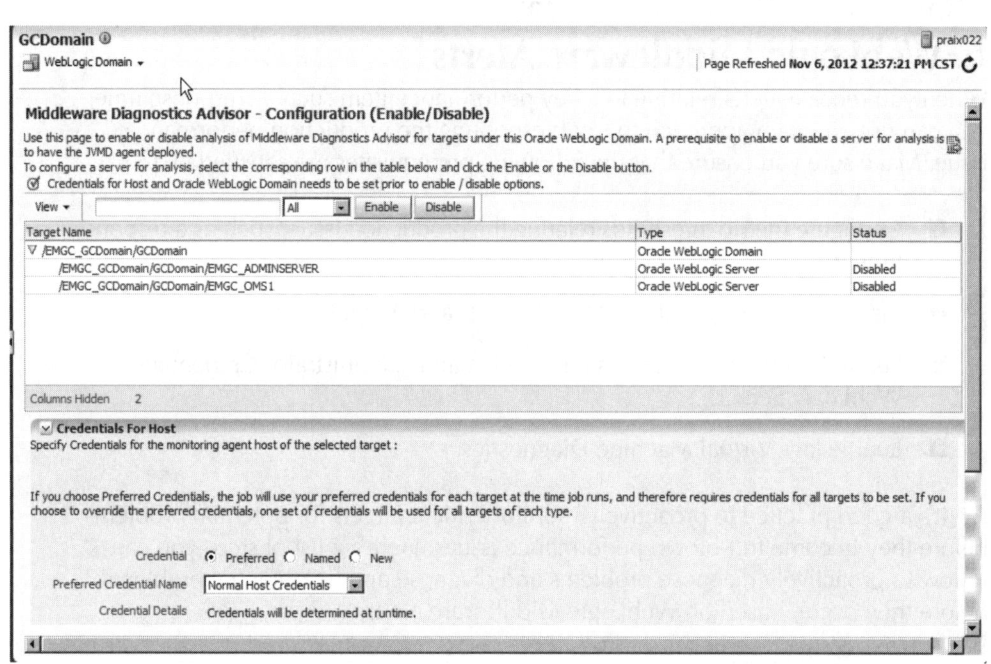

FIGURE 11-9. *The Middleware Diagnostics Advisor – Configuration page*

When to Use the Middleware Diagnostics Advisor

Oracle recommends that you monitor the Advisor's findings during peak load times and during times when you notice a high CPU, memory, or I/O utilization. The Middleware Diagnostics Advisor can generate useful findings because it has access to all the configuration information for the entire middleware environment, as well as the performance metrics and dependency data for all the components. This allows the Advisor to perform an analysis of your entire middleware stack. You can glean information about pending problems by viewing information on the diagnostic findings that occur most frequently during a given time period, such as the last 24 hours. Each finding has summary information, and the Analysis Information table provides detailed information and the Related Targets table shows the targets involved in this finding. The Suggestion column contains the recommendations to fix the problem, for example asking you to consider tuning the SQL statements to improve performance.

Diagnosing Problems Related to WebLogic Middleware Alerts

When you receive alerts relating to a key performance item such as response time, you can use a certain approach to troubleshooting the production performance issue. Make sure you ensure that the following prerequisites are satisfied first.

- Configure metric thresholds relating the production issue, such as a response time threshold.
- Install and configure the JVMD Manager and Agent.
- Set up Preferred Credentials for the host and Administrator Credentials for WebLogic Server.
- Enable Java Virtual Machine Diagnostics.

It's a good practice to proactively monitor critical targets for potential problems before they become full-blown performance issues. Here's a list of steps you can follow to proactively diagnose problems and diagnose and fix potential problems before they occur, based on WebLogic Middleware alerts.

1. When you see a critical alert for a domain on the Middleware Home page, click the link for the domain.
2. In the WebLogic Home page, select Middleware Diagnostics Advisor. You do this by selecting Diagnostics from the WebLogic Domain drop-down menu and selecting Middleware Diagnostics Advisor.
3. We're assuming you've already configured one or more servers for diagnostic analysis. If not, you must first deploy the JVM Diagnostic Agent and refresh the domain so the JVM's status reflects the deployment of the Agent. Once you deploy the Agent, enter the credentials and enable the target for diagnostic analysis by the Middleware Diagnostics Advisor.
4. In the Diagnostics Findings section on the Middleware Diagnostics Advisor page, click on a finding and the Finding Details page appears. The presence of a finding clearly indicates that Cloud Control has discovered a critical issue through its comprehensive analysis of your entire middleware stack.
5. Check the Analysis Information table and the related targets table to understand the finding and find out the targets that are impacted by the finding.
6. For example, you may see "Possible memory leak in the application code" under Suggestions if there's a JVM memory leak. Alternatively, you may see a finding such as "Thread Lock," meaning there are threads that are holding

locks over a long time. You can then drill down to find the specific threads holding and waiting on the locks. The Suggestions column may recommend a redesign of the code to prevent the locking. You can take proactive action based on the advice presented in the Suggestions column.

Transaction Diagnostics and Root-Cause Analysis

Real-time troubleshooting of slow-performing applications is not an easy task using traditional measures, as you need to spend critical time reviewing logs and other indicators of performance issues. OEM Cloud Control 12*c* offers powerful instrumentation that lets you search transactions based on their message content and time of arrival, thus helping quickly identify and fix technical exceptions or slow performance conditions. By letting you drill down to the root cause of problems through the precise transaction based on the message content and context (time of arrival, customer ID, and so on) as well as by correlating application invocations, Cloud Control 12*c* dramatically reduces the time to diagnose run-time issues, as well as the mean time to repair.

What makes Cloud Control's root cause analysis capabilities really powerful is its ability to handle a wide array of causes, ranging from high-level causes such as application faults and exceptions, to low-level issues caused by bad data, for example. You can choose from this wide variety of potential exceptions, following which Cloud Control will monitor the system traffic and catch the exceptions as soon as they occur. As you can imagine, this is a vastly superior method of tracking exceptions and failed transactions, when compared with the traditional "method" of poring over hard-to-access log files. Cloud Control automatically aggregates messages from all the components involved in serving the application and tags the exceptions and faults in real time. It's this ability to offer speedy diagnostic data that enables administers to quickly analyze and repair performance problems.

Diagnostic Snapshots

You can diagnose performance data for a JVM target in the offline mode by creating *diagnostic snapshots*. A diagnostic snapshot captures live performance data for a specific period and allows you to perform offline diagnostics on the captured data. Use the Diagnostic Snapshots page to create diagnostic snapshots and export the diagnostic data to a file that you can then export to a different host. You can also view a diagnostic snapshot from this page. The View option lets you view summary information such as the targets, target types, and the diagnostic information collected for a specific diagnostic snapshot. By clicking Analyze on this page, you can analyze a snapshot from the Analyze Diagnostic Snapshot page. By analyzing a diagnostic snapshot, you can view details about a JVM such as the thread stack, CPU, and heap utilization and garbage collection. You can also view a graph for active threads.

The ability to create a diagnostic snapshot means that you can focus on fixing the performance problem at hand and analyze the captured details later on to isolate the root cause. Usually there's no time to diagnose performance problems when you're in the throes of the problem. Your priority during that time is going to be the restoration of the application to its normal performance so users can continue their work.Often, you may want to capture a set of diagnostics in your production environment for use later on either by you or by Oracle support. Oracle Enterprise Manager's Diagnostic Snapshots feature enables you to create performance snapshots that capture JVM operational data relating to the memory and CPU usage, threads, and garbage collection, along with the WebLogic logging information. Generally, a diagnostic snapshot contains all the data necessary to resolve a performance issue. The specific diagnostic data differs based on the type of target, but as long as you pick any Fusion Middleware component, diagnostic log message data is included in the diagnostic snapshot. You can generate a snapshot for any target, including a Fusion Middleware farm. You can send these snapshots to Oracle Support or export them to another OEM Cloud Control. Thus, diagnostic snapshots offer yet another means of drilling down to the root cause of performance issues in middleware applications.

Creating Diagnostic Snapshots You can create a diagnostic snapshot in the context of one or multiple Fusion Middleware farms. You can create a diagnostic snapshot by going to Targets | Middleware and choosing Manage Diagnostic Snapshots from the Middleware Features menu. Initially you'll notice the message "No Diagnostic Snapshots Available" under the Diagnostic Snapshots section. In the Diagnostic Snapshots section, click Create to create a diagnostic snapshot. Figure 11-10 shows

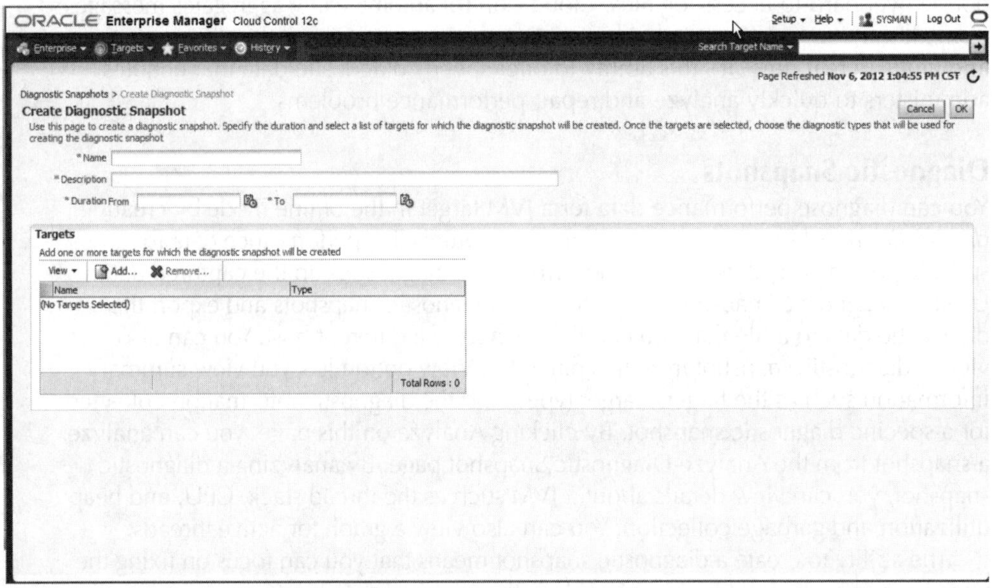

FIGURE 11-10. *Creating a diagnostic snapshot*

the Create Diagnostic Snapshot page. You can select the targets for generating the snapshot, the duration of the period during which Cloud Control collects the data, and choose to import the snapshot data into a local Enterprise Manger instance or export it to a file(s) for import to a different Enterprise Manager instance.

Once you create a new diagnostic snapshot and click OK, you'll get a confirmation from OEM Cloud Control, letting you know that the diagnostic snapshot creation completed successfully, as shown in Figure 11-11.

Managing Diagnostic Snapshots In the Middleware Home page, choose Manage Diagnostic Snapshots from the Middleware Features menu, to display and manage diagnostic snapshots. The page displays all available diagnostic snapshots in a tabular form. You can view and analyze the diagnostic snapshots from this page. You can also import and export the diagnostic snapshots into a different Enterprise Manager Instance from this page.

In order to analyze a diagnostic snapshot, select a diagnostic snapshot and click Analyze. The Analyze Diagnostic Snapshot page, shown in Figure 11-12, presents a summary of all diagnostic types of the diagnostic snapshot and a summary of the diagnostic snapshot.

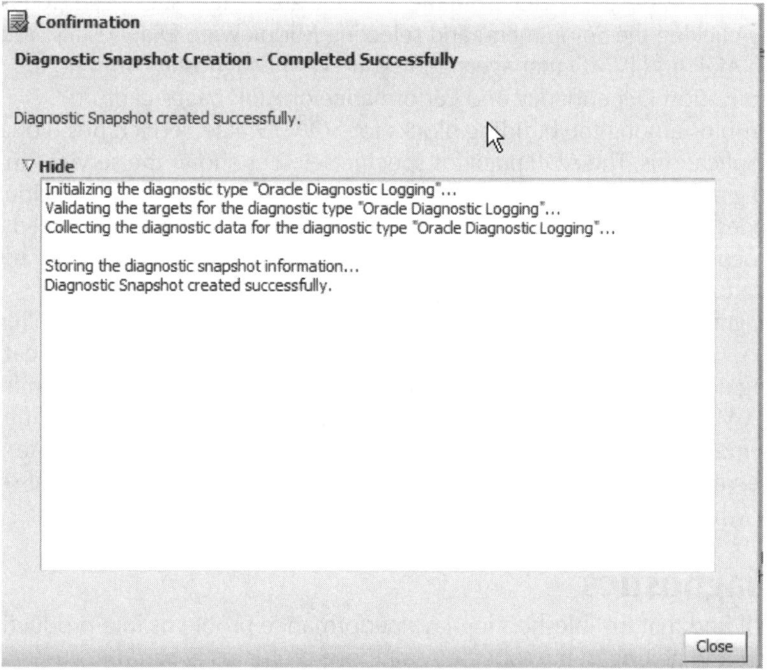

FIGURE 11-11. *Confirmation following a successful diagnostic snapshot creation*

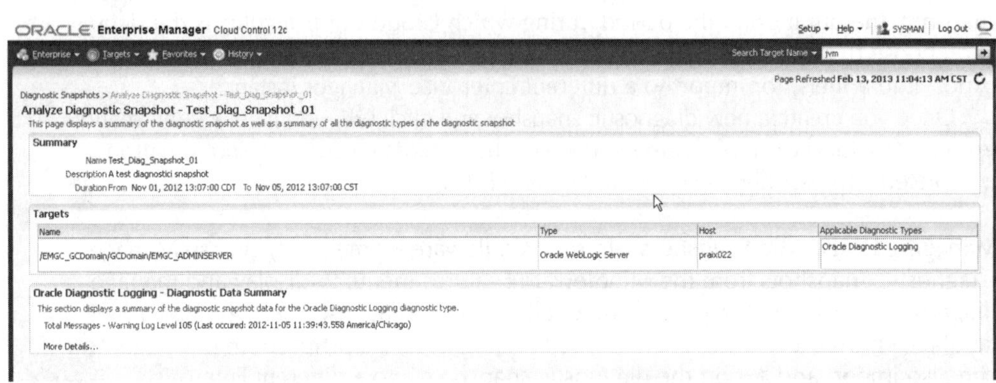

FIGURE 11-12. *Analyzing a diagnostic snapshot*

JVM Diagnostics and Application Dependency and Performance Managers

You can monitor the Application Dependency and Performance Manager (ADP) and JVM Diagnostics Manager (JVMD) from the Middleware Diagnostics page. You access this page by clicking the Setup menu and selecting Middleware Diagnostics. You can deploy both ADP and JVMD managers and set up JVM Diagnostics from here.

The Application Dependency and Performance or ADP pages capture interrelationships among the building blocks for SOA, Oracle Service Bus, Portal, and ADF applications. The ADP page for specific services shows the services in both tabular and graphic form. It also shows a performance summary of the individual pipeline nodes. You need to deploy the ADP Manager to a dedicated managed server and deploy ADP agents on servers running critical SOA, IOSB, Portal, and ADF applications.

JVM Diagnostics (JVMD) helps you diagnose problems suffered by Java applications such as SOA, Oracle Service Bus, Portal, ADF, or even proprietary Java applications, by providing detailed diagnostics going down to the Java thread level. With minimal overhead, JVMD provides powerful diagnostic services designed to resolve hung threads, memory leaks, and so on. You deploy the JVM Manager on a separate managed server or servers (for high availability) and then deploy JVMD agents on each server where you need thorough diagnostic visibility inside applications.

JVM Diagnostics

Often, you'll find that troubleshooting Java performance problems in a production environment and getting to the root cause of those problems is hard because you can't reproduce the problem in a test environment. Cloud Control's JVM Diagnostics

(JVMD) provides critical help in troubleshooting these problems. JVMD provides detailed diagnostics for any JVM running in your environment by providing "live" insight into the thread stacks. JVMD consists of a JVMD Manager and a JVMD Agent. The JVMD Manager is in the form of an EJB object that runs on a WebLogic managed server instance. In order to troubleshoot production Java problems, you must deploy the JVMD Agent on the JVM running the production WebLogic server. The Agent collects performance data and transmits it to the Management Repository so you can view this information through Enterprise Manager Cloud Control.

Since JVMD's diagnostics operate at a native level, there is a trivial amount of performance overhead totaling less than 1 percent, thus making it ideal for real-time production diagnostics.

Downloading the JVM Diagnostics Components

You can download necessary JVM-related binaries, such as the Agent and Manager software, and deploy them. To download the binaries, go to Setup | Middleware Diagnostics first. In the Middleware Diagnostics Home page, on the right-hand side, click Setup JVM Diagnostics. When you click the Downloads tab, the page shows you a list of JVM Diagnostics components that you can download, as shown in Figure 11-13.

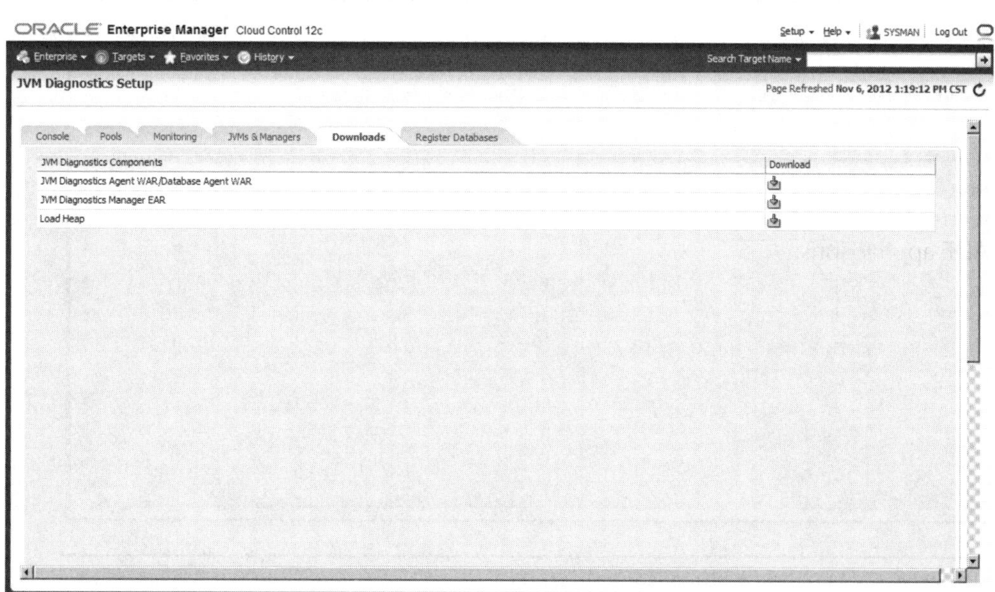

FIGURE 11-13. *Downloading the JVM Diagnostics components*

Installing JVM Diagnostics

In order to install the JVM Diagnostics Manager, go to Setup | Middleware Diagnostics in the EM Cloud Control Console. The Middleware Diagnostics page is mainly useful for deploying and managing the JVM Diagnostics Manager, including its status and availability on various hosts. Click Setup JVM Diagnostics. Figure 11-14 shows the JVM Diagnostics Setup page.

You must deploy the JVMD Manager on a managed server that's part of your EM Cloud Control domain.

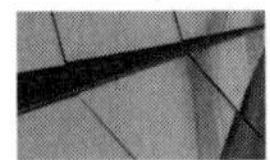

NOTE
Oracle recommends that you dedicate a WebLogic Server–managed server instance exclusively for running the JVMD Manager.

Before you can deploy the JVMD Agent, you must ensure that the JVMD Manager is running in the Active state.

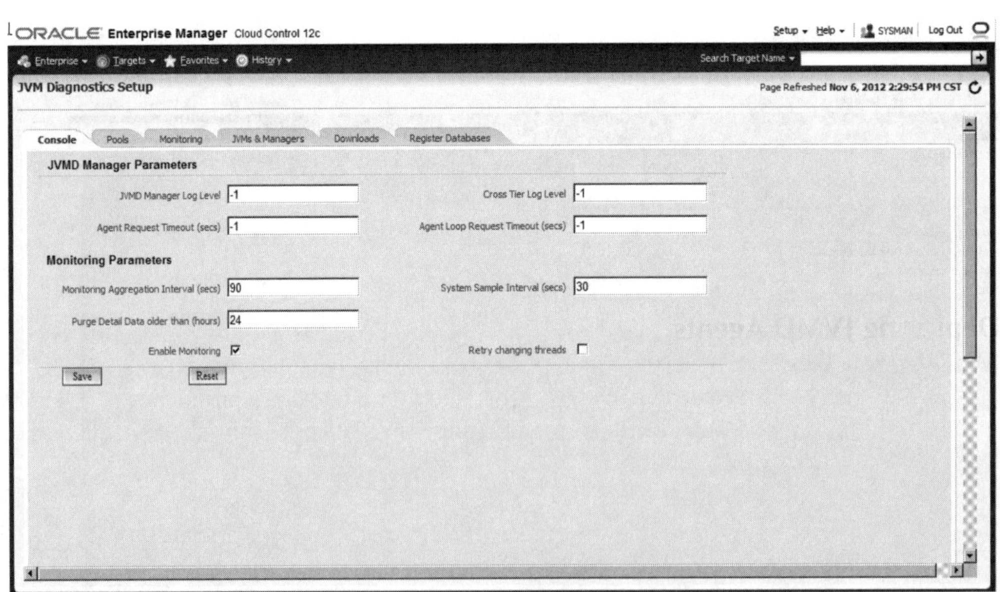

FIGURE 11-14. *The JVM Diagnostics Setup page*

Deploying the JVMD Manager

The JVMD Manager is the brain of the JVMD monitoring system and it collects run-time data from the JVMD agents through periodic requests and stores that data in a repository. As mentioned earlier, the JVMD Manager is actually an EJB application running on WebLogic Server.

Perform the following steps to deploy the JVMD Manager on a host that's running the OMS.

1. Log in to EM Cloud Control as the user SYSMAN.
2. Select Middleware Diagnostics from the Setup menu.
3. Click Deploy JVM Diagnostics Manager in the Middleware Diagnostics page.
4. In the Deploy JVM Diagnostics page shown in Figure 11-15, select "Create a managed server." You must enter the following information:
   - An OMS server from the Host drop-down list.
   - A name for a new WebLogic Server–managed server, in the Managed Server Name field.
   - Port numbers for the new managed server's listen port (Managed Server Listen Port) and SSL listen port (Managed Server SSL Listen Port).
5. Provide credentials for the following:
   - Oracle Management Server
   - Oracle WebLogic Domain
6. Click Deploy.

Deploying JVMD Agents

JVMD Agents collect the data and transmit it for use by the JVMD Manager. You must install the JVMD Agent on each target managed server where a production JVM is running. The data that the Agents collect includes data pertaining to JVM threads, stacks, heap, and CPU usage.

Follow these steps to deploy a JVMD Agent to a WebLogic server.

1. Select Middleware from the Targets menu.
2. Click the Oracle Fusion Middleware farm that you're interested in, to view all the managed servers available in that domain.

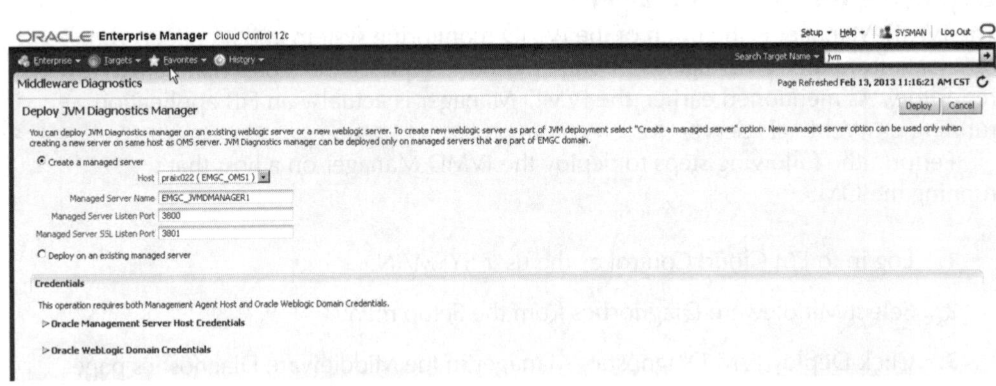

FIGURE 11-15. *Deploying the JVM Diagnostics Manager*

3. Select a specific WebLogic domain from the target Navigation pane on the left-hand side of the page. From the WebLogic Domain menu, select Diagnostics and click Setup Diagnostics Agents to deploy the JVMD Agent on the selected managed server(s).
4. On the Deploy Diagnostics Agents page, select the managed server on which you want to deploy the JVMD Agent. Figure 11-16 shows the Deploy Diagnostics Agents page. Note that that any managed servers that aren't running are deselected by default in the list of managed servers you can choose from.
5. The next step is to enter the properties for the agents in the Diagnostics Agent Configuration section. Select the JVMD Manager (we only have one) from the JVMD Manager list.
6. Provide the credentials for the following:
   - Oracle Management Server
   - Oracle WebLogic Domain
7. Click Deploy.

You can verify that the installation was successful by going to the Middleware Diagnostics page (by selecting Middleware Diagnostics from the Setup menu) and monitoring the current status and availability of the JVMD Manager that you've installed.

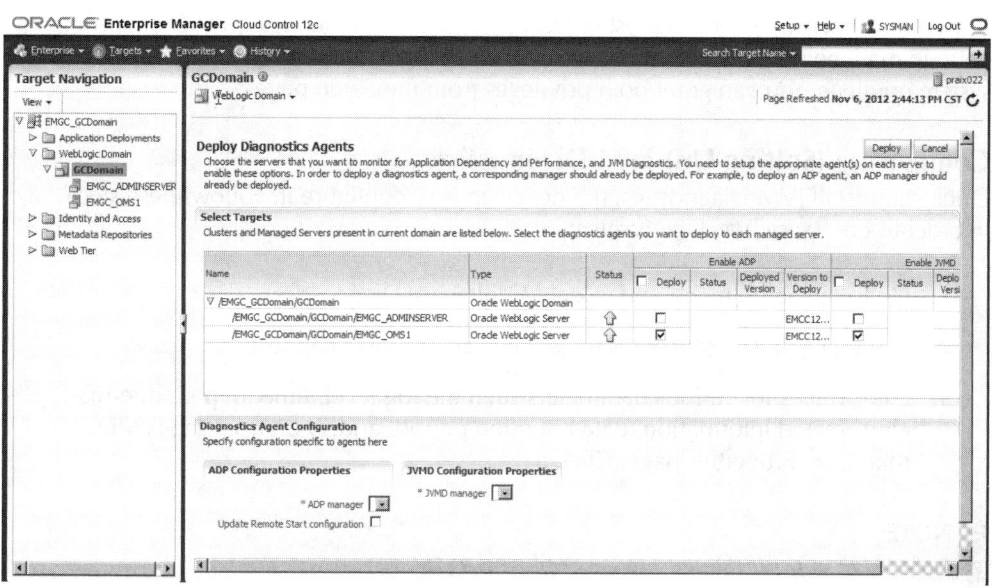

FIGURE 11-16. *The Deploy Diagnostics Agents page*

Verifying That the JVMD Agent Is Correctly Installed

In order to verify the Agent installation, first select Middleware from the Targets menu. On the home page, select the domain where you installed the JVMD Agent. From the Target Navigation section on the left, click Java Virtual Machine Pools. The JVMD targets you see here correspond to a managed server where you've deployed a JVMD Agent. You should also be able to see an application named javadiagnosticagent_<*managed_server_name*> on the targeted managed server when you view the applications from the WebLogic Server Administration Console in the domain where you deployed a JVMD Agent.

Monitoring the Diagnostic Managers

You can monitor various attributes such as Status and Availability and Host of both diagnostics managers—the ADP Manager and the JVMD Manager. In order to monitor various diagnostic manager–related attributes, select Middleware Diagnostics from the Setup menu. You can view the manager-related diagnostics, such as the Manager Name, Port Version, Status and Availability, on the Diagnostic Manager page.

You can monitor both ADP and JVMD Managers by going to the Middleware Diagnostics page (Setup | Middleware Diagnostics). From here, you can check the availability and status of the two managers.

User Roles

A user must have the JVM Diagnostics User system privilege to view JVM Diagnostics data. To manage the JVM operations, a user must be granted the JVM Administrator system privilege. You can grant both privileges from the Setup pages.

Configuring (Setting Up) JVM Diagnostics

Once you install JVM Diagnostics, the next step is to configure it. Follow these steps in order to configure JVM Diagnostics.

1. Go to the Setup menu and select Middleware Diagnostics.
2. In the Diagnostic Managers page, click Setup JVM Diagnostics.
3. Enter values for various parameters such the log level, timeout period, e-mail alert-related information, data retention period, and so on from the JVMD Managers Properties page. Click Save.

NOTE
Since ADP and JVMD need to be deployed to dedicated managed servers, Oracle recommends that you deploy these only when you need deep diagnostic visibility and not as a matter of course.

Application Dependency and Performance

As Java EE, SOA, and Portal applications become increasingly important delivery mechanisms for mission-critical functions throughout the enterprise, they are also becoming progressively more complex. OEM Cloud Control 12c's new Application Dependency and Performance (ADP) feature gives you the capability to capture interrelationships among the components of complex applications in an Application Schema model. You can utilize ADP to monitor performance of Java EE applications and Middleware components such as Oracle SOA Suite 11g, Oracle Service Bus, Oracle WebLogic Portal, and Oracle WebCenter. You can achieve the following through the use of ADP:

- Help manage complex Java EE, Portal, and SOA applications by delivering a service-oriented view across heterogeneous environments.
- Reduce dependence on Java EE and other application experts by using self-customization and the capability to evolve over time.
- Reduce inefficient manual operations.
- Set up and maintain a powerful APM environment without relying on Java EE experts.

The key to understanding the interrelationships among components such as Servlets, JSPs, and the underlying SQL calls is to understand the metadata that defines these relationships. Using the metadata captured from the various containers, OEM builds views for both standard and non-standard Java components. OEM shows you the relationships between the JSPs Servlets and Web Services and the components such as EJBs and JDBC calls that underlie the high-level components.

For any given URL, you can view the invocation counts for, say, a servlet and its components, thus clarifying the flow of the context for the URL. Using the delay analysis metric, you can find the time spent in each of the servlet's components. This allows you to focus on those components that are taking the most time and understand the reasons for such behavior. Context is considered a crucial element in Java EE applications, and the ability to trace the flow of the application's context and analysis of component dependency, delay distribution, and SQL performance based on context provides true end-to-end visibility into your applications, all the way to the SQL being executed. You can identify the specific class or SQL statement that's causing a URL to respond slowly. Once again, you're going to spend less time diagnosing the problem while also being more accurate in your performance diagnosis.

The Architecture of Application Dependency and Performance

The ADP Manager, the ADP Java Agent, the ADP Database, and the ADP User Interface (UI) constitute the key components of ADP. Let's discuss these key components in the following sections. The ADP Java Agents are the workhorses of ADP—they collect and summarize performance data and submit the raw data in a summarized form to the ADP, where the data is further processed by the ADP Manager. The ADP data is stored in the Management Repository in a separate ADP schema. The ADP user interface (ADP UI) is the way ADP users get to access all of ADP's features in order to set their service level objectives and analyze data. You can access the ADP UI by going to Targets | Middleware and selecting Application Dependency and Performance from the Middleware Features menu on the Middleware page. Figure 11-17 shows the Application Dependency and Performance page.

The ADP Operational Dashboard

For each component in the managed environment, the Operation Dashboard displays the following health indicators:

- Performance
- Availability
- Errors
- Load

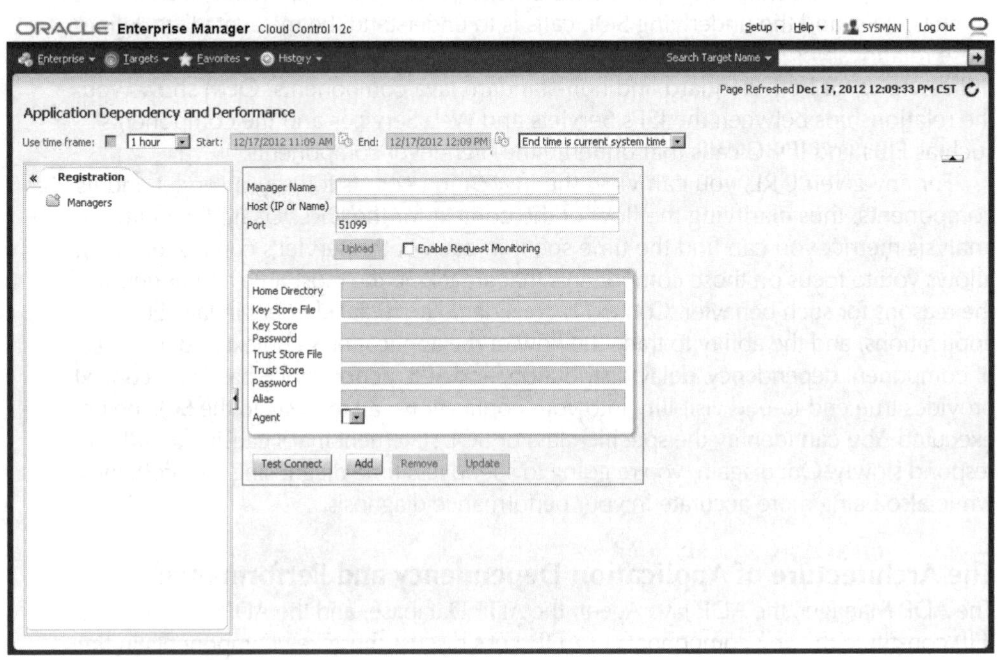

FIGURE 11-17. *The Application Dependency and Performance page*

ADP Timeframes You can specify the length of time over which to display the information. You can drill down to view details of a performance issue for a narrow range of time. ADP displays its information in the form of tables and graphs.

By right-clicking the ADP Main Display Window and selecting Create Comparative View, you can compare the performance statistics captured for two different time periods using the analytical tool.

ADP Metrics The Application Schema model determines the precise performance metrics that ADP will capture and analyze. You also have the ability to customize the monitoring by configuring your own metrics if they're needed to throw light on the root causes of key performance issues.

If you've followed the best practice recommendation of always capturing baseline performance statistics, those statistics could help you over and over in assessing a current performance issue. To create custom metrics, click on Custom Metric Configuration in the Configuration tab.

There are four major types of metrics provided by ADP:

- **Snapshot Count** These are metrics such as Active Sessions, Pending Requests, and Completions, which are counts of an entity at a point in time.
- **Aggregated Count** These metrics aggregate the number of times a monitored event has occurred from the beginning of the display time window. The metrics include Requests Serviced, Total Sessions, and Processes Aborted.
- **Average Timing** Timing-based metrics are calculated by computing the average time taken to complete a unit of work and includes metrics such as Response Time and Connection Delay.
- **Minimum and Maximum Response Time Measurement** These metrics capture the minimum and maximum response times observed during each collection sampling interval.

Application Schema Visualization Application Schema Visualization is the way ADP represents metric data it has captured and stored. There are three ways in which ADP can let you view the metric data:

- **Functional view** This view shows how the business functions are assembled with functional building blocks. For example, the Pageflow functional view shows the logical flow associated with a Struts pageflow.
- **Topology view** This view shows how the applications, server instances, and shared resources come together in forming an application environment. In each Topology view, the interconnecting lines show the calls made among the various entities.
- **Architecture view** You use this view to understand the module and component-level structure interrelationships among Java EE, SOA, and Portal applications.

Exporting ADP Data

While ADP stores its performance data in its internal data repository, you can also store this data in a historical data repository of your own. You can make use of ADP data in external databases by exporting the ADP data to the external targets. There are three different ways to export ADP data:

- Export row performance data in the form of comma-separated values (CSV) files

- Export the data directory to a database in the form of data stored in relational tables
- Export its aggregated data as a set of CSV files

Oracle provides you with scripts, such as the runexportMetric.sh script (located in the bin directory on the ADP Manager), to export metrics to CSV files. Following is an example that shows how to execute this script.

```
./runExportMetric.sh <path to export.xml configuration> <start time>
<end time>
```

Oracle recommends as a best practice that you deploy ADP and JVMD if you need deeper visibility into your application diagnostics.

Installing Application Dependency and Performance

Oracle recommends that you deploy the ADP in your environment. Doing this involves the deployment of the Application Dependency and Performance Manager application and the ADP agents that enable you to monitor the ADP application.

Installing the ADP Manager

The Middleware Diagnostics page lets you deploy and monitor the ADP Manager. You can deploy the ADP Manager only on managed servers that belong to a Cloud Control–managed domain.

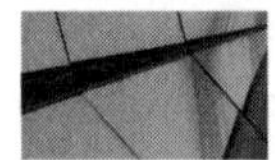

TIP
Oracle recommends that you choose an exclusive managed server for hosting the ADP Manager.

The following steps show how to deploy ADP Manager on the same host as OMS. Note that while this example shows how to deploy the ADP Manager on the OMS server, you can also deploy it on an existing managed server.

1. Select Middleware Diagnostics from the Setup menu.
2. Click Deploy ADP Manager in the Middleware Diagnostics page.
3. Select "Create a managed server" in the Deploy ADP Manager page and enter the following details:
   a. Managed Server Name: Example EMGC_ADPMANAGER1
   b. Port Numbers for Listen Port, SSL Listen Port, ADP Manager Registry Port, and so on. You can accept the default values for the port numbers if you wish.

4. If you selected the same host as the Administration Server (EMGC_OMS1), you must now provide the credentials for the server hosting the WebLogic Administration Server and the WebLogic domain credentials. If you selected a different host (EMGC_OMS2), you must also provide the credentials for the host machine where the Managed Server is running.
5. Select "Deploy on an existing managed server" and click Deploy in the upper right-hand side. You'll see an ADP Deployment Status page—click on the provided link to view the status of the deployment. Figure 11-18 shows the ADP Manager deployment status.

If you've done everything correctly, you should now see the new JVMD Manager when you click Middleware Diagnostics from the Setup menu.

Deploying the ADP Agent

For any server that you want to monitor with ADP, you must set up the ADP Agent on that server. However, before you can deploy the ADP Agent, you must first

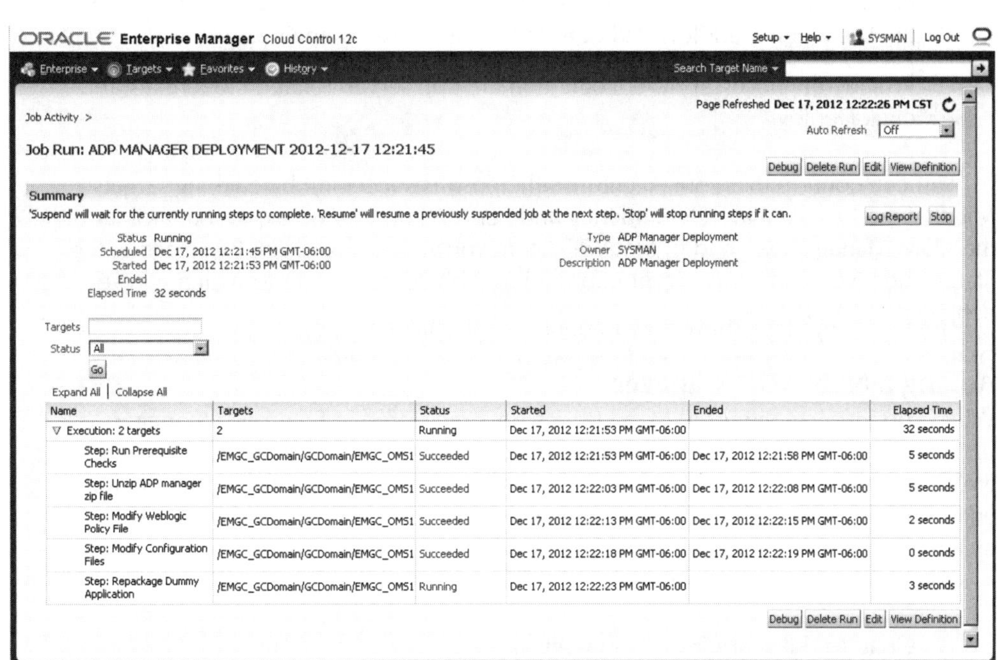

FIGURE 11-18. *Deployment status of the ADP Manager*

deploy the ADP Manager. Once you've installed the ADP Manager, you must deploy the ADP Agent by following these steps.

1. Select Middleware from the Targets menu.
2. Click Oracle WebLogic Domain in the Middleware page. You must select a managed server that's not part of the Enterprise Manager Cloud Control domain (EMGC_DOMAIN).
3. Select Diagnostics from the WebLogic Domain menu and click Setup Diagnostic Agents.
4. In the Deploy Diagnostics Agents page, select the managed server where you want to deploy the ADP Agent. Ensure that the managed servers you choose are up and running.
5. For each Agent, enter configuration properties in the Diagnostics Agent Configuration section.
6. You may see an Additional Configuration section if the Management Agent discovers a monitored WebLogic domain that isn't Java Required Files (JRF)–enabled. If so, you must enter the absolute paths to the WebLogic Home and the WebLogic Middleware home of the monitored domain.
7. Provide the necessary WebLogic domain and server–related credentials and click Deploy.

You can confirm that your Agent installation was successful by clicking Targets | Middleware | Application Dependency and Performance. Here, expand the folder of the ADM Manager assigned to the ADP Agent you've just deployed. By selecting the Status node, you can verify Agent Information table for the server to which you've deployed the ADP Agent.

Adding a New ADP Manager

When you install a new ADP Manager, it's only registered in Enterprise Manager until you enable the manager for monitoring. Monitoring a manager provides you greater visibility and lets you pinpoint the application deployments responsible for end-user performance issues. Once you enable a manager for monitoring, ADP creates and sets up the targets for request performance data collection.

You can enable the monitoring of an ADP Manager by following these steps.

1. Go to Middleware from the Targets menu.
2. Click Application Dependency and Performance in the Related Links section.

3. Click Managers in the Registration tab and enter the ADP Manager information in the Main Display window.
4. Enable monitoring for a manager and click Upload to send the manager properties to the ADP target in Request Monitoring.
5. Click Test Connect and then click Add.

How ADP Monitors Middleware Targets

When you select a specific Middleware target such as an Oracle WebLogic Server domain or an Oracle SOA Suite cluster, ADP automatically discovers the configuration of the specific target, as well as other useful information, such as the deployed applications on that target. For example, you can monitor Java EE application performance by performing the following steps:

1. Go to Application Dependency and Performance.
2. Select Middleware and click Java EE Application on the Middleware page.
3. Select Summary region on the Home tab and click the Application Dependency and Performance link.
4. Click the Monitoring tab and select the application.
5. ADP will discover Java EE components such as servlets, JSPs, and EJBs.
6. By selecting a node such as Applications, Web Services, or Services, you can view the performance data for the component.

Viewing JVM Diagnostics Threshold Violations

Any time a threshold violation occurs in one of the managed Middleware entities, an event is generated. Use these steps to view the generated event.

1. Select Monitoring from the drop-down menu on the home page of the WebLogic Server domain. Under Monitoring, select Incident Manager.
2. Click Events without Incidents in the Views panel to view any outstanding JVMD threshold violations.
3. In order for a specific threshold violation to be promoted to an incident, click on the link in the Target Name column of the Java Diagnostic Event in the Incident Manager: Events without Incidents page.

NOTE
You can't view an incident for an event if that event wasn't promoted to the status of an incident.

Cross-Tier Diagnostics

OEM Cloud Control's JVM diagnostics can find cross-tier issues by correlating Java threads to database sessions wherever possible. You aren't limited to viewing the status and class tack of a JVM's active threads in isolation, because the Cross-Tier Diagnostics capability means that you see the threads in the execution context of user requests. Often, Java threads are stuck because of locks. If a thread is locked because it's waiting for a database lock, you can isolate the Java code where the thread is stuck and also the SQL that's being executed in the database. By thus drilling down to the level of the table lock itself, you can communicate the locking information to the Oracle DBA and let them release the table lock so the stuck Java threads can continue their work.

Analyzing Heap Snapshots

You can take advantage of the JVM Diagnostics memory analysis to find the dangling references causing memory leaks. In order to track memory usage patterns and identify the sources of memory leaks, you need snapshots of the JVM memory heap, called *heap snapshots*, over a period of time. Each heap snapshot captures the relationships among the objects in the JVM heap. You can take these snapshots without affecting your application performance. You can view a heap snapshot by going to Middleware | JVM (or a JVM Pool) and in the JVM Home page, selecting Heap Snapshots. From the list of available heaps, select a heap and click the heap's Details page. You can find out information about the size and usage of the heap from here.

Taking a Heap Snapshot

You can take a heap snapshot by following these steps:

1. Go to Targets | Middleware.
2. Click on a JVM target to display the JVM Home page.
3. In the JVM Home page, select Heap Snapshots from the Java Virtual Machine menu.
4. Click Create in the Available Heaps page.
5. In the Heap Snapshot page, choose the option to create the heap snapshot. Or, you can optionally create the snapshot and load it into the repository automatically by executing the loadheap script.

6. Enter credentials for the host, database user, and the JVM Diagnostic Agent.
7. Click Take Snapshot after entering the schedule for the snapshot.

Differential Heap Analysis

Analyzing memory usage and pinpointing memory leaks is an extremely tedious job for Oracle WebLogic Server administrators. Using Cloud Control's differential heap analysis, you can compare and contrast heap dumps from two time periods and the tool highlights those Java classes that have grown in size over time.

In order to compare two heap snapshots, go to Targets | Middleware | JVM (or JVM Pool) and select Heap Snapshots. Click the Compare Heaps tab and select the second heap for comparison (the first is selected already from the list of available heaps). Cloud Control will present a comparison table for the two heaps in the Diff Heaps page, with data from the two heaps for things such as the number of reachable objects, the difference in the total, and adjusted reachable memory. You can then click on the root-set with the most growth in memory to identify the source of the memory leak.

Uploading Trace Diagnostics Images and Heap Data

You can upload both trace and heap data to a file for use later on. You can upload trace diagnostic images (trace data) to the OMS or to a local machine. In order to perform the upload, select Middleware and click on a Java Virtual Machine or a JVM Pool target. Click the Thread Snapshots menu option and click Upload. In the Upload Trace Diagnostic Images page, select either the local machine or the OMS as the destination for the image upload.

A heap snapshot captures the state of the JVM memory at a certain time point, and you can analyze these snapshots to detect JVM memory leaks. The upload procedures for a heap snapshot are similar to those for the trace diagnostic images. Just choose the Take Heapshot option in the Upload Trace Diagnostic Images page to take a snapshot of the JVM memory. Click the Load icon to load a specific heap snapshot to the database. Once the loading is completed, you can view the Diagnostic Image Analysis page by clicking the Loaded Successfully, Goto Snapshot link. The page displays details about garbage collections and the JVM heap memory usage and details about all the objects in the heap.

Viewing Real-Time Data for a JVM

You can view the real-time performance data for any JVM by following these steps. Make sure you have registered the target with the JVMD Manager and that the JVMD Agent is running on the server where the JVM is initiating the requests.

1. Go to Targets | Middleware and click on a JVM target.
2. Select JVM Diagnostics from the menu and click Live Thread Analysis.

3. You'll see a list of threads, along with their status. You can view details such as the thread name and the request it's currently processing, the current lower-level user method being executed, and the line number in the method being executed. You'll also see a section that examines the current state of the thread, which could be a database, Remote Method Invocation (RMI), or network wait state. If the thread is in a wait state of some type, you can click on a link such a DB Wait state to view the details and drill down to the application request causing the database wait event.

4. You can trace specific threads by clicking Trace Thread. There are other tables on this page as well, such as the Details for Method table, which shows details of the selected method, and the Lock Held table, which shows the locks currently held by the current thread. By clicking Trace Active Threads, you can start a high-frequency monitoring of all active threads for a short time period.

Managing JVM Pools

In order to make your management of the JVMs easier, you can create JVM pools to group together related JVMs in your environment. Following are the steps to create a JVM Pool in the WebLogic domain.

1. From the Setup menu, select Middleware Diagnostics.
2. Click the Pools tab.
3. Click New Pool. Enter information such as the name of the new JVM Pool and the pool interval, and click Save.

The JVM Pool Home page shows information about the JVM Pool such as any current incidents and alerts, pool configuration, status and the Realtime Thread States, which is the current state of the various threads in the JVM.

Updating Pool Thresholds

You can edit JVM Pool thresholds by clicking the Pools tab and viewing the Show JVM Pools page, and by clicking Edit for a specific JVM Pool, you can get to the Edit JVM Pool Information page. Click Set Thresholds and in the Edit Thresholds for JVM Pool page, enter the threshold level, the name of the metric that's being measured, and its threshold. You must also specify an Action URL, which is the URL that Cloud Control will invoke when an alert's threshold is exceeded. Following is a sample URL template for Tracing Threads:

```
http://localhost/jvmTraceActive.jsp?traceThread=allactive&JVM_THREAD_ID=&JVM_ID=1&
JVM_MACHINE=machine_name&JVM_PORT=8080&pollInterval=50&pollDuration=10&samplesfile
name=traceactive&detailsfile=on
```

Setting the Monitoring Status for a Pool of JVMs

Once you've set up and configured a JVM Pool, you must enable monitoring for the JVMs in that pool. You do this by selecting Middleware Diagnostics from the Setup menu and clicking Setup JVM Diagnostics in the Diagnostic Managers page. Click the Monitoring tab and then click Start Monitoring.

Any idle thread won't be monitored and you can add threads to an Idle Thread Rule to mark them idle. You create the rule by clicking New Rule. For example, you can select the Current Call rule type to ignore threads that are making calls to a predetermined function. Here's an example of this type of rule:

```
weblogic.socket.PosixSocketMuxer->processSockets.
```

Viewing JVM Historical Performance Data

It's very easy to view historical data for any JVM running in your environment. From the JVM Home page for a specific JVM target, you can click the Diagnostics Summary page to access the following server state charts for a specific JVM.

- Active Threads
- CPU Utilization by JVM
- Heap Utilization by JVM

You can filter the displayed data according to various criteria, such as the Method Name, Thread State, and DBState. Cloud Control also provides detailed server state charts such as Active Threads by JVM, Top Requests, To SQLs, and Top Methods for this JVM. View the thread data by clicking the Threads tab and compare data between two different times by selecting the Compared With checkbox.

You can also use the following links from the Diagnostics Summary page:

- **View Snapshots** View trace data for the JVM.
- **Export to File** Export trace data to a file.
- **Memory Analysis** View details about the JVM heap utilization and garbage collection and objects utilizing the heap. You can also clock Configure Heap Dump to load heap snapshots into the repository.
- **Offline Diagnostics** Create diagnostic snapshots for immediate or later usage.

You can do all of these things for a JVM Pool instead of a specific JVM, by choosing a JVM Pool target at the beginning, instead of a specific JVM.

Viewing the JVM Home Page

You can view summary information for all JVMs by going to the JVM Home page, which you can get to by clicking on the JVM Target in the Middleware Home page. You can view information such as the JVM's pool information, thresholds and alerts issued for this JVM, availability status, and recent configuration changes. You can also get the number of active threads in the last 24 hours, and the status and details of each active thread (real-time thread state).

Viewing Real-Time Data for a JVM Pool

In order to view real-time data for a JVM Pool, go to Targets | Middleware and click on the JVM Pool you want to analyze. In the JVM Pool Home page, select the Live Thread Analysis option. You'll see the list of JVMs in the pool and details about each of the JVMs, such as its status, percentage of its heap memory in use, the number of threads waiting for database or network activity to complete, and which threads are actually on the CPU (runnable threads). You can view pie charts depicting thread and heap behavior in a specific JVM. You'll also find the threads grouped into separate charts based on criteria such as whether the threads are in the runnable state, network wait state, or object wait state, for example.

Tracing Active Threads

Analyzing active Java thread behavior is sometimes quite hard, especially when you're trying to find out the time spent by threads waiting on locks or the time spent by them on database-related waits. It's also hard to see the effect of one thread's activity on activity in the other threads in the JVM. Cloud Control lets you trace all the active threads in a JVM and create a periodic thread activity sampling based on a comprehensive trace file containing highly useful diagnostic information relating the thread state, usage of resources, and call stack details.

You need to follow these steps to trace active threads in a JVM.

1. Go to the Middleware Home page from the Targets menu.
2. Select a JVM target and in the JVM's Home page, click Thread Snapshots | Take Snapshot.
3. Specify the time interval between samples and the duration of the trace in the Trace Active Threads page. If you want to trace idle threads as well, in addition to the active ones, select the parameter *Trace All Threads*.
4. To generate a trace file, click Start Trace.
5. Once the trace file is created, click the Go to Saved Trace link to review the data. On the Diagnostic Image Analysis page, you'll see several sections, each focusing on an area such as Resource Usage (CPU, heap, and garbage collection), Top States (shows the JVM Trace Analysis, including DB waits), Top Methods, Threads by State, Requests by State, and Methods by State.

You can view a list of all available traces by going to the JVM or JVM Pool Home page and selecting Thread Snapshots on that page. Using the trace ID, date, and the JVM's name, you can pick a thread and click Details to access the Diagnostic Image Analysis page, which contains an analysis of the trace file's contents.

Using the Support Workbench

When you open a service request (SR) with Oracle Support, the Oracle support personnel will often request tons of diagnostic data from you to help them get to the bottom of the issue and make useful recommendations to you. Use the Support Workbench to ease your burden of collecting and sending this diagnostic data to Oracle Support. Using the workbench, you can gather data, request an SR number, and upload the diagnostic data to Oracle Support, thus helping you reduce the time it takes to resolve critical production issues.

You can get to the Support Workbench page from a domain's Home page by clicking on the WebLogic Domain drop-down and selecting Diagnostics | Support Workbench. The Support Workbench summary page aggregates the Support Workbench diagnostic information across all WebLogic servers that are members of this target. The workbench shows a incident summary of problems and incidents, and any new problems within the last 24 hours. Figure 11-19 shows the Support Workbench page in Cloud Control.

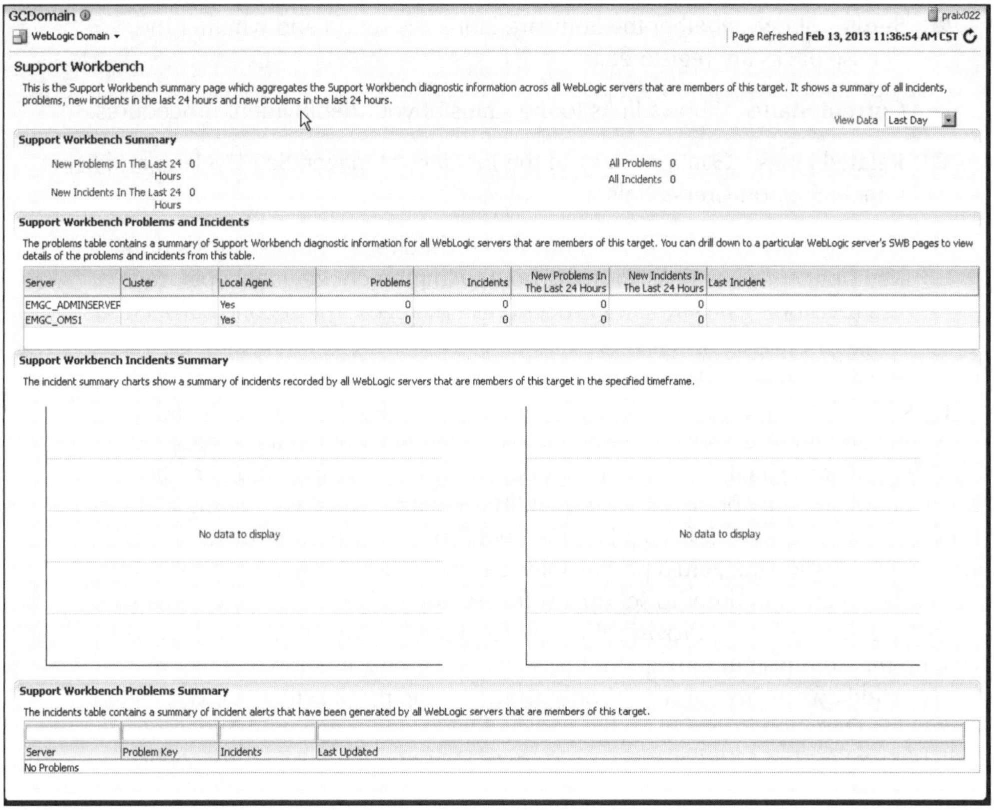

FIGURE 11-19. *The Support Workbench page*

Provisioning Middleware Through Cloud Control 12*c*

Often, Middleware administrators need to clone a WebLogic domain or a Middleware home. OEM Cloud Control 12*c* offers efficient Middleware Provisioning deployment procedures, letting you automate your middleware provisioning operations. You can clone a WebLogic domain or a Middleware home from an existing installation. You can also use the WebLogic Domain Provisioning Profile to clone a domain. You can also create and use a Middleware Home Gold Image for cloning a middleware home.

The Middleware Provisioning Page in EM Cloud Control

The Middleware Provisioning page is the central page for all middleware provisioning actions. Following are the key sections on this page.

- **Setup** Shows whether the Software Library is set up and whether the license packs are registered.
- **Current Status** Shows links to the status of your deployment procedures.
- **Related Links** Contains links to the Incident Manager, Self Update, and My Oracle Support Credentials.
- **Getting Started** This section has two subsections. The first subsection, Key Concepts, has links showing how to implement key concepts, such as Provisioning Profiles and Procedures Privileges. The second subsection, Common Tasks, contains information about tasks such as setting up the software library, for example.

A software library stores representations of reference gold images, application software, software patches, and their associated directive scripts. You can choose an Oracle-supplied entity or create your own library entity. Once you define a library entity, you can reference it from a Deployment Procedure in order to easily patch, provision, or deploy the actual parent software. You must configure at least one upload file location in order to set up a software library. You can create a software library by going to Setup | Provisioning and Patching | Software Library. This will bring up the Administration page for the Software Library, as shown in Figure 11-20.

The Middleware Provisioning Profile shows all the profiles that you've created. By clicking Downloads Profile and accessing Updates Home, you can download an available profile. The Middleware Provisioning Deployment Procedures section

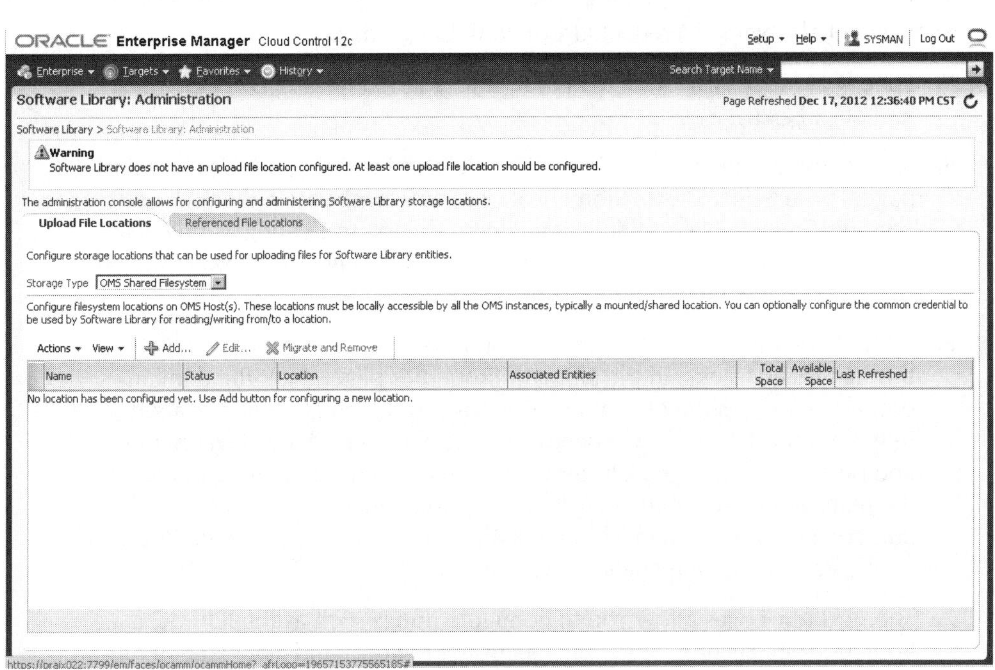

FIGURE 11-20. *The Software Library Administration page*

shows all the Oracle-supplied deployment procedures. You can run a deployment procedure, create a copy, or delete or edit a deployment procedure from here.

The Provision Middleware Wizard lets you clone and configure both Oracle Middleware homes and WebLogic domains, either through using profiles from the Software Library or by cloning from an existing installation.

Cloning from an Existing Installation

You can clone both a WebLogic domain and a Middleware home from a current installation. The following two sections show how to perform both of these tasks.

Cloning a Domain Once Cloud Control discovers a WebLogic domain, you can clone it easily by going through the following steps.

1. Select Middleware from the Targets menu.
2. Right-click on the WebLogic domain you want to clone, select Provisioning, and then Clone WebLogic Domain.

3. In the Host Credentials section, select one of the three options: Preferred Credentials, Named Credentials, or New Credentials.

4. Specify a directory to store temporary files in the Working Directory field and click Next.

5. Specify the destination host in the Middleware Provisioning: Destinations page. In the Select Destination Locations section, choose either of two options: Create a New Middleware Home or Use an Existing Middleware Home, in order to specify the new location of the new Middleware Home. Also specify the JDK Home location. Click Next.

6. In the Middleware Provisioning: Domain Configuration page, you'll go through several steps. In the Domain Properties page, enter the domain properties such as the Domain Name, Password, and Domain Location. In the Administration Server page, enter details such as the server name and port numbers. In the Cluster page, enter the cluster address to identify the managed servers in that cluster. In the Machines page, you can add configuration for a machine. Finally, in the Servers page, enter the configuration for the managed server(s).

7. The next few pages allow you to configure things such as the JDBMC Data Sources, JMS, Security Store, and Security Providers and any external files.

8. Once you complete all of your configuration work, using the Schedule page, choose whether to run the procedure immediately or later. Click Next.

9. In the Review page, review the deployment procedure details and click Submit.

Cloning a Middleware Home Once Cloud Control discovers an Oracle Middleware home, you can clone that home by executing the following steps.

1. Select Middleware from the Targets menu.

2. Right-click on the WebLogic domain you're interested in and select Provisioning | Clone Middleware Home.

3. Follow Steps 3 through 7 in the previous section on cloning a WebLogic domain.

4. Specify a Deployment instance name in the Schedule page and specify whether you want to run the cloning procedure immediately or later on.

5. On the Review page, review the details and click Submit to start the cloning process.

Cloning from a Profile or a Middleware Gold Image

You can clone either a WebLogic domain or a Middleware home from a profile, provided you first create the profile and store it in the Software Library. You can choose between a stored Middleware Profile and an existing Middleware home, both from the Software Library.

Cloning a Domain from a WebLogic Domain Provisioning Profile When you want to ensure that all your WebLogic domains follow specific standards regarding their configuration, you can use a WebLogic Domain Provisioning Profile as the source for creating new domains. The first thing you must do in order to use a profile from the Software Library as the basis for a new domain is to create that profile. A WebLogic Domain Provisioning Profile includes the Middleware home, binaries (software from Middleware home), and the configuration information for the domain (from the domain home).

To create an Oracle Middleware Profile, follow these steps:

1. Select Provisioning and Patching from the Enterprise menu.
2. Select Software Library.
3. Create a folder for storing the profiles.
4. Select the folder from the Actions menu.
5. Select Create Entity.
6. Select Component and choose the WebLogic Domain Provisioning Profile component. Click Continue.
7. In the WebLogic Domain Provisioning Profile: Describe page, enter the name and description of the new profile and the values for product and vendor attributes. Click Next.
8. In the Create WebLogic Domain Provisioning Profile: Configure page that appears, click the Search icon next to the WebLogic Domain field and select a WebLogic domain from which you want to create the profile.
9. In the Working Directory field, specify the directory path on the host where Cloud Control should temporarily store the files needed for creating the profile.
10. Enter either Preferred or Named Credentials in the host Credentials section for the machine where the WebLogic Server domain's Administration Server is installed. You can also specify New Credentials to override the Preferred Credentials by entering them in the New Credentials box. Click Next.
11. In the Review page, after reviewing, click Save and Upload.

You can now go to the Job Activity page and monitor the job status. Once the job completes, to ensure that you've done everything currently, look for your new profile by going to Provisioning and Patching | Middleware Provisioning. Once you see your new profile there, it's ready for your use in creating a new WebLogic domain.

Once you create a profile and store it in the Software Library, as shown in the previous section, you're ready to clone a new domain with the profile acting as the source. Here are the steps to create a domain with a profile as its basis.

1. Select Provisioning and Patching and choose Middleware Provisioning.
2. Click Provision after selecting the profile you want to base your new domain on. Make sure you see the component in the Source Information section. Click Next.
3. Specify the destination where you want the domain to be created, on the Middleware Provisioning: Destinations page.
4. Select a host after clicking Add Hosts. You can specify a set of either Preferred or Named Credentials for the destination host. You can also override the Preferred Credentials if you wish, by choosing New Credentials.
5. In the Select Destinations Locations section, specify a location for the Middleware home on the Host machine. In the Middleware Home Directory field, enter the path for the directory where you want to create the Middleware home. Enter the absolute path to the JDK directory in the JDK Home Location field, but only if the JDK home is not installed in the Middleware home.
6. Specify a temporary directory for cloning related files in the Working Directory field. Click Next.

Cloning a Middleware Home from a Middleware Home Gold Image You can also create an Oracle Middleware Home Gold Image, in a fashion similar to creating a provisioning profile for cloning domains. You can then save this gold image in the Software Library and use it as the basis for new Middleware homes. Here are the steps to create a Middleware Home Gold Image.

1. Select Software Library after selecting Provisioning and Patching from the Enterprise menu.
2. From the Actions menu, select Create Entity and then select Component.
3. In the Create Component window, select Oracle Middleware Home Gold Image. Click Continue.

4. In the Describe page, enter the name, description, and product version, and so on. Click Next.
5. In the Create Middleware Home Gold Image: Configure page, select the Middleware home you want to use as the basis for the gold image.
6. Specify the directory in the Working Directory field. This is the directory on the destination host that temporarily stores files required during the creation of the gold image.
7. In the Host Credentials page, select one of Preferred, Named, or New Credentials. Click Next.
8. Click Save and Upload. Check the Middleware Provisioning page under Provisioning and Patching to ensure that you can see the new gold image there.

Scaling Up/Scaling Out Oracle Middleware

WebLogic domains may consist of a set of independent managed servers or a cluster that consists of a set of managed servers. It's quite common for organizations to deploy WebLogic Server clusters rather than individual managed servers in production environments for meeting scalability as well as reliability requirements. You can expand a WebLogic Server cluster consisting of multiple managed servers that are linked together in two ways. You can create new WebLogic managed servers on an existing machine or add new machines to your cluster, where you can install additional WebLogic Server instances. The first method is called a domain *scale-up* strategy, and the second, a *scale-out* type of deployment. OEM Cloud Control 12*c* makes it very easy to perform both scale-out and scale-up middleware deployments. The Scale Up/Scale Out Wizard lets you add server instances to a cluster on the same machine. It also allows you to add machines to the cluster, so you run more managed servers on the new machines.

Besides having the usual read and write permissions, the user performing a scale-up/scale-out middleware deployment procedure must ensure that the following prerequisites are satisfied.

- You must first discover the WebLogic domain that you're scaling up or scaling out with OEM Cloud Control.
- Ensure that you have enough free space on the destination machine to hold a new Middleware home.
- Ensure that the new Middleware Home directory is either brand new or empty.
- You must install the Management Agent on the destination and source machines.

There are a few precautions you must take to ensure that all goes well with your scaling deployment operations. Make sure that you don't attempt any configuration changes on the source domain while performing a scaling-up/scaling-out operation. You must also ensure that the listener port and SSL port numbers are different in the source and destination servers. In addition, any externally staged applications on the source server must be manually deployed to the new server(s). If you're scaling up the same server as the source server, take care to provide different values for the working directory names for the source and target directories. Finally, it's a good practice to ensure unique farm prefixes because the prefix helps to uniquely identify domains.

Scaling Up and Scaling Out a WebLogic Domain

Following is a list of steps that you need to take in order to perform a scale-up or scale-out of a WebLogic domain through Cloud Control 12c.

NOTE
You must not change any configuration on the source domain or perform any patching of software while executing the deployment procedures. If you do so, the managed server may not respond properly to requests.

1. Select Middleware from the Targets menu.
2. Right-click on the WebLogic domain you want to scale up or scale out.
3. Once you select Provisioning and Scale up/Scale out WebLogic Domain from the menu, the WebLogic Domain Scale Up: Source page appears. Enter the credentials (these can be Preferred, Named, or New) for the Administration Server Console and Host Credentials.
4. Specify a temporary directory for the scale up–related file storage, in the Working Directory field. Click Next.
5. In the WebLogic Domain Scale Up: Managed Servers page, select a domain or cluster. By clicking on the Add Server tab on the left side, you can configure a new server, including the configuration of the machine you want to associate with the new Managed Server. If you want to copy an existing server, you can do so by clicking the Clone Server tab and selecting a server from the list.
6. Specify a Deployment Instance name in the Schedule page. You can also specify whether you want to run the procedure immediately or later on. Click Next.

7. Click Submit on the Review page when you're satisfied with the details of the deployment procedure that are presented on this page.

8. You can view the progress of the job execution in the Procedure Activity page. You can choose to debug the execution or stop the procedure execution from this page.

Note that the custom Java applications are supported by the deployment procedures listed here, but only in the staged mode. If you've used external stage mode for staging any applications, you must manually deploy those applications.

Both after scaling out and cloning a WebLogic domain on which you've deployed an Oracle Fusion Middleware component such as the SOA Suite, you must set the STARTSCRIPTENABLED=TRUE parameter in the nodemanager.properties file. This ensures that you can start the Administration Server from the Console.

Java EE Application Deployment and Undeployment

Oracle Enterprise Manager Cloud Control supports the deployment, undeployment, and redeployment of Java EE applications. Instead of logging in to a separate WebLogic server or the Oracle Fusion Middleware Administration Console, you can perform all your deployment work from a central location. You must make sure to preconfigure the Java EE applications before you can deploy them to a WebLogic domain through Cloud Control. That is, the archives (.jar files and .war files) must be in the Software Library. The ability to store Java EE applications in the Software Library allows the quick simultaneous deployment of apps to various domains or to the cloud. The deployments can use the deployment plans for creating necessary data sources and the configuring of services such as JMS. You can also undeploy the application across domains. Since the Software Library stores previous incarnations of all applications, if you have to roll back an application deployment, you can simply redeploy the original application version.

Creating Java EE Components

Before you can deploy a Java EE application component, you must first create it. The components contain the archive files, deployment files, and post-deployment scripts required for deploying an application. Follow these steps to create a Java EE Application component.

1. After selecting Provisioning and Patching from the Enterprise menu, select Software Library.

2. Select Create Entity and then select Component.

3. Select Java EE Application from the Create Entity: Component window. Click Continue.

4. Enter a name and description for the application in the Create Java Application page. Click Next.
5. Select the files for the application in the Create Entity: Select Files page. You must configure a minimum of one upload file location. Select either an OMS Shared File System or an OMS Agent File System in the Specify Destination section.
6. Add the standard Java EE archive files (.ear, .jar, .war, .rar) and the execution plan and pre- and post-deployment scripts. Upload the files either from the local filesystem or from a remote filesystem monitored by the management Agent, called the Agent Filesystem. Once you complete the file section, click OK.
7. Specify the file types in the Type field in the Create Entity: Select Files page and click Next.
8. Review the information and click Save and Upload.

Deploying a Java Application

Deploying Java EE applications is straightforward with Cloud Control. Use the following steps to deploy a Java EE application.

1. Select Provisioning and Patching and then Middleware Provisioning.
2. Right-click on the WebLogic domain and select Provisioning, and then Deploy/Undeploy Java EE Applications.
3. Select the Java EE Application Provisioning procedure in the Deployment Procedure Manager page and click Launch.
4. Choose Deploy in the Deploy/Undeploy Java EE Applications: Select Targets page. Select the WebLogic domains and then select the targets to which you want to deploy the Java EE applications. Click Next.
5. Click Add in the Deploy/Undeploy Java EE Applications: Select Applications page to add the archives and other files you've created earlier in the Software Library.
6. In the Type field, select one or more from Archive, Plan, Pre Deploy Script, and Post Deploy Script. Once you complete selecting the deployment files, enter a name for the application. You can also select the "Deploy this archive as library" option if you want to deploy the application as a shared library.

7. You can enter a name for the application and specify a Staging Mode, which can be the default staging mode for the all targets or the Stage or No Stage options, depending on whether you want the archive files to be moved to the destination machine.
8. You have three options for the selection of the Start mode for deployment:
   - **Full mode** Make the application available to all users.
   - **Admin mode** Make the application available only to the Administrators.
   - **Do not start** Deploy the application but don't start it, pending the completion of post-deployment configuration activities.
9. Click OK. Click Next if this is the only application you want to add.
10. Click the Lock icon to lock the configuration information. Click Next.
11. Supply credentials for each domain and the host on which the Administration Server is running—choose from Preferred, Named, and New Credentials. Click the Lock icon again.
12. Schedule the deployment of the application in the Schedule Deployment page. Click Next.
13. Review the details and click Submit.

Redeploying a Java EE application involves similar steps as the deployment procedures described here—choose the Redeploy operation in the Select Targets page to redeploy an application. To *undeploy* an application, of course, you must choose the Undeploy option from the same page.

Provisioning SOA Artifacts and Composites

In addition to provisioning Java EE applications, you can also provision SOA Artifacts and Composites using OEM Cloud Control. Deploying SOA artifacts can include the provision of SOA composites, Web Service policies, and policy and credential stores. The SOA infrastructure domain that contains the soa-infra binaries is the key WebLogic domain for SOA.

Provisioning Procedures

As with a WebLogic Domain and a WebLogic Home, you can provision SOA artifacts from a reference installation, or from a gold image. You can use either method by navigating to Enterprise | Provisioning and Patching | Procedure Library | Deployment Procedure Manager | SOA Artifacts Provisioning. Once you select Launch and then click Go, you'll see the Select Source page of the Deployment Procedure. Here, you must choose either Provision from Reference Environment or

Provision from Gold Image. The next step is to use the Select Artifacts page to choose the type of SOA artifacts you want to provision—you must select from SOA Composites, Web Services Policies, and Java Platform Security Configuration.

Deploying SOA Composites

Once you've provisioned Oracle SOA Suite 11*g* and its WebLogic domain and have also deployed the SOA Composites as explained in the previous section, you're ready to provision the SOA composites.

1. Navigate to Enterprise | Provisioning and Patching | Procedure Library | Deployment Procedure Manager. Select Deploy SOA Composites in the Procedure Library sub-tab. Select Launch and Go.
2. In the Select Destination page, select the Oracle WebLogic domain from the Destination Domain Name field.
3. Choose Preferred Credentials in the Credentials section. Click Next.
4. On the Source page, click Add in the Composites section and choose either Software Library or File System as the source, depending on where you stored them.
5. Select "Verify adapter dependencies" if you wish to ignore the missing adapters in the destination domain. Click Next.
6. Schedule the deployment in the Schedule page.
7. Review the deployment details in the Review page and click Submit.

You can access the SOA Home page by going to Targets | Middleware and selecting SOA Home from the Middleware Features drop-down menu. The SOA Home shows a list of all the currently monitored SOA composites, as well as all BPEL Processes and OSB and Web Services. Critical metrics for these services are provided to view and compare the values.

Using Oracle Exalogic Elastic Cloud

You can monitor various aspects of Exalogic Elastic Cloud from OEM Cloud Control 12*c*. Note that the Exalogic Elastic Cloud is considered a system target, not a group target. Following are the different types of Exalogic Elastic cloud targets you can manage from OEM Cloud Control 12*c*.

- Application deployments
- WebLogic domains

- IB switch
- Coherence clusters

Using the Exalogic Elastic Cloud Discovery Wizard

One important thing you must understand when you're planning to add any Exalogic targets to EMCC is that, unlike in the case of other targets such as databases and middleware, the Exalogic Elastic Cloud Discovery Wizard doesn't actually discover or add the targets to EMCC. In order to monitor Exalogic targets through EMCC, you must have first made targets out of all the individual components that are part of the Exalogic Elastic Cloud. Once you've done this, you can then run the Exalogic Elastic Cloud Discovery Wizard, which maps the targets it sees in the Exalogic Elastic Cloud and maps them to existing EM targets before adding those targets as members of the Exalogic Elastic Cloud.

You can access and use the Exalogic Elastic Cloud Discovery Wizard by following these steps.

1. Select Exalogic Elastic Cloud from the Add drop-down page on the Systems page. Click Go.
2. You'll see the Discover Exalogic Elastic Cloud page. Enter the name of the Oracle Exalogic Target you want to monitor in the Name field.
3. Specify the Management Agent you wish to perform the discovery. Click Next.
4. You'll see the Discover Oracle Exalogic Targets: Discovered targets page next. This page shows all hosts that were discovered. Click Finish, which will end the discovery process.
5. The new target is now displayed in the Systems page, and you'll receive a confirmation about the addition of the target to the Exalogic Elastic Cloud instance.

Using the Exalogic Elastic Cloud Home Page and Dashboard

You can view performance metrics as well as alert information for the following targets in the Exalogic Elastic Cloud:

- Application deployments
- WebLogic domains

- Coherence clusters
- Hosts

In addition, by accessing the Hardware tab, you can also access information regarding the hardware and infrastructure of the Exalogic Elastic Cloud itself.

To access the Exalogic Elastic Cloud Dashboard, go to the Systems page and choose Exalogic Elastic Cloud from the Search field drop-down list. Click Go to display the Exalogic Elastic Cloud Home page. Choose a component name, such as a WebLogic domain, from the drop-down menu. Let's say you did select the WebLogic Domains Summary page. You'll then see charts that show the status of WebLogic Servers, Request Processing Time metric information, CPU Usage, Requests per minute, and Heap Usage data. You can view general information about an Exalogic target by choosing General Information from the drop-down menu. Similarly, the Application Deployments, the Hosts page, and the Coherence Clusters page show details about the hosted applications, the hosts, and the Coherence Clusters, respectively. For example:

- The Application Deployments page lets you view details about the applications hosted on the hosts running on the Exalogic Elastic Cloud target.
- The Coherence Clusters page shows details about the Coherence targets hosted on the virtual machines running on the Exalogic Elastic Cloud target.
- The Hosts page shows details about the host targets hosted on the virtual machines running on the Exalogic Elastic Cloud target.

Configuration and Change Management

One of the biggest headaches of a system administrator working in large environments is the sheer magnitude of the change tracking work one needs to perform. Ensuring compliance with company regulations becomes a tough task, due to large uncoordinated deployments of applications. OEM Cloud Control offers highly useful configuration management capabilities to reduce your burden in ensuring compliance.

Tracking Assets

Tracking enterprise-wide IT assets and their detailed configuration information for those assets is traditionally a labor-intensive manual process, with the information tracked in documents such as spreadsheets. You can use OEM Cloud Control to automatically collect configuration information for Oracle WebLogic

Server as well as the operating system and the server it runs on. OEM periodically collects configuration information such as:

- Oracle WebLogic Server installations and their patch levels
- Configuration information for Oracle WebLogic Server
- Kernel parameter settings and installed packages
- Hardware information for CPU, memory, storage, and network

You can customize the default configuration templates if you want OEM to track only specific configuration items for WebLogic Server and the operating system and server.

Summary

As you have seen in this chapter, Oracle Enterprise Manager Cloud Control is an ideal platform for monitoring and managing middleware. It is ideal for managing Oracle's WebLogic middleware, but can also be used to manage other middleware products as well. In this chapter you have seen how to discover middleware targets and configure them for monitoring as well as managing these targets. In addition, you have seen how to provision middleware through Cloud Control. As with other target types, OEM Cloud Control does an excellent job monitoring and managing middleware.

PART III

Notable Management Packs

CHAPTER 12

Lifecycle Management Pack

Oracle Enterprise Manager Cloud Control 12*c* has been enhanced to provide support for the management of the entire lifecycle of the targets that it is managing. This includes the ability not only to deploy the software necessary for running the targets, such as OS, database, middleware, and applications, but also to handle monitoring, change management, patching, configuration management, and compliance management. These abilities of OEM Cloud Control 12*c* provide complete lifecycle management capabilities.

Oracle Enterprise Manager Cloud Control 12*c* has provided a number of tools for lifecycle management to deliver the following solutions:

- **Discovery** OEM Cloud Control will determine software deployments that can become managed targets within Cloud Control via either automated discovery or manual discovery. Installs Agent software in order to manage those targets. Includes a workflow in order to easily, efficiently, and accurately deploy management software.
- **Provisioning** Used to discover bare metal servers and existing target servers. Can be used to provision Linux OS on bare metal servers or hypervisors with Oracle VM. Provisions database software as well as application software such as middleware and application servers. Supports upgrading Oracle databases, including Oracle Real Application Clusters (RAC).
- **Patching** Provides a patching framework that incorporates patch plans to patch Oracle databases in an automated and efficient manner. Compares current configuration and patch sets, notifies you when patches are available, and recommends specific patches. Validates patch plans and notifies you of potential issues and problems. Provides the option for out-of-place patching, in-place patching, and rolling patches.
- **Change Management** Captures database configurations and provides the ability to compare systems or compare a system with a previous incarnation. Propagates changes from one system to another system based on these changes. Can be used to compare local and remote databases.
- **Configuration Management** Captures and compares configuration information throughout the enterprise. Monitors change activity throughout the enterprise. Creates relationships between managed entities.
- **Compliance Management** Evaluates compliance of targets and systems. Advises how to correct compliance issues. Allows you to customize your own compliance framework.

The provisioning and patch automation packs that were included in Oracle Enterprise Manager 10*g*/11*g* have now been enhanced and their functionality has been rolled into the Lifecycle Management Pack. These are the components of Oracle Enterprise Manager Cloud Control 12*c* that are used to automate the application of patches, deploy components such as databases and middleware, and even for the deployment of operating systems on bare metal hardware. The provisioning functionality is one of the most powerful components of Cloud Control and is related to the patch automation pack as well as the Cloud Control Software Library.

The previous chapter covered the configuration and change management components of the Lifecycle Management Pack. This chapter will continue with the provisioning and patch automation components of the Lifecycle Management Pack.

Discovery

The discovery process of Cloud Control targets has been greatly enhanced and improved over the OEM Grid Control 11*g* product. OEM Cloud Control automatically discovers software deployments using IP scanning with NMAP (Network Mapper). NMAP is used to discover hosts and services on a computer network, creating a map of the network. This provides an automated and efficient method of discovering targets and using this information to automate the deployment of Agent software. Configuring and deploying Agents is covered in Chapter 5; however, the discovery process is reviewed in this chapter.

To initiate Auto Discovery, invoke the Configure Auto Discovery tool by selecting Add Target | Configure Auto Discovery from the Setup menu. This will invoke the Configure Auto Discovery tool, as shown in Figure 12-1.

This tool includes a number of options for Auto Discovery including Hosts and Virtual Discovery using IP Scan and the ability to scan for target software using existing targets by invoking the discovery modules. To initiate a scan, do the following steps:

1. Click the Hosts and Virtual Server Discovery Using IP Scan link. This invokes the Host Discovery (Agentless) screen.
2. Click the Create icon to invoke the Host Discovery Specification: Create screen. Here you can add the discovery range.
3. Select the Agent to be used for the IP Range Scan. This will then return you to the Host Discovery Specification: Create screen, now allowing you to enter an IP range as seen in Figure 12-2.
4. Enter the IP Address range and optionally enter ports. Click Save and Submit IP Scan to begin the scan. The scan will then be scheduled.

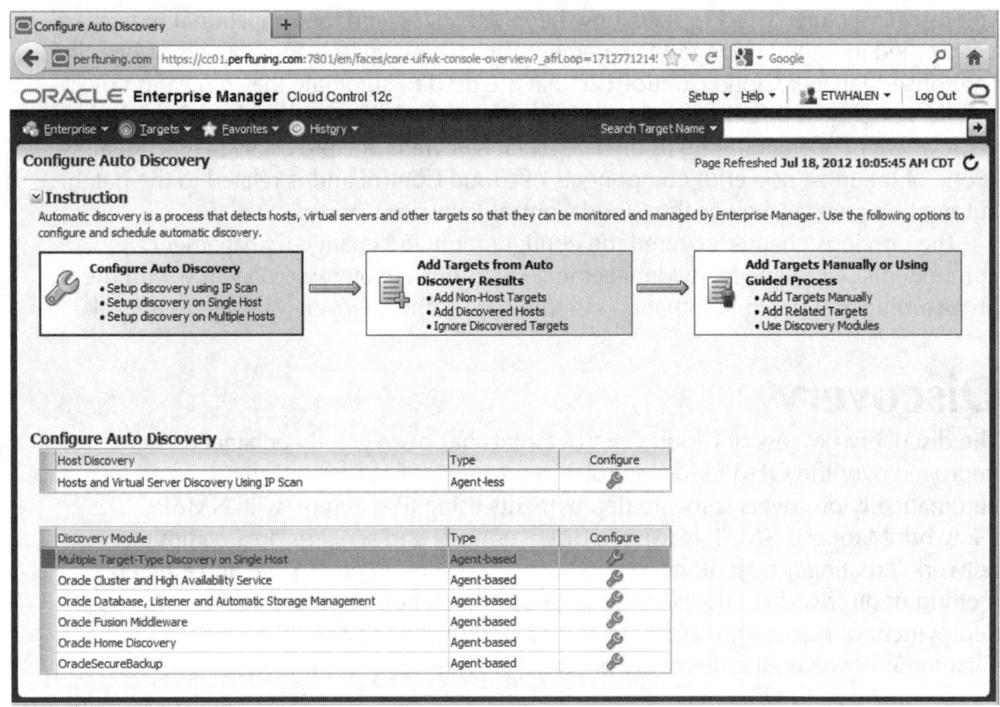

FIGURE 12-1. *The Configure Auto Discovery screen*

Once the auto discovery has run, you can view the result of the auto discovery by selecting Add Target | Auto Discovery Results from the Setup menu. Here you will see lists of Host Targets, Non-Host Targets, and Ignored Targets as shown in Figure 12-3.

This allows you to then take these targets and promote each to a managed target by adding an Agent. To do this, select one or more targets and click the Promote button. This will allow you to then deploy the Agent to this newly found target.

ORACLE Enterprise Manager Cloud Control 12c Help

Host Discovery Specification: Create

Save and Submit IP Scan | Cancel

* Name Host Discovery 07/18/12 10:11:03

Description

Scan Details | Job Details

IP Ranges for Scan

Use this section to select an agent that performs the IP scan, and for each agent, specify the IP ranges for the scan. The following formats are supported: host name, IP address, IP range (including CIDR notation). Use space to separate values. (For example: hostname.com 192.168.0.1 128.16.10.0/24 10.0.0-255.1-250,254)

Advanced

To perform host discovery scans, configure the hosts of the scanning agents with Sudo Privilege Delegation, and use credentials that have Run As 'root' attribute set.

View | Add | Remove

Agent to Perform Scan	IP Ranges for Scan	Host Name
cc01.perftuning.com:3872	192.168.60.1-254	cc01.perftuning.com

Configure Ports: cc01.perftuning.com:3872

Agentless discovery automatically scans for a list of default ports to detect services. To extend each scan to other ports, specify service name and port value(s). Use dash-separated

View | Add | Remove

Service Name	Ports
Telnet	23

FIGURE 12-2. *The Host Discovery Specification: Create screen*

NOTE

On Linux, to run `nmap`*, you must have both libssl .so.4 and libcrypto.so.4 libraries installed. If they are not already installed, use* `yum` *to install libssl-devl by running* `yum install openssl-devel`*. Next, change the directory to /usr/lib64. Perform the following symbolic links: ln -s ../../lib64/libssl .so.0.9.8e libssl.so.4 ln -s ../../lib64/libcrypto .so.0.9.8e libcrypto.so.4 Once this is completed,* `nmap` *should run properly. Follow the instructions preceding this note for running the automatic host discovery.*

Adding a host target manually is covered in Chapter 4. Adding nonhost targets is covered throughout the book in the chapter relating to that particular target type.

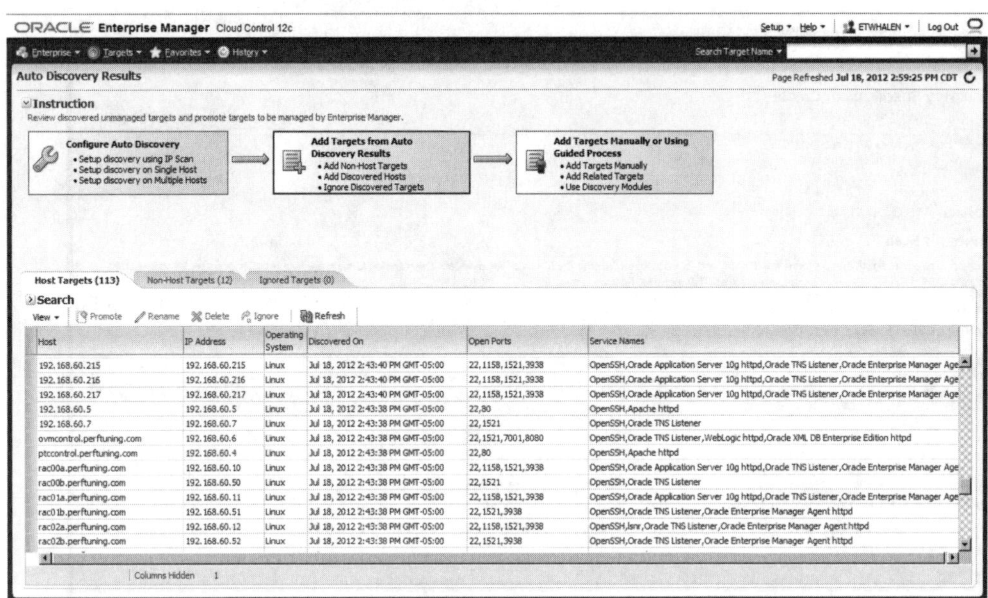

FIGURE 12-3. *The Auto Discovery Results screen*

Introduction to the Provisioning and Patch Automation

The provisioning component of Cloud Control provides the ability to provision software and databases on systems in your enterprise that are configured under the control of OEM Cloud Control. Using the Cloud Control infrastructure, it is able to push software out to these systems and configure that software. In addition, it includes the ability to perform cloning and database configuration as well.

The patch automation component of Cloud Control provides the ability to configure patches for automatic download from Oracle and for the automatic deployment of those patches, if desired. These patches can be put into bundles and deployed as a unit. In addition, the lifecycle management features allow these patch bundles to be pushed to various lifecycle stages such as test, dev, QA, UAT, and production.

The provisioning component of Cloud Control includes the ability to download the provisioning components from Oracle directly from within Cloud Control. Before any of this can be done, however, the Software Library must be configured. This is covered in the next section.

Configuring the Software Library

The Software Library is the Cloud Control Repository that is used to store objects such as patches, images such as virtual appliance images and gold images, as well as application software and their associated scripts. It is the intermediary area on disk that stores these files that have been uploaded and are available for deployment within Cloud Control. The Software Library is required for many of the provisioning functions including where Agent software is staged for downloading to client systems.

The Software Library is a filesystem directory (Unix and Linux) or a Windows folder (Microsoft Windows). This folder must be created before the Software Library can be configured. The process for configuring the Software Library is as follows:

1. Create the directory to be used as the Software Library Repository. This is done by using OS commands. The Software Library can be stored locally or on network storage. For this example we created the directory /u01/app/OracleHomes/SWLib01. This location should be on a shared filesystem such as OCFS2 or on an NAS drive so that it is accessible from all OMS systems.
2. From the Setup menu, select Provisioning and Patching | Software Library. The Software Library: Administration screen will be displayed as shown in Figure 12-4.
3. Click Add.

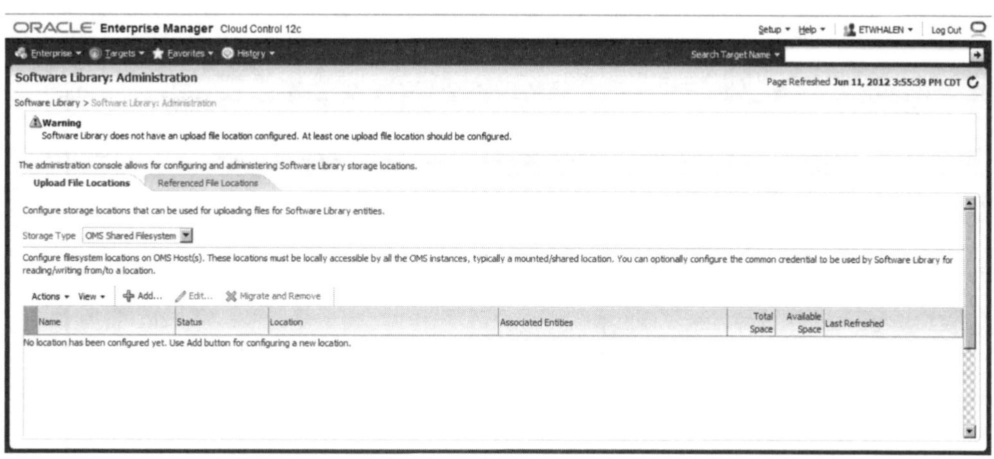

FIGURE 12-4. *The Software Library: Administration screen*

4. In the popup window, you will see entries for name and location for the Software Library. Choose a name that is descriptive, such as SWlib or SWlib01. Enter the directory that you had created in Step 1 for the location. This is shown in the following illustration.

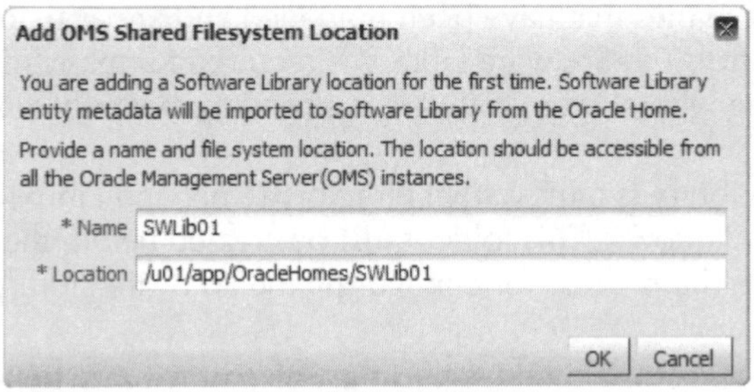

5. You will be notified when the Software Library configuration has completed and it will appear in the Software Library: Administration screen as shown earlier, but now with the Software Library configured, as shown in Figure 12-5.

Once the Software Library has been configured, you will be able to perform many of the self-maintenance functions of Cloud Control including updating, configuring provisioning, downloading additional management agents, and configuring patching.

The Software Library should be accessible from all OMS servers. If you have only one OMS, it can be placed on a standalone filesystem; however, if you add another OMS server, that location must be converted into a shared location.

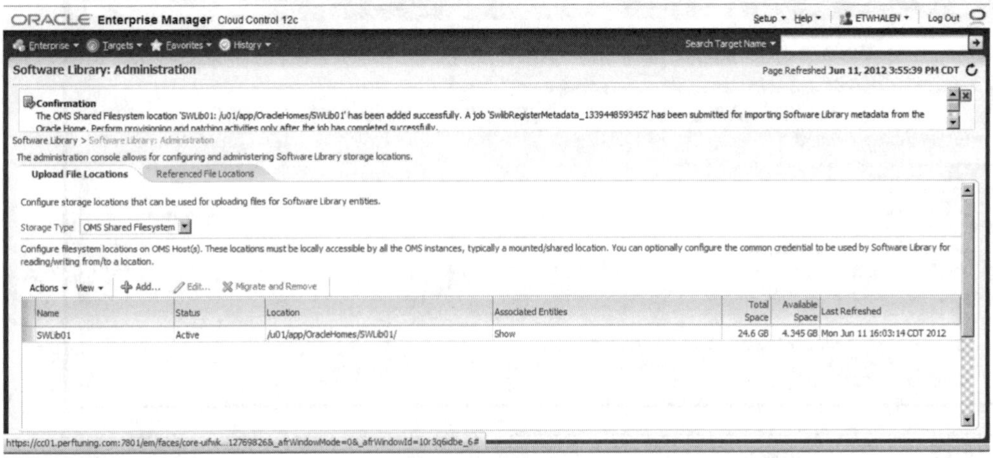

FIGURE 12-5. *The Software Library: Administration screen*

Populating the Software Library with Application Software

In order to use the Software Library to install software, such as the Oracle Grid Infrastructure or the Oracle Database Server, you must first install that software into the Software Library. To populate the Software Library with these components, start with the main Software Library screen by selecting Enterprise | Provisioning and Patching | Software Library. This brings up the main Software Library screen as shown in Figure 12-6.

From the Actions drop-down list, select Create Entity | Component. This is shown in the following illustration.

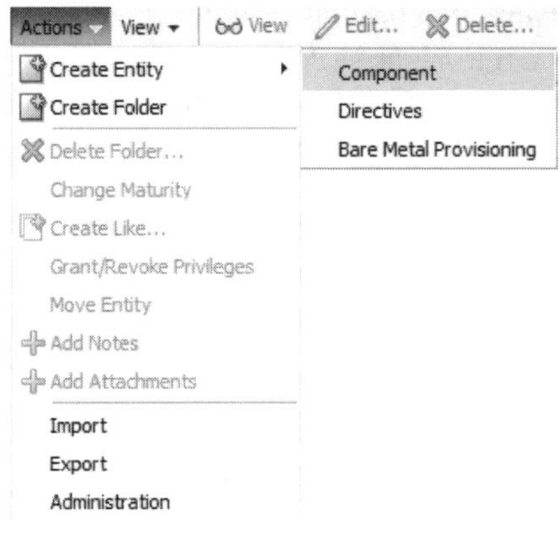

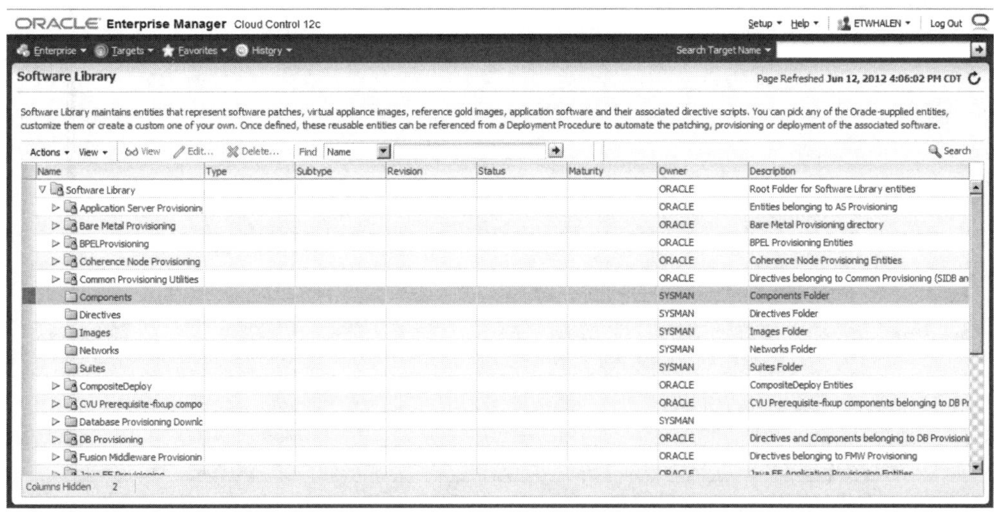

FIGURE 12-6. *The Software Library screen*

From the Create Entity: Component popup, shown in the following illustration, select Installation Media from the drop-down list.

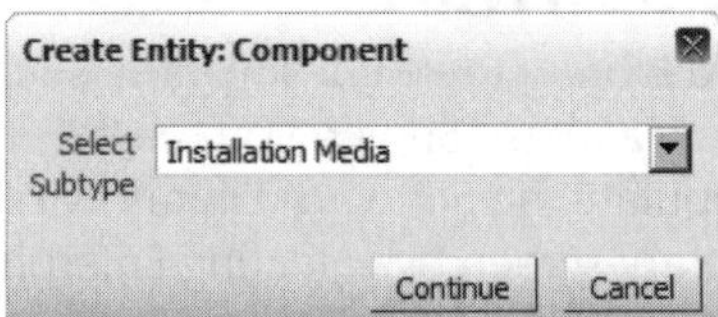

Click the Continue button to continue installing the Oracle installation media. Clicking Continue will invoke the Create Installation Media: Describe screen. This screen is used to describe the installation media and select its location. Fill in the Name, Description, and any attachments or notes that you would like to add (such as README files), as shown in Figure 12-7.

Click Next to continue to the Create Installation Media: Configure screen. Here you select the Product, Platform, and Version from the drop-down menus, as shown in Figure 12-8.

Fill in the proper values from the drop-down menus and click Next to continue. This will bring you to the Create Installation Media: Select Files screen as shown in Figure 12-9. Here you can either upload files or refer to files. Specify the upload

FIGURE 12-7. *The Create Installation Media: Describe screen*

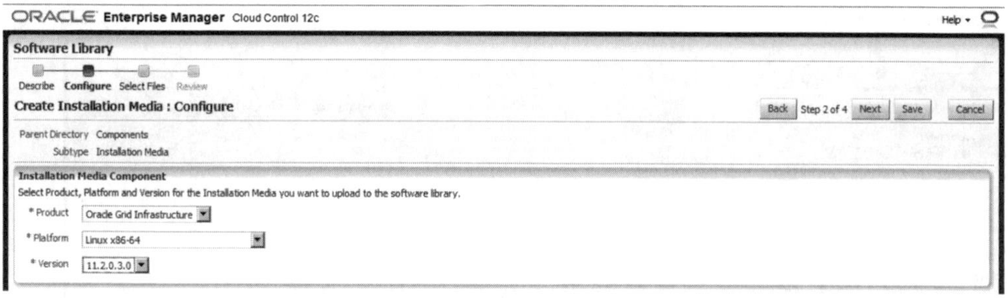

FIGURE 12-8. *The Create Installation Media: Configure screen*

location and the file source. The upload location should be the Software Library. The file source can be the local box you are running the browser from or an Agent server including the OMS server. Use the popup window to browse to and select the file.

Clicking Next takes you to the Create Installation Media: Review screen as shown in Figure 12-10. Review your selections and click the Save and Upload button to upload the installation media to the Software Library. This section should be repeated for all of the software components that need to be uploaded to the Software Library.

Once the files have been uploaded to the Software Library, you will see the Components listed in the Software Library. This is shown in Figure 12-11.

Once the installation media has been uploaded, it can be used in provisioning.

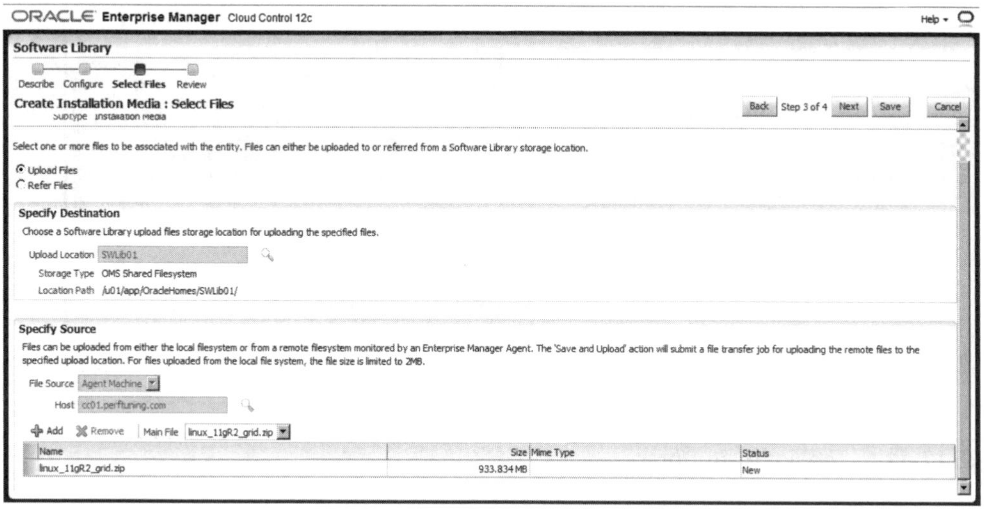

FIGURE 12-9. *The Create Installation Media: Select Files screen*

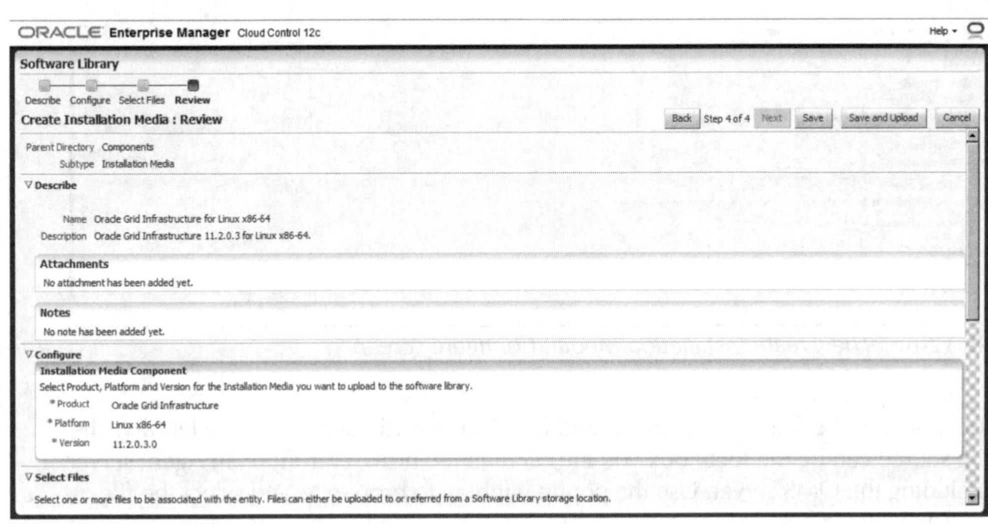

FIGURE 12-10. *The Create Installation Media: Review screen*

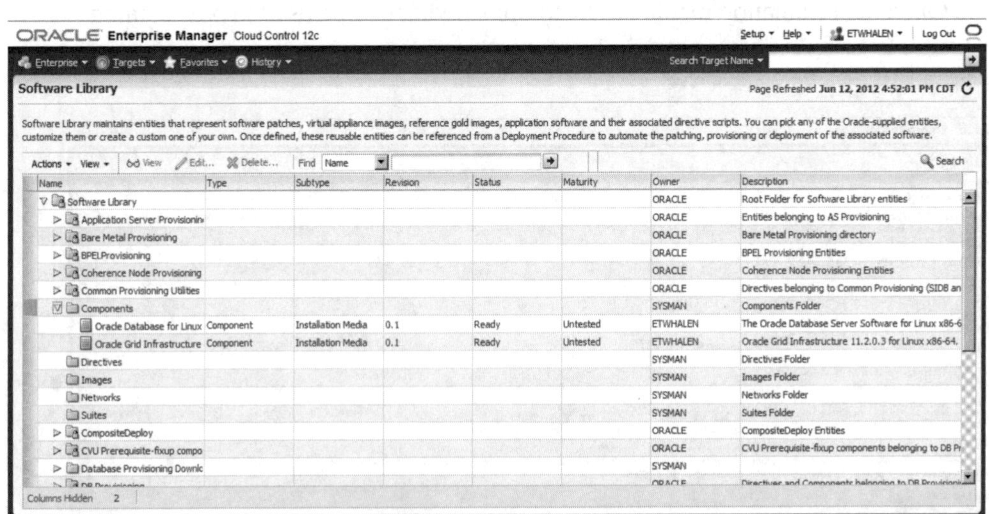

FIGURE 12-11. *The Software Library*

The Procedure Library

Oracle Enterprise Manager Cloud Control provides the ability to deploy software by using predefined deployment procedures. These procedures are used for the deployment of software, applications, and patching. By using these procedures to perform these tasks, risk is reduced and implementation is optimized. The provisioning, deployment procedures, and patch plans offered by OEM Cloud Control cover many phases of the system lifecycle.

To invoke a procedure, select Enterprise | Provisioning and Patching | Procedure Library. This will invoke the Deployment Procedure Manager as shown in Figure 12-12. You can see that numerous procedures can be selected.

Select a procedure by clicking the radio button next to the procedure that you want to create. For this example I've selected Provision Oracle Database. From the top or bottom of the screen, select Launch to start the procedure. The Create Like button can be used to create a copy of the procedure.

Once you have selected Launch, the Provision Oracle RAC Database: Select hosts screen will appear. For this example you can select options such as to Deploy software (Deploy Grid Infrastructure and Deploy Database software), and Configure

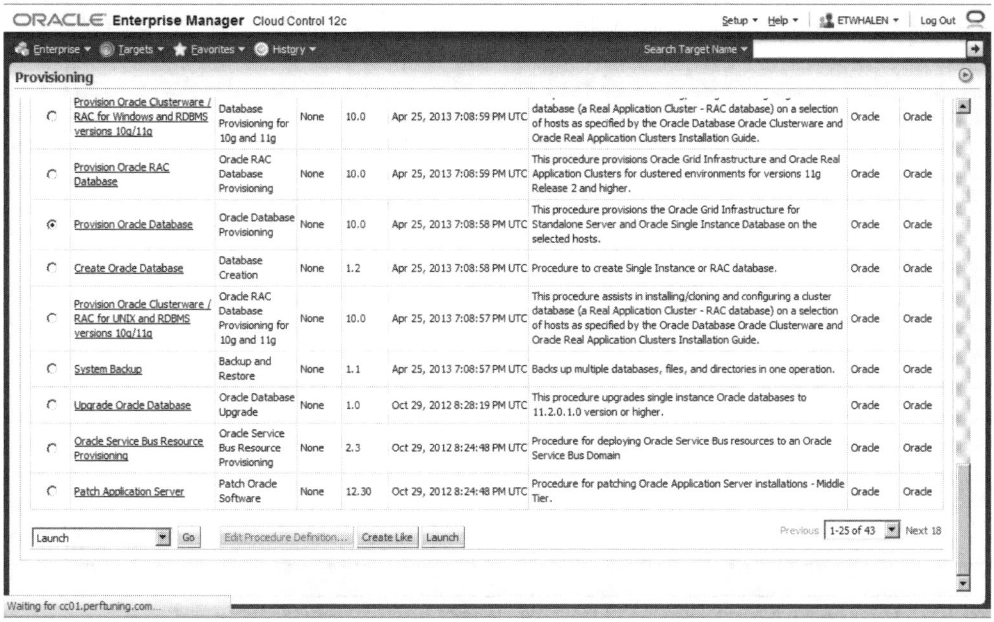

ORACLE Enterprise Manager Cloud Control 12c | Setup ▾ Help ▾ | ETWHALEN ▾ | Log Out

Enterprise ▾ Targets ▾ Favorites ▾ History ▾ | Search Target Name ▾

Provisioning

○	Provision Oracle Clusterware / RAC for Windows and RDBMS versions 10g/11g	Database Provisioning for 10g and 11g	None	10.0	Apr 25, 2013 7:08:59 PM UTC	database (a Real Application Cluster - RAC database) on a selection of hosts as specified by the Oracle Database Oracle Clusterware and Oracle Real Application Clusters Installation Guide.	Oracle	Oracle
○	Provision Oracle RAC Database	Oracle RAC Database Provisioning	None	10.0	Apr 25, 2013 7:08:59 PM UTC	This procedure provisions Oracle Grid Infrastructure and Oracle Real Application Clusters for clustered environments for versions 11g Release 2 and higher.	Oracle	Oracle
◉	Provision Oracle Database	Oracle Database Provisioning	None	10.0	Apr 25, 2013 7:08:58 PM UTC	This procedure provisions the Oracle Grid Infrastructure for Standalone Server and Oracle Single Instance Database on the selected hosts.	Oracle	Oracle
○	Create Oracle Database	Database Creation	None	1.2	Apr 25, 2013 7:08:58 PM UTC	Procedure to create Single Instance or RAC database.	Oracle	Oracle
○	Provision Oracle Clusterware / RAC for UNIX and RDBMS versions 10g/11g	Oracle RAC Database Provisioning for 10g and 11g	None	10.0	Apr 25, 2013 7:08:57 PM UTC	This procedure assists in installing/cloning and configuring a cluster database (a Real Application Cluster - RAC database) on a selection of hosts as specified by the Oracle Database Oracle Clusterware and Oracle Real Application Clusters Installation Guide.	Oracle	Oracle
○	System Backup	Backup and Restore	None	1.1	Apr 25, 2013 7:08:57 PM UTC	Backs up multiple databases, files, and directories in one operation.	Oracle	Oracle
○	Upgrade Oracle Database	Oracle Database Upgrade	None	1.0	Oct 29, 2012 8:28:19 PM UTC	This procedure upgrades single instance Oracle databases to 11.2.0.1.0 version or higher.	Oracle	Oracle
○	Oracle Service Bus Resource Provisioning	Oracle Service Bus Resource Provisioning	None	2.3	Oct 29, 2012 8:24:48 PM UTC	Procedure for deploying Oracle Service Bus resources to an Oracle Service Bus Domain	Oracle	Oracle
○	Patch Application Server	Patch Oracle Software	None	12.30	Oct 29, 2012 8:24:48 PM UTC	Procedure for patching Oracle Application Server installations - Middle Tier.	Oracle	Oracle

Launch | Go | Edit Procedure Definition... | Create Like | Launch | Previous | 1-25 of 43 | Next 18

Waiting for cc01.perftuning.com...

FIGURE 12-12. *The Deployment Procedure Manager*

software (Configure Grid Infrastructure and Create a new database). These options are used to decide how to deploy the procedure. In addition, you are required to add the destination hosts from a list of hosts with Agents on them as shown in Figure 12-13.

Once you have clicked the Next button, you will be taken to the Provision Oracle Database: Configure screen. The next few screens allow you to configure various components by selecting individual component configuration options as shown in Figure 12-14 in the Provision Oracle Database: Configure screen.

You will go through each of the task links until you have configured each of the necessary components. Depending on which procedure you choose, you might get a different set of tasks. When all of the tasks are completed, you can proceed with the provisioning of the procedure that you have selected. Once this has started, you can watch the job status to see how it is going. If you leave the job status screen, you can find it again by selecting Enterprise | Provisioning and Patching | Procedure Activity from the Enterprise menu.

Here you can see the currently running procedures are listed, as shown in Figure 12-15.

The provisioning procedure might run for quite a long time. When it has completed, you should see a success message in the Procedure Activity screen.

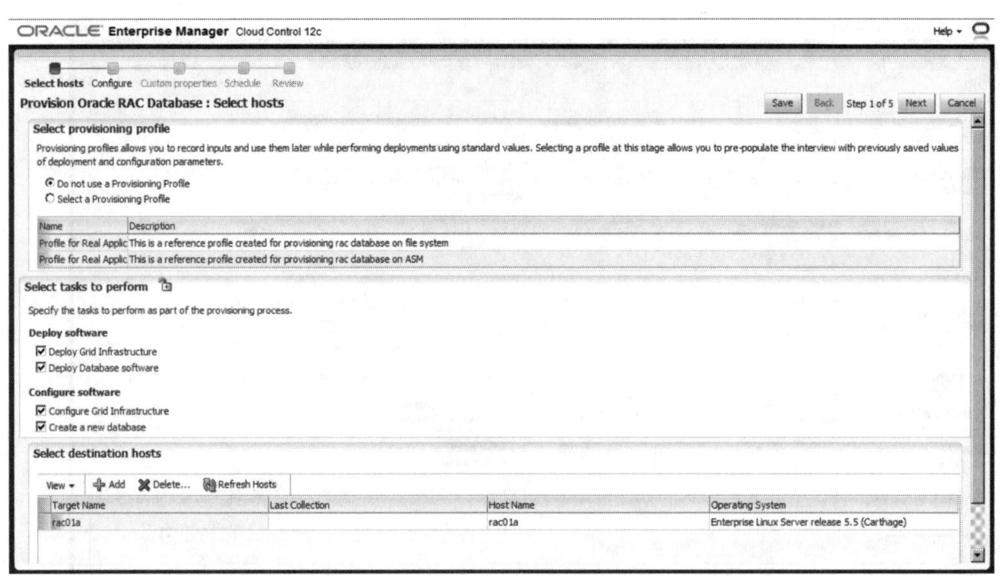

FIGURE 12-13. *The Provision Oracle Database: Select hosts screen*

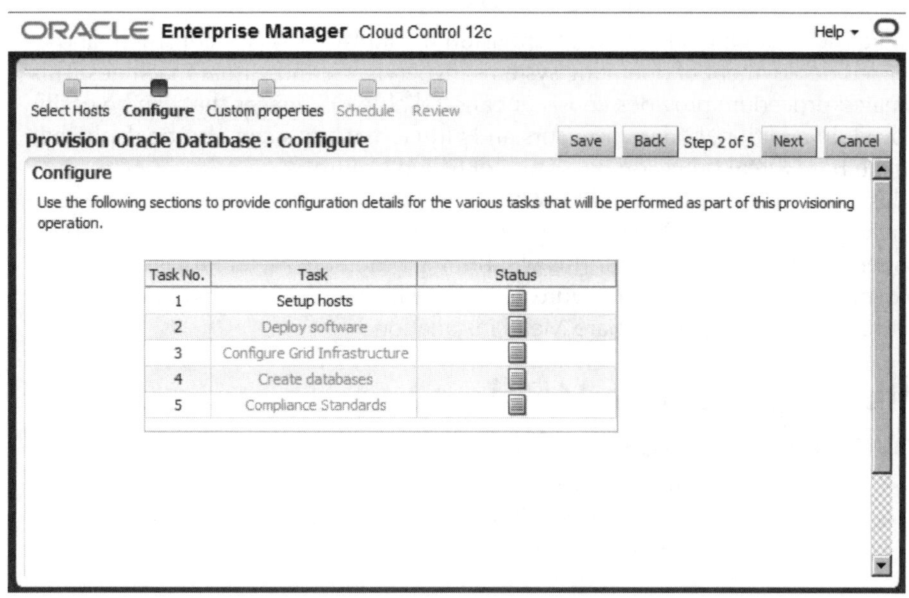

FIGURE 12-14. *The Provision Oracle Database: Configure screen*

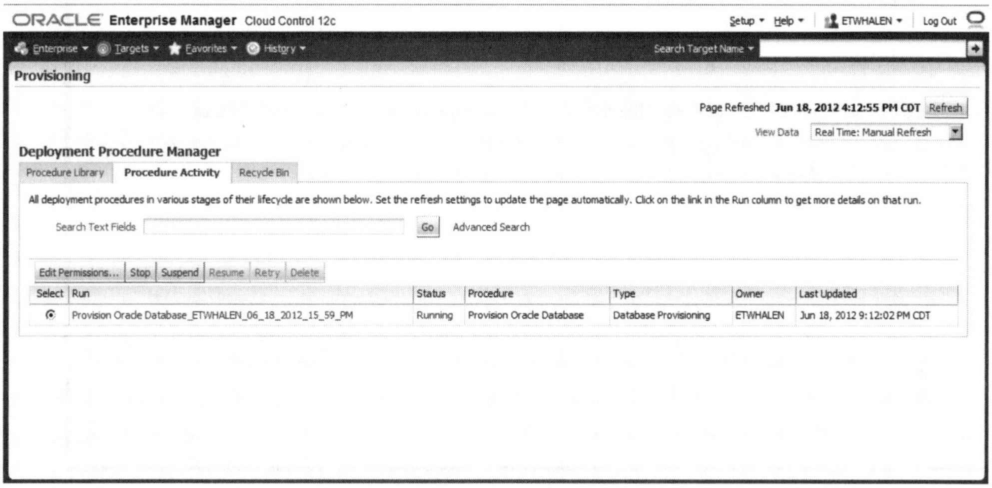

FIGURE 12-15. *The Deployment Procedure Manager: Procedure Activity screen*

Bare Metal Provisioning

The Bare Metal or Operating System provisioning utility allows for consistent and optimized deployment of operating systems, hypervisors, and virtual machines. This automated procedure provides consistent and reliable OS images that can be easily deployed. In addition, both hypervisors and virtual machines can also be deployed using the Bare Metal provisioning feature of Cloud Control.

This utility requires the use of boot servers, image servers, and DHCP servers. To begin the process, select Provisioning and Patching | Bare Metal Provisioning from the Enterprise drop-down menu. This will bring up the Bare Metal Provisioning: Deployments page as shown in Figure 12-16. Notice the warning that the OMS server has not been set up for Bare Metal installation.

Setting Up the Bare Metal Provisioning Infrastructure

There are several things that need to be set up before you can attempt bare metal provisioning. Click the Infrastructure tab to see the items that can be configured as part of the bare metal installation infrastructure, as shown in Figure 12-17.

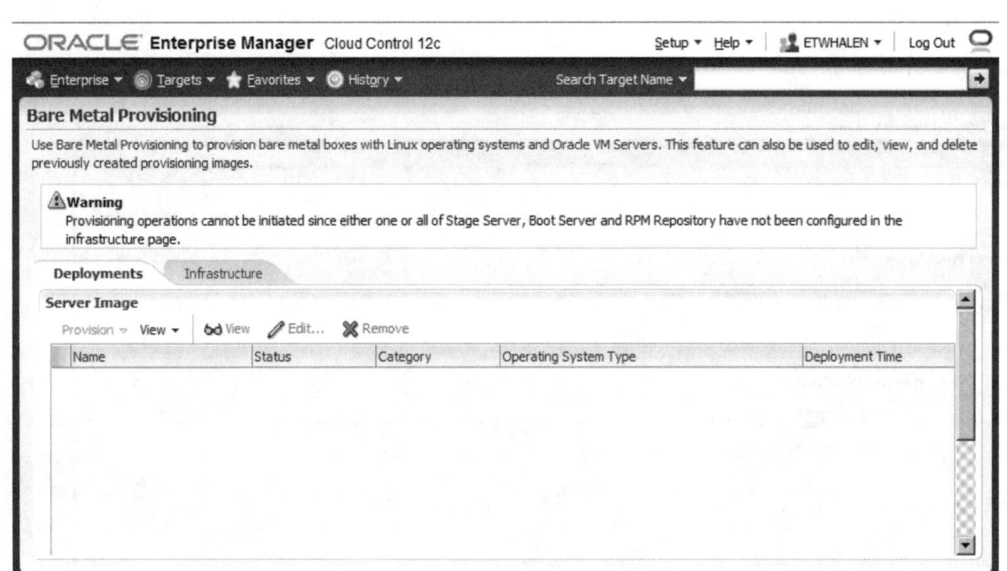

FIGURE 12-16. *Bare Metal Provisioning: Deployments*

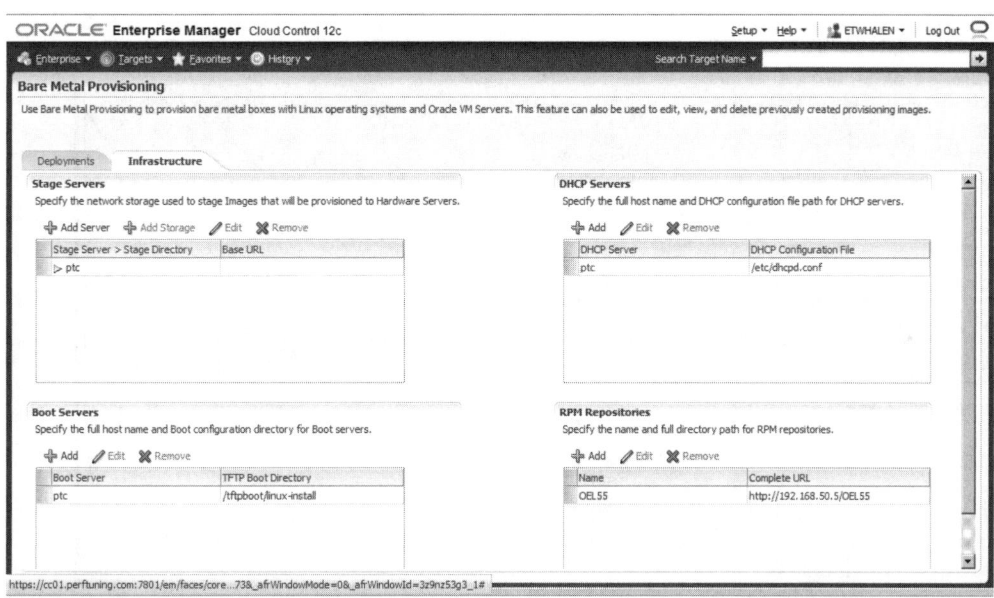

FIGURE 12-17. *Bare Metal Provisioning: Infrastructure*

In this screen you can set up the stage servers, DHCP servers, boot servers, and RPM Repository servers. All of these have to be set up so that the bare metal provisioning can work properly. All of these configurations have to be filled out before you can begin provisioning with the Lifecycle Management Pack.

Bare Metal Provisioning Deployments

Once the infrastructure has been configured, the Provision button will become available. This will allow you to select it and drop down into the list. Select Operating System. This will invoke the Provision Operating System Wizard as shown in Figure 12-18.

Fill in the required fields and continue to the next screen. Follow the next seven screens to specify Deployment Options, Basic OS Details, Additional OS Details, Disk Layout, Network, Schedule, and Credentials for the job, and finally a review of your selections. At this point you can submit the job and it will run as an OEM Cloud Control job to provision the new server using PXE boot. Turn on the server and it will boot into PXE boot with TFTP and load the OS onto the new hardware.

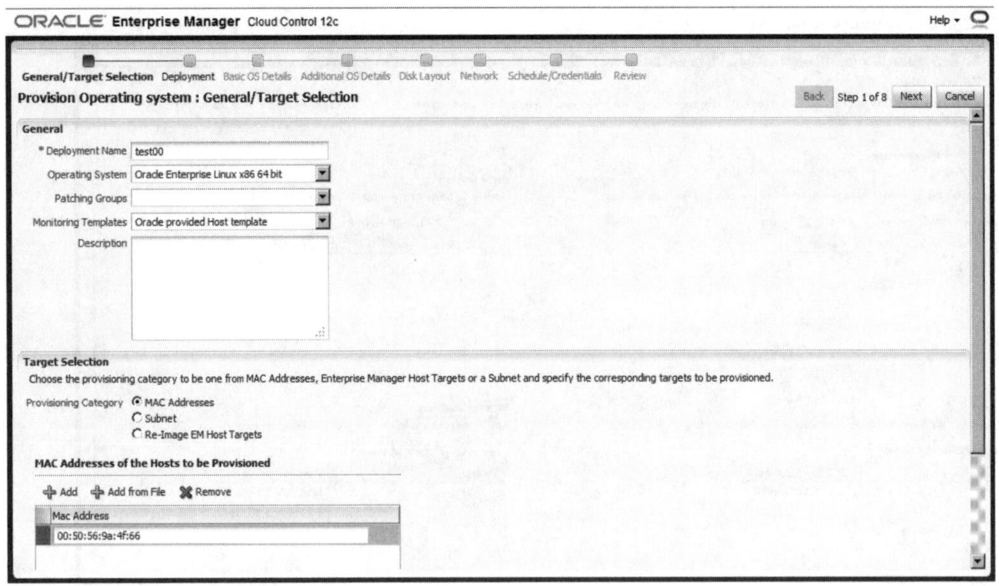

FIGURE 12-18. *The Provision Operating System screen*

Database Provisioning

To perform database provisioning, select Provisioning and Patching | Database Provisioning from the Enterprise drop-down list. This will invoke the Database Provisioning screen. This screen has a number of sections that allows for quick access to Setup, Target Host Setup, Current Status, Related Links, Profiles, and Deployment Procedures as seen in Figure 12-19.

The Database Provisioning Wizard contains both profiles and procedures. The profiles are similar to procedures, but have a little more reference configurations built into them. However, essentially all of the database profiles and procedures end up in the same Database Procedure Wizard that you saw in the earlier example. Thus, database provisioning is simply an easier way to get to the same procedures that are available in the procedure library.

The Database Procedure Wizard guides you through the process of configuring the deployment via a series of configuration settings that must be imputed. Once all of these are done, the job will launch and perform the provisioning of the Oracle database. Options include standalone instance or RAC, ASM, or filesystem and a number of other options.

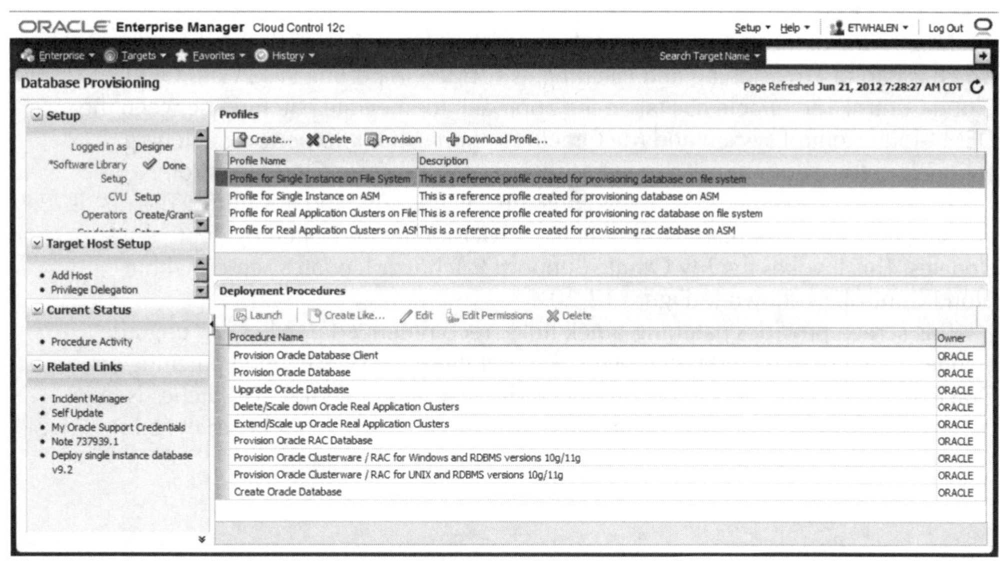

FIGURE 12-19. *The Database Provisioning screen*

NOTE

Provisioning is a great way to deploy software; however, be aware that you can also easily clone an Oracle home from an existing Oracle home and clone a database from an existing database. This is available in the Database screen under Oracle Database | Provisioning | Clone Database Home and Oracle Database | Provisioning | Clone Database.

Middleware Provisioning

Middleware provisioning is similar to database provisioning in that it is simply a number of shortcuts to the Procedure Library middleware items. The middleware provisioning can be done using a number of different methods, including cloning from an existing cluster or by using software stored in the Software Library. Middleware provisioning options and procedures will vary widely based on which middleware component you choose to provision.

Patching

Patching is one of the most important duties of the Oracle DBA. This is why patching, which is part of Provisioning and Patching, is such an important task. With OEM Cloud Control 12*c* Oracle has taken the approach to integrate patching between the OEM Cloud Control system and My Oracle Support (MOS). To perform patching of Oracle software, you must use the MOS integration within Cloud Control.

There are several methods of invoking the Patches and Updates utility. The first is by using the Enterprise menu and selecting Provisioning and Patching | Patches & Updates. This invokes the My Oracle Support: Patches & Updates screen within Cloud Control, as shown in Figure 12-20.

This screen provides patching quick links, recommended patches, an upgrade planner, patch search, and patch plans. Each of these are of use when patching an Oracle database or other Oracle products. The first step in deploying patches is to create a patch plan. Once the patch plan has been created, it can be analyzed and deployed.

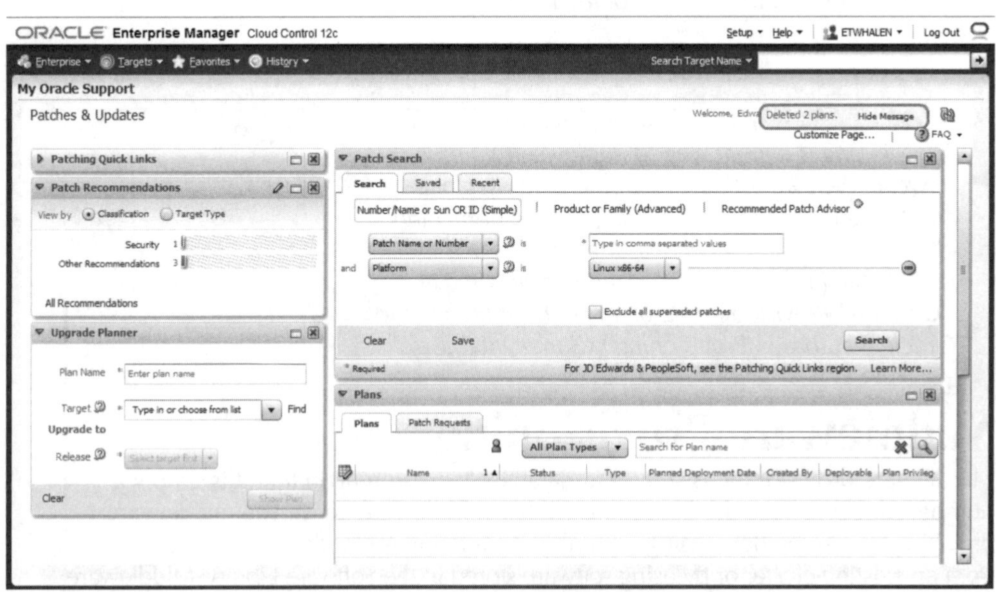

FIGURE 12-20. *The My Oracle Support: Patches & Updates screen*

Creating a Patch Plan

Here you can search for patches and updates and create patch plans. The second option is to take recommended patches. In the Patches & Updates screen on the left side and in the Enterprise summary screen at the bottom left side, you will find Patch Recommendations as shown in the following illustration. These recommendations are based on OEM Cloud Control's connection to MOS and your current inventories. In this case we only have one database system (the EM Repository), so there aren't very many patches.

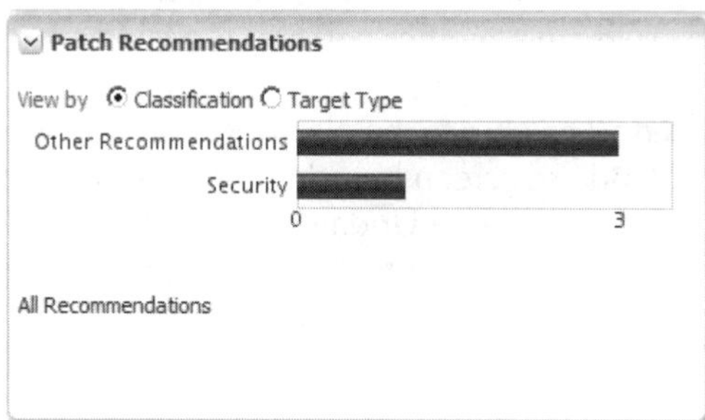

Click the All Recommendations link and you will be connected with MOS again, this time with recommended patches. The recommended patches are listed along with the target that each affects, as shown in Figure 12-21.

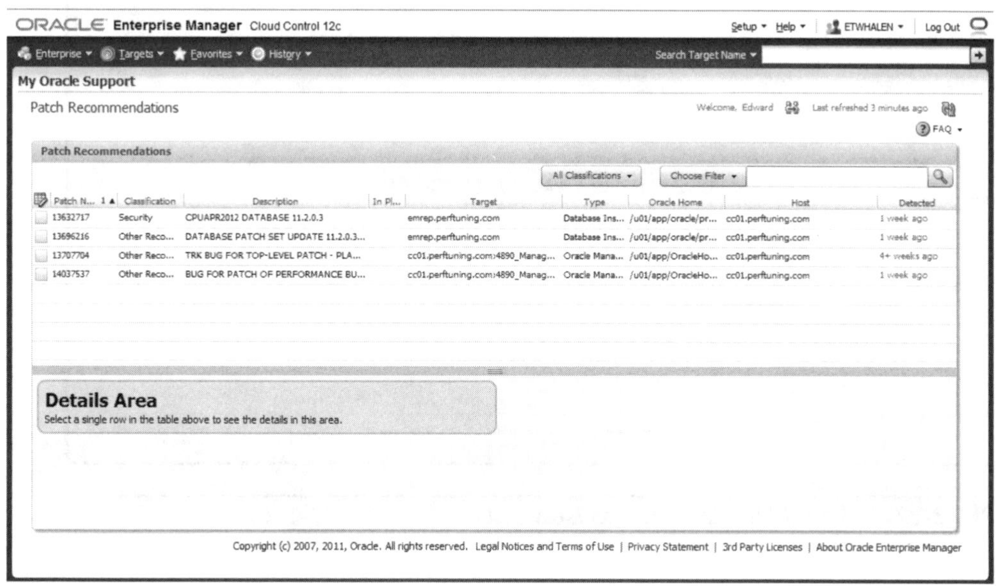

FIGURE 12-21. *The My Oracle Support: Patch Recommendations screen*

Here you will select the patches that you want to apply by checking the box to the left of the patch number. Once you have checked the box, the options will appear below the line that the patch is on. Click Add to Plan and Add to New as shown in Figure 12-22.

You will be prompted to give the patch plan a name via a dialog box. This name should be descriptive enough to identify the plan and know where it should be applied. Once you have several patch plans, having a descriptive name is useful.

A patch plan is a group of patches that have been selected to be applied for a target or set of targets. Once you have selected a patch plan, you can add more patches to that plan by selecting another patch and clicking Add to Plan | Add to Existing.

Once you have added all patches to the plans that you want from recommendations, return to the Patches & Updates screen by using the Enterprise menu and selecting Provisioning and Patching | Patches & Updates. This will bring you to the Patches & Updates screen as shown earlier in Figure 12-20, but now the Plans section is populated with the patch plan that you had just created.

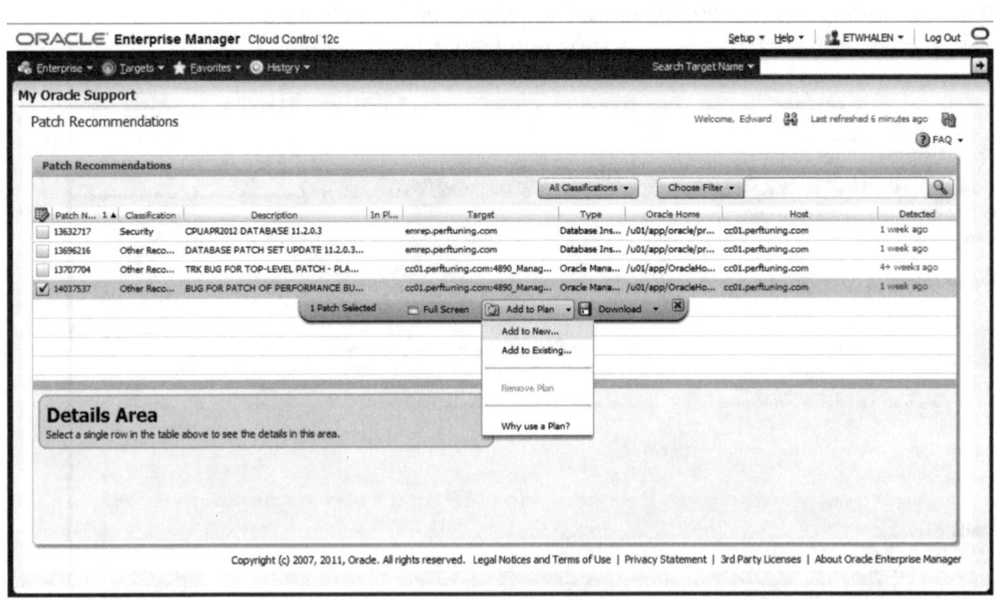

FIGURE 12-22. *The Add to Plan | Add to New option*

Validating and Deploying the Patch Plan

Once the patch plan has been created, it should be validated and configured for deployment in your Cloud Control environment. Click the patch plan in the Patches & Updates window. This will invoke the Patches & Updates Plan Wizard. This is a multistep process. You might be brought to either the first or second step.

Step 1: Plan Information From the Plan Information screen, you change the patch plan name, provide a description, and allow other groups and users to access this plan set. In addition, you can set the schedule for deployment of this patch plan. This is shown in Figure 12-23.

Step 2: Patches Here you will see the patches that are part of this patch plan. Figure 12-24 shows the screen where you can also add additional patches to the patch plan.

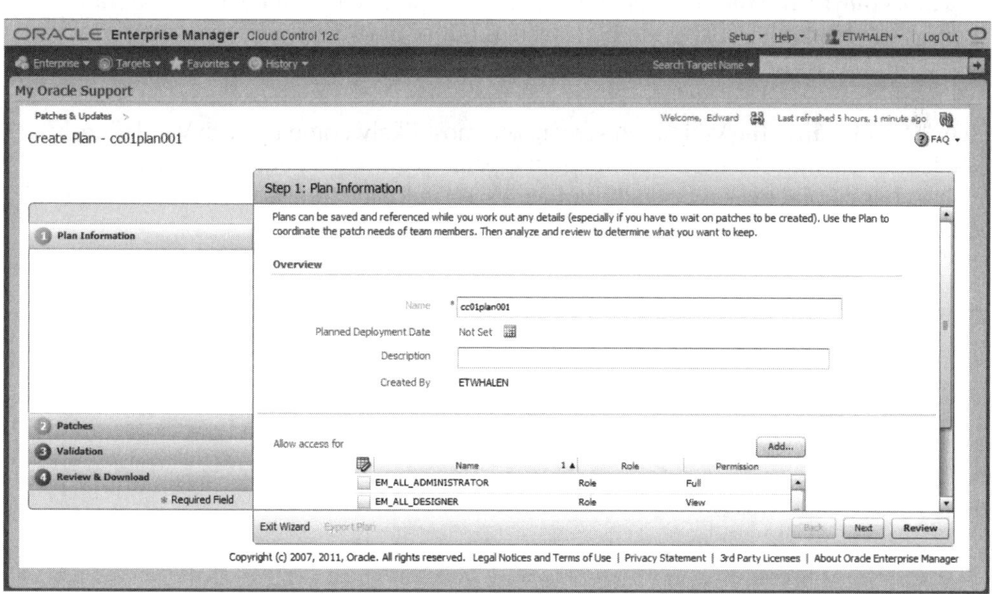

FIGURE 12-23. *The Create Plan: Plan Information screen*

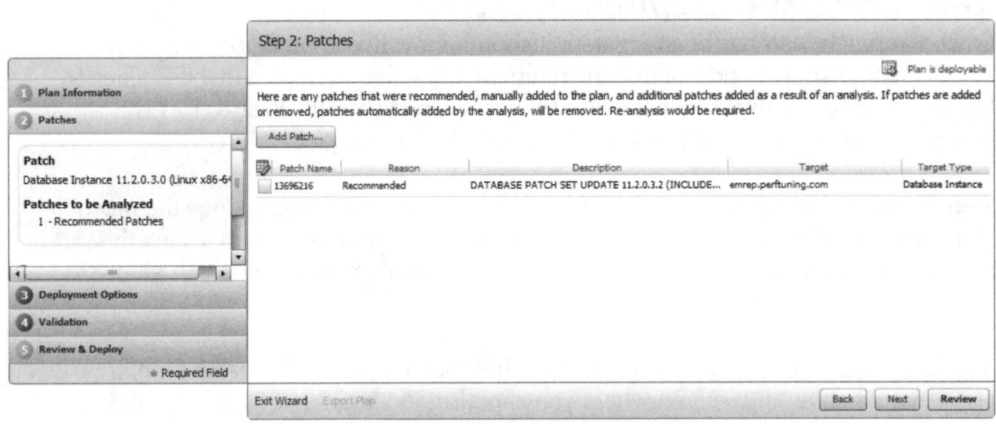

FIGURE 12-24. *The Create Plan: Patches screen*

Step 3: Deployment Options Depending on the type of patch, there might be some additional information, such as in-place versus out-of-place upgrades, credentials, and so on. This is shown in Figure 12-25.

Step 4: Validation The Validation screen will most likely come up with Validation Needed. Click the Validation button and the patch plan will be analyzed. When the analysis has completed successfully, you will see the Ready for Deployment message as shown in Figure 12-26.

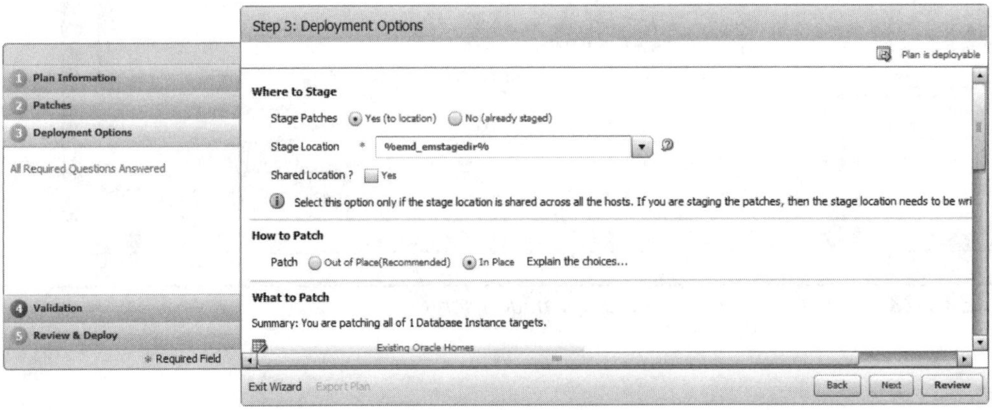

FIGURE 12-25. *The Create Plan: Deployment Options screen*

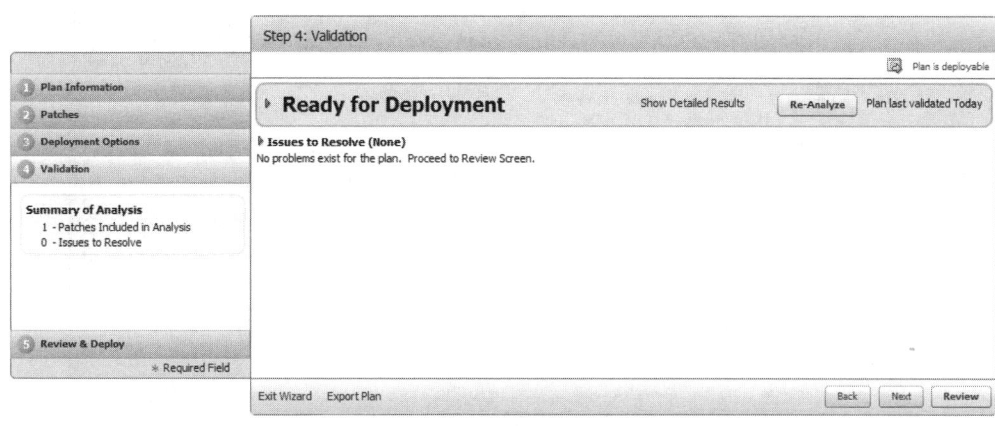

FIGURE 12-26. *The Create Plan: Validation screen*

Enabling OS Authentication

In some cases, for a database upgrade or patch, OS authentication must be enabled for the database upgrade to succeed. You will be informed of this during the validation. To enable OS authentication for the oracle user, do the following:

1. Find the value for the os_authentic_prefix (usually ops$) by doing a `show parameters` from SQL+Plus.
2. Set `remote_os_authent=true` in the SPFILE and restart the Oracle instance.
3. Create the oracle user in SQL+Plus by doing the following:

   ```
   SQL> create user ops$oracle identified externally;
   ```

4. Give privileges to the oracle user (decide which role based on your security requirements):

   ```
   SQL> grant dba to ops$oracle
   ```

5. Test:

   ```
   $ sqlplus /
   ```

You should be able to connect as the oracle user without SYSDBA and without providing database credentials.

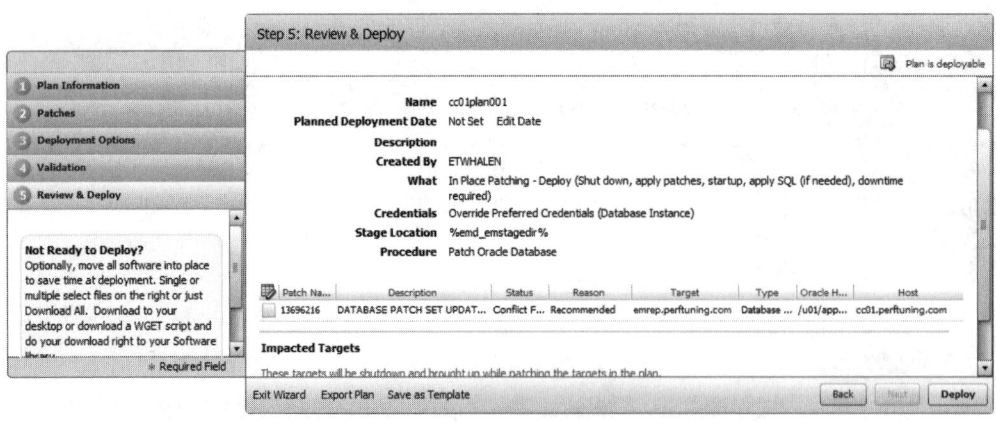

FIGURE 12-27. *The Create Plan: Review & Deploy screen*

Step 5: Review & Deploy The final screen is the Review & Deploy screen, shown in Figure 12-27. Here you can validate all of your choices, the patch plan validation and the impacted targets. When you are satisfied, click the Deploy button. This will begin deploying the patch.

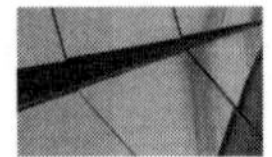

NOTE
Do not attempt to update the OMS server. During the upgrade process, the OMS and Repository database will become unavailable and the upgrade/patch might fail. Updating the OMS server should be done manually.

When the process has completed, the patch/upgrade should show a successful conclusion.

Linux Patching

Linux patching is available for Cloud Control 12c because of the close integration between Oracle and Linux. The Cloud Control Linux patching system is tightly integrated with the Unbreakable Linux Network in the same way that database patching is integrated with My Oracle Support. The steps necessary to set up Linux patching are fairly straightforward. The steps are as follows:

1. Create a Linux RPM Repository from the ULN (Unbreakable Linux Network) channels that you have selected.
2. Download the patches from ULN to the RPM Repository.

3. Create Linux Patching Groups in order to set up the Linux hosts that you want to patch.
4. Apply Patches to the Patching Groups.

These steps are pretty straightforward, but do require some setup. Once you have set up the RPM Repository and configured Linux patching, things can be done in a very automated fashion. The steps are described in detail in the following sections.

Linux RPM Repository Server Prerequisites

There are a few things that need to be done in order to set up the RPM Repository server. They are necessary for a successful configuration and installation of the RPM packages.

1. Configure the RPM server with `up2date` or `yum`. It must be connected to the Oracle Unbreakable Linux Network (ULN) in order to download the RPM packages.
2. The RPM server must be set up as a Web server. The `httpd` package must be installed and running. The RPM Repository will be installed in /var/www/html/yum. If you want it to go somewhere else, such as /u01/html/yum, create a symbolic link from /var/www/html/yum to /u01/html/yum.
3. During the validation process, the script is expecting to find the packages in the /yum tree. Create a symbolic link from /yum to /u01/html/yum.

The third step is most likely the result of a bug in the Oracle deployment scripts. That step might not be necessary in later releases.

Create Linux RPM Repository from ULN

The first step in setting up the Linux RPM Repository is to choose a Repository server and install and configure `YUM` or `up2date`. If the Linux RPM Repository server is going to be Oracle Enterprise Linux (OEL) 5 or earlier, you can use either `YUM` or `up2date`. With OEL 6 or newer, `up2date` has been deprecated in lieu of `YUM`. If it is not installed, you must install `YUM` on the Repository server.

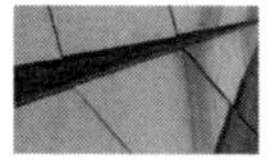

NOTE
For the examples in this chapter, Oracle Enterprise Linux (OEL) 5 is used for the Linux RPM Repository.

From the Setup menu, select Provisioning & Patching | Linux Patching. This will bring you to the Patching Setup screen as shown in Figure 12-28.

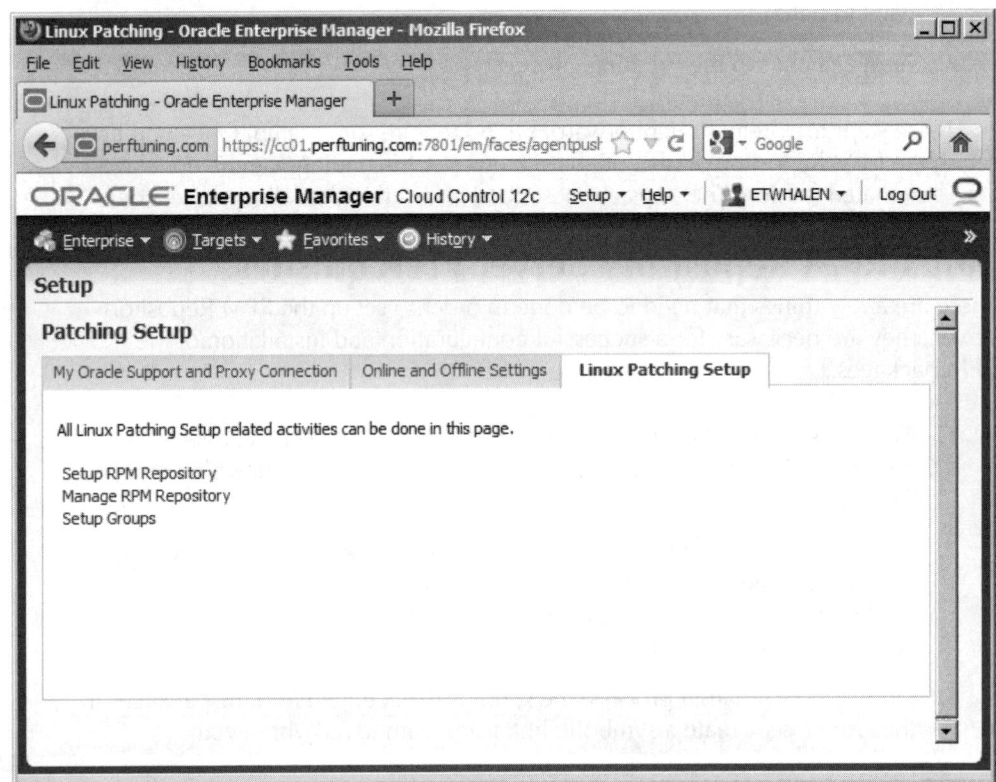

FIGURE 12-28. *The Setup | Provisioning & Patching | Patching Setup screen*

Click the Setup RPM Repository link to begin the RPM Repository setup process.

Fill in the RPM Repository server name by selecting it from the available hosts (that have Agents installed), the normal and privileged host credentials.

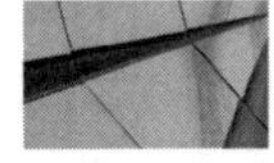

NOTE
If this Agent is newly installed, don't forget to set the privilege delegation from Setup | Security | Privilege Delegation.

Once you have filled out this screen, as shown in Figure 12-29, click Apply. This will start a job to create the Linux RPM Repository server.

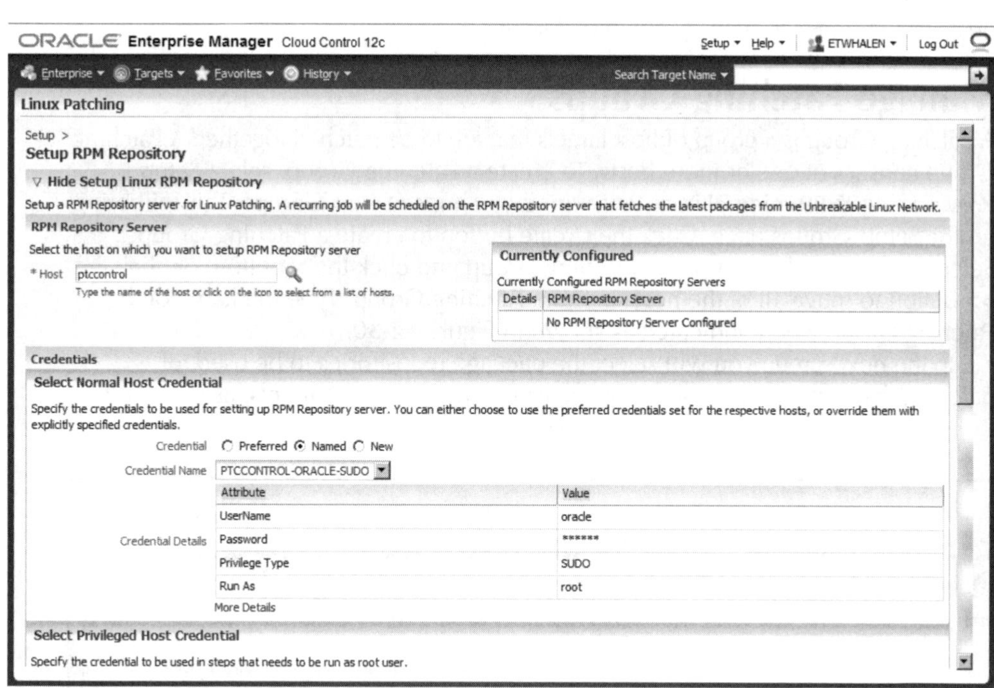

FIGURE 12-29. *The Setup RPM Repository screen*

During the RPM Repository setup process, you will be prompted several times for confirmation of steps that must be run manually. These include the `up2date` registration and ULN subscription additions. Once the process has completed, the RPM Repository should be set up and ready to use.

NOTE

Because of an Oracle bug, you might see the following message during the validation stage:

```
ERROR: Error occurs while reading the
content of File "/yum/EnterpriseLinux/EL5/
oracle/x86_64/repodata/primary.xml.gz".
```

The workaround is to change the permissions on the /yum directory tree to 777 (`chmod -R 777 /yum`) and run the step again. This is a problem regardless of the account used to create the Linux RPM Repository.

Once the Repository creation has completed, you are ready to move on to the next step, which is to manage Patching Groups.

Manage Patching Groups

A Patching Group is a group of host targets that are to be patched together. A Patching Group consists of one or more hosts. To create a Patching Group, select Setup | Provisioning & Patching | Linux Patching, then choose Setup Groups. This will bring up the Setup Groups page. Click the Create button to create a Patching Group. Select the hosts to be part of the Patching Group and click the > button, or click the >> button to move all of the hosts into the Patching Group. Type the name of the Patching Group where indicated as shown in Figure 12-30.

In the next screen you will select the package repositories to be used for patching these hosts. Select as many package repositories (channels) as you want.

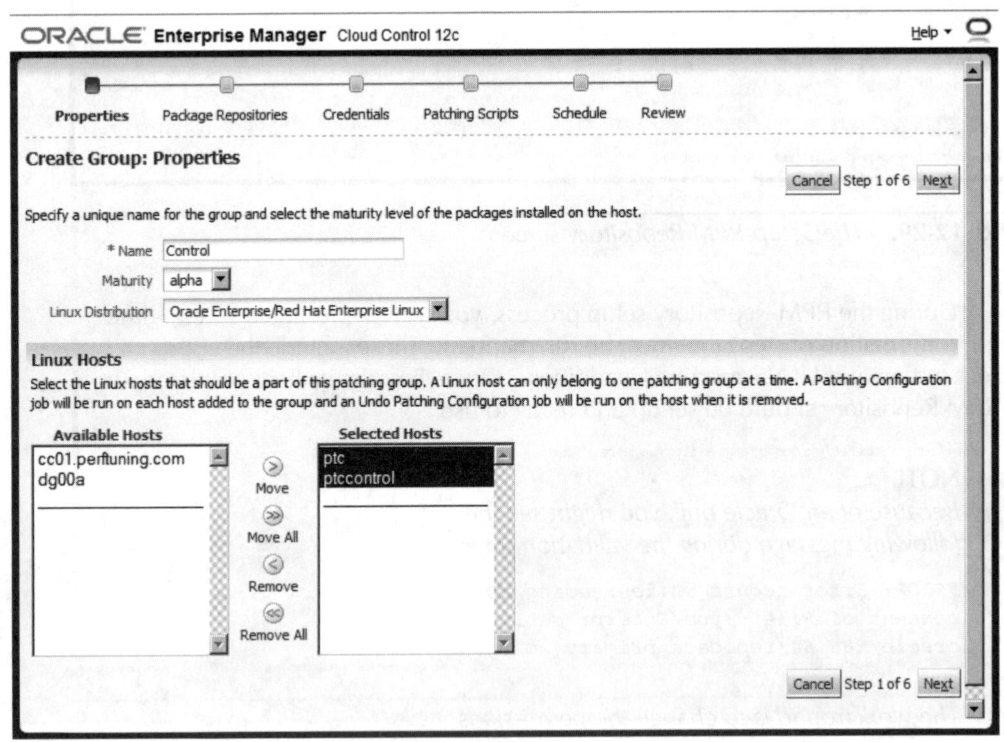

FIGURE 12-30. *The Create Group: Properties screen*

Also select the staging area. You can also choose to apply the patches automatically or manually by checking the Automatically Update Hosts checkbox. You also have some choices about rogue packages and whether to update specific patches only when the host reboots. This screen is shown in Figure 12-31.

You will then be taken to the Create Group: Credentials screen, where you will be able to select the credentials needed for patching. This is shown in Figure 12-32.

Clicking Next takes you to the review screen. When you are satisfied with your selections, you can create the Patching Group by clicking the Finish button. Once the Patching Group has been created, you will be taken back to the Linux Patching screen. This screen will now show the Patching Group as well as the jobs that are currently running as part of this configuration, as shown in Figure 12-33.

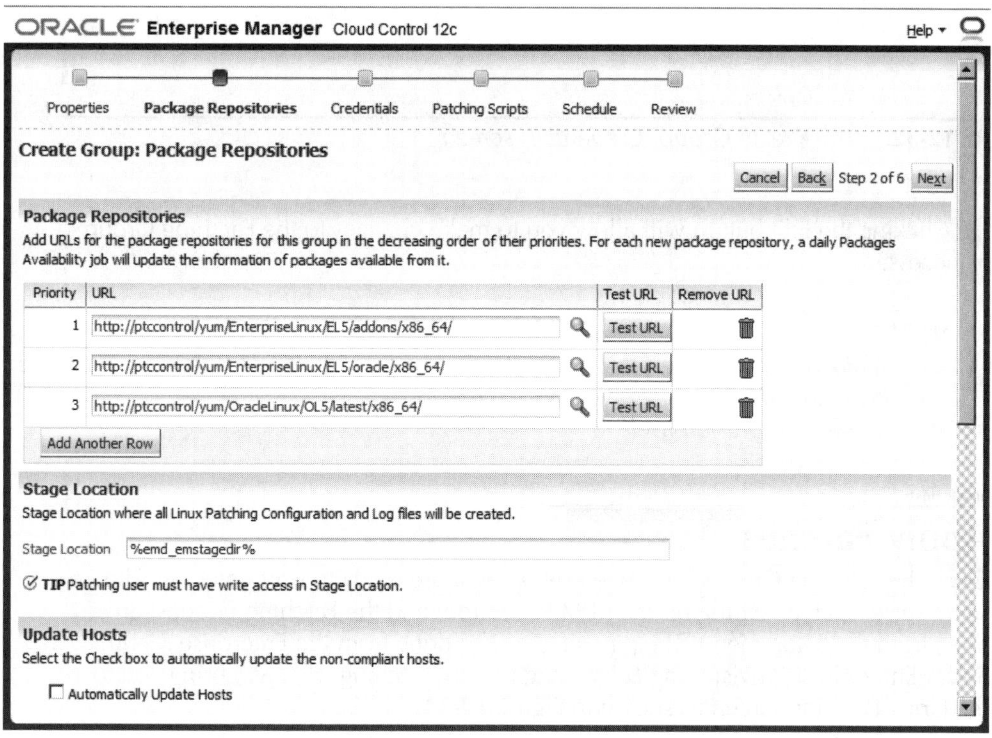

FIGURE 12-31. *The Create Group: Package Repositories screen*

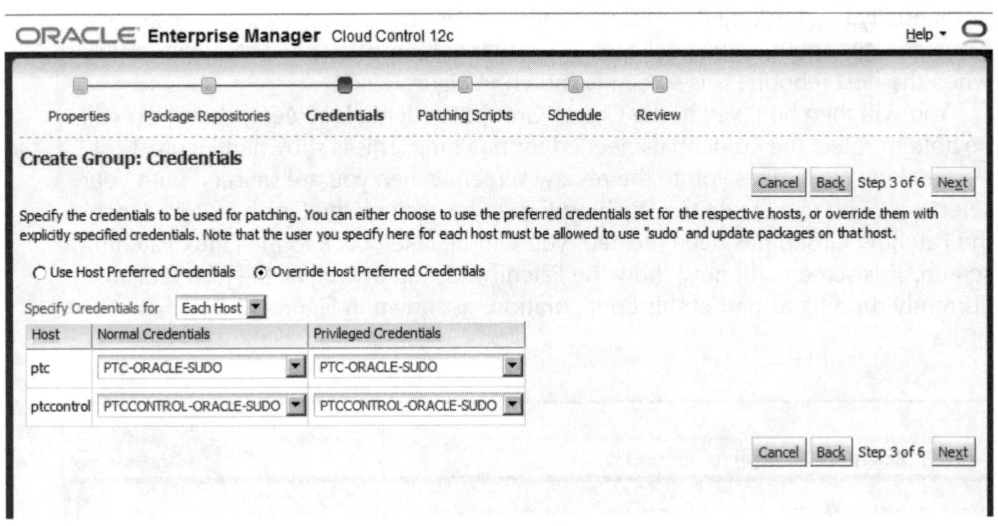

FIGURE 12-32. *The Create Group: Credentials screen*

Clicking the Edit button will allow you to make changes to the Patching Group as necessary.

NOTE
You should not choose the OMS system(s) for patching within the Linux Patching system because of the dependency upon itself.

Apply Patches

Once the Patching Groups have been set up, you are ready to start patching. The setup steps, such as setting up the RPM Repository and the Patching Groups, are done from the Setup menu. The patching itself is done from the Enterprise Menu. Select Enterprise | Provisioning & Patching | Linux Patching. This will bring you to the Linux Patching screen as shown in Figure 12-34.

You will now see the Compliance Home tab, which shows the patchable Linux groups and hosts as well as the compliance report and jobs. Select a Patching Group from the radio buttons and click the Schedule Patching button to launch the

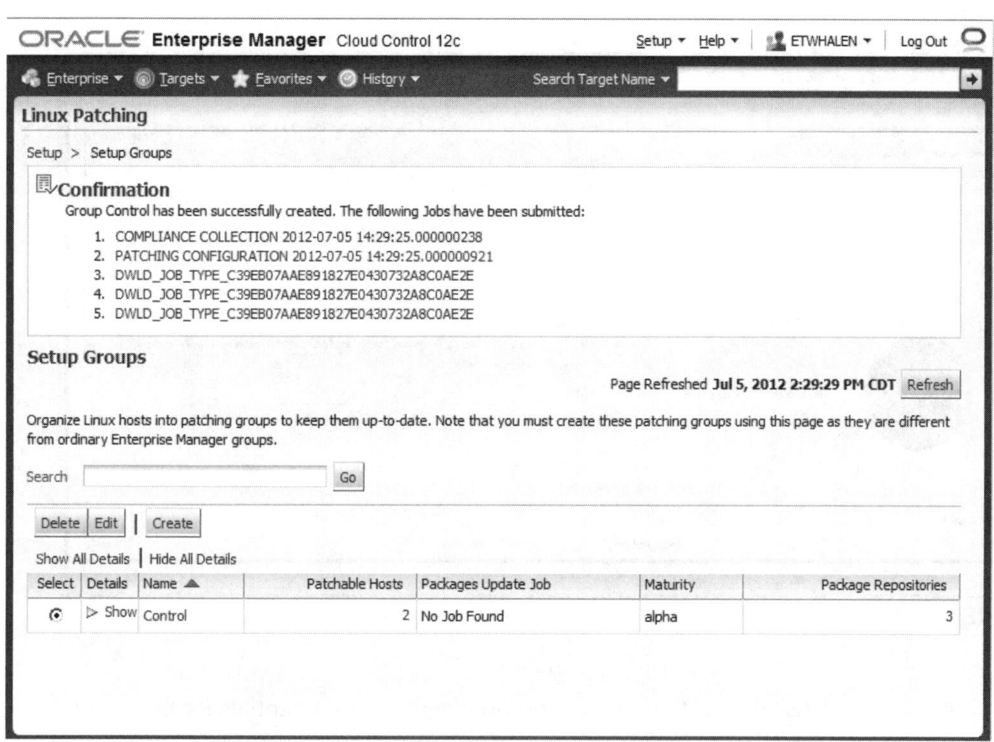

FIGURE 12-33. *The Linux Patching screen*

patching process. This will invoke the Patch Wizard. There are several steps to the Patch Wizard, as covered here:

1. **Package Repository** Here you are prompted to select the type of Linux and whether to use `YUM` or `up2date` as the method of patching. You can also change the staging location and the package repositories that you want to use for the patching operation. Click Next to continue.
2. **Select Updates** This is where you actually select the updates to be applied. There is a checkbox to hide obsolete updates, a place to search for specific updates, and a section where you can choose from the thousands of packages to update your Linux host with. Click Next to Continue.
3. **Select Hosts** Here you select the Patching Groups to be the target of the patching process, or you can expand a Patching Group and select a specific host. Click Next to continue.

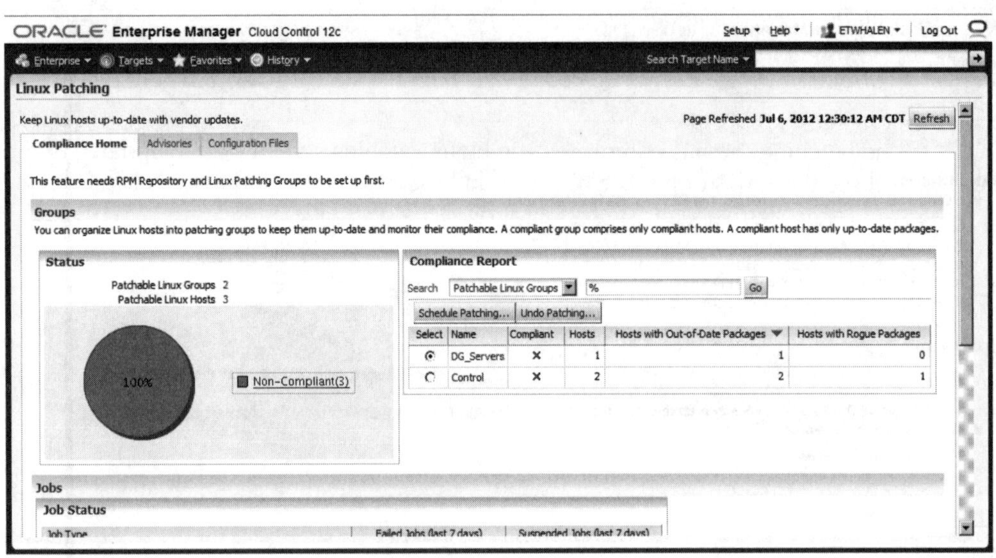

FIGURE 12-34. *The Linux Patching: Compliance Home screen*

4. **Credentials** Select the normal and privileged host credentials for the target systems. Click Next to continue.
5. **Pre/Post Scripts** You can specify any scripts to run before and/or after the patching. This is useful for shutting down applications or databases and restarting them after the process has completed. Click Next to continue.
6. **Schedule** You can run immediately, at a later time, or set up a repeating schedule. This allows for a great deal of flexibility in scheduling the patch updates. Click Next to continue.
7. **Review** Review your patching choices and click Finish when you are satisfied, or click Back to go to a previous screen.

This will start the patching process. Depending on the amount of patching to do, this could take a while. Once you have clicked Finish, you will be brought to the Deployment Procedure Manager. You can watch the steps by clicking on the job and drilling down into the steps.

NOTE
Many patches have a manual reboot step. You will have to click on this step and confirm that the reboot has occurred. Then the job will continue.

Once the patching job has completed, the Linux Patching screen will be updated and you will see the status of the Patching Group hosts.

You can see the status of Linux Patching procedures by selecting Enterprise | Provisioning and Patching | Procedure Activity. This will show a list of the currently running and past procedures. Clicking on the procedure will drill into that procedure.

Manage the RPM Repository

Once the RPM Repository has been created, channels can be managed via the ULN URL (http://linux.oracle.com). You can also manage and view the channels via OEM Cloud Control by selecting Setup | Provisioning & Patching | Linux Patching, and then Manage RPM Repository.

Configuration Management

Oracle Enterprise Manager Cloud Control is constantly taking inventory of the configuration of the targets that it is monitoring. This information is saved and is available for instant access and comparison. Information is collected on database configuration, host configuration, middleware, storage, and so on.

Cloud Control can then be used to search for specific configuration information, compare configurations, and view latest and saved configurations as well as usage details. It can also be used to monitor configuration history for changes and to perform root cause analysis and impact analysis.

Configuration Searches

To perform a configuration search, select Configuration | Search from the Enterprise Menu. This will invoke the Configuration Search Library utility as shown in Figure 12-35. Here you will see the saved configuration searches that can be used to find and display configuration information.

You can select a configuration by clicking on one of the searches, then either clicking on the Run icon or Create Like. In this example we clicked on the Database Tablespaces search and clicked Run. This brought up the Database Tablespaces search as shown in Figure 12-36. Here you can click a target hyperlink to go to the target home screen or provide more search criteria to narrow the search.

Information is shown about the database tablespaces. This provides a quick and easy view of the database tablespaces or other search criteria.

https://cc01.perftuning.com:7801/em/faces/core-uifwk-console-overview?_afrLoop=2086...indowId=null#%2Fcore-ecm-search-searchLibrary%40%3F_adf.ctrl-state%3D17q44d59b_82

Setup ▾ Help ▾ | ETWHALEN ▾ | Log Out

Enterprise ▾ Targets ▾ Favorites ▾ History ▾ Search Target Name ▾

Configuration Search Library

Page Refreshed **Jul 22, 2012 6:00:17 PM CDT**

Search

View ▾ Run Edit... Delete... | Create... Create Like...

Search Name	Target Type	Owner	Modified Date	Created Date
Database Tablespaces	Database Instance	SYSMAN	Sun, May 27, 2012 at 09:04:36	Sun, May 27, 2012 at 09:04:36
Initialization Parameter Settings	Database Instance	SYSMAN	Sun, May 27, 2012 at 09:04:36	Sun, May 27, 2012 at 09:04:36
Database Datafiles	Database Instance	SYSMAN	Sun, May 27, 2012 at 09:04:36	Sun, May 27, 2012 at 09:04:36
IBM WebSphere Application Server : Web Modules	IBM WebSphere Application Server	SYSMAN	Sun, May 27, 2012 at 09:03:55	Sun, May 27, 2012 at 09:03:55
IBM WebSphere Application Server : JDBC Providers	IBM WebSphere Application Server	SYSMAN	Sun, May 27, 2012 at 09:03:55	Sun, May 27, 2012 at 09:03:55
IBM WebSphere Application Server : Data Sources	IBM WebSphere Application Server	SYSMAN	Sun, May 27, 2012 at 09:03:54	Sun, May 27, 2012 at 09:03:54
IBM WebSphere Application Server : Deployed Applications	IBM WebSphere Application Server	SYSMAN	Sun, May 27, 2012 at 09:03:54	Sun, May 27, 2012 at 09:03:54
IBM WebSphere Application Server : EJB Modules	IBM WebSphere Application Server	SYSMAN	Sun, May 27, 2012 at 09:03:54	Sun, May 27, 2012 at 09:03:54
Oracle WebLogic Server : Data Sources	Oracle WebLogic Server	SYSMAN	Sun, May 27, 2012 at 09:03:54	Sun, May 27, 2012 at 09:03:54
JBoss Application Server : Protocols	JBoss Application Server	SYSMAN	Sun, May 27, 2012 at 09:03:54	Sun, May 27, 2012 at 09:03:54
JBoss Application Server : JVM Information	JBoss Application Server	SYSMAN	Sun, May 27, 2012 at 09:03:54	Sun, May 27, 2012 at 09:03:54
Oracle WebLogic Server : Deployed Applications	Oracle WebLogic Server	SYSMAN	Sun, May 27, 2012 at 09:03:54	Sun, May 27, 2012 at 09:03:54
Oracle WebLogic Server : EJB Modules	Oracle WebLogic Server	SYSMAN	Sun, May 27, 2012 at 09:03:54	Sun, May 27, 2012 at 09:03:54
Oracle WebLogic Server : Ports	Oracle WebLogic Server	SYSMAN	Sun, May 27, 2012 at 09:03:54	Sun, May 27, 2012 at 09:03:54
Oracle WebLogic Server : Web Modules	Oracle WebLogic Server	SYSMAN	Sun, May 27, 2012 at 09:03:54	Sun, May 27, 2012 at 09:03:54
WebCache Configuration Search	Web Cache	SYSMAN	Sun, May 27, 2012 at 09:03:54	Sun, May 27, 2012 at 09:03:54
Search Patchsets installed in Oracle Homes	Oracle Home	SYSMAN	Sun, May 27, 2012 at 09:00:29	Sun, May 27, 2012 at 09:00:29
Search Patches Applied on Oracle Products	Oracle Home	SYSMAN	Sun, May 27, 2012 at 09:00:28	Sun, May 27, 2012 at 09:00:28
Search Oracle Products installed in Oracle Homes	Oracle Home	SYSMAN	Sun, May 27, 2012 at 09:00:28	Sun, May 27, 2012 at 09:00:28
Search Host Operating System and Hardware Summaries	Host	SYSMAN	Sun, May 27, 2012 at 09:00:02	Sun, May 27, 2012 at 09:00:02
Search NIC Configurations on Hosts	Host	SYSMAN	Sun, May 27, 2012 at 09:00:02	Sun, May 27, 2012 at 09:00:02
Search Hosts for Operating System Components	Host	SYSMAN	Sun, May 27, 2012 at 09:00:02	Sun, May 27, 2012 at 09:00:02
Search File Systems on Hosts	Host	SYSMAN	Sun, May 27, 2012 at 09:00:02	Sun, May 27, 2012 at 09:00:02

Total Number of Rows : 25

FIGURE 12-35. *The Configuration Search Library utility*

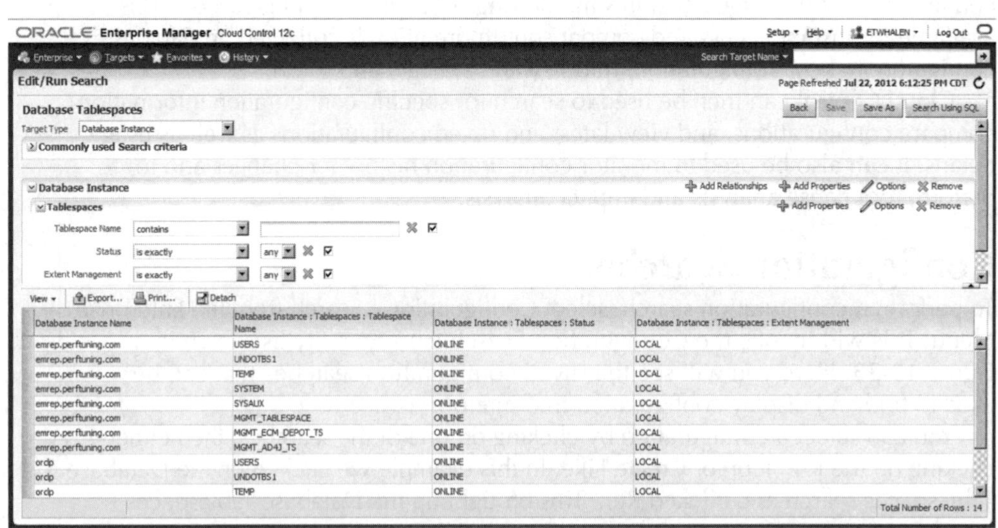

FIGURE 12-36. *The Database Tablespaces Search screen*

The Configuration Browser

The configuration browser allows you to browse configuration data from the available targets that are monitored under Cloud Control 12*c*. To invoke the configuration browser, select All Targets from the Targets drop-down menu. In this menu, right-click on the target for which you want to browse configuration data. From the pop-up menu, select Configuration | Last Collected or "Target Type" | Configuration | Last Collected.

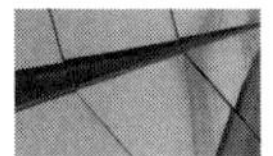

NOTE
The Database Instance target requires the selection Oracle Database | Configuration | Last Collected. The option to select Configuration | Last Collected is not available for some target types.

This will invoke the Latest Configuration screen. The Latest Configuration for a database is shown in Figure 12-37. Here you can see configuration information about the database as well as additional tabs that show relationships, member of, uses, and used by.

This is very convenient for quickly and efficiently viewing configuration data.

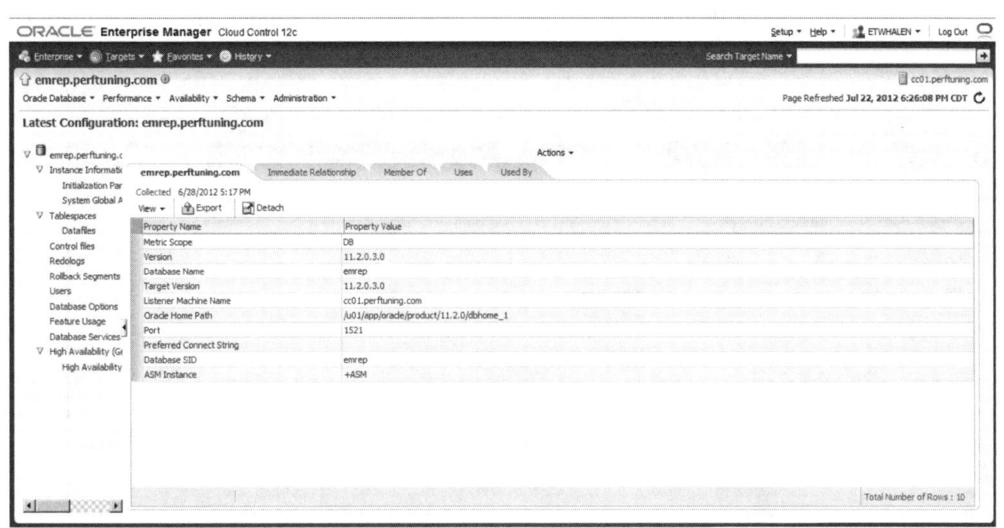

FIGURE 12-37. *The Latest Configuration screen*

Configuration History

From the same Configuration menu selection, you can choose History to show a history of configuration changes. These changes are shown in the Configuration Changes tab as shown here in Figure 12-38. This is extremely useful for seeing what changes have been made to the configuration over the lifetime of the target.

Click the History Records hyperlink to view the change records, or perform a comparison as shown in the next section.

Configuration Comparisons

To compare configurations from the same Configuration menu, select Compare. This will invoke the multistep Configuration Comparison Wizard. To perform configuration comparisons, you must have saved a configuration.

1. Select the first configuration to compare.
2. Select a configuration to compare it to.
3. Select a configuration Template (if desired). Select template settings.
4. Select a comparison schedule and who to notify (via e-mail when the comparison job has completed).
5. Review your settings for the comparison.
6. Click the Submit button. The comparison job will be submitted.

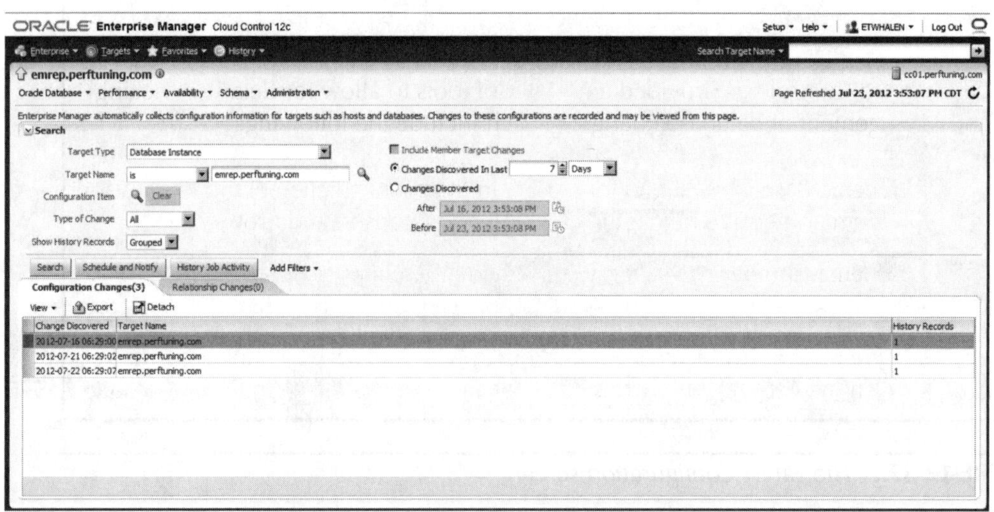

FIGURE 12-38. *Configuration History*

Once the comparison job has completed, you can view the changes that have been made to the target between the configuration collections.

Other Configuration Activities

In addition to the configuration activities shown earlier, the Configuration menu includes the following options:

- **Topology** Shows the configuration topology relationships.
- **Comparison Job Activity** Shows the configuration jobs and their status.
- **Save** Used to save configurations.
- **Saved** Used to show saved configurations.

Configuration management is an important part of lifecycle management and is closely related to change management, which is covered in the next section.

Change Management

Change management is an important part of lifecycle management. In previous releases of OEM Grid Control this capability was part of the Change Management Pack. This is now part of the Lifecycle Management Pack. Change management allows you to track and report changes that have been made to targets under management of Cloud Control. This includes both host and nonhost targets.

Database change management is an important part of the lifecycle of the database. Databases do not remain constant. They tend to change over time, from both a software perspective and a schema perspective. It is important to keep track of these changes so that the systems can be properly upgraded and maintained. OEM Cloud Control has provided a number of tools to allow for detailed tracking and management of database changes, which include the following:

- **Schema Baseline** Allows for a point-in-time configuration of the database and schema objects to be captured for later comparison and browsing.
- **Schema Comparison** Allows for schema baselines to be compared both within the same target at different points in time or between different targets.
- **Schema Synchronization** Allows the process of taking changes that have been made to a schema on one target and propagating them to another target.
- **Schema Change Plans** Allows you to promote specific changes from one target to another target.
- **Data Comparison** Allows you to compare row data from one database target to another database target.

These tools are extremely valuable for the management of the database lifecycle and for maintaining a healthy database.

Schema Baselines

Schema baselines allow you to take a snapshot of the configuration of the database schema and parameters. This is valuable for recording the configuration at a specific point in time. The schema baseline can be used to compare itself against a later point in time or against other databases.

To take a schema baseline, select Change Management | Schema Baselines from the Schema menu within the Database Target screen or from within All Targets (by right-clicking on the database target). This will invoke the Schema Baselines utility. From this screen you can either import or create a schema baseline.

To create a schema baseline, click the Create button. This will invoke the Create Schema Baseline Wizard. The steps to create a schema baseline are as follows:

1. **Source** Name the schema baseline and choose the source database. Optionally, provide a description.
2. **Objects** Choose the baseline objects. You can choose nonschema objects, such as tablespaces, rollback segments, and so on, as well as schema objects and initialization parameters. Also select schemas to include.
3. **Job Options** As with most tasks that we have seen in this book, the baseline creation process uses the Cloud Control job system.
4. **Review** Review your options and configuration.
5. **Submit** Click the Submit button to create the schema baseline.

Once the Schema Baseline Wizard has completed, you will see the Submit Job Successful message and you'll be able to monitor the schema baseline creation process.

Schema Comparison

With a minimum of two schema baselines, you can perform a schema comparison operation. This allows you to view the differences between two target schemas. You can compare parameters, schema objects, and database structures such as tablespaces. The schema comparison operation is invoked by selecting Change Management | Schema Comparison from the Schema menu. This will invoke the Schema Comparison screen. Select Create to invoke the Schema Comparison Wizard.

Once the Schema Comparison Wizard has been invoked, follow these steps in order to compare two schema baselines.

1. **Left Source** Name the schema comparison and choose the left source database from either an instance or a baseline. Optionally, provide a description.
2. **Right Source** Choose the right source database from either an instance or a baseline.
3. **Objects** Choose the comparison objects. You can choose nonschema objects, such as tablespaces, rollback segments, and so on, as well as schema objects and initialization parameters. Also select schemas to include.
4. **Rules** Here you can choose to include or exclude things such as physical attributes, partitioning, statistics, and so on.
5. **Job Options** As with most tasks that we have seen in this book, the baseline creation process uses the Cloud Control job system.
6. **Review** Review your options and configuration.
7. **Submit** Click the Submit button to create the schema baseline.

Once the Schema Comparison Wizard has completed, you will see the Submit Job Successful message and you'll be able to monitor the schema comparison creation process.

Eventually, the schema comparison output will be available in the Schema Comparison screen. Click it and select View to see the results of the comparison.

Schema Synchronizations

The schema synchronization feature allows you to take a database target and synchronize another database with that schema. Synchronizations can occur from either an existing database instance, a baseline, or a change plan instance (discussed in the next section). This allows the target database to be synchronized with the source, ensuring that the schemas are identical.

The schema synchronization operation is invoked by selecting Change Management | Schema Synchronizations from the Schema menu. This will invoke the Schema Synchronizations screen. Select Create to invoke the Schema Synchronization Wizard.

Once the Schema Synchronization Wizard has been invoked, follow these steps to synchronize the target with the source.

1. **Source** Choose the source database, baseline, or change plan instance to be used for the synchronization.
2. **Destination** Choose the database target that is to be synchronized. This must be a database target.
3. **Objects** Here you can choose to include or exclude things such as physical attributes, partitioning, statistics, and so on. You must include at least one schema.
4. **Rules** Here you can choose to include or exclude things such as physical attributes, partitioning, statistics, and so on.
5. **Mode** Here you can choose either unattended or Interactive mode. For unattended mode you must provide credentials.
6. **Job** As with most tasks that we have seen in this book, the baseline creation process uses the Cloud Control job system. This includes both source and target database credentials.
7. **Review** Review your options and configuration.
8. **Submit** Click the Submit button to create the schema synchronization.

Once the Schema Synchronization Wizard has completed, you will see the Submit Job Successful message and be able to monitor the schema synchronization creation process.

Eventually the schema comparison output will be available in the Schema Synchronization screen. Click it and select View to see the results of the synchronization.

Schema Change Plans

The schema change plan feature allows you to take a database target and update another database with specific schema objects. Once the change plan has been created, it can be used to synchronize the target database using the database synchronization feature described earlier in this section. This allows for the target database to be synchronized with the source, ensuring that the selected schema objects are identical.

The schema synchronization operation is invoked by selecting Change Management | Schema Change Plans from the Schema menu. This will invoke the Create Change Plan screen. Select Create from Comparison to invoke the Change Plan Wizard.

Once the Change Plan Wizard has been invoked, follow these steps in order to create the change plan.

1. **Comparison** Choose the comparison from previously created schema comparisons to be used for the change plan. Here you can also choose to create the change plan from the left side of the comparison or the right side.
2. Click OK to continue.
3. **View** Once the change plan has been created, click View to edit the changes. The change plan includes Drop and Add values. Select ones that you do not want to execute and delete them.
4. **Create Synchronization from Change Plan** Click the Create Synchronization from Change Plan button to create the schema synchronization.

You can then use this synchronization to synchronize a target database with this change plan.

Data Comparison

The Data Comparison feature allows you to compare row data between database targets. This is very useful for determining changes that have been made to the actual data in the database. Select Change Management | Data Comparisons from the Schema menu. This will invoke the Data Comparisons screen. Select Create from Data Comparisons to invoke the Create Data Comparison Wizard.

Once the Create Data Comparison Wizard has been invoked, follow these steps in order to create the data comparison.

1. **Create Data Comparison** Name the Data Comparison and provide a description if desired. Choose the Reference Database and Candidate Database. Click OK to continue.
2. **Comparison Items** Select the items to be compared either by selecting candidate pairs from the Actions menu or by adding schema mappings from the Schema Mappings section.
3. **Submit Comparison Job** Once you have selected the comparison items, click the Submit Comparison Job from the Data Comparisons screen.
4. **View Results** Once the job has completed, you can view the results by selecting the comparison and clicking the View Results button.

This feature is very useful if it is important to compare data and/or indexes in different incarnations or different schemas.

Compliance Management

Oracle Enterprise Manager Cloud Control Compliance Management has two separate pieces: monitoring of compliance to business best practices and monitoring of real-time configuration changes. Monitoring of compliance to business best practices is a process where the system is regularly analyzed and deviations from compliance to business best practices are reported. This allows for decisions to be made and issues remediated. Real-time monitoring allows for immediate reporting of changes to the system that might be problematic.

Compliance and Best Practices

Compliance to business best practices is an important job of the IT staff. Oracle Enterprise Manager Cloud Control provides the ability to determine if the targets are adhering to business best practices by determining if targets and systems have valid configuration settings and whether there are vulnerabilities. In addition, Cloud Control will advise how to bring these systems into compliance.

Accessing the compliance features of OEM Cloud Control is done using the Enterprise menu. Select Compliance | Results, Compliance | Library, or Compliance | Real Time Observations from the Enterprise Menu.

If you select Compliance | Results from the Enterprise menu, you will see the Compliance Results page. From this page you will see a summary of the Compliance Standards being evaluated and a summary of the compliance results showing both Target Evaluations and Violations. Highlight the compliance standard and click the Show Results button to show the compliance results details and Security Recommendations for Oracle Products as shown in Figure 12-39.

Here you will see security violations. By clicking the Target Compliance tab, you will see compliance violations based on host targets. To determine the specific compliance violations, you can browse to that specific target and drill down into the compliance violation or security recommendations.

Real-Time Configuration Monitoring

In order to view real-time compliance standards and best practices, select Compliance | Real-time Observations from the Enterprise menu. This will bring up the Real-time Observations utility. From here you can browse observations by compliance frameworks, browse observations by system targets, or search observations. By selecting the hyperlinks you can browse the observations that are discovered in real time. This provides the ability to perform regular audits and determine the real-time state of the systems.

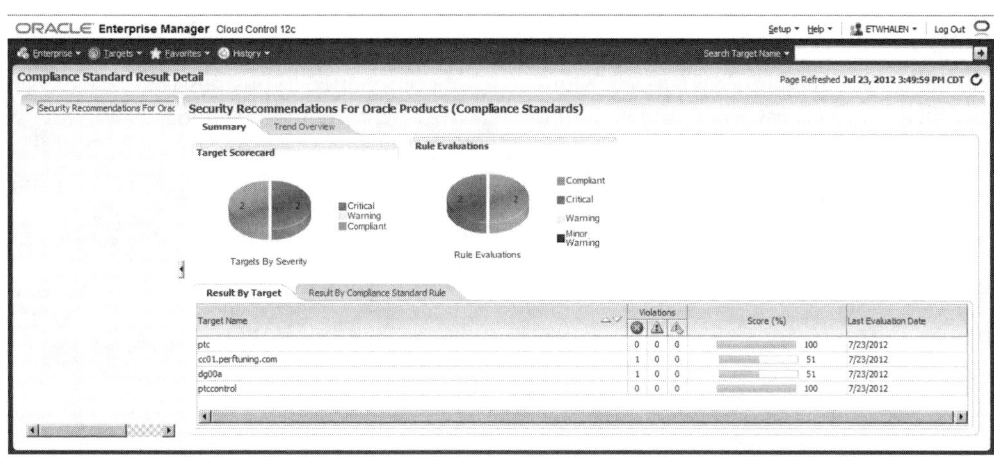

FIGURE 12-39. *Security Recommendations for Oracle Products screen*

Summary

Oracle Enterprise Manager Cloud Control 12*c* has been enhanced to provide support for the management of the entire lifecycle of the targets that it is managing. As you have seen, this includes the ability to deploy the software necessary not only for running the targets—such as OS, database, middleware, and applications—but also for monitoring, change management, patching, configuration management, and compliance management. These abilities of OEM Cloud Control 12*c* provide complete lifecycle management capabilities.

The capabilities for Provisioning and Patching within Oracle Enterprise Manager Cloud Control 12*c* are extensive. The Lifecycle Management Pack provides a number of tools for provisioning bare metal servers, Oracle databases, and application servers as well as the ability to patch these products. The provisioning pack is tightly integrated with My Oracle Support and can download patches as well as providing metadata about those patches in order to advise the administrator of patching needs. Linux Patching provides the ability to work in conjunction with the Unbreakable Linux Network in order to download and deploy patches on an Enterprise basis. These are powerful tools in the Cloud Control product.

CHAPTER 13

Oracle Virtualization Plug-In

Virtualization has become an integral part of Oracle's direction for the future. Oracle has introduced several products to provide virtualization support including Oracle VM for x86. In addition to the Oracle VM Manager that is available as a core component of Oracle, VM for x86 native support has been provided in Oracle Enterprise Manager Cloud Control 12*c* for supporting Oracle VM for x86.

NOTE
For the remainder of this chapter, Oracle VM for x86 (Oracle's official name) will be shortened to Oracle VM. Unless otherwise noted, any reference to Oracle VM is actually referencing Oracle VM for x86.

This chapter provides information on Oracle VM and how to manage an Oracle VM Server Farm from OEM Cloud Control. The chapter provides an overview and introduction to Oracle VM, how to manage the virtual Server Farm from Oracle VM, and how to manage Virtual Machines (VMs) from OEM Cloud Control.

Virtualization has become a dominant technological force and has established a foothold in every major corporation and field. Virtualization is one of the core components of the cloud and has revolutionized the way we do computing. Oracle has responded to the need for virtualization technology with Oracle VM, their premier virtualization product. In addition to Oracle VM for x86, which is a type 1 hypervisor, Oracle has several other virtualization products including Oracle VM for SPARC and Oracle VM Virtual Box. OEM Cloud Control support for virtualization is designed for Oracle VM for x86, which is the focus of this chapter.

What Is Virtualization?

Virtualization is the abstraction of computer hardware resources. This definition is very general; however, the broad range of virtualization products, both hardware and software, makes a more specific definition difficult. There are hardware products that support virtualization, software products that create virtual systems, and hardware that assists with software virtualization. All of these products and options perform essentially the same function: they separate the operating system and applications from the underlying hardware.

A number of different types of virtualization are available, including the following:

- Hardware virtualization
- Full software virtualization
- Paravirtualization
- Hardware-assisted software virtualization

Although virtualization allows you to abstract resources away from the hardware layer, you'll still discover some limitations. With today's commercially available technology, virtualization—or at least the most popular types of virtualization—allows you to abstract only similar architectures. For example, if you use software virtualization that runs on x86 or x86_64 architecture, you can run only virtual hosts with either an x86 or x86_64 operating system. In other words, you can't virtualize a SPARC system on an x86 or x86_64 architecture.

At this time, several major virtualization products are on the market:

- VMware was one of the first companies to offer a fully virtualized hardware platform environment, including a range of products with fully virtualized environments. VMware was founded in 1988 and was acquired by EMC in 2003. In addition to hardware virtualization, VMware also offers some paravirtualized drivers.

- Microsoft Hyper-V was recently released. Hyper-V provides both fully virtualized and guest-aware (paravirtualized) virtualization (if you are running a Windows guest).

- Xen Hypervisor is an open-source standard for virtualization and runs on multiple platforms. The first public release of Xen was in 2003, and the company was acquired by Citrix in 2007. Xen currently supports both HVM (Hardware Virtual Machine) and PV (paravirtualized machine). Xen does not offer any paravirtualized drivers.

- Oracle VM is a free, next-generation server virtualization and management solution from Oracle that makes enterprise applications easier to deploy, manage, and support. The Oracle VM hypervisor is an open-source Xen project with Oracle enhancements that make it easier, faster, and more efficient. In addition, Oracle VM is currently the only virtualization product supported for the Oracle Relational Database Management System (RDBMS) and other Oracle products. Oracle VM supports both HVM and PV and provides a set of paravirtualized drivers for both Windows and Linux PVHVM (Paravirtualized Hardware Virtual Machines).

In addition, numerous proprietary hardware and software products allow you to virtualize specific vendors' hardware and operating systems.

Overview of Virtualization Technologies

Virtualization has been around for quite a while now; however, its mass appeal has only been realized with the extensive improvements that have appeared in the last few years. In virtualization's early days, you had to purchase very expensive hardware;

now, due to its ability to use commodity PC servers, you can download free virtualization software to get started.

A number of different virtualization technologies are available in the market today, including the following:

- Full software virtualization
- Hardware-assisted software virtualization or Hardware Virtual Machine (HVM)
- Paravirtualization or paravirtualized machine (PV)
- Hardware-assisted software virtualization with paravirtual drivers (PVHVM)
- Component or resource virtualization

Depending on your situation, you might be able to take advantage of one or more of these virtualization types. In this section, I'll explore each virtualization type, along with their pros and cons. Each type has its own attributes, which provide specific benefits. The type of virtualization that you choose depends on your needs. Oracle VM supports hardware-assisted software virtualization, paravirtualization, and the hybrid PVHVM.

Full Software Virtualization

In *full software virtualization,* all the hardware is simulated by a software program. Each device driver and process in the guest OS "believes" it is running on actual hardware, even though the underlying hardware is really a software program. Software virtualization even fools the OS into thinking that it is running on hardware.

One of the advantages of full software virtualization is that you can run any OS on it. It doesn't matter if the OS in question understands the underlying host hardware or not. Thus, older OSs and specialty OSs can run in this environment. The architecture is very flexible because you don't need a special understanding of the OS or hardware.

The OS hardware subsystem discovers the hardware in the normal fashion. It believes the hardware is really hardware. The hardware types and features that it discovers are usually fairly generic and might not be as full-featured as actual hardware devices, though the system is functional.

Another advantage of full software virtualization is that you don't need to purchase any additional hardware. With hardware-assisted software virtualization, you need to purchase hardware that supports advanced VM technology. Although this technology is included in most systems available today, some older hardware does not have this capability. To use this older hardware as a virtual host, you must use either full software virtualization or paravirtualization.

NOTE
Only hardware-assisted software virtualization requires advanced VM hardware features; full software virtualization does not. Oracle VM and VMware ESX work on older hardware that does not have any special CPU features. This type of virtualization is also known as emulation.

Unfortunately, full software virtualization adds overhead. This overhead translates into extra instructions and CPU time on the host, resulting in a slower system and higher CPU usage. With full software virtualization, the CPU instruction calls are trapped by the Virtual Machine Monitor (VMM) and then emulated in a software program. Therefore, every hardware instruction that would normally be handled by the hardware itself is now handled by a program.

For example, when the disk device driver makes an I/O call to the "virtual disk," the software in the VM system intercepts it, then processes it, and finally makes an I/O to the real underlying disk. The number of instructions to perform an I/O is greatly increased.

With networking, even more overhead is incurred since a network switch is simulated in the software. Depending on the amount of network activity, the overhead can be quite high. In fact, with severely overloaded host systems, you could possibly see network delays from the virtual switch itself. This is why sizing is so important.

Hardware-Assisted Software Virtualization

Hardware-assisted software virtualization is available with CPU chips with built-in virtualization support. Recently, with the introduction of the Intel VT and AMD-V technology, this virtualization type has become commoditized. This technology was first introduced on the IBM System/370 computer. It is similar to software virtualization, with the exception that some hardware functions are accelerated and assisted by hardware technology. Similar to software virtualization, the hardware instructions are trapped and processed, but this time using hardware in the virtualization components of the CPU chip.

By using hardware-assisted software virtualization, you get the benefits of software virtualization, such as the ability to use any OS without modifying it, and, at the same time, achieve better performance. Because of virtualization's importance, significant effort is going into providing more support for hardware-assisted software virtualization. Hardware-assisted virtualization also supports any operating system.

Using hardware-assisted software virtualization, Oracle VM lets you install and run Linux and Solaris x86-based OSs as well as Microsoft Windows. With other virtualization techniques, Oracle VM only allows Linux OSs. This technique also makes migrating from VMware systems to Oracle VM easier.

As mentioned earlier, both Intel and AMD are committed to support for hardware-assisted software virtualization. They both introduced virtualization technology around the mid-2005–2006 period, which is not that long ago, and their support has improved the functionality and performance of virtualization. Intel and AMD do not yet fully support paravirtualization. Hardware-assisted software virtualization components are changing at a very fast pace, however, with new features and functionality being introduced continually.

NOTE
Hardware-assisted virtualization is really the long-term virtualization solution. Applications such as Xen will be mainly used for management.

Intel

Intel supports virtualization via its VT-x technology. The Intel VT-x technology is now part of many Intel chipsets, including the Pentium, Xeon, and Core processors families. The VT-x extensions support an Input/Output Memory Management Unit (IOMMU) that allows virtualized systems to access I/O devices directly. Ethernet and graphics devices can now have their DMA and interrupts directly mapped via the hardware. In the latest versions of the Intel VT technology, extended page tables have been added to allow direct translation from guest virtual addresses to physical addresses.

AMD

AMD supports virtualization via the AMD-V technology. The AMD-V technology includes a rapid virtualization indexing technology to accelerate virtualization. This technology is designed to assist with the virtual-to-physical translation of pages in a virtualized environment. Because this operation is one of the most common, by optimizing this function, performance is greatly enhanced. AMD virtualization products are available on both the Opteron and Athlon processor families.

The virtual machine that uses the hardware-assisted software virtualization model has become known as the Hardware Virtual Machine or HVM. This terminology will be used throughout the rest of this chapter and refers to the fully software virtualized model with hardware assist.

Paravirtualization

In *paravirtualization,* the guest OS is aware of and interfaces with the underlying host OS. A paravirtualized kernel in the guest understands the underlying host technology and takes advantage of that fact. Because the host OS is not faking the guest 100 percent, the amount of resources needed for virtualization is greatly reduced. In addition, paravirtualized device drivers for the guest can interface with the host system, reducing overhead. The idea behind paravirtualization is to reduce both the complexity and overhead involved in virtualization. By paravirtualizing both the host and guest operating system, very expensive functions are offloaded from the guest to the host OS.

The guest essentially calls special system calls that then allow these functions to run within the host OS. When using a system such as Oracle VM, the host operating system acts in much the same way as a guest operating system. The hardware device drivers interface with a layer known as the hypervisor. The hypervisor, which is also known as the Virtual Machine Monitor (VMM), was mentioned earlier in this chapter. There are two types of hypervisor: The type 1 hypervisor runs directly on the host hardware; the type 2 or hosted hypervisor runs in software.

Hybrid Virtualization Technology

Since Oracle Enterprise Linux (OEL5), Oracle has provided the ability to create a Hardware Virtualized Machine (HVM) that uses a few specific paravirtualized device drivers for network and I/O. This hybrid virtualization technology provides the benefits of a paravirtualized virtual machine with the additional hardware accelerations available within the Hardware Virtual Machine (HVM). This technology is still new but might be the future of virtualization.

The Hypervisor

The hypervisor is what makes virtualization possible. The hypervisor is the component that translates the virtual machines into the underlying hardware. The type of hypervisors that we are concerned with are the type 1 and type 2 hypervisors.

Type 1 Hypervisor

The *type 1* (or *embedded*) hypervisor is a layer that runs directly on the host hardware, interfacing with the CPU, memory, and devices. Oracle VM and VMware ESX Server both use the type 1 hypervisor. The hypervisor treats the host OS in much the same way as a guest OS. The host OS is referred to as Domain 0 or dom0 and guests are referred to as Domain U or domU, as shown in Figure 13-1. Here you can see that that all virtual machines must go through the hypervisor to get to the hardware. The dom0 domain is a virtual system just like the domU virtual machines (but has more capabilities, as covered later in this chapter). Currently, the type 1 hypervisor is considered the most efficient and is the most recommended hypervisor.

NOTE

Even though Oracle VM and VMware both use a type 1 hypervisor, these hypervisors are significantly different. VMware handles device drivers directly in the hypervisor; Xen handles them in dom0 or a driver domain.

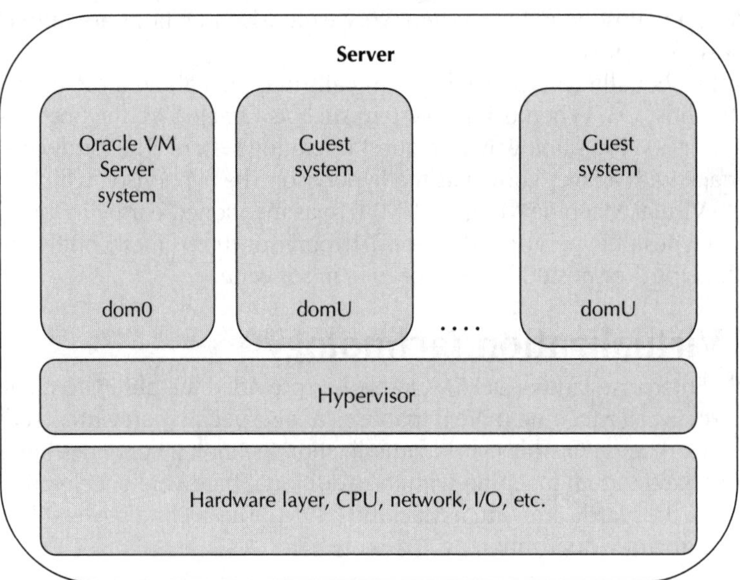

FIGURE 13-1. *The type 1 hypervisor represented graphically*

As you can see from Figure 13-1, the dom0 domain does not differ much from other domains in the virtual environment, except that you access it differently and it is always enabled by default. In addition, dom0 has unlimited rights to hardware, whereas domU only has access through a layer of indirection and only to what dom0 grants it. Because the type 1 hypervisor is essentially part of the OS, it must be installed on the hardware itself and support the devices installed on the system.

Type 2 Hypervisor

The *type 2* or *hosted* hypervisor runs as a program and is used for software virtualization. Because the type 2 hypervisor runs as a program, it neither has the same priority as the type 1 hypervisor, nor does it have the ability to access the hardware directly. Its main advantage is that you can install it on a variety of host systems without modification. The type 2 hypervisor works with both full software virtualization and hardware-assisted software virtualization. VMware Server is an example of a type 2 hypervisor.

Recently Oracle has released a new product, Oracle VM VirtualBox. Oracle VM VirtualBox is a type 2 hypervisor–based product.

Introduction to Oracle VM

In recent years, virtualization has changed the way we look at computing. Instead of using many different computer systems for different tasks, with virtualization, we can use a single system to host many applications. Not only has virtualization increased in popularity, but it has also sparked new hardware CPU innovation, including Intel VT-x and AMD-V technologies. Over the next few years, virtualization will be a core technology in every data center. Oracle VM, although a relatively new entry in the virtualization market, is based on stable and proven technology.

Oracle is relatively new to the virtualization arena, but Oracle's technology is based on a relatively long history of virtualization. Oracle VM was introduced at the Oracle World conference in 2007. The product was made available for download shortly after that. This was touted by Oracle as one of their largest software announcements in the history of the company. The Oracle VM product consists of two major components: the Oracle VM Server and the Oracle VM Manager.

Oracle VM 3.*x* was introduced at the Oracle OpenWorld conference in 2011. This product introduced a completely new user interface and provides a more stable platform for virtualization.

History of Oracle VM

Oracle VM is a relative newcomer, considering that the biggest competition, VMware, was introduced in 1998 and is majority owned by EMC. VMware introduced their first virtualization product for the desktop in 1999 and their first server product in 2001. It was really not until 2003 that VMware introduced the VMware Virtual Center, the VMotion and Virtual SMP technology. This is what made virtualization a viable product for server consolidation in the Enterprise. Prior to that, VMware was primarily used only as a test or training platform. In 2004 VMware introduced their 64-bit support. This is also the year that EMC acquired VMware.

As with Oracle VM, VMware is supported on the Intel/AMD x86 platforms only. This in part has led to the race for both Intel and AMD to focus their efforts on providing an extensive set of features that optimize virtualization on their platforms. With both Oracle VM and VMware, fully virtualized systems are supported. In addition, Oracle VM supports paravirtualization, whereas the underlying operating system realizes that it is running on a virtual system and makes intelligent choices based on that knowledge. VMware provides replacement drivers for video and I/O, but it isn't the same as paravirtualization. Both products also support any OS that will run on the x86 platform in a fully virtualized guest.

The third major player in the virtualization market is Microsoft with their Hyper-V product. The Microsoft Hyper-V virtualization solution is a hypervisor-based virtualization product that was introduced in 2008. This product appears to be primarily targeted to the Microsoft Windows environment.

One final player in the virtualization market is Citrix. Citrix recently purchased XenSource, but isn't pushing it as a dominant platform in virtualization. Citrix tends to focus more on the desktop replacement rather than on the virtualization environment.

These products do not represent the entirety of the virtualization market and virtualization products, but represent the main competition to Oracle VM, which is the focus of this book. There are many other virtualization products, including hardware virtualization, that will not be covered here.

Even though Oracle VM is a relative newcomer to virtualization, the technology is not. Oracle VM is based on the Xen hypervisor, which is a proven and stable technology. So, in order to understand the history of Oracle VM, you must first look at the history of the Xen hypervisor.

History of Xen

The Xen virtualization product began around the same time as VMware. It started at the University of Cambridge Computer Laboratory and released its first version in 2003. The leader of the project then went on to found XenSource. Unlike both VMware and Hyper-V, Xen is maintained by the open source community under the GNU General Public License. In 2007 XenSource was acquired by Citrix Systems.

Whereas VMware and Hyper-V only support the x86 architecture, Xen supports x86, x86_64, Itanium, and Power-PC architectures. The Xen architecture is based on a hypervisor, as mentioned earlier in this chapter. This hypervisor originally only allowed Linux, NetBSD, and Solaris operating systems to operate in a paravirtualized environment. However, since the introduction of the virtualization support in hardware and Xen 3.0, unmodified OSs can now operate in Xen.

Oracle VM 2.2 is based on the Xen 3.4 kernel. In order to fully appreciate where the Xen 3.4 kernel is, let's look at a brief history of the Xen hypervisor. The following table gives a brief timeline of the Xen history:

Date	Development
2002	Development begins on the Xen hypervisor.
2003	The first release of Xen was made available.
2004	The second release of Xen was made available and the first Xen developers' summit was held.
2005	XenSource was founded and version 3.0 was released.
2006	XenEnterprise was released. This was also when Linux began adding enhancements for virtualization. This was also when VMware and Microsoft begin adopting paravirtualization as well. In addition, this year marked the launch of the Amazon EC2 (Enterprise Cloud 2).

Date	Development
2007	XenSource was acquired by Citrix. Oracle announced Oracle VM based on the Xen hypervisor. The original version was Oracle VM 2.1.
2008	Xen began showing up as embedded in Flash.
2009	Oracle released Oracle VM 2.2 based on Xen 3.4.
2011	Oracle released Oracle VM 3.x at the Oracle OpenWorld conference.

This long history of Xen virtualization has allowed Oracle to quickly enter the virtualization market with a stable and proven technology.

Components of Oracle VM

Oracle VM is made up of two main components: the VM Server and the VM Manager. The VM Server is the hardware on which the hypervisor and virtual machines reside. The VM Server is made up of a Domain 0 or Dom0, which hosts the VM Agent and virtual machines. It is the Agent that communicates with the VM Manager in order to configure and manage the VM Server and VM Server Farm.

The VM Manager is a piece of software that runs on any Linux system and is used to manage the VM Server Farm. From the VM Manager, both the VM Servers and virtual machines are managed. The VM Manager is a required component, even if OEM Cloud Control is being used to manage the VM Server Farm. OEM Cloud Control uses the VM Manager via an API to manage the VM Server Farm.

Oracle VM Templates

One of the main advantages of Oracle VM is the vast library of preconfigured VM templates that are available from Oracle's Web site. These templates can be downloaded and installed on Oracle VM, thus allowing for quick deployment of virtual machines that include preconfigured software, such as Oracle E-Business Suite or PeopleSoft.

Oracle is constantly updating the library of templates. Please check Oracle's Web site to get the latest list of templates that are available for Oracle VM.

Configuring OEM Cloud Control for Oracle VM

In order to manage Oracle VM from OEM Cloud Control, you must first have an Oracle VM Manager system configured and available. OEM Cloud Control uses the VM Manager API to communicate with and manage the Oracle VM environment. Before attempting to install OEM support for Oracle VM for x86, verify that the VM

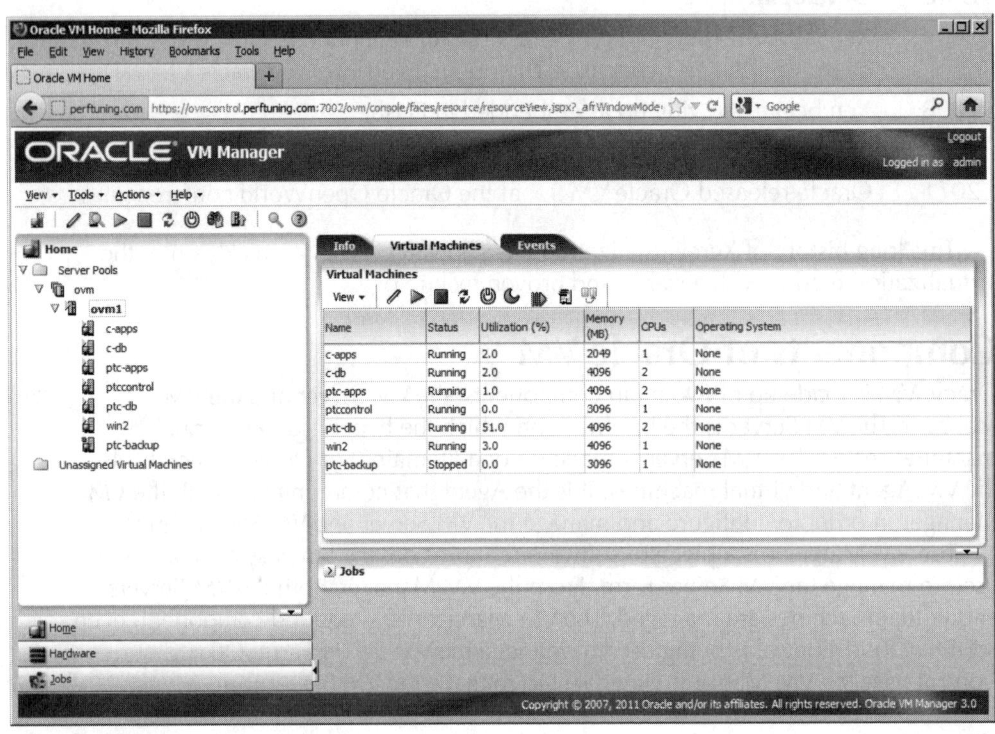

Name	Status	Utilization (%)	Memory (MB)	CPUs	Operating System
c-apps	Running	2.0	2049	1	None
c-db	Running	2.0	4096	2	None
ptc-apps	Running	1.0	4096	2	None
ptccontrol	Running	0.0	3096	1	None
ptc-db	Running	51.0	4096	2	None
win2	Running	3.0	4096	1	None
ptc-backup	Stopped	0.0	3096	1	None

FIGURE 13-2. *The OVM Manager screen*

Manager is up and running properly and that you are able to access it with a valid username and password. The OVM Manager screen is shown in Figure 13-2.

Once you have verified that the OVM Manager is functioning properly, you are ready to begin configuring OEM Cloud Control for OVM management. Depending on the version of OEM Cloud Control 12*c* that you have installed, you might have to perform some configuration steps in order for Oracle VM management to be available.

The first step is to set up the Oracle Virtualization plug-in in OEM Cloud Control 12*c*. The second step is to configure Oracle VM Management.

Configure the Oracle Virtualization Plug-in

From the OEM Cloud Control Console, select Setup | Extensibility | Self Update. Here you should see the Self Update screen as shown in Figure 13-3.

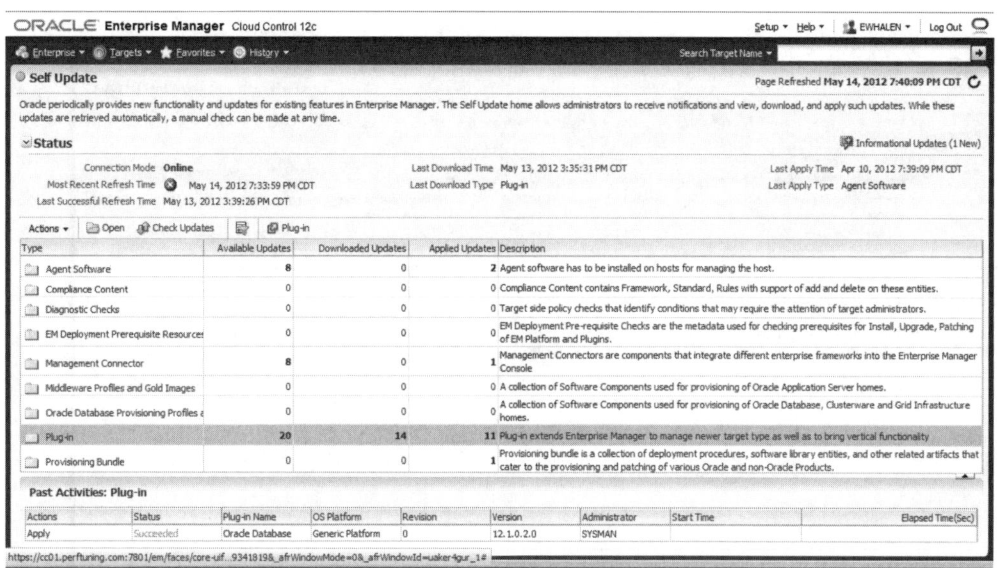

FIGURE 13-3. *The Self Update screen*

From the Self Update screen, click the Plug-in link. This will open the Plug-in Updates screen. Scroll down until you see Oracle Virtualization. This might be already installed, or might show as available, as in Figure 13-4.

Select the line with Oracle Virtualization and click the Download button. A dialog box will pop up asking whether to download immediately or to schedule the download. It is your choice. Choose Select to continue. Eventually the software will be downloaded to the Software Library and show as Downloaded. At that point, it can be installed.

In order to install Oracle Virtualization support, select the line that contains Oracle Virtualization (which now shows Downloaded Status) and click the Apply button. This will take you to the Plug-ins screen. To get to the Plug-ins screen directly, select Setup | Extensibility | Plug-ins. Expand Servers, Storage and Network so that you can see the Oracle Virtualization option as shown in Figure 13-5.

Select the Deploy On drop-down and select Management Servers. You will be prompted for the Repository Sys password in the pop-up box. Enter the sys password and click Continue. Once the prerequisite checks have completed successfully, click Next to continue. You will receive a warning that there will be some management server downtime. Check the box that you have backed up the Repository and OMS,

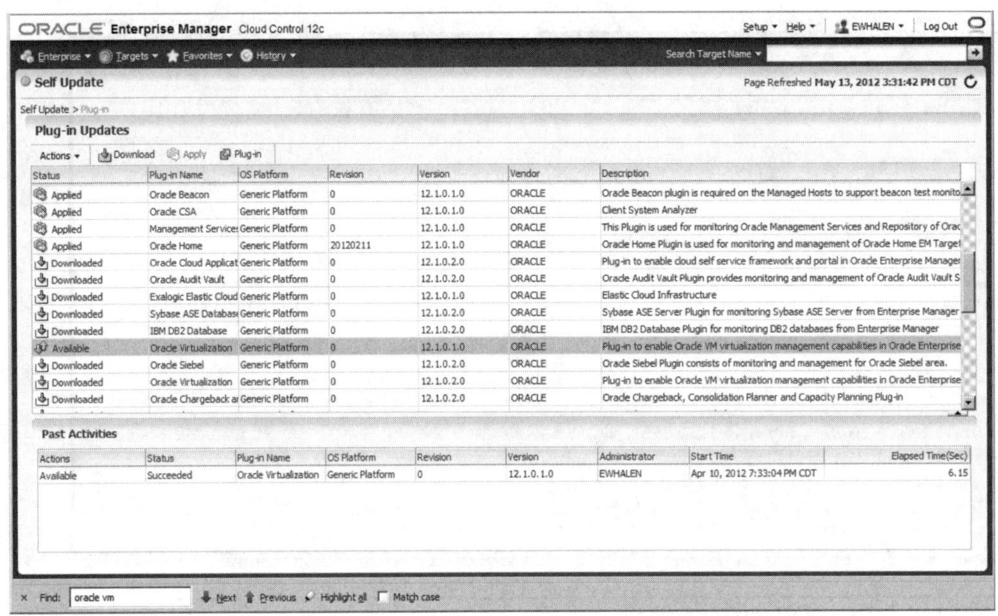

FIGURE 13-4. *The Plug-in Updates screen*

and click the Deploy button to continue. You will be informed that the deployment is in progress.

NOTE
During the deployment, the OMS server will become unavailable for several minutes.

To determine the status of the deployment, the following command can be used:

```
$ emctl status oms -details
```

An example of this command is shown here:

```
[oracle@cc01 ~]$ emctl status oms -details
Oracle Enterprise Manager Cloud Control 12c Release 12.1.0.1.0
Copyright (c) 1996, 2012 Oracle Corporation.  All rights reserved.
```

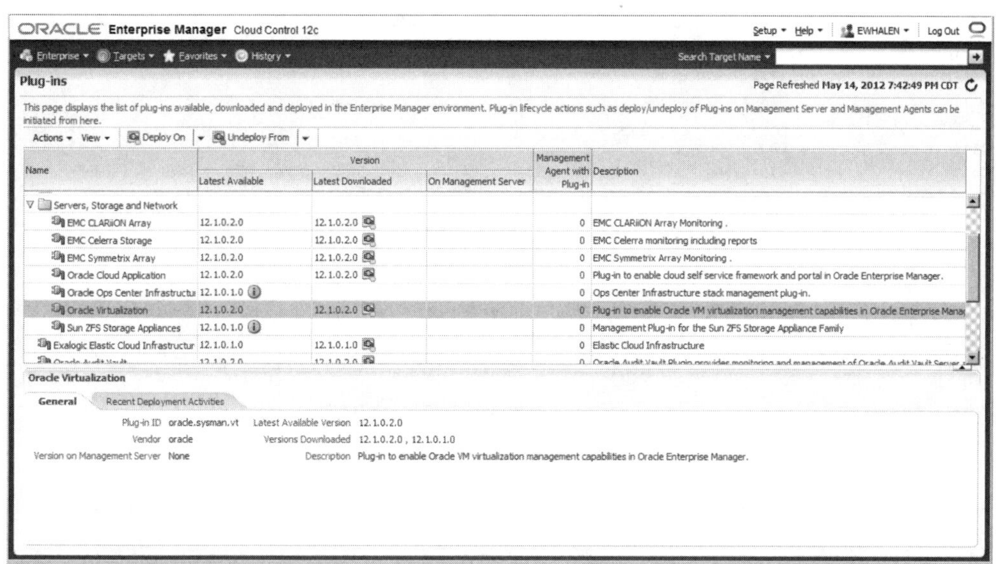

FIGURE 13-5. *The Plug-ins screen*

```
Enter Enterprise Manager Root (SYSMAN) Password :
Console Server Host : cc01.perftuning.com
HTTP Console Port   : 7789
HTTPS Console Port  : 7801
HTTP Upload Port    : 4890
HTTPS Upload Port   : 4901
OMS is not configured with SLB or virtual hostname
Agent Upload is locked.
OMS Console is locked.
Active CA ID: 1
Console URL: https://cc01.perftuning.com:7801/em
Upload URL: https://cc01.perftuning.com:4901/empbs/upload

WLS Domain Information
Domain Name      : GCDomain
Admin Server Host: cc01.perftuning.com

Managed Server Information
Managed Server Instance Name: EMGC_OMS1
Managed Server Instance Host: cc01.perftuning.com

Oracle Management Server is down, may be due to the following plugin being deployed/undeployed on
the server:
```

```
Plugin Deployment/Undeployment Status

Destination          : OMS - cc01.perftuning.com:4890_Management_Service
Plugin Name          : Oracle Virtualization
Version              : 12.1.0.2.0
ID                   : oracle.sysman.vt
Content              : Plugin
Action               : Deployment
Status               : Deploying
Steps Info:
---------------------------------------- ------------------------- ----------
Step                                     Start Time                End Time
Status
---------------------------------------- ------------------------- ----------
Start deployment                         5/14/12 7:49:05 PM CDT    5/14/12 7:49:05 PM CDT    Success

Initialize                               5/14/12 7:49:19 PM CDT    5/14/12 7:49:25 PM CDT    Success

Install software                         5/14/12 7:49:26 PM CDT    5/14/12 7:49:27 PM CDT    Success

Validate plug-in home                    5/14/12 7:49:27 PM CDT    5/14/12 7:49:27 PM CDT    Success

Perform custom pre-configuration         5/14/12 7:49:27 PM CDT    5/14/12 7:49:29 PM CDT    Success

Check mandatory patches                  5/14/12 7:49:29 PM CDT    5/14/12 7:49:29 PM CDT    Success

Generate metadata SQL                    5/14/12 7:49:29 PM CDT    5/14/12 7:49:42 PM CDT    Success

Pre-configure repository                 5/14/12 7:49:42 PM CDT    5/14/12 7:49:42 PM CDT    Success

Pre-register DLF                         5/14/12 7:49:42 PM CDT    5/14/12 7:49:42 PM CDT    Success

Stop management server                   5/14/12 7:49:42 PM CDT    5/14/12 7:50:28 PM CDT    Success

Configure repository                     5/14/12 7:50:28 PM CDT    5/14/12 7:52:47 PM CDT    Success

Register DLF                             5/14/12 7:52:47 PM CDT    5/14/12 7:53:59 PM CDT    Success

Configure middle tier                    5/14/12 7:53:59 PM CDT    N/A                       Running

---------------------------------------- ------------------------- ---------
```

Once the deployment has completed, the OEM Cloud Control Console will once again become available.

This process must now be repeated in order to deploy the Oracle Virtualization Plug-in on a Management Agent. From the Plug-ins screen, select Oracle Virtualization again. This time, from the Deploy On drop-down menu, select Management Agent. You will see the Deploy Plug-in on Management Agent screen, as shown in the following illustration.

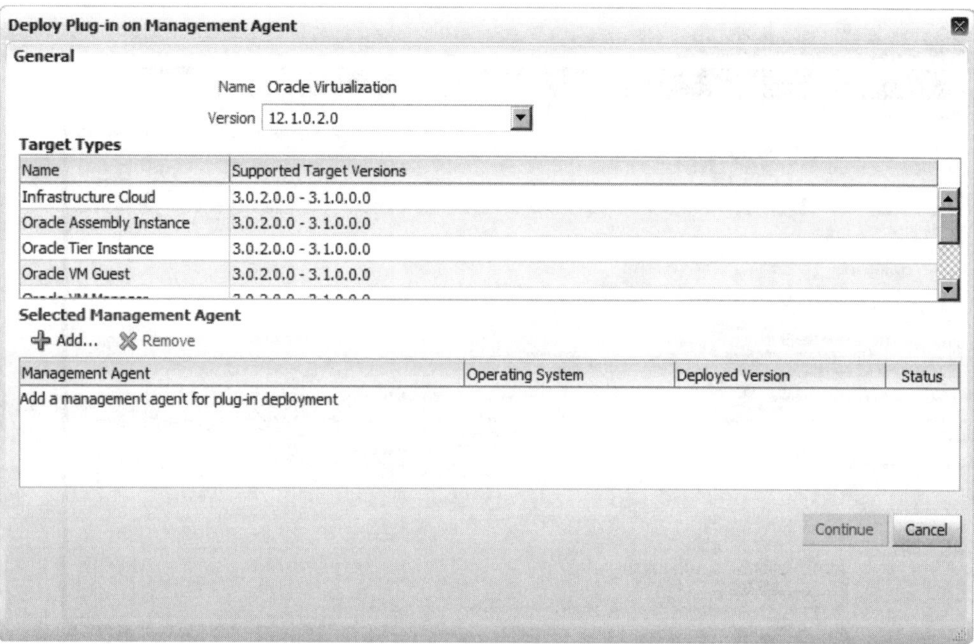

Click the Add button and add a Management Agent to be used to communicate with the OVM Manager. In this example, we have chosen the OEM Cloud Control OMS Agent. Click Continue to proceed. After the prerequisite checks have completed successfully, click Next. After reviewing the details, click Deploy to proceed. In a few minutes the Agent Plug-in will be complete and you are ready to configure Virtualization Management within OEM Cloud Control.

Configure Oracle Virtualization Management

Once the Oracle Virtualization Plug-in has been deployed, it can be accessed via the OEM Cloud Control Console. Select Enterprise | Infrastructure Cloud | Home from the main menu. This will invoke the Infrastructure Cloud Home screen as shown in Figure 13-6. As you can see, at this point nothing has been configured.

In order to use the Infrastructure Cloud features of Cloud Control, you must configure them. The first step is to register an Oracle VM Manager system. From the Infrastructure Cloud drop-down menu, select Register OVM Manager. This will bring up the OVM Manager Registration screen as shown in Figure 13-7 (filled in).

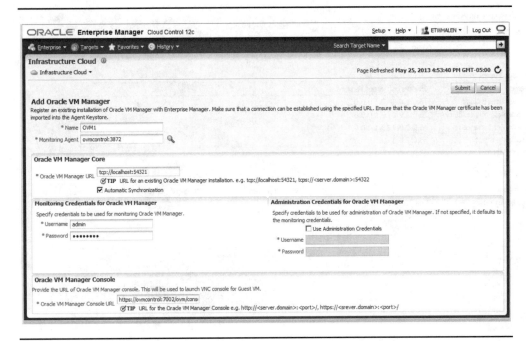

FIGURE 13-6. *The Infrastructure Cloud Home screen*

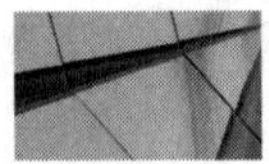

NOTE

The URL for the VM Manager Core does not include /ovm/manager on the end. In this example, Oracle VM Manager Core is https://ovmcontrol.perftuning.com:7002 and Oracle VM Manager Console is https://ovmcontrol.perftuning.com:7002/ovm/console.

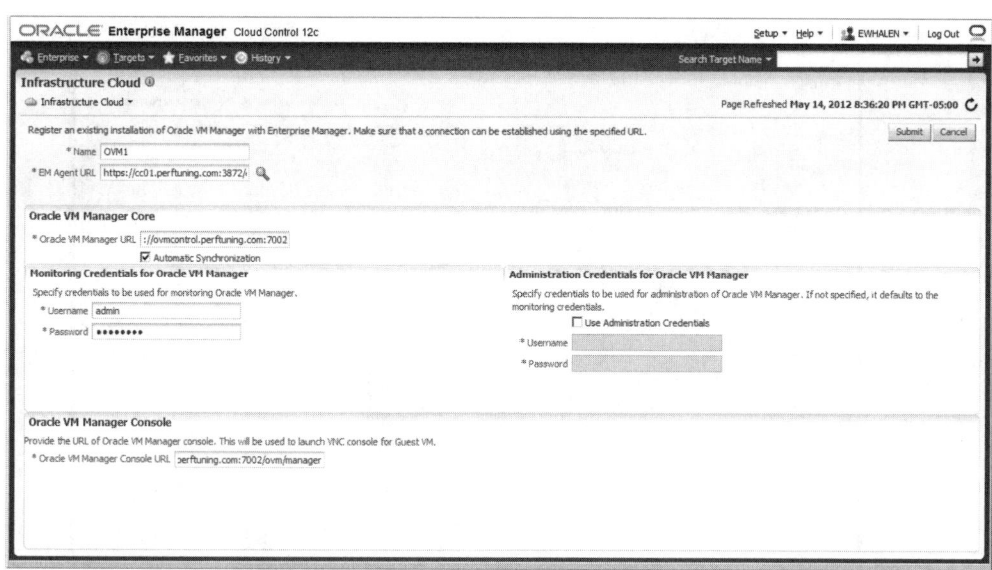

FIGURE 13-7. *The Infrastructure Cloud OVM Manager Registration screen*

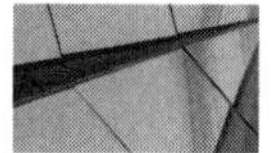

NOTE

Newer versions of OEM Cloud Control 12c require the URL for the VM Manager Core to use the form tcps://<server.domain>:port, where port is 54321 for tcp and 54322 for tcps. In this example, Oracle VM Manager Core is tcps://ovmcontrol:54322 and Oracle VM Manager Console is https://ovmcontrol .perftuning.com:7002/ovm/console. However, we personally had problems with the VM Manager Core URL in the latest plug-in (12.1.0.4.0) when trying to use anything but tcp://localhost:54321 for the VM Manager Core URL.

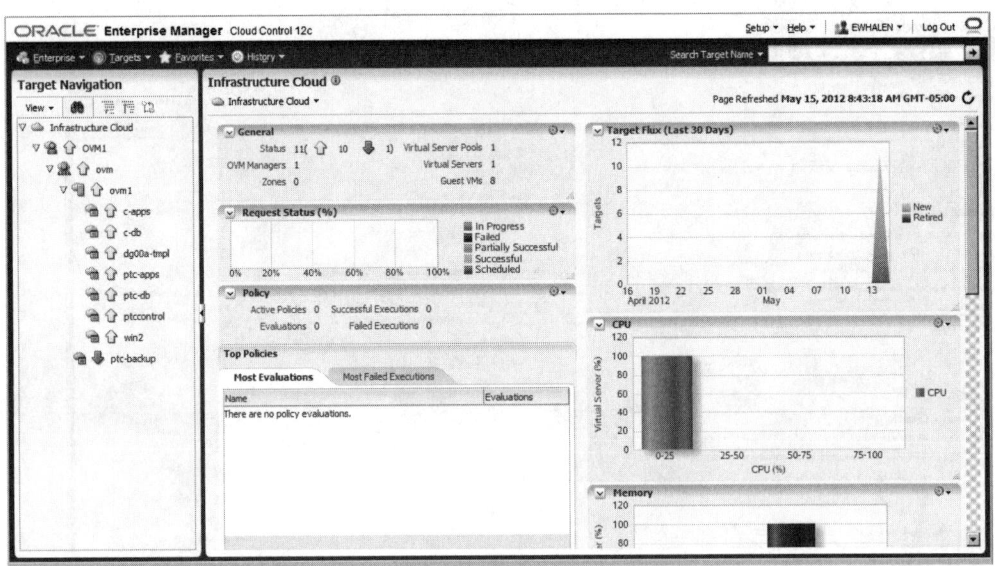

FIGURE 13-8. *The Infrastructure Cloud screen*

After you submit the job, it will take a few minutes for the Infrastructure Cloud monitoring to begin. Eventually the Infrastructure Cloud screen will become populated as shown in Figure 13-8.

At this point, the OEM Cloud Control server has been configured to allow management of Oracle VM for x86 hosts and virtual machines. In the next section you will see how to use this tool to manage and monitor the OVM systems.

Managing the Oracle VM Manager from OEM Cloud Control

Using OEM Cloud Control to manage the VM Infrastructure is fairly straightforward and easy to do. Depending on which level of focus you have selected from the Target Navigation menu, you will see the VM Manager, VM Server Pool, or VM Server management screens. Each of these screens lets you manage a different part of the Infrastructure Cloud. This section will explore those three levels of management.

Managing the VM Manager

Select the VM Manager in the Target Navigation pane in order to manage the VM Manager. This will bring up the VM Manager screen as shown in Figure 13-9.

The VM Manager screen is only the starting point for the Oracle VM Manager management and monitoring. The VM Manager drop-down menu contains a number of tools that can be accessed by selecting them from this drop-down. They include the following:

- **Home** The VM Manager Home screen.
- **Monitoring**
  - **All Metrics** This is where you will find access to all of the VM Manager metrics and view the current values.
  - **Metric and Collection Settings** From this page you can easily find and modify all of the metric thresholds for VM Manager monitoring.
  - **Metric Collection Errors** Provides a list of metric collection errors.

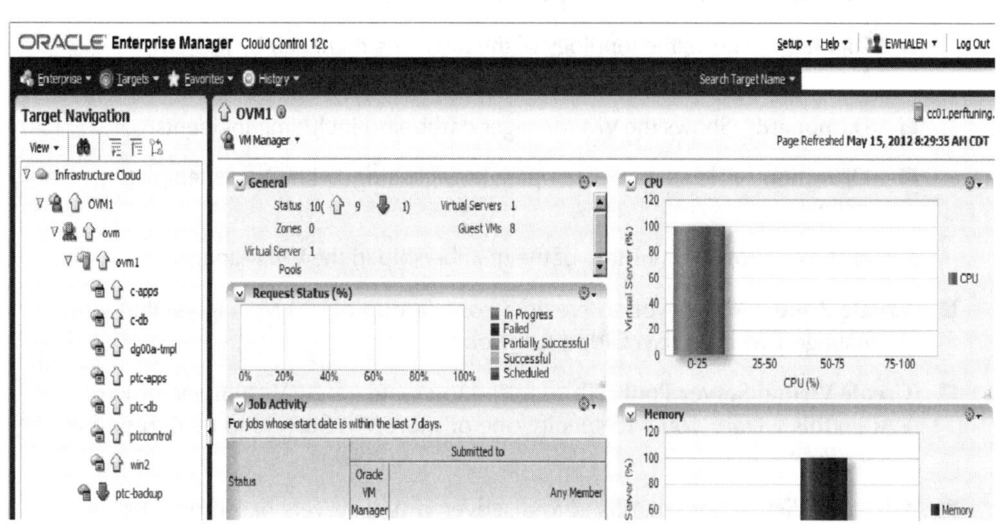

FIGURE 13-9. *The VM Manager screen*

  - **Status History** Provides information on the availability of the VM Manager.
  - **Incident Manager** This is a link directly to the Incident Manager.
  - **Alert History** This provides a graphical display of the Alert History for the VM Manager.
  - **Blackouts** In this screen you can view current blackouts and create new blackouts for VM Manager objects.
- **Control**
  - **Create Blackout** Allows you to create a blackout.
  - **End Blackout** Allows you to end a previously created blackout.
- **Job Activity** Shows job activity for the current VM Manager.
- **Information Publisher Reports** This brings up all of the reports related to the VM Manager. Here you will find a number of reports that you can run on the state of the VM Manager as well as its configuration.
- **Members**
  - **Show All** Shows all of the members that are managed by this VM Manager.
  - **Topology** Shows the topology of the members managed by this VM Manager.
  - **Dashboard** Shows the VM Manager dashboard including incidents.
  - **Operation** Allows you to compare target settings with Oracle template settings.
  - **History** Provides a history of the membership in the VM Manager.
- **Create Zone** Allows you to create a zone (group of VM Managers) that will be managed within OEM Cloud Control.
- **Create Virtual Server Pool** This is used to create a new Virtual Server Pool. Within this wizard you will specify one or more VM Servers to be part of the Server Pool.
- **Discover Virtual Server** Used to discover virtual servers based on a list of one or more IP addresses or long host names.
- **Synchronize** Synchronizes the OEM Infrastructure Cloud information with the Oracle VM Manager.

- **Administration**
  - **Network** Used to manage Networks, VLAN Groups, and Virtual Network Interface Cards.
  - **Storage** Used to manage file servers and storage arrays.
  - **Storage Repository** This is where you go to manage the Storage Repositories that are defined within the Server Pool.
  - **Yum Repository** Here you can manage the Yum Repository on the VM Servers.
  - **Unowned Virtual Server** This screen will show any unowned VM Servers.
- **Configuration**
  - **Last Collected** Shows the latest collected VM Manager configuration information.
  - **Topology** Shows the current VM Manager topology.
  - **Search** Provides a list of search criteria that is used to view specific VM Manager components.
  - **Compare** Used to compare different VM Managers.
  - **Comparison Job Activity** Provides a list of currently running comparison jobs.
  - **History** Provides a list of previously run jobs.
  - **Save** Used to save the current configuration of a VM Manager.
  - **Saved** Lists all saved configurations.
- **Compliance**
  - **Results** Provides a list of current compliance violations.
  - **Standard Associations** Provides a list of compliance standards that are associated with the target.
  - **Real-time Observations** Provides a list of real-time compliance standards violations.
- **Target Setup**
  - **Edit VM Manager** This is a link to the setup for OEM Cloud Control configuration for the VM Manager.
  - **Monitoring Configuration** Used to view or modify the monitoring configuration of the VM Manager target.
  - **Administrator Access** Used to grant administrator access to the VM Manager instance target.

- **Remove Target** Used to remove the VM Manager target.
- **Add to Group** Used to add the VM Manager target to a group.
- **Properties** Used to view and modify the VM Manager target properties.

- **Target Information** Provides a quick link to basic VM Manager status information.

Unlike in previous versions of OEM, most screens are now accessed via the drop-down menus rather than the related links. This provides a much quicker and easier method of navigating OEM Cloud Control 12*c*.

Managing the VM Server Pool

Select the VM Server Pool in the Target Navigation pane in order to manage the VM Server Pool. This will bring up the VM Server Pool screen as shown in Figure 13-10.

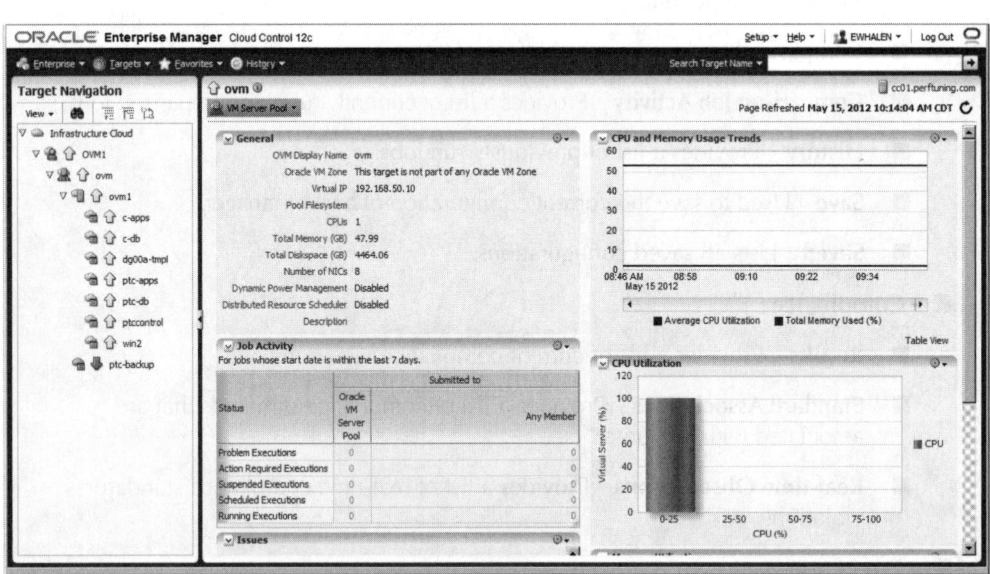

FIGURE 13-10. *The VM Server Pool screen*

The VM Server Pool screen is only the starting point for the Oracle VM Server Pool management and monitoring. The VM Server Pool drop-down menu contains a number of tools that can be accessed by selecting them from this drop-down. Many are the same as for the VM Manager drop-downs, but there are several differences. They include the following:

- **Home** The VM Server Pool Home screen.
- **Monitoring**
  - **All Metrics** This is where you will find access to all of the VM Server Pool metrics and view the current values.
  - **Metric and Collection Settings** From this page you can easily find and modify all of the metric thresholds for VM Server Pool monitoring.
  - **Metric Collection Errors** Provides a list of metric collection errors.
  - **Status History** Provides information on the availability of the VM Server Pool.
  - **Incident Manager** This is a link directly to the Incident Manager.
  - **Alert History** This provides a graphical display of the Alert History for the VM Server Pool.
  - **Blackouts** In this screen you can view current blackouts and create new blackouts for VM Server Pool objects.
- **Control**
  - **Create Blackout** Allows you to create a blackout.
  - **End Blackout** Allows you to end a previously created blackout.
- **Job Activity** Shows job activity for the current VM Server Pool.
- **Information Publisher Reports** This brings up all of the reports related to the VM Server Pool. Here you will find a number of reports that you can run on the state of the VM Server Pool as well as its configuration.
- **Members**
  - **Show All** Shows all of the members that are managed by this VM Server Pool. For the VM Server Pool, members are made up of virtual machines.
  - **Topology** Shows the topology of the members managed by this VM Server Pool. These include VM Servers and virtual machines.
  - **Dashboard** Shows the VM Server Pool dashboard including incidents.

  - **Operation** Allows you to compare target settings with Oracle template settings.
  - **History** Provides a history of the membership in the VM Manager.
- **OVM Events** This provides a list of events (failures and so on) that have occurred within the VM Server Pool.
- **Manage DRS/DPM Policies** Provides a screen where you can manage DRS (Distributed Resource Scheduler) and DPM (Distributed Power Management) policies.
- **Deploy**
  - **Assembly** Used to deploy an assembly. An assembly is like a template, but it can include multiple virtual machines and the relationship between them.
  - **Template** Used to deploy a virtual machine from a template.
  - **ISO** Used to deploy a virtual machine from an ISO image.
  - **PXE** Used to deploy a virtual machine using PXE boot.
- **Configuration**
  - **Last Collected** Shows the latest collected VM Server Pool configuration information.
  - **Topology** Shows the current VM Server Pool topology.
  - **Search** Provides a list of search criteria that is used to view specific VM Server Pool components.
  - **Compare** Used to compare different VM Server Pools.
  - **Comparison Job Activity** Provides a list of currently running comparison jobs.
  - **History** Provides a list of previously run jobs.
  - **Save** Used to save the current configuration of a VM Server Pool.
  - **Saved** Lists all saved configurations.
- **Compliance**
  - **Results** Provides a list of current compliance violations.
  - **Standard Associations** Provides a list of compliance standards that are associated with the target.
  - **Real-time Observations** Provides a list of real-time compliance standards violations.

- **Target Setup**
  - **Edit VM Server Pool** This is a link to the setup for OEM Cloud Control configuration for the VM Server Pool. Here you can add and remove virtual servers.
  - **Monitoring Configuration** Used to view or modify the monitoring configuration of the VM Server Pool target.
  - **Administrator Access** Used to grant administrator access to the VM Server Pool instance target.
  - **Remove Target** Used to remove the VM Server Pool target.
  - **Add to Group** Used to add the VM Server Pool target to a group.
  - **Properties** Used to view and modify the VM Server Pool target properties.
- **Target Information** Provides a quick link to basic VM Server Pool status information.

Managing VM Server

Select the VM Server in the Target Navigation pane in order to manage the VM Server. This will bring up the VM Server screen as shown in Figure 13-11.

The VM Server screen is only the starting point for the Oracle VM Server management and monitoring. The VM Server drop-down menu contains a number of tools that can be accessed by selecting them from this drop-down. They include the following:

- **Home** The VM Server Home screen.
- **Monitoring**
  - **All Metrics** This is where you will find access to all of the VM Server metrics and view the current values.
  - **Metric and Collection Settings** From this page you can easily find and modify all of the metric thresholds for VM Server monitoring.
  - **Metric Collection Errors** Provides a list of metric collection errors.
  - **Status History** Provides information on the availability of the VM Server.
  - **Incident Manager** This is a link directly to the Incident Manager.
  - **Alert History** This provides a graphical display of the Alert History for the VM Server.
  - **Blackouts** In this screen you can view current blackouts and create new blackouts for VM Server objects.

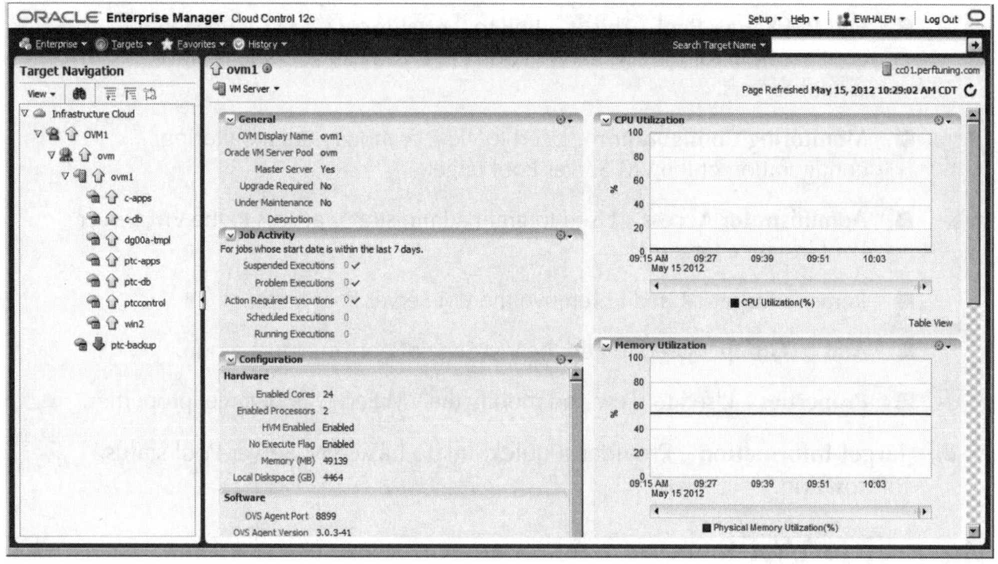

FIGURE 13-11. *The VM Server screen*

- **Control**
  - **Start** Starts the VM Server if it is currently in the Stopped state.
  - **Stop** Stops the VM Server if it is currently in the Running state
  - **Restart** Restarts the VM Server system.
  - **Create Blackout** Allows you to create a blackout.
  - **End Blackout** Allows you to end a previously created blackout.
- **Job Activity** Shows job activity for the current VM Server.
- **Information Publisher Reports** This brings up all of the reports related to the VM Server. Here you will find a number of reports that you can run on the state of the VM Server as well as its configuration.

- **Members**
  - **Show All** Shows all of the members that are managed by this VM Server.
- **OVM Events** This provides a list of events (failures and so on) that have occurred within the VM Server Pool.
- **Start Maintenance** Places the VM Server system into maintenance mode.
- **Stop Maintenance** Takes the VM Server system out of maintenance mode.
- **Rediscover Virtual Server** The Rediscover Virtual Server job will synchronize the OEM Infrastructure Cloud with the VM Manager.
- **Upgrade** Performs a Yum upgrade on the VM Server System.
- **Deploy**
  - **Assembly** Used to deploy an assembly. An assembly is like a template, but it can include multiple virtual machines and the relationship between them.
  - **Template** Used to deploy a virtual machine from a template.
  - **ISO** Used to deploy a virtual machine from an ISO image.
  - **PXE** Used to deploy a virtual machine using PXE boot.
- **Configuration**
  - **Last Collected** Shows the latest collected VM Server configuration information.
  - **Topology** Shows the current VM Server topology.
  - **Search** Provides a list of search criteria that is used to view specific VM Server components.
  - **Compare** Used to compare different VM Servers.
  - **Comparison Job Activity** Provides a list of currently running comparison jobs.
  - **History** Provides a list of previously run jobs.
  - **Save** Used to save the current configuration of a VM Server.
  - **Saved** Lists all saved configurations.
- **Compliance**
  - **Results** Provides a list of current compliance violations.

- **Standard Associations** Provides a list of compliance standards that are associated with the target.
- **Real-time Observations** Provides a list of real-time compliance standards violations.

- **Target Setup**
  - **Edit VM Server** This is a link to the setup for OEM Cloud Control configuration for the VM Server.
  - **Monitoring Configuration** Used to view or modify the monitoring configuration of the VM Server target.
  - **Administrator Access** Used to grant administrator access to the VM Server instance target.
  - **Remove Target** Used to remove the VM Server target.
  - **Add to Group** Used to add the VM Server target to a group.
  - **Properties** Used to view and modify the VM Server target properties.
- **Target Information** Provides a quick link to basic VM Server status information.

Now that you have configured the VM Server systems, the VM Server Pool, and the VM Manager, you are ready to start administering the virtual machines themselves.

Managing Virtual Machines from OEM Cloud Control

Managing the virtual machines is really the main task of the VM Administrator. Within OEM Cloud Control, there are several methods of managing the virtual machine themselves, but all perform the same tasks. The first method is to click on the virtual machine in the Target Navigation pane. This will bring up the VM Guest screen as shown in Figure 13-12.

The second method is to right-click on the VM in the Target Navigation screen and use the drop-down menu as shown here in the illustration.

Either method will allow you to perform the basic VM management tasks and both methods will be described in the next few sections.

Home
Monitoring
Control
Job Activity
Information Publisher Reports
OVM Events
Migrate...
Move...
Clone...
Save as Template...
VNC Console...
Configuration
Compliance
Target Setup
Target Information

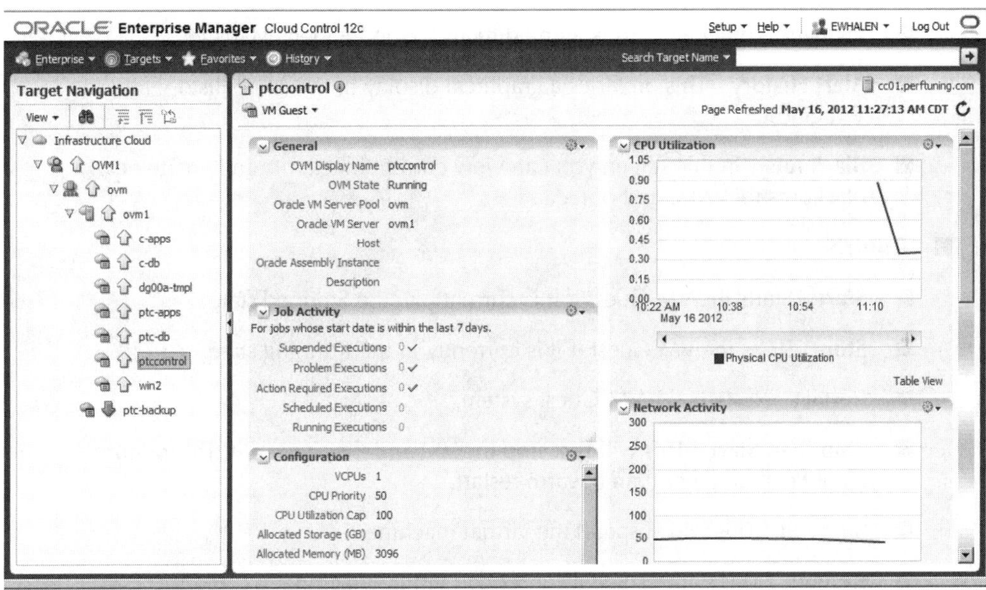

FIGURE 13-12. *The VM Guest screen*

Using the VM Guest Screen Menu

On the VM Guest screen, you can monitor and manage a single VM Guest image. Management is done by using the VM Guest drop-down menu. The VM Guest drop-down menu contains a number of tools that can be accessed by selecting them from this drop-down. They include the following:

- **Home** The VM Guest Home screen.
- **Monitoring**
  - **All Metrics** This is where you will find access to all of the VM Guest metrics and view the current values.
  - **Metric and Collection Settings** From this page you can easily find and modify all of the metric thresholds for VM Guest monitoring.
  - **Metric Collection Errors** Provides a list of metric collection errors.

- **Status History** Provides information on the availability of the VM Guest.
- **Incident Manager** This is a link directly to the Incident Manager.
- **Alert History** This provides a graphical display of the Alert History for the VM Guest.
- **Blackouts** In this screen you can view current blackouts and create new blackouts for VM Guest objects.

- **Control**
  - **Start** Starts the VM Guest if it is currently in the Stopped state.
  - **Stop** Stops the VM Guest if it is currently in the Running state.
  - **Restart** Restarts the VM Guest system.
  - **Stop then Start** This will first stop the VM and then restart it. This performs a cold restart rather than a warm restart.
  - **Suspend** This will suspend the virtual machine.
  - **Resume** This will resume a suspended virtual machine.
  - **Power Off** Powers off the virtual machine.
  - **Create Blackout** Allows you to create a blackout.
  - **End Blackout** End a blackout.
- **Job Activity** Shows job activity for the current VM Guest.
- **Information Publisher Reports** This brings up all of the reports related to the VM Guest. Here you will find a number of reports that you can run on the state of the VM Guest as well as its configuration.
- **OVM Events** This provides a list of events (failures and so on) that have occurred within the VM Guest Pool.
- **Migrate** Performs a live migration between VM Servers in the same Server Pool.
- **Move** Moves the virtual machine storage to another repository.
- **Clone** Clones the VM Guest to a new VM Guest image.
- **Save as Template** Saves the VM Guest as an Oracle VM Template.
- **VNC Console** Starts the VNC Console for this Virtual Machine.

- **Configuration**
  - **Last Collected** Shows the latest collected VM Guest configuration information.
  - **Topology** Shows the current VM Guest topology.
  - **Search** Provides a list of search criteria that is used to view specific VM Guest components.
  - **Compare** Used to compare different VM Guests.
  - **Comparison Job Activity** Provides a list of currently running comparison jobs.
  - **History** Provides a list of previously run jobs.
  - **Save** Used to save the current configuration of a VM Guest.
  - **Saved** Lists all saved configurations.
- **Compliance**
  - **Results** Provides a list of current compliance violations.
  - **Standard Associations** Provides a list of compliance standards that are associated with the target.
  - **Real-time Observations** Provides a list of real-time compliance standards violations.
- **Target Setup**
  - **Edit VM Guest** This is a link to the setup for OEM Cloud Control configuration for the VM Guest.
  - **Monitoring Configuration** Used to view or modify the monitoring configuration of the VM Guest target.
  - **Administrator Access** Used to grant administrator access to the VM Guest instance target.
  - **Remove Target** Used to remove the VM Guest target.
  - **Add to Group** Used to add the VM Guest target to a group.
  - **Properties** Used to view and modify the VM Guest target properties.
- **Target Information** Provides a quick link to basic VM Guest status information.

Using the VM Guest Drop-Down Menu

The options in the VM Guest drop-down menu will be available depending on the state of the VM Guest. Some options will be unavailable if the VM Guest is running. The menu items are shown in the following illustration.

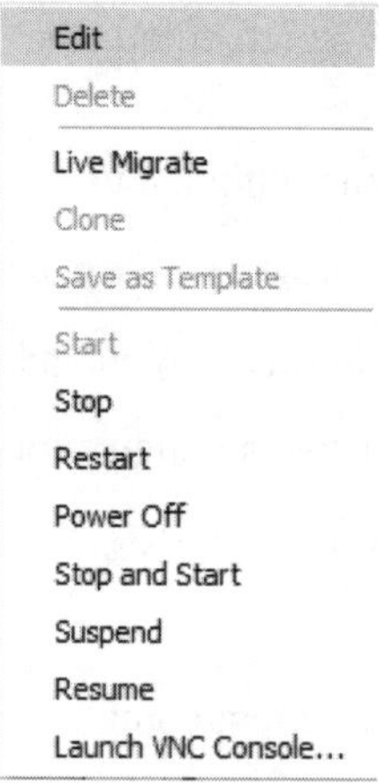

The control options are similar to the available options in the Control section of the VM Guest screen, with a few additions. The menu items available are as follows:

- **Edit** Here you can edit the VM Guest configuration. Not all options are available for edit if the VM Guest is running.
- **Delete** Delete the VM Guest (if it's not running).
- **Live Migrate** Performs a live migration between VM Servers in the same Server Pool.
- **Clone** Clones the VM Guest to a new VM Guest image (if not running).
- **Save as Template** Saves the VM Guest as an Oracle VM Template (if not running).
- **Start** Starts the VM Guest if it is currently in the Stopped state.
- **Stop** Stops the VM Guest if it is currently in the Running state.
- **Restart** Restarts the VM Guest system.
- **Power Off** Powers off the virtual machine.

- **Stop and Start** This will first stop the VM and then restart it. This performs a cold restart rather than a warm restart.
- **Suspend** This will suspend the virtual machine.
- **Resume** This will resume a suspended virtual machine.
- **Launch VNC Console** Starts the VNC Console for this virtual machine.

Using the menus makes it easier to manage the virtual machine than by using hyperlinks, since several steps can now be avoided. The menu system within OEM Cloud Control has simplified many of the tasks and made finding the right control easier than in previous releases.

Summary

This chapter has provided an overview of Oracle VM and how OEM Cloud Control can be used to manage the Oracle VM Server Farm and virtual machines. As you have seen in this chapter, Oracle VM is a stable and robust virtualization technology based on a long history of Xen virtualization technology. OEM Cloud Control can easily and quickly be configured to be used to manage the Oracle VM Server Farm and virtual machines.

By using OEM Cloud Control for managing Oracle VM, the management has now been moved to a centralized Console, thus providing more efficiency and ease of use. OEM Cloud Control has now provided the ability to manage both virtual machine cloud computing as well as the database cloud. This provides built-in support for cloud computing into OEM Cloud Control.

Index

B

C

D

E

F

G

H

I

M

N

O

P

Q

R

T

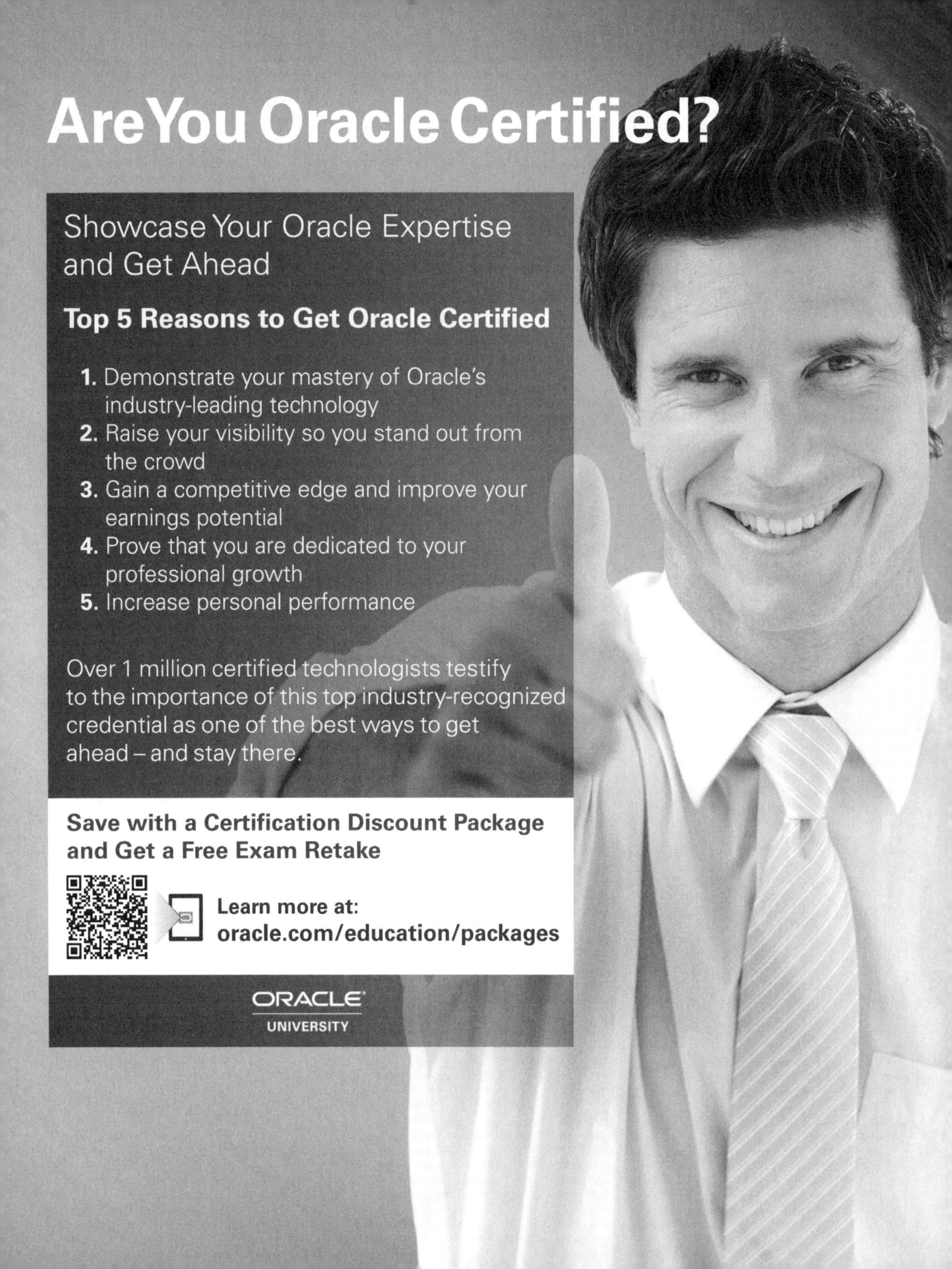
Are You Oracle Certified?
Showcase Your Oracle Expertise and Get Ahead
Top 5 Reasons to Get Oracle Certified
1. Demonstrate your mastery of Oracle's industry-leading technology
2. Raise your visibility so you stand out from the crowd
3. Gain a competitive edge and improve your earnings potential
4. Prove that you are dedicated to your professional growth
5. Increase personal performance
Over 1 million certified technologists testify to the importance of this top industry-recognized credential as one of the best ways to get ahead – and stay there.
Save with a Certification Discount Package and Get a Free Exam Retake
Learn more at:
oracle.com/education/packages
ORACLE
UNIVERSITY

Reach More than 700,000 Oracle Customers with Oracle Publishing Group

Connect with the Audience that Matters Most to Your Business

Oracle Magazine
The Largest IT Publication in the World
Circulation: 550,000
Audience: IT Managers, DBAs, Programmers, and Developers

Profit
Business Insight for Enterprise-Class Business Leaders to Help Them Build a Better Business Using Oracle Technology
Circulation: 100,000
Audience: Top Executives and Line of Business Managers

Java Magazine
The Essential Source on Java Technology, the Java Programming Language, and Java-Based Applications
Circulation: 125,000 and Growing Steady
Audience: Corporate and Independent Java Developers, Programmers, and Architects

For more information or to sign up for a FREE subscription:
Scan the QR code to visit Oracle Publishing online.